THIRD EDITION

LONGMAN PREPARATION COURSE FOR THE TOEFL iBT® TEST

TOEFL iBT® is the registered trademark of Educational Testing Service (ETS®). This publication is not endorsed or approved by ETS.

DEBORAH PHILLIPS

ALWAYS LEARNING

PEARSON

Longman Preparation Course for the TOEFL iBT® Test: Third Edition

Pearson Education, 10 Bank Street, White Plains, NY 10606

Staff credits: The people who made up the *Longman Preparation Course for the TOEFL iBT® Test, 3e* team, representing editorial, production, design, and manufacturing, are: Rhea Banker, Tracey Cataldo, Dave Dickey, Warren Fischbach, Pam Fishman, Patrice Fraccio, Michael Kemper, Christopher Leonowicz, Julie Molnar, Jane Townsend, and Kenneth Volcjak.

Contributing authors: Helen Ambrosio, Amy Bramhall, Diego Connelly, Tammy Gilbert, Christopher Kilmer, Elizabeth Mariscal, Megan Moriarty, William Trudeau, Sarah Wales-McGrath

Project & development editor: Helen Ambrosio
Development editor: Tammy Gilbert
Text composition: ElectraGraphics, Inc.
Cover and text photography credits appear on p. xxvi.

Library of Congress Cataloging-in-Publication Data
Phillips, Deborah, 1952-
  [Longman preparation course for the TOEFL test]
  Longman preparation course for the TOEFL iBT test / Deborah Phillips. — Third Edition.
    pages cm
  ISBN 978-0-13-324802-9 (without Answer Key) — ISBN 0-13-324802-X (without Answer Key) — ISBN 978-0-13-324812-8 (with Answer Key) — ISBN 0-13-324812-7 (with Answer Key)
  1. English language—Textbooks for foreign speakers. 2. Test of English as a Foreign Language—Study guides. 3. English language—Examinations—Study guides. I. Title.
  PE1128.P445 2014
  428.0076--dc23
                                                                              2014011173

Printed in the United States of America

ISBN 10: 0-13-324802-X (without Answer Key)
ISBN 13: 978-0-13-324802-9 (without Answer Key)

1 2 3 4 5 6 7 8 9 10—V011—20 19 18 17 16 15 14

ISBN 10: 0-13-324812-7 (with Answer Key)
ISBN 13: 978-0-13-324812-8 (with Answer Key)

1 2 3 4 5 6 7 8 9 10—V011—20 19 18 17 16 15 14

CONTENTS

INTRODUCTION

ABOUT THIS COURSE

PURPOSE OF THE COURSE

This course is intended to prepare students for the TOEFL iBT® test (Internet-Based Test). It is based on the most up-to-date information available on the TOEFL iBT® test. This third edition has been updated to feature test-length reading and listening passages, more at-level items, and the latest question types found on the TOEFL iBT® test.

Longman Preparation Course for the TOEFL iBT® Test, 3E can be used in a variety of ways, depending on the needs of the reader:

- It can be used as the *primary classroom text* in a course emphasizing preparation for the TOEFL iBT® test.

- It can be used as a *supplementary text* in a more general ESL/EFL course.

- Along with the free audio program on mp3 files, it can be used as a tool for *individualized study* by students preparing for the TOEFL iBT® test outside of the ESL/EFL classroom.

WHAT IS IN THE BOOK

The book contains a variety of materials that together provide a comprehensive TOEFL test preparation course:

- **Diagnostic Pre-Tests** for each section of the TOEFL iBT® test (Reading, Listening, Speaking, Writing) measure students' level of performance and allow students to determine specific areas of weakness.

- **Language Skills** for each section of the test provide students with a thorough understanding of the language skills that are regularly tested on the TOEFL iBT® test.

- **Test-Taking Strategies** for each section of the test provide students with clearly defined steps to maximize their performance on the test.

- **Exercises** provide practice of one or more skills in a non-TOEFL test format.

- **TOEFL Exercises** provide practice of one or more skills in a TOEFL test format.

- **TOEFL Review Exercises** provide practice of all of the skills taught up to that point in a TOEFL test format.

- **TOEFL Post-Tests** for each section of the test measure the progress that students have made after working through the skills and strategies in the text.

- Eight **Mini-Tests** allow students to simulate the experience of taking actual tests using shorter versions (approximately 1.5 hours each) of the test.

- Two **Complete Tests** allow students to simulate the experience of taking actual tests using full-length versions (approximately 3.5 hours each) of the test.

- **Scoring Information** allows students to determine their approximate TOEFL test scores on the Diagnostic Pre-Tests, Post-Tests, Mini-Tests, and Complete Tests.

- **Skill-Assessment Checklists** and **Diagnostic Charts** allow students to monitor their progress in specific language skills on the Pre-Tests, Post-Tests, Mini-Tests, and Complete Tests so that they can determine which skills have been mastered and which skills require further study.

- **Grammar and Structure** practice exercises provide students with the necessary foundation and a reference for key grammar points.

WHAT IS ON THE WEBSITE

COMPLETE AUDIO RECORDINGS NOW INCLUDED ON WEBSITE

NEW! The complete audio program to accompany this book is now included as mp3 files on the text's website at www.pearsonelt.com/TOEFLiBT. The website contains all of the recorded materials from the Listening, Writing, and Speaking sections as well as the Mini-Tests and Complete Tests.

AUDIO TRANSCRIPTS

All audio transcripts are now available to download or print from the website.

ANSWER KEY

The answer keys are available on the website only for those who have purchased the text with access to the answer keys.

WHAT IS ON THE MyEnglishLab FOR THE TOEFL iBT® TEST

NEW! This text comes with access to the *MyEnglishLab for the TOEFL iBT® Test*, an online component designed to provide additional interactive practice for the test. A range of activities are provided to master the skills necessary to succeed on the TOEFL iBT® Test. Both skill-specific activities and authentic test-style questions are incorporated, providing maximum exposure to the specific question types students will encounter. Special features include tips for answering question types, correct and incorrect answer feedback, and video presentations covering the material students will encounter on the test. Timed and untimed practice tests and mini-tests allow for teacher assessment and self-study assessment.

OTHER AVAILABLE MATERIALS

Pearson publishes a full suite of materials for TOEFL iBT® test preparation. Materials are available for the TOEFL iBT® test at both intermediate and advanced levels. Please visit Pearson's website at www.pearson.com for a complete list of available TOEFL iBT® test products.

ABOUT THE TOEFL IBT® TEST

OVERVIEW OF THE TOEFL iBT® TEST

The TOEFL iBT® test is an exam to measure the English proficiency and academic skills of nonnative speakers of English. It is required primarily by English-language colleges and universities. Additionally, institutions such as government agencies, businesses, or scholarship programs may require this test.

DESCRIPTION OF THE TOEFL iBT® TEST

The TOEFL iBT® test currently has the following four sections:

- The **Reading** section consists of three long passages and questions about the passages. The passages are on academic topics; they are the kind of material that might be found in an undergraduate university textbook. Students answer questions about stated and unstated details, inferences, sentence restatements, sentence insertion, vocabulary, pronoun reference function, fact and negative fact, and overall organization of ideas.

- The **Listening** section consists of six long passages and questions about the passages. The passages consist of two campus conversations and four academic lectures or discussions. The questions ask the students to determine main ideas, details, function, stance, inferences, and overall organization.

- The **Speaking** section consists of six tasks, two independent tasks and four integrated tasks. In the two independent tasks, students must answer opinion questions about some aspect of academic life. In the two integrated reading, listening, and speaking tasks, students must read a passage, listen to a passage, and speak about how the ideas in the two passages are related. In the two integrated listening and speaking tasks, students must listen to long passages and then summarize and offer opinions on the information in the passages.

- The **Writing** section consists of two tasks, one integrated task and one independent task. In the integrated task, students must read an academic passage, listen to an academic passage, and write about how the ideas in the two passages are related. In the independent task, students must write a personal essay.

The format of a TOEFL iBT® test is outlined in the following chart:

	iBT	APPROXIMATE TIME
READING	3 passages and 36–42 questions	60 minutes
LISTENING	6 passages and 34 questions	60 minutes
SPEAKING	6 tasks and 6 questions	20 minutes
WRITING	2 tasks and 2 questions	60 minutes

It should be noted that at least one of the sections of the test will include extra, uncounted material. Educational Testing Service (ETS) includes extra material to try out material for future tests. If you are given a longer section, you must work hard on all of the materials because you do not know which material counts and which material is extra. (For example, if there are four reading passages instead of three, three of the passages will count and one of the passages will not count. It is possible that the uncounted passage could be any of the four passages.)

HOW THE TEST IS SCORED

Students should keep the following information in mind about the scoring of the TOEFL iBT® test:

- The TOEFL iBT® test is scored on a scale of 0 to 120 points.

- Each of the four sections (Reading, Listening, Speaking, and Writing) receives a scaled score from 0 to 30. The scaled scores from the four sections are added together to determine the overall score.

- After students complete the Pre-Tests, Post-Tests, Mini-Tests, and Complete Tests in the book, it is possible for them to estimate their scaled scores. A description of how to determine the scaled scores of the various sections is included on pages 591–598.

HOW TO PREPARE FOR THE TOEFL IBT® TEST

The TOEFL iBT® test is a standardized test of English and academic skills. To do well on this test, you should improve your knowledge of the language and academic skills and test-taking strategies covered on the test. This book can familiarize you with the English language skills, academic skills, and test taking strategies necessary for the TOEFL iBT® test, and it can also provide a considerable amount of test practice. A generous amount of additional practice can be found on MyEnglishLab for the TOEFL iBT® Test.

HOW TO USE THIS BOOK

Following these steps can help you to get the most out of this book:

1. Take the Diagnostic Pre-Test at the beginning of each section. Try to reproduce the conditions and time pressure of a real TOEFL test. Take each section without interruption. Time yourself to experience the time pressure of an actual test. Play the audio one time only during the test. (Play it more times when you are reviewing.)

2. After you complete the Reading or Listening Diagnostic Pre-Test, diagnose your errors and record your results. Complete the Diagnosis and Scoring Charts on pages 591–598 to determine which language skills you have mastered and which need further study. Record your results on the Test Results charts on pages 595 and 598.

3. After you complete the Speaking or Writing Diagnostic Pre-Test, assess, score, and record your results. Complete the checklists on pages 599–604 to assess the skills used. Score your results using the Speaking Scoring Criteria on pages 605–606 or the Writing Scoring Criteria on pages 613–614. Record your scores on pages 608–609 and page 616.

4. Work through the presentations and exercises, paying particular attention to the skills that caused you problems in a Pre-Test. Each time that you complete a TOEFL-format exercise, try to simulate the conditions of a real test. For reading questions, allow yourself one-and-a-half minutes for one question. For listening questions, play the audio one time only during the exercise. Do not stop the audio between the questions. For speaking, allow yourself 15 to 20 seconds to prepare your response and 45 to 60 seconds to give it. For writing, allow yourself 20 minutes to write an integrated writing response and 30 minutes to write an independent writing response.

5. Complete the Appendix exercises for areas that you need to improve.

6. When you have completed all the skills exercises for a section, take a Post-Test. Follow the directions above to reproduce the conditions and time pressure of a real TOEFL test and to diagnose your answers and record your results.

7. Periodically schedule Mini-Tests and Complete Tests. As you take each one, follow the directions above to reproduce the conditions and time pressure of a real test and to score, diagnose, and record your results.

HOW TO GET THE MOST OUT OF THE SKILLS EXERCISES IN THE BOOK

The skills exercises are a vital part of the TOEFL iBT® test preparation process presented in this book. Maximum benefit can be obtained from the exercises if the students are properly prepared for the exercises and if the exercises are carefully reviewed after completion. Here are some suggestions:

- Be sure that the students have a clear idea of the appropriate skills and strategies involved in each exercise. Before beginning each exercise, review the skills and strategies that are used in that exercise. Then, when you review the exercises, reinforce the skills and strategies that can be used to determine the correct answers.

- As you review the exercises, be sure to discuss each answer, the incorrect answers as well as the correct answers. Discuss how students can determine that each correct answer is correct and each incorrect answer is incorrect.

- In this new edition, all of the exercises are designed to be as challenging as the actual test. It is important to keep students under time pressure while they are working on the exercises. An equal amount of time should be spent in reviewing the exercises once they have been completed.

HOW TO GET THE MOST OUT OF THE TESTS IN THE BOOK

There are four different types of tests in this book: Diagnostic Pre-Tests, Post-Tests, Mini-Tests, and Complete Tests. When the tests are given, it is important that the test conditions be as similar to actual TOEFL iBT® test conditions as possible; each section of the test should be given without interruption and under the time pressure of the actual test. Giving the speaking tests in the book presents a unique problem because the students need to respond individually during the tests. Various ways of giving speaking tests are possible; you will need to determine the best way to give the speaking tests for your situation. Here are some suggestions:

- You can have the students come in individually and respond to the questions as the teacher listens to the responses and evaluates them.

- You can have a room set up where students come in individually to take a speaking test and record their responses on a computer or audio recording device. Then either the teacher or the student will need to evaluate the responses.

- You can have a room set up where students come in in groups of four to take a speaking test and record the responses on four computers or audio recording devices, one in each corner of the room. Then either the teacher or the students will need to evaluate the responses.

- You can have the students sit down in an audio lab or computer lab where they can record their responses on the system. Then either the teacher or the students will need to evaluate the responses.

Review of the tests should emphasize the function served by each of these different types of tests:

- While reviewing the Diagnostic Pre-Tests, you should encourage students to determine the areas where they require further practice.

- While reviewing the Post-Tests, you should emphasize the language skills and strategies involved in determining the correct answer to each question.

- While reviewing the Mini-Tests, you should review the language skills and test-taking strategies that are applicable to the tests.

- While reviewing the Complete Tests, you should emphasize the overall strategies for the Complete Tests and review the variety of individual language skills and strategies taught throughout the course.

HOW MUCH TIME TO SPEND ON THE MATERIAL

You may have questions about how much time it takes to complete the materials in this course. The numbers in the following chart indicate approximately how many hours it takes to complete the material:

	BOOK SKILLS	HOURS		BOOK SKILLS	HOURS
READING SKILLS	Pre-Test	2	MINI-TEST 3	Speaking	1
	Skills 1–2	8		Writing	1
	Skills 3–4	8	MINI-TEST 4	Reading	1
	Skills 5–6	8		Listening	1
	Skills 7–8	8		Speaking	1
	Skills 9–10	8		Writing	1
	Post-Test	2	MINI-TEST 5	Reading	1
LISTENING SKILLS	Pre-Test	1		Listening	1
	Skills 1–2	6		Speaking	1
	Skills 3–4	6		Writing	1
	Skills 5–6	6	MINI-TEST 6	Reading	1
	Post-Test	1		Listening	1
SPEAKING SKILLS	Pre-Test	2		Speaking	1
	Skills 1–4	5		Writing	1
	Skills 5–8	5	MINI-TEST 7	Reading	1
	Skills 9–12	5		Listening	1
	Skills 13–15	4		Speaking	1
	Skills 16–18	4		Writing	1
	Post-Test	2	MINI-TEST 8	Reading	1
WRITING SKILLS	Pre-Test	2		Listening	1
	Skills 1–8	12		Speaking	1
	Skills 9–15	12		Writing	1
	Post-Test	2	COMPLETE TEST 1	Reading	2
MINI-TEST 1	Reading	1		Listening	2
	Listening	1		Speaking	2
	Speaking	1		Writing	2
	Writing	1	COMPLETE TEST 2	Reading	2
MINI-TEST 2	Reading	1		Listening	2
	Listening	1		Speaking	2
	Speaking	1		Writing	2
	Writing	1	APPENDIX		33
MINI-TEST 3	Reading	1			**200 hours**
	Listening	1			

HOW TO DIVIDE THE MATERIAL

You may need to divide the materials in this course so that they can be used over a number of sessions. The following is one suggested way to divide the materials into two sessions:

SESSION 1	BOOK	HOURS
READING SKILLS	Pre-Test	2
	Skills 1–2	8
	Skills 3–4	8
	Skills 5–6	8
LISTENING SKILLS	Pre-Test	1
	Skills 1–2	6
	Skills 3–4	6
SPEAKING SKILLS	Pre-Test	2
	Skills 1–4	5
	Skills 5–8	5
WRITING SKILLS	Pre-Test	2
	Skills 1–8	12
MINI-TEST 1	Reading	1
	Listening	1
	Speaking	1
	Writing	1
MINI-TEST 2	Reading	1
	Listening	1
	Speaking	1
	Writing	1
MINI-TEST 3	Reading	1
	Listening	1
	Speaking	1
	Writing	1
MINI-TEST 4	Reading	1
	Listening	1
	Speaking	1
	Writing	1
COMPLETE TEST 1	Reading	2
	Listening	2
	Speaking	2
	Writing	2
APPENDIX		12
		101 hours

SESSION 2	BOOK	HOURS
READING SKILLS	Skills 7–8	8
	Skills 9–10	8
	Post-Test	2
LISTENING SKILLS	Skills 5–6	6
	Post-Test	1
SPEAKING SKILLS	Skills 9–12	5
	Skills 13–15	4
	Skills 16–18	4
	Post-Test	2
WRITING SKILLS	Skills 9–15	12
	Post-Test	2
MINI-TEST 5	Reading	1
	Listening	1
	Speaking	1
	Writing	1
MINI-TEST 6	Reading	1
	Listening	1
	Speaking	1
	Writing	1
MINI-TEST 7	Reading	1
	Listening	1
	Speaking	1
	Writing	1
MINI-TEST 8	Reading	1
	Listening	1
	Speaking	1
	Writing	1
COMPLETE TEST 2	Reading	2
	Listening	2
	Speaking	2
	Writing	2
APPENDIX		21
		99 hours

The following is a suggested way to divide the materials into three sessions:

SESSION 1	BOOK	HOURS
READING SKILLS	Pre-Test	2
	Skills 1–2	8
	Skills 3–4	8
LISTENING SKILLS	Pre-Test	1
	Skills 1–2	6
SPEAKING SKILLS	Pre-Test	2
	Skills 1–4	5
MINI-TEST 1	Reading	1
	Listening	1
	Speaking	1
	Writing	1
MINI-TEST 2	Reading	1
	Listening	1
	Speaking	1
	Writing	1
MINI-TEST 3	Reading	1
	Listening	1
	Speaking	1
	Writing	1
APPENDIX		21
		65 hours

SESSION 2	BOOK	HOURS
READING SKILLS	Skills 5–6	8
	Skills 7–8	8
LISTENING SKILLS	Skills 3–4	6
SPEAKING SKILLS	Skills 5–8	5
	Skills 9–12	5
WRITING SKILLS	Pre-Test	2
	Skills 1–8	12
MINI-TEST 4	Reading	1
	Listening	1
	Speaking	1
	Writing	1
MINI-TEST 5	Reading	1
	Listening	1
	Speaking	1
	Writing	1
COMPLETE TEST 1	Reading	2
	Listening	2
	Speaking	2
	Writing	2
APPENDIX		6
		68 hours

SESSION 3	BOOK	HOURS
READING SKILLS	Skills 9–10	8
	Post-Test	2
LISTENING SKILLS	Skills 5–6	6
	Post-Test	1
SPEAKING SKILLS	Skills 13–15	4
	Skills 16–18	4
	Post-Test	2
WRITING SKILLS	Skills 9–15	12
	Post-Test	2
MINI-TEST 6	Reading	1
	Listening	1
	Speaking	1
	Writing	1
MINI-TEST 7	Reading	1
	Listening	1
	Speaking	1
	Writing	1
MINI-TEST 8	Reading	1
	Listening	1
	Speaking	1
	Writing	1
COMPLETE TEST 2	Reading	2
	Listening	2
	Speaking	2
	Writing	2
APPENDIX		6
		67 hours

ACKNOWLEDGMENTS

The publisher would like to thank the following contributors, reviewers, focus group, and survey participants:

Stephen Abbot, Universidad del Valle de México, Mexico • **Adekemi Allou**, Master Executive English, Mexico • **Maria Teresa Avila**, Universidad del Valle de México, Mexico • **Robin Babcock**, UMass, Boston, North Eastern, MA, USA • **Rocio Bayod**, Universidad de la Comunicación, Mexico • **Vera Laurenti Bianchin**, Fundacao Richacd Hugh Fisk, Brazil • **Virginia L. Blanford**, ELT Specialist, NY, USA • **Veronica Montaño Bonilla**, Anglo Mexicano de Coyoacan, Mexico • **Ricardo Gabriel Cedillo**, Escuela Medico Naval, Mexico • **Itzel Rosas Colmenares**, Quill Language Learning, Mexico • **Silvia Helena R. D. Correa**, Alumni (Binational Ctr), Brazil • **Alma Isabel de la Garza**, Universidad de la Comunicación, Mexico • **Teresa del Valle**, Global Language Instruction, Mexico • **Lou Di Giacomo**, CA International Univ., CA, USA • **Marta Olga Dmytrenko**, ELI, Wayne State Univ., MI, USA • **Olufemi Elugbaju**, Top Tutors, Brazil • **Miriam Leticia Felix**, Escuela Medico Naval, Mexico • **Lin Fenno**, Boston Academy of English, MA, USA • **Marilena Fernandes**, Alumni (Binational Ctr), Brazil • **Paul Fraccalvieri**, Baruch Colege, LaGuardia CC, NY, USA • **Marcos Freddi**, Speed Up English, Brazil • **Ilan Genegger**, ICBEU, Brazil • **Todd Hannig**, Bunker Hill CC, MA, USA • **Francisco Hernández**, Universidad del Valle de México, Mexico • **Kyle Hess**, ELS Language Centers, MI, USA • **Manuel Hidalgo**, Quill Language Learning, Mexico • **Jacklyn Janeksela**, Kingsborough CC, Lehman College, NY, USA • **Lavaughn John**, Top Tutors, Brazil • **Ana Virginia Kesselring**, Virginia Center School, Brazil • **Christopher Kilmer**, Colorado School of English, CO, USA • **Jane Kirsch**, ELI, Geo. Mason Univ., VA, USA • **Edgar Leija**, Quill Language Learning, Mexico • **Thomas Leverett**, So. Illinois University, IL, USA • **Patricia Macip**, Instituto Las Americas, Mexico • **Paulo Marao**, Flextime Language Ctr, Brazil • **Elizabeth Mariscal**, Univ of CA, San Diego, CA, USA • **Seabrook Mendoza**, CA State San Marcos, CA, USA • **Paul Metzger**, Kingsboro CC, NY, USA • **Eugenio Mirisola**, Up Language Consultants, Brazil • **Nora Fonseca Morales**, Anglo Mexicano de Coyoacan, Mexico • **Megan Moriarty**, ELT Specialist, CA, USA • **Verónica Elisa Perez Puebla**, La Salle, Mexico • **Briana Raissi**, GEOS Language Institute, NY, USA • **Frederick Reece**, Koc Univ, Istanbul, Turkey • **Lauren J. Rogener**, ASC English, MA, USA • **Helen Roland**, Miami-Dade College, FL, USA • **Rodrio Marín Rougan**, Centro Universitario Cultural, Mexico • **Nilhan Selcuk**, Koc Univ, Istanbul, Turkey • **Mario Z. Souza**, Baruch College, NY, USA • **Nilufer Ulker**, Istanbul Tech. Univ, Istanbul, Turkey • **Linda Van Doren**, Colorado School of English, CO, USA • **Rebecca Vogel**, St. Mary's University of Minnesota, MN, USA • **P. Monique Ward**, Gwinnett Tech. College, GA, USA • **Cinar Yildiz**, Tobb Univ of Economics & Tech., Ankara, Turkey • **Lorelai Zuñiga**, Instituto Las Americas, Mexico

NOTE TAKING

Note taking is critical to success on the TOEFL iBT® test. Take notes on all the passages in the Listening section, and on both the reading and listening passages for the integrated tasks in the Speaking and Writing sections. Even if you understand these passages clearly as you are reading and listening, your notes will help you remember the information and use it later to answer questions, record spoken responses, and write effective responses and essays.

Although everyone develops their own style of note taking, there are some practical strategies that can be applied to tasks. One method is to take notes using a "T-chart." A T-chart is a graphic organizer that helps you organize information for your notes. You draw a chart with two columns and label the columns based on what information you need.

Look at the sample material that follows. First read the sample passages and transcripts, and then study how the example T-charts were created based on the sample passages.

LISTENING

For the **Listening tasks**, there are various ways to organize your notes, such as by labeling the columns of a T-chart for cause and effect or for problems and solutions, by using the two columns for comparing and contrasting two different topics, or for listing advantages and disadvantages of the same topic or situation. You can also use a basic outline to organize listening notes into topic, main points, and supporting ideas. It is important that note taking on the Listening portion of the test be brief, and that your focus remains on listening to the passage.

> TIP: Don't try to write down everything from the listening passage and the reading passage word for word.

Listening Sample Excerpt

(narrator)	Listen to part of a lecture in an astronomy class.
(professor)	Well, certainly in popular culture—science fiction movies, fictional stories, even people who claim to have been kidnapped by aliens—the possibility of life on the red planet has been explored and confirmation is presumed to be within our grasp. But, no matter what we might imagine or believe, the fact remains that there has never been any verifiable proof of life on Mars. Now . . . scientific investigations have been ongoing for decades, including telescopic observations in the late 1800s by Percival Lowell, and the orbiting *Mariner* spacecrafts of the 1960s and 1970s. But only in the twenty-first century—I know as a young student, this would have been beyond my wildest dreams—umm . . . NASA and the Mars Science Laboratory, or MSL, have been able to collect geochemical samples directly from the surface of Mars. And what have they found? No, not little gray or green beings, however, they did find some of the elements necessary to support life . . .

Notes

Aliens ? = pop culture belv life on Mars

Investigatns	Findngs
—Telescop obs 1800s Perc Lowell	—X verifybl proof
—Mariners crft 1960s-70s	—X little gray/ grn being
—21st cent- nasa collct geochems fr surfc mars	—Rovers missns discvr chems & mins nec 4 life

Abbreviations and Symbols

Abbreviations (shortened words) and symbols are used so that you can the reduce time and the amount you write in the notes.
Abbreviate by following these guidelines:
Delete the ending of a word or use only the first syllable (topic = top; listening = list)
Delete vowels from a word if it doesn't lead to confusion (discover = dscvr; child = chld)
Use acronyms (initials, letters) for names or common terms (Theodore Roosevelt = TR; homework= HW; main points = MPs)

SPEAKING

For the **integrated Speaking tasks**, a T-chart should be organized so that one side lists the topic and main points of the Listening lecture and the other side lists the topic and three main points of the Reading passage.

Speaking Sample Excerpt from Reading Passage

A notice from the office of the university president

Effective Monday, November 11th, no pets will be allowed on the university campus. This applies to all university professors, administrators, students, and visitors alike. This policy is being put in place for the comfort and safety of everyone on campus and because buildings on campus are not built to accommodate pets. The only exception to this rule is the use of animals such as seeing-eye dogs that are trained for use in assisting persons with disabilities. Any other pets, no matter how large or small, are unequivocally not allowed. Anyone who fails to follow this policy will face immediate action by the university.

Speaking Sample Excerpt from Listening Passage

(narrator)	Now listen to two students as they discuss the notice.
(man)	What's the deal with the new policy on pets?
(woman)	Oh, you saw that? I guess one of the professors has a pet snake that got loose and ended up in the president's office. I heard the president kind of freaked out.
(man)	What? Just because of one incident? It's not fair for the president to penalize everyone just because one professor was careless.
(woman)	Yeah, it's a pretty harsh reaction.
(man)	I think it's too strict. You know, a lot of local people, not students, who live off campus use the paths on the campus to walk their dogs. It's not a safety issue because they control their dogs. If the university makes them stop, it'll cut down the interaction between people on campus and off.
(woman)	I guess I do see a lot of people walking their dogs, and they are pretty considerate about it.
(man)	Exactly. I've talked with a few of them and they've actually been really interesting people. It sort of helps the university be part of the neighborhood.
(woman)	It does seem kind of pointless to drive them away from the campus.
(man)	I'll bet the president hasn't really thought this through.

Notes

Reading Passage	Listening Passage
Top: X pets on campus!	Op (opinion):
MPs:	M— X like policy X pets
—4 comf/safe, bldg X accom	W— reas = prof's snake in pres off
—excp disabil	R4 (reasons for opinion):
—X follow = immed act by univ	M: — X fair, pres punish all, ++strict
	— people off camp walk dogs, control, safe
	— ↓ interact btw camp & neigh

&, +	and; also	**b/f or b/4**	before	*****	important
++	more	**aft**	after	**M**	man/men
w/	with	**@**	at	**W**	woman/women
w/o	without	**→**	leads to; causes	**4**	for
=	equals, is, means, is same as	**←**	comes from; result of	**2**	to
≠	unequal to, is not the same as	**↓**	decrease	**ppl**	people
X	no, not	**↑**	increase	**/**	per
b/c	because	**$**	dollars	**" "**	ditto; repeated information
>	greater than, bigger than, more than	**ex., e.g.**	example	**re**	regarding; about
<	fewer than, smaller than, less than	**K**	thousand	**ft**	feet
1st, 2nd, 3rd	first, second, third	**%**	percent	**yr**	year

NOTE TAKING

WRITING

For the **integrated Writing tasks**, a T-chart should be organized so that one side lists the topic and main points of the Reading passage and the other side lists the topic and main points of the Listening lecture.

Writing Sample Excerpt from Reading Passage

In most democracies, decisions on parenting are left to the parents. However, due to serious issues such as child abuse, neglect, and an increase in crimes committed by youth, several countries are considering implementing mandatory parenting classes for all prospective parents. Proponents believe mandatory parenting classes will provide essential information about childcare to uninformed parents, leading to a reduction in child abuse and neglect cases. In addition, supporters believe that raising the standard of parenting ensures that the future generation is not burdened with anti-social behaviors, thus reducing the costs of existing child support systems that respond to crises. Finally, it is thought that since the classes would provide current and standardized information from a variety of professionals, the quality of parenting will increase.

Writing Sample Excerpt from Listening Passage

(professor) I'd like to point out that the idea of mandatory parenting classes is not without controversy. Opponents point out that there is no data linking the implementation of parenting education to a decline in child abuse or neglect. Before governments institute such a policy, there should be broad-scale studies with verifiable proof of its ability to significantly reduce violence towards and neglect of children. Critics also feel that potential cost reduction is not a valid reason for the intrusion of the government into the role of parenting. This leads us to the final reason why mandatory parenting is being contested. Standardized practices disregard the unique beliefs and customs of the individual family.

Notes

Reading Notes	Listening Notes
Top: Parenting class shld be mandatory 4 all prspctv prnts	Top: Parenting class shld X be mandatory 4 prspctv prnts
MPs:	MPs:
—provide essntl info abt child care to prvnt abuse & neglct	—X data links ↓ parental abuse + neglect w/ prnt ed
—↑ standrd of parenting = future gen X burdnd w/ anti-social behvr → < cost of child spprt systms	—Prnts know best, X ok 4 gov 2 intrfr w/ role of prnt
—Classes = stndrdzd info frm ++ profsnls, → qulty prntng	—Stndrdzd practs X = unique blfs & cstms of fam, X 2 child need same prning

&, +	and; also	b/f or b/4	before	*	important
++	more	aft	after	M	man/men
w/	with	@	at	W	woman/women
w/o	without	→	leads to; causes	4	for
=	equals, is, means, is same as	←	comes from; result of	2	to
≠	unequal to, is not the same as	↓	decrease	ppl	people
X	no, not	↑	increase	/	per
b/c	because	$	dollars	" "	ditto; repeated information
>	greater than, bigger than, more than	ex., e.g.	example	re	regarding; about
<	fewer than, smaller than, less than	K	thousand	ft	feet
1st, 2nd, 3rd	first, second, third	%	percent	yr	year

NOTE TAKING STRATEGIES

1. Be brief.

2. **Use symbols and abbreviations.** Create your own abbreviation list or add to the list below.

3. **Write key words and phrases.** Content words are those that hold meaning. Avoid writing function words. Function words are words that don't hold meaning, such as articles, prepositions, forms of the verb *be* (*am, is, are, was, were*), and auxiliary verbs (*be, have, do*).

4. Draw arrows or connecting lines between related ideas if they will remain clear to you.

5. After noting the main ideas, indent details, supporting ideas, or examples.

6. Leave space between topics or ideas in case you want to fill in information later.

7. Write down important names and dates.

8. Write clearly.

9. Use a T-chart or another type of graphic organizer.

10. **Paraphrase.** For example, this sentence *"Even though the first few years of life are a time when learning is at its highest and tremendous amounts of information are processed, people seem to remember basically nothing from this period."* can be paraphrased, *"Memories from infancy and the toddler years are almost non-existent in adults, despite the fact that these were periods of intense learning."*

Symbol	Meaning	Symbol	Meaning	Symbol	Meaning
&, +	and; also	**b/f or b/4**	before	*****	important
++	more	**aft**	after	**M**	man/men
w/	with	**@**	at	**W**	woman/women
w/o	without	**→**	leads to; causes	**4**	for
=	equals, is, means, is same as	**←**	comes from; result of	**2**	to
≠	unequal to, is not the same as	**↓**	decrease	**ppl**	people
X	no, not	**↑**	increase	**/**	per
b/c	because	**$**	dollars	**" "**	ditto; repeated information
>	greater than, bigger than, more than	**ex., e.g.**	example	**re**	regarding; about
<	fewer than, smaller than, less than	**K**	thousand	**ft**	feet
1st, 2nd, 3rd	first, second, third	**%**	percent	**yr**	year

CREDITS

Cover: (left) Moritz Wussow/Fotolia, (middle) Kzenon/Fotolia, (right) michaeljung/Fotolia.

Page 143 alexsalo images/Shutterstock; p. 144 Blend Images/Alamy; p. 147 mangostock/Shutterstock; p. 149 Blend Images/Alamy; p. 152 (left) Alexander Raths/Shutterstock, (right) Goodluz/Shutterstock; p. 153 (left) Pearson Learning Group, (right) Paylessimages/Fotolia; p. 154 wavebreakmedia/Shutterstock; p. 156 auremar/Shutterstock; p. 158 Goodluz/Shutterstock; p. 160 alexsalo images/Shutterstock; p. 161 paylessimages/Fotolia; p. 162 (top) Monkey Business Images/Shutterstock, (bottom left) Sergiy Goruppa/Hemera/Thinkstock, (bottom right) Zoonar RF/Thinkstock; p. 163 Pearson Learning Group; p. 164, 165, 166 Purestock/Thinkstock; p. 167, 168 Hutchings Photography; p. 170 wavebreakmedia/Shutterstock; p. 171 Pearson Learning Group; p. 172 (top) Photodisc/Thinkstock, (bottom left) Gary Unwin/Shutterstock, (bottom right) Ivan Kuzmin/Shutterstock; p. 173 Hutchings Photography; p. 175, 176, 177 Pearson Learning Group; p. 178, 179 Jack Hollingsworth/Photodisc/Thinkstock; p. 181 (left & right) Pearson Learning Group; p. 182 (left) Goodshoot/Thinkstock, (right) Andres Rodriguez/Fotolia; p. 183 Hutchings Photography; p. 185 (top left) Jack Hollingsworth/Digital Vision/Thinkstock, (middle right) BMJ/Shutterstock, (bottom left) Martin Lehmann/Shutterstock; p. 187 Monkey Business Images/Shutterstock; p. 190 Hutchings Photography; p. 193 bikeriderlondon/Shutterstock; p. 194 Stokkete/Shutterstock; p. 195 bikeriderlondon/Shutterstock; p. 196 Hutchings Photography; p. 198 Diego Cervo/Shutterstock; p. 200 Hutchings Photography; p. 203 (left) Pearson Learning Group, (right) Hutchings Photography; p. 204 Hutchings Photography; p. 205 Monkey Business Images/Shutterstock; p. 206 Stokkete/Shutterstock; p. 208 Hutchings Photography; p. 211 Pearson Learning Group; p. 212 Robert Kneschke/Fotolia; p. 217 Mike Good/Dorling Kindersley; p. 218 (top) Hutchings Photography, (bottom) Anton Gvozdikov/Shutterstock; p. 219 wavebreakmedia/Shutterstock; p. 252 East/Shutterstock; p. 254 Hutchings Photography; p. 256 (top) Monkey Business Images/Shutterstock, (bottom) wavebreakmedia/Shutterstock; p. 257 Riccardo Piccinini/Shutterstock; p. 266 Kzenon/Shutterstock; p. 271 Monkey Business Images/Shutterstock; p. 272 Africa Studio/Fotolia; p. 274 apops/Fotolia; p. 275 (top) WavebreakmediaMicro/Fotolia, (bottom) diego cervo/Fotolia; p. 284 contrastwerkstatt/Fotolia; p. 285 Monkey Business Images/Shutterstock; p. 287 Riccardo Piccinini/Shutterstock; p. 289 (top) Monkey Business Images/Shutterstock, (middle) Riccardo Piccinini/Shutterstock, (bottom) Edyta Pawlowska/Fotolia; p. 298 wavebreakmedia/Shutterstock; p. 300 Datacraft Co., Ltd/Pearson; p. 301 Paylessimages/Fotolia; p. 303 Jack Hollingsworth/Photodisc/Thinkstock; p. 304 (top) Goodshoot/Thinkstock, (bottom) paylessimages/Fotolia; p. 313 bikeriderlondon/Shutterstock; p. 315 Zurijeta/Shutterstock; p. 316 Karramba Production/Shutterstock; p. 317 (top) Hutchings Photography, (bottom) Hutchings Photography; p. 321 Jack Hollingsworth/Photodisc/Thinkstock; p. 330 Goodshoot/Thinkstock; p. 332 Jack Hollingsworth/Photodisc/Thinkstock; p. 334 (top) paylessimages/Fotolia, (bottom) taka/Fotolia; p. 335 Robert Kneschke/Fotolia; p. 353 Wavebreak Media/Thinkstock; p. 374 Top Photo Group/Thinkstock; p. 381 ONOKY/Photononstop/Alamy; p. 382 Maridav/Fotolia; p. 385 Maridav/Fotolia; p. 386 Jon Barlow/Pearson Education Ltd; p. 388 wavebreakmedia/Shutterstock; p. 394 Goodluz/Shutterstock; p. 395 Jenner/Fotolia; p. 397 contrastwerkstatt/Fotolia; p. 398 Monkey Business Images/Shutterstock; p. 406 Alexander Raths/Shutterstock; p. 407 Monkey Business Images/Shutterstock; p. 410 Riccardo Piccinini/Shutterstock; p. 411 paylessimages/Fotolia; p. 413 Image Source/Alamy; p. 419 Pius Lee/Fotolia; p. 420 Diego Cervo/Shutterstock; p. 423 paylessimages/Fotolia; p. 424 wavebreakmedia/Shutterstock; p. 432 alexsalo images/Shutterstock; p. 433 Creatas Images/Thinkstock; p. 436 Jupiter Images/liquidlibrary/Thinkstock; p. 437 Alexander Raths/Shutterstock; p. 439 Paylessimages/Fotolia; p. 446 Sergey Nivens/Shutterstock; p. 447 (top) Jack Hollingsworth/Digital Vision/Thinkstock, (middle) Eric Isselee/Shutterstock, (bottom left) Stephen Inglis/Shutterstock, (bottom right) In Green/Shutterstock; p. 450 Blend Images/Alamy; p. 451 Brocreative/Shutterstock; p. 459 Pearson Learning Group; p. 460 Jack Hollingsworth/Photodisc/Thinkstock; p. 463 Diego Cervo/Shutterstock; p. 464 Andres Rodriguez/Fotolia; p. 466 Maridav/Fotolia; p. 472 mangostock/Shutterstock; p. 473 Wavebreak Media/Thinkstock; p. 476 Karramba Production/Shutterstock; p. 477 Fuse/Thinkstock; p. 492 Pius Lee/Fotolia; p. 493 Goodshoot/Thinkstock; p. 494 Odua Images/Shutterstock; p. 495 Pearson Learning Group; p. 496 (top left) Africa Studio/Shutterstock, (top right) Bettmann/Corbis, (middle) Photos.com/Thinkstock, (bottom) guynamedjames/Fotolia; p. 498 (top) taka/Fotolia, (bottom) TIM SHAFFER/Associated Press/Newscom; p. 500 Monkey Business Images/Shutterstock; p. 501 contrastwerkstatt/Fotolia; p. 502 Zurijeta/Shutterstock; p. 503 bikeriderlondon/Shutterstock; p. 506 wavebreakmedia/Shutterstock; p. 520 alexsalo images/Shutterstock; p. 521 Andres Rodriguez/Fotolia; p. 522 taka/Fotolia; p. 523 Purestock/Thinkstock; p. 524 (top left) paylessimages/Fotolia, (top right) Doug Meek/Shutterstock, (middle left) Tips Images/Tips Italia Srl a socio unico/Alamy, (middle right) Daniele Silva/Shutterstock, (bottom) Anton_Ivanov/Shutterstock; p. 526 bikeriderlondon/Shutterstock; p. 529 Monkey Business Images/Shutterstock; p. 530 (top) Wavebreak Media/Thinkstock, (bottom) Zurijeta/Shutterstock; p. 531 Karramba Production/Shutterstock; p. 533 Brian Enright/Fotolia.

READING

READING DIAGNOSTIC PRE-TEST

30 minutes

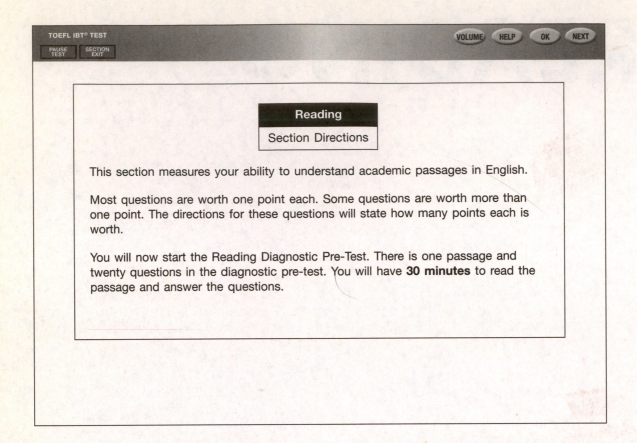

VOLUME HELP OK NEXT

PAUSE TEST SECTION EXIT

Reading

Section Directions

This section measures your ability to understand academic passages in English.

Most questions are worth one point each. Some questions are worth more than one point. The directions for these questions will state how many points each is worth.

You will now start the Reading Diagnostic Pre-Test. There is one passage and twenty questions in the diagnostic pre-test. You will have **30 minutes** to read the passage and answer the questions.

Read the passage and answer the questions that follow.

Paragraph

Aggression

1►   Aggressive behavior is any behavior that is intended to cause injury, pain, suffering, damage, or destruction. While aggressive behavior is often thought of as purely physical, verbal attacks such as screaming and shouting or belittling and humiliating comments aimed at causing harm and suffering can also be a type of aggression. What is key to the definition of aggression is that whenever physical or verbal harm is inflicted, it is intentional.

2►   Aggression was likely an early survival mechanism for humans, much in the same way it was for animals. Despite this, it is generally thought that aggressive behavior was not named as such before the seventeenth century, when the term was used to refer to an unprovoked physical attack. The term expanded beyond the description of purely physical aggression to include a psychological dimension in the early twentieth century, as psychiatrists put more emphasis on aggressive behavior and its potential motives.

3►   Questions about the causes of aggression have long been of concern to both social and biological scientists. Theories about the causes of aggression cover a broad spectrum, ranging from those with biological or instinctive emphases to those that portray aggression as a learned behavior.

4►   Numerous theories are based on the idea that aggression is an inherent and natural human instinct. **9A** Aggression has been explained as an instinct that is directed externally toward others in a process called displacement, and it has been noted that aggressive impulses that are not channeled toward a specific person or group may be expressed indirectly through socially acceptable activities such as sports and competition in a process called catharsis. **9B** Biological, or instinctive, theories of aggression have also been put forth by ethologists, who study the behavior of animals in their natural environments. **9C** A number of ethologists have, based upon their observations of animals, supported the view that aggression is an innate instinct common to humans. **9D**

5►   Two different schools of thought exist among those who view aggression as instinct. One group holds the view that aggression can build up spontaneously, with or without outside provocation, and violent behavior will thus result, perhaps as a result of little or no provocation. Another suggests that aggression is indeed an instinctive response but that, rather than occurring spontaneously and without provocation, it is a direct response to provocation from an outside source.

6►   In contrast to instinct theories, social learning theories view aggression as a learned behavior. This approach focuses on the effect that role models and reinforcement of behavior have on the acquisition of aggressive behavior. Research has shown that aggressive behavior can be learned through a combination of modeling and positive reinforcement of the aggressive behavior and that children are influenced by the combined forces of observing aggressive behavior in parents, peers, or fictional role models and of noting either positive reinforcement for the aggressive behavior or, minimally, a lack of negative reinforcement for the behavior. While research has provided evidence that the behavior of a live model is more influential than that of a fictional model, fictional models such as those seen in movies and on television, do still have an impact on behavior. **19A** On-screen deaths or acts of violent behavior in certain television programs or movies can be counted in the tens, or hundreds, or even thousands; while some have argued that this sort of fictional violence does not in and of itself cause violence and may even have a beneficial cathartic[1] effect, studies have shown correlations between viewing of violence and incidences of aggressive behavior in both childhood and adolescence. **19B** Studies have also shown that it is not just the modeling of aggressive behavior in either its real-life or fictional form that correlates with increased acts of violence in youths; a critical factor in increasing aggressive behaviors is the reinforcement of the behavior. **19C** If the aggressive role model is rewarded rather than punished for violent behavior, that behavior is more likely to be seen as positive and is thus more likely to be imitated. **19D**

GLOSSARY

1. *cathartic*—providing emotional release; therapeutic

1. Which of the following is NOT defined as aggressive behavior?
   - Ⓐ inflicting pain accidentally
   - Ⓑ making insulting remarks
   - Ⓒ destroying property
   - Ⓓ trying unsuccessfully to injure someone

2. The author mentions "belittling and humiliating comments" in paragraph 1 in order to
   - Ⓐ demonstrate how serious the problem of aggression is
   - Ⓑ clarify the difference between intentional and unintentional aggression
   - Ⓒ provide examples of verbal aggression
   - Ⓓ illustrate the nature of physical aggression

3. The word "intentional" in paragraph 1 is closest in meaning to
   - Ⓐ deliberate
   - Ⓑ estimated
   - Ⓒ forbidden
   - Ⓓ intermittent

4. According to paragraph 2, which of the following is true about aggression?
   - Ⓐ Aggression was not a typical behavior for humans before the seventeenth century.
   - Ⓑ There was probably no specific term to describe aggressive behavior until the seventeenth century.
   - Ⓒ Animals were much more likely to display aggressive behavior than humans, at least until recently.
   - Ⓓ The psychological definition of aggression has been around as long as the physical one has.

5. Which of the sentences below best expresses the essential information in the highlighted sentence in paragraph 3? *Incorrect* choices change the meaning in important ways or leave out essential information.
   - Ⓐ Biological theories of aggression emphasize its instinctive nature.
   - Ⓑ Theories that consider aggression biological are more accepted than those that consider it learned.
   - Ⓒ Various theories about aggression attribute it to either natural or learned causes.
   - Ⓓ Various theories try to compare the idea that aggression is biological with the idea that it is learned.

6. According to paragraph 4, "displacement" is
   - Ⓐ internally directed aggression
   - Ⓑ a modeled type of aggression
   - Ⓒ aggression that is unintentional
   - Ⓓ aggression that is directed outward

7. It can be inferred from paragraph 4 that "catharsis"
   - Ⓐ is a positive process
   - Ⓑ involves channeling aggression internally
   - Ⓒ is studied by ethologists
   - Ⓓ should be negatively reinforced

8. An ethologist would be most likely to study
   - Ⓐ learned catharsis in a certain species of monkey
   - Ⓑ the evolution of a certain type of fish
   - Ⓓ the bone structure of a certain type of dinosaur
   - Ⓓ how a certain male lion fights other male lions

9. Look at the four squares [■] that indicate where the following sentence could be added to paragraph 4.

   One may, for example, release aggression by joining a football team or a debate team or even a cooking competition.

   Where would the sentence best fit? Click on a square [■] to add the sentence to the passage.

10. The phrase "schools of thought" in paragraph 5 is closest in meaning to
    - Ⓐ institutions of higher learning
    - Ⓑ lessons to improve behavior
    - Ⓒ methods of instruction
    - Ⓓ sets of shared beliefs

11. It is NOT mentioned in paragraph 5 that some believe that instinctive aggression may occur
    - Ⓐ without being provoked
    - Ⓑ in order to cause provocation
    - Ⓒ in response to minor provocation
    - Ⓓ in response to clear provocation

12. The word "it" in paragraph 5 refers to
    - Ⓐ aggression
    - Ⓑ an instinctive response
    - Ⓒ provocation
    - Ⓓ a direct response

13. The author begins paragraph 6 with the expression "In contrast to instinct theories" in order to
    - Ⓐ introduce the instinct theories that will be presented in paragraph 6
    - Ⓑ indicate that paragraph 6 will present two contrasting theories
    - Ⓒ contrast instinctive theories of aggression with biological theories of aggression
    - Ⓓ provide a transition to the idea that will be presented in paragraph 6

14. It is NOT mentioned in paragraph 6 that aggression can be learned by observing
    - Ⓐ others of the same age
    - Ⓑ violent programs on TV
    - Ⓒ one's mother or father
    - Ⓓ professional football games

15. The word "that" in paragraph 6 refers to

Ⓐ research
Ⓑ evidence
Ⓒ the behavior
Ⓓ a live model

16. What is stated in paragraph 6 about the modeling of aggressive behavior?

Ⓐ Fictional models are as likely to cause aggressive behavior as are live models.
Ⓑ Little correlation has been found between viewing of aggressive behavior on television and acting aggressively.
Ⓒ Aggression in works of fiction may cause aggressive behavior.
Ⓓ Aggression in society has an effect on the type of violence in movies and on television.

17. The phrase "in and of itself" in paragraph 6 is closest in meaning to

Ⓐ internally
Ⓑ single-handedly
Ⓒ genuinely
Ⓓ semi-privately

18. The word "critical" in paragraph 6 could best be replaced by

Ⓐ negative
Ⓑ considerate
Ⓒ crucial
Ⓓ studied

19. Look at the four squares [■] that indicate where the following sentence could be added to paragraph 6.

Thus, it is more common for a youth to imitate aggressors who have been rewarded than those who have been punished.

Where would the sentence best fit? Click on a square [■] to add the sentence to the passage.

20. The word "imitated" in paragraph 6 is closest in meaning to

Ⓐ repeated
Ⓑ copied
Ⓒ exhibited
Ⓓ initiated

21. Which situation would most likely result in increased aggressive behavior in children?

Ⓐ witnessing TV shows in which the aggressor gets away without being punished
Ⓑ watching two friends compete in a wrestling match
Ⓒ viewing a verbal argument between parents
Ⓓ viewing TV shows in which the hero defeats the agressor

READING

22.

> **Directions:** An introductory sentence for a brief summary of the passage is provided below. Complete the summary by selecting the THREE answer choices that express the most important ideas in the passage. Some sentences do not belong in the summary because they express ideas that are not presented in the passage or are minor ideas in the passage. **This question is worth 2 points** (2 points for 3 correct answers, 1 point for 2 correct answers, and 0 points for 1 or 0 correct answers).

Aggression, which causes harm to those affected by it, has been accounted for by numerous theories.

- •3
- • 5
- • 6

Answer Choices (choose 3 to complete the chart):

(1) Various theories indicate that learned aggression occurs as a result of observation of this type of behavior and reward for it.
(2) Various theories indicate aggression is neither instinctive nor learned.
(3) Various theories indicate that instinctively caused aggression is always cathartic.
(4) Various theories indicate that instinctively caused aggression may occur with or without provocation.
(5) Various theories indicate that aggression may be instinctive or learned.
(6) Various theories indicate that learned aggression results from displacement of anger.

Turn to pages 591–595 to diagnose your errors and *record* your results.

READING DIAGNOSTIC PRE-TEST   5

The first section on the TOEFL iBT® test is the Reading section. This section consists of three passages*, and each passage is followed by 12–14 questions. Most of the questions accompanying a passage are worth one point each. However, the last question in each set has multiple answers, and is worth 2–4 points, depending on its length. Test takers are given a total of 60 minutes to complete the whole Reading section. While it is advisable to allow approximately 20 minutes to answer the questions for each passage, test takers are not given the passages in separately timed, 20-minute blocks. In other words, for a three-passage Reading section, the test taker is given 60 minutes at the beginning of the section. It is the test taker's responsibility to monitor the time and use it to answer the questions accordingly.

- The **passages** are lengthy readings (approximately 700 words each) on academic topics.

- The **questions** cover the following areas: fact and negative fact, vocabulary; pronoun reference; sentence restatement; where sentences can be inserted into the passage; stated and unstated details; inferences; rhetorical purpose; and overall organization of ideas.

Reading Section	Approximate Passage Length	Number of Questions
Passage 1	700 words	12–14 questions
Passage 2	700 words	12–14 questions
Passage 3	700 words	12–14 questions

*Some tests have four reading passages instead of three. 80 minutes is given for the test taker to complete a four-passage Reading section.

The following strategies can help you in the Reading section.

STRATEGIES FOR READING

1. **Be familiar with the directions.** You can look at a sample test on the ETS website by using this link: http://www.ets.org/toefl to see the directions. The directions on every test are the same, so it is not necessary to spend time reading them when you take the test. Dismiss the directions as soon as they come up. Click on `Continue` as soon as it appears and use your time on the passages and questions.

2. **Do not worry if a reading passage is on a topic that is not familiar to you.** All of the information that you need to answer the questions is included in the passages. You do not need any special background knowledge to answer the questions.

3. **Scroll to the end of the passage to see the questions.** Use the scrollbar on the right side of the box containing the passage. Once you get to the end of the passage, click on `Next` in the top right-hand corner of the screen. The first question should appear. You can move back and forth among questions for each reading passage by clicking on `Next` and `Back` in the top right-hand corner. If you skip a question, write the number down so you remember to return to it later.

4. **Do not spend too much time reading the passages.** You may not have time to read each passage in depth, and it is quite possible to answer some of the questions correctly without first reading the passages in detail.

5. **Skim each passage and its questions to determine the main idea and overall organization of ideas in the passage.** You do not need to understand every detail in each passage to answer the questions correctly. Skimming the questions will help you understand what information you need to look for. Most of the questions are asked in the order that information appears in the passage, except for the final chart or table question. In addition, many of the questions indicate where you need to look for information in the passage by using highlighted words/phrases or arrows pointing to a particular section. Using these location hints in the passage and questions can save you time when reading for information.

6. **Look at each question to determine what type of question it is.** The type of question tells you how to proceed to answer the question. Refer to the chart at the end of this section for more information.

   - For *vocabulary questions,* the targeted word will be highlighted in the passage. Find the highlighted word, and read the context around it.

   - For *referent questions,* the targeted word will be highlighted in the passage. Find the highlighted target word, and read the context preceding it.

   - For *paraphrasing questions,* the targeted sentence will be highlighted in the passage. Read the highlighted sentence carefully. It may also be helpful to read the context around the highlighted sentence.

   - For *sentence insertion questions,* there will be darkened squares indicating where the sentence might be inserted. Read the context around the darkened squares carefully.

   - For *factual information questions* (including detail and unstated detail questions) and *negative factual information questions* the paragraph number will be included in the question. Skim the paragraph for key words from the question and read the sentences around the key words in the paragraph. For *negative factual information questions,* the words NOT and EXCEPT will be included in the questions.

   - For *inference questions,* choose a key word from the question, and skim for the key word (or a related idea) in order in the passage. Read the part of the passage around the key word (or related idea).

   - For *rhetorical purpose questions,* the targeted word or phrase will be highlighted in the passage. Read the highlighted word or phrase and the context around it to determine the rhetorical purpose.

   - For *overall ideas questions,* such as summary information and organizational (schematic) table questions, focus on the main ideas rather than minor details of the passages. The main ideas and important details are most likely explained in the introductory paragraph and at the beginning or end of each supporting paragraph.

7. **Choose the best answer to each question.** You may be certain of a particular answer, or you may eliminate any definitely incorrect answers and choose from among the remaining answers.

8. **Do not spend too much time on a question you are completely unsure of.** If you do not know the answer to a question, simply guess and go on. You can return to this question later (while you are still working on the same passage) if you have time.

9. **Monitor the time carefully on the title bar of the computer screen.** The title bar indicates the time remaining in the section, the total number of questions in the section, and the number of the question that you are working on.

10. **Guess to complete the section before time is up.** It can only increase your score to guess the answers to questions that you do not have time to complete. (Points are not subtracted for incorrect answers.)

11. **Remember the information from previous questions.** Information used to answer earlier questions can help you answer later questions, especially chart or table questions. Remember that the information in one question may have a connection to other questions, and help to connect the ideas in the passage. Understanding and using these connections will help to increase your score.

Improving Reading Comprehension

The following tips will assist you in improving your overall reading comprehension abilities. Making use of these tips will help to increase your score on the Reading section of the test.

- **Read in English every day.** Choose academic material that is typical of what is covered on the TOEFL iBT® test: history, anthropology, social and other sciences, literature, music, and the arts. Major newspapers and topic-specific magazines have articles in these areas that often use vocabulary and some sentence structures used on the TOEFL iBT® test.

- **Read out loud sometimes.** For some people, reading out loud forces them to pay attention to the words they are reading. It is not practical to do this on the actual test, but reading out loud can help you improve overall comprehension, which will help you on the test.

- **Look at any titles, subheadings or questions given along with a reading.** Titles and subheadings provide information about the topic and how it is broken down. Questions that are given with the reading tell you what information you can expect to be answered in the reading.

- **Ask yourself questions about the reading.** Use the *wh-* question words to make up the questions (i.e., Who is involved in the action? What is the main point of this paragraph? When is the passage taking place?).

- **Pay attention to transition words and phrases.** Words and phrases such as *in addition, however, on the other hand*, and *so on* provide important information about the relationship between ideas. They provide especially important information about the organization of ideas (cause-effect, comparison-contrast, chronological, etc.). Understanding the relationships will help you to understand the reading more effectively.

- **Summarize the main points of the reading.** When you finish reading the material you have chosen, spend a few minutes summarizing the main points of the reading for yourself. Use the questions you make up to help you summarize. If you are hesitant about a main point, go back and re-read that part of the passage.

- **Time yourself.** A native speaker of English reads around 250 words per minute on average. This means that it would take him just under three minutes to read a TOEFL iBT® test passage. Although the TOEFL iBT® test does give more time for you to read the passage, you should still try to increase your reading speed to meet this average. It will be very helpful for you in your future academic studies. Time yourself regularly on passages similar to the TOEFL iBT® test in length (around 700 words). Practice the strategies above until you are using them more easily and have increased your speed.

Improving Vocabulary Skills

As with reading comprehension, you must study and use new vocabulary regularly in order to improve.

- **Set aside a certain amount of time each day to study.** Pick a regular time when you are free (at least 20 minutes), and commit yourself to studying during that time. Review words using flash cards, smartphone applications (apps), or other tools.

- **Practice vocabulary at the level you need to do well on the TOEFL iBT® test.** A good place to start is with the Academic Word List, which can be found on the Internet. The words on this list and their synonyms appear often in all of the sections of the test.

- **Study the entire word family.** Don't just study a single part of speech (noun, adjective, verb, adverb) for a word. Many words in English, especially at the academic level, can be formed into different parts of speech by, for example, adding *suffixes* to the end of the word: communicate (verb); communic*ation* (noun); communic*ative* (adjective). It is important for you to understand all of the different forms and how they are used in sentences.

- **Learn synonyms instead of definitions.** The TOEFL iBT® test consistently uses synonyms in its reading and listening passages. Therefore, it is not enough to learn just a word and its definition; you need to understand what other words with the same meaning can replace that word. For example the verb *to stress* can be replaced by *to emphasize*.

- **Study words in the context of a sentence.** It is not enough to know the meaning or synonym of a word; you must also understand *how the word is used* to express ideas. Many words have different meanings depending on how they are used. For example, the noun *house* means a building to live in, while the verb *house* means to provide shelter or provide a living space. In addition, many words that may be synonyms in one context are not synonyms in another context. Reading and hearing words in the correct context help you to understand when and how to use them effectively.

- **Listen to and say the word.** Since the TOEFL iBT® test recycles vocabulary throughout the test, it is important that you can both recognize and use a word by knowing how it's pronounced.

- **Don't focus on technical words.** Don't spend a lot of time studying words from specific disciplines, such as biology or astronomy. Words that are specific to a field are often explained in context on the test or they are defined for you in a pop-up glossary. Once you begin your area of study in college, then you can focus on the words specific to that area.

READING

Type of Question	Frequency per Reading Passage on the Test	Point Value	How to Identify the Question
Vocabulary	3–5 questions	1	The word or phrase ". . ." is closest in meaning to . . .
Referents	0–2 questions	1	The word ". . ." in the passage refers to . . .
Paraphrasing	Usually 1 question	1	Which of the sentences below best expresses the essential information . . . ?
Sentence Insertion	1 question	1	Where would the sentence best fit? Click on a square [■] to add the sentence to the passage.
Factual Information/ Negative Factual Information	3–6 questions	1	According to paragraph X . . . ? In paragraph X, (where, what, when, etc.) . . . ? It is stated in paragraph X . . . It is indicated in paragraph X . . . What is implied in paragraph X . . . ? In paragraph X it can be inferred that . . . It is implied in paragraph X . . . It is suggested in paragraph X . . . It is most likely that . . . What probably happened . . . ? According to the passage, which of the following is NOT true . . . ? All of the following are mentioned EXCEPT . . . ?
Rhetorical Purpose	0–3 questions	1	Why does the author . . . ? What is the function of . . . ? The author mentions X in order to . . .
Summary Chart	0–1 question	0–2	An introductory sentence for a brief summary of the passage is provided below. Complete the summary by selecting THREE answer choices that express the most important ideas in the passage.
Schematic Table	0–1 question	0–3	Complete the table below to summarize information about X in the passage. Match the appropriate statements to X.

READING SKILLS

The following skills will help you to implement the strategies in the Reading section of the TOEFL iBT® test.

VOCABULARY AND REFERENCE

Reading Skill 1: UNDERSTAND VOCABULARY FROM CONTEXT

Vocabulary questions test your understanding of English, as well as your ability to use context clues to help you determine the meaning of a word or phrase. Vocabulary is one of the most important skills to develop for the entire TOEFL iBT® test. Vocabulary questions are the most common questions found on the Reading section. In addition, vocabulary used in the Reading section is also used in the other sections of the test.

The vocabulary tested in the Reading section may be words that you haven't seen before, or words that are familiar to you, but that have more than one meaning and are being used in the context of the reading passage in ways that are not familiar to you. Therefore, it is important to develop the skill of using context to help you guess successfully at the meaning of a word.

Strategies to Improve Context Skills

- Read the entire sentence with the target vocabulary word in it. See if you can determine a potential definition of the word by using the words in the sentence around the target vocabulary item (context).

- Determine what part of speech the word is. Try to understand its function in the sentence. (Is it the subject? the verb? modifying a noun?) Is the word singular or plural in form? If it is a verb, what is the tense (present, past, future)? Is it active or passive?

- Determine if you have seen or heard the word before. If you have, what was the context? Does the meaning you are familiar with seem to fit into the context in the reading passage?

- Determine if the word looks similar to another word you might know. What part of the word looks similar (the prefix, the root, or the suffix)? Does a meaning similar to the word you know seem to fit into this context?

- Determine if there are any conjunctions of similarity or contrast, such as *and* or *but* that connect this word to other words in the sentence. Use your knowledge of the other words and their relationship to this word to make a guess about the meaning. Is it a synonym (same meaning) for another word in the sentence? Is it an antonym (opposite meaning)?

- If you cannot get enough information from the sentence with the word in it, read one or two sentences before and after the word. See if there are synonyms, antonyms, or conjunctions that will help you establish the relationship between the target vocabulary word and other words or phrases in the previous or following sentence that can help you determine the meaning of the vocabulary word.

Look at the underlined word in each sentence or pair of sentences below. Use the **Strategies to Improve Context Skills** in this section to help you guess the best synonym to replace each underlined word.

1. interval—The researcher spent three-month intervals in Antarctica for each of the past four winters in order to complete his experiments.
   Ⓐ travels   Ⓑ periods of time   Ⓒ research methods

2. persist—The young man has practiced his guitar daily for the past two years. If he persists with this schedule, he will definitely become a successful musician.
   Ⓐ practices   Ⓑ continues   Ⓒ observes

3. immense—The television program featured an immense whale, spotted in the Atlantic Ocean. The narrator said the whale's size broke all previous records that had been set.
   Ⓐ massive   Ⓑ tiny   Ⓒ common

4. encompass—These bamboo trees now encompass the entire house. There is no area around the house where they don't grow.
   Ⓐ surround   Ⓑ invade   Ⓒ rise

5. hue—The beautiful <u>blue</u> hue of Margaret's dress matches her eyes.
      Ⓐ shape   Ⓑ color   Ⓒ size

6. diminish—When someone feels anger at another person, the emotion can be strong in the beginning. However, it should <u>diminish</u> as time passes, so the person begins to calm down.
      Ⓐ get larger   Ⓑ express   Ⓒ decrease

7. merge—If the two companies are <u>merged</u> with each other, they can control the majority of the market for this particular product.
      Ⓐ combined   Ⓑ divided   Ⓒ sold

8. replication—*West Side Story* is a modern <u>replication</u> of the story from *Romeo and Juliet*. However, it uses almost all of the themes from the original play, and *West Side Story* is set in twentieth-century United States.
      Ⓐ substitution   Ⓑ copy   Ⓒ comparison

> Be aware of all of a word's parts of speech. A word may have different meanings, depending on whether it is a noun or a verb.

Example

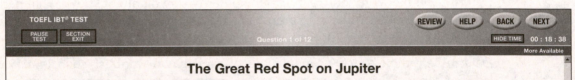

The Great Red Spot on Jupiter

1▶ One distinctive feature of the planet Jupiter is the Great Red Spot, a massive oval of swirling reddish-brown clouds. Although it is not known exactly how long the spot has been in existence, it was first observed nearly 400 years ago, when telescopic lenses became effective enough to pick it out of the night sky. Since that first discovery, the phenomenon has been observed and measured at various intervals to gather more information both about the spot and the planet Jupiter.

2▶ The Great Red Spot draws the attention of scientists, especially astronomers, because it is considered the most powerful storm in the entire solar system. It is a high-pressure storm much like a hurricane on Earth, but it is much larger and has persisted for far longer than any storms on our planet. The storm turns in a counter-clockwise direction, and completes a full rotation in about six days. Scientists speculate that one reason it may have endured for so long is that it does not pass over land areas, which would cause it to weaken and break apart. They also suggest that the storm is controlled by Jupiter's considerable amount of internal heat, which also allows it to continue on indefinitely.

3▶ The spot's immense size is clearly one of its notable aspects. While the size of the spot has fluctuated over the centuries, growing and shrinking in width and length, it can still easily encompass the entire Earth within its area. And, although the size remains impressive, it seems to have steadily declined in recent decades. A century ago, it measured almost 25,000 miles (40,000 kilometers) in surface area; it is now approximately half that size. If it continues at its current pace of decrease, scientists predict it will shrink so much that its shape will change from an oval to more of a circle by the middle of the twenty-first century.

4▶ It's not just the size, but also the color of the spot that fascinates amateur and professional astronomers alike. The spot is generally described as reddish-brown, but in fact, it varies in hue across its entire area. The reddest area is in the center of the spot, which is also the warmest part. As one moves away from the center, the color diminishes to lighter shades of red, pale salmon, and finally, white. The variation in color has led astronomers to establish various theories of how the spot has been formed. The relationship of heat to color seems to back the influence of environmental factors on the spot's development. Another widely accepted theory, related to the composition of the spot, suggests that it is composed of complex organic molecules along with various sulfur compounds.

5▶ Modern astronomers are getting a hand in tracing the development of the Great Red Spot through another storm that began to form more recently and has been nicknamed by many "Red Spot, Junior." This new spot first appeared in 2000, when three smaller storms merged

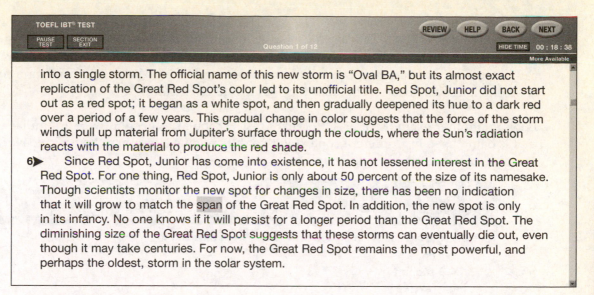

TOEFL iBT® TEST
PAUSE TEST   SECTION EXIT
REVIEW   HELP   BACK   NEXT
Question 1 of 12
HIDE TIME   00 : 18 : 38
More Available

into a single storm. The official name of this new storm is "Oval BA," but its almost exact replication of the Great Red Spot's color led to its unofficial title. Red Spot, Junior did not start out as a red spot; it began as a white spot, and then gradually deepened its hue to a dark red over a period of a few years. This gradual change in color suggests that the force of the storm winds pull up material from Jupiter's surface through the clouds, where the Sun's radiation reacts with the material to produce the red shade.

6▶   Since Red Spot, Junior has come into existence, it has not lessened interest in the Great Red Spot. For one thing, Red Spot, Junior is only about 50 percent of the size of its namesake. Though scientists monitor the new spot for changes in size, there has been no indication that it will grow to match the span of the Great Red Spot. In addition, the new spot is only in its infancy. No one knows if it will persist for a longer period than the Great Red Spot. The diminishing size of the Great Red Spot suggests that these storms can eventually die out, even though it may take centuries. For now, the Great Red Spot remains the most powerful, and perhaps the oldest, storm in the solar system.

Look at an example of a TOEFL iBT® test vocabulary question with a familiar word that is being used in a different context with a different meaning than the typical, everyday meaning of the word. (See paragraph 2.)

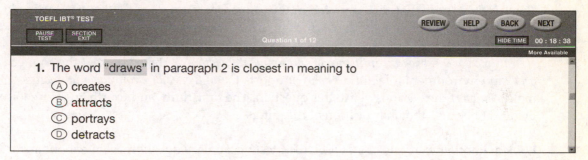

TOEFL iBT® TEST
PAUSE TEST   SECTION EXIT
REVIEW   HELP   BACK   NEXT
Question 1 of 12
HIDE TIME   00 : 18 : 38
More Available

1. The word "draws" in paragraph 2 is closest in meaning to

Ⓐ creates
Ⓑ attracts
Ⓒ portrays
Ⓓ detracts

This question asks about the meaning of the word "draws." It is likely that you usually connect the word "draw" to creating some kind of picture. However, if you read the sentence carefully, you can see that *attention* is the object of the verb *draw*, not a word that means *picture*: *The Great Red Spot draws the attention of scientists . . .* There is also a cause/effect relationship in the sentence that helps you to understand the word: *. . . because it is considered the most powerful storm . . .* Therefore, you can understand that it is the *powerful storm* that *draws the attention of scientists*. Putting these context clues together tells you that the best answer for this question is the second answer choice: *attracts*.

Now look at an example of a TOEFL iBT® test vocabulary question asking about a word you may not be familiar with. (See paragraph 3.)

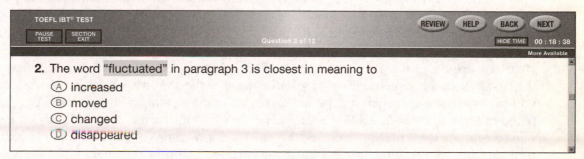

TOEFL iBT® TEST
PAUSE TEST   SECTION EXIT
REVIEW   HELP   BACK   NEXT
Question 2 of 12
HIDE TIME   00 : 18 : 38
More Available

2. The word "fluctuated" in paragraph 3 is closest in meaning to

Ⓐ increased
Ⓑ moved
Ⓒ changed
Ⓓ disappeared

The third answer choice is correct. This question asks about the meaning of the word "fluctuated." You are not expected to know the meaning of this word. However, you should note that "fluctuated" is the verb, and it is connected to "size" in the sentence: *. . . the size of the* *spot has fluctuated over the centuries. . . .* You should also pay attention to the phrase *growing and shrinking in width and length* in the sentence. This is a description of what has happened to the size, and a clue to the meaning of *fluctuated*. Based on these context clues, you can determine that *fluctuated* is closest in meaning to *changed*. The first, second, and fourth answer choices are incorrect because they have different meanings.

Look at another example of a TOEFL iBT® test vocabulary question with a familiar word that is being used in a different context with a different meaning than the typical, everyday meaning of the word. (See paragraph 4.)

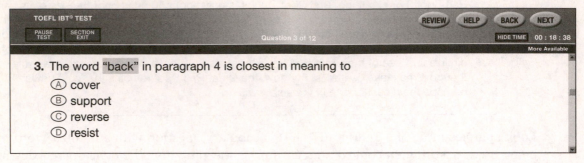

The second answer choice is correct. This question asks about the meaning of the word "back." First, note that *back* is a verb in this sentence, but it does not have a participle such as *away* or *up* following it, both of which give *back* the meaning of moving in a reverse direction. *Relationship* is the subject connected to *back* and *influence* is the object. The *relationship of heat to color . . . back the influence of environmental factors . . .* tells you that the connection of *heat*, an environmental factor, to *color* <u>supports</u> *the influence of environmental factors. . .* This makes *support* the best answer to this question. The first, third, and fourth answer choices are incorrect because they have different meanings.

Look at another example of a TOEFL iBT® test vocabulary question asking about a word you may not be familiar with. (See paragraph 6.)

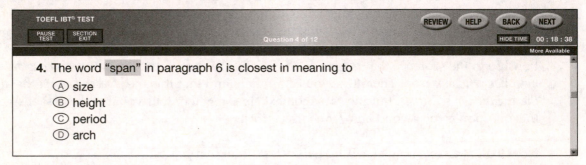

The first answer choice is correct. In this question, you are asked about the meaning of the word "span." It is important to note that *span* is acting as a noun in this sentence, not a verb (as it sometimes can). The context of the sentence also tells you that the word is connected to a characteristic of the Great Red Spot, and that it is something that can grow: . . . *that it will grow to match the span of the Great Red Spot.* This information, along with the information in the first half of the sentence: *Though scientists monitor the new spot for changes in size . . .* tells you that *span* is a synonym for the word *size*, since the size of the new spot is being compared to the size of the Great Red Spot. Therefore, *size* is the correct answer for this question. The second answer choice is incorrect because it is a measure of elevation, but specifically from bottom to top, which does not fit the context. The third answer choice is incorrect because although it can fit the sentence, it does not match the meaning of the word in this situation. The fourth answer choice is incorrect because although it is one definition of the word, it is not the correct meaning in this context.

The following chart outlines the key points that you should remember about Vocabulary from Context questions.

KEY POINTS FOR QUESTIONS ABOUT UNDERSTANDING VOCABULARY FROM CONTEXT	
FREQUENCY	3–5 questions per reading passage
WHERE TO FIND THE ANSWER	The word is highlighted in the passage. Most of the information needed to answer the question is in the context of the sentence in which the word is located. Occasionally, you may need to read a sentence before or after the highlighted word to help you choose the best answer.
HOW TO ANSWER THE QUESTION	1. Read the entire sentence that the highlighted vocabulary word is in; see if the meaning is easy to understand. 2. Determine the function of the word (part of speech) in the sentence and its relationship to other words. 3. Identify any conjunctions or transitional words or phrases that can clarify the meaning of the highlighted word or its relationship to other words. 4. Identify any words or phrases in the sentence that might be synonyms or antonyms of the word in the question. 5. When necessary, read the sentences immediately before and after the highlighted word for more information.

In the exam, you may be able to eliminate incorrect answer choices by understanding what is wrong with them.

For vocabulary questions, incorrect answer choices may:
- be one definition of the word, but not the correct one in the context of the passage, which is using another definition of the word.
- be an antonym.
- be another word that could fit into the sentence, but does not match the actual meaning of the word in the question.

READING EXERCISE 1: Study each of the passages and choose the best answers to the questions that follow.

PASSAGE ONE (Questions 1–8)

Paragraph   **Air Pollution**

1▶   While air pollution is not entirely restricted to man-made substances, in the vast majority of areas where it is a problem, human activity has been the primary cause. The Industrial Revolution, which took place from the late eighteenth to the early nineteenth century, generated the first notable increase of air pollution. As the use of coal became widespread to fuel factories and heat homes during this period, residents of large cities began to notice a smoky haze that hung over their heads. This haze was termed "smog" in the early twentieth century by Dr. Henry Antoine Des Voeux, who spoke at a public health meeting about the combination of smoke and fog that had adversely affected the health of London citizens.

2▶   Further modernization, especially of transportation, has led to smog being introduced into suburban and

> While context clues can help you determine which answer choice is correct, it is not the only vocabulary skill you should rely on. The TOEFL iBT® test does include vocabulary questions in which they expect you to already know the meaning of the highlighted word without the use of context clues.

rural environments. The extensive rail system that started expanding in the late 1800s across the United States conveyed people and cargo to distant locations while the trains simultaneously puffed clouds of coal-produced smog along their path. The introduction of automobiles with oil as their fuel source compounded the issue by allowing individuals to add to the steadily increasing amount of air pollution. Personal vehicles permitted couples and families to travel long distances more easily, and promoted the settlement of previously untouched areas. An ever-growing global network of roads, and the proliferation of affordable vehicles have allowed air pollution to impact areas once considered safe from its effects.

3▶ Today, the oxidation of exhaust gases from cars and trucks is one of the primary sources of the world's pollution. This foggy vapor, poised over some of the world's largest cities, and growing to include smaller ones, is more accurately called "photochemical smog." It results from chemical reactions that take place in the air, using the energy of sunlight. The production of smog begins when gases are created in the cylinders of vehicle engines. In these cylinders, oxygen and nitrogen gas combine as the fuel burns to form nitric oxide (NO), a colorless gas. The nitric oxide is forced out into the air through the vehicle tailpipe along with other gases.

> Don't read the sentence containing the target vocabulary word only for the word's meaning. Pay attention to the information the sentence is telling you about the topic. This can help you answer other questions on the test.

4▶ When the gas reaches the air, it comes into contact with available oxygen from the atmosphere and combines with the oxygen to produce nitrogen dioxide (NO_2), which is a gas with a brownish hue. This nitrogen dioxide plays a role in the formation of acid rain in wetter or more humid climates and tends to decompose back into nitric acid as it releases an oxygen atom from each molecule; the released oxygen atoms quickly combine with oxygen (O_2) molecules to form ozone (O_3). The brownish colored nitrogen dioxide is partially responsible for the brown color in smoggy air; the ozone is the toxic substance that causes irritation to eyes.

5▶ In actuality, smog is far more hazardous in warm, sunny, dry weather than during rainy weather. This is because the air in the upper part of the atmosphere can become warm enough in these types of climatic conditions to prevent vertical circulation. Warm air tends to rise, so when the upper atmosphere is cooler than the lower, it pushes the cool air down and the warm air up, carrying whatever pollutants are trapped in the lower level up and away from people. However, when the upper layer of air is as warm as, or warmer than the lower level, the air does not circulate vertically and the impurities remain in the lower level of air that people breathe. The issue is made worse for cities that are in the basins of valleys, surrounded by mountain ranges, because the mountains act as an additional barrier to air movement. Thus, cities that sit in valleys, and are in climates where it is warm and dry for much of the year, such as Los Angeles, suffer the harmful effects of air pollution more than other locales.

6▶ As smog has become an international issue, especially in connection with the potential of global warming—still a controversial and debated concept—attempts to limit its production have intensified. The Kyoto Protocol, named after the Japanese city where it was initially adopted, is the most well-known of recent efforts. The protocol called for member nations of the United Nations to establish policies that would contain, and ultimately reduce, emissions that lead to smog. However, the protocol has had mixed results. While 191 nations signed and ratified the protocol, some did not ratify, or formally agree to, the policy.

1. The word "notable" in paragraph 1 is closest in meaning to

ⓐ written
ⓑ significant
ⓒ measured
ⓓ ordinary

2. The word "adversely" in paragraph 1 is closest in meaning to

ⓐ carefully
ⓑ accidentally
ⓒ medically
ⓓ negatively

3. The word "promoted" in paragraph 2 is closest in meaning to

Ⓐ encouraged
Ⓑ announced
Ⓒ blocked
Ⓓ lifted

4 The word "poised" in paragraph 3 is closest in meaning to

Ⓐ interacting
Ⓑ sitting
Ⓒ blowing
Ⓓ poisoning

5. The word "hue" in paragraph 4 is closest in meaning to

Ⓐ color
Ⓑ odor
Ⓒ thickness
Ⓓ smoke

6. The word "hazardous" in paragraph 5 is closest in meaning to

Ⓐ healthy
Ⓑ safe
Ⓒ dangerous
Ⓓ visible

7. The word "intensified" in paragraph 6 is closest in meaning to

Ⓐ calmed
Ⓑ lengthened
Ⓒ aggravated
Ⓓ strengthened

8. The word "protocol" in paragraph 6 is closest in meaning to

Ⓐ manners
Ⓑ agreement
Ⓒ law
Ⓓ preciseness

READING

PASSAGE TWO (Questions 9–16)

Paragraph

Autism

1▶ Autism is one of a group of developmental disorders that are characterized by severe behavioral abnormalities across the following primary areas of functioning: social development, communication, and behavior. While it is a complex syndrome that is not currently well understood, autism seems to affect the processing of information in the brain by somehow disrupting the organization of the nervous system and the connections within it. In addition, there appears to be a genetic component to autism. However, it is not clear whether the causes of autism are gene mutations or highly unusual combinations of typical genetic variants. What is clear is that autistic sufferers perceive and react to normal stimuli in ways that are not thought of as typical by most of society.

2▶ The uncertain origins of autism often lead to controversy regarding its diagnosis. Part of the problem with diagnosing autism is that many of its defining traits commonly occur in the general population. For example, autistic toddlers, ages one to three, tend to make less eye contact and show lower ability to express themselves nonverbally than other young children of the same age. However, two- to three-year olds that have been raised in a highly stressful environment often display similar symptoms, making it difficult to attribute the behavior to a definite cause. In addition, older children and young adults demonstrate behaviors similar to responses connected with other disorders, such as anxiety disorders. Consequently, medical experts look for a broad range of symptoms that typically overlap the three areas of social development, communication, and behavior. When diagnosing autism, medical experts typically observe impaired social function, which manifests itself by a deficiency in social intuition. Autistics tend to smile less often, show decreased instances of eye contact, and respond less often when their own names are called. In addition, they demonstrate lower levels of social bonding, although they are likely to become very attached to their primary caretakers. This lack of social connection means they face

> Some words, such as *beneficial* and *violent* have positive or negative meanings associated with them. Understanding whether a word is positive, negative, or neutral in meaning can help you eliminate incorrect answer choices.
> Become familiar with Coxhead's Academic Word List (http://www.victoria.ac.nz/lals/resources/academicwordlist/). It will help you understand the TOEFL iBT® test passages better, and more specifically, help you to answer the vocabulary questions.

challenges in terms of making and maintaining friendships, which can result in higher levels of loneliness for them than their non-autistic peers.

3▶   An inability to develop sufficient natural speech to communicate at a level that meets their needs is another common symptom of the disorder. This symptom can often present itself in the first year of an infant's life, and is characterized by lower levels of common infant sounds, known as babbling, as well as unusual body language and reduced response to speech and movement directed at the autistic infant. The lack of communication skills may intensify as the child approaches the second and third year of life, displaying itself in lower levels of consonant, and word formation, along with less integration of words and corresponding movements. At this stage, many sufferers of autism may simply repeat the words they hear, a condition called echolalia, rather than spontaneously forming responses to speech directed at or around them.

4▶   Another hallmark of the condition is that autistic toddlers tend to engage in repetitive behavior that may be limited in scope. These behaviors can become ritualistic or compulsive in nature, meaning that the sufferer has to follow certain patterns of behavior in a certain arrangement, in order to maintain a sense of comfort and security in his environment. This tendency to repeat behaviors is often linked to a resistance to change, whether it is of schedules, immediate surroundings, or even objects within particular surroundings. In about 30 percent of autistic cases, certain behaviors can cause injury to the autistic or those around him, such as striking out or banging parts of his body against other objects.

5▶   In some cases, autistic children appear to develop normally in their first year, and then regress, though this is not common. Regardless of how the initial stage starts, once it begins, autism progresses consistently throughout childhood without remission. Obvious signs gradually show themselves in the first year of a child's life and become rooted between the second and third years; the disorder persists throughout adulthood, though it may present in a less obvious manner.

9. The word "component" in paragraph 1 is closest in meaning to
   - Ⓐ element
   - Ⓑ arrangement
   - Ⓒ ornament
   - Ⓓ disease

10. The word "controversy" in paragraph 2 is closest in meaning to
   - Ⓐ discussion
   - Ⓑ research
   - Ⓒ agreement
   - Ⓓ debate

11. The word "attribute" in paragraph 2 is closest in meaning to
   - Ⓐ pull
   - Ⓑ attach
   - Ⓒ take
   - Ⓓ commend

12. The word "primary" in paragraph 2 could best be replaced by
   - Ⓐ elementary
   - Ⓑ main
   - Ⓒ introductory
   - Ⓓ primitive

13. The word "sufficient" in paragraph 3 is closest in meaning to
   - Ⓐ important
   - Ⓑ abundant
   - Ⓒ enough
   - Ⓓ successive

14. The word "spontaneously" in paragraph 3 is closest in meaning to
   - Ⓐ intentionally
   - Ⓑ naturally
   - Ⓒ irregularly
   - Ⓓ repeatedly

15. The phrase "engage in" in paragraph 4 could best be replaced by
   - Ⓐ protest
   - Ⓑ start
   - Ⓒ use
   - Ⓓ determine

16. The word "persists" in paragraph 5 is closest in meaning to
   - Ⓐ lessens
   - Ⓑ worsens
   - Ⓒ stops
   - Ⓓ continues

Parasitic Plants

Paragraph

1►   Parasitic plants are plants that survive by using food from a host plant rather than producing their own food from the sun's energy. Because they do not need sunlight to survive, parasitic plants are generally found in shaded areas as opposed to areas exposed to direct sunlight. The plants can be classified in various ways; one of the most prevalent methods is by determining whether the plant depends wholly on its host (holoparasite) or has some degree of photosynthesis[1] ability (hemiparasite), which allows it to provide some of its own nutrients when necessary. Regardless of which classification a parasitic plant falls under, it does rely on a host plant for its primary means of sustenance. At times it may overtake its host, although the parasitic plant will rarely destroy the host entirely.

> Do not worry about understanding technical words. The TOEFL iBT® test does not ask questions about technical words. In fact, it generally provides definitions (see the glossary following this passage) for words that are specific to a passage.

2►   In addition to whether the parasite is a holoparasite or a hemiparasite, another important method of classification exists to differentiate various plants. This classification is used to recognize how the plant attaches itself to its host. A stem parasite connects to the host stem, often wrapping itself around the stem, whereas a root parasite joins with the root of the host. In both instances, the parasites attach themselves to the host plant by means of their own modified root system, a haustorium. The haustorium penetrates into the host plant and creates a vascular system that channels nutrients from the host plant to the parasite.

3►   In order for the parasitic plant to have the opportunity to thrive, it has to germinate, or sprout seeds close to the host plant whose nutrients it wishes to draw from. This can happen in multiple ways. New seeds may drop from existing plants adjacent to current host plants and their seedlings, creating an expanding area for new parasitic plants to bloom. In some cases, insects, birds, or small animals may transport tiny seeds from the parasites to new regions, where they may end up in proximity to new host plants that they can attach to for survival.

4►   Once the seeds are in the vicinity of a host plant, they also need a method to determine in which direction to grow to reach the host. Root parasitic plants generally use chemical clues dispersed into the soil by the host plant to determine the direction. For most root plants, they can only grow three to four millimeters without nutritional provision from the host plant, so it is imperative that root seeds fall in very close proximity to the host. Stem parasites, on the other hand, can grow several centimeters on their own, before requiring an attachment to the host plant. Thus, stem parasites do not need to sprout as close to the host as a root parasite does. In addition, while scientists have concluded that root parasites use chemical clues as a guide, they believe that stem parasites rely on odor and light to turn them in the appropriate direction.

5►   Seeds from the dodder, a stem parasite, can remain dormant for up to five years before they look for a host plant. Once awakened, the seed germinates above ground and then rapidly sends out stems in search of a host. A dodder seed has enough autonomous resources within its seed to survive for about six days. During this time, its stems can branch out up to six centimeters to reach a host plant. After the host plant is located, the dodder stem wraps itself around the host stem, moving in an upward direction and attaching its haustoria to several locations along the host plant's stem. In experiments performed with dodders and a variety of compatible host plants, experts have suggested dodders have a means to seek out plants with higher levels of sugar in them, which raises the parasite plant's chances of survival.

6►   There is an additional way in which parasitic plants can be categorized. Certain parasitic plants are considered generalists, attaching themselves to a diversity of host plants, while other parasites specialize in just a few, or even a single, type of host plants. The dodder is a generalist, choosing among several kinds of hosts. The world's heaviest

READING

flower, a species of rafflesia, is a specialist parasite that flourishes among, and lives off of, only the roots of jungle vines. Each of its ponderous blooms can weigh up to 15 pounds (7 kilograms) and can measure up to 3 feet (1 meter) across.

GLOSSARY

1. *photosynthesis*—a process in which green plants convert water and carbon dioxide into food when exposed to light

17. The phrase "as opposed to" in paragraph 1 is closest in meaning to
    - Ⓐ in conflict with
    - Ⓑ instead of
    - Ⓒ on the other side of
    - Ⓓ away from

18. The word "sustenance" in paragraph 1 is closest in meaning to
    - Ⓐ sunlight
    - Ⓑ protection
    - Ⓒ maturity
    - Ⓓ food

19. The word "channels" in paragraph 2 is closest in meaning to
    - Ⓐ carries
    - Ⓑ penetrates
    - Ⓒ creates
    - Ⓓ prevents

20. The word "adjacent" in paragraph 3 is closest in meaning to
    - Ⓐ connected
    - Ⓑ remote
    - Ⓒ away
    - Ⓓ near

21. The word "dispersed" in paragraph 4 could best be replaced by
    - Ⓐ contained
    - Ⓑ limited
    - Ⓒ spread
    - Ⓓ dug

22. The phrase "branch out" in paragraph 5 could best be replaced by
    - Ⓐ decline
    - Ⓑ collect
    - Ⓒ modify
    - Ⓓ extend

23. The word "compatible" in paragraph 5 could best be replaced by
    - Ⓐ suitable
    - Ⓑ related
    - Ⓒ inappropriate
    - Ⓓ solid

24. The word "diversity" in paragraph 6 could best be replaced by
    - Ⓐ uniformity
    - Ⓑ variety
    - Ⓒ adaptation
    - Ⓓ likeness

PASSAGE FOUR (Questions 25–32)

Paragraph

Edna Ferber

1▶ Edna Ferber (1887–1968) was a popular American novelist in the first half of the twentieth century. Growing up as the daughter of an immigrant father and U.S.-born mother, her Jewish heritage caused her to encounter numerous incidences of discrimination, though none were severe enough to hinder her from pursuing and achieving renown as an author. However, it was Ferber's gender more than her background that caused astonishment among the early readers of her stories. Many assumed from reading her first works that the author was a man hiding behind a female pseudonym, a false name, and were genuinely surprised to find out that the author was indeed female. This mistaken identity was a source of pride for Ferber, since she believed that it showed her work to be equal in quality to that of any man, and further reinforced her popularity as she consistently produced stories of the same high level.

2▶ Ferber initially planned to be a journalist and embarked on her career by working as a newspaper reporter in Wisconsin. While she was recovering from a period of sickness during this point in her career, Ferber decided to try her hand at writing fiction. Her first novel, *Dawn O'Hara, the Girl Who Laughed*, was published in 1911, when she was only 24 years old. By the following year, the prolific author's short stories were being collected and marketed in book form.

3▶   Although Ferber achieved rapid preliminary success with her fictional writing, it was not enough to sustain a living, so she continued in her career in journalism for a number of years after her early stories came out. During this time she was able to expand her newspaper writing beyond the local level to the national level. She covered major media events such as both the Democratic and Republican National Conventions of 1920, which preceded the presidential election of that same year. This work, in addition to her fiction writing, not only permitted her to support herself, but also bolstered her reputation as a flexible writer.

4▶   Her big break came with the novel *So Big* (1924), which was awarded the Pulitzer Prize in Literature in the subsequent year and was quickly adapted into a silent film. The main conflict in the novel is between a mother who places a high value on work and honor and a son who repudiates his mother's values, instead preferring the easier path to fortune and celebrity. Like many of Ferber's novels, this novel features a tenacious female protagonist with strong character who struggles to deal with ethical dilemmas about the importance of status and money. Also like many of Ferber's writings, it contains a male character of markedly lesser moral strength who plays a prime role in the struggle of the female heroine.

5▶   Probably the best known of Ferber's novels was *Show Boat* (1926), which tells the story of a Southern woman married to a charismatic but irresponsible man who leaves her with a daughter she must take great pains to support. In 1927, the novel was made into a musical that has endured to the present; yet this was a production that Ferber at first declined. Her fear was that the tone and meaning of her novel would be made light of in the contemporary style of musicals being produced. It was only when the producer, Jerome Kern, assured her that the production would convey the original intent of her novel, that she agreed to collaborate on the musical.

6▶   In addition to *So Big*, well-known novels by Ferber that were made into films include *Cimarron* (1930), which won an Academy Award, and *Giant* (1952). Both *So Big* and *Cimarron* have been remade, with the first "talkie" version of *So Big* in 1932 and a more prominent version in 1953, and a remake of *Cimarron* in 1960.

7▶   One can speculate on whether Ferber's tendency to write novels with weak males was a reflection of what she observed in her own life or whether the strength of the female leads necessitated an equilibrium found by creating male counterparts for them that were lacking in their morals and work ethic. No definite link has been drawn from Ferber's personal life to that of her characters, since she never married and had no children. Nevertheless, it would certainly not be unreasonable to hypothesize that, within the framework of her writing, Ferber desired to present female role models of strength and independence to young women of her time, role models that they could aspire to become like.

25. The word "incidences" in paragraph 1 is closest in meaning to

ⒶⒶ occurrences
Ⓑ issues
Ⓒ problems
Ⓓ effects

26. The word "consistently" in paragraph 1 is closest in meaning to

Ⓐ occasionally
Ⓑ stubbornly
Ⓒ regularly
Ⓓ rarely

27. The phrase "embarked on" in paragraph 2 is closest in meaning to

Ⓐ took a trip to
Ⓑ started out on
Ⓒ improved upon
Ⓓ had an opinion about

28. The word "bolstered" in paragraph 3 is closest in meaning to

Ⓐ changed
Ⓑ damaged
Ⓒ strengthened
Ⓓ started

29. The word "repudiates" in paragraph 4 is closest in meaning to

Ⓐ refuses to accept
Ⓑ lives up to
Ⓒ tries to understand
Ⓓ makes the best of

30. The word "endured" in paragraph 5 is closest in meaning to

Ⓐ lasted
Ⓑ tested
Ⓒ waited
Ⓓ limited

31. The word "convey" in paragraph 5 is closest in meaning to

Ⓐ support
Ⓑ differentiate
Ⓒ transport
Ⓓ communicate

32. The word "equilibrium" in paragraph 7 could best be replaced by

Ⓐ balance
Ⓑ uniformity
Ⓒ distinction
Ⓓ similarity

Reading Skill 2: RECOGNIZE REFERENTS

The TOEFL iBT® test tests your ability to make connections between ideas through the use of pronouns and adjectives. The ideas you are asked to connect may be in the same sentence or may be in two consecutive sentences. You may be asked to determine the referent for a particular pronoun or adjective (the noun or noun phrase to which a pronoun or adjective refers is the referent). The referent usually comes before the pronoun or adjective being used, so it is important to pay careful attention to the context around both the pronoun or the adjective and the referent. Even though there aren't many referent questions in the Reading section—usually 1–2 per test—this is an important skill to develop to help you produce clear responses to the speaking and writing tasks on the test.

Reference Words	
Type of Word	**Examples**
third-person subject pronoun	*he, she, it, they*
third-person object pronoun	*him, her, it, them*
third-person possessive adjective	*his, her, its, their*
third-person possessive pronoun	*his, hers, theirs*
demonstrative pronoun*	*this, that, these, those*
relative pronoun	*who, whose, which, where, when, that*
quantifier*	*one, some, a few, many, several, few*
clause subordinator	*what, when, which*

* These words may sometimes be followed in the question by a noun that is included in the phrase (i.e., *this fact; many kinds*).

Strategies to Answer Referent Questions

- Determine what kind of reference word is being used (i.e., third-person pronoun, demonstrative pronoun, quantifier, etc.); eliminate any referents in the answers that do not match the type of pronoun or adjective in the question.

- Determine whether the reference word is singular or plural; eliminate any referents in the answers that do not match in number. For example, *this = the theory* is correct; *these ≠ the theory* (incorrect).

- Establish the context around both the referent and the reference word.

- Replace your answer choice with the reference word in the sentence where it is located to double check your answer.

Example

TOEFL IBT® TEST

PAUSE TEST SECTION EXIT

REVIEW HELP BACK NEXT

Question 1 of 12

HIDE TIME 00 : 18 : 38

More Available

Tornadoes

1▶ A tornado requires patterns of both cold and warm air in the same region in order to form. The most likely time for this to occur is during warm or hot weather when a thunderstorm is approaching. The tornado is created when warm, moist air rises from the ground and comes into contact with a mass of colder air at the bottom of a thundercloud. The rising air pushes against the colder air, and the rotation of the earth causes the air to spin, in much the same way that water in a sink spins as it goes down a drain.

2▶ As mentioned, tornadoes generally, but not always, develop in conjunction with a thunderstorm. Thunderstorms that result in tornadoes are referred to as supercells. Not all thunderstorms create tornadoes, but they do increase the risk, especially when other conditions, such as a cold front or low-level converging winds are also present. Because thunderstorms include the presence of large, often dark, clouds, these clouds get caught up in the tornado's swirling wind, which creates the menacing funnel that most people associate with danger and destruction of property.

3▶ The formation of a tornado occurs in an organized series of steps. The first stage occurs just before the onset of a thunderstorm, when the wind changes direction and increases its speed. As the wind moves faster and higher in altitude, it begins an invisible horizontal spin. Once the thunderstorm starts, rising air inside of the storm causes the spinning wind to become vertical, or to shift from side to side to an up and down position. The thunderstorm then surrounds this area of rotating air, which can vary in length. Clouds that have formed in the lower part of the thunderstorm convert into a wall of clouds that spins around the circling wind. Shortly after the completion of the previous step, the tornado develops.

4▶ A tornado is fed by warm, moist air in the atmosphere. The more warm, moist air there is, the longer the tornado can last. This phase of the tornado is referred to as its "mature" stage and can last from a few minutes to well over an hour. However, as the tornado uses up the warm, moist air, cooler air begins to wrap around the tornado. Once the cooler air completely surrounds the violent storm, it prevents the tornado from pulling in more warm air; as a result, the tornado weakens and eventually breaks apart.

5▶ The most perilous stage of the tornado is its mature stage. The pressure at the center of a tornado is much lower than that in the air surrounding the tornado. The low pressure creates a funnel in the middle of the tornado, which causes destruction by acting much like a vacuum cleaner and sucking up whatever is in its path. During this time, it has the force to tear apart buildings and toss large vehicles in the air as though they were sheets of paper. In many cases, people are alerted to the fact that a tornado is coming, either by watching the way clouds in the sky are forming, or by listening for a specific sound of the wind associated with tornadoes, which sounds very similar to a loud train whistle. Being aware of these warning signs allows people time to find shelter, though in some cases, the storm arrives with only a few minutes of warning before it begins its path of destruction.

6▶ Unfortunately, not all tornadoes provide such a clear indication of their arrival. The funnel clouds created can be completely hidden by heavy rain or dust that the wind picks up from the ground. When the funnels are concealed by these elements, it makes it very difficult, even for experts, to see the impending danger. Relatively weak tornadoes may even appear to be invisible, with the only sign of their existence being swirling clouds of dirt or debris at the bottom of the funnel, near the ground. These tornadoes are weaker because there is less moisture and fewer clouds in the air, yet they can still cause considerable damage to the areas they strike. In addition, people usually do not realize these types of weaker tornadoes have arrived until the damage begins, making escape more difficult.

7▶ Despite the obvious dangers of these powerful storms, their formation, strength, and size are of great interest to many people. Some amateurs and experts alike are referred to as "stormchasers" because they literally chase the storms in vehicles as they attempt to record their power and devastation.

READING

Look at an example of a referent question with a third-person subject pronoun. (See paragraph 2.)

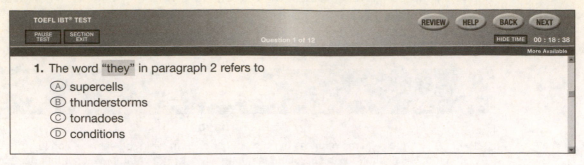

The second answer choice is correct. The sentence reads *Not all thunderstorms create tornadoes, but they do increase the risk. . . .* Both *thunderstorms* and *tornadoes* are plural nouns, but when you think about the logical meaning, it makes more sense that thunderstorms increase the risk of tornadoes. The first, third, and fourth answer choices are incorrect because, although they are plural nouns, they do not logically answer the question.

> Remember that on the TOEFL iBT® test, almost all referents are located before the pronouns or adjectives that refer back to them.

Now look at an example of a referent question with a relative pronoun. (See paragraph 3.)

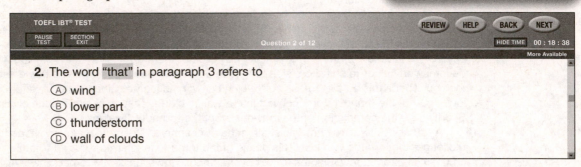

The fourth answer choice is correct. The sentence reads *clouds that have formed in the lower part of the thunderstorm convert into a wall of clouds that spins around. . . .* Looking at the context of the sentence, you can see *that* functions as a relative pronoun, introducing an adjective clause. The verb that follows, *spins*, is singular, so you must replace *that* with a singular noun. By looking at the context carefully, you can see that the most logical replacement is to say that the *wall* (of clouds) *spins around*. Therefore, the correct choice is *wall*. The first, second, and third answer choices are incorrect because, while they are all singular nouns, they do not logically answer the question.

Now look at an example of a referent question with a third-person possessive adjective. (See paragraph 4.)

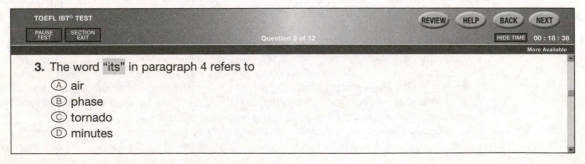

The third answer choice is correct. It is the tornado's *mature stage* that is being referred to, so the correct choice is *tornado*. The second answer choice is incorrect because the sentence reads *this phase of the tornado is referred to as its "mature" stage. . . .* Both *phase* and *stage* are synonyms, so logically *phase* doesn't fit. The first and fourth answer choices are incorrect because they do not logically answer the question.

Look at another example of a referent question with a relative pronoun. (See paragraph 5.)

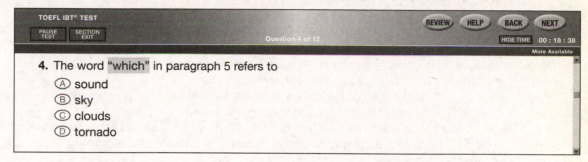

The first answer choice is correct. The sentence reads *. . . which sounds very similar to a loud train whistle.* By reading this part of the sentence, you can see that *sounds* is a singular verb that refers to making a noise like *a loud train whistle.* By reading the part of the sentence in front of this adjective clause *. . . either by watching the way clouds in the sky are forming, or by listening for a specific sound of the wind associated with tornadoes . . . ,* the logical context indicates that it is the *sound*, being used in this part of the sentence as a noun, that makes the noise. Therefore, the correct choice is *sound*. The third answer choice is incorrect because it is a plural noun. The second and fourth answer choices are incorrect because, while they are both singular nouns, they do not logically answer the question.

The following chart outlines the key points that you should remember about Referent Questions.

KEY POINTS FOR QUESTIONS ABOUT RECOGNIZING REFERENTS	
FREQUENCY	0–2 questions per reading section
WHERE TO FIND THE ANSWER	The word is highlighted in the passage. Most of the information for the answer is in the highlighted sentence. Occasionally, you may need to read a sentence before or after the highlighted word to help choose the best answer.
HOW TO ANSWER THE QUESTION	1. Read the entire sentence with the word in it; see if the referent is easy to understand. 2. Determine what kind of reference word is being used. 3. Determine whether the word is singular or plural. 4. Establish the context around both the referent and the reference word. 5. Plug in your answer choice in place of the reference word to double check your answer.

In the exam, you may be able to eliminate incorrect answer choices by understanding what is wrong with them.

For referent questions, incorrect answer choices may:
- not match the pronoun or adjective in number.
- not match pronoun or adjective in type (i.e., relative pronoun referring to an object vs. referent referring to a person).
- have the wrong meaning based on the context of the sentence.

READING EXERCISE 2: Study each of the passages and choose the best answers to the questions that follow.

PASSAGE ONE (Questions 1–8)

Paragraph   **Collective Behavior**

1▶   Many types of animals combine the advantages of family association with those conferred by membership in still larger groups. Bees congregate in hives; some fish move in schools; ants gather in mounds; wolves live in packs; deer associate in herds. This type of congregational, or collective, behavior gives animals such as these distinct advantages over other species that rely on more solitary behaviors. While defense of the group is a clear benefit for animals that gather in groups, another way collective species profit is through their system of foraging for food. Congregational species have developed methods, ranging from straightforward to complex, of searching for, obtaining, and transporting nutrients back to the "home" spot.

> When you are reading, always practice connecting pronouns and adjectives to their referents. This helps with general comprehension as well as with answering referent questions.

2▶   The behavior in which a group of social animals (or insects) imitates or copies the behavior of others is referred to as allelomimesis. During this behavioral activity, one member, or a small group, of the species discovers the initial food source. Through signals already familiar to the group, the location of the nutrient source is communicated to a larger group of the community. This group follows the signal to the food source, and if required, in turn communicates the location to yet another group. For example, bee colonies often send out small groups of bees that scout—look for—flowers that contain the essential nutrients they require. These scouts then return to the hive and through a complicated "dance" communicate the location of the flowers to others in the hive that can use the scout's information to obtain their own food. Allelomimesis is a commonly observed phenomenon in studies of insects such as bees, ants, and others.

3▶   Scientists and other experts have long assumed that certain collective species follow allelomimesis almost exclusively, but this is inaccurate. The original assumption resulted in the adoption of set parameters to describe this group behavior. Actions that fell within the parameters reinforced the notion that allelomimesis was the predominant foraging behavior, yet, this is, in fact, not the case. More recent research by scientists indicates that allelomimesis is not always the prevalent form of behavior for collective groups; individuals within these species do, at times, differ in their actions, even when working toward the common purpose of acquiring nutrients. Thus, foraging behaviors have now been more accurately categorized into what are known as explorative and sedentary strategies.

4▶   The differentiation of foraging strategies within a particular group seems to depend on factors such as the availability of adequate nutrients in the food supply. In other words, when a species detects an imbalance in nutrients, either instinctively, or through other natural mechanisms, their foraging strategy adapts in an attempt to compensate for this lack. For some members of a species, this displays itself through a more active role in searching for food, whereas in others, it results in a more passive reaction.

5▶   One species that has been studied in some detail regarding this phenomenon is the social caterpillar. When food sources are adequately balanced, the species follows the pattern of allelomimesis; each member of the group maintains a consistent level of foraging activity with others in the search for food. In contrast, when the source becomes imbalanced the species separates into two distinguishable categories of foragers: exploratory and sedentary. The observation of this phenomenon is fascinating, in that it shows behavior contradictory to what might be assumed. The more active caterpillars, the ones that take responsibility for finding food, spend less time consuming nutrients than their less active counterparts. These sedentary caterpillars move more moderately than the active caterpillars, yet they take in more food.

6▶   While it may seem that the more passive caterpillars take advantage of the active caterpillars, those that expend less energy in fact serve a vital function: maintaining group cohesion. One study, at least, suggests that colonies consisting of more active, as opposed to passive, caterpillars demonstrate less unity within their groups than when there are more passive than active ones. Apparently, because the active caterpillars tend to divide their resources among various plants to find nutrients, they lose focus on the group as a whole. On the other hand, the more sedentary caterpillars usually focus on one food source at a time. Therefore, they are able to keep the groups within the colony intact. Consequently, it seems a balanced proportion of active and passive caterpillars in a colony ensure that both the nutritional and communal needs of the colony are met.

1. The word "those" in paragraph 1 refers to
   Ⓐ types
   Ⓑ animals
   Ⓒ advantages
   Ⓓ groups

2. The word "they" in paragraph 2 refers to
   Ⓐ small groups
   Ⓑ flowers
   Ⓒ nutrients
   Ⓓ bee colonies

3. The word "others" in paragraph 2 refers to
   Ⓐ studies
   Ⓑ insects
   Ⓒ bees
   Ⓓ ants

4. The word "their" in paragraph 3 refers to
   Ⓐ collective groups
   Ⓑ species
   Ⓒ scientists
   Ⓓ individuals

5. The phrase "this lack" in paragraph 4 refers to
   Ⓐ imbalance in nutrients
   Ⓑ natural mechanisms
   Ⓒ foraging strategy
   Ⓓ attempt

6. The word "what" in paragraph 5 refers to
   Ⓐ foragers
   Ⓑ observation
   Ⓒ phenomenon
   Ⓓ behavior

7. The word "ones" in paragraph 6 refers to
   Ⓐ resources
   Ⓑ colonies
   Ⓒ caterpillars
   Ⓓ groups

8. The word "they" in paragraph 6 refers to
   Ⓐ active caterpillars
   Ⓑ resources
   Ⓒ groups
   Ⓓ sedentary caterpillars

PASSAGE TWO (Questions 9–16)

Paragraph   **The Smartphone Revolution**

1▶   Smartphones have rapidly increased their dominance in the mobile phone market in recent years, accounting for more than half of all mobile phones sold globally. These multifunctional devices have revolutionized the way in which users communicate, correspond, and interact with the world, and others, around them. Since smartphones have combined the tasks of previously separate devices into one exceptionally efficient product, their appeal to consumers cannot be overestimated. Prior to the modern development of the smartphone, people required a combination of machines, such as computers, televisions, PDAs (Personal Digital Assistants), and cameras to accomplish all of the functions that are currently handled with a single piece of technology.

2▶   While smartphones have only been in existence since the 1990s, the original concept was introduced in 1973 by Theodore Paraskevakos. In that year, the innovative entrepreneur obtained a patent for his idea of uniting the functions of data processing activities, intelligent applications, and visual displays with those of a telephone. At that time, Paraskevakos made note of such tasks as banking and bill paying in his outline; two commonplace activities many users today perform with their smartphones. Paraskevakos may have come up with his concept of an advanced phone as a result of his earlier success with transmitting electronic data through telephone lines, a process that became the foundation for the "Caller ID (Identification)" function available on virtually all contemporary phones. Since beginning his engineering work in 1968, Paraskevakos has obtained over 20 patents worldwide which are based on this technology.

3▶ Despite the fact that it took almost 20 years to bring the first smartphone to market, once it appeared, subsequent generations of enhanced versions have emerged with increasing frequency, offering consumers a variety of brands from which to choose. In 1992, the IBM Corporation demonstrated a prototype of a phone that incorporated PDA capabilities with traditional phone functions. A couple of years later, an improved version was put on the market for the public. By this time, several competitors were working on their own adaptations of what would later be called a "smartphone," and by the end of the first decade of the twenty-first century, the popularity of the smartphone approached that of its predecessor, the "feature" phone.

4▶ Though mobile phones are divided into three categories—those that provide only basic phone and text services, feature phones, and smartphones—the line between a feature phone and a smartphone is still somewhat blurred. In general, a feature phone differs from a smartphone in that it provides access to less functions than the smartphone does, although it does have a variety of functions over and above those of a basic mobile phone. One of the challenges of distinguishing between feature phones and smartphones is that, with the rapid evolution of successive generations of phones, the features exclusive to yesterday's smartphones are often found on today's feature phones. So while modern feature phones may still be behind in terms of the capabilities of their smartphone contemporaries, they may in fact be more advanced than smartphones of just a few years ago. For example, in the early part of the first decade of the twenty-first century, functions such as GPS (Global Positioning System) and Wi-Fi (Wireless Fidelity) access belonged solely to smartphones, whereas, by the end of that decade, many feature phones had evolved to include these functions.

5▶ One characteristic that most people agree differentiates smartphones from feature phones is the use of "apps," application programs designed specifically for the individual operating systems of smartphones. These apps are programs that can be downloaded directly onto the smartphone, or downloaded through a website. Apps have become one of the most popular features of smartphones in recent years, and cover a wide range of fields. Some apps, such as word processing or spreadsheet programs, help users complete tasks. Other apps provide information, such as weather or location. Still others are a source of entertainment, allowing for books and music to be downloaded, or for games to be played on the smartphone screen. For example, Angry Birds, one of the most popular apps on the market when it was created, was a game first devised for the Apple iPhone. Its enormous fame led to versions being devised for other smartphone operating systems, and then for other devices, such as computers and gaming consoles.

9. The word "their" in paragraph 1 refers to
   - (A) smartphones
   - (B) tasks
   - (C) separate devices
   - (D) consumers

10. The word "those" in paragraph 2 refers to
    - (A) intelligent applications
    - (B) functions
    - (C) data processing activities
    - (D) displays

11. The word "this technology" in paragraph 2 refers to
    - (A) contemporary phones
    - (B) telephone lines
    - (C) electronic data
    - (D) Caller ID

12. The phrase "an improved version" in paragraph 3 refers to
    - (A) a variety
    - (B) a phone
    - (C) a PDA
    - (D) a prototype

13. The word "its" in paragraph 3 refers to
    - (A) the first decade
    - (B) the public
    - (C) the smartphone
    - (D) the feature phone

14. The word "they" in paragraph 4 refers to
    - (A) feature phones
    - (B) capabilities
    - (C) contemporaries
    - (D) functions

15. The word "others" in paragraph 5 refers to

Ⓐ programs
Ⓑ tasks
Ⓒ apps
Ⓓ books

16. The word "Its" in paragraph 5 refers to

Ⓐ Angry Birds
Ⓑ the market
Ⓒ the Apple iPhone
Ⓓ a game

PASSAGE THREE (Questions 17–24)

Paragraph   **New World Epidemics**

1▶   When colonists from Europe traveled across the Atlantic to explore the New World, they never imagined what they would find, nor did they envision the devastation suffered by the native tribes of the Americas because of diseases that they carried with them. Though it was surely unintentional, these diseases effectively reduced well over half the population of Native American tribes, with some estimates claiming the loss of up to 95 percent of the original inhabitants of the New World.

> Some referent words have more than one function or meaning, such as *that*. Whenever you see these words, make sure you understand which meaning they express in the passage. This will help you to determine their referents.

2▶   This huge loss of life resulted from the introduction of Old World diseases into the Americas in the early sixteenth century. The inhabitants of the Americas were separated from Asia, Africa, and Europe by rising oceans following the Ice Ages, and, as a result, they were isolated by means of this watery barrier from numerous virulent epidemic diseases that had developed across the ocean, such as measles, smallpox, pneumonia, and malaria. While Pre-Columbian Americans did transmit infections among their own people, their living environment, which allowed them plenty of fresh air and wide-open spaces, meant they had a relatively disease-free environment when compared with residents of distinctly more crowded cities and towns in Europe. As a result of the lack of exposure to these more serious infections, native tribes lacked the antibodies needed to protect them from bacteria and viruses introduced into their environment by European settlers.

3▶   The most prevalent and deadly disease of this time period that affected Native Americans was probably smallpox. Smallpox is an infection that results in fever, painful sores, and ultimately death, without proper medication. Once this phenomenon was observed by Europeans, reactions varied from fascinated scientific interest to compassion, which led to educating the natives or conversely, to a calculated strategy for conquering the land by purposely spreading the disease. At least one British general, Lord Jeffrey Amherst, took advantage of the compromised immune systems of Native Americans to spread the disease. He employed the strategy during the French and Indian War (1756–1763) by distributing blankets that had been used by previous smallpox sufferers to unsuspecting Native Americans, who were likely grateful for what they viewed as a kindness shown to them.

4▶   Even though other Europeans may not have shared the brutal perspective of Amherst, nor his intentions to eliminate the New World's inhabitants, many believed they possessed innately superior immune systems to those of the Native Americans. Ignorant of the reality of how the human body develops resistance to infection and disease, Europeans were often convinced that their relative health in the New World was a spiritual indication that they were destined to conquer the land. This viewpoint was further reinforced as the Europeans witnessed the natives' often futile attempts to overcome the sickness with their natural remedies. The indigenous tribes attempted to adapt their homegrown medicines composed of plants, berries, tree bark, and other organic substances, but they often failed in these attempts. Used to living in communal environments, whether in small or large groups, Native Americans were slow to realize that quarantine, or isolation of the sick, was one of the most effective methods to slow or stop the spread of the disease. Eventually, compassionate

Europeans educated the native people and assisted them in finding better ways to combat the fatal infection, but not before a vast majority of them had been wiped out.

5►   Although smallpox may have been the most devastating disease, it was not the only one Native Americans contracted from Europeans. Colonists brought a variety of infections to the New World with them, including measles, tuberculosis, diphtheria, and influenza. Each of these presented new and seemingly insurmountable challenges to Native American populations, and each had its own tragic effect on the mortality rate of indigenous tribes. As with smallpox, the transfer of these diseases likely started slowly, rapidly increasing as more settlers arrived on the shores of the Americas and gradually pushed further inland. A widespread consensus among experts exists that indicates these various diseases reduced far greater numbers of native people in the New World than the many battles that were fought to gain control over the land.

17. The word "them" in paragraph 1 refers to
  Ⓐ native tribes
  Ⓑ diseases
  Ⓒ colonists
  Ⓓ Americas

18. The word "they" in paragraph 2 refers to
  Ⓐ the inhabitants
  Ⓑ epidemic diseases
  Ⓒ rising oceans
  Ⓓ the Ice Ages

19. The word "that" in paragraph 2 refers to
  Ⓐ a disease-free environment
  Ⓑ this watery barrier
  Ⓒ virulent epidemic diseases
  Ⓓ the ocean

20. The word "which" in paragraph 3 refers to
  Ⓐ scientific interest
  Ⓑ compassion
  Ⓒ reactions
  Ⓓ phenomenon

21. The word "who" in paragraph 3 refers to
  Ⓐ Lord Jeffrey Amherst
  Ⓑ sufferers
  Ⓒ blankets
  Ⓓ Native Americans

22. The word "those" in paragraph 4 refers to
  Ⓐ Europeans
  Ⓑ intentions
  Ⓒ immune systems
  Ⓓ inhabitants

23. The word "them" in paragraph 4 refers to
  Ⓐ effective methods
  Ⓑ Europeans
  Ⓒ native people
  Ⓓ better ways

24. The word "these" in paragraph 5 refers to
  Ⓐ Europeans
  Ⓑ colonists
  Ⓒ measles
  Ⓓ infections

PASSAGE FOUR (Questions 25–32)

Paragraph
Horatio Alger, Jr.

1►   Horatio Alger, Jr. (1832–1899) was the author of more than 100 books for boys in the second half of the nineteenth century; books that focused on the theme of success coming to those who work hard to achieve it. The majority of Alger's stories highlighted a "rags-to-riches" triumph based on integrity of character and persistent personal effort, a tendency that may have been influenced by Alger's childhood. Though Alger grew up as the eldest son of a respectable Massachusetts family, his early years were marked by financial struggle. As the namesake of his father, Horatio Alger, Sr., Alger's professional course was determined while he was still a youth: he was to follow in the path of his father, a Unitarian minister. Ultimately, Alger was not able to follow his father's wishes, instead becoming a highly popular writer of books for juvenile boys.

2►   Initially, Alger set out to be a minister, for which his father had prepared him. He graduated with honors from Harvard in 1852 and graduated from the Cambridge Divinity School eight years later. Alger did in fact serve as a minister in a congregation in Massachusetts for a short time, but his term of service ended abruptly in early 1866. This event resulted in Alger permanently moving to New York City in 1866 to devote his time to writing inspirational books for boys.

3▶ As an author, Alger established a recurring theme in virtually all of his stories. Typically, he wrote about the poor and homeless children of the slums of New York City, seeing them as unfortunate pawns of society, who, if only given the opportunity, could improve their lot. A general plotline that followed often was of a poor boy who managed to achieve a respectable and successful life by working hard and taking advantage of opportunities presented. Though his writing style was characterized by simplicity and repetition, it was at first well received by his target audience; his books were enormously popular, selling millions of copies well into the first few decades of the twentieth century.

4▶ There is widespread belief that Alger created his stories not only from his childhood observations, but also as a direct result of the environment he found himself in as an adult. Both in his ministry and his ensuing work as a tutor, the prominent author came across boys from opposite ends of the social classes. His constant championing of the poor youth rising above his circumstances through honesty, hard work and the generosity of an affluent benefactor may have stemmed from his hope of inspiring the youth around him to reach across social barriers and benefit one another. In his own life, Alger informally adopted young boys, usually impoverished, and took delight in their successes as they escaped the poor surroundings they had been born into.

5▶ Unfortunately for Alger, during the latter part of his lifetime, his novels experienced a decline in popularity, when he was criticized for his formulaic writing style, which critics claimed invariably presented the same plot, differing only in the settings and minor details, such as the names and occupations of the various characters. The writer added a darker tone of violence in an attempt to appeal to the new generation of youth he wanted to reach. However, this backfired on him, and as a result, librarians across the country declared his new works inappropriate for young boys, and called for restrictions on who could read his novels. By the end of Alger's life, his viewpoint had become so inconsequential that his death went nearly unnoticed outside of the circle of family and friends.

6▶ However, after Alger's death, a resurgence in the popularity of his work occurred in the early part of the twentieth century, with a bulk of his book sales coming from the first two decades of the 1900's. This revival of his popularity in turn inspired a number of organizations that recognize the extraordinary accomplishments of struggling youth. Thus, in spite of the fact that his works are rarely read in current times, his influence lives on through these groups that offer acknowledgement to individuals who persevere through adversity to achieve the "American Dream" of prosperity, one that is based on the principles outlined in Alger's writings.

25. The word "it" in paragraph 1 refers to
(A) the second half
(B) nineteenth century
(C) theme
(D) success

26. The phrase "this event" in paragraph 2 refers to
(A) serve as a minister
(B) congregation
(C) term of service ended
(D) moving to New York City

27. The word "them" in paragraph 3 refers to
(A) books
(B) children
(C) slums
(D) stories

28. The word "it" in paragraph 3 refers to
(A) simplicity
(B) style
(C) repetition
(D) audience

29. The word "his" in paragraph 4 refers to

Ⓐ poor youth
Ⓑ Alger
Ⓒ tutor
Ⓓ prominent author

30. The word "which" in paragraph 5 refers to

Ⓐ lifetime
Ⓑ popularity
Ⓒ writing style
Ⓓ plot

31. The word "this" in paragraph 5 refers to

Ⓐ names and occupations
Ⓑ a darker tone of violence
Ⓒ attempt to appeal to a new generation
Ⓓ youth he wanted to reach

32. The phrase "one" in paragraph 6 refers to

Ⓐ youth
Ⓑ adversity
Ⓒ the American Dream
Ⓓ prosperity

READING EXERCISE (Skills 1–2): Read the passage.

Paragraph

Coral Colonies

1▶   Coral colonies require a series of complicated events and circumstances to develop into the characteristically intricate reef structures for which they are known. These events and circumstances involve physical and chemical processes as well as delicate interactions among various animals and plants for coral colonies to thrive.

2▶   The basic element in the development of coralline reef structures is a group of animals from the Anthozoa class, called stony corals, that is closely related to jellyfish and sea anemones. These small polyps[1] (the individual animals that make up the coral reef), which are for the most part only a fraction of an inch in length, live in colonies made up of an immeasurable number of polyps clustered together. Each individual polyp obtains calcium from the seawater where it lives to create a skeleton around the lower part of its body, and the polyps attach themselves both to the living tissue and to the external skeletons of other polyps. Many polyps tend to retreat inside of their skeletons during hours of daylight and then stretch partially outside of their skeletons during hours of darkness to feed on minute plankton from the water around them. The mouth at the top of each body is surrounded by rings of tentacles used to grab onto food, and these rings of tentacles make the polyps look like flowers with rings of clustered petals; because of this, biologists for years thought that corals were plants rather than animals.

3▶   Once these coralline structures are established, they reproduce very quickly. They build in upward and outward directions to create a fringe of living coral surrounding the skeletal remnants of once-living coral. That coralline structures are commonplace in tropical waters around the world is due to the fact that they reproduce so quickly rather than the fact that they are hardy life-forms easily able to withstand external forces of nature. They cannot survive in water that is too dirty, and they need water that is at least 72° F (or 22° C) to exist, so they are formed only in waters ranging from 30° north to 30° south of the equator. They need a significant amount of sunlight, so they live only within an area between the surface of the ocean and a few meters beneath it. In addition, they require specific types of microscopic algae for their existence, and their skeletal shells are delicate in nature and are easily damaged or fragmented. They are also prey to other sea animals such as sponges and clams that bore into their skeletal structures and weaken them.

4▶   Coral colonies cannot build reef structures without considerable assistance. The many openings in and among the skeletons must be filled in and cemented together by material from around the colonies. The filling material often consists of fine sediments created either from the borings and waste of other animals around the coral or from the skeletons, shells, and remnants of dead plants and animals. The material that is used to cement the coral reefs comes from algae and other microscopic forms of seaweed.

GLOSSARY

1. *polyps*—simple sea animals with tube-shaped bodies

5▶	An additional part of the process of reef formation is the ongoing compaction and cementation that occurs throughout the process. Because of the soluble and delicate nature of the material from which coral is created, the relatively unstable crystals of corals and shells break down over time and are then rearranged as a more stable form of limestone.

6▶	The coralline structures that are created through these complicated processes are extremely variable in form. They may, for example, be treelike and branching, or they may have more rounded and compact shapes. What they share in common, however, is the extraordinary variety of plant and animal life-forms that are a necessary part of the ongoing process of their formation.

1. The word "they" in paragraph 1 refers to
   (A) coral colonies
   (B) events and circumstances
   (C) intricate reef structures
   (D) chemical processes

2. The word "that" in paragraph 2 refers to
   (A) the basic element
   (B) the development of coralline reef structures
   (C) a group of animals
   (D) the Anthozoa class

3. The phrase "an immeasurable number" in paragraph 2 is closest in meaning to
   (A) an exact integer
   (B) a huge quantity
   (C) a surprising total
   (D) a changing sum

4. The word "minute" in paragraph 2 could best be replaced by
   (A) tiny
   (B) light
   (C) timely
   (D) soft

5. The phrase "once-living" in paragraph 3 is closest in meaning to
   (A) aging
   (B) dead
   (C) growing
   (D) solitary

6. The word "hardy" in paragraph 3 is closest in meaning to
   (A) difficult
   (B) fragile
   (C) scarce
   (D) rugged

7. The word "They" in paragraph 3 refers to
   (A) coralline structures
   (B) upward and outward directions
   (C) skeletal remnants
   (D) external forces of nature

8. The word "them" in paragraph 3 refers to
   (A) sea animals
   (B) sponges and clams
   (C) skeletal structures
   (D) many openings

9. The word "borings" in paragraph 4 is closest in meaning to
   (A) dull pieces
   (B) strange creations
   (C) living beings
   (D) powdery remnants

10. The word "ongoing" in paragraph 5 is closest in meaning to
    (A) mobile
    (B) continuous
    (C) increasing
    (D) periodic

11. The phrase "break down" in paragraph 5 is closest in meaning to
    (A) cease functioning
    (B) interrupt
    (C) descend
    (D) decompose

12. The word "that" in paragraph 6 refers to
    (A) variety
    (B) life-forms
    (C) part
    (D) process

13. The word "their" in paragraph 6 refers to
    (A) coralline structures
    (B) complicated processes
    (C) rounded and more compact shapes
    (D) plant and animal life-forms

SENTENCES

Reading Skill 3: RECOGNIZE PARAPHRASES

Paraphrasing is the skill of communicating the same primary information in a different way, often using synonyms and changing the word and clause order in a sentence. It is an important skill to know for every section of the TOEFL iBT® test. In the Reading section of the test, you are asked to recognize sentence paraphrases. A sentence is highlighted in the passage and four possible answer choices are provided. You need to choose the paraphrase from the answers that is closest in meaning to the original sentence.

Because the sentences are almost always complex, an effective strategy is to look at the sentence in parts. (See the answer explanation for example question 1 below.)

Strategies to Answer Paraphrase Questions

- Use punctuation, such as commas, to break the sentence down into parts that are easier to understand.

- Identify any transitional words or phrases that can indicate time (*before, after, meanwhile, first, during, until, finally*); contrast (*however, but, similarly, instead, on the other hand*); addition (*also, in addition, moreover, as well as*); and so on.

- Look at the parts one by one and identify important information in each one.

Example

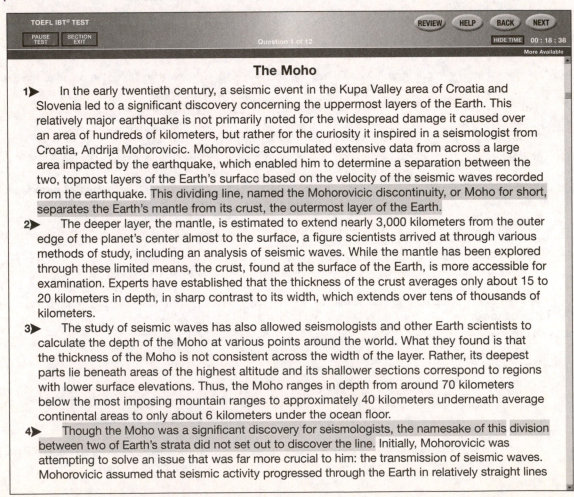

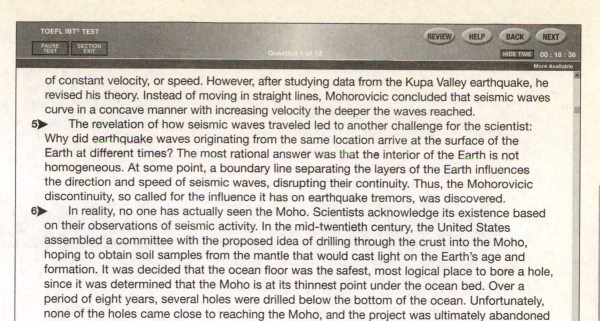

TOEFL IBT® TEST

PAUSE TEST   SECTION EXIT

REVIEW   HELP   BACK   NEXT

Question 1 of 12

HIDE TIME   00 : 18 : 38

More Available

of constant velocity, or speed. However, after studying data from the Kupa Valley earthquake, he revised his theory. Instead of moving in straight lines, Mohorovicic concluded that seismic waves curve in a concave manner with increasing velocity the deeper the waves reached.

5▶   The revelation of how seismic waves traveled led to another challenge for the scientist: Why did earthquake waves originating from the same location arrive at the surface of the Earth at different times? The most rational answer was that the interior of the Earth is not homogeneous. At some point, a boundary line separating the layers of the Earth influences the direction and speed of seismic waves, disrupting their continuity. Thus, the Mohorovicic discontinuity, so called for the influence it has on earthquake tremors, was discovered.

6▶   In reality, no one has actually seen the Moho. Scientists acknowledge its existence based on their observations of seismic activity. In the mid-twentieth century, the United States assembled a committee with the proposed idea of drilling through the crust into the Moho, hoping to obtain soil samples from the mantle that would cast light on the Earth's age and formation. It was decided that the ocean floor was the safest, most logical place to bore a hole, since it was determined that the Moho is at its thinnest point under the ocean bed. Over a period of eight years, several holes were drilled below the bottom of the ocean. Unfortunately, none of the holes came close to reaching the Moho, and the project was ultimately abandoned due to its excessive cost.

Now look at an example that asks you to choose the best paraphrase of a highlighted sentence in the passage. (See paragraph 1.)

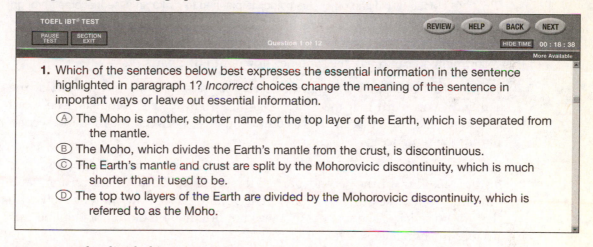

TOEFL IBT® TEST

PAUSE TEST   SECTION EXIT

REVIEW   HELP   BACK   NEXT

Question 1 of 12

HIDE TIME   00 : 18 : 38

More Available

1. Which of the sentences below best expresses the essential information in the sentence highlighted in paragraph 1? *Incorrect* choices change the meaning of the sentence in important ways or leave out essential information.

Ⓐ The Moho is another, shorter name for the top layer of the Earth, which is separated from the mantle.

Ⓑ The Moho, which divides the Earth's mantle from the crust, is discontinuous.

Ⓒ The Earth's mantle and crust are split by the Mohorovicic discontinuity, which is much shorter than it used to be.

Ⓓ The top two layers of the Earth are divided by the Mohorovicic discontinuity, which is referred to as the Moho.

This sentence can be divided into several parts.

- *This dividing line* refers to information in the previous sentence: *a separation between the two, topmost layers of the Earth's surface.* You learn from this information that the highlighted sentence states something about the separation.

- . . . *named the Mohorovicic discontinuity, or Moho for short*, tells you the name of the separation: "the Mohorovicic discontinuity." It also gives you another, shorter name for it: "Moho."

- . . . *separates the Earth's mantle from its crust*, indicates what two parts are being separated. You learn that the mantle and the crust are divided by the Moho.

- . . . *the outermost layer of the Earth* describes a characteristic of the crust. You learn in this part that the crust is the outer part of the Earth, which means that the mantle is the second layer of the Earth.

Therefore, the fourth answer choice is correct. The first answer choice is incorrect because the top layer of the Earth is the crust. It also mentions *Moho* as an abbreviation, but this is not essential information in the sentence. The second answer is incorrect because it confuses *discontinuity* with *discontinuous*. The third answer is incorrect because the sentence does not mention the length of the Moho.

Try to paraphrase the sentence for yourself before you look at the answer choices, then look for the answer that most closely matches the paraphrase you thought of.

Look at another example. (See paragraph 4.)

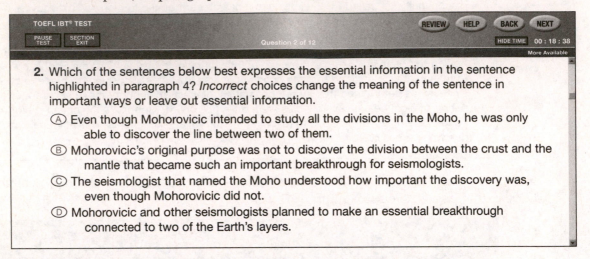

In this example, you can break the sentence down into two parts.

- *Though the Moho was a significant discovery for seismologists.* In this part of the sentence, you learn that the Moho was important to seismologists. The word "Though" indicates that there is a contrast in ideas between the first and second part of the sentence.

- *. . . the namesake of this division between two of the earth's strata did not set out to discover the line.* In the second part of the sentence, both "this division" and "the line" refer back to "the Moho." The second part of the sentence tells you that Mohorovicic ("the namesake") was not originally looking for the line that divides the two layers.

Therefore, the second answer choice is correct. The first answer choice is incorrect because *all the divisions in the Moho* inaccurately describes the Moho, and is not mentioned in the sentence. The third answer choice is incorrect because the seismologist that discovered it and Mohorovicic are the same person. The fourth answer choice is incorrect because the sentence states that Mohorovicic did not intend to discover the division.

Sometimes, the highlighted sentence refers to information in preceding or following sentences. In this case, you may need to read one or two sentences before or after the highlighted statement in order to have enough information to choose the correct answer.

The following chart outlines the key points that you should remember about how to Recognize Paraphrase questions.

KEY POINTS FOR QUESTIONS ABOUT RECOGNIZING PARAPHRASES

FREQUENCY	Never more than one question per reading passage (some passages do not contain this question type).
WHERE TO FIND THE ANSWER	The sentence is highlighted in the passage. Most of the information for the answer is in the highlighted sentence. Occasionally, you may need to read 1 or 2 sentences before or after the highlighted sentence to help you to choose the best answer.
HOW TO ANSWER THE QUESTION	1. Use punctuation, such as commas, to break the sentence down into parts that are easier to understand. 2. Identify any transitional words or phrases that can indicate time, contrast, addition, and so on. 3. Look at the parts one by one and identify important information in each one. 4. When necessary, read sentences immediately before and after the highlighted sentence for more information.

In the exam, you may be able to eliminate incorrect answer choices by understanding what is wrong with them.

For Recognizing Paraphrases questions, incorrect answer choices may:
- leave out important information.
- contain false information.
- add in information that may be true, but is not included in the original sentence.
- use many of the same words or terms but not relate the information accurately.

READING EXERCISE 3: Study each of the passages and choose the best answers to the questions that follow.

PASSAGE ONE (Questions 1–4)

Paragraph

Camouflage

1▶   Most people recognize camouflage for its utility as military protection. Camouflage is widely used to disguise soldiers on the front lines of a conflict from their opponents, and therefore, save the lives of the soldiers. However, camouflage as protection for soldiers is a relatively recent military innovation, and one that originated through imitating nature.

2▶   Camouflage did not originate with humans; rather, it is a highly varied adaptation copied from nature. As with many ideas that are considered modern and innovative, the concept of camouflage came about from observing how animals acted in the wild. As animals, insects, and other species evolved, weaker, slower prey developed creative means to avoid the predators that chased and killed them. For example, certain animals change their coats, the fur covering their skin, while other species take on the appearance or even sometimes the behavior of their predators to evade capture and death.

3▶   Camouflage is one of the most effective ways for animals to avoid attack in the treeless Arctic. However, the summer and winter landscapes there are so diverse that a single protective color scheme would, of course, prove ineffective in either one season or the other. Thus, many of the inhabitants of the Arctic tundra change their camouflage twice a year. The arctic fox is a clear-cut example of this phenomenon; it sports a brownish-gray coat in the summer which then turns white as cold weather sets in, and the process reverses itself in the springtime. Its brownish-gray coat blends in with the barren tundra landscape in the months without snow, and the white coat naturally blends in with the landscape of the frozen winter tundra.

4▶   Camouflaging falls under three broad categories: mimesis, crypsis, and dazzling, each of which provides a distinct advantage to the creature who has a specific adaptation, and each of which has evolved within particular species based on their requirements for survival. In mimesis, which is also referred to as "masquerade," the entire animal is disguised as some other creature or object which is of no interest to its enemy, such as when a grasshopper mimics an edible dry leaf. While mimesis is commonly practiced by animals targeted for prey, there are instances when a predator will take advantage of it; for example, the flower mantis, an insect, can successfully replicate the appearance of a certain flower, which allows this predator to draw in and devour its prey. The advantage of mimesis is that it allows animals to hide as they move around in the open.

5▶ Crypsis is a more diverse form of camouflage than mimesis. Crypsis allows the animal to hide by blending in with the background, making it extremely difficult to perceive the animal, especially when it stays still. Many insects and reptiles have this adaptation, changing color to blend into a background of leaves, trunks, or desert rocks. There are several other ways, in addition to changing color to melt into the background, that crypsis works in the wild. Animals such as leopards and giraffes use disruptive patterning, the bold marks on their coat, to blend into the trees of the forest or jungle. Other animals have evolved in such a way that they can eliminate the shadow from around their bodies; shadow is a definite indicator of the presence of an animal or object and may be a key element that predators track. The horned lizard, for instance, has developed a wide and flat body that allows it to lie virtually undetected against the ground of its natural habitat.

6▶ Dazzling is a less common form of camouflage than mimesis and crypsis that allows the animal to hide while in motion. Dazzling resembles the disruptive patterning of crypsis, but serves as a greater advantage to animals while they move. Whereas disruptive pattern may make an animal such as a giraffe more conspicuous when in motion, dazzling creates an illusion of distance and speed, a clear advantage for an animal being chased. Perhaps the most well-known example of an animal that makes use of dazzling is the zebra. It is often fairly simple to spot a single zebra while it is standing still. However, the distinctive black and white stripes can create a tremendous amount of confusion for a hunter pursing a fleeing herd of zebras. In a large group, the pattern of each zebra's stripes blends in with the stripes of the zebras around it, thus making it difficult for the predator to select a specific target, thus allowing the striped animals a greater chance of escape.

1. Which of the sentences below best expresses the essential information in the highlighted sentence in paragraph 2? *Incorrect* choices change the meaning in important ways or leave out essential information.
   Ⓐ Evolution resulted in strengthening aggressive animals and insects.
   Ⓑ Evolution of vulnerable species resulted in protective adaptations.
   Ⓒ A variety of species developed predatory abilities.
   Ⓓ By observing other species, weak animals and insects developed creative defense strategies.

2. Which of the sentences below best expresses the essential information in the highlighted sentence in paragraph 3? *Incorrect* choices change the meaning in important ways or leave out essential information.
   Ⓐ Opposite conditions in summer and in winter necessitate different protective coloration for Arctic animals.
   Ⓑ The coloration of the summer and winter landscapes in the Arctic fails to protect the Arctic tundra.
   Ⓒ In a single season, protective coloring schemes are ineffective in the treeless Arctic.
   Ⓓ For many animals, a single protective coloring scheme effectively protects them during summer and winter months.

3. Which of the sentences below best expresses the essential information in the highlighted sentence in paragraph 4? *Incorrect* choices change the meaning in important ways or leave out essential information.
   Ⓐ Mimesis is a popular strategy for predators, such as the flower mantises, who can more easily see their prey when they take on the appearance of particular flowers.
   Ⓑ Mimesis is usually used by animals being hunted, but sometimes hunters are able to employ the adaptation, as when the flower mantis disguises itself as a flower to catch its victim.
   Ⓒ Both predators and prey use mimesis as a means of disguise: the flower mantis is the most successful animal at disguising itself to catch its prey.
   Ⓓ Mimesis is generally used by prey to escape their predators; when predators such as the flower mantis use mimesis, the prey trap and eat the hunter.

4. Which of the sentences below best expresses the essential information in the highlighted sentence in paragraph 6? *Incorrect* choices change the meaning in important ways or leave out essential information.

Ⓐ A zebra in a large group is specifically targeted by predators due to its individual pattern of stripes.

Ⓑ Zebras can sometimes escape their pursuers because the pattern of stripes of the herd mixes together and confuses predators.

Ⓒ Predators have difficulty finding a herd of zebras because their stripes blend into the background.

Ⓓ The combined patterns of zebras' stripes can give the predators a greater chance of choosing the ones that can't escape.

PASSAGE TWO (Questions 5–9)

Paragraph

Post-it® Notes

1▶ One of the world's most well-known, and seemingly simple, products took several years and a series of unexpected yet fortunate events to come to light. The start of what would become Post-it® Notes came in the late 1960s at the 3M company in Minnesota quite by accident. Researchers at 3M were working on developing different types of adhesives, and one particularly weak adhesive, a compound of acrylate copolymer microspheres, was formulated. Employees at 3M were asked if they could think of a use for weak adhesive, which, provided it did not get dirty, could be reused. For several years the adhesive was shelved, as employees of the organization could not find a suitable, marketable use for the sticky substance. Yet, the mild adhesive stayed on the workers' minds, and years later, their persistence would pay off.

2▶ It wasn't until the mid-seventies that a 3M researcher thought of a practical and convenient use for the adhesive. Tired of losing his place in a book he used often, the researcher suggested his associate's sticky innovation could be applied to a piece of paper to be used as a bookmark that would stay in place in a book. Another use was found when the product was attached to a report that was to be sent to a coworker with a request for comments on the report; the colleague made his comments on the paper attached to the report and returned the report. Thus, the idea for Post-it® Notes was born.

3▶ It was decided within the company that there would be a test launch of the product in 1977 in four American cities. Sales of this innovative product in test cities were less than stellar, most likely because the product, while innovative, was also quite unfamiliar. A final attempt was then made in the city of Boise to introduce the product. In this attempt, 3M salesmen gave demonstrations of the product in offices throughout Boise while simultaneously offering free samples of the sticky notes to their audiences. When the salesmen returned a week later to the sites where the product had initially been demonstrated and handed out, a huge percentage of the office workers, having noted how useful the tiny adhesive pieces of paper were, showed great interest in purchasing the Post-it® Notes.

4▶ Interestingly, the use of yellow for the early notes also came about through chance. In their rush to test the original paper, 3M employees picked up scrap paper that had been discarded by another department and applied the adhesive to the back of the sheets. When testing and first taking the product to market, the company continued the use of canary yellow as the color of the notes, perhaps for consistency's sake, or perhaps because the bright color made it easy to distinguish when laid against the typical white of most book and report pages of the era.

5▶ Over time, 3M came to understand the huge potential of this new product, and over the next few decades more than 400 varieties of Post-it® products—in varying colors, shapes, and sizes—have been promoted, most with success that has paralleled the original product's showing in Boise. Other competitors noticed the remarkable success of the Post-it® products as well. When 3M's original patent on Post-Its® expired in the 1990s, rival companies flooded the market with products similar to those 3M had exclusively marketed for years. While the competitors are allowed to replicate the formula and general design of Post-it®Notes, there are two elements of the product that are off-limits: the name Post-it®, which has been copyrighted by 3M, and the initial color of original Post-its®, canary yellow, which 3M also claims sole use of.

6▶   Today, the use of Post-it®Notes has expanded beyond their primary functions as a convenient marker for extra notes and memos, and a placeholder for readers. Artists of all types have imagined diverse roles for the notes and have made them the central components of more than one art exhibit. The tiny colorful pieces of paper have been used to create art images, or served as the canvasses for portraits and murals. In the early 2000s, the play *Inside a Bigger Box* was opened in conjunction with an international art show consisting entirely of works inspired by or created with Post-it®Notes.

> Try to paraphrase the sentence part by part. Write down the main point of each part so you don't forget it when you move on to the next part.

5. Which of the sentences below best expresses the essential information in the highlighted sentence in paragraph 1? *Incorrect* choices change the meaning in important ways or leave out essential information.

Ⓐ Of the many adhesives that were being developed at 3M, one was not a particularly strong adhesive.

Ⓑ Researchers at 3M spent many years trying to develop a really weak adhesive.

Ⓒ Numerous weak adhesives resulted from a program to develop the strongest adhesive of all.

Ⓓ Researchers were assigned to develop different types of uses for acrylate copolymer microspheres.

6. Which of the sentences below best expresses the essential information in the highlighted sentence in paragraph 2? *Incorrect* choices change the meaning in important ways or leave out essential information.

Ⓐ The 3M company suggested applying for a patent on the product in a report prepared by a colleague.

Ⓑ One unexpectedly discovered use for the adhesive was in sending and receiving notes attached to documents.

Ⓒ A note was attached to a report asking for suggestions for uses of one of 3M's products.

Ⓓ A colleague who developed the new product kept notes with suggestions by other workers.

7. Which of the sentences below best expresses the essential information in the highlighted sentence in paragraph 3? *Incorrect* choices change the meaning in important ways or leave out essential information.

Ⓐ When the salesmen went back to the places where they had demonstrated Post-it® Notes, they discovered that many office workers had already purchased the product.

Ⓑ Though office workers found the small adhesive notes to be useful, the salesmen left after demonstrating and handing out the product.

Ⓒ Salesmen who showed the Post-it® Notes and left samples for office workers returned a week later to sell the product.

Ⓓ Many office workers wanted to buy the practical tiny sticky notes that salesmen had demonstrated and left samples of a week earlier.

8. Which of the sentences below best expresses the essential information in the highlighted sentence in paragraph 4? *Incorrect* choices change the meaning in important ways or leave out essential information.

Ⓐ The company tested the canary yellow color, but ultimately decided to continue to sell the notes in white, which was easier to distinguish at that time.

Ⓑ The canary yellow color showed itself to be popular in tests for books and reports, so the company used the same color for the Post-it® Notes when they first went to market.

Ⓒ The company had a choice of colors for the first Post-it® Notes but decided to use the bright yellow paper it had first chosen, since it would be consistent.

Ⓓ The company kept using the bright yellow for Post-it® Notes, even when the product was first sold, possibly because it wanted to keep the same color or maybe because it was a good contrast color for the notes.

9. Which of the sentences below best expresses the essential information in the highlighted sentence in paragraph 5? *Incorrect* choices change the meaning in important ways or leave out essential information.

Ⓐ Although competitors can replicate Post-it® Notes, they must change the colors and names of their products so they are not the same as those of 3M.

Ⓑ Competitors can use the same adhesive and shape of Post-it® Notes, but they are not allowed to use the name or the yellow color, both of which belong to 3M alone.

Ⓒ Competitors can produce notes like Post-it® Notes, but they cannot use the name, color, shape, or formula of the original.

Ⓓ Because Post-it® Notes are so competitive, only the shape and adhesive remain the same; the yellow color and name has changed.

Paragraph

The Pulitzer Prize

1▶   The Pulitzer Prize came about as part of an attempt by newspaperman Joseph T. Pulitzer to upgrade the profession of journalism. Pulitzer, the owner of the *New York World* and the *St. Louis Post-Dispatch*, made a proposal in 1903 to Columbia University to make a $2 million bequest to the university for the dual purposes of establishing a school of journalism at the university and also awarding prizes for exceptional work in journalism and other fields. However, the university did not initially respond as one might expect to such a seemingly generous offer.

2▶   Interestingly, Columbia University was not immediately amenable to the proposal by Pulitzer inasmuch as journalism was not held in high regard in general and Pulitzer's papers were more known for their sensationalization of the news than for the high quality of the journalism. The trustees of the university were not at all sure at first that they wanted a school of journalism because newspaper reporting was considered more of a trade than a profession at the time, and they did not want to diminish the academic prestige of their institution. It took years of discussion and negotiation to agree on the terms for establishing the school of journalism and the prizes bearing Pulitzer's name, and it was not actually until the year after Pulitzer's death in 1911 that construction began on the building to house Columbia's new school of journalism. The school of journalism opened in 1913, and the first prizes were awarded in 1917, for work done the previous year.

3▶   The method for selecting Pulitzer Prize winners and the categories for prizes have changed slightly over the years. Today, more than twenty-one different awards are given in three different areas, with the majority of awards going to journalists; fourteen of the awards are from various aspects of journalism (i.e., news reporting, feature writing, cartoons, and photography), six awards are given in letters (fiction, nonfiction, history, drama, poetry, and biography), and one award in music. Award categories are reevaluated and modified as modes of written communication have altered. Categories that become obsolete are eliminated; the category for telegraphic reporting, based on the telegram, was discontinued once the telegraph fell out of widespread use. Conversely, categories have expanded to include written work produced and presented through advancements in technology. For example, in 2008, the first online-only submissions were accepted for review. Prior to that, any work that was considered had to come originally from a printed source.

4▶   The process to achieve an award has several steps. First, the Pulitzer Prize hopeful submits his work for consideration. Anyone who has published work that meets the conditions for entry is allowed to submit his work, and the prize committees will not look at any publications that have not been formally entered. Columbia University appoints nominating juries comprising experts in each field, who carefully review each of the entries. The juries select the top three entries in each category that they feel are most qualified and they submit these nominations to the Pulitzer Prize Board, which makes the final decisions and awards the prizes. While there are various nominating juries for the different categories, a single board makes the decisions for all of the categories.

5▶   Because of its prestige, the Pulitzer Prize is one of the most sought after awards in writing. Winners are considered the best writers in their respective fields, and for this reason, thousands of authors submit their work each year, even though the monetary compensation for winning is relatively small. Past winners have used the positive publicity and reputation generated by the award to launch or strengthen their writing careers.

6▶   The award is not without its detractors, however. One of the most famous opponents of the award was Robert R. "Colonel" McCormick, former editor and publisher of the

A strong knowledge of synonyms, antonyms, and transitional words is essential for recognizing paraphrases. For example:
Synonyms: *significant = noteworthy, considerable, remarkable, memorable, important*
Antonyms: *significant ≠ superficial, unimportant, meaningless*
Transitional phrases: *however, in contrast, although, similarly, as a result, in fact, in addition*

READING

Chicago Tribune. He disputed the validity of the prize, feeling that it was little more than a bribe. As a result, McCormick would not honor any *Chicago Tribune* journalists who were named as winners. His stance against the Pulitzer Prize continued throughout his tenure at the newspaper, ending in 1961.

10. Which of the sentences below best expresses the essential information in the highlighted sentence in paragraph 1? *Incorrect* choices change the meaning in important ways or leave out essential information.

Ⓐ Joseph Pulitzer generously offered to donate a large sum of money to Columbia University for two specific purposes.

Ⓑ In 1903, an attempt was made by Joseph Pulitzer to halt the movement of the school of journalism and the journalism prizes from Columbia University.

Ⓒ Joseph Pulitzer requested that Columbia University donate a large sum of money to the *New York World* and the *St. Louis Post-Dispatch* for the purpose of establishing journalism scholarships and prizes.

Ⓓ In 1903, Joseph Pulitzer decided to give up his position as head of two newspapers to take over the department of journalism at Columbia University.

11. Which of the sentences below best expresses the essential information in the highlighted sentence in paragraph 2? *Incorrect* choices change the meaning in important ways or leave out essential information.

Ⓐ While the university immediately appreciated Pulitzer's proposal, they did not agree completely with him about the need to create a trade school for journalism.

Ⓑ University officials were unhappy about Pulitzer's offer because they believed the newspaper reports would damage the image of journalism at their institution.

Ⓒ Initially, the university was not interested in working with Pulitzer to establish journalism as a course of study because they did not consider newspaper reporting to be an acceptable profession, or one that would enhance the school's reputation.

Ⓓ The trustees were unclear about how the exchange of reporting with the Pulitzer newspapers would increase the quality of what was being taught in Columbia University's school of journalism.

12. Which of the sentences below best expresses the essential information in the highlighted sentence in paragraph 3? *Incorrect* choices change the meaning in important ways or leave out essential information.

Ⓐ Telegraphic reporting, an unpopular category, was taken off the list of prizes.

Ⓑ Categories that are no longer relevant, such as telegraphic reporting, are removed from the types of prizes awarded.

Ⓒ When a mode of written communication goes out of style, as telegraphic reporting did, its reward is significantly decreased.

Ⓓ It was nearly impossible to eliminate the telegraphic reporting category from the prize list once it was established.

13. Which of the sentences below best expresses the essential information in the highlighted sentence in paragraph 4? *Incorrect* choices change the meaning in important ways or leave out essential information.

Ⓐ The prize committee only evaluates official entries, though anyone who is eligible is allowed to enter.

Ⓑ Anyone who is a writer can ask the committee to look at his work.

Ⓒ Only certain writers that meet the strict conditions for entry can submit their work.

Ⓓ The prize committee selects works from the public to examine and award prizes to.

14. Which of the sentences below best expresses the essential information in the highlighted sentence in paragraph 5? *Incorrect* choices change the meaning in important ways or leave out essential information.

Ⓐ Though the amount of money won for the prize is pretty small, struggling writers still appreciate the financial recognition.

Ⓑ Writers who win the prize become the best in their field of writing, despite the lack of money won.

Ⓒ Winning writers become well-known for their work and gain a large financial windfall from the award.

Ⓓ Writers mainly submit their work for the boost it gives to their writing reputation, and not for the prize money.

Competition and Cooperation

Paragraph

1▶   Once viewed as two disparate behavioral patterns largely independent of one another, explanations of the interrelationship between competition and cooperation have evolved over time. Early research into competition and cooperation defined each of them in terms of the distribution of rewards related to each. Competition was defined as a situation in which rewards are dispensed unequally on the basis of performance; cooperation, on the other hand, was defined as a situation in which rewards are distributed in a primarily equitable manner on the basis of mutual interactive behavior among individuals. By this definition, a competitive situation requires at least one competitor to fail for each competitor that wins, while a cooperative situation offers a reward only if all members of a group receive it.

2▶   Researchers have found definitions of these two conditions based upon rewards inadequate, primarily due to the fact that definitions of these two concepts with reward distribution as the distinctive difference have depicted competition and cooperation as opposites. In current understanding, competition is not viewed as the opposite of cooperation; instead cooperation is perceived as an integral component of competition. Cooperation is necessary among team members, perhaps in a sporting event or in a political race, in order to win the competition. To take the idea a step further, cooperation is of great significance between opposing teams as well, inasmuch as the competing sides need to be in agreement regarding the basic ground rules of the game or election that each are striving to win.

3▶   Interestingly, the word "competition" is derived from a Latin verb which means "to come together." An understanding of the derivation of the word "competition" further supports the understanding that cooperation, rather than evoking a characteristic at the opposite extreme of human nature from competition, is in reality a necessary factor in competition. If the structure of a competition is analyzed more deeply, it is easily seen that, in fact, virtually all competitions require that two or more parties meet in order to begin the contest. This, in and of itself, requires a sense of cooperation to achieve.

4▶   A societal expectation of social cohesion also influences the state of competition and its connection to cooperation. While the vast majority of people have an inherent sense of individual self-interest, this desire to put one's own wants and needs ahead of those of others is softened by the desire for social connection and acceptance. In other words, although a person may want to make accomplishing his goals and "winning" his competitions the priority, he realizes that doing so may destroy social connections with friends and family, connections that he values more than achieving his individual goals. For this reason, people often modify their competitive nature to allow for more cooperative actions, so that others in their social circles have the chance to achieve at relatively similar levels of success.

5▶   However, even with the motivation of social cohesion influencing the competitive mindset and moving it more toward a collaborative way of thinking, this does not mean that competitors always become strictly cooperative within their close social circles. Although a competitor may moderate his achievements to remain inside the socially acceptable levels of his circle of family and friends, he may still want to be at the top of that circle. This typically translates to competition within the circle in which a competitor or group of competitors attains the position of "winner" within the social grouping and then maintains a stable level of achievement so as not to outshine the group by too much. Another option is that the "winner" becomes more cooperative with others of his group in order to help them reach his level; subsequently, the competitors can begin a new round of competition to reach higher goals.

6▶   In social groupings where a competitor violates these intrinsic guidelines, whether intentionally or by accident, the competitor can find himself isolated from the rest of the group. In this scenario, the competitor has a few options to choose from: he can alter his behavior to bring him back to a level found suitable by the rest of the group; he can accept the terms of the isolation as a necessary sacrifice for satisfying his individual self-interest;

or he can seek out a new social group that he is more compatible with. However, even within the new group, the competitor has to adjust himself to the balance of cooperation and competition modeled by this group as a whole.

15. Which of the sentences below best expresses the essential information in the highlighted sentence in paragraph 1? *Incorrect* choices change the meaning in important ways or leave out essential information.

    Ⓐ Unequal rewards for competition should be distributed equally to achieve cooperation.

    Ⓑ Earlier definitions of competition and cooperation described them in basically the same way.

    Ⓒ Competition and cooperation were seen as opposites, with rewards distributed equally to those who competed and unequally to those who cooperated.

    Ⓓ Competition was defined in terms of unequal distribution of rewards and cooperation in terms of equal distribution of rewards.

16. Which of the sentences below best expresses the essential information in the highlighted sentence in paragraph 2? *Incorrect* choices change the meaning in important ways or leave out essential information.

    Ⓐ It does not work well to define competition and cooperation in terms of rewards because definitions of this type incorrectly indicate that the two are opposites.

    Ⓑ Researchers tend to define competition and cooperation on the basis of rewards because this shows how the two differ.

    Ⓒ Researchers are looking for ways to define cooperation and competition in terms of rewards but have so far not been able to come up with definitions.

    Ⓓ Research has shown that the optimal definitions of competition and cooperation are those indicating that the two are opposites.

17. Which of the sentences below best expresses the essential information in the highlighted sentence in paragraph 3? *Incorrect* choices change the meaning in important ways or leave out essential information.

    Ⓐ "Competition" and "cooperation" are virtually synonyms due to the origins of each word.

    Ⓑ Despite the meaning of "competition," research has shown that it is the extreme opposite in meaning to "cooperation."

    Ⓒ One can recognize that cooperation is closely connected to competition though examining the origins of the word "competition."

    Ⓓ People with characteristics at the opposite ends of human nature have found an essential connection by understanding the beginnings of the word "competition" and the principle of cooperation.

18. Which of the sentences below best expresses the essential information in the highlighted sentence in paragraph 4? *Incorrect* choices change the meaning in important ways or leave out essential information.

    Ⓐ People who show a strong sense of self-interest are more likely to have weak social connections and acceptances.

    Ⓑ Although it is difficult for inherently selfish people to develop close, accepting social relationships, they manage to connect to others.

    Ⓒ People who demonstrate less self-interest typically do not connect with those who demonstrate more self-interest.

    Ⓓ Even though most people want to take care of their own needs first, the desire for a connection to, and acceptance from others helps them to be less selfish.

19. Which of the sentences below best expresses the essential information in the highlighted sentence in paragraph 5? *Incorrect* choices change the meaning in important ways or leave out essential information.

    Ⓐ However, social cohesion encourages competitors to move in the direction of more cooperative actions within their social circles.

    Ⓑ Nevertheless, competitors do not become exclusively cooperative in their actions within their close social group, in spite of the effect of social cohesion on behavior.

    Ⓒ In contrast, competitors move closer to social cohesion within their circle of friends and family by being strictly cooperative in their actions.

    Ⓓ Competitors influence the bond of social cohesion within the group through their cooperative behavior, although it is not always strictly collaborative.

Reading Skill 4: INSERT SENTENCES INTO THE PASSAGE

TheTOEFL iBT® test asks you to insert a sentence into the passage to assess your skill at understanding the logical organization of a passage as well as the logical and grammatical connections between sentences in a passage. On the test, you are given a choice of four locations indicated by black squares where you can insert the bolded sentence from the question. The locations are at the beginning or the end of sentences. Usually the sentences are in the same paragraph, but occasionally they may be in two consecutive paragraphs, typically at the end of one paragraph and the beginning of the next one. To insert the sentence, click on a square. The sentence will be placed at the location of that square and highlighted.

Strategies to Answer Sentence Insertion Questions

- Read the sentence to determine if it is stating a general idea or is talking about a specific example or detail. General ideas usually occur toward the beginning of the paragraph; an example or detail will typically be one of the sentences after the main idea sentence of a paragraph.

- Look for referents, pronouns, or adjectives within the sentence that can be connected to an idea(s) in one of the sentences marked with a black square (refer to the Reference Words chart on page 22 in Reading Skill 2 for more information on these words).

- Look for connections between singular and plural nouns or pronouns in the bolded sentence in the question to be inserted and the marked sentences in the passage.

- Look for transitional words or phrases (see chart below) that establish a relationship between ideas in the sentence in the question and the marked sentences in the passage.

- Once you click on the black square where you think the bolded sentence should be placed and it is inserted into the paragraph, read the sentence before the inserted sentence, and the sentence after to double check that you have placed it in the best location.

Transitional Words and Phrases	
Contrast	*however; although; contrary to; on the contrary; in contrast to; on the other hand*
Similarity	*similarly; likewise; in the same way; like; as*
Addition of Ideas	*and; also; as well; in addition; further; furthermore; moreover*
Examples	*for example; for instance*
Sequence	*first; next; afterward; subsequently; then; finally*
Result	*therefore; as a result; consequently; thus; hence*

Example

Games

1▶   Games and competitive activities have been an integral part of many societies for thousands of years. Though the exact date of when games started is impossible to trace, it is assumed that they were initiated as a means of entertainment and relaxation. They may also have developed as a method of distinguishing which members of a group had superior skills, whether physical or mental, which could contribute to the survival and prosperity of the entire group.

2▶   **1A** Games fall under two broad categories: those that primarily require physical skills, such as wrestling or soccer, or those that focus more on mental skills, like board games or cards. **1B** Certainly physical competitions involve the use of intelligent strategy to plan out the best moves to make, such as calculating how to get a ball past the opponents' team to the goal. **1C** In a similar way, games that emphasize mental abilities may also require some sort of physical skill, especially in terms of making quick moves. **1D** Therefore, it is fair to say that, though there are distinct categories of games, there are shared similarities among most games.

3▶   In general, for a game to exist, an individual or group must be competing against something, typically another individual or group. Each competition involves guidelines that all players must adhere to in order to advance in the game. **2A** Virtually all games have some sort of ranking system, many of these involving the awarding of points for attaining a certain level or goal. **2B** Competitors who use successful strategies while following the rules of the game get more points or a higher ranking. **2C** Likewise, unsuccessful tactics cause players to fall behind their competitors. **2D** Finally, almost every game involves some sort of risk. The risk involved in ancient games may be relatively small by today's standards, as in a gain or loss of status or reputation within a group, or it may have been larger, involving a gain or loss of power, money, or possessions. This risk, which most likely originated as a method to promote survival, is what today still motivates players to do their best in the competition.

4▶   **3A** Card games are a prime example of how societies evolve over time. **3B** Many experts trace the origin of cards back to ancient China, around the time the Chinese began using sheets of paper for writing instead of rolls of paper. **3C** The smaller sheets of paper made it convenient to develop portable card games in which the pieces could be easily replicated and carried from place to place. **3D** This portability permitted the transfer of card games across multiple cultures as traders and travelers from various countries would meet and pass the time together sharing games on the road.

5▶   Card games also reveal cultural values. One common similarity among card games is that there are suits, or sets of cards, within each deck. Each suit has a certain amount of cards with the same symbol, though the number of symbols on each card might vary. For example, the traditional American deck of cards has four suits of 13 cards each: hearts, spades, clubs, and diamonds. **4A** In some cultures the suits are represented with money symbols, and in others, with deities or objects considered valuable or spiritually significant. **4B** Some experts argue that examining cards from a certain era of a particular society can be a window into what the society viewed as necessary or worthy.

6▶   **4C** When cards were first created, they had to be made by hand, a time consuming process. It was also expensive, which meant that, initially, card games were a privilege of the rich. **4D** The invention of the printing press resulted in an easier and much cheaper reproduction of cards, which made them more accessible and more popular among the working classes of society as well. The accessibility of cards not only accounted for the widespread circulation of card games, but also brought along with it the symbols of importance within a culture. For instance, as Europeans brought cards to the Americas, the cards retained the powerful images of kings, queens, and princes on cards of higher value. These symbols remain a reminder of the original power structures that were common in many countries in the Western Hemisphere.

Look at an example of a sentence that can be inserted into the passage. (See paragraph 2.)

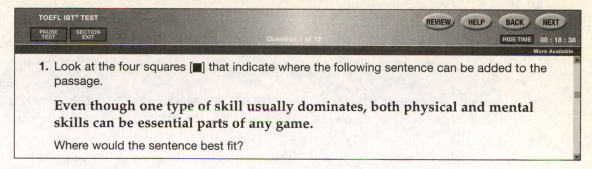

To answer this question, you need to decide the best place in paragraph 2 *to add* the sentence.

When you read the sentence, you will notice that the first part of the sentence says, *Even though one type of skill* (physical or mental) *usually dominates. . . .* Therefore, a connection to the previous sentence can be made in which physical and mental skills are mentioned separately.

The last part of the sentence mentions that *both physical and mental skills are essential parts of any game*. Therefore, a connection can be made to the sentences following this one, which explain how a physical game uses mental skills and a mental game uses physical skills.

Using this information, and looking at the context of the paragraph, you can see that the best choice to place this sentence is (1B). You should click on (1B) to insert the sentence in the correct location.

Look at another example of a sentence that can be inserted into the passage. (See paragraph 3.)

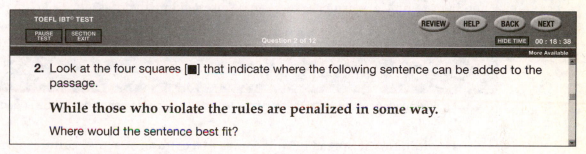

To answer this question, you need to decide the best place in paragraph 3 *to add* the sentence.

The first words of this sentence are *While those* [people] *who*, which indicate a contrast to the people who were mentioned in a previous sentence by using the word "While." It also indicates that this sentence is expressing a detail, not a main idea, and might be less appropriate as the first sentence.

The phrase *the rules* is also a clue. Since this sentence does not describe specifically what kind of rules, it means that the rules were probably mentioned in a previous sentence as well.

The sentence following (2C) says, *Likewise unsuccessful tactics cause players to fall behind their competitors.* "Likewise" in this context connects this sentence to the insertion sentence because *those* (players) *who . . . are penalized in some way* for not following the rules are like those players who use unsuccessful tactics in that both of them will fall behind their competitors. In other words, both of these types of players are being compared and these sentences can be connected by understanding the use of the transitional word "Likewise." Therefore, this sentence needs to be placed between (2B) and (2C). You should click on (2C) to insert the sentence in the correct location.

Look at another example of a sentence that can be inserted into the passage. (See paragraph 4.)

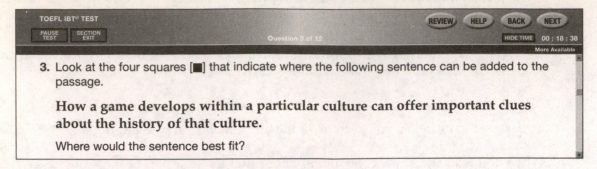

TOEFL IBT® TEST

PAUSE TEST   SECTION EXIT

REVIEW   HELP   BACK   NEXT

Question 3 of 12

HIDE TIME   00 : 18 : 38

More Available

3. Look at the four squares [■] that indicate where the following sentence can be added to the passage.

How a game develops within a particular culture can offer important clues about the history of that culture.

Where would the sentence best fit?

To answer this question, you need to decide the best place in paragraph 4 *to add* the sentence.

The first words of this sentence are *How a game develops*, which tells us that we are describing a method. To understand whether this sentence refers to a main idea or details, you need to skim the sentence choices in paragraph 4. All of the sentence choices discuss a specific category of games (*card games*).

Since the sentence you are inserting mentions games in general, it is a main idea sentence, and should be placed at the beginning of the paragraph, in front of sentence (3A). You should click on (3A) to insert the sentence in the correct location. You will also notice the insertion sentence mentions *the history of that culture* which connects it to the idea of *societies* evolving or changing *over time* in the sentence following (3A).

Look at another example of a sentence that can be inserted into the passage. (See paragraphs 5–6.)

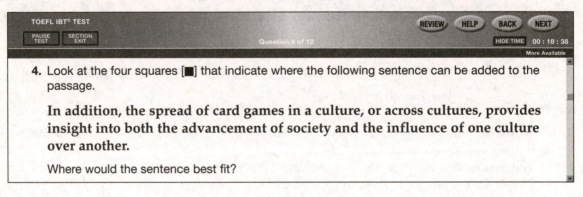

TOEFL IBT® TEST

PAUSE TEST   SECTION EXIT

REVIEW   HELP   BACK   NEXT

Question 4 of 12

HIDE TIME   00 : 18 : 38

More Available

4. Look at the four squares [■] that indicate where the following sentence can be added to the passage.

In addition, the spread of card games in a culture, or across cultures, provides insight into both the advancement of society and the influence of one culture over another.

Where would the sentence best fit?

To answer this question, you need to decide the best place in paragraph 5 or 6 *to add* the sentence.

The beginning of the sentence reads *In addition, the spread of card games . . . In addition* tells you that this is not the first idea discussed about the *spread of card games*. The latter part of the sentence mentions *both the advancement of society and the influence of one culture over another*. This indicates that this sentence should come in front of examples of how card games helped society move forward, as well as how cultures influenced one another through card games. The sentence introduces the two above mentioned concepts, so it is a main idea sentence and therefore, would most likely be at the beginning of a paragraph.

When you read and understand the context of the sentences where you can choose to place the insertion sentence, you see that paragraph 6 provides an example of society advancing when it mentions how card games spread through societal classes (*The . . . printing press . . . made them more accessible . . . among the working classes . . .*). In paragraph 6, another example also mentions how cultures transferred important values (*The accessibility of the cards . . . also brought along with it the symbols of importance . . .*).

The best place to insert this sentence is at the beginning of paragraph 6, choice (4C). You should click on (4C) to insert the sentence in the correct location.

The following chart outlines the key points that you should remember about Inserting Sentences.

KEY POINTS FOR QUESTIONS ABOUT INSERTING SENTENCES	
FREQUENCY	Every reading passage includes just one.
WHERE TO FIND THE ANSWER	The squares are clearly marked in the passage. The test also usually automatically scrolls to the paragraph(s) with the squares.
HOW TO ANSWER THE QUESTION	1. Read the sentence to determine if it is stating a general idea or is talking about a specific example or detail. General ideas usually occur toward the beginning of the paragraph; an example or detail will typically follow the main idea sentence of a paragraph. 2. Look for referents, pronouns, or adjectives within the sentence that can be connected to an idea(s) in one of the sentences marked with a black square. 3. Look for connections between singular and plural nouns or pronouns in the sentence to be inserted and the marked sentences in the passage. 4. Look for transitional words or phrases (see chart above) that establish a relationship between ideas in the sentence in the question and the marked sentences in the passage. 5. Click on the square in front of the sentence in the passage where you want to place the insertion sentence. The insertion sentence is automatically placed in the passage and highlighted for you to see. 6. Once you click on the black square where you think the bolded sentence should be placed and it is inserted into the paragraph, read the sentence before, the inserted sentence, and the sentence after to double check that you have placed it in the best location. If you want to change the location, click on a different square and the insertion sentence will be moved.

In the exam, you may be able to eliminate incorrect answer choices by understanding what is wrong with them.

For Sentence Insertion questions, adding the sentence in incorrect locations may:
• interrupt the flow of ideas and separate sentences that belong together.
• insert referents, pronouns, adjectives, or transitional words and phrases that do not connect logically with the previous sentence.

READING EXERCISE 4: Study each of the passages and choose the best answers to the questions that follow.

PASSAGE ONE (Questions 1–4)

Pararaph   **Popcorn**

1▶   **1A** Popcorn was first discovered and harvested in the Central American region of present-day Guatemala thousands of years ago. Today, it has become a worldwide favorite, inspiring various added flavors and methods of heating the kernels so they "pop" into the fluffy softened texture that can easily be eaten. **1B** The Native Americans who brought popcorn to the attention of European explorers believed that the individual corn kernels contained spirits. **1C** For those long-ago tribes, popcorn was considered an essential and nutritious part of the diet; for popcorn-eaters today, the treat is thought of as more of a snack than a necessary element of healthy eating. **1D**

2▶   **2A** This traditional Native American dish was quite a novelty to newcomers to the Americas. Columbus and his sailors found natives in the West Indies wearing popcorn necklaces, and explorer Hernando Cortes described the use of popcorn amulets in the religious ceremonies of the Aztecs. **2B** The Aztecs may have believed that wearing the amulets brought them favor in the eyes of their gods. **2C** Bringing popcorn to the Thanksgiving celebration symbolized the respect these Native Americans had for the new settlers and the hope they had for unity with them. **2D** According to legendary descriptions of the celebratory meal, Quadequina, the brother of Chief Massasoit, contributed several deerskin bags of the popped treat to the celebration.

3▶   Popcorn differs from the corn generally eaten directly off the cob, also known as "sweet" corn, in that the kernels of popcorn have a hard nonporous exterior than is practically impenetrable by moisture and a dense starchy center. This combination of factors allows for the buildup of intense pressure inside each kernel when it is heated sufficiently which consequently causes an explosive pop that forces the center of each kernel out of the hull, or outside covering, and into a variety of popcorn "flakes," as popped kernels are known as. In contrast, sweet corn has a much softer, porous hull which moisture can penetrate quite easily, thus preventing sweet corn kernels from achieving the amount of internal pressure necessary to make them pop.

4▶   **3A** The popping of corn started with relatively primitive techniques that involved some sort of roasting of the kernels over an open fire. **3B** One method of popping corn involved skewering an ear of corn on a stick and roasting it until the kernels popped off the ear. **3C** Corn was also popped by first cutting the kernels off the cob, throwing them into a fire, and gathering them as they popped out of the fire. **3D** In another method for popping corn, sand and unpopped kernels of corn were mixed together in a cooking pot and heated until the corn popped to the surface of the sand in the heated pot. As can be imagined, these techniques resulted in significant amounts of popcorn being overcooked, lost to the open environment, or going unpopped.

5▶   Modern methods of popping corn have removed many of the frustrations of earlier methods. **4A** Households developed more efficient methods of popping corn in small amounts with the development of indoor stoves on which metal kettles and pots could be placed. **4B** Electric air poppers were introduced in the twentieth century as a healthy alternative to popcorn steeped in oil over the stove's heat. **4C** As microwave oven use became more widespread in the late part of the twentieth century, microwaving popcorn became one of the most convenient and favored methods of making the snack. **4D**

6▶   In addition to the rise in popularity of making popcorn at home, the commercial market also took on the challenge of figuring out ways to produce it in larger quantities. A commercial breakthrough for popping corn in large amounts was made in the latter part of the nineteenth century, with Charles Cretors's invention of a large-scale popcorn machine. Cretors's invention increased the uniform heating of the kernels in mass numbers, which allowed for fewer unpopped kernels and more profit for vendors. His popcorn machine served as the prototype for many commercial machines used at large venues, such as stadiums and movie theaters. Alongside the introduction of this new popcorn machine, which made way for freshly popped corn to be served at public events, F.W. Rueckheim presented the first flavored popcorn, caramel corn. This flavor maintains its popularity today, partly due to his brother Louis's modification of the recipe, which created the first commercially packaged flavored popcorn, Cracker Jack®.

1. Look at the four squares [■] that indicate where the following sentence could be added to the first paragraph of the passage.

Consequently, the ancient peoples gave the popped food positions of honor in various religious ceremonies in addition to enjoying its taste.

Where would the sentence best fit? Click on a square [■] to add the sentence to the passage.

2. Look at the four squares [■] that indicate where the following sentence could be added to the second paragraph of the passage.

A century after the early explorers, the Pilgrims at Plymouth may have been introduced to popcorn at the first Thanksgiving dinner by the Wampanoag tribe.

Where would the sentence best fit? Click on a square [■] to add the sentence to the passage.

3. Look at the four squares [■] that indicate where the following sentence could be added to the fourth paragraph of the passage.

This tasty treat has been popped for at least 5,000 years, using a variety of different methods.

Where would the sentence best fit? Click on a square [■] to add the sentence to the passage.

4. Look at the four squares [■] that indicate where the following sentence could be added to the fifth paragraph of the passage.

It remains a very popular method for preparing the snack, since the treat pops up ready-to-eat in just a few minutes.

Where would the sentence best fit? Click on a square [■] to add the sentence to the passage.

PASSAGE TWO (Questions 5–8)

Paragraphs

Lions

1▶ Something unusual about lions is that they hunt in groups. **5A** This may be in part because lions in particular are more social than other species; they travel and live together in a group called a pride, which is usually composed of related individuals. Prides range anywhere from 5 to 30 members, though they are more likely to fall on the smaller end of this range than the larger. **5B** Group hunting is beneficial to lions because it means that much larger prey can be captured by the lions. **5C** It also means that individual lions expend much less energy during a hunt. **5D**

2▶ There is a standard pattern to the process of hunting in groups. The process is initiated by a single female, who positions herself at a raised elevation to serve as a lookout to spot potential prey. **6A** When prey is spotted, a group of young lionesses advances on the herd and pushes the herd in the direction of a different lioness that has hidden herself downwind. **6B** It is up to this concealed female to choose the weakest member of the herd for the kill. **6C** Once the kill is made, the hunters decide whether to consume it on the spot or take it back to share with the other members of the pride. **6D** This decision is based on the size of the kill: smaller prey is devoured by the hunters immediately after the attack, while larger prey can be dragged back to be shared by the rest of the group.

3▶ The younger and stronger females are the ones that go on the attack for food. **7A** Although these females are at the peak of their health, speed, and strength, when compared to other creatures of the wild, their stamina is not as enduring. **7B** Therefore, it is imperative that the females are in close proximity to their prey before they charge in the final attack. **7C** Coordinating their movements to lead the victim downwind toward the main attacker lets the lionesses conserve their energy and strength for the final rush before the kill. **7D** It is also the reason that lionesses plan the hunts strategically, typically hunting under the cover of darkness or in areas where they are not easily spotted.

> Sentences that you insert into the passage do not change the meaning of the paragraph they are placed in. However, they can help you understand the ideas in that paragraph in more detail.

4▶ As can be seen from this description of the process, it is the females rather than the male or males in the pride that take part in the kill. There are several reasons why the females take the lead in the hunt for food. First, the typical pride consists of only 1 to 2 males, with the rest being females and cubs. As male cubs mature, they are pushed out of the pride, becoming solitary nomads, or joining other prides lacking male lions. On occasion, a male lion will make a solitary kill, one in which the single male takes down and consumes the prey. On these occasions, the male will not share his kill with other lions, though he does tend to insure that any larger kills brought back to the group by females are shared with the young cubs.

5▶ Another important factor that hinders males from hunting is their anatomy, specifically the large mane that flows from the top of their head down across their shoulders. The voluminous amount of fur is thick and heavy, not only weighing down the lion more than the mane-free females, but also increasing their body heat. This increase in body temperature can be hazardous during hunts, especially in the warm climates that most lions inhabit. Higher body temperatures can lead to exhaustion, depleting the energy of the male lion and providing a means of escape for its prey while at the same time leaving him vulnerable to attack from other animals.

6▶ **8A** The male lions, along with the older and weaker females that are no longer eligible to hunt, stay behind and protect the pride from intruders as the hunt is carried out. **8B** This is especially important when there are young cubs present that have not learned the skills to evade attack or appropriately protect themselves from outsiders. **8C** The male lions present an intimidating presence to other animals watching the pride, and the males will rise to the occasion and attack when necessary in order to protect the group for which they are responsible. **8D**

5. Look at the four squares [■] that indicate where the following sentence could be added to the first paragraph of the passage.

Other cats do not.

Where would the sentence best fit? Click on a square [■] to add the sentence to the passage.

6. Look at the four squares [■] that indicate where the following sentence could be added to the second paragraph of the passage.

This is usually accomplished by knocking the prey to the ground and breaking its neck.

Where would the sentence best fit? Click on a square [■] to add the sentence to the passage.

7. Look at the four squares [■] that indicate where the following sentence could be added to the third paragraph of the passage.

It is primarily for this reason that the females hunt in groups and spend a long time stalking their prey before the attack.

Where would the sentence best fit? Click on a square [■] to add the sentence to the passage.

8. Look at the four squares [■] that indicate where the following sentence could be added to the sixth paragraph of the passage.

Thus, the males have a defensive rather than an offensive role.

Where would the sentence best fit? Click on a square [■] to add the sentence to the passage.

PASSAGE THREE (Questions 9–12)

Paragraph   **Accidental Inventions**

1▶ The term "serendipity" is often defined as a "happy accident" or "pleasant surprise." Throughout the course of human innovation and invention, serendipity has played almost as significant a role in the discovery and application of new products as intentional planning and long-term experimentation has. A number of products that we commonly use today were developed quite by accident. There are many examples of this concept that came about when an insightful person realized a potential benefit in a negative situation.

2▶ One of these accidental inventions is the leotard, a close-fitting, one-piece garment worn today by dancers, gymnasts, and acrobats, as well as practitioners of Pilates, yoga, and other forms of exercise. **9A** In 1828, a circus performer named Nelson Hower was faced with the prospect of missing his performance because his costume was at the cleaners. **9B** Instead of canceling his part of the show, he decided to perform in his long underwear. Prior to Hower's wearing of the comparatively form-fitting underwear, acrobats and dancers wore more modest, looser fitting attire in which to perform, and even rehearse. **9C** Soon after the debut of Hower's outfit, other circus performers began performing the same way. **9D** When popular acrobat Jules Leotard adopted the style, it became known as the leotard.

Look for relationships between the key words in the highlighted sentence in the answer and transitional words in the sentences marked by the black squares that indicate comparison, contrast, or additional ideas.

3▶ The inventions of various new foods and beverages have also come about through serendipity. One example is the Popsicle®. **10A** In 1905, 11-year-old Frank Epperson stirred up a drink of fruit-flavored powder and soda and then mistakenly left the drink, with the spoon in it, out on the back porch until the next morning. **10B** As the temperature dropped overnight, the soda water froze around the spoon, creating a tasty treat. **10C** Years later, remembering how enjoyable the treat had been, Epperson went into business producing Popsicles. **10D**

4▶ Another success story involving food and chance is the invention of the chocolate chip cookie, today considered the most well-known type of cookie in the United States. Yet, it has only been around since about 1930 when Ruth Wakefield substituted broken pieces of chocolate bars for the baker's chocolate that she traditionally used but had run out of for making her already famous chocolate cookies. Instead of melting into the sweet, buttery cookie dough, as Wakefield had hoped, the small bits of chocolate remained separate from the rest of the dough, making a new delicious type of cookie that quickly gained popularity throughout the nation.

5▶ Some accidental discoveries have resulted in improvements to already existing products that increase their functionality or practical use for individual consumers. **11A** The inventor of Teflon®, a nonstick coating frequently applied to the surface of cooking implements to prevent food from sticking, had the original intention of devising a new refrigerant for producing cool temperatures. **11B** As the inventor, Roy Plunkett, experimented with the different properties of chemicals to create the cooling substance, he noticed an odd reaction occurring in one of the pressure bottles containing the chemical mixture. **11C** After cutting open the bottle to investigate further, Plunkett observed a waxy substance that was slippery to the touch. **11D** Though far from what he had intended to produce, the material sparked an idea in Plunkett and his employers, and Teflon was trademarked in 1945.

6▶ Like Teflon, Super Glue® started from the concept of something entirely different than the resulting product. During World War II, scientists were striving to create materials to make plastic gunsights for soldiers that provided exceptionally clear visibility. **12A** In the course of their research, they manufactured a substance, cyanoacrylates, that stuck to everything it touched. **12B** Initially rejected as completely useless because of its strong adhesive quality, the cyanoacrylates were set aside as a failure. **12C** However, less than a decade later, researchers working for the company Eastman Kodak rediscovered the formulation, creating the popular glue that went on to be advertised as strong enough to attach and hang a car from a crane. **12D**

9. Look at the four squares [■] that indicate where the following sentence could be added to the second paragraph of the passage.

They enjoyed the comfort of performing in underwear rather than costumes.

Where would the sentence best fit? Click on a square [■] to add the sentence to the passage.

10. Look at the four squares [■] that indicate where the following sentence could be added to the third paragraph of the passage.

It was a taste sensation that stayed on his mind.

Where would the sentence best fit? Click on a square [■] to add the sentence to the passage.

READING

11. Look at the four squares [■] that indicate where the following sentence could be added to the fifth paragraph of the passage.

Teflon is a prime example of this.

Where would the sentence best fit? Click on a square [■] to add the sentence to the passage.

12. Look at the four squares [■] that indicate where the following sentence could be added to the sixth paragraph of the passage.

The iconic commercial remains an important symbol of the product to this day.

Where would the sentence best fit? Click on a square [■] to add the sentence to the passage.

PASSAGE FOUR (Questions 13–16)

Paragraph

Neon

1►   Neon is a nonmetallic chemical element revealed when air is liquefied and then heated. It is the second-lightest of the noble gases—the Group 18 gases of the periodic table of elements—falling only behind helium. While the most prevalent commercial use for neon remains in the manufacturing of neon advertising signs, it is also utilized in certain types of lasers and as a cryogenic refrigerant.

2►   **13A** In the 1770s, researchers discovered that oxygen and nitrogen were present in air, and in fact made up 99 percent of it. Up until that decade, air was believed to be a single element. **13B** In 1894, the chemical element argon was identified as a third component of air by Sir William Ramsay. **13C** However, it represented only 0.934 percent of air, leaving 0.034 percent still a mystery. **13D** Ramsay and Travers continued to research the tiny amounts of gas that remained after nitrogen, oxygen, and argon were removed.

3►   **14A** In 1898, Sir Ramsay and William Travers discovered neon as another component of air. (Ramsay later went on to win the Nobel Prize in Chemistry for discovering all of the noble gases.) They named it for the Greek word *neos*, which means *new*. Although neon is a colorless gas under normal conditions, when an electrical discharge is passed through it, it generates an incredibly bright reddish-orange hue. **14B** Ramsay and Travers observed this by chilling air until it became a liquid, and then heating the liquid to catch the gases that boiled off. **14C** Adding the electrical discharge to the new gas in a rudimentary version of a mass spectrometer produced the glowing light. **14D** Neon actually discharges the most intense light at normal currents and voltages of all the noble gases.

4►   It is a monatomic element, comprised of a single atom (it forms no compounds). Neon has three stable isotopes, all of which are produced in the formation of stars. **15A** In the universe, neon is the fifth most abundant gas, but it is comparatively rare on Earth, comprising only 1 part in 65,000 of Earth's atmosphere. **15B** This is due to its relative lightness, which allows it to escape into outer space. **15C** Much smaller amounts are believed to exist deep within the Earth's crust. **15D** Interestingly, an increased amount of Ne-20 is found in diamonds. Researchers believe this suggests a solar neon reservoir inside Earth.

5►   **16A** In the early 1900s, George Claude of France produced large quantities of neon as a byproduct of his air liquefaction company. **16B** But its commercial application wasn't fully realized until 1912, when Claude's business associate Jacques Fonseque demonstrated an electrified sealed neon tube that could be used in advertising. **16C** The first neon sign was displayed at a Paris barbershop in 1912. **16D** Neon signs soon gained in popularity throughout the United States, especially demonstrated by their prevalence in the city of Las Vegas, Nevada. Another commercial use of neon is in cryogenic refrigeration, which cools items to very low temperatures. It has 40 times the refrigerating capacity of liquid helium, and 3 times that of liquid hydrogen. Other uses of the element include the production of high-voltage indicators and—prior to the advent of LCD flat screens—television tubes.

13. Look at the four squares [■] that indicate where the following sentence could be added to the second paragraph of the passage.

But after the determination that air was composed of multiple elements, new measuring techniques evolved, allowing scientists to recognize that there was something else besides the two known elements present in air.

Where would the sentence best fit? Click on a square [■] to add the sentence to the passage.

14. Look at the four squares [■] that indicate where the following sentence could be added to the third paragraph of the passage.

This process of separating out parts of a mixture through collection of vapors is called fractional distillation.

Where would the sentence best fit? Click on a square [■] to add the sentence to the passage.

15. Look at the four squares [■] that indicate where the following sentence could be added to the fourth paragraph of the passage.

The stable isotopes of neon are Ne-20, Ne-21, and Ne-22.

Where would the sentence best fit? Click on a square [■] to add the sentence to the passage.

16. Look at the four squares [■] that indicate where the following sentence could be added to the fifth paragraph of the passage.

The first American equivalent was lit in 1923 at a Los Angeles Packard car dealership.

Where would the sentence best fit? Click on a square [■] to add the sentence to the passage.

READING EXERCISE (SKILLS 3–4): Read the passage and choose the best answers to the questions that follow.

Paragraph

Theodore Dreiser

1▶ **1A** Theodore Dreiser, the American author best known for the novel *Sister Carrie* (1912), introduced a powerful style of writing that had a profound influence on the writers that followed him, from Steinbeck to Fitzgerald and Hemingway. **1B** *Sister Carrie* challenged the conventional writings of the period, which focused on a higher moral ground. **1C** It was here that Theodore Dreiser created the fictional account that laid bare the harsh reality of life in the big city, which established him as the architect of a new genre. **1D**

2▶ Dreiser was born in 1871 into a large family whose fortunes had in the recent past taken a dramatic turn for the worse. Before Theodore's birth, his father had built up a successful factory business, only to lose it to a fire. **4A** The family was rather abruptly thrust into poverty, and Theodore spent his youth moving from place to place in the Midwest as the family tried desperately to reestablish itself financially. **4B** He left home at the age of 16. **4C** After earning some money, he spent a year at Indiana University but left school and returned to Chicago, yearning for the glamour and excitement that it offered. **4D** At the age of 22, he began work as a reporter for a small newspaper in Chicago, the *Daily Globe,* and later worked on newspapers in Pittsburgh, Cleveland, Saint Louis, and New York City. In his work as a reporter, he was witness to the seamier side of life and was responsible for recording events that befell the less fortunate in the city, the beggars, the alcoholics, the prostitutes, and the working poor.

3▶ **5A** Dreiser first tried his hand at fiction by writing short stories rather than novels, and the first four short stories that he wrote were published. **5B** Based on this, he was encouraged to write a novel that would accurately depict the harsh life of the city, and the novel *Sister Carrie* was the result of his effort. **5C** This novel chronicles the life of Carrie Meeber, a small-town girl who goes to Chicago in a quest for fame and fortune. **5D** As Carrie progresses from factory worker to Broadway star by manipulating anyone in her path, Dreiser sends a clear message about the tragedy of life that is devoted purely to the quest for money.

4▶ *Sister Carrie,* unfortunately for Dreiser, did not achieve immediate success. **7A** The novel was accepted for publication by Doubleday, but Dreiser was immediately asked to make major revisions to the novel. **7B** When Dreiser refused to make the revisions, Doubleday published only a limited number of copies of the book and refused to promote or advertise it. **7C** Published in limited release and without the backing of the company, the novel was a dismal failure, selling fewer than 500 copies. **7D**

5▶ After the failure of the novel that was so meaningful to him, Dreiser suffered a nervous breakdown; he was depressed, stricken with severe headaches, and unable to sleep for days on end. Having sunk to a point where he was considering suicide, he was sent by his brother to a sanatorium in White Plains, New York, where he eventually recovered. **10A** After leaving the sanatorium, he took a position as an editor for Butterick's. **10B** He was successful in this position, and was eventually able to purchase a one-third interest in a new publishing company, B.W. Dodge, which republished Dreiser's novel *Sister Carrie.* **10C** This new release of the novel proved considerably more successful than the first release had been. **10D** In its first year, the reissued version of *Sister Carrie* sold 4,500 copies, with strong reviews, and the next year it sold more than 10,000 copies. The recognition that accompanied the success of the novel was based not only on the power of the description of the perils of urban life but also on the new trend in literature that Dreiser was credited with establishing.

1. Look at the four squares [■] that indicate where the following sentence could be added to paragraph 1.

This forceful first novel set a new path for American novels at the end of the nineteenth century.

Where would the sentence best fit? Click on a square [■] to add the sentence to the passage.

2. Which of the sentences below best expresses the essential information in the first highlighted sentence in paragraph 2? *Incorrect* choices change the meaning in important ways or leave out essential information.

Ⓐ Dreiser's family had formerly been rich before it had become poor.
Ⓑ Dreiser was, unfortunately, born into an overly dramatic family.
Ⓒ The fortunes of Dreiser's family had recently increased.
Ⓓ Members of Dreiser's family suffered from the serious effects of a disease.

3. Which of the sentences below best expresses the essential information in the second highlighted sentence in paragraph 2? *Incorrect* choices change the meaning in important ways or leave out essential information.

Ⓐ Dreiser served as a witness in a number of trials that involved beggars, alcoholics, and prostitutes.
Ⓑ Dreiser observed and wrote about the underprivileged as part of his newspaper job.

Ⓒ In New York City, during Dreiser's time, there were many people who were less fortunate than Dreiser.
Ⓓ Dreiser's work involved working with beggars, alcoholics, and prostitutes.

4. Look at the four squares [■] that indicate where the following sentence could be added to paragraph 2.

At this young age, he moved alone to Chicago and supported himself by taking odd jobs.

Where would the sentence best fit? Click on a square [■] to add the sentence to the passage.

5. Look at the four squares [■] that indicate where the following sentence could be added to paragraph 3.

It was rather unusual for a novice writer to achieve so much so quickly.

Where would the sentence best fit? Click on a square [■] to add the sentence to the passage.

6. Which of the sentences below best expresses the essential information in the highlighted sentence in paragraph 3? *Incorrect* choices change the meaning in important ways or leave out essential information.

Ⓐ Dreiser devoted his life primarily to trying to become rich.
Ⓑ In Dreiser's novel, Carrie succeeds by moving from a low-level job to stardom.
Ⓒ Dreiser used one of his characters to demonstrate the negative aspects of lust for money.
Ⓓ Dreiser tried to warn Carrie that she was taking the wrong path in life.

7. Look at the four squares [■] that indicate where the following sentence could be added to paragraph 4.

These changes were intended to tone down some of the starker and more scandalous descriptions.

Where would the sentence best fit? Click on a square [■] to add the sentence to the passage.

8. Which of the sentences below best expresses the essential information in the first highlighted sentence in paragraph 5? *Incorrect* choices change the meaning in important ways or leave out essential information.

Ⓐ Dreiser recovered from an attempted suicide at a sanatorium.

Ⓑ Dreiser's brother went to a sanatorium after attempting suicide.

Ⓒ After being sent to a sanatorium, Dreiser considered committing suicide.

Ⓓ Dreiser's brother stepped in to help Dreiser after Dreiser became depressed.

9. Which of the sentences below best expresses the essential information in the second highlighted sentence in paragraph 5? *Incorrect* choices change the meaning in important ways or leave out essential information.

Ⓐ In Dreiser's novels, he recognized the power of urban life and new trends that existed in it.

Ⓑ The success of Dreiser's novel went unrecognized because it represented such a new trend in literature.

Ⓒ Dreiser credited his urban upbringing and literary background for the success that his novel achieved.

Ⓓ Dreiser achieved acclaim because his writing was so powerful and because he established a new trend.

10. Look at the four squares [■] that indicate where the following sentence could be added to paragraph 5.

This company was one that published magazines to promote sewing and the sale of clothing patterns.

Where would the sentence best fit? Click on a square [■] to add the sentence to the passage.

READING REVIEW EXERCISE (SKILLS 1–4): Read the passage and choose the best answers to the questions that follow.

Paragraph   **Pulsars**

1▶   There is still much for astronomers to learn about pulsars. Based on what is known, the term *pulsar* is used to describe the phenomenon of short, precisely timed radio bursts that are emitted from somewhere in space. Though all is not known about pulsars, they are now believed in reality to emanate from spinning neutron stars, which are highly reduced cores of collapsed stars that are theorized to exist.

2▶   Pulsars were discovered in 1967, when Jocelyn Bell, a graduate student at Cambridge University, noticed an unusual pattern on a chart from a radio telescope. What made this pattern unusual was that, unlike other radio signals from celestial objects, this series of pulses had a highly regular period of 1.33730119 seconds. Because day after day the pulses came from the same place among the stars, Cambridge researchers came to the conclusion that they could not have come from a local source such as an Earth satellite.

3▶   **5A** A name was needed for this newly discovered phenomenon. **5B** The possibility that the signals were coming from a distant civilization was considered, and at that point the idea of naming the phenomenon *L.G.M.* (short for Little Green Men) was raised. **5C** However, after researchers had found three more regularly pulsing objects in other parts of the sky over the next few weeks, the name *pulsar* was selected instead of L.G.M. **5D**

4▶   As more and more pulsars were found, astronomers engaged in debates over their nature. It was determined that a pulsar could not be a star inasmuch as a normal star is too big to pulse so fast. The question was also raised as to whether a pulsar might be a white dwarf star, a dying star that has collapsed to approximately the size of the Earth and is slowly cooling off. However, this idea was also rejected because the fastest pulsar known at the time pulsed around 30 times per second and a white dwarf, which is the smallest known type of star, would not hold together if it were to spin that fast.

5▶   The final conclusion among astronomers was that only a neutron star, which is theorized to be the remaining core of a collapsed star that has been reduced to a highly dense radius of only around 10 kilometers, was small enough to be a pulsar. Further evidence of the link between pulsars and neutron stars was found in 1968, when a pulsar was found in the middle of the Crab Nebula. The Crab Nebula is what remains of the supernova[1] of the year 1054. Several hypotheses have been developed around the concept that neutron stars are what form after a supernova explosion, which results in a subsequent implosion of the remaining matter. This intense implosion brings about an inward contraction of neutrons packed so densely together that they no longer resemble normal matter, and are thus referred to as neutron stars. A neutron star is believed to be what formed and survived after the Crab Nebula supernova explosion.

6▶   The generally accepted theory for pulsars is the lighthouse theory, which is based upon a consideration of the theoretical properties of neutron stars and the observed properties of pulsars. According to the lighthouse theory, a spinning neutron star emits beams of radiation that sweep through the sky, and when one of the beams passes over the Earth, it is detectable on Earth. The radiation is contained within a field of radio waves created by the immensely powerful magnetic field of a neutron star, a magnetic field said to be about one trillion times the strength of the Earth's magnetic field. The radio waves are dispersed through the north and south poles of the pulsar. In order for the beam to pass over the Earth, the pulsar has to be aligned in such a way that these poles face the direction of the Earth. It is known as the lighthouse theory because the emissions from neutron stars are similar to the pulses of light emitted from lighthouses as they sweep over the ocean. For this reason, some believe that the name *lighthouse* is actually more appropriate than the name *pulsar.*

GLOSSARY

1. *supernova*—a star that explodes due to the intense nuclear energy contained within

1. The phrase "emanate from" in paragraph 1 is closest in meaning to
   - (A) develop from
   - (B) revolve around
   - (C) wander away from
   - (D) receive directions from

2. Which of the sentences below best expresses the essential information in the highlighted sentence in paragraph 2? *Incorrect* choices change the meaning in important ways or leave out essential information.
   - (A) It was unusual for researchers to hear patterns from space.
   - (B) It was unusual for celestial objects to emit radio signals.
   - (C) It was unusual that the pattern of the pulsars was so regular.
   - (D) It was unusual that the period of pulses was only slightly more than a second in length.

3. The word "they" in paragraph 2 refers to
   - (A) day after day
   - (B) the pulses
   - (C) the stars
   - (D) Cambridge researchers

4. The word "raised" in paragraph 3 could best be replaced by
   - (A) lifted
   - (B) suggested
   - (C) discovered
   - (D) elevated

5. Look at the four squares [■] that indicate where the following sentence could be added to paragraph 3.

   This name was selected because it indicates a regularly pulsing radio source.

   Where would the sentence best fit? Click on a square [■] to add the sentence to the passage.

6. The phrase "engaged in" in paragraph 4 could best be replaced by
   - (A) became attached to
   - (B) were disappointed in
   - (C) made promises about
   - (D) took part in

7. The word "their" in paragraph 4 refers to
   - (A) weeks
   - (B) pulsars
   - (C) astronomers
   - (D) nature

8. Which of the sentences below best expresses the essential information in the highlighted sentence in paragraph 4? *Incorrect* choices change the meaning in important ways or leave out essential information.

Ⓐ Pulsars could not be white dwarfs because the frequency of the pulsars is too high.

Ⓑ Pulsars cannot spin very fast because they will fall apart if they spin fast.

Ⓒ White dwarfs cannot be dying stars because they cannot pulse at around 30 times per second.

Ⓓ White dwarfs cannot contain pulsars because white dwarfs spin much faster than pulsars.

9. The word "Further" in paragraph 5 is closest in meaning to

Ⓐ distant
Ⓑ irrelevant
Ⓒ additional
Ⓓ unreliable

10. Which of the sentences below best expresses the essential information in the highlighted sentence in paragraph 5? *Incorrect* choices change the meaning in important ways or leave out essential information.

Ⓐ Several theories suggest that a supernova explodes and then collapses inward, creating a neutron star.

Ⓑ It is believed that a neutron star explodes, creating a supernova that subsequently implodes.

Ⓒ Most hypotheses have proven that a supernova explosion produces several neutron stars.

Ⓓ A supernova explodes and then collapses outward, which forms the hypotheses that explain neutron stars.

11. The word "properties" in paragraph 6 is closest in meaning to

Ⓐ lands
Ⓑ characteristics
Ⓒ masses
Ⓓ surroundings

Reading Skill 5: FIND FACTUAL INFORMATION

Finding factual information assesses your ability to recognize and understand the details and examples that support main ideas. It is one of the most important skills on the TOEFL iBT® test. Because of this, questions asking about factual information in a passage are one of the most common types of questions given in the Reading section.

The information needed to answer factual information questions is found directly stated in the passage. However, the answers are often restatements that use synonyms and different sentence structures from what is stated in the passage. Usually factual information questions indicate the paragraph in which you can find the information, or they have key words that are easy to scan for in the passage.

Strategies to Answer Factual Information Questions

- Look for any indications in the question that tell you where the answer is located (i.e., According to paragraph 2 . . . ; Paragraph 4 states that . . . ; What is stated in paragraph 3 about . . .).

- Remember that the questions are generally given in order of how the information is presented. This means that the information to answer the second question will probably be found after the information used to answer the first question.

- Look for clear key words—such as dates, names, and locations—to help you scan for information and to eliminate wrong answers.

Look at the following passage and examples of factual information questions.

Example

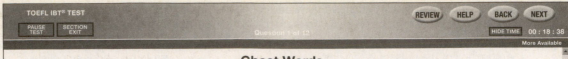
Ghost Words

1▶ A ghost word is a previously nonexistent word that has made its way into a reference work by mistake. Walter Skeat, a lexicographer,[1] first used the term "ghost word" in the late nineteenth century to explain the existence of words that appeared in certain dictionaries and other sources, but in fact had no etymological[2] basis. Ghost words have come into being through a variety of errors, typographical and proofreading mistakes, misunderstandings, and mistranslations.

2▶ Many ghost words are the result of typographical errors. One well-known example of a ghost word is the word "Dord," which appeared in a 1934 American dictionary defined as density, as it is used in physics and chemistry. "Dord" was added to the dictionary when a typesetter who was making entries into the dictionary misread the entry "D or d" and typed it as "Dord." In reality, the letter "d" (or its capitalized version "D") was used to refer to density in physics or chemistry. When the error was discovered over a decade later, the ghost word "Dord" was removed from the dictionary.

3▶ Not all ghost words are recognized as errors, removed from reference works, and forgotten. One example of a well-established ghost word is the word "syllabus." The Roman writer Cicero had correctly used the Latin word *sittabus* in his writings to refer to the title and author label on a manuscript. In a 1470 edition of Cicero's works, *sittabus* was miswritten as "syllabus"; the miswritten ghost word "syllabus" has now achieved status as a commonly used word referring to an outline of the contents of a course.

4▶ Other terms that originated as ghost words but remain in use have come about from mistranslations. Both "scapegoat" and "gravy" are two words that enjoy widespread acceptance but originated as translation errors. "Scapegoat" owes its existence to a scribe who was translating the Bible from Hebrew into English in the 1500s. The translator misunderstood the original Hebrew word and thought it meant "a goat that escapes" and so, came up with the term "scapegoat." However, later examination of the original word showed that it should have been translated as a type of rugged mountain, not an animal. Today, the term refers to a person who is blamed for something bad that happens, even if it is not his or her fault. "Gravy" came into existence from a mistranslation that happened even earlier than that of "scapegoat." In the 1300s, a writer translating a French cookbook changed the word "grane," which was a general reference to cooking ingredients, to "gravy," which is now used to refer to types of meat sauces.

5▶ Ghost words have also arisen due to verbal reconstructions, either because of pronunciation differences or limited literacy skills. "Tweed" is one such example. In modern times, "tweed" is a type of thick wool cloth that comes from twill (a woven textile design)."Tweed" became a word when English speakers misheard the Scottish pronunciation of "twill" as "tweed." Another ghost word whose acceptance spread verbally is "okay." Though its exact origins are unknown, it is believed that it developed due to a lack of literacy skills among certain members of society. Today, it is almost universally used to express acceptance or adequacy.

6▶ The survival of ghost words within the English language seems to be influenced by two factors. One is the length of time between the first use of the word and the discovery of the mistake that created it. Words such as "Dord," which are discovered relatively soon after they appear in dictionaries, are generally quickly removed from use and forgotten. Other words, like "scapegoat," that take centuries to be corrected, may never be erased from the language. The second factor is how far the term spreads before its incorrectness is revealed. "Syllabus" is an example of a word that, though known to be a mistake, has been used by such a wide range of people and in so many contexts that it would be almost impossible to remove from the language.

7▶ There are English words and phrases that have been intentionally created with no etymological history, but some experts do not include these words under the umbrella of ghost words. "Before math" (meaning, what precedes or produces a particular result; events that have yet to happen) is an example of a word that was intentionally derived from another word "aftermath" (meaning, the time after an important or bad event). Many lexicographers refer to this type of word as a back formation, meaning it was created backward from another source.

GLOSSARY

1. *lexicographer*—a person who writes, edits, or gathers words for a dictionary
2. *etymological*—related to the history or origin of words

Look at an example of a question that asks you to find factual information. (See paragraph 1.)

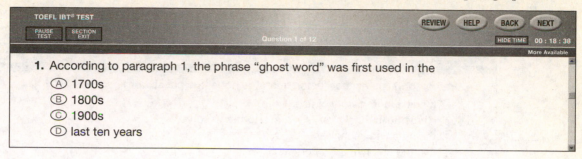

1. According to paragraph 1, the phrase "ghost word" was first used in the
   Ⓐ 1700s
   Ⓑ 1800s
   Ⓒ 1900s
   Ⓓ last ten years

Paragraph 1 states that *Walter Skeat . . . first used the term "ghost word" in the late nineteenth century. . .* The nineteenth century refers to the 1800s, so the correct answer choice is the second answer choice, *1800s.*

Look at another example of a question that asks you to find factual information. (See paragraph 4.)

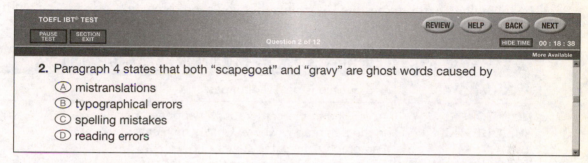

2. Paragraph 4 states that both "scapegoat" and "gravy" are ghost words caused by
   Ⓐ mistranslations
   Ⓑ typographical errors
   Ⓒ spelling mistakes
   Ⓓ reading errors

The second sentence of paragraph 4 states *both "scapegoat" and "gravy". . . originated as translation errors*, which means they were translated incorrectly. The correct answer choice is the first choice, *mistranslations.*

Look at another example of a question that asks you to find factual information. (See paragraph 6.)

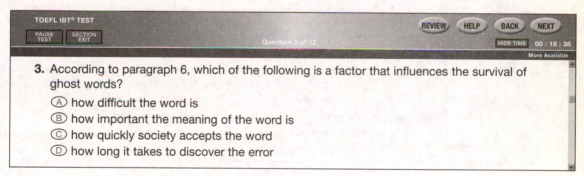

3. According to paragraph 6, which of the following is a factor that influences the survival of ghost words?
   Ⓐ how difficult the word is
   Ⓑ how important the meaning of the word is
   Ⓒ how quickly society accepts the word
   Ⓓ how long it takes to discover the error

The correct answer choice is the fourth choice, *how long it takes to discover the error.* In paragraph 6, the first sentence states that the survival of ghost words . . . *are . . . influenced by two factors.* The second sentence mentions that one factor is the length of time between the first use . . . *and the discovery of the mistake . . .* The fifth sentence says the second factor is how far the term spreads before its incorrectness is revealed. One of the factors mentioned in the passage discusses a relationship between time and the word being discovered as a mistake, so you should choose an answer that includes both pieces of information. The third and fourth answer choices both discuss time, but only the fourth answer choice mentions discovery of a mistake or error.

Look at another example of a question that asks you to find factual information. (See paragraph 7.)

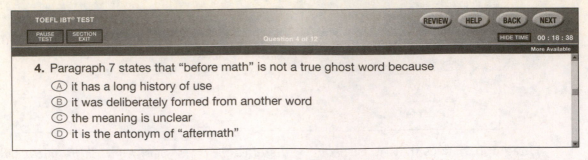

Paragraph 7 discusses reasons why certain words are not ghost words (. . . *but some experts do not include these words under the umbrella of ghost words*). The second sentence states that *"beforemath" . . . was intentionally derived from another word. . . .* The correct choice is the second choice, *it was deliberately formed from another word.*

The following chart outlines the key points that you should remember about Factual Information questions.

KEY POINTS FOR QUESTIONS ABOUT FINDING FACTUAL INFORMATION	
FREQUENCY	3–6 questions per reading passage
HOW TO IDENTIFY THE QUESTION	According to the paragraph, X happened because . . . In the paragraph, (where, what, when, etc.) . . . ? Paragraph X indicates/states . . . In paragraph X, what does the author say about . . . ? What reason is given in the paragraph for . . . ? In the paragraph, X is an example of . . . Which statement in paragraph X best explains/describes . . . ? In the paragraph, which of the following . . . ?
WHERE TO FIND THE ANSWER	Usually the question will tell you in what paragraph(s) to look for the answer. The questions are also generally in the order of the information presented in the passage.
HOW TO ANSWER THE QUESTION	1. Look for any indications in the question that tell you where the answer is located (i.e., *According to paragraph 2 . . .*). 2. Look for clear key words — such as dates, names, and locations—to help you scan for information and to eliminate wrong answers. 3. Look for synonyms in the answer choices that match the information in the passage. Be careful of sentence structure. 4. Be aware of transitional signals that indicate a relationship between ideas and may indicate comparison, contrast, cause/effect, and so on.

In the exam, you may be able to eliminate incorrect answer choices by understanding what is wrong with them.

For Factual Information questions, incorrect answer choices may:
• include details from the passage, but use them in a way that is not accurate according to the passage.
• contain false information or information that contradicts that in the passage.
• use details mentioned in the passage, but that do not answer the question.

READING EXERCISE 5: Study each of the passages and choose the best answers to the questions that follow.

PASSAGE ONE (Questions 1–8)

Paragraph

Lake Baikal

1▶   Crescent-shaped Lake Baikal, in Siberia, is only the ninth largest lake in area at 395 miles (620 kilometers) in length and 46 miles (74 kilometers) in width, yet it is easily the largest body of fresh water in the world. It holds one-fifth of the world's fresh water, which is more than the total of all the water in the five Great Lakes, a group of lakes located on the border between Canada and the United States. It holds so much fresh water despite its less-than-impressive area because it is by far the world's deepest lake. The average depth of the lake is 1,312 feet (400 meters) below sea level, and the Olkhon Crevice, the lowest known point of the lake, is more than 5,250 feet (1,600 meters) deep.

2▶   Lake Baikal, which today is located near the center of the Asian peninsula, is most likely the world's oldest lake. It began forming 25 million years ago as Asia started splitting apart in a series of great faults. The Baikal Valley dropped away, eventually filling with water and creating the deepest of the world's lakes. Underneath the lake, below a sediment layer of 4.3 miles (7 kilometers), the earth's crust continues to separate at a rate of about 2 centimeters per year. The fault zone also has continual seismic activity with the regular recording of earthquakes every 3 to 4 years. The lake is singular among large high-latitude lakes due to the fact that its sediments have not been scoured clean by any continental ice sheets that flowed over the area, giving researchers a very specific record of climactic changes over the previous 250,000 years.

3▶   Surrounded by mountains, this large body of freshwater is located in a region where average temperatures range from below freezing in the winter to a cool 14 degrees Celsius (57 degrees Fahrenheit) in the summer months. Before convenient modes of transportation around and across the lake became common, those who were daring could cross the lake on foot during the deep winter freezes. However, these adventurous travelers put themselves at great risk for frostbite and hypothermia, since the large, flat open expanse of the lake allowed the cold wind to blow unhindered across its surface.

4▶   At the turn of the twentieth century, the Trans-Siberian Railroad was completed, which opened up travel to and around the lake. As more people came into contact with the lake, its potential as a commercially profitable resource was explored. This led a variety of investors, ranging from those interested in tourism and environmental preservation to those looking to develop new energy resources, to survey the area and introduce a wide range of commercial opportunities into the region. As a result, today the area has been developed to include hotels, resorts, and trails. In addition, although prior proposals to exploit the region for fossil fuel and nuclear energy sources have been largely restricted to preserve the natural beauty of the area, many predict that it is only a matter of time before large corporations will be permitted to fully utilize the abundant natural resources of the lake valley.

5▶   A number of environmental concerns have been raised as development of the Lake Baikal area progresses. One such concern involved the Bayalsk Pulp and Paper Mill, constructed in 1966. Because it was built right on the shoreline, it discharged chemical waste directly into the lake. Decades of protest from area residents had little effect in changing the conditions of the plant. Though it closed in 2008 due to lack of revenue, and with a promise from the owner that the plant would never reopen, it in fact resumed production in 2010, with support from the federal government, which created legislation permitting the mill operation, despite its polluting of the lake.

6▶   Residents and concerned environmentalists had more luck with the proposed oil pipeline that a major Russian corporation planned to route through the Lake Baikal Valley. Environmental activists and concerned local citizens worked together to keep the pipeline out of the valley. These groups pointed out that the consistent seismic activity in the area could cause a catastrophic oil spill that would be capable of destroying the ecological balance of the region. However, in spite of the numerous public protests, it was not until the government stepped in and requested that the oil company reroute the pipeline that the corporation agreed to honor the wishes of the protestors. Ultimately, the pipeline was diverted completely away from the federal and public natural reserves that surround Lake Baikal.

> Build your vocabulary, so you can easily recognize synonyms of words in the passage that are used for important words in the answer.

1. What is stated in paragraph 1 about the shape of Lake Baikal?
   Ⓐ It is wider than it is long.
   Ⓑ It is circular in shape.
   Ⓒ Its width is one-half of its length.
   Ⓓ It is shaped like a new moon.

2. According to paragraph 1, Lake Baikal
   Ⓐ holds one-fifth of the world's water
   Ⓑ holds five times the water of the Great Lakes
   Ⓒ holds one-ninth of the world's water
   Ⓓ holds 20 percent of the world's fresh water

3. According to paragraph 1, the Olkhon Crevice is
   Ⓐ outside of Lake Baikal
   Ⓑ 400 meters below sea level
   Ⓒ the deepest part of Lake Baikal
   Ⓓ 5,000 meters deep

4. It is mentioned in paragraph 2 that Lake Baikal
   Ⓐ is not as old as some other lakes
   Ⓑ formed when sections of the Earth were moving away from each other
   Ⓒ was fully formed 25 million years ago
   Ⓓ is today located on the edge of the Asian peninsula

5. Paragraph 3 states that Lake Baikal
   Ⓐ is protected from the weather by mountains
   Ⓑ never gets cooler than 14 degrees Celsius
   Ⓒ is frozen enough to walk on in the summer
   Ⓓ was dangerous to cross in the winter

6. According to paragraph 4, the lake region
   Ⓐ has provided economic opportunity for tourists
   Ⓑ has had its abundant natural resources fully exploited
   Ⓒ has been commercially developed by investors
   Ⓓ has had its natural beauty destroyed

7. Paragraph 5 mentions the Bayalsk Pulp and Paper Mill as an example
   Ⓐ of a progressive and productive company
   Ⓑ of a company that is an environmental hazard
   Ⓒ of an unsuccessful lake area investment
   Ⓓ of a company that responds to citizen concerns

8. According to paragraph 6, activists and citizens
   Ⓐ protested government involvement in building the oil pipeline near Lake Baikal
   Ⓑ wanted the new oil pipeline near Lake Baikal to be made safer
   Ⓒ endured several earthquakes during their protests
   Ⓓ cooperated to prevent the construction of the oil pipeline near Lake Baikal

PASSAGE TWO (Questions 9–16)

The Postage Stamp

Paragraph

1▶ The postage stamp has been around for only a relatively short period of time. The use of stamps for postage was first proposed in England in 1837, when Sir Rowland Hill published a pamphlet entitled "Post Office Reform: Its Importance and Practicability" to put forth the ideas about postal rates. He stated that they should not be based on the distance that a letter or package travels but should instead be based on the weight of the parcel and that fees for postal services should be collected in advance of the delivery, rather than after, through the use of postage stamps.

2▶ Prior to Hill's revolutionary suggestion, postal fees were usually charged to the recipient of the mail, as opposed to the sender, which created severe problems for the postal service. One of the most critical was that the British postal service had no effective method of collecting postal fees if the recipient refused to pay for the mail being delivered. Another issue was that of limiting the size and number of packages sent from one location to the other; there was no incentive for people sending mail to put restrictions on the size or amount of parcels, since they were not the ones that were charged for the delivery.

This created cumbersome loads of mail for postal workers to deliver, and the issue was compounded if the recipient refused to pay, which rendered the mail undeliverable.

3▶ Fortunately, the ideas proposed by Hill went into effect in England almost immediately after the publication of his pamphlet. The first English stamp, which featured a portrait of then Queen Victoria, was printed in 1840. This stamp, the "penny black," came in sheets with an adhesive backing that needed to be separated with scissors and provided enough postage for a letter weighing 14 grams or less to any destination. Another more expensive stamp, the "two pence blue" was put on sale within days of the first stamp's introduction to provide for the delivery of heavier pieces of mail.

4▶ Other countries noted the success of the new system of postal delivery and followed suit within a few years of the inception of the English stamp. In 1843, Brazil was the next nation to produce national postage stamps, and various areas in what is today Switzerland also produced postage stamps later in the same year. Postage stamps in five- and ten-cent denominations were first approved by the U.S. Congress in 1847, and by 1860 postage stamps were being issued in more than ninety governmental jurisdictions worldwide. Most original postage stamps followed a pattern similar in design and structure to England's "penny black"; the stamps were rectangular in shape and typically depicted images of queens, presidents, or other political figures prominent in the respective nations. One primary exception was the Brazilian stamp; the government of Brazil opted to put an abstract image on the postage in order to prevent their leader's image being marred by a postmark, a necessary mark indicating the stamp had been paid for.

5▶ As postage stamps became more widespread in their use, innovations occurred to improve the convenience and appeal of the stamps. About a decade or so after the stamp's initial appearance, perforations between the individual stamps were included on the sheets of multiple stamps. These small holes dividing the postage greatly increased the ease and speed of separating individual stamps. Instead of needing scissors to carefully cut between the stamps, the postage could now be separated by tearing along the perforated lines. Another innovation involved the images on the stamps. As time progressed, countries moved away from solely depicting national leaders on the small squares and began to use the stamps to display other images of national pride, including plants and wildlife, celebrities, and even icons symbolizing the nation. In the United States for example, stamps have been issued with famous cartoon characters, such as Mickey Mouse and Bart Simpson.

6▶ It is these diverse images that have caused stamps to become popular as collectibles. Serious collectors track down stamps with diverse images, especially stamps that have not been separated from their sheets, or stamps that have a clean postmark. Stamps issued in limited runs, which restrict their circulation, are particularly sought after, and can be worth much more than their face value.

9. According to paragraph 1, postage stamps were first suggested

Ⓐ in the first half of the eighteenth century
Ⓑ in the second half of the eighteenth century
Ⓒ in the first half of the nineteenth century
Ⓓ in the second half of the nineteenth century

10. It is indicated in paragraph 1 that Sir Rowland Hill believed that postage fees

Ⓐ should be paid before delivery
Ⓑ should be related to distance
Ⓒ should have nothing to do with how heavy a package is
Ⓓ should be collected after the package is delivered

11. According to paragraph 2, prior to the use of postage stamps

Ⓐ mail carriers refused to deliver heavy pieces of mail
Ⓑ the receiver often paid to have mail returned to the sender
Ⓒ the sender would limit the amount and number of packages sent
Ⓓ the size and volume of packages sent were problems for the postal service

12. What is stated in paragraph 3 about the first English postage stamp?

Ⓐ It was designed by Queen Victoria.
Ⓑ It contained a drawing of a black penny.
Ⓒ It was produced in sheets of fourteen stamps.
Ⓓ It could be used to send a lightweight letter.

13. According to paragraph 4, Brazil introduced postage stamps

   Ⓐ before England
   Ⓑ before Switzerland
   Ⓒ after the United States
   Ⓓ after Switzerland

14. It is mentioned in paragraph 4 that in 1847

   Ⓐ postage stamps were in use in ninety different countries
   Ⓑ it cost fifteen cents to mail a letter in the United States
   Ⓒ two different denominations of postage stamps were introduced in the United States
   Ⓓ the U.S. Congress introduced the "penny black" stamp

15. Which of the following is an innovation in the production of stamps mentioned in paragraph 5?

   Ⓐ Scissors were no longer included with each sheet of stamps to assist in separating them.
   Ⓑ Stamp images of national leaders and heroes were introduced.
   Ⓒ Small holes were punched into the sheets of stamps to make the stamps easier to separate.
   Ⓓ A single sheet of stamps included stamps with various images.

16. It is mentioned in paragraph 6 that some stamps

   Ⓐ preserved in complete sheets are considered more valuable to collectors
   Ⓑ have decreased in value
   Ⓒ duplicate images to appeal to collectors
   Ⓓ have unlimited circulation

PASSAGE THREE (Questions 17–24)

The Clovis Culture

Paragraph

1▶ From its first discovery in the early part of the twentieth century, an ancient indigenous people referred to as the Clovis culture was considered to be the earliest native culture in the Americas. While this claim has been discredited due to more recent discoveries of earlier groups of people, the fact remains that the Clovis people were influential in the development of tribes, or groups of people that lived, socialized, and created family units, across the North American continent. Several later tribes are thought to have derived from the Clovis, based on the similarity of cultural artifacts that have been analyzed. Precise dating of the origin of this New World culture cannot be determined, but many experts estimate that the Clovis people lived between 13,000–13,500 years ago.

2▶ The Clovis people were initially identified and grouped together by the tools that archeologists found at various sites. They were named the Clovis people after the site near Clovis, New Mexico, where the first tools of this sort were discovered in 1932. The tools are quite sophisticated and are unlike any tools that have been found in the Old World. Their development indicates a relatively superior knowledge and use of the technology available to people at that time. One distinct and commonly found indicator of the Clovis culture is the spear point used in their weapons; the point is fluted, thinned down by chipping away small flakes, on both sides, an advantage for hunting, and presumably, for protection from invaders.

3▶ In the years since the first tools of this sort were discovered in New Mexico, archeologists have discovered Clovis tools in areas ranging from Mexico to Montana in the United States and Nova Scotia in Canada. All of the Clovis finds date from approximately the same period, a fact that suggests that the Clovis spread rapidly throughout the North American continent. From the evidence that has been discovered, some archeologists have concluded that the Clovis were a mobile culture. They traveled in groups of 40 to 50 individuals, migrating seasonally and returning to the same hunting camps each year. Their population increased rapidly as they spread out over the continent, and they were quite possibly motivated to develop their sophisticated hunting tools to feed their rapidly expanding populace.

4▶ However, another theory has been proposed to explain the wide proliferation of the tools that were used in the Clovis culture. Rather than a single group of indigenous people that dispersed rapidly and broadly across the vast expanse of the Americas, some researchers suggest that the tools created by the original tribe were rapidly adopted by neighboring tribes. Thus, instead of the Clovis people dominating the region, perhaps the initial tribe remained relatively small and stationary, while their tools were passed and replicated from tribe to tribe. This replication could have been accomplished through several methods: trade with neighboring tribes, invasions and conflicts, or less likely, through intermarriage between the Clovis and other tribes.

5▶   Just as the knowledge of how the tools of the Clovis culture spread is uncertain, so the manner in which the Clovis people disappeared remains a mystery. One prevalent theory hypothesizes that the decline in availability of both the vegetation and animals that the Clovis consumed resulted in their eventual extinction. Another hypothesis is that a period of climactic cooling, lasting approximately 1,500 years, created inhabitable conditions which made it impossible for the Clovis to survive. A third, less supported idea, is that a comet struck the earth in the area where the Clovis dwelled and destroyed their culture.

6▶   Even though there is much that is controversial about the origin, evolution, and eventual disappearance of the Clovis culture, archeologists have agreed on a few significant points. The first point is that the tools used by the people allowed for mobility and superior methods of obtaining food. The second is that many tribes using the Clovis tools traveled in relatively small groups and returned annually to the same sites. Yet another point of agreement is that the Clovis people were able to successfully pass on their culture quite rapidly throughout North, Central, and parts of South America. These points of concession bolster the reputation of the Clovis as a dominant force in their era, and provide essential information about the evolution of native tribes in the Western hemisphere.

17. Paragraph 1 states that the Clovis people
    Ⓐ were the first people to live on the American continents
    Ⓑ originated less than 13,000 years ago in North America
    Ⓒ evolved from several other New World tribes
    Ⓓ were preceded by other tribes in the Americas

18. What is stated in paragraph 2 about Clovis tools?
    Ⓐ They date from around 10,000 B.C.
    Ⓑ They were used to help identify the Clovis people.
    Ⓒ They have been found at only one location.
    Ⓓ They were discovered by archeologists hundreds of years ago.

19. It is indicated in paragraph 2 that the tools found near Clovis, New Mexico, were
    Ⓐ very rudimentary
    Ⓑ similar to others found prior to 1932
    Ⓒ rather advanced
    Ⓓ similar to some found in Africa and Europe

20. It is mentioned in paragraph 3 that it is believed that the Clovis people
    Ⓐ lived in familial groups of four or five people
    Ⓑ had a relatively stable population
    Ⓒ lived only in New Mexico
    Ⓓ spent summers and winters in different places

21. According to paragraph 4, an alternative theory states that
    Ⓐ the Clovis tribes may have not have moved around very much
    Ⓑ isolated themselves from other tribes
    Ⓒ were dominated by another, more powerful tribe
    Ⓓ did not engage in trade

22. The theory mentioned in paragraph 4 also states that
    Ⓐ the Clovis tools spread after the extinction of the Clovis people
    Ⓑ there was not a rapid spread of the Clovis tools
    Ⓒ the tools made by the Clovis people were used by other tribes
    Ⓓ the Clovis offered their tools to their neighbors

23. According to paragraph 5
    Ⓐ the reason for the extinction of the Clovis people is that they were unable to grow enough food
    Ⓑ how and why the Clovis people disappeared remain unsolved
    Ⓒ the spread of the Clovis people was limited by the impact of a comet
    Ⓓ the cooling period that destroyed the Clovis culture has not been determined

24. What does paragraph 6 state is TRUE about the Clovis culture?
    Ⓐ The Clovis people moved more rapidly than other tribes.
    Ⓑ The Clovis people had a strong influence on their era.
    Ⓒ The Clovis people quickly adapted to other cultures around them.
    Ⓓ The Clovis people significantly changed the evolution of native tribes.

Paragraph

Brown Dwarfs

1▶   A brown dwarf is a celestial body that has never quite become a star. A typical brown dwarf has a mass that is 8 percent or less than that of the Sun. The mass of a brown dwarf is too small to generate the internal temperatures capable of igniting the nuclear burning of hydrogen to release energy and light.

2▶   A brown dwarf contracts at a steady rate, and after it has contracted as much as possible, a process that takes about 1 million years, it begins to cool off. Its emission of light diminishes with the decrease in its internal temperature, and after a period of 2 to 3 billion years, its emission of light is so weak that it can be difficult to observe from Earth.

3▶   Because of these characteristics of a brown dwarf, it can be easily distinguished from stars in different stages of formation. A brown dwarf is quite distinctive because its surface temperature is relatively cool and because its internal composition—approximately 75 percent hydrogen—has remained essentially the same as it was when first formed. A white dwarf, in contrast, has gone through a long period when it burns hydrogen, followed by another long period in which it burns the helium created by the burning of hydrogen and ends up with a core that consists mostly of oxygen and carbon with a thin layer of hydrogen surrounding the core.

4▶   Another factor that is used to distinguish brown dwarf stars from other stars, especially those with a low mass similar to these celestial bodies, is the presence of lithium in the atmosphere surrounding the star. Typically, most stars burn off lithium as they heat up, so the chemical element is depleted as the stars age. However, brown dwarfs almost never reach an internal temperature high enough to burn off the majority of the lithium so its presence in more than trace amounts signals to scientists that they are likely observing a brown dwarf candidate. Yet, this is not a foolproof test since some very young stars, that are not brown dwarfs, may still have significant amounts of lithium in their atmosphere. Likewise, a few brown dwarfs may reach a temperature intense enough to burn off lithium without being hot enough to ignite hydrogen. Therefore, other tests are used in conjunction with the lithium assessment to verify whether a star is actually a brown dwarf.

5▶   It is even more difficult to discriminate between brown dwarfs and large planets. Though planets are not formed in the same way as brown dwarfs, they may in their current state have some of the same characteristics as a brown dwarf. The planet Jupiter, for example, is the largest planet in our solar system with a mass 317 times that of our planet and resembles a brown dwarf in that it radiates energy based on its internal energy. In addition, Jupiter has more or less the same radius as most brown dwarfs. It is the mechanism by which it was formed that distinguishes a planet such as Jupiter from a brown dwarf.

6▶   While there is no exact standard to determine the difference between a brown dwarf and a planet based on mass, the International Astronomical Union (IAU) has established loose guidelines to define the difference. In general, if a body in space is more than ten times the mass of Jupiter, experts estimate its likelihood of being a planet to be very small. The likelihood decreases even further if the body reaches more than 13 times the mass of Jupiter, which is the cutoff point the IAU recommends for defining an outer space body as a brown dwarf.

7▶   As the mass of a brown dwarf climbs, the method through which its volume is governed changes. Those that are above a mass 65 times that of Jupiter have their volume controlled by the same process that controls the volume of stars. Those at the low end of brown dwarf mass, closer to only ten times the mass of Jupiter, have their volume controlled much in the same way that planets do. Those that fall within the range have their volume controlled by a combination of factors that are similar to the mechanisms used to control the volume of both planets and stars. The consequence of these various control methods is that the volume of all brown dwarfs remains relatively constant, rarely varying more than 10 to 15 percent in the radius of each of these celestial objects.

25. It is stated in the passage that the mass of an average brown dwarf
    Ⓐ is smaller than the mass of the Sun
    Ⓑ generates an extremely high internal temperature
    Ⓒ is capable of igniting nuclear burning
    Ⓓ causes the release of considerable energy and light

26. According to paragraph 2, a brown dwarf cools off
    Ⓐ within the first million years of its existence
    Ⓑ after its contraction is complete
    Ⓒ at the same time that it contracts
    Ⓓ in order to begin contracting

27. What is stated in paragraph 2 about a brown dwarf that has cooled off for 2 to 3 billion years?
    Ⓐ Its weak light makes it difficult to see from Earth.
    Ⓑ It no longer emits light.
    Ⓒ Its weak light has begun the process of restrengthening.
    Ⓓ Scientists are unable to study it.

28. It is indicated in paragraph 3 that
    Ⓐ the amount of hydrogen in a brown dwarf has increased dramatically
    Ⓑ a brown dwarf had far more hydrogen when it first formed
    Ⓒ about three-quarters of the core of a brown dwarf is hydrogen
    Ⓓ the internal composition of a brown dwarf is always changing

29. What is stated in paragraph 4 about lithium's relationship to brown dwarfs?
    Ⓐ It indicates a lower mass than other stars.
    Ⓑ It is easily burned off by the heat of the brown dwarfs.
    Ⓒ It takes more heat to burn off than to ignite hydrogen.
    Ⓓ It tends to be present in higher amounts in the atmosphere around brown dwarfs than other stars.

30. It is indicated in paragraph 5 that both large planets and brown dwarfs
    Ⓐ share the same mass
    Ⓑ are formed in the same way
    Ⓒ have some of the same features
    Ⓓ produce a large amount of internal energy

31. According to paragraph 6, the IAU
    Ⓐ has been in existence for over ten years
    Ⓑ is the only astronomy group dedicated to the study of brown dwarfs
    Ⓒ has developed guidelines to distinguish brown dwarfs from large planets
    Ⓓ has established an exact definition of brown dwarfs and large planets

32. What is mentioned in paragraph 7 about the volume of brown dwarfs?
    Ⓐ It is controlled by the same process in all brown dwarfs.
    Ⓑ It remains fairly consistent, regardless of mass.
    Ⓒ It has never been accurately measured.
    Ⓓ It has no relationship to the radius.

Reading Skill 6: IDENTIFY NEGATIVE FACTS

Identifying negative facts tests your ability to distinguish between two types of information: true versus false information, and details provided in the passage versus information that is not provided. To answer this question correctly, you must choose the answer that is incorrect according to the passage. This means that three of the answer choices will be *stated* or *true* based on the passage; one answer choice will not.

Like factual information questions, negative questions tell you where to look for the information. Often, the information needed is found in a single paragraph, however, you may also need to scan multiple paragraphs.

Strategies to Answer Negative Fact Questions

- Look for any indications in the question that tell you where the answer is located (i.e., *According to paragraph 2 . . .*).

- Remember that the questions are generally given in the same order as the information is presented in the passage. This means that the information to answer the second question will probably be found after the information used to answer the first question.

- Look for key words in the answer choices to help you scan for information and to eliminate answers found in the passage.

- Remember that there are two kinds of answer choice sets for this type of question: (1) Three true answers and one that is *not true* according to the passage, or (2) three true answers and one that is *not stated or not mentioned* in the passage.

Example

Moonbows

1▶ Almost everyone is familiar with the colorful arch of a rainbow, but not many people have heard of its counterpart, the moonbow. Rainbows are caused by the reflection of sunlight off water droplets in the air, usually in the form of rain. The sunlight hits the droplets and bounces back, creating an array of colors[1]. A rainbow is visible when the Sun is low in the sky behind the observer and the water droplets are in the atmosphere in front of the observer. Light from the Sun reflects off the inside surfaces of raindrops and is bent as it travels through them. It appears as a band of colors because each of the colors in sunlight is bent to a different angle.

2▶ The formation of a moonbow shares similarities with that of a rainbow; however, unlike rainbows, moonbows do not reflect the light directly from the Sun through the droplets. Instead, the light is first reflected off of the surface of the Moon, then from the Moon through the water droplets. This means that the observer of a moonbow must be situated so he is between the Moon and the droplets, rather than the Sun and the water droplets. Yet, as is the case with the position of the Sun for observing a rainbow, the Moon must be behind the moonbow viewer in order for it to be visible.

3▶ Other conditions must also be met for a moonbow to be visible. Typically, the Moon must be full or almost full, so that its light is at its brightest. The Moon must also be low in the sky—no higher than 42 degrees—and the sky has to be extremely dark. These rare conditions, along with the necessity of water in the atmosphere opposite the Moon, mean that moonbows are sighted much less often than rainbows. Moonbows are usually most visible during a full moon, two to three hours before sunrise, and from a location far from other sources of light.

4▶ Even though all of the physical conditions for a moonbow may be met, there is still no guarantee that an observer will be able to witness its full effect with his own eyes. Since light from the Moon is not as intense as sunlight, the bow appears muted in its display of colors. Unless the Moon is exceptionally bright, the moonbow appears as a white or grayish-white band of light to the naked eye. An extremely bright Moon in an exceptionally dark sky may produce a faint band of different colors. Colors may also be more visible in fall and winter, when the air is drier, allowing for light to travel more easily to the water droplets. However, most people rely on long exposure photographs to capture the moonbow and provide an image of its colors.

5▶ In some locales, people have to depend on rain for the chance of a moonbow to appear, but in locations where there are waterfalls, the phenomenon can be viewed more often, through the mist from the waterfalls. In the United States, there are a few well-known places to catch sight of a moonbow. One is Yosemite Falls in California. Another is Cumberland Falls, located in Kentucky. Officials that monitor Cumberland Falls make a unique claim about moonbows and the falls: they claim that Cumberland Falls is the only location in the Western Hemisphere where the emergence of a moonbow can be accurately predicted.

6▶ A phenomenon commonly mistaken for a moonbow is a corona, a colored circle that occasionally appears around the Moon. Though they appear to be the same, coronas are formed when light reflects off droplets or ice crystals in clouds, not through mist or water droplets in the air.

GLOSSARY

1. *array of colors*—an impressive group or collection of colors

Look at an example that asks you to find the one answer that is *not true*. (See paragraph 1.)

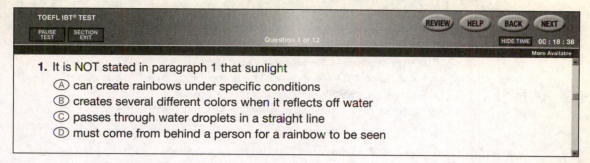

The third answer choice is correct. In line 6 of paragraph 1, it is stated that *light . . . is* <u>bent</u> *as it travels through water droplets.* The only information that is NOT true is the third answer choice: it is NOT stated that sunlight *passes through water droplets in a* <u>straight</u> *line.* The first answer choice is incorrect because it is true. Line 2 of paragraph 1 says that *rainbows are caused by the reflection of sunlight . . . ,*

The second answer choice is incorrect because it is true. Line 3 states that the *sunlight* creates *an array of colors.* The fourth answer choice is incorrect because it is true. Line 4 states that the *Sun is . . . behind the observer.*

> Most negative fact answer choices refer to information that is not found in the passage. Once you have found three answer choices that are mentioned in the passage, you don't need to look for the fourth; it is the answer.

Look at another example that asks you to find the one answer that is *not true* and for which you will need to scan the entire passage. (See entire passage.)

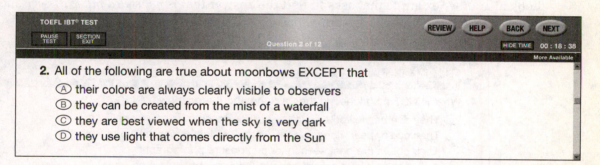

The first answer choice is correct. The only answer choice that is NOT true about moonbows is *that their colors are always clearly visible to observers.* Paragraph 4 (lines 3 to 4) says *unless the Moon is exceptionally bright, the moonbow appears as a white or grayish-white band of light.* The second answer choice is true. Paragraph 5 (line 3) says that moonbows *can be viewed . . . through the mist from the waterfalls.* The third answer choice is true. In paragraph 2 (line 1), it states that *moonbows do not reflect light directly from the Sun.* The fourth answer choice is true. Paragraph 3 (line 3) states that *the sky has to be extremely dark* for moonbows to be seen.

Look at an example that asks to find the answer that is *not stated in the passage.* (See paragraph 3.)

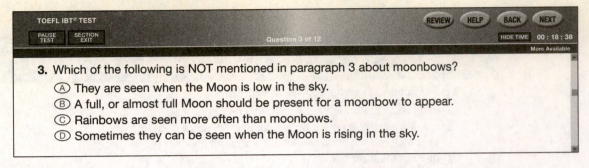

3. Which of the following is NOT mentioned in paragraph 3 about moonbows?

Ⓐ They are seen when the Moon is low in the sky.
Ⓑ A full, or almost full Moon should be present for a moonbow to appear.
Ⓒ Rainbows are seen more often than moonbows.
Ⓓ Sometimes they can be seen when the Moon is rising in the sky.

- The first sentence of paragraph 3 states that *conditions must . . . be met* to see a moonbow.

- Line 2 tells you that *the Moon must . . . be low in the sky*, so the first answer choice is stated in the paragraph.

- Line 5 states that moonbows *are . . . at their . . . most visible during a full Moon*, so the second answer choice is stated in the paragraph

- Line 4 says *moonbows are sighted much less often than rainbows*, so the third answer choice is stated in the paragraph

The paragraph does **not** mention whether or not a moonbow can be seen when the Moon is <u>rising</u>.

Therefore, the correct answer choice is the fourth one because it is NOT mentioned in the paragraph that *sometimes they can be seen when the Moon is rising in the sky.*

Look at another example that asks to find the answer that is *not stated in the passage* and for which you will need to scan the entire passage. (See entire passage.)

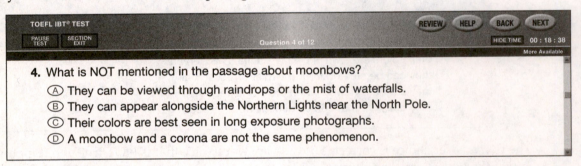

4. What is NOT mentioned in the passage about moonbows?

Ⓐ They can be viewed through raindrops or the mist of waterfalls.
Ⓑ They can appear alongside the Northern Lights near the North Pole.
Ⓒ Their colors are best seen in long exposure photographs.
Ⓓ A moonbow and a corona are not the same phenomenon.

The second answer choice is correct. There is no mention of the Northern Lights or the North Pole in the passage. Therefore, it is NOT mentioned in the passage that moonbows can appear alongside the Northern Lights near the North Pole.

The first answer choice is incorrect because in paragraph 5, lines 1–2 state that in some locales, people have to depend on rain for the chance of a moonbow to appear, but in locations where there are waterfalls, the phenomenon can be viewed more often.

The third answer choice is incorrect because in paragraph 4, lines 7–8 tell you most people *. . . rely on long exposure photographs to capture the moonbow and provide an image of its colors.* The fourth answer choice is incorrect because paragraph 6 states that one phenomenon commonly mistaken for a moonbow is a corona.

The following chart outlines the key points that you should remember about Negative Fact questions.

KEY POINTS FOR QUESTIONS ABOUT IDENTIFYING NEGATIVE FACTS

FREQUENCY	1–2 questions per reading passage
HOW TO IDENTIFY THE QUESTION	It is NOT stated/mentioned/discussed/indicated . . . It is NOT true . . . All of the following are true EXCEPT . . . Which of the following is NOT given as a reason . . .? Which of the following is NOT mentioned . . .?
WHERE TO FIND THE ANSWER	Usually the question will tell you in what paragraph(s) to look for the answer. The questions are also generally in the order of the information presented in the passage. Questions that require you to scan the entire passage for an answer usually come later in the set of questions related to the passage.
HOW TO ANSWER THE QUESTION	1. Look for any indications in the question that tell you where the answer is located (i.e., *According to paragraph 2* . . .). 2. Look for clear key words—such as dates, names, and locations—to help you scan for information and to eliminate wrong answers. 3. In order to eliminate answers that are true or mentioned in the passage, look for synonyms in the answer choices that match the information in the passage.

In the exam, you may be able to eliminate incorrect answer choices by understanding what is wrong with them.

For Negative Fact questions, incorrect answer choices may:
• include information that is mentioned or true according to the passage.
• contain false information.
• use other details mentioned in the passage or paragraph.

READING EXERCISE 6: Study each of the passages and choose the best answers to the questions that follow.

PASSAGE ONE (Questions 1–8)

Paragraph

Flatfish

1▶ At first glance, flatfish might seem to be an awkward anomaly of evolution, because of one distinctive feature present in virtually no other living organism: the presence of both eyes on one side of the head. Nevertheless, this asymmetrical feature is of great benefit to flatfish, the majority of whom spend their lives on the bottom of the ocean floor. At birth, the eyes start out in the common symmetrical position of one eye on each side of the head; as the fish develops, one eye migrates to the left or right side of the head, depending on which side the fish faces toward the surface and away from the sandy ocean bed.

2▶ Members of the flatfish family, sand dabs and flounders, have an additional evolutionary advantage over many colorfully decorated ocean neighbors in that they are able to adapt their body coloration to different environments. These aquatic chameleons have flattened bodies that are well-suited to life along the ocean floor in the shallower areas of the continental shelf that they inhabit. They also have remarkably sensitive color vision that registers the subtlest gradations on the sea bottom and in the sea life around them. Information about the coloration of the environment is carried through the nervous system to chromatophores, which are pigment-carrying skin cells on the upper side of the fish. These chromatophores are able to accurately reproduce not only the colors but also the texture of the ocean floor. Each time that a sand dab or flounder finds itself in a new environment, the pattern on the body of the fish visible to potential predators adapts to fit

READING EXERCISE 6   73

in with the color and texture around it. However, the underside of a flatfish is generally pale or colorless.

3► Not all flatfish live exclusively along the bottom of the sea floor; some flatfish hunt for prey in the mid-levels of the ocean in which they dwell, with some types of flatfish breaking the surface of the water in pursuit of food. These flatfish that travel to higher levels in the water may not show the extremes of asymmetry that those that reside solely on the floor display. For example, while flounders, which occasionally hunt at mid-ocean level, have well-developed teeth on both sides of the jaw, their relatives, the soles, live almost exclusively at the bottom of the ocean, feed primarily on boneless prey and tend to have teeth on only one side of the jaw.

4► These oddly developed fish actually start out in similar fashion to other, commonly symmetrical fish. Flatfish spawn eggs that hatch into larvae and disperse away from the floor, floating throughout the water as plankton[1]. During this initial stage of development, the fish have protection in the form of spines covering the head, gills, and fins. As the fish mature into their adult form, one eye moves across the head to join with its counterpart; the protective spines drop away and the fish sinks to the bottom of the water, with its blind vulnerable side turned to the floor. Depending on the species and gender, flatfish may take several years to reach full maturity.

5► There are several types of flatfish that range in size and desirability for human consumption. One of the smallest types of flatfish is the *Tarphops oligolepsis,* with a span of just 1.8 inches (4.5 centimeters) and a weight of less than an ounce (2 grams). On the opposite end of the spectrum is the Atlantic halibut, which can reach a length of 8.2 feet (2.5 meters) and a weight of 700 pounds (316 kilograms). Fishermen hoping to reel in flatfish usually focus on the species that rise to mid-level or above from the bottom, as these present less of a challenge to catch. Thus, flounder and halibut are much more sought after, and caught, than sole. When sole are caught by fishermen, it is most likely in water only a few hundred feet deep, close to the edge of a reef or coastline.

> Since most factual questions ask you to choose information that is true according to the passage, it is easy to get confused when answering negative fact questions. Remember NOT to choose an answer choice that mentions true information from the passage. You are looking for *false* information.

GLOSSARY
1 *plankton*—very small plants and animals that live in the sea and are consumed by fish

1. What is NOT mentioned in the passage regarding the eyes of flatfish?
   - Ⓐ The symmetry of the eyes changes according to surface of the ocean bottom.
   - Ⓑ The eyes are originally formed on both sides of the head.
   - Ⓒ One eye moves to the other side as the fish mature.
   - Ⓓ The asymmetry helps the flatfish.

2. It is NOT stated in the passage that sand dabs
   - Ⓐ are a type of flatfish
   - Ⓑ are in the same family as flounders
   - Ⓒ are found in shallower water
   - Ⓓ are colorless all over their bodies

3. All of the following are stated about the vision of sand dabs and flounders EXCEPT that they are
   - Ⓐ able to spot distance movements
   - Ⓑ able to see colors
   - Ⓒ able to see the sea bottom
   - Ⓓ able to distinguish other organisms

4. It is NOT true that chromatophores
   - Ⓐ are skin cells
   - Ⓑ carry pigment
   - Ⓒ adapt to surrounding colors
   - Ⓓ change shape on the ocean floor

5. The passage does NOT mention that
   - Ⓐ some flatfish do not live solely on the ocean floor
   - Ⓑ all flatfish display the same level of asymmetry
   - Ⓒ the asymmetry influences the teeth as well as the eyes of flatfish
   - Ⓓ some flatfish may come above the surface of the water to hunt

6. The passage mentions everything EXCEPT the following about the development of flatfish.
   - Ⓐ Flatfish are initially spawned like other species of fish.
   - Ⓑ Flatfish lose their protective spines as they mature.
   - Ⓒ Flatfish grow to adulthood relatively quickly.
   - Ⓓ Flatfish fall to the ocean floor as they grow.

7. According to the passage, what is NOT true about the development of flatfish?

Ⓐ They float in the water as plankton.
Ⓑ They are spawned away from the ocean floor.
Ⓒ They start out with spines to protect the head, fins, and gills.
Ⓓ The eyeless side faces the bottom of the ocean.

8. All of the following are true about flatfish EXCEPT

Ⓐ some flatfish are better for eating than others
Ⓑ flatfish vary greatly in size and weight
Ⓒ the Atlantic halibut is a very large type of flatfish
Ⓓ sole is considered easier to catch than flounder or halibut

PASSAGE TWO (Questions 9–16)

Paragraph
Limestone Caves

1▶ Caves, natural cavities formed within the earth, can be formed from varied substances, but the largest caves, measured by depth and length, are commonly created out of limestone. Limestone primarily derives from the hard outer shells of marine organisms, and was originally formed on ancient sea beds or at the bottom of oceans. Limestone caves are known as "solutional" caves since the limestone is dissolved, opening up a slowly expanding hole, which results in the creation of the cave. These caves can be spectacular structures filled with giant stalactites and stalagmites.

2▶ Limestone caves are formed in one of two ways. For a long time, it was accepted that all the caves were made by rainwater, a weak acid, when it dissolves calcite, or lime, out of limestone. Carbonic acid is formed when the rainwater combines with atmospheric carbon dioxide. Over time, the acid-laden water drips down into cracks, enlarging them into caves. However, more recently, it was revealed that some well-known caves, including the Carlsbad Caverns in New Mexico, were not formed by carbonic acid, but instead, by sulfuric acid. Apparently, microorganisms far beneath the earth's surface consume oil and generate hydrogen sulfide. This hydrogen sulfide mixture rises to the earth's surface and mixes with water, producing the sulfuric acid that eats away at the limestone. Thus, both methods involve water combining with another substance to form an acid that erodes the limestone, creating the caves.

3▶ Regardless of which type of acid initiates the erosion process, the liquid substances carry the dissolved limestone particles to other parts of the caves and deposit them. These deposits become "speleothems," the structures that grow from the floors and ceilings, and cover the walls of the caves. These deposits can also form structures known as stalactites and stalagmites. All of the formations are created as the water evaporates on the surfaces of the cave, leaving behind the solid limestone grains that build up and create often unique and eye-catching shapes.

4▶ Stalactites, which extend down from cave ceilings, are formed in limestone caves when groundwater containing dissolved lime drips from the roof of the cave and leaves a thin deposit as it evaporates. Stalactites generally grow only a fraction of an inch each year, but over time a considerable number may grow to be several yards long. In cases where the supply of water is seasonal, they may actually have growth rings resembling those on tree trunks that indicate how old the stalactites are.

5▶ Stalagmites are formed on the floor of a limestone cave where water containing dissolved lime has dripped either from the cave ceiling or from a stalactite above. They develop in the same way as stalactites, when water containing dissolved limestone evaporates. The deposits of limestone gradually build up over hundreds or thousands of years. One of the tallest stalagmites, the Great Dome in Carlsbad Cavern, is over 67 feet (21 meters) high. Using currently accepted growth-rate calculations, it is estimated that the stalagmite reached this height in just under 4,000 years.

6▶ In some limestone caves with mature limestone development, stalactites and stalagmites grow together, creating limestone pillars that stretch from the cave floor to the cave ceiling. These pillars are referred to as "columns" due to their resemblance to the manmade structures used to support the roofs and ceilings of buildings. The growth rate of stalagmites and stalactites has proven difficult to measure with any consistency, making it hard to predict when the formations with the possibility of merging into columns might actually do so.

7▶   A fourth type of speleothem is called flowstone. Flowstone forms as the water flows or drips down the walls of a cave, leaving behind the limestone sediment. Flowstone, while having an irregular surface, develops much more smoothly and evenly than stalagmites and stalactites because of the large area that the water has to flow over.

8▶   In some caves, experts have determined that a lack of moisture will prevent further growth of the formations, while in others, rates of growth have varied depending on the amount of moisture and the speed of dripping or flowing water. While the growth rate of the cave formations is virtually imperceptible from one year to the next, an evaluation of thousands of years worth of data give scientists the ability to estimate a yearly growth rate. In some caves, these estimations may take decades to confirm, and in others, they may never be validated since the dry conditions of those caves today hinder further growth of the structures.

9. Paragraph 1 states all of the following about caves EXCEPT
   - Ⓐ most caves, of all sizes, are made of limestone
   - Ⓑ caves are measured by how deep and how long they are
   - Ⓒ they are natural holes created in the earth
   - Ⓓ they can be formed from different substances

10. It is indicated in paragraph 2 that all of the following are part of the process of forming limestone caves EXCEPT that
   - Ⓐ rainwater dissolves lime from limestone
   - Ⓑ the acidic water seeps into breaks in the ground
   - Ⓒ the lime in the water evaporates
   - Ⓓ the cracks in the ground develop into caves

11. Which of the following is NOT true about speleothems?
   - Ⓐ They are made from limestone particles.
   - Ⓑ They cover only the floors and ceilings of the caves.
   - Ⓒ They include stalactites and stalagmites.
   - Ⓓ They create unusual and interesting formations.

12. According to paragraph 4, it is NOT true that stalactites
   - Ⓐ enlarge cave ceilings
   - Ⓑ are found in limestone caves
   - Ⓒ grow in a downward direction
   - Ⓓ grow quite slowly

13. It is NOT mentioned in paragraph 4
   - Ⓐ how long stalactites may grow
   - Ⓑ how the age of a stalactite is determined
   - Ⓒ what one of the effects of a limited water supply is
   - Ⓓ what causes stalactites to disappear

14. What is NOT true about stalagmites?
   - Ⓐ They are formed by the same method as stalactites.
   - Ⓑ They grow in the same direction as stalactites.
   - Ⓒ They can join a stalactite to form a single structure.
   - Ⓓ Some stalagmites have grown over thousands of years.

15. Which of the following is NOT a speleothem?
   - Ⓐ a stalagmite
   - Ⓑ a stalactite
   - Ⓒ a limestone grain
   - Ⓓ a flowstone

16. What is NOT mentioned in paragraph 8 about moisture and its relationship to speleothems?
   - Ⓐ The pace of growth depends on the amount of moisture.
   - Ⓑ Without moisture, the formations will not grow.
   - Ⓒ A lack of moisture has sped up the formation of speleothems.
   - Ⓓ The growth rate of speleothems is hard to determine in caves that have dried up.

PASSAGE THREE (Questions 17–24)

Paragraph

Chewing Gum

1▶   Throughout the course of history, chewing gum has come from multiple sources. In fact, chewing gum and automobile tires share an odd commonality: at one time, both included resin from the rubber tree, a material prized for its flexible yet durable qualities. However, this resinous substance was not the only, or even the first, material to be used as chewing gum. Gum from 5,000 years ago has been uncovered, with teeth imprints still visible, that came from the tar[1] of birch tree bark. Today, chewing gum is more likely to be made from synthetic forms of rubber, or latex, since these can be produced more easily and abundantly than the natural rubbery sap that is drawn from trees.

2▶   Historically, chewing gum has served a valuable purpose cosmetically. The ancient Aztecs produced a type of gum from chicle, an organic rubber source, which the women in this culture frequently—more so than the men—used as a breath freshener, a common use for gum today. Besides adding freshness to the breath by promoting the production and circulation of saliva[2], the stickiness of gum removes food particles from between the teeth that contribute to bad breath, as well as reducing cavities or holes in the teeth caused by decay. Both of these advantages improve the health and appearance of the mouth and extend the life of teeth, which in ancient times was a clear symbol of youth and attractiveness. Unfortunately, in modern times, this benefit is diminished by gum that is high in sugar, so most contemporary health professionals recommend sugarless gum.

3▶   Chewing gum has also been shown to provide medical benefits, especially in treating conditions that have an effect on the digestive system. Studies have indicated that chewing gum after specific types of stomach surgery may reduce recovery time. It also appears to benefit certain patients suffering from other stomach-related diseases. The chewing of gum seems to enhance production of saliva, which stimulates the digestive system in both instances, and that in turn encourages the secretion of digestive juices. The digestive juices help to neutralize potentially harmful stomach acid, and aid in the elimination of undigested particles in the digestive tract. In addition to benefiting the digestive system, some research has concluded that chewing gum may also alleviate stress and reduce jaw pain.

4▶   Despite providing medical benefits, chewing gum, and its close relative, bubble gum, are mainly promoted as a recreational habit, primarily to young people. Bubble gum, a popular treat with children, was invented by the Fleer Chewing Gum Company. An accountant for the company, Walter Diemer, was experimenting with recipes when he noticed one that was less sticky and stretched more easily than regular chewing gum. He colored it pink, his favorite color, and it was eventually marketed as Double Bubble. It was instantly successful, due in part to the strategy of teaching all salespeople how to blow bubbles.

5▶   The founder of one of the most popular American brands of chewing gum, Wrigley's, ironically did not set out to sell gum. Wrigley's chewing gum was actually developed as a premium to be given away with other products rather than as a primary product for sale. William Wrigley Jr. initially sold soap as a wholesaler, giving baking soda away as a premium, and using a cookbook to promote each deal. Over time, the baking soda and cookbook became more popular than the soap, so Wrigley began a new operation selling baking soda. He began hunting for a new premium item to give away with sales of baking soda; he soon decided on chewing gum.

6▶   Once again, Wrigley realized that demand for the premium was stronger than the demand for the original product. Consequently, he created the Wm. Wrigley Jr. Company to produce and sell chewing gum. Wrigley started out with two brands of gum, Vassar and Lotta Gum, and soon introduced Juicy Fruit and Spearmint. The latter two brands grew in popularity, while the first two were phased out. Juicy Fruit and Spearmint are two of Wrigley's main brands to this day.

GLOSSARY

1 *tar*—a sticky, thick substance produced from the heating of organic material, such as wood
2 *saliva*—the liquid that is produced naturally in the mouth

17. It is NOT stated in paragraph 1 that chewing gum

Ⓐ is flexible and long-lasting
Ⓑ from thousands of years ago was discovered
Ⓒ is made today from mostly natural materials
Ⓓ can be made more easily from synthetic rubber

18. According to paragraph 2, among the Aztecs chewing gum was

Ⓐ used for cosmetic purposes
Ⓑ more popular among men than women
Ⓒ made from chicle
Ⓓ used to eliminate bad breath

19. It is NOT indicated in paragraph 2 that a benefit of chewing gum is

Ⓐ encouraging the production of saliva
Ⓑ removing small pieces of food from the teeth
Ⓒ increasing sugar levels in the mouth
Ⓓ promoting a healthy mouth

20. All of the following are mentioned as medical benefits of gum EXCEPT

Ⓐ decreasing levels of depression
Ⓑ reducing recovery time after surgery
Ⓒ stimulating the digestive system
Ⓓ relieving jaw discomfort

21. In paragraph 4, all of the following are stated about bubble gum EXCEPT that

Ⓐ it was invented by an employee of a chewing gum company
Ⓑ it proved to be habit-forming
Ⓒ demonstrations assisted in its sales
Ⓓ its color was based on a personal preference

22. It is NOT mentioned in paragraph 5 that Wrigley later

Ⓐ sold baking soda
Ⓑ used chewing gum as a premium to sell baking soda
Ⓒ sold chewing gum
Ⓓ used baking soda as a premium to sell chewing gum

23. According to paragraph 6, the Wm. Wrigley Jr. Company did all of the following EXCEPT

Ⓐ begin with two brands of gum
Ⓑ add new brands to the original two
Ⓒ phase out the last two brands
Ⓓ phase out the first two brands

24. According to the passage, it is NOT true that

Ⓐ gum originally shared something in common with another widely used product
Ⓑ gum is primarily valued for its medical benefits in modern times
Ⓒ both chewing and bubble gum target young people in their advertisements
Ⓓ gum showed itself to be more popular than products it was used to promote

Negative fact questions that refer to the whole passage are generally found near the end of the questions, so you will have had the chance to read most of the passage before answering this type of negative fact question. Remembering answers to previous questions may help you answer this type of negative fact question more quickly.

PASSAGE FOUR (Questions 25–31)

Paragraph

Dissociative Identity Disorder

1▶ Dissociative identity disorder (DID), previously called multiple personality disorder, is a psychological condition in which a person's identity dissociates, or fragments, thereby creating distinct independent identities within one individual. Each separate personality can be distinct from the other personalities in a number of ways, including posture, manner of moving, tone and pitch of voice, gestures, facial expressions, and use of language. Personalities can even differ in gender, with a biological female exhibiting male personalities and vice versa. What is perhaps more astounding is that the alternate personalities, called "alters," may also have dissimilar physiological characteristics, displaying different allergies, right- or left-side dominance, or vision, which could mean that one person may require multiple eyeglass prescriptions to accommodate the varying alters.

2▶ A person suffering from DID may have a large number of independent personalities or perhaps only two or three. There is documented evidence of a single DID sufferer displaying 100 personalities, but that is uncommon; the average number of alters for a DID patient is around 10. These alternate personalities tend to become fixed over time, and may negatively affect a person's life for years. At times, alters develop that may have a tendency to be aggressive, either toward people in the sufferer's environment, or the other alters themselves.

3▶ Two stories of actual women suffering from dissociative identity disorder have been extensively recounted in books and films that are familiar to the public. One of them is the story of a woman with twenty-two separate personalities known as Eve. In the 1950s, a book by Corbett Thigpen and a motion picture starring Joanne Woodward, each of which was titled *The Three Faces of Eve,* presented her story; the title referred to three faces, when the woman known as Eve actually experienced twenty-two different personalities, because only three of the personalities could exist at one time. Two decades later, Carolyn Sizemore, Eve's twenty-second personality, wrote about her experiences in a book entitled *I'm Eve.* The second well-known story of a woman suffering from dissociative personality disorder is the story of Sybil, a woman whose sixteen distinct personalities emerged over a period of forty years. A book describing Sybil's experiences was written by Flora Rheta Schreiber and was published in 1973; a motion picture based on the book and starring Sally Field followed, although the validity of the Sybil accounts later became contested.

4▶   DID is a controversial psychiatric disorder and consensus on its diagnosis and treatment has yet to be reached, with some critics claiming that many observed cases of DID in the latter part of the twentieth century may have been induced during therapy for other conditions. One dilemma is that the term "dissociative" does not have a precise, clear definition in the psychiatric community. Thus, the term "dissociative" has been used on people suffering from a range of symptoms: from periodic inability to pay attention, which may be quite normal, to prolonged episodes of amnesia, where the sufferer cannot remember anything that occurred in prior days, weeks, or months. There is also disagreement about the root of the disorder, though the most popular theories center around some sort of trauma or extremely upsetting incident that happened in the patient's life from which he must dissociate, or disconnect.

5▶   Sufferers of DID usually seek psychiatric help for other issues in their life, such as depression, anxiety, or loss of memory or time, and are not aware that they, in fact, have the disorder until it is diagnosed. The appearance of DID is not exclusive to adults; some research has shown that the average age for the onset of an initial alter is slightly less than six years old. Most children who acquire DID are believed to have suffered a trauma of some kind and used the dissociation to protect themselves from the pain. These children also exhibit depression, along with anxiety, behavior problems, and hallucinations, seeing things that aren't actually present.

6▶   Treatment generally revolves around psychotherapy and often includes some form of hypnosis. Frequently, the therapist's goal is to become familiar with each of the personalities and attempt to uncover the root of the dissociation or find a common thread that will allow all of the personalities to unite into a single, pervasive personality. As can be imagined, this is a difficult, often impossible task, and typically requires several years of treatment and a diverse combination of therapy and perhaps prescribed medicine to achieve. As with other disorders, the earlier it is diagnosed, the better the prognosis; children tend to respond to treatment more successfully than adults.

25. It is NOT stated in paragraph 1 that someone suffering from dissociative identity disorder has

- Ⓐ a psychological condition
- Ⓑ a fragmented identity
- Ⓒ a number of independent identities
- Ⓓ has different vision in the left and right eyes

26. It is indicated in paragraph 1 that distinct personalities can differ in all of the following ways EXCEPT

- Ⓐ manner of dressing
- Ⓑ manner of moving
- Ⓒ manner of speaking
- Ⓓ manner of gesturing

27. It is indicated in paragraph 3 that it is NOT true that Eve

- Ⓐ suffered from dissociative identity disorder
- Ⓑ starred in the movie about her life
- Ⓒ had twenty-two distinct personalities
- Ⓓ had only three distinct personalities at any one time

28. It is NOT stated in paragraph 3 that *The Three Faces of Eve*

- Ⓐ was based on the life of a real woman
- Ⓑ was the title of a book
- Ⓒ was the title of a movie
- Ⓓ was made into a movie in 1950

29. All of the following are mentioned in paragraph 3 about Carolyn Sizemore EXCEPT that she

   Ⓐ wrote *I'm Eve*

   Ⓑ was one of Eve's personalities

   Ⓒ wrote a book in the 1970s

   Ⓓ was familiar with all twenty-two personalities

30. According to paragraph 3, it is NOT true that Sybil

   Ⓐ was a real person

   Ⓑ suffered from dissociative identity

   Ⓒ developed all her personalities over sixteen years

   Ⓓ developed sixteen distinctive personalities over a long period of time

31. It is NOT mentioned in paragraph 5 that sufferers of DID

   Ⓐ are often accurately diagnosed at the age of five

   Ⓑ demonstrate periods of forgetfulness

   Ⓒ likely experienced an emotionally disturbing event

   Ⓓ are often unaware of their condition

READING EXERCISE (Skills 5–6): Study the passage, and choose the best answers to the questions that follow.

Paragraph

John Muir

1▶ John Muir (1838–1914), a Scottish immigrant to the United States, is today recognized for his vital contributions in the area of environmental protection and conservation of the wilderness. As such, he is often referred to as the unofficial "Father of National Parks."

2▶ Muir came to his role as an environmentalist in a rather circuitous way, meandering through many unrelated jobs and activities before ending up as a conservationist. Born in Dunbar, Scotland, Muir came to the United States with his family at the age of eleven. The family settled on a Wisconsin farm, where Muir was educated at home rather than in public school because his father felt that participation in an education in a public school would violate his strict religious code. Young Muir did read considerably at home and also developed some interesting mechanical devices by whittling them from wood; when some of his inventions were put on display at a state fair, they were noted by officials from the University of Wisconsin, and Muir was invited to attend the university in spite of his lack of formal education. He left the university after two and a half years. Later, while working in a carriage factory, he suffered an injury to his eye. His vision did recover, but following the accident he decided that he wanted to spend his life studying the beauty of the natural world rather than endangering his health working in a factory. He set out on a 1,000-mile walk south to the Gulf of Mexico, and from there he made his way to Yosemite, California, lured by a travel brochure highlighting the natural beauty of Yosemite.

3▶ He arrived in California in 1868, at the age of thirty, and once there, he took a number of odd jobs to support himself, working as a laborer, a sheepherder, and—after he had become familiar with the wilderness area—a guide. He also began a writing campaign to encourage public support for the preservation of the wilderness, particularly the area around Yosemite. He married in 1880, and for the years that followed he was more involved in family life and in running the ranch given to him and his wife by her parents than in preservation of the environment.

4▶ He had been away from the environmentalist movement for some time when, in 1889, he was asked by an editor of the magazine *The Century* to write some articles in support of the preservation of Yosemite. The editor, well aware of Muir's talent as a writer and his efforts in the 1870s to support the conservation of Yosemite, took Muir camping to areas of Yosemite that Muir had not seen for years, areas that had been spoiled through uncontrolled development. Because of the experience of this trip, Muir agreed to write two articles in support of the institution of a National Parks system in the United States with Yosemite as the first park to be so designated. These two articles in *The Century* initiated the Yosemite National Park campaign.

5▶ The campaign was indeed successful. The law creating Yosemite National Park was enacted in 1890, and three additional national parks were created soon after. A year later, a bill known as the Enabling Act was passed; this was a bill that gave U.S. presidents the right to reserve lands for preservation by the U.S. government. Pleased by this success but keenly aware of the need to continue the effort to preserve wilderness areas from undisciplined development, Muir established an organization in 1892, the Sierra Club, with the expressed goal of protecting the wilderness, particularly the area of the Sierra Nevada mountain range where Yosemite is located.

6▶   From then until his death in 1914, Muir worked assiduously[1] on his writing in an effort to build recognition of the need for environmental protection. His writings from this period include *The Mountains of California* (1894), *Our National Parks* (1901), *My First Summer in the Sierra* (1911), and *My Boyhood and Youth* (1913).

7▶   A century later, the results of what John Muir was instrumental in initiating are remarkable. The National Park Service is now responsible for more than 350 parks, rivers, seashores, and preserves. More than 250 million people visit these parks each year, and the Sierra Club has more than 650,000 members.

GLOSSARY

1 *assiduously*—diligently; with great care

> Answers for factual information questions are often related to other questions, such as vocabulary, inference, and chart questions. Remembering the information you used to answer factual questions can help you answer others.

1. According to paragraph 1, Muir was born
   - Ⓐ in the first half of the eighteenth century
   - Ⓑ in the second half of the eighteenth century
   - Ⓒ in the first half of the nineteenth century
   - Ⓓ in the second half of the nineteenth century

2. It is stated in paragraph 1 that Muir is known for
   - Ⓐ his contributions to immigration reform
   - Ⓑ his explorations of the wilderness
   - Ⓒ his efforts to maintain natural areas
   - Ⓓ his extensive studies of the national parks

3. It is indicated in paragraph 2 that Muir's early education
   - Ⓐ was conducted at home
   - Ⓑ took place in a religious school
   - Ⓒ violated his father's wishes
   - Ⓓ was in a public school

4. It is NOT mentioned in paragraph 2 that Muir
   - Ⓐ whittled wood
   - Ⓑ was taught how to whittle by his father
   - Ⓒ created mechanical devices
   - Ⓓ was admitted to the university because of his whittling

5. According to paragraph 2, after Muir left the university, it is NOT true that he
   - Ⓐ took a job in a factory
   - Ⓑ suffered an irreversible injury
   - Ⓒ made a decision to quit his job
   - Ⓓ embarked on a long walking tour

6. All of the following are mentioned in paragraph 3 as jobs that Muir held EXCEPT
   - Ⓐ a laborer
   - Ⓑ an animal tender
   - Ⓒ a wilderness guide
   - Ⓓ a travel writer

7. It is stated in paragraph 3 that in the years after 1880, Muir
   - Ⓐ took some odd jobs
   - Ⓑ devoted a lot of time to his family
   - Ⓒ gave his wife's parents a ranch
   - Ⓓ spent most of his time preserving the environment

8. It is NOT mentioned in paragraph 4 that Muir
   - Ⓐ had been uninvolved with environmentalists for a period of time
   - Ⓑ was contacted by an editor for *The Century*
   - Ⓒ worked as an editor for *The Century*
   - Ⓓ wrote two articles for *The Century*

9. The camping trip that is discussed in paragraph 4
   - Ⓐ occurred in the 1870s
   - Ⓑ led Muir to areas that he had never before seen
   - Ⓒ took place in areas that were in their natural state
   - Ⓓ helped to convince Muir to write the articles

10. It is stated in paragraph 5 that the Enabling Act
    - Ⓐ allowed the president to set aside lands to conserve them
    - Ⓑ became law in 1890
    - Ⓒ called for the establishment of the first three national parks
    - Ⓓ preserved lands for government use

11. According to paragraph 5, it is NOT true that the Sierra Club was founded

   Ⓐ after the passage of the Enabling Act
   Ⓑ by John Muir
   Ⓒ before the turn of the century
   Ⓓ to move Yosemite to the Sierra Nevada

12. It is mentioned in paragraph 6 that, for the last decades of his life, Muir

   Ⓐ spent a considerable amount of time in Yosemite
   Ⓑ wrote a number of new laws
   Ⓒ changed his mind on the need for environmental protection
   Ⓓ devoted himself to increasing public awareness of the environment

13. It is NOT indicated in paragraph 7 that early in the twenty-first century

   Ⓐ hundreds of locations are part of the National Park Service
   Ⓑ numerous parks, rivers, seashores, and preserves are being developed
   Ⓒ a quarter of a billion people visit these parks each year
   Ⓓ more than a half a million people belong to the Sierra Club

READING REVIEW EXERCISE (Skills 1–6): Read the passage and answer the questions that follow.

Paragraph

Caretaker Speech

1▶   Children learn to construct language from those around them. Until about the age of three, children tend to learn to develop their language by modeling the speech of their parents, but from that time on, peers have a growing influence as models for language development in children. It is easy to observe that, when adults and older children interact with younger children, they tend to modify their language to improve communication with younger children, and this modified language is called caretaker speech.

2▶   Caretaker speech is used often quite unconsciously; few people actually study how to modify language when speaking to young children but, instead, without thinking, find ways to reduce the complexity of language in order to communicate effectively with young children. **5A** A caretaker will unconsciously speak in one way with adults and in a very different way with young children. **5B** Caretaker speech tends to be slower speech with short, simple words and sentences which are said in a higher-pitched voice with exaggerated inflections and many repetitions of essential information. **5C** It is not limited to what is commonly called baby talk, which generally refers to the use of simplified, repeated syllable expressions such as "ma-ma," "boo-boo," "bye-bye," "wa-wa," but also includes the simplified sentence structures repeated in sing-song inflections. **5D**

3▶   Caretaker speech serves the very important function of allowing young children to acquire language more easily. The higher-pitched voice and the exaggerated inflections tend to focus the small child on what the caretaker is saying, the simplified words and sentences make it easier for the small child to begin to comprehend, and the repetitions reinforce the child's developing understanding. Then, as a child's speech develops, caretakers tend to adjust their language in response to the improved language skills, again quite unconsciously. Parents and older children regularly adjust their speech to a level that is slightly above that of a younger child; without studied recognition of what they are doing, these caretakers will speak in one way to a one-year-old and in a progressively more complex way as the child reaches the age of two or three.

4▶   It is thought by some linguists that this adaptation of speech to the corresponding verbal ability of a child is in fact a response to cues from the young child that may also be processed unconsciously. For instance, as a caretaker speaks to an infant, the infant may respond with smiles, laughter, or other vocal sounds. This signals to the caretaker that the infant is responding positively to the speech. Even an intense gaze at the speaker by the infant indicates that the infant understands that a message is being conveyed, which in turn encourages the speaker to continue to adjust the speech with repetitions, exaggerated expressions, or other appropriate means in order to communicate more effectively. As the child grows, the caretaker continues to process the changes in the child's unconscious cues and adapts speech directed at the child accordingly.

5 ▶ **13A** An important point to note is that the function covered by caretaker speech, that of assisting a child to acquire language in small and simple steps, is an unconsciously used but extremely important part of the process of language acquisition and as such is quite universal. **13B** Studying cultures where children do not acquire language through caretaker speech is difficult because such cultures are difficult to find. **13C** The question of why caretaker speech is universal is not clearly understood; instead, proponents on either side of the nature vs. nurture debate argue over whether caretaker speech is a natural function or a learned one. **13D** Those who believe that caretaker speech is a natural and inherent function in humans believe that it is human nature for children to acquire language and for those around them to encourage their language acquisition naturally; the presence of a child is itself a natural stimulus that increases the rate of caretaker speech among those present. In contrast, those who believe that caretaker speech develops through nurturing rather than nature argue that a person who is attempting to communicate with a child will learn by trying out different ways of communicating to determine which is the most effective from the reactions to the communication attempts; a parent might, for example, learn to use speech with exaggerated inflections with a small child because the exaggerated inflections do a better job of attracting the child's attention than do more subtle inflections. Whether caretaker speech results from nature or nurture, it does play an important and universal role in child language acquisition.

1. According to paragraph 1, children over the age of three
   Ⓐ learn little language from those around them
   Ⓑ are no longer influenced by the language of their parents
   Ⓒ are influenced more and more by those closer to their own age
   Ⓓ first begin to respond to caretaker speech

2. The word "modeling" in paragraph 1 could best be replaced by
   Ⓐ demonstrating
   Ⓑ mimicking
   Ⓒ building
   Ⓓ designing

3. Which of the sentences below best expresses the essential information in the highlighted sentence in paragraph 2? *Incorrect* choices change the meaning in important ways or leave out essential information.
   Ⓐ Most people are quite aware of the use of caretaker speech because of thorough study and research about it.
   Ⓑ The unconscious use of caretaker speech involves a reduction in the complexity of language, while the conscious use of caretaker speech involves an increase in complexity.
   Ⓒ Young children tend to use caretaker speech quite unconsciously in order to reduce the complexity of their thoughts to language that they can express.
   Ⓓ People generally seem to be able to adapt their language to the level of a child's language without thinking consciously about it.

4. The word "It" in paragraph 2 refers to
   Ⓐ caretaker speech
   Ⓑ a higher-pitched voice
   Ⓒ essential information
   Ⓓ baby talk

5. Look at the four squares [■] that indicate where the following sentence could be added to paragraph 2.

   Examples of these are expressions such as "Say bye-bye" or "Where's da-da?"

   Where would the sentence best fit? Click on a square [■] to add the sentence to the passage.

6. All of the following are mentioned in paragraph 3 as characteristics of caretaker speech EXCEPT
   Ⓐ overemphasized inflections
   Ⓑ the use of rhyming sounds
   Ⓒ the tendency to repeat oneself
   Ⓓ the use of easier words and structures

7. It is indicated in paragraph 3 that parents tend to
   Ⓐ speak in basically the same way to a one-year-old and a three-year-old
   Ⓑ use language that is far above the language level of a child
   Ⓒ speak in a progressively less complex way as a child matures
   Ⓓ modify their speech according to the language development of a child

8. The word "processed" in paragraph 4 could best be replaced by

- (A) advanced
- (B) developed
- (C) figured out
- (D) proceeded

9. Which of the sentences below best expresses the essential information in the highlighted sentence in paragraph 4? *Incorrect* choices change the meaning in important ways or leave out essential information.

- (A) The caretaker uses his own gaze to adjust the level of speech in order to help the infant understand better.
- (B) Infants communicate through exaggerated facial expressions, which are understood and adjusted to by the speaker to communicate more clearly.
- (C) Even though the infant looks intently at the speaker, the infant cannot usually understand that a message is being shared between the speaker and infant.
- (D) By interpreting the way an infant is looking at the person speaking, caretaker speech can be modified to make it clearer to the infant.

10. The word "that" in paragraph 5 refers to

- (A) an important point
- (B) the function
- (C) caretaker speech
- (D) a child's reading skills

11. According to paragraph 5, it is NOT expected that someone who believes in nurture over nature

- (A) would believe that caretaker speech is more of a learned style of language than a natural one
- (B) would use different styles of caretaker speech with children in response to what is working best
- (C) would learn to use different styles of caretaker speech with different children
- (D) would use less caretaker speech than do those who believe in nature over nurture

12. The phrase "trying out" in paragraph 5 is closest in meaning to

- (A) experimenting with
- (B) bringing about
- (C) throwing away
- (D) taking over

13. Look at the four squares [■] that indicate where the following sentence could be added to paragraph 5.

It is not merely a device used by English-speaking parents.

Where would the sentence best fit? Click on a square [■] to add the sentence to the passage.

Reading Skill 7: MAKE INFERENCES FROM STATED FACTS

Making inferences tests your ability to draw conclusions and make logical guesses about information that is not directly stated in the passage. For example, in this sentence: "Tina left the classroom with tears in her eyes and slammed the door shut, nearly breaking the glass," one can infer that the woman was upset based on her appearance (crying) and actions (slamming the door shut in a very hard or angry way). In order to make an inference, you must look at the information, or evidence, that you do find in the passage, and then use critical thinking skills to come up with an answer that is reasonable and can be supported by that information. Making inferences is a very important skill on the TOEFL iBT® test, and is a skill that is tested or that you will need to use on every section of the test.

In addition, the ability to use critical thinking skills to make inferences is essential for success in academic life at universities and colleges in the United States.

Look at the chart for some examples of how making inferences can be useful.

Type of Inference	Usefulness in Academic Settings
predicting future events	business; science *We are going to go out tonight for dinner after work. Our co-worker, John, has a cold and is at home resting.* **Prediction:** *John won't be joining us tonight for dinner.*
determining the probable cause/effect of a relationship	sociology; business; science *Susan has been using her car for years to commute to her job in a city far away, but now she is complaining that it isn't working well.* **Effect:** *Susan will probably need to buy a new car.* **Cause:** *Her current car is getting old and worn out due to the fact she has been driving it long distances for a long time.*
determining the likelihood of an event in the past	history; anthropology; astronomy
measuring the accuracy of a statement	sociology; law; business

Inference Exercise

Read each sentence or group of sentences below. Determine which inference can best be drawn from the information provided.

determining the probable cause/effect of a relationship
EX. After looking through the window, the man grabbed his umbrella before he headed out the door.

_____ The man expected the weather to be pleasant.
__X__ It was raining outside.
_____ The man was late for work.

measuring the accuracy of a statement
1. Bats are nocturnal creatures. They are most active at night, and are rarely seen in daylight.

_____ Bats sometimes hunt during the day.
_____ Bats have excellent night vision.
_____ Bats sleep during the day.

determining the likelihood of an event in the past
2. Recent dietary guidelines have established that people need to eat five to nine servings of fruits and vegetables each day. Former guidelines had suggested only four to six servings per day. However, concerns about people's health led experts to increase this amount.

_____ People were probably not eating enough fruits and vegetables in the past.
_____ The former guidelines were more accurate than the current guidelines.
_____ People enjoy eating fruits and vegetables.

measuring the accuracy of a statement

3. The first computer had to be housed in an enormous room. It has only been relatively recently that computers have become portable enough to carry around from place to place. Newer tablet or laptop models make computers even more convenient to transport.

_____ Older computers were smaller than newer computers.

_____ Portable computers function better than desktop computers.

_____ Tablet computers are smaller than previous models of computers.

determining the probable cause/effect of a relationship

4. Clothing has undergone quite an evolution over time. Early garments were crude coverings made of animal skin or plants, which were made by hand using a time-consuming process. Nowadays, a large percentage of clothing is sewn by machine and uses synthetic materials.

_____ In the past, people worked together to make clothing.

_____ The use of plants for clothing led to man-made fabrics.

_____ Clothing is made more quickly today than in the distant past.

determining the probable cause/effect of a relationship

5. As oil becomes more scarce, the cost of fuel made from oil increases. This additional expense is passed on from the oil refinery to the fuel distributor to the fuel consumer at the end of the line. The result is a decrease in the consumption of this type of fuel, if not a decrease in the use of energy overall.

_____ Consumers probably use other types of fuel in place of oil.

_____ Consumers are angry that they have to pay more for fuel.

_____ Fuel distributors have begun to pressure oil refineries to lower prices.

predicting a future event

6. Many native tribes of people have been severely affected by the rapid march of modern development into their traditional locales. Some have been able, with government support, to slow down the destruction of their traditional ways of life while others, lacking the power or resources to do so, face an uncertain future.

_____ Modern society will soon destroy all native tribal structures.

_____ Some native tribes may be forced to give up their traditions.

_____ Government support may be slow in coming to native tribes.

Strategies to Answer Inference Questions

- Look for any indications in the question that tell you where the answer is located (i.e., *According to paragraph 2 . . .*).

- Look for information in the passage that contradicts an answer choice and eliminate that answer choice.

- Remember that for some answers, you may need to analyze several details from the passage to reach a conclusion.

- Look for clear key words—such as dates, names, and locations—to help you skim for information and to eliminate wrong answers.

- Do not choose an answer based only on the fact that it appears to be true. The correct answer will not be stated directly and must be inferred.

Example

TOEFL IBT® TEST
REVIEW · HELP · BACK · NEXT
PAUSE TEST · SECTION EXIT
Question 1 of 12
HIDE TIME · 00 : 18 : 38
More Available

The History of Money

1▶ Virtually every known country in the world has a system of currency, but the actual understanding of how and why money developed as a means of obtaining goods and services has not received much attention in recent history. Money is more than just a system of banknotes and coins that transfer economic value. There is a psychology of defining needs and developing trust that has assisted in the evolution of monetary systems.

2▶ Prior to the use of money, people in most civilizations used to trade, or barter, for goods, but this was not a completely satisfactory arrangement for everyone. First, in order to barter with someone, a person needed something of value to barter with. In an agricultural society, this often meant trading grains or food crops in exchange for animals. However, within such a system, if a person was not fortunate enough to possess something of value, he would be unable to get what he needed in return. In addition to having something of value to offer, traders also needed to find someone who wanted what they were offering. In other words, if one person had grain to trade for cattle, he had to find a trading partner with cattle who also wanted and needed grain for his animals. If the cattle owner already had sufficient grain, or needed wood to build a new shelter for his animals instead, then neither side would be able to trade for what they wanted.

3▶ The introduction of nonperishable substances as money was an important solution to this dilemma. Early societies began introducing stones, shells, or metals that they considered valuable as payment for perishable goods like food, seeds, and animals. By allowing a farmer to accept gold for his cattle instead of grain, societies made trade a more flexible process. For example, if the farmer sold his extra cattle in the spring in exchange for a certain amount of gold, the farmer could use that same gold in the winter for grain when his supply ran out. Those who possessed talents, such as carpentry or writing, instead of goods, also reaped the benefits of using gold. A skilled carpenter, or even less skilled crop gatherer, could trade his services for gold that could be saved until he needed it to obtain goods or services for himself.

4▶ The use of money as a concrete form of payment was beneficial for international trade as well. When perishable goods were exchanged, they could not be taken long distances. This meant the circle of trade was mostly local. Once more durable materials began to be used as money, merchants and travelers could take the money to towns further away and bring back goods that were previously unknown in their local area. The ability to cross the borders of a different country and conduct business led to the introduction of even more exotic goods into a particular town or village.

5▶ Expansion into international trade meant the materials for money had to be standardized for wider acceptance. While some cultures had previously used shells, simple metals, or even durable rice grains as units of monetary exchange within their own societies, some of these early forms of money were rejected by outside cultures. Over time as trade advanced, it became clear that the materials being used for money had to meet specific criteria for value on which a wide range of people could agree.

6▶ The materials used for money had to exhibit three characteristics to be considered suitable for use: scarcity, indestructibility, and portability. Scarcity meant that the materials were not easily available to many people. They had to exist in relatively small amounts, or be somewhat difficult to obtain. In addition, the substances used for money needed to be durable and almost impossible to destroy. No one wanted to trade goods or services for a material that would not be long lasting. Finally, the materials used had to be portable, small and light enough to travel with over distances. As a result, silver and gold became popular monetary units. The metals were not commonly available, and it was easy to mold and separate them into small, convenient pieces, such as roughly shaped coins for travel. Best of all, while the metals can be melted down, it is practically impossible to destroy them entirely, which means they retain their value over long periods of time.

> Practice understanding inferences in your everyday reading. When you see words such as *suggest*, *imply*, *likely*, or *probably*, ask yourself what conclusion you can make from the information you are reading.

READING

Look at an example of an inference question. (See paragraph 2.)

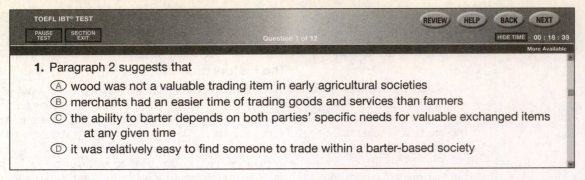

The third answer choice is correct. Paragraph 2 tells you *in an agricultural society, this often meant trading grains or food crops in exchange for animals.* The next sentence mentions . . . *if a person was not fortunate enough to possess something of value* . . . by which you can infer that grains, animals, and crops had value. The first and fourth answer choices are incorrect because they contradict the information in the paragraph. The second answer choice is incorrect because merchants are not mentioned in the paragraph.

Look at another example of an inference question.(See paragraph 3.)

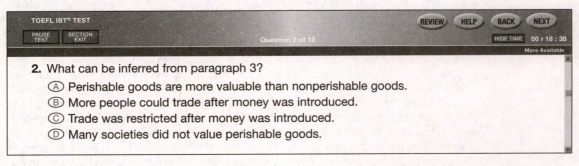

Paragraph 3 first gives examples of nonperishable goods (line 2) by contrasting a few with perishable goods: *Early societies began introducing stones, shells, or metals . . . as payment for perishable goods like food, seeds, and animals.* Subsequent lines in the paragraphs give examples of the types of people that could use money for trade: farmers could *accept gold for . . . cattle* (line 4). Carpenters and crop gatherers *could trade [their] services for gold* (lines 8–9).

These examples indicate that more people enjoyed the benefits of using money, which means the correct answer choice is the second choice, *more people could trade after money was introduced.*

Look at another example of an inference question. (See paragraph 5.)

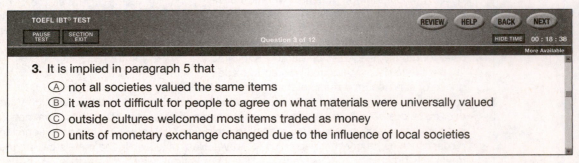

Paragraph 5 states in lines 1–2 that . . . *the materials for money had to be standardized for wider acceptance.* In lines 3–4, it also tells you that . . . *some of these early forms of money were rejected by outside cultures . . . .* Lines 4–5 state that . . . *money had to meet specific criteria . . . on which a wide range of people could agree.* Therefore, the correct answer is the first choice, *not all societies valued the same items.*

Look at another example of an inference question. (See paragraph 6.)

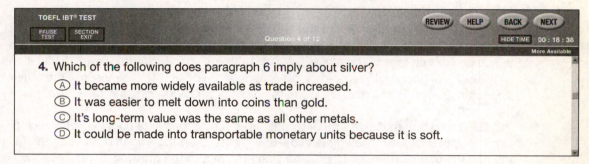

The fourth answer choice is correct. The first sentence of paragraph 6 states . . . *materials used for money had to exhibit three characteristics . . . scarcity, indestructibility, and portability.*

The following chart outlines the key points that you should remember about Inferences from Stated Facts questions.

KEY POINTS FOR QUESTIONS ABOUT MAKING INFERENCES	
FREQUENCY	1–3 questions per reading passage
HOW TO IDENTIFY THE QUESTION	What can be inferred from paragraph X about . . . ? Which of the following is suggested in paragraph X? What is implied by the author in paragraph X . . . ? In paragraph X, it can be inferred that . . . Paragraph X implies . . . Paragraph X suggests . . .
WHERE TO FIND THE ANSWER	Usually the question will tell you in what paragraph(s) to look for the answer. The questions are also generally in the order of the information presented in the passage.
HOW TO ANSWER THE QUESTION	1. Look for any indications in the question that tell you where the answer is located (i.e., *According to paragraph 2 . . .*). 2. Look for clear key words—such as dates, names, and locations—to help you scan for information and to eliminate wrong answers. 3. Look for information in the passage that contradicts an answer choice; eliminate that choice. 4. Do not choose an answer based only on the fact that appears to be true. The correct answer will not be stated directly and must be inferred.

In the exam, you may be able to eliminate incorrect answer choices by understanding what is wrong with them.

For Inferences from Stated Facts questions, incorrect answer choices may:
- manipulate the stated details.
- contain false information.
- contradict direct information given in the paragraph.
- suggest a conclusion that is not reasonable or logical.

READING EXERCISE 7: Study each of the passages and choose the best answers to the questions that follow.

PASSAGE ONE (Questions 1–8)

Paragraph   **Tiger Moths**

1▶   One of the most beautiful of the 100,000 known species in the order *Lepidoptera*[1] are the tiger moths, moths known for the striking appeal of their distinctive coloration, which can match that of the closely related butterfly species. More than 200 variations of the colorful tiger moth exist in North America. In addition to their visually attractive appearance, tiger moths can be identified by their heavy bodies and their slow, purposeful flight patterns.

2▶   Similar to butterflies and other moths, tiger moths begin as eggs, which develop into caterpillar larvae.[2] The egg is laid—usually in the spring—so that it will attach to the surface of a plant that can provide vital nutrients to the growing larva. Once the egg hatches, the larva immediately begins feeding on the plant. Depending on the type of tiger moth, it can feed on a variety of plants or rely solely on a single plant species. One well-known single-plant feeder is the milkweed tussock moth, which both feeds off of and gets its name from the milkweed plant. In contrast, the banded woolly bear moth, another type of tiger moth, obtains its nutrients from a wider variety of plant species, including several types of herbs.

3▶   Both categories of tiger moths, single-plant and multiple-plant feeders, spend the spring and summer feeding in an attempt to gorge themselves with nutrients that will carry them through the cold months of winter. During these months, most tiger moth caterpillars find a safe place to hide so that they can regulate their body processes in a state of torpor, a sleep-like phase of inactivity similar to that of hibernation in larger species. During this stage, the caterpillars depend entirely on their internal store of nutrients.

4▶   Once winter passes and warmer weather returns, the caterpillars emerge and prepare for the pupa stage. During this stage, the caterpillar once again attaches itself to a plant, this time to form a protective covering, or cocoon around itself. Inside the cocoon, the caterpillar transforms into a pupa, and in a short time, emerges from the cocoon as an adult moth. It is important to note that the adult moth's development is not quite complete as soon as it comes out of the cocoon; it needs time to pump blood to its wings so that they can fully form and open. After the caterpillar enters the pupa stage, and once it becomes a moth, it no longer requires feeding.

5▶   Tiger moths, once they reach maturity, only have a few days of life left, during which the prime focus is to find a mate and lay eggs that will hatch into the next generation of moths. This is perhaps the most vulnerable period of a tiger moth's life. Its wings are extremely delicate, and can easily be damaged or torn off. Since it has evolved to not consume food during the moth stage of life, its energy stores become depleted, causing it to age and die in a few short days. However, what would seem to be two of the biggest threats to a tiger moth's existence—its heavy body and slow speed—are almost negligible in the danger they pose to the creature. In fact, the tiger moth has few, if any, predators seeking to eat it.

6▶   The reason the tiger moth is unappealing to predators is that it is covered with highly conspicuous orange-and-black or yellow-and-black patterns of spots and stripes. Such boldly patterned color combinations are commonplace in the animal world, serving the function of forewarning potential predators of unpleasant tastes and smells. This is unquestionably the function served by the striking coloration of the garden tiger moth, which is quite visually attractive but is also poisonous to predators. Certain glands in the garden tiger moth produce strong toxins that circulate throughout the insect's bloodstream, while other glands secrete bubbles that produce a noxious warning smell.

The tiger moth, indeed, is a clear example of a concept that many predators intuitively understand, that creatures with the brightest coloration are often the least suitable to eat.

GLOSSARY

1 *Lepidoptera*—the family of insects that includes moths and butterflies
2 *caterpillar larvae* (singular *larva*)—a small, wingless insect with long rounded body and many short legs that develops into a butterfly or moth

1. It is implied in paragraph 1 about the order *Lepidoptera* that
   (A) all members of the order are moths
   (B) there may be more than 100,000 species in this order
   (C) all members of the order are brightly colored
   (D) there are most likely fewer than 100,000 species in this order

2. It can be inferred from paragraph 1 that butterflies are
   (A) not colorful
   (B) larger than most tiger moths
   (C) also part of the order *Lepidoptera*
   (D) competitors of the tiger moth

3. What is implied about the eggs of tiger moths in paragraph 2?
   (A) They are generally laid in warmer seasons.
   (B) Only some of them grow into large caterpillars.
   (C) Not all of the eggs hatch at the same time.
   (D) They are slower to develop than butterfly eggs.

4. What can be inferred about the plants mentioned in paragraph 2?
   (A) They can be poisonous to moth eggs.
   (B) They provide shelter for moth larva.
   (C) They are essential for the development of the moth larva.
   (D) There is only one type that moths attach to.

5. It is implied in paragraph 3 that
   (A) both butterflies and tiger moths hibernate
   (B) caterpillars do not consume additional food during the winter
   (C) caterpillars store food in a secure hiding place
   (D) other species of moths also stock up on food in warmer months

6. Paragraph 4 suggests that
   (A) caterpillars need to eat to get ready for the pupa stage
   (B) the moth completes its full development inside a cocoon
   (C) the tiger moth cocoon allows the pupa to survive during development
   (D) plants are not vital to the pupa stage

7. What can be inferred from paragraph 5?
   (A) An adult tiger moth can produce many generations throughout its short life.
   (B) Most tiger moths die without laying eggs.
   (C) Tiger moths are threatening to predators due to their large bodies.
   (D) The size and speed of tiger moths are not disadvantages.

8. What would most likely happen to a predator that wanted to eat a tiger moth?
   (A) The predator would be unable to catch it.
   (B) The predator would capture it by poisoning it.
   (C) The predator would be unable to find it.
   (D) The predator would back away from it.

PASSAGE TWO (Questions 9–16)

Paragraph

The Cambrian Explosion

1▶   Many of the major phyla of animals arose during the Cambrian Period, in what is called the Cambrian Explosion. Prior to the Cambrian Period, some scientists believe that the majority of organisms were simple one-celled creatures that in certain instances would organize themselves into colonies. These same scientists propose that an explosion of evolutionary diversification occurred about 580 million years ago, and lasted approximately 70–80 million years. During this period of rapid evolutionary growth, the pre-Cambrian single-celled organisms developed into the multicelled predecessors of

> Inference questions on the TOEFL iBT® test usually have a lot of support from information in the passage. Often, the answer is the most logical, obvious choice from the reading.

many of today's organisms. The new, more complicated organisms spread throughout the Earth and formed complex communities.

2▶   One theoretical explanation for the rapid diversification that occurred during the Cambrian Period is known as the theory of polar wander. According to this theory, the rapid diversification occurred because of an unusually rapid reorganization of the Earth's crust during the Cambrian Period. This change in the Earth's top layer initiated evolutionary change inasmuch as change in the environment serves to trigger a concurrent change in evolutionary development.

3▶   Because the Cambrian Period occurred so long ago, it is practically impossible to say with absolute certainty how accurate the claims of scientists who support this theory of the explosion of life are. The primary evidence accumulated in support of the Cambrian Explosion is fossils. Multiple samples of fossils, pre- and post-Cambrian Period, that were preserved in the sediment layers of the Earth have been dug out and examined. Proponents of the Cambrian Explosion use the predominance of single-celled fossils prior to the explosion, and the corresponding rise in multicelled fossils during and after the Cambrian Explosion, to validate their theories on the development of life during this time.

4▶   However, a debate has been fueled over the impact of Cambrian Explosion due to the discovery of fossils dating back over a billion years ago. These fossils show evidence of the complex types of cells that are considered to be the building blocks of all animals, plants, and fungi that exist in our modern era, thus throwing into doubt that all multicelled development originated from the Cambrian Explosion. This and other discoveries have given rise to a different theory of evolutionary development. This competing theory states that the evolution of life occurred in phases that began millions, even billions, of years before the Cambrian Explosion. During these phases, there was a short rapid period of evolutionary growth, followed by long periods of rest during which organisms remained relatively stable, without much evolutionary progress.

5▶   There are obvious problems that arise in determining which theory is more accurate. One of the most apparent concerns is the validity of dating techniques. There is no doubt that methods used to discover the Earth's true age have become increasingly sophisticated with advances in technology. However, the fact that scientists have to project further and further back in time as new investigations of the Earth's layers reveal more clues leaves more room for error. In other words, the older the Earth appears to be, the more gaps appear in definitively pinpointing its age.

6▶   Another issue arises with the use of fossil evidence. Despite fossils being the most reliable source for dating the Earth, especially regarding life forms, their scarcity makes gathering an abundance of evidence for various time periods a challenge. Fossilization is a complex process that the smallest adversity can render incomplete or useless. First, living organisms have to die relatively intact, and quickly be buried in a sediment layer before they decay beyond recognition. Then, the sediment layers require protection from erosion that could eat away at the fossils. These two factors heavily influence the preservation of fossils, and the further back in time scientists investigate, the fewer the fossils that are uncovered.

7▶   Technology has remedied somewhat the difficulty of finding and preserving fossils as it has improved methods of dating the Earth. In fact, it is technological advances that have helped spark the debate involving the Cambrian Explosion theory and other theories of the late twentieth century. The discoveries giving rise to the theory behind the Cambrian Explosion came to light in the mid-1800s, whereas theories regarding the earlier development of multicelled organisms were proposed over a century later with the help of technological improvements in research methods.

9. It can be inferred from paragraph 1 that
   Ⓐ some major phyla developed during periods other than the Cambrian Period
   Ⓑ many other phyla of animals became extinct during the Cambrian Explosion
   Ⓒ descriptions of various animal phyla were created during the Cambrian Period
   Ⓓ the major phyla of animals that came about during the Cambrian Period died out in the Cambrian Explosion

10. It can be inferred from paragraph 2 that one basis for the theory of polar wander is that
   Ⓐ relatively little change in the Earth's crust took place during the Cambrian Period
   Ⓑ rapid diversification was not possible because of the changes in the Earth's crust
   Ⓒ the Earth's crust changed more slowly in other periods
   Ⓓ evolutionary changes are the cause of environmental changes

11. Paragraph 3 suggests that
   Ⓐ most fossils found in sediment are from the Cambrian Period
   Ⓑ other types of evidence besides fossils have also supported the theory of the explosion of life during the Cambrian Period
   Ⓒ single-celled fossils were more common during the Cambrian Period
   Ⓓ scientists supporting the Cambrian Explosion theory are uncertain about the dates of fossil evidence

12. It can be inferred from paragraph 4 that
   Ⓐ the earliest fossils indicate that evolution occurred slowly over long periods of time
   Ⓑ scientists have conclusively shown that multicelled development occurred after the Cambrian Explosion
   Ⓒ no fossils exist prior to the Cambrian Explosion
   Ⓓ multicelled organisms may have evolved in phases

13. Paragraph 5 implies that
   Ⓐ it is easy to come up with the precise age of the Earth
   Ⓑ technology has not yet succeeded in perfecting methods of dating the Earth
   Ⓒ current research has not provided new information about the Earth's crust
   Ⓓ as scientists look further back into the history of the Earth, it becomes easier to predict its age

14. It can be inferred from paragraph 6 that
   Ⓐ finding intact fossils is the main challenge in validating one of the theories
   Ⓑ fossils are abundant in supply, giving scientists a clear look at the past
   Ⓒ fossilization is a fragile process that can quickly fall apart
   Ⓓ most organisms die relatively intact before they fossilize

15. It can be inferred from paragraph 6 that
   Ⓐ scientists are challenged when recreating life forms from a specific time period
   Ⓑ scientists depend on fossils to help them date the Earth
   Ⓒ scientists can preserve fossils and protect them from erosion
   Ⓓ erosion has destroyed most fossil evidence found on the Earth

16. Paragraph 7 suggests that
   Ⓐ technology has made it more difficult to study the Earth's age
   Ⓑ technology has no effect on scientific research related to the Cambrian Period
   Ⓒ the Cambrian Explosion was responsible for improvements in technology
   Ⓓ the technology of the 1800s was not as advanced as later technology

PASSAGE THREE (Questions 17–24)

Paragraph

The Golden Age of Comics

1▶   The period from the late 1930s until after the end of World War II is known as the Golden Age of Comics. The modern comic book came about in the early 1930s in the United States as a giveaway premium to promote the sales of a whole range of household products such as cereal and cleansers. The comic books, which were printed in bright colors to attract the attention of potential customers, proved so popular that some publishers decided to produce comic books that would come out on a monthly basis and would sell for a dime each. Though comic strips had been reproduced in publications prior to this time, the *Famous Funnies* comic book, which was started in 1934, marked the first occasion that a serialized book of comics was attempted.

2▶   The precise event that initiated the Golden Age of Comics has been debated for decades; nevertheless, virtually all comic book experts agree that the introduction of Superman in 1938 changed the concept of comic books, as well as their perception in the eyes of the public. Previously, comic books had focused on reprints of already existing comic strips. However, the enormous popularity of Superman ushered in an entire generation of original characters known as superheroes, many of which remain popular today. Shortly after Superman arrived on the scene, Batman, The Flash, The Green Lantern, and Wonder Woman were created, along with a host of others. The superheroes varied widely in their backgrounds, appearances, and superpowers, yet all shared one characteristic in common: a noble compulsion to protect the United States—and later the world—against evil.

3▶   At the start of the Golden Age of Comics, many Americans were in despair and only slowly recovering from the effects of the Great Depression. Comics debuted as an inexpensive way to entertain children and young adults who were not able to afford the cost of a movie ticket. Perhaps because of their impoverished target audience, the first "villains" were often the wealthy owners of industry or powerful politicians. These prominent figures were portrayed as corrupt and unconcerned about the "common man," and were almost always thoroughly defeated by the end of the comic book issue. Although some villains were able to escape after their losses to return in a later storyline, ultimately the conquering superhero always came out on top.

4▶   As the United States entered into World War II, new characters emerged that reflected the struggles Americans faced with their opposition overseas. The superheroes were recruited to battle against the same foreign forces American soldiers faced, though in the comic books, the negative characteristics of the opposing militaries were exaggerated and embellished in order to make the adventures more dramatic and thrilling for readers at home. Popular storylines exhibited patriotism and presented the ultimate resolution of good defeating evil.

5▶   The post-war demand for comic books fell off sharply from previous years, though this did not necessarily mean a decrease in the popularity of superheroes. While Superman, Batman, and other superheroes continued to be featured in traditional comic book formats, they also began to come to life in other media, especially films and television shows. Thus, even as the Golden Age of Comics began its inevitable decline, the enormous contribution of its superheroes to the popular culture of the United States has ensured that its significance will not be forgotten.

17. It can be inferred from paragraph 1 that, at the beginning of the 1930s, comic books most likely cost
(A) nothing
(B) five cents
(C) ten cents
(D) twenty-five cents

18. Comic books would least likely have been used to promote
(A) soap
(B) cookies
(C) jewelry
(D) bread

19. It is implied in paragraph 2 that
(A) the start of the comic book's popularity has been precisely determined
(B) Superman was not a popular figure when he first came out
(C) it took decades for comic books to reach their Golden Age
(D) not everyone agrees on what first caused comic books to gain popularity

20. From the information in paragraph 2, it appears that Superman most likely
(A) was introduced sometime after Batman
(B) was a character that first appeared in a comic book
(C) first appeared in the early 1930s
(D) was the most popular superhero of his time

21. It can be inferred from paragraph 3 that the villains in comic books

Ⓐ were eventually regarded as heroes by people after the Great Depression

Ⓑ sometimes defeated the superheroes in early comic books

Ⓒ were ones people in the 1930s liked to see defeated

Ⓓ were always killed at the end of a fight in comic books during their golden age

22. It can be inferred from the passage that

Ⓐ comic book storylines were influenced by Americans' real-life struggles

Ⓑ comic books helped Americans understand the reality of the world around them

Ⓒ comic books remain as popular today as they were decades ago

Ⓓ comic books had no lasting impact once the Golden Age ended

23. Paragraph 4 suggests that

Ⓐ comic books promoted Americans' devotion to their country

Ⓑ comic books depicted the domestic troubles in the U.S. at the time

Ⓒ comic books reached their height of excellence after World War II was over

Ⓓ overseas popularity of military-themed comic books was highest during World War II

24. What is implied in paragraph 5?

Ⓐ Superman remains the most popular superhero.

Ⓑ Superheroes became less popular as comic books declined.

Ⓒ Superheroes remain popular in modern times.

Ⓓ Films and television have influenced the popularity of superheroes more than comic books.

PASSAGE FOUR (Questions 25–32)

Paragraph

The Filibuster

1▶ The term "filibuster" has been in use since the mid-nineteenth century to describe the tactic of delaying legislative action in order to prevent the passage of a bill. The word comes from the Dutch *freebooter,* or pirate, and most likely developed from the idea that someone conducting a filibuster is trying to steal away the opportunity that proponents of a bill have to make it successful.

2▶ In the earlier history of the U.S. Congress, filibusters were used in both the House of Representatives and in the Senate, but they are now much more a part of the culture of the Senate than of the House. One reason is that the House began creating and enforcing rules to limit the time a representative could speak as early as 1842. As membership in the House grew in proportion to the increasing U.S. population, the rules restricting speech became even stricter. As a result, the filibuster has been effectively eliminated as a mechanism for delaying legislation in the House.

3▶ The Senate, the smaller of the two bodies, has established rules that can constrain but not totally eliminate filibusters. The Senate adopted its first cloture rule in 1917, a rule that requires a vote of two-thirds of the Senate to limit debate to one hour on each side. The rule was changed in 1975 and now requires a vote of three-fifths of the members to invoke cloture in most situations.

4▶ Though the cloture rule was enacted in 1917, it did not completely eliminate the filibuster as a tactic used by senators opposed to a particular bill. Senator Huey Long conducted a filibuster in 1937 in support of his political views, reciting Shakespeare and reading recipes in an effort to consume time. In 1953, Senator Wayne Morse filibustered for 22 hours and 26 minutes in a single session in protest of oil legislation being considered by the Senate. This record was broken just a few years later by Senator Strom Thurmond, who spoke continuously for 24 hours and 18 minutes during his filibuster against passage of civil rights legislation in 1957. Thurmond held the floor of the Senate by lecturing on the law and reading from court decisions and newspaper columns.

5▶ Ironically, early on in the establishment of the Senate, a motion similar to the cloture rule was voted into existence in 1789. However, a prominent leader of that time, Aaron Burr, successfully argued that the rule was unnecessary. Consequently, it was struck down at the beginning of the nineteenth century, allowing for the potential of a filibuster from that point on. Although this potential existed, it was not put into practice until the late 1830s, with the first Senate filibuster occurring in 1837.

6▶   Filibustering has met with mixed success in the Senate. Some of the most passionate filibustering has been done in attempts to deter civil rights legislation. A filibuster was successful in blocking legislation against discrimination in employment, contained in a bill introduced by Senator Dennis Chavez in 1946. Although Senator Chavez had enough votes to secure passage of the measure, the filibuster, which continued for weeks, forced him to finally remove the bill from consideration. However, Senator Thurmond's attempt to block passage of a civil rights bill in 1957 ultimately failed, despite his astoundingly lengthy address. Similarly, an attempt by southern Democratic senators in the early 1960s to block passage of important civil rights legislation fell short, despite the fact that the filibuster lasted 75 hours. It ended when the Senate invoked the cloture rule, only the second time it had done so since 1927.

7▶   In modern times, the threat of filibusters has gained popularity as a strategy used by the minority political party to influence legislation. Along with rising threat has come a concurrent rise in the number of cloture motions filed. In the 1960s, an individual senate term of six years documented no more than seven cloture motions being filed. In the first decade of the twenty-first century, this number had risen to no *fewer* than 49 cloture motions per Senate term, and a record of 112 cloture votes was set in 2008.

25. It can be inferred from the information in paragraph 1 that around 1800
   Ⓐ the first filibuster took place
   Ⓑ legislative action was never delayed
   Ⓒ the term "filibuster" was not in use in the U.S. Congress
   Ⓓ the Dutch introduced the term *freebooter*

26. It can be inferred from paragraph 1 that a *freebooter* was most likely someone who
   Ⓐ served in the Senate
   Ⓑ robbed passing ships
   Ⓒ enacted legislation
   Ⓓ served in the Dutch government

27. It is implied in paragraph 2 that, in its early years, the House
   Ⓐ had no rules against filibusters
   Ⓑ had few filibusters
   Ⓒ had fewer filibusters than the Senate
   Ⓓ had the longest filibuster on record

28. Based on the information in paragraph 3, a vote of cloture would most likely be used to
   Ⓐ initiate filibusters
   Ⓑ break filibusters
   Ⓒ extend filibusters
   Ⓓ encourage filibusters

29. It is implied in paragraph 4 that Senator Thurmond was opposed to
   Ⓐ filibusters
   Ⓑ lecturing on the law
   Ⓒ speaking in the Senate
   Ⓓ a civil rights bill

30. Paragraph 5 suggests that
   Ⓐ Aaron Burr felt filibusters would encourage debate in the Senate
   Ⓑ filibusters were common practice in the Senate as early as 1789
   Ⓒ Aaron Burr had a lot of influence on Senate decisions
   Ⓓ filibusters were a prominent strategy for Aaron Burr

31. In paragraph 6, the information provided implies that
   Ⓐ Dennis Chavez successfully blocked a filibuster
   Ⓑ Strom Thurmond filibustered only to break a previous record
   Ⓒ Most senators of the 1950s and 1960s supported civil rights legislation
   Ⓓ A filibuster's success depends on how long it lasts

32. It can be inferred from paragraph 7 that
   Ⓐ filibusters are more frequent today than cloture motions
   Ⓑ both filibuster threats and cloture motions have become more common in the past few years
   Ⓒ the highest number of cloture motions was recorded in the 1960s
   Ⓓ the majority party uses filibusters as often as the minority party

Reading Skill 8: INFER RHETORICAL PURPOSE QUESTIONS

The term *rhetoric* refers to the ability to use language in an effective manner to express ideas.

Rhetorical purpose questions test your ability to understand the relationship of words and phrases to the ideas being communicated in a passage.

Rhetorical purpose may be used to:

- provide an example of something familiar to the reader in order to explain something that may not be known.

- provide a definition of an unfamiliar concept, object, or idea.

- to emphasize, clarify, or develop ideas.

- provide a point of comparison or contrast for another idea(s).

- criticize or provide an argument for or against something in order to persuade the reader.

When you are asked a rhetorical purpose question, you must infer the relationship that the highlighted words or phrases in the passage have to the ideas around them. To do this, you must look for logical connections between the highlighted information and the sentences around it or for logical connections between paragraphs.

Strategies to Answer Rhetorical Purpose Questions

- Read the sentence that contains the highlighted information.

- Look for signal words or phrases (i.e., *one example; rather than*) that establish a relationship between the highlighted word(s) and other ideas.

- Read one to two sentences around the key sentence to clearly understand the relationship between the highlighted word(s) and the other ideas being presented.

Example

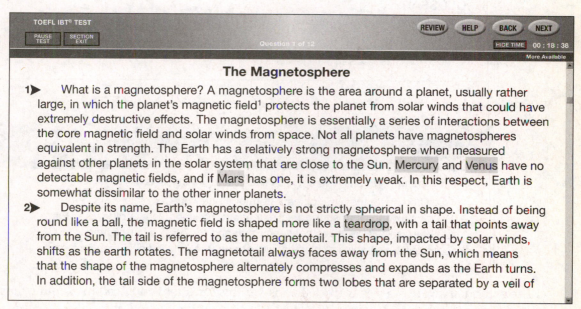

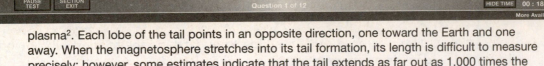

plasma[2]. Each lobe of the tail points in an opposite direction, one toward the Earth and one away. When the magnetosphere stretches into its tail formation, its length is difficult to measure precisely; however, some estimates indicate that the tail extends as far out as 1,000 times the Earth's radius.

3▶ The side of the magnetosphere that faces the sun is quite different in appearance from the magnetotail. First, the solar winds compress the sunward side so that it is only about 6 to 10 times the Earth's radius in length. As can be imagined, the compression condenses the particles within the magnetosphere into a much smaller area. This compression also changes the shape of the magnetosphere on the sunward facing side. Rather than being dragged out like a tail, the magnetic field is pushed in by the solar winds, looking much like a bow that shoots an arrow. This bow shape is called the "bow shock" of the magnetosphere.

4▶ Beneath the bow shock area of Earth's magnetosphere lay the magnetosheath and magnetopause. The magnetosheath is formed mostly by solar wind that has been pushed back from penetrating closer to the Earth. Basically, this layer is a cushion that shields the Earth from the flow of pressure from both the solar winds moving in from the outside and the Earth's own magnetic field pushing outward from the Earth's core. It works with the magnetopause to protect the earth from too much solar wind. The magnetopause is below the magnetosheath. This area balances the pressure received from the solar winds and the Earth's magnetic field. While the pressure from the Earth's magnetic field remains constant, the pressure from the solar winds fluctuates with the Earth's rotation, which results in related changes in the thickness of the magnetopause.

5▶ These layers of the magnetosphere ensure that solar winds do not unduly disrupt the Earth's magnetic field, which remains an essential factor to the survival of many of Earth's species. Although there is currently not any substantial evidence that humans respond innately to the magnetic field, the presence of a certain protein found in the human retina of the human eye indicates the possibility. This protein, cryptochrome, has been taken from humans and implanted into the fly *Drosophila*. In tests with the fly, it has been shown that the protein enables the fly to sense and respond to the magnetic field. It is theorized that the light sensitive protein detects changes in the pressure of solar winds and the corresponding change in the magnetic field. Additionally, migratory animals have shown a clear dependence on their ability to sense the magnetic field. One such animal, the sea turtle, relies on its perception of the magnetic field to guide its long migratory trek. Several species of birds that regularly migrate also depend on their innate ability to respond to the Earth's magnetic field in order to safely reach their destinations.

GLOSSARY

1 *magnetic field*—an area in which a physical force makes objects pull towards or push apart from each other

2 *plasma*—a gas that exists at very high temperatures, for example in stars, which consists of ions and electrons and reacts to a magnetic field

Look at an example of a rhetorical purpose question. (See paragraph 1.)

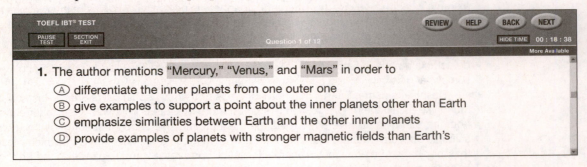

TOEFL IBT® TEST · REVIEW · HELP · BACK · NEXT

PAUSE TEST · SECTION EXIT · Question 1 of 12 · HIDE TIME · 00 : 18 : 38

More Available

1. The author mentions "Mercury," "Venus," and "Mars" in order to
   - Ⓐ differentiate the inner planets from one outer one
   - Ⓑ give examples to support a point about the inner planets other than Earth
   - Ⓒ emphasize similarities between Earth and the other inner planets
   - Ⓓ provide examples of planets with stronger magnetic fields than Earth's

The second answer choice is correct. To answer this question, you need to examine the information around the words *Mercury, Venus,* and *Mars* in the first paragraph.

- The sentence before the key sentence (lines 5–6) states that *the Earth has a relatively strong magnetosphere when measured against other planets . . . close to the Sun.*

- The sentence mentioning the three planets in the question states *Mercury and Venus have no detectable (measurable) magnetic field* and *any potential field that Mars might have is extremely weak.*

- The sentence following the key sentence tells you that *Earth . . . is . . . dissimilar to the other inner planets.*

From this, you can infer that the three planets, *Mercury, Venus,* and *Mars* are mentioned to support information that is not true about the Earth.

Look at another example of a rhetorical purpose question. (See paragraph 2.)

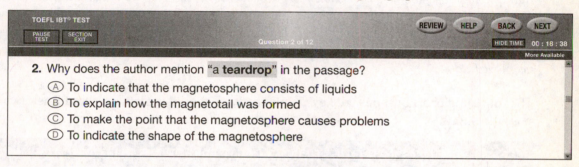

The fourth answer choice is correct. To answer this question, you need to read the information around *a teardrop* in the second paragraph to understand why it is relevant to the information in the paragraph. The sentence containing the key word (lines 1–2) contrasts the teardrop shape with the shape of a ball to explain how the magnetosphere looks: *Instead of being round like a ball, the magnetic field is shaped more like a teardrop.*

Look at another example of a rhetorical purpose question. (See paragraph 3.)

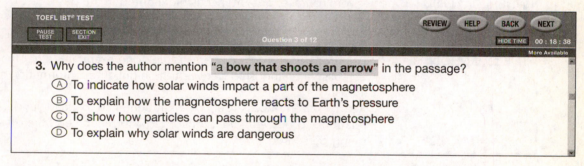

The first answer choice is correct. To answer this question, you need to examine the information around *a bow that shoots an arrow* in the third paragraph. The sentence before the key sentence tells you that the paragraph is describing the shape of the magnetic field *on the sunward facing side.* The key sentence states *. . . the magnetic field is pushed in by the solar winds, looking much like a bow that shoots an arrow,* indicating the effect solar winds have on this part of the magnetosphere.

Look at another example of a rhetorical purpose question. (See paragraph 5.)

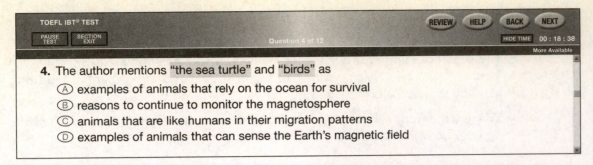

4. The author mentions "the sea turtle" and "birds" as

    Ⓐ examples of animals that rely on the ocean for survival

    Ⓑ reasons to continue to monitor the magnetosphere

    Ⓒ animals that are like humans in their migration patterns

    Ⓓ examples of animals that can sense the Earth's magnetic field

The fourth answer choice is correct. To answer this question, you need to look at the information in paragraph 5 around the sentences in which *the sea turtle* and *birds* are mentioned (lines 10–11). In the sentence before the animals are first mentioned (lines 9–10), it tells you that . . . *migratory animals have shown . . . dependence on their ability to sense the magnetic field.* The following sentence gives an example of one animal that depends on this ability: . . . *the sea turtle, relies on . . . the magnetic field to guide its migratory trek.* The next sentence gives another example: . . . *birds that . . . migrate also depend on their . . . ability to respond to the Earth's magnetic field . . .*

The following chart outlines the key points that you should remember about Rhetorical Purpose questions.

KEY POINTS FOR QUESTIONS ABOUT INFERRING RHETORICAL PURPOSE	
FREQUENCY	1–2 questions per reading
HOW TO IDENTIFY THE QUESTION	Why does the author mention/discuss . . . ? What is the function of . . . ? The author mentions X in order to . . . Why does the author compare X to Y . . . The author uses X as an example of . . .
WHERE TO FIND THE ANSWER	The word, phrase, or sentence is highlighted in the passage.
HOW TO ANSWER THE QUESTION	1. Read the sentence that contains the highlighted information. 2. Look for signal words or phrases (i.e., *one example*, *rather than*) that establish a relationship between the highlighted information and other ideas. 3. Read 1–2 sentences around the key sentence to clearly understand the relationship between the highlighted information and the other ideas being presented.

In the exam, you may be able to eliminate incorrect answer choices by understanding what is wrong with them.

For Rhetorical Purpose questions, incorrect answer choices may:
- contain information that is not relevant to the purpose.
- contain false information.
- contain information that contradicts the purpose.

READING EXERCISE 8: Study each of the passages and choose the best answers to the questions that follow.

PASSAGE ONE (Questions 1–8)

Paragraph

Xerography

1▶   One more familiar use of electrochemistry that has made its way into the mainstream is xerography, a process for replicating documents that is dependent on photoconductive materials. A photoconductive material is an insulator in the dark but becomes a conductor when exposed to bright light. When a photocopy is being made, an image of a document is projected onto the surface of a rotating drum, and bright light causes the photoconductive material on the surface of the drum to become conductive.

2▶   As a result of the conductivity, the drum loses its charge in the lighted areas, and toner (small grains to which dry ink adheres) attaches itself only to the darker parts of the image. The grains are then carried to a sheet of paper and fused with heat. When a laser printer is used, the image is projected by means of a laser beam, which creates a brighter light and a greater contrast between lighter and darker areas and therefore results in sharper printed images.

3▶   Xerography has gone through a series of innovations since its invention in the late 1930s by Chester Carlson. One of the most notable alterations was to the name of the process. When Carlson first developed the technique, he called it "electrophotography" since it used both photography and electrostatic printing in the procedure. Later the name was changed to "xerography" in recognition of the fact that the process reproduces documents without the use of liquid chemicals, instead using a powdered toner to replicate the images.

4▶   A more significant change was made to the instruments that actually created the copies. Initially, the procedure took several steps to complete, and necessitated the use of flat plates that were manipulated by hand through the various copying stages. From the beginning, Carlson and others involved with the process realized how inconvenient and time-consuming it was to make a copy, and they worked continuously on ideas to make the process faster and more efficient. Eighteen years after the original machine was introduced to the public, they devised a suitable solution to the flat plates: a cylindrical rotating surface that allowed the process to be entirely automatic, except for a push of the "start" button.

5▶   The revolutionary invention of the rotating drum meant the copier was now viable as a commercial product. The first commercial automatic copier, the Xerox 914, came onto the market in 1960. This first generation of copiers was cumbersome by today's standards; not many households would be able to dedicate the necessary space it would take to have one of these early machines. Fortunately, continuing innovations in both the xerographic process and other types of technology have greatly decreased the size of machines capable of making copies. Today, the vast majority of copy machines, as well as many laser and LED printers, make use of Carlson's ingenious idea.

6▶   Photocopying through xerography involves several steps. First, an electrostatic charge is evenly spread over the surface of the rotating drum, or cylinder. The distributed charge is positive or negative depending on what type of copy is being made and what type of copier is being used. Standard copiers generally distribute a positive charge, while digital copiers use a negative charge. Next, the document being duplicated is exposed to light by flash lamps. At the same time, a combination of lenses and mirrors projects the original image through a lens, so that it is projected onto and synchronized with the rotating drum.

7▶   The third and fourth steps of the process concern the development and transfer of the image. In the development stage, a form of static electricity propels toner powder to coat the image that was projected onto the drum in the previous step. Then, in the transfer step, the toner from the drum, now in the form of the image, is transferred onto paper as the paper passes through the copying mechanism. The transfer is achieved through a blend of pressure on the paper and electrostatic attraction of the toner powder to the paper.

8► The remaining steps of the copying process finalize the image onto the paper. After the image has been transferred, the next step is to neutralize the electric charge on the paper and separate the paper from the drum surface. After that, the toner is permanently bonded to the paper using heat or a radiant fusing process, both of which ensure that the toner particles are permanently affixed to the paper. Finally, any remaining toner on the drum is cleaned off through a process that typically includes some type of suction to remove the particles. Usually, this toner is carried to a container in the machine for later disposal, though some machines will recycle the toner for use in subsequent copies.

1. The author begins the first paragraph with "One more familiar use of electrochemistry" in order to
   - (A) explain that xerography is one of the less familiar uses of electrochemistry
   - (B) make it clear that electrochemistry requires photoconductive materials
   - (C) show that xerography is the only known use for electrochemistry
   - (D) indicate that other less familiar uses have already been discussed

2. Why does the author explain that "A photoconductive material is an insulator in the dark but becomes a conductor when exposed to bright light"?
   - (A) It gives an explanation of a property that is necessary for xerography.
   - (B) It indicates that bright light is required for insulation to take place.
   - (C) It gives one example of a successful xerographic process.
   - (D) It explains the role of insulation in xerography.

3. The author mentions "small grains to which dry ink adheres" in order to
   - (A) provide information that contradicts the previous statement
   - (B) provide another example of conductivity
   - (C) provide further detail information about toner
   - (D) provide an alternate explanation for the effectiveness of toner

4. Why does the author mention "a laser printer" in the passage?
   - (A) It is an alternative to xerography.
   - (B) It is a way of duplicating without using electrochemistry.
   - (C) It is a second example of xerography.
   - (D) It is a less effective type of xerography than is a photocopier.

5. Why does the author include the phrase "except for a push of the 'start' button"?
   - (A) to explain the one step of the process that Carlson had no control over
   - (B) to indicate that it is not necessary to push a button to begin the copying process
   - (C) to emphasize that improvements to the copying process reduced the amount of work people had to do
   - (D) to show that Carlson had thought of almost every step necessary in the copying process

6. The author mentions that "not many households would be able to dedicate the necessary space" for a copier in order to
   - (A) explain that copiers remain exclusively a product for businesses
   - (B) emphasize how large the first automatic copiers were
   - (C) illustrate the dislike most households had for copiers when they were first introduced
   - (D) explain how households have increased in size since 1960

7. Why is "a blend of pressure on the paper and electrostatic attraction of the toner powder" mentioned?
   - (A) to summarize the final step of the copying process
   - (B) to illustrate how toner is propelled in the development stage
   - (C) to explain how the drum is coated with powder
   - (D) to explain how the image is transferred onto paper

8. Why does the author discuss suction in paragraph 8?
   - (A) to provide an explanation of how the last part of the copying process is achieved
   - (B) to illustrate the neutralization process
   - (C) to give an example of how toner is recycled
   - (D) to explain how the toner adheres to the paper

Paragraph   **Demographic Change**

1▶   A visitor transported from the early twentieth century to modern times would most likely be amazed by the vast changes in the demographics of the United States over the course of 100 years. The shifts include not only the size of the population and primary residential areas for most Americans, but also notable changes in the age of the population, and even the ratio of men to women. All of these shifts have led to the composition of the United States being startlingly different from what it was just a short century ago.

2▶   The United States had already been gradually moving away from being a country of mainly rural communities to one of more metropolitan centers by the latter part of the 1800s. Nonetheless, in the early part of the twentieth century, over 70 percent of the population still lived in farm communities. The census of 1910 documented approximately 28 percent of U.S. citizens living in urban areas while the rest were dwelling in rural ones. However, by the beginning of the current century, according to the census of 2000, this proportion had reversed itself: 80 percent of the population reported living in urban or suburban areas, leaving only 20 percent residing in rural locales.

3▶   Another significant change is the overall increase in population. According to U.S. census statistics, the population of the United States grew to three times its size over the course of 100 years. In 1900, the official count was 76 million people, while the 2000 census showed a population record of 281 million people, which some people estimate to be much higher, since illegal immigrants tend to avoid being counted in the official census. Additionally, based on census statistics, the decade of the 1990s saw the biggest population explosion—32.7 million people—in any 10-year span of the last century.

4▶   An additional factor that may come as a shock to some is how the United States has aged from 1900 to today. In the beginning of the twentieth century, half of the population was under the age of 23. When compared to data from the 2000 census which shows that half of the population in modern times is over the age of 35, a difference of 12 years, a substantial shift in ages can be seen. Some of this change has been influenced by improvements in health care, and some has been the result of fluctuations in the birthrate over the course of the century. Birthrates were initially lower at the beginning of the century, "booming" immediately after World War II, and tapering off again in the last half of the century. In fact, the "baby boom" generation not only impacted birthrates from the 1940s to the 1960s, it also affected age when measured in five-year increments. In both the beginning and middle of the century, the largest age group of U.S. citizens was under the age of five. In contrast, due to the impact of the baby boom generation, the 2000 census documented that the two largest, five-year age groups were over the age of 30: from 35–39 years of age and 40–44 years of age.

5▶   Another shift that a North American from a century ago would not likely have predicted is the change in the ratio of men to women in the United States. At the beginning of the twentieth century, males outnumbered females in virtually every part of the United States. However, as the proportion of males to females (measured per 100 births) steadily declined in every decade from 1910 until 1980, the predominance of men to women reversed itself; by the turn of the new century, women outnumbered men in all regions of the United States, except the West. Only seven states out of the 50 recorded a higher ratio of men to women, with all of those states being located in the western United States.

6▶   One development that may not be considered such a surprise is the change in racial demographics, especially since the United States has been regarded as a nation of immigrants. Although in the first years of the nation, the vast majority of voluntary settlers to the United States came from Caucasian, or "white" origins, the past century has seen a large influx of other races, including African, Asian, and especially Hispanic (those of Spanish origin or from Spanish-speaking countries) races. As a result, the face of the United States has quite literally been changing. Whereas only two states outside of the southern region of the United States claimed a minority population of more than 10 percent in 1900, 26 states recorded a minority proportion of over 10 percent in 2000. In fact, three states, California, Hawaii, and New Mexico, documented a population comprised of more than 50 percent minorities in the 2000 census.

9. The author mentions "A visitor transported from the early twentieth century to modern times" in order to emphasize

Ⓐ how travel has changed over the past century
Ⓑ the popularity of the United States for tourists
Ⓒ that life has not changed much in the United States since the early twentieth century
Ⓓ the enormous changes in demographics over the past century

10. The author uses the word "Nonetheless" in paragraph 2 in order to

Ⓐ indicate that many people still lived in rural areas despite a growing shift to city living
Ⓑ emphasize how tremendously the rural population was increasing
Ⓒ point out that there had been a 70 percent rise in rural communities since the late 1800s
Ⓓ argue that no real change had taken place in rural and urban communities, despite census numbers

11. The author includes the phrase "this proportion had reversed itself" in paragraph 2 in order to

Ⓐ explain how the population of cities had decreased by the end of the 1900s
Ⓑ highlight the continually changing residences of Americans
Ⓒ reinforce the fact that a majority of the population had moved out of rural areas by the late twentieth century
Ⓓ to emphasize that demographic changes were common in 2000

12. "Illegal immigrants" are mentioned in paragraph 3 as an example of

Ⓐ a population that is unlikely to grow
Ⓑ a population that is not always counted on the U.S. census
Ⓒ a population that accounts for the largest increase of people according to the U.S. census
Ⓓ a population that usually has no influence on the demographics of the United States

13. Why does the author mention "improvements in health care" in paragraph 4?

Ⓐ It helps to explain why the birthrate is continuing to increase.
Ⓑ It is an example of a factor that contributed to variations in the birthrate.
Ⓒ It helps to explain why the population is younger today.
Ⓓ It is an example of a factor that contributed to a rise in the age of the majority population.

14. The author mentions the "'baby boom' generation" in paragraph 4 because they

Ⓐ changed the way the census was conducted in the 1940s
Ⓑ were responsible for a higher percentage of children younger than five years old
Ⓒ influenced how the total population of the United States aged in the last half of the twentieth century
Ⓓ had an impact on how the total population aged in the first half of the twentieth century

15. The word "However" is used in paragraph 5 to introduce the concept that

Ⓐ more women than men currently live in the United States
Ⓑ more men than women currently live in the United States
Ⓒ women outnumber men in the western part of the United States
Ⓓ women outnumber men in all 50 states

16. The author states "the face of the United States has quite literally been changing" in paragraph 6 to emphasize that

Ⓐ the demographic changes in the United States are no longer surprising
Ⓑ minority populations are increasing in the United States
Ⓒ the descendants of the first U.S. settlers are now the minority race
Ⓓ minorities make up more than 10 percent of the population in only two states

PASSAGE THREE (Questions 17–24)

The Hubble Telescope

Paragraph

1▶   The Hubble telescope, named after the prominent astronomer Edwin Hubble, was launched into space with great fanfare on April 25, 1990. Although there are many powerful telescopes at various locations on Earth, the Hubble telescope was expected to be able to provide considerably better information because it would be able to operate from the vacuum of space, without interference from the Earth's atmosphere. By launching the Hubble telescope into space, NASA (the National Aeronautics and Space Administration) was, in essence, placing an observatory above the Earth's atmosphere.

2▶   The Hubble telescope is distinct from other orbiting telescopes in that, to date, it has been the only telescope designed for maintenance and repair while it is orbiting in space.

A major part of the design concept for the telescope was planned around the ability to send astronauts up to the telescope to service it at necessary intervals, as opposed to removing the telescope from orbit, thus potentially losing precious images during the time that the telescope would be grounded for repairs. Therefore, both the design and the orbit path for the telescope needed to be carefully orchestrated to ensure the greatest ease of access for astronauts, while simultaneously allowing for the best path for the telescope to travel in order to reflect images, many of which have been extremely illuminating to scientists as they study outer space.

3▶ It has been fortunate that the designers of the Hubble telescope planned in advance for in-orbit repairs. Shortly after the telescope was launched, a malfunction in the main mirror was revealed, which led to a distortion of the images that the telescope reflected back to researchers on Earth. Though scientists realized the problem with the main mirror almost immediately after the launch of the telescope, it was not until 1993 that the first repair mission was sent to the telescope. During this mission, the mirror was repaired in a unique fashion: rather than replacing the mirror, an impossibility while the telescope was in orbit, new optical components were added to the telescope to correct the reflection of the primary mirror. In a sense, these additions to the mirror acted as "eyeglasses" by correcting what the main mirror "sees."

4▶ The mission to repair the mirror was not the only trip arranged by NASA to maintain the Hubble telescope at its optimal operating capacity. Four subsequent missions took place after that first mission, the last occurring in 2009. During each mission, astronauts fixed, updated, and replaced components essential to the operating success of the telescope. The final mission's goal was to make sure the telescope would operate successfully until at least 2014. This mission occurred only after some controversy. Initially, it was canceled because of safety concerns surrounding the space shuttle program. However, after much public debate, NASA approved the rescheduling of the mission, to the dismay of the mission's opponents.

5▶ Delays were not new to the Hubble team. Originally, the telescope was completed and scheduled to be sent into orbit in 1983, but the catastrophic accident of another space shuttle set the launch back several years. The United States' confidence had been deeply shaken in the space program and no one wanted to push a space project that would require manned service trips on a regular basis. NASA first had to demonstrate significant improvement in its safety systems before it was permitted to launch the telescope. In addition, once launched, the initial transfer of images back to Earth was delayed by a mathematical miscalculation. Astronomers working on the instructions for orienting the telescope relied on data from charts prepared in the 1950s. These charts proved to be inaccurate, and caused the astronomers to misdirect the aim of the Hubble.

6▶ Despite the difficulties and risks involved in undertaking such an ambitious project, most of the people that participated, as well as the researchers that study the telescope's images, would likely deem the project worth the hardships that were endured. The field of astrophysics, in particular has benefited from the images sent back. One of the most remarkable feats aided by the telescope is the ability of astrophysicists to predict the rate at which the universe is expanding to a far more accurate degree than has ever been possible. Not only has the telescope assisted with numerous scientific breakthroughs, it has also greatly improved public relations for astronomy. Many of its breathtaking images have been released to the public, creating a stronger interest in the field of astronomy.

17. Why does the author mention "many powerful telescopes at various locations on Earth" in paragraph 1?

Ⓐ to emphasize the need for telescopes at various locations on Earth
Ⓑ to show that the Hubble telescope was different from existing telescopes
Ⓒ to indicate how the atmosphere improves the quality of information from space
Ⓓ to emphasize the similarities between the Hubble telescope and other telescopes

18. The author uses the phrase "in essence" in paragraph 1 in order to indicate that the information that follows the phrase

Ⓐ provides a simplified description of a previously stated situation
Ⓑ indicates the cause of a previously stated effect
Ⓒ provides further details about a previously stated main idea
Ⓓ indicates the classification to which previously stated examples belong

19. Why does the author use the phrase "as opposed to" in paragraph 2?
   (A) to show that the Hubble telescope operates in a different way than other telescopes
   (B) to explain that NASA's design to repair the telescope in orbit did not have support
   (C) to contrast two different methods of repairing the telescope
   (D) to emphasize that repairing the telescope in orbit was dangerous

20. The author includes the phrase "in a unique fashion" in paragraph 3 in order to
   (A) describe the astronaut's unusual uniforms
   (B) to highlight the unusual approach to repairing the mirror
   (C) to explain how the telescope continued to reflect images during the repair
   (D) to indicate that the method used to repair the telescope was strange

21. "Why does the author use the term "eyeglasses" in paragraph 3?
   (A) to explain an effect the telescope has on images
   (B) to describe the telescope's importance to NASA
   (C) to demonstrate that the Hubble telescope extends for long distances
   (D) to help the reader understand the function of the telescope's main mirror

22. The author includes the phrase "to the dismay of the mission's opponents" in order to
   (A) show that NASA's decision to send up another repair team was fully supported
   (B) emphasize that some people were not pleased about NASA's decision to send up another repair team

   (C) indicate that opponents to NASA's decision continued to fight against it
   (D) explain that the astronauts were reluctant to repair the telescope

23. Why does the author mention "Delays were not new to the Hubble team"?
   (A) to emphasize the many delays in constructing the telescope
   (B) to explain how the Hubble aged during a waiting period
   (C) to introduce more examples of setbacks first mentioned in the previous paragraph
   (D) to explain the reason for the Hubble creators' frustration

24. In paragraph 6, the author includes the phrase "in particular" in order to emphasize
   (A) the detailed images sent back from the telescope for study by astronomers
   (B) the precision of repairs made to the telescope by the astronauts
   (C) the field of study that has benefited from the telescope's discoveries
   (D) the specific problems encountered by astrophysicists working on the telescope

Learn to quickly identify words and phrases that signal an example is being presented: *for example, for instance, such as, like.*

PASSAGE FOUR (Questions 25–32)

Territoriality

Paragraph

1▶   In many species, members of the species exhibit aggressive behavior toward one another, often with a focus on territoriality, the fight for exclusive control of a particular area. The level of violence in territorial aggression varies widely from species to species. Some species rely on nonlethal contests for control of territory that involves noisemaking maneuvers such as roaring or hissing or aggressive posturing or gestures. Other species, however, value their territory to the point of being willing to seriously injury or even kill other members of their own species.

2▶   Two common factors that inspire territoriality in animals are feeding and mating. Animal species search out habitats that are the most appropriate for providing their essential survival needs, especially in terms of food. Once a particular species has found this habitat, it often becomes necessary to defend it against other members of the same species that are also looking for the ideal location. At the same time the animal is attempting to push out encroachers, those that move in on its territory, it must also attract suitable mates to the area. Therefore, the animal tends to use specific behaviors to control the level of appeal of its environment. Its sounds or postures will change to reflect how the animal views another in its territory; appealing, gentle displays will be aimed at potential mates, whereas more aggressive behavior will be directed toward animals seen as threats.

3▶ Other reasons for defending a territory in addition to feeding and mating are shelter and the protection of the young. When an animal chooses its territory, it will often build a home there, particularly if it intends to mate. This homebuilding process is referred to as "nesting," even though the structure may not actually be a nest for the animal's babies. Nesting adds value to the territory because the animal has expended time and energy in making it more livable. If newborn or infant animals are being cared for, the area has additional value to the protective parent. As the value of the territory increases, the animal may correspondingly increase its territorial behaviors to defend the area from others. In other words, an animal may concede its territory to a competitor more easily if it has no young to protect; the presence of the young might compel the animal to defend its home with more ferocity.

4▶ Most bird species, for example, are known to be territorial to some degree, though the territorial behaviors exhibited by most species are limited to singing contests, which can go on for days, or threatening postures with wings lifted or extended. The swan, on the other hand, is quite unlike other birds in this respect. The swan may seem particularly elegant and serene as it glides across the surface of a lake; however, male swans are, in reality, quite territorial and will fight other male swans for the exclusive use of a lake no matter how large the lake is. Males will engage in ferocious contests, with their necks entwined as they attempt to cause mortal injury to each other.

5▶ Species not only defend their territory against members of their own kind, but are often faced with the need to wage battle against other species for the same area. In this situation, when different species are involved, other factors come into play besides food, mates, shelter, and protection of the young. One common model used to measure the intensity of territorial fights between different species is the "hawk[1] versus dove[2]" game, in which the "hawk" represents a species known to be more aggressive and a "dove" symbolizes a typically nonconfrontational species. In this model, the tendencies of the involved species (whether they are likely to fight or simply prefer to posture in some way) are analyzed to predict the victor. For example, when a "hawk" and a "dove" come into conflict, it is almost certain that the hawk will prevail, due to its more aggressive nature.

6▶ However, when two "hawks" or two "doves" confront one another, the outcome is far less predictable based on the animals' tendencies. In these situations, other components are measured as well, such as the relative size of the animals, which are currently in possession of the territory, the proximity of other suitable territories, and the maturity of each contender. For instance, when two "doves" are battling for the same location, the younger nesting dove has a clear advantage over the older dove that has just entered the territory.

GLOSSARY

1. *hawk*—a predatory species of bird characterized by a short, hooked beak, broad wings, and curved claws
2. *dove*—a small, non-predatory bird, related to the pigeon, and often used to symbolize peace

25. Why does the author include "the fight for exclusive control of a particular area" in paragraph 1?

Ⓐ It presents an argument against a previously stated point.

Ⓑ It provides a definition of a previously stated term.

Ⓒ It presents a second area of focus of aggressive behavior.

Ⓓ It introduces a new idea to be further developed in the paragraph.

26. In paragraph 2, the author mentions "appealing, gentle displays" with "aggressive behavior" in order to

Ⓐ explain how different animals protect their territory

Ⓑ give an example of successful and unsuccessful defense strategies

Ⓒ illustrate how animals change behavior depending on purpose

Ⓓ show that animals have no control over their behavior

27. Why does the author mention "nesting" in paragraph 3?

  (A) To provide a name for the animal homebuilding process
  (B) To emphasize that only birds engage in territorial behavior
  (C) To compare how different a bird's nest is from other animal homes
  (D) To explain that birds are not the only animals that build nests

28. The author uses the phrase "In other words" in paragraph 3 to

  (A) introduce a new example
  (B) explain a previous point in an alternative way
  (C) suggest that previous examples were not adequately explained
  (D) focus the reader's attention on the main idea of the paragraph

29. Why does the author mention "singing contests" in paragraph 4?

  (A) to demonstrate that birds create beautiful sounds
  (B) to provide an example of unusual behavior by birds
  (C) to show how violently aggressive some bird behavior is
  (D) to demonstrate that some types of territorial behaviors are not very aggressive

30. The author mentions "their necks entwined" in paragraph 4 in order

  (A) to indicate that swans are really rather affectionate
  (B) to emphasize how long swans' necks are
  (C) to make the point that the swans are only pretending to hurt one another
  (D) to create a mental image for the reader of fighting swans

31. The author mentions the "'hawk versus dove' game" in paragraph 5 in order

  (A) to entertain readers during the passage
  (B) to introduce the framework for predicting the result of a territorial fight
  (C) to reinforce the idea that only certain species are territorial
  (D) to provide examples of two species that are aggressive while competing for a territory

32. Why does the author mention "the relative size of the animals" in paragraph 6?

  (A) to highlight the fact that animals will only fight other animals that are similar in size
  (B) to explain that animals similar in size are commonly related to one another
  (C) to indicate that size is not a factor in a territorial fight
  (D) to explain that size can play a part in some territorial battles

READING EXERCISE (Skills 7–8): Read the passage and answer the questions that follow.

Ella Deloria

Paragraph

1▶ It was not until her posthumous novel *Waterlily* was published in 1988 that Ella C. Deloria became known for her literary ability in addition to her already-established reputation in the academic arena of linguistics[1] and ethnology[2]. During her lifetime, she was recognized for the linguistic ability and cultural sensitivity that went into the production of a collection of traditional short stories entitled *Dakota Texts* (1932). After her death, her versions of a number of longer traditional stories and the novel *Waterlily* were published; with the publication of *Waterlily* came the recognition of her true literary ability and the awareness that it was the strength of her literary ability, in addition to her linguistic expertise and her deep cultural understanding, that had made her versions of traditional stories so compelling.

2▶ Ella Cara Deloria was born into a Nakota[3]-speaking family in 1889; however, she grew up among the Lakota people in North Dakota, where her father was a leader in the Episcopal Church. Her father, the son of a traditional Nakota medicine man, valued both the cultural traditions of his family and those of the country of his citizenship. As a result, Deloria primarily spoke Nakota at home and Lakota when she was out in the community. She was well versed there in the cultural traditions of her Sioux ancestors (with a complex kinship structure in which all of a child's father's brothers are also considered fathers, all of a child's mother's sisters are also considered mothers, and all of the children of all these mothers and fathers are considered siblings). Her education, however, was in English,

GLOSSARY

1 *linguistics*—the study of language
2 *ethnology*—the study of different races
3 *The Lakota, Nakota,* and *Dakota* are related groups of people that are part of the Sioux nation.

at the Episcopalian Saint Elizabeth Mission School and the All Saints School. After high school, she attended Oberlin College in Ohio for one year, and then she transferred to Columbia University to study linguistics under Franz Boas, the founder of American Indian linguistics.

3▶   After graduating from Columbia, she was encouraged by Boas to collect and record traditional Lakota stories. She was in a unique position to take on this task because of her fluency in the Lakota language as well as in English, her understanding from childhood of the complexities and subtleties of Lakota culture, and her linguistic training from Columbia. The result of her research was the *Dakota Texts,* a bilingual collection of 64 short stories. To create this remarkable work, Deloria was able to elicit stories from venerable Sioux elders, without need for translators and with an awareness of appropriately respectful behavior. She listened to the stories as numerous generations had before her, and then, unlike previous generations, recorded them in writing—initially in Lakota and later in English. She transcribed them essentially as they were told but with her own understanding of the nuances of what was being told.

4▶   In addition to the shorter stories that were published in *Dakota Texts,* Deloria spent 1937 working on transcribing a number of longer and more complicated texts, which were not published until after her death. "Iron Hawk: Oglala Culture Hero" (1993) presents the diverse elements of the culture-hero genre; "The Buffalo People" (1994) focuses on the importance of tribal education in building character; "A Sioux Captive" (1994) tells the story of a Lakota woman who rescued her husband from the Crow; "The Prairie Dogs" (1994) describes the sense of hope offered by the Sioux warrior-society ceremonies and dances.

5▶   Her novel *Waterlily,* which was first published 40 years after it was completed and 17 years after her death, reflects her true literary talent as well as her accumulated understanding of traditional culture and customs. The novel recounts the fictional story of the difficult life of the title character, with a horrendous childhood experience as witness to a deadly enemy raid and a first marriage terminated by the untimely death of her husband in a smallpox epidemic, and comes to a close with the hopeful expectations of an impending second marriage. At the same time, it presents a masterful account of life in a nineteenth-century Sioux community with its detailed descriptions of interpersonal relationships and attitudes, everyday tasks and routines, and special ceremonies and celebrations.

1. It can be inferred from paragraph 1 that, while she was alive, Ella Deloria

   (A) did little to make use of her education in linguistics

   (B) achieved acclaim more for her transcriptions than for her novel

   (C) was the published author of a number of types of fiction and nonfiction

   (D) was recognized for the literary maturity of her novel

2. Why does the author use the word "however" in paragraph 2?

   (A) to emphasize that she was born in an earlier century

   (B) to clarify the differences between the Lakota and the Dakota

   (C) to show that she was raised in a different environment from the one where she was born

   (D) to demonstrate that she was very different from other members of her family

3. Why does the author include in paragraph 2 the information "with a complex kinship structure in which all of a child's father's brothers are also considered fathers, all of a child's mother's sisters are also considered mothers, and all of the children of all these mothers and fathers are considered siblings"?

   (A) to provide details to emphasize how the Nakota and the Lakota differed

   (B) to introduce the idea that Deloria's education in English was completely different from her home life

   (C) to provide an alternate explanation for Deloria's use of Nakota at home and Lakota in the community

   (D) to provide an example of one cultural tradition of the Sioux

4. Why does the author begin paragraph 3 with "After graduating from Columbia"?

  (A) to indicate that paragraph 3 follows paragraph 2 in chronological order
  (B) to clarify that paragraph 3 describes Deloria's education at Columbia
  (C) to recognize the importance of education throughout Deloria's life
  (D) to demonstrate that paragraph 3 provides examples of a concept presented in paragraph 2

5. It is implied in paragraph 3 that *Dakota Texts* was written

  (A) only in English
  (B) only in Dakota
  (C) in Dakota and Lakota
  (D) in Lakota and English

6. Why does the author mention "an awareness of appropriately respectful behavior" in paragraph 3?

  (A) to show one way that Deloria was qualified to elicit stories from Sioux elders
  (B) to show that Deloria's linguistic training had been effective
  (C) to show the difference between Deloria's transcriptions and her novel
  (D) to show why Deloria needed to work with a translator

7. It can be inferred from paragraph 4 that "Iron Hawk: Oglala Culture Hero" was published

  (A) in the same year that it was written
  (B) just prior to Deloria's death
  (C) long after it was transcribed
  (D) long before *Waterlily* was published

8. Why does the author discuss "The Prairie Dogs" in paragraph 4?

  (A) It was written by Deloria.
  (B) It describes Deloria's own life story.
  (C) It provides insight into rituals and dances.
  (D) It was one of the earliest short stories that Deloria transcribed.

9. It can be inferred from the passage that *Waterlily* was completed

  (A) in 1937
  (B) in 1948
  (C) in 1954
  (D) in 1988

10. Why does the author mention "the untimely death of her husband in a smallpox epidemic" in paragraph 5?

  (A) It provides a harsh example of Waterlily's difficult life.
  (B) It provides evidence of the historical existence of Waterlily.
  (C) It demonstrates how unusual Waterlily's life in a nineteenth-century Sioux community was.
  (D) It reinforces the overall message of hopelessness of Waterlily.

READING REVIEW EXERCISE (Skills 1–8): Read the passage.

Early Autos

Paragraph

1▶   America's passion for the automobile developed rather quickly in the beginning of the twentieth century. At the turn of that century, there were few automobiles, or horseless carriages, as they were called at the time, and those that existed were considered frivolous playthings of the rich. **5A** They were rather fragile machines that sputtered and smoked and broke down often; they were expensive toys that could not be counted on to get one where one needed to go; they could only be afforded by the wealthy class, who could afford both the expensive upkeep and the inherent delays that resulted from the use of a machine that tended to break down time and again. **5B** These early automobiles required repairs so frequently both because their engineering was at an immature stage and because roads were unpaved and often in poor condition. **5C** Then, when breakdowns occurred, there were no services such as roadside gas stations or tow trucks to assist drivers needing help in their predicament. **5D** Drivers of horse-drawn carriages considered the horseless mode of transportation foolhardy, preferring instead to rely on their four-legged "engines," which they considered a tremendously more dependable and cost-effective means of getting around.

2▶   Automobiles in the beginning of the twentieth century were quite unlike today's models. Many of them were electric cars, even though the electric models had quite a limited range and needed to be recharged frequently at electric charging stations; many others were powered by steam, though it was often required that drivers of steam cars be certified steam engineers due to the dangers inherent in operating a steam-powered machine. The early automobiles also lacked much emphasis on body design; in fact, they were often little more than benches on wheels, though by the end of the first decade of the century they had progressed to leather-upholstered chairs or sofas on thin wheels that absorbed little of the incessant pounding associated with the movement of these machines.

3▶   In spite of the rather rough and undeveloped nature of these early horseless carriages, something about them grabbed people's imagination, and their use increased rapidly, though not always smoothly. In the first decade of the last century, roads were shared by the horse-drawn and horseless variety of carriages, a situation that was rife with problems and required strict measures to control the incidents and accidents that resulted when two such different modes of transportation were used in close proximity. New York City, for example, banned horseless vehicles from Central Park early in the century because they had been involved in so many accidents, often causing injury or death; then, in 1904, New York State felt that it was necessary to control automobile traffic by placing speed limits of 20 miles per hour in open areas, 15 miles per hour in villages, and 10 miles per hour in cities or areas of congestion. However, the measures taken were less a means of limiting use of the automobile and more a way of controlling the effects of an invention whose use increased dramatically in a relatively short period of time.

4▶   Just before the turn of the twentieth century in 1893, the first automobile company was established: the Durvea Motor Wagon Company. Despite being the first, this company never really made a lasting mark on the automobile industry. Other companies founded in the next decade, such as Oldsmobile (1902) and Ford (1903) outpaced the Durvea Company soon after they started. The companies that dominated the automobile industry at the beginning of the last century employed mass production techniques that resulted in dramatic reductions in the cost of a car. This, in turn, allowed more average wage-earners to take advantage of the new transportation technology, leading to ever growing cycles of demand and production. Before 1910, the cost of a Ford was around $850; by 1915, it dropped to under $500. Fewer than 5,000 automobiles were sold in the United States for a total cost of approximately $5 million in 1900, while considerably more cars, 181,000, were sold for $215 million in 1910, and by the middle of the 1920s, automobile manufacturing had become the top industry in the United States and accounted for 6 percent of the manufacturing in the country.

1. Based on the information in paragraph 1, who would have been most likely to own a car in 1900?
   Ⓐ a skilled laborer
   Ⓑ a successful investor
   Ⓒ a scholarship student
   Ⓓ a rural farmer

2. The word "frivolous" in paragraph 1 is closest in meaning to
   Ⓐ trivial
   Ⓑ delicate
   Ⓒ essential
   Ⓓ natural

3. It is indicated in paragraph 1 that it was necessary to repair early autos because of
   Ⓐ the elaborate engines
   Ⓑ the lack of roads
   Ⓒ the immature drivers
   Ⓓ the rough roads

4. The author refers to "four-legged 'engines'" in paragraph 1 in order to indicate that
   Ⓐ early autos had little more than an engine and wheels
   Ⓑ it was foolish to travel on a four-legged animal
   Ⓒ horses were an effective mode of transportation
   Ⓓ automobile engines were evaluated in terms of their horsepower

5. Look at the four squares [■] that indicate where the following sentence could be added to paragraph 1.

   These horrendous road conditions forced drivers to use their automobiles on grooved, rutted, and bumpy roads.

   Where would the sentence best fit? Click on a square [■] to add the sentence to the passage.

6. The phrase "many others" in paragraph 2 refers to

   (A) automobiles in the beginning of the twentieth century
   (B) today's models
   (C) electric models
   (D) electric charging stations

7. It is stated in paragraph 2 that the owners of steam-powered cars

   (A) sometimes had to demonstrate knowledge of steam engineering
   (B) had to hire drivers to operate their cars
   (C) often had to take their automobiles to charging stations
   (D) were often in danger because of the limited range of their automobiles

8. Why does the author mention "benches on wheels" in paragraph 2?

   (A) to show how remarkably automobile design had progressed
   (B) to show that car designs of the time were neither complex nor comfortable
   (C) to indicate that early automobiles had upholstered chairs or sofas
   (D) to emphasize how the early automobiles were designed to absorb the pounding of the machine on the road

9. The word "incessant" in paragraph 2 is closest in meaning to

   (A) heavy
   (B) bothersome
   (C) jolting
   (D) continual

10. The phrase "rife with" in paragraph 3 could be replaced by

    (A) full of
    (B) surrounded by
    (C) dangerous due to
    (D) occurring as a result of

11. It can be inferred from paragraph 3 that the government of New York State believed that

    (A) all horseless vehicles should be banned from all public parks
    (B) strict speed limits should be placed on horse-drawn carriages
    (C) horseless and horse-drawn vehicles should not travel on the same roads
    (D) it was safer for cars to travel faster where there was less traffic and there were fewer people

12. Which of the sentences below best expresses the essential information in the highlighted sentence in paragraph 3? *Incorrect* choices change the meaning in important ways or leave out essential information.

    (A) It was necessary to take a measured approach in dealing with inventions such as the automobile.
    (B) The various laws were needed because the use of automobiles grew so fast.
    (C) The dramatic look of the automobile changed considerably over a short period of time.
    (D) It was important to lawmakers to discover the causes of the problems relating to automobiles.

13. What can be inferred about the Durvea Motor Wagon Company from paragraph 4?

    (A) It was more successful than Ford or Oldsmobile.
    (B) It provided a business model that later car companies copied.
    (C) It did not use mass production methods to produce automobiles.
    (D) It lacked the engine technology to create cars that would last a long time.

14. In paragraph 4, why does the author compare the price of a car before 1910 with the price of a car in 1915?

    (A) to demonstrate that cars were becoming more affordable
    (B) to show that the quality of cars declined in the early 1900s
    (C) to provide evidence of the impact of inflation on prices in the United States
    (D) to support the idea that cars were only for the wealthy

15. According to paragraph 4, it is NOT true that

    (A) the total cost of the automobiles sold in the United States in 1900 was around $5 million
    (B) sales of cars increased by more than 175,000 from 1900 to 1910
    (C) automobile manufacturing was the top U.S. industry in 1920
    (D) automobile manufacturing represented more than 5 percent of total U.S.manufacturing by 1925

Reading Skill 9: Select Summary Information

Summary information questions evaluate your ability to determine which details in the passage are major supporting ideas and should be included in the summary and which details are only minor and therefore, do not belong in the summary. When this type of question occurs, it always appears as the last question in the set of questions, and it is organized in a chart form. The thesis statement, or main idea of the entire passage, is given to you. You must choose the most important ideas that support this thesis from a list of six options following the chart. For this question, you must choose only three answers. This means that three of the answer choices provided will be not be used to fill in the summary chart. Because the question has more than one answer choice, it is worth multiple points; you will receive 0 to 2 points depending on how many correct answers you choose. When you decide you want to place an answer into the summary, click on the answer and then drag the answer to the space in the summary where you want to place it. Your answers may be placed in any order in the chart. By selecting the correct answers, you are completing a summary of the reading passage. You can click back and forth between the question and the passage while you are answering this question.

Since the summary question is at the end of the set of questions, you can use information from previous questions to help you determine the most important ideas.

Strategies to Answer Summary Chart Questions

- Read the thesis statement that is provided. Understanding this statement will help you to select answers that are related only to the main idea of the passage.

- Quickly read the topic statements (the first sentences) of each paragraph.

- Look for three answer choices from the six provided that are the main topics of paragraphs.

- In the answer choices, be aware that the information in the correct answers may be paraphrased using synonyms and alternate syntax or sentence order. The correct answers will not repeat exact information from the passage, but rather will synthesize or combine different pieces of information.

- Eliminate choices that are definitely false or not discussed in the passage.

- Eliminate choices that describe minor details or examples.

Example

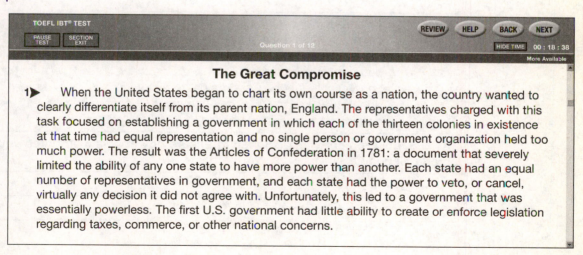

TOEFL IBT® TEST

PAUSE TEST   SECTION EXIT

Question 1 of 12

REVIEW   HELP   BACK   NEXT

HIDE TIME   00 : 18 : 38
More Available

2▶   Within a few years, government representatives realized the seriousness of the situation and reconvened at the Constitutional Convention of 1787 to come up with a solution. Defining this solution was not an easy process. Smaller states still insisted that each state have an equal number of representatives in the legislature. On the other hand, more populous states felt that a fairer solution would be to assign representatives on the basis of population, which meant that larger states would ostensibly have more influence in the government. These states' argument put an emphasis on representing each citizen equally, as opposed to representing each state equally.

3▶   Ultimately, the gentlemen assembled at the convention came up with "The Great Compromise," a strategy designed to provide some degree of satisfaction to everyone. To do this, they looked back to their motherland for inspiration and divided the legislative branch of the government into two parts, known as a "bicameral congress." In the upper house of Congress, the Senate, each state was to be represented by two legislators. However, in the lower house, the House of Representatives, the number of lawmakers per state was to be based on the population of a respective state. Thus, today, California, one of the most populous states, has over fifty representatives in the U.S. Congress, while Wyoming, the least populous state, has only a single representative.

4▶   To prevent one house from becoming more powerful than the other, the representatives at the convention in 1787 also mandated that the two houses had to work together to create laws. The Senate could not enact a law without the House's approval and vice versa. Whichever house came up with a law and passed it first must submit that law to the other house for passage as well. This tradition, which carries on into modern times, meant that members of both houses of Congress were required to build close working relationships founded on compromise and the best interests of the people they mutually represented.

5▶   This spirit of checks and balances, whereby one group "checks" the work of the other, accurately reflects the overall philosophy agreed upon by the founders of the United States: no one group can assert unlimited authority over another. In practical terms, this means any government decision or piece of legislation has to pass through a complex procedure before it is put into action or becomes law. The typical process works in the following manner: first, a member of the House or Senate—the legislative branch—introduces a bill they want to become a law. Once it passes in the first house, it is sent to the second house for approval. The bill then goes to the executive branch—the president—to be signed into law. However, it still needs to be judged constitutionally appropriate by the judicial branch—the Supreme Court. When all three branches have signaled their approval of the bill, then it officially becomes a law. At any time during this process, one of the branches—legislative, executive, or judicial—can indicate their disapproval of the bill. When this happens, the bill is either returned to Congress for revisions or canceled.

6▶   One point of controversy surrounding this method of lawmaking is that the vastly larger population of the United States today makes it a time-consuming and unwieldy process. As the multiplication of states from thirteen to fifty has occurred, the Congress has swelled to well over 500 members. Critics of the system complain that so many voices cause harmful delays and unnecessary expense in creating new legislation.

Directions: An introductory sentence for a brief summary of the passage is provided below. Complete the summary by selecting the THREE answer choices that express the most important ideas in the passage. Some sentences do not belong in the summary because they express ideas that are not presented in the passage or are minor ideas in the passage. **This question is worth 2 points** (2 points for 3 correct answers, 1 point for 2 correct answers, and 0 points for 1 or 0 correct answers).

The U.S. government was designed to ensure power was distributed equally among all people.

-
-
-

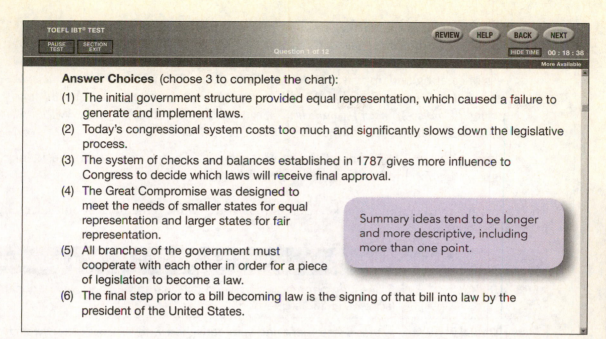

Answer Choices (choose 3 to complete the chart):

(1) The initial government structure provided equal representation, which caused a failure to generate and implement laws.

(2) Today's congressional system costs too much and significantly slows down the legislative process.

(3) The system of checks and balances established in 1787 gives more influence to Congress to decide which laws will receive final approval.

(4) The Great Compromise was designed to meet the needs of smaller states for equal representation and larger states for fair representation.

> Summary ideas tend to be longer and more descriptive, including more than one point.

(5) All branches of the government must cooperate with each other in order for a piece of legislation to become a law.

(6) The final step prior to a bill becoming law is the signing of that bill into law by the president of the United States.

Since the main idea of the entire passage is given in the bolded sentence, you must choose the three supporting ideas that best reinforce this main idea. The ideal choices are sentences that mention broad and important ideas, are accurate based on the passage, and are reinforced by more specific details from the passage.

- **Choice 1:** This is one of the summary ideas: The first paragraph states that each of the thirteen colonies . . . had equal representation and this led to a government that was essentially powerless. In addition, the first paragraph states: *The first U.S. government* [initial government structure] *had little ability* [caused a failure] *to create or enforce legislation* [to generate or implement laws] *regarding taxes, commerce, or other national concerns.*

- **Choice 2:** This is NOT one of the summary ideas: It is mentioned as an argument in paragraph 6 (lines 4–5), and is a specific detail, not a broadly stated fact: *Critics . . . complain . . . so many voices cause harmful delays and unnecessary expense. . . .* In addition, it is not a main idea related to the bolded thesis statement about ensuring that "power was distributed equally among all people."

- **Choice 3:** This is NOT one of the summary ideas: Paragraph 5 (lines 1–3) states that *this spirit of checks and balances . . . means . . . no one group can assert unlimited authority over another,* which makes this statement false. In other words, Congress does not have more power or influence over the laws than the other branches of government; the system of "checks and balances," in fact, indicates the opposite: *When all three branches have signaled their approval of the bill, then it officially becomes a law.*

- **Choice 4:** This is one of the summary ideas: Paragraph 2 (lines 3–5) tells you *smaller states still insisted that each state have an equal number of representatives* while *more populous states* wanted *to assign representatives on the basis of population.* Lines 1–2 of paragraph 3 state that they *came up with "The Great Compromise,". . . to provide some degree of satisfaction to everyone.* Lines 5–6 say that in *the Senate, each state was to be represented by two legislators* [to meet the needs of smaller states for equal representation.] *However, in . . . the House of Representatives, the number of lawmakers per state was to be based on the population of a respective state* [to meet the needs of . . . larger states for fair representation].

READING SKILL 9 115

- **Choice 5:** This is one of the summary ideas: Lines 1–2 of paragraph 4 state that The Great Compromise *mandated that the two houses* (the Senate and the House of Representatives) *had to work together to create laws*. Paragraph 5 describes the process of creating and approving a law and says (lines 9–11): *When all three branches have signaled their approval of the bill, then it officially becomes a law. At any time during this process, one of the branches . . . can indicate their disapproval . . . When this happens, the bill is either returned to Congress for revisions or canceled.*

- **Choice 6:** This is NOT one of the summary ideas. The process of the president signing the bill into law is a specific detail.

The following chart outlines the key points that you should remember about Select Summary questions.

KEY POINTS FOR QUESTIONS ABOUT SELECTING SUMMARY INFORMATION	
FREQUENCY	1 question per reading passage (alternated with an organizational [schematic] table question)
HOW TO IDENTIFY THE QUESTION	A thesis statement and summary chart with six possible answer choices are given.
WHERE TO FIND THE ANSWER	Throughout the entire passage.
HOW TO ANSWER THE QUESTION	1. Read the thesis statement that is provided. 2. Quickly read the topic statements (the first sentences) of each paragraph. 3. Look for answer choices from the six provided that are the main topics of paragraphs. 4. In the answer choices, be aware that the information in the correct answers may be paraphrased using synonyms and alternate syntax or sentence order. The correct answers will not repeat exact information from the passage, but rather will synthesize or combine different pieces of information. 5. Eliminate choices that are definitely false or not discussed in the passage. 6. Eliminate choices that describe minor details or examples.

In the exam, you may be able to eliminate incorrect answer choices by understanding what is wrong with them.

> For Select Summary Information questions, incorrect answer choices may:
> - contain minor details or examples.
> - contain information not discussed in the passage.
> - contain information that is false or inaccurate based on the passage.
> - use transition words and syntax to confuse the ideas.

READING EXERCISE 9: An introductory sentence for a brief summary of each passage is provided below each passage. Complete the summary by selecting the answer choices that express the most important ideas in the passage. Some sentences do not belong in the summary because they express ideas that are not presented in the passage or are minor ideas in the passage.

PASSAGE ONE (Question 1)

Paragraph

Island Plant Life

1▶ Islands are geographical formations that are completely surrounded by water, yet many islands are covered with a rich assortment of plant life. It may seem surprising that so much plant life exists on many islands, yet there are surprisingly simple explanations as to how the vegetation has been able to establish itself there. Principles for the development of plant life on an island have been established that take into account factors such as island size, distance from larger landmasses, and whether the island was formerly attached to land or whether it emerged independently from the water. Other elements that influence plant life on islands include existing animal life on and around the island, as well as the migration patterns of birds.

2▶ One generally accepted principle about island plant life is that larger islands support a wider diversity of plant life than smaller islands. An obvious reason for this is that larger islands have more land area to support plant life, but this does not entirely explain the variety of species that are found on them in comparison to those on smaller islands. Larger islands also have a broader diversity of soil types, which can support different kinds of plants. These varying soil types occur with more frequency on larger islands than on smaller islands, permitting plant species to root and grow in multiple areas, which in turn, reduces the chances of plant extinction. For example, if a plant can only grow in one area on a small island, a catastrophic event that destroys that area will wipe out the species on that island. In contrast, if a plant species is growing in several areas on a larger island, the probability of a destructive occurrence happening to every area where it grows is dramatically decreased, so the plant species has a greater likelihood of survival.

3▶ Proximity to larger landmasses, usually mainland regions, also has a positive impact on the development of plant species on islands. Islands in extremely close proximity benefit from wind and weather patterns that transport seeds from the mainland. Even islands that are a little further away, but are relatively easy to reach from the mainland, have the potential for seed transfer to occur through visits from people, especially if the islands are inhabited by people or are popular tourist destinations. However, a danger occurs with this means of seeding the island, since people from other locations can unknowingly introduce plant life considered exotic to the island, and which can adversely affect some of the native species. A third means by which islands receive the benefits of seed transfer is through bird migration. As birds fly over or rest on islands, they also drop seeds from their bodies that they picked up on the mainland.

4▶ Some islands are created when rising water levels or flooding occurs, cutting off a piece of land from a larger mass. These islands that used to be part of a mainland tend to retain the same plant species they had before the islands were separated from the larger landmass. This makes sense in that the soil type and climate of both land areas remain virtually the same. In addition, the newly formed islands may also have the same animal species as the mainland has, which means that patterns of seed transfer and fertilization will mimic what occurs on the mainland and sustain the plant life that already exists. One such example of this type of island is Kangaroo Island off the coast of Australia. It was separated from Australia approximately 10,000 years ago because of rising sea levels. Its closest point to the mainland is only 8 miles (13 kilometers). Although the human inhabitants eventually died off after the island became isolated, several native species, both plant and animal, continued to thrive and are still present on the island today.

5▶ Conversely, islands with the least amount of plant species and diversity are those that emerge from the ocean in isolated areas far from other landmasses. These islands generally form from volcanic activity. As the lava from a volcano cools, it changes composition and becomes capable of supporting plant life. This process can take centuries before a measurable amount of plant species are seen. While these islands can be seeded from wind and bird migration, the diversity and amount of seeds being carried decreases the farther out the island is from larger landmasses.

This question is worth 2 points (2 points for 3 correct answers, 1 point for 2 correct answers, and 0 points for 1 or 0 correct answers).
Simple principles govern the amount and variety of plant life on an island.
•
•
•

Answer Choices (choose 3 to complete the chart):

(1) Larger islands have a greater variety of plant life than smaller islands.
(2) Islands that emerge in the ocean are usually created by active volcanoes.
(3) Distance from the mainland affects plant life on islands.
(4) Birds sometimes carry seeds to islands.
(5) Some islands were created when rising water cut them off from larger areas of land.
(6) Islands once part of a large mass generally have more and varied plant life than those formed independently.

PASSAGE TWO (Question 2)

Ben and Jerry's

Paragraph

1▶   A detailed examination of Ben and Jerry's Homemade, Inc., a company widely known for its unconventional ice cream flavors and business tactics, reveals that creativity has been the cornerstone, leading to the organization's tremendous success. All successful businesses are not established and run in the same way, with formal business plans, traditional organizational structures, and a strong focus on profits. Ben Cohen and Jerry Greenfield, the entrepreneurs responsible for the highly successful ice cream business that bears their names, were businessmen with a rather unconventional approach.

2▶   Ben and Jerry, friends since middle school, were rather unusual individuals even from the beginning of their careers. They chose not to begin their entrepreneurial careers by attending one of the elite business schools in the United States, rather, opting to take a five-dollar correspondence course from Pennsylvania State University. This short course was specifically about how to make ice cream, and was offered by Pennsylvania State's Creamery, the largest university creamery in the country.

3▶   Since the two men had little financial backing to start their business, they had to cut corners wherever they could. With an initial investment of just $12,000, the only location they could afford for the startup of their business was a gas station that they converted to an ice cream production factory. Though this start-up was rather untraditional, they were strongly committed to creating the best ice cream possible, which soon made the community ice cream shop a local favorite. In 1979, on the first anniversary of their opening, Ben and Jerry held their first annual free-cone day, when the two proprietors personally served free cones to every customer that came in and requested one as a token of gratitude for the success they had achieved. This early success has grown, due to the partners' persistence in learning their business and their commitment to the quality of their product.

4▶   Even though they became extremely successful, Ben and Jerry did not convert to a more conventional style of doing business. In an era where companies were measured on every penny of profit that they managed to squeeze out, Ben and Jerry had a strong belief that business should give back to the community; thus, they began a tradition of donating 7.5 percent of their pretax profit to social causes that they believed in. They also lacked the emphasis on executive salary and benefits packages that so preoccupy other corporations, opting instead for a five-to-one policy in which the salary of the employee receiving the highest pay could never be more than five times the salary of the employee receiving the lowest pay. This salary structure remained a standard of the company until the mid-1990s, when the owners were forced to modify it in order to attract business expertise from outside of the company.

5▶   Eventually, the business grew beyond the scope of the two men's ability to run it effectively, but neither of them wanted to eliminate the community and environmentally conscious aspects that they had incorporated into the business. Consequently, in their negotiations with large corporations interested in buying the business, the founders insisted on certain conditions before agreeing to sell. These conditions included a demonstrable commitment to improving the communities in which Ben and Jerry shops are located, as well as dedication to being environmentally responsible in the production, packaging, and distribution of its ice cream flavors. This responsibility encompassed both an agreement to use only hormone-free milk and packaging methods that lessened the use of environmentally damaging products and techniques.

6▶   The new parent company, Unilever, which purchased the ice cream company in 2000, complied with Ben and Jerry's conditions, agreeing to run the ice cream division separately from their more traditionally organized subsidiaries. Over time, the parent organization has not been able to maintain all of the initial agreements, especially in regards to environmental responsibility. However, Ben and Jerry's is still known for its active support of charitable events, relatively natural ingredients, and commitment to the environment. And while Ben and Jerry lost official authority to make decisions for the company after it was sold, they still involved themselves in the production and promotion of new flavors.

> **This question is worth 2 points** (2 points for 3 correct answers, 1 point for 2 correct answers, and 0 points for 1 or 0 correct answers).
>
> **Ben Cohen and Jerry Greenfield followed an unconventional approach with their company.**
>
> •
>
> •
>
> •

Answer Choices (choose 3 to complete the chart):

(1) They tried to ensure that their company would continue to benefit the community after it was sold.
(2) They began their business with little background knowledge and minimal investment.
(3) The new owners of Ben and Jerry are not as committed to social causes.
(4) They had a salary structure that limits the salaries of high-level executives.
(5) They supported community and environmental causes with their business profits.
(6) They borrowed a large amount of money to start their business.

PASSAGE THREE (Question 3)

Paragraph   **The Bald Eagle**

1▶   Prior to the bald eagle becoming the national symbol of the United States in 1782, it had already been honored as a prominent creature, along with its cousin the golden eagle, in many Native American cultures. In the Native American tribes that honor the bald eagle, it is largely seen as a messenger between the world of the living and the "spirit" world, carrying prayers from this world and messages from the other. The bald eagle was particularly revered in the Pacific Northwest where the great majority of bald eagles lived and where they shared a fondness for salmon with tribes of that region.

2▶   When the United States, recognizing the strength and power that the bald eagle represented, adopted the bird as its national symbol in the late eighteenth century, it is estimated that there were as many as 75,000 nesting pairs in North America. Most of these pairs were concentrated in what is now known as Canada, and further northwest, in present-day Alaska. However, bald eagles were also found further south, as far as the northern part of Mexico, and while they were primarily seen on the West Coast, they spread their habitats inland across the continent, with sightings all the way to Florida in the southern United States. Bald eagles can establish habitats near most lakes, rivers, and other bodies of water that supply the necessary provision of fish that the eagles require as their primary food source.

3▶   The term "bald" in the bald eagle's name is somewhat misleading, since, in fact, the heads of bald eagles are covered with a profusion of white feathers. Experts speculate that the bird received its odd moniker for one of two reasons: First, the term "bald" originally meant a visible white spot, perhaps in reference to the natural whitening of hair as people age. This definition provides an apt name for the eagle with its white head feathers contrasting sharply with its typically darker-hued body feathers. Another reason that people cite for the name of the eagle is that the multitude of white feathers covering the eagle's head do make it appear bald or without any feathers on its head from a distance.

4▶   The feathers of a bald eagle are fascinating in and of themselves. Each eagle has approximately 7,000 feathers over its entire body, and the feathers are used for several purposes. The most obvious purpose is for enabling bald eagles to fly; the birds use the feathers to help them soar and dive, and also to control their speed and stability as they swoop down on prey or come in for a landing. Yet, the feathers, which are hollow, but surprisingly strong and pliable, serve other purposes as well. They provide waterproof protection from wet weather and greatly assist the eagles in regulating their body temperature during both hot and cold weather. The feathers also act as a source of protection. Eagles will often "puff themselves up," or expand the space between their feathers, in order to make themselves appear larger and more intimidating to their potential enemies. This expansion is also useful during "preening," which is a technique bald eagles use to attract mates. In most cases, especially for males, appearing larger is an appealing characteristic to a potential partner. Humans as well admire the eagle's feathers; they are still prized by Native American tribes, who, even today, award feathers to members of their tribes that demonstrate exceptional strength and courage.

5▶   Though the bald eagle gained national importance as the symbol of the United States, something tragic happened to the vast population that originally numbered well above 100,000. By the early 1960s, the number of nesting pairs had been reduced to an estimated low of around 450. The demise of the bald eagle is generally attributed to the harmful effects of the pesticide DDT (dichloro-diphenyl-trichloroethane), a chemical used in farming, and of widespread hunting of the bird, for its feathers and other sought after parts.

6▶   As a result of the drastic decline of the bird, the bald eagle is now protected by federal laws. It was originally protected by the Bald Eagle Act of 1940 and later by the Endangered Species Act of 1973. However, it is not just the laws directly related to endangered species that aided in the resurgence of the bald eagle; its resurgence has also been widely attributed to the banning of DDT in 1972. Today there are more than 5,000 pairs of bald eagles, a tenfold increase over the low point of 450, which has led to it being removed from the Endangered Species List, though it is still protected by other laws such as the Bald and Golden Eagle Protection Act.

This question is worth 2 points (2 points for 3 correct answers, 1 point for 2 correct answers, and 0 points for 1 or 0 correct answers).
The bald eagle has been honored in United States history for its unique attributes, yet it has not always been protected.
•
•
•

Answer Choices (choose 3 to complete the chart):

(1) Bald eagles were once the most numerous and widespread birds in North America.

(2) The term "bald" originally referred to a white spot on the top of older eagles' heads.

(3) The bald eagle is a powerful symbol to present-day Americans, as well as Native Americans.

(4) The bald eagle, named for the white feathers on its head, has feathers on its body with several useful features.

(5) Two different pieces of endangered species legislation were enacted 33 years apart.

(6) Since the extreme decrease in the bald eagle population, due to a pesticide and hunting, legislation has been enacted to specifically protect the bird.

PASSAGE FOUR (Question 4)

Paragraph

Modernism in Art

1▶ A proliferation of varying styles characterized the world of American art and architecture in the period starting from the late 1800s through the first several decades of the following century. In spite of the fact that these various styles often had little in common with each other, they are traditionally clustered under the label of *modernism*. It is thus rather difficult to give a precise definition of modernism, one that encompasses all the characteristics of the artists and architects who are commonly grouped under this label. Despite this inability to definitively describe what is and is not modernism, modernist works share a few vital characteristics.

2▶ One fundamental characteristic of modernism is a demonstration of progressive innovation. In general, a modernist is someone who tries to develop an individual style by adding to or improving upon the style of immediate predecessors. The modernist belief was in starting with the ideas of the mainstream movement and then innovating from the mainstream to improve upon the ideas of predecessors rather than in breaking away from the mainstream to create something entirely new. However, because there were varying ideas on what constituted the mainstream and because the potential innovations emanating from the mainstream were infinite, modernism under this definition could take a myriad of directions.

3▶ However, a unifying, and central, component of the diversion away from the mainstream involved the artists' reaction to changes in the world around them, particularly changes in science. Thus, modernism includes not just the styles of art being expressed, but also the ideology, or underlying ideas, which brought about the new artistic expression. Modernists were responding to new developments occurring around them, especially scientific discoveries that stripped away previously held notions of reality and its foundations. Prominent and respected scientists of the day, such as Darwin and Freud, made people question the very origins of life and how it should be perceived. Certain longstanding "truths" had been challenged, leaving people far less certain of their vision of the world. Modernists responded to this new age of uncertainty by discarding intellect and replacing it with intuition, perception not based on facts, in an attempt to portray the world beyond its physical surface.

4▶ The biological sciences were not the only field that helped to shape modernist work; advances in technology heavily influenced this period of artistic expression as well. As modernists observed the increased use of machines in both industry and daily life, they took the spirit of innovation responsible for the new devices and applied that in their depiction of art, for pieces they designed for functional use and entertainment. Modernists turned away from traditional conventions of display, instead reworking subjects, colors, and compositions in their attempts to define their own visual expression of the new world around them.

5▶ Another essential characteristic of modernism was the belief that art could and should reflect the reality of modern life and would not, for example, focus on the lives of society's most privileged members or on otherworld entities such as angels and sprites. Though there was agreement among modernists as to the need for art to reflect modern life, there was far less agreement on what actually constituted modern life. For some it involved advancements in technology and transportation. For others, increased wealth and the subsequent rise in consumerism became their focus. Still others highlighted greater personal freedoms and a sense of shaking off the traditions of the past. Thus, modern artists and architects reflect very different aspects of modern life in their works.

6▶   In addition to the various emphases chosen by individual artists, a reliance on personal intuition as opposed to intellectual rationalization accounts for the great variety of expression throughout the movement. Two different artists could observe the same phenomenon, for example, and note its impact on the life of the general public. Yet, their individual intuitive understanding of the reach of this impact and its importance to the public, along with each artist's preferred medium of artistic expression, would likely result in strikingly different depictions of the phenomenon. Perhaps due to the rapid and varied changes happening in the world around them, the artists and architects of the modernist period cycled through several styles of expression over a relatively short period of time, yet they somehow still managed to convey a strong sense of the reality of the eras in which they lived.

This question is worth 2 points (2 points for 3 correct answers, 1 point for 2 correct answers, and 0 points for 1 or 0 correct answers).
Though modernism in art shares certain characteristics, these characteristics can be difficult to define precisely.
•
•
•

Answer Choices (choose 3 to complete the chart):

(1) A reflection of the reality of modern life is one aspect of modernism.
(2) There is no universal agreement as to exactly what makes up modern life.
(3) Science and technology had a large influence on modernist expression.
(4) Modernism stresses the importance of the individual intellect.
(5) Many different styles are part of modern art.
(6) It can be difficult to define what the mainstream is.

Reading Skill 10: Complete Organizational (Schematic) Tables

Organizational or schematic table questions evaluate your ability to outline the key information from a passage. You must be able to recognize overall organization of the information in the passage and major points in the passage. The question always appears as the last question in the set of questions (alternating with a summary question), and it is organized in a table format. Category headings from two or three of the broad ideas from a passage are provided in the table. You must choose the ideas that correspond to each category from a list of usually seven answer choices following the table. For this question, you must choose only five answer choices. This means that two of the answer choices provided will be not be used to fill in the schematic table. Because the question has more than one answer choice, it is worth multiple points; you will receive 0 to 3 points depending on how many correct answers you choose. When you decide you want to place an answer into a category, click on the answer and then click in the space in the category where you want to place the answer. By placing the answers into the correct categories, you are completing an outline of the reading passage. You can click back and forth between the question and the passage while you are answering this question.

Since the organizational (schematic) table is at the end of the set of questions, you can jot down quick notes from previous questions to help you outline the key ideas.

Strategies to Answer Organizational (Schematic) Table Questions

- Identify the categories that are provided.

- Scan each paragraph that discusses the related categories in the table for information that corresponds to the answer choices.

- In the answer choices, be aware that the information may be paraphrased using synonyms and alternate syntax. Scan to find the information quickly. Remember, the wording in the correct answers will differ.

- Eliminate choices that are definitely false or not discussed in the passage.

- Eliminate choices that are not relevant to the categories in the table.

Transitional Words and Phrases	
Contrast	*however; although; contrary to; on the contrary; in contrast to; on the other hand*
Similarity	*similarly; likewise; in the same way; like; as*
Addition of Ideas	*and; also; as well; in addition; further; furthermore; moreover*
Examples	*for example; for instance*
Sequence	*first; next; afterward; subsequently; then; finally*
Result	*therefore; as a result; consequently; thus; hence*

Example

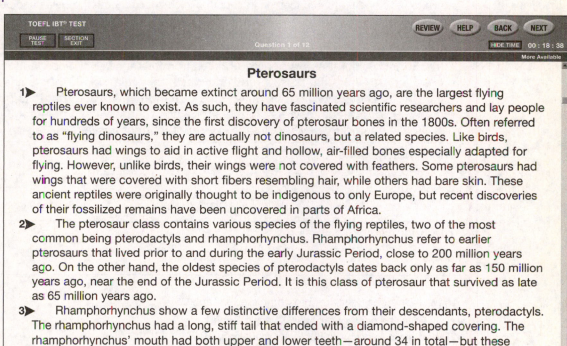

TOEFL IBT® TEST

PAUSE TEST | SECTION EXIT | Question 1 of 12 | HIDE TIME 00 : 18 : 38

REVIEW | HELP | BACK | NEXT

More Available

Pterosaurs

1▶ Pterosaurs, which became extinct around 65 million years ago, are the largest flying reptiles ever known to exist. As such, they have fascinated scientific researchers and lay people for hundreds of years, since the first discovery of pterosaur bones in the 1800s. Often referred to as "flying dinosaurs," they are actually not dinosaurs, but a related species. Like birds, pterosaurs had wings to aid in active flight and hollow, air-filled bones especially adapted for flying. However, unlike birds, their wings were not covered with feathers. Some pterosaurs had wings that were covered with short fibers resembling hair, while others had bare skin. These ancient reptiles were originally thought to be indigenous to only Europe, but recent discoveries of their fossilized remains have been uncovered in parts of Africa.

2▶ The pterosaur class contains various species of the flying reptiles, two of the most common being pterodactyls and rhamphorhynchus. Rhamphorhynchus refer to earlier pterosaurs that lived prior to and during the early Jurassic Period, close to 200 million years ago. On the other hand, the oldest species of pterodactyls dates back only as far as 150 million years ago, near the end of the Jurassic Period. It is this class of pterosaur that survived as late as 65 million years ago.

3▶ Rhamphorhynchus show a few distinctive differences from their descendants, pterodactyls. The rhamphorhynchus had a long, stiff tail that ended with a diamond-shaped covering. The rhamphorhynchus' mouth had both upper and lower teeth—around 34 in total—but these did not extend fully to the tip of the jaw. Instead, the toothless portion of the mouth formed a hooked beak. Both the shape of the jaw and the lack of front teeth indicate that this pterosaur subsisted on a diet of primarily small insects and fish. The skull was somewhat short and lacked any type of crest or raised structure on the top. In general, rhamphorhynchus were smaller in size than pterodactyls, with a lesser wing span as well. There is evidence that in flight, the rhamphorhynchus tended to hold its head parallel to the ground, to aid in balance. In addition, certain studies also suggest that these earlier pterosaurs were nocturnal, meaning they were active during the night and slept during the day.

TOEFL IBT® TEST

PAUSE TEST   SECTION EXIT

REVIEW   HELP   BACK   NEXT

Question 1 of 12

HIDE TIME   00 : 18 : 38

More Available

4▶ Pterodactyls, as the later members of the pterosaur family are called, evolved to compensate for issues the rhamphorhynchus may have had trouble with. The wingspan of a pterodactyl was typically larger than that of a rhamphorhynchus, reaching up to 59 inches (1.5 meters) in length in the largest of the species. The longer wingspan allowed the pterodactyls to fly longer distances and more efficiently swoop down for fish. Although the mouth of a pterodactyl ended in a beak, similar to its predecessor, the beak tip was much shorter and included teeth all the way to the tip. The extension of the teeth to the front of the jaw, and the larger number of teeth—up to 90—demonstrate that the pterodactyl was not only able to feed on fish, but could also supplement its diet with small animals. Pterodactyls, as with some other species of pterosaurs were diurnal: active during the day. And unlike rhamphorhynchus, pterodactyls flew with their head in a downward angle, instead of parallel to the ground. This downward position helped them to spot prey on the ground more easily.

5▶ As technological advances have improved scientific research methods, further refinements of the classification of pterosaurs has occurred. Fossil specimens once classified under the category of pterodactyls have been organized into further subcategories. These categories are determined by increasingly detectable physical differences and lifestyle patterns in later animals. One such example is

> When reading, develop the habit of organizing a schematic chart in your own mind. When you notice several separate details that seem to describe a broader idea, create a picture in your mind of the entire idea and how the separate details fit into the picture.

the ctenochasma family. One significant physical difference animals from this family have from pterodactyls is their jaw structure. A pterosaur belonging to the ctenochasma family is now known to have had up to 400 teeth in its mouth, which covered both the inside and outside of the upper and lower jaws, creating a comblike appearance. In addition, the ctenochasma operated on a nocturnal schedule, similar to its ancestor, the rhamphorhynchus.

Directions: Select the appropriate phrases from the answer choices, and match them to the type of reptile to which they relate. TWO of the answer choices will not be used. **This question is worth 3 points** (3 points for 5 correct answers, 2 points for 4 correct answers, 1 point for 3 correct answers, and 0 points for 2, 1, or 0 correct answers).

rhamphorhynchus	• • •
pterodactyls	• •

Answer Choices (choose 5 to complete the table):

(1) lived in the early part of the Jurassic Period
(2) had teeth in both the back and front of the jaw
(3) had wings covered in feathers
(4) were inactive during the day
(5) lacked teeth in the front of the jaw
(6) had short tails and short heads
(7) were active during the day

To answer this question correctly, you must skim the passage to find the paragraphs that discuss rhamphorhynchus (paragraphs 2–3) and the ones that discuss pterodactyls (paragraphs 2, 4–5, 6). Then you need to scan these paragraphs to match the listed details with the appropriate category.

REMEMBER: Not all the answers are used, so if you do not find an answer when you are scanning quickly, then skip that choice.

- Choice 1: Rhamphorhynchus: Paragraph 2 (lines 2–3): *Rhamphorhynchus . . . lived prior to and during the early Jurassic Period . . .*

- Choice 2: Pterodactyls: Paragraph 4 (line 7): *The extension of the teeth to the front of the jaw . . .*

- Choice 3: NEITHER: refers to birds, which were mentioned in paragraph 1.

- Choice 4: Rhamphorhynchus: Paragraph 3 (lines 10–11): *these earlier pterosaurs were nocturnal . . . active during the night and slept during the day.*

- Choice 5: Rhamphorhynchus: Paragraph 3 (lines 2–4): *The rhamphorhynchus' mouth had both upper and lower teeth . . . but these did not extend fully to the tip of the jaw.*

- Choice 6: NEITHER: refers to ctenochasmas in paragraph 6.

- Choice 7: Pterodactyls: Paragraph 4 (lines 10–11): *Pterodactyls . . . were diurnal: active during the day.*

The following chart outlines the key points that you should remember about Organizational (Schematic) Table questions.

KEY POINTS FOR QUESTIONS ABOUT COMPLETING ORGANIZATIONAL (SCHEMATIC) TABLES	
FREQUENCY	1 question per reading passage (alternated with a summary chart question)
HOW TO IDENTIFY THE QUESTION	5 categories are provided in a table with 7 possible answers following the table.
WHERE TO FIND THE ANSWER	Identify the paragraphs that discuss the categories given.
HOW TO ANSWER THE QUESTION	1. Identify the categories that are provided. 2. Scan each paragraph that discusses the related categories in the table for information that corresponds to the answer choices. 3. In the answer choices, be aware that the information may be paraphrased using synonyms and alternate syntax. Information from the passage will not be repeated in exactly the same way in the answer choices. 4. Eliminate choices that are definitely false or not discussed in the passage. 5. Eliminate choices that are not related to the categories given in the table.

In the exam, you may be able to eliminate incorrect answer choices by understanding what is wrong with them.

For Complete Organizational (Schematic) Table questions, incorrect answer choices may:
- contain information that is not relevant to the categories given.
- contain information not discussed in the passage.
- contain information that is false based on the passage.

READING EXERCISE 10: Study each passage, and complete the table that follows by matching the answer choice to its appropriate position in the table. Some answer choices do not belong in the table because they express ideas that are not presented in the passage or are minor ideas in the passage.

PASSAGE ONE (Question 1)

Paragraph   **Sand Dunes**

1▶   Dunes are defined as mounds, or hills, of sand that are built up by either wind or water flow. While dunes have been observed underwater, for practical reasons, most dune tracking is done on dry ground. These dunes can be found along some coastal areas, usually in single or multiple sets that are parallel to the shore and directly inland from the beach. However, the largest accumulations of dunes have been discovered in dry areas, often deserts, further inland. The vast majority of these inland dunes have formed in and around lake or seabeds that dried up long ago.

2▶   Since the structure of sand dunes is heavily influenced by wind direction and speed, along with the amount of sand present, dunes are not uniform in shape or size. In areas where the wind blows in one direction, sand dunes often form in long straight or curved lines. Winds that crisscross or blow in from multiple directions will change this basic shape by deepening or eliminating curves or by pushing the sand upward to enhance the height of the dune instead of its width.

3▶   Ridge dunes form where there are large amounts of sand, generally in the interiors of deserts, and winds blow in one direction. Under these conditions, parallel ridges of sand, known as transverse dunes, form at right angles to the wind. Because they form perpendicular to the blowing of the wind, ridge or linear, dunes create wavy ridges at the top. This formation makes ridge dunes less stable than other types of dunes, and creates the potential of ridge dunes breaking down into crescent dunes over time.

4▶   When the direction of the wind changes so that it comes from different directions, star-shaped dunes form from the massive amounts of sand in desert interiors. Star-shaped dunes are relatively stable dunes that can reach incredible heights in some deserts, and are quite common in massive deserts such as the Sahara. The reason that these dunes reach such high altitudes is that the multidirectional winds prevent the dunes from spreading out too far in any one direction, instead pushing the sand upward. Usually star-shaped dunes resemble a pyramid in shape, with angled faces on at least three of the arms that extend from the center of the mound. Because of the way they are formed, star-shaped dunes are considered the tallest dunes on Earth; the Badain Jaran Desert in China contains the highest dunes to be measured, at up to 500 meters tall.

5▶   Crescent dunes form on the edges of deserts where there is less sand and where the winds blow mainly in one direction. As their name suggests, crescent dunes are typically curved, and are molded into shape by winds that blow consistently from the same direction. In general, crescent dunes are wider than they are long. These dunes, which are also known as barchan dunes, are less stable than star-shaped dunes and can shift as much as 20 meters per year as winds blow over the outer curves of the crescent in the direction of the pointed ends. Dunes in Egypt and China have been documented as moving more than 100 meters per year.

6▶   Sand dunes perform several functions necessary for ecological balance. For example, dunes found along coastlines act as natural barriers against damage that may be caused by storm waves rushing inland. Dunes in many locations are also host to a variety of plants and animals, some of which are extremely rare and face extinction if their dune habitats are destroyed, which makes their destruction, due to the expanding use of dune areas by people an important environmental concern.

7▶   The disappearance of sand dunes becomes more common year after year, as the increasing world population compels people to take over areas once considered uninhabitable. Either the dunes are leveled in order to make room for homes or recreational use, or they are destroyed to prevent their sand from blowing into areas now developed for people. A prime example of this is Golden Gate Park in San Francisco. Called the largest man-made park in the world for decades after its construction, Golden Gate Park was built atop an area of sand dunes that stretched for miles. Initially promoted as a project to provide more recreational space for the city's residents, the area where it was built was deliberately chosen to encourage housing developments in order to expand the city westward.

> **Directions:** Select the appropriate ideas from the answer choices, and match them to the appropriate type of dune. TWO of the answer choices will not be used. **This question is worth 3 points** (3 points for 5 correct answers, 2 points for 4 correct answers, 1 point for 3 correct answers, and 0 points for 2, 1, or 0 correct answers).

ridge dunes	•
	•
star-shaped dunes	•
crescent dunes	•
	•

Answer Choices (choose 5 to complete the table):

(1) usually have greater width than length
(2) do not always retain their original dune formation
(3) have a U-shaped form that is very stable
(4) form when winds from various directions blow over large volumes of sand
(5) most commonly occur near oceans
(6) are characterized by wavy ridges
(7) can shift large distances over time

PASSAGE TWO (Question 2)

Paragraph

The Etymology of Words

1▶   Since English is the current *lingua franca*—the accepted language of global communication, especially in areas of commerce and political discourse—its origins and development are of interest to a widespread audience. English originated from a collection of Germanic dialects, which eventually evolved into a primarily Germanic language with substantial contributions based on both Latin and Greek roots. Over the centuries, as English speakers began to travel, explore, and settle in other parts of the world, the language was influenced by other nearby languages, such as French, Spanish, and Italian—known as the "Romance languages"—along with those that were not Latin-based, such as Japanese and Arabic.

2▶   The etymologies[1] of many English words today can be traced back to their word parts in their original language, particularly those of Latin, Greek, or Germanic origin. These word parts can consist of: a prefix, a word part that precedes the main part of the word; the root, the part that contains the primary meaning of the word; and a suffix, the part attached to the end of the word. By understanding the meaning of each word part, one can frequently guess the meaning of the word. For example, a very common word part is "ology," which means "the study of." When one combines this suffix with the root "bio," which means "life" or "living" to form the word "biology," it conveys the meaning of "the study of life" or "the study of living things." When this suffix is connected to the root "graph" ("writing"), it means "the study of writing." In turn, if the root "graph" is joined to the prefix "auto," which means "self," it creates "autograph," literally "self writing." "Auto," "bio," and "graph" are also connected to form the English term "autobiography," a story that is written about one's own life, as opposed to "biography," which is a story an author writes about another person's life.

GLOSSARY

1 *etymology*—the study of the origins, history, and meanings of words or a description of the origins of a particular word

3►   However, not all etymologies are as easily traceable; some modern words owe their meaning to the context in which they were originally used or to the traditions from which they first came, rather than to the literal meaning. One such word is "escape" which derives from Latin and literally meant "out of cape." Centuries ago, in Roman times, capes were a common piece of clothing worn, draped around the shoulders or neck, by men. When Roman men were being pursued by their enemies, their enemies would grab onto the Roman's capes in an attempt to catch and hold onto to the men. The Romans, however, would slip out of their capes and run away, thus "escaping" from their enemies and avoiding capture. Another example is the word "cheer," which originates from the Greek word for "face." The expressions "cheer up" and "be of good cheer" began as a way to encourage people to wear happy expressions on their faces, but expanded over time to now convey a more general sense of emotional happiness. Likewise, the word "ballot," which today refers to the means by which a voter chooses a candidate in an election, is related to its original definition "small ball or pebble" through tradition, not its precise meaning. In earlier times, Italians used a tiny ball or pebble called a "ballot" in the Italian language to cast their vote. As the voting process modernized to include paper ballots and voting by electronic means, the term "ballot" retained the primary meaning of its original function, but not its literal meaning.

4►   Still other words in English have strayed even farther from their original connotations. In English, the term "hazard" is defined in modern times as "danger," yet this is a connotation that developed gradually. The word itself comes from the Arabic "al zahr," meaning "the dice[2]." In the Middle Ages, European crusaders and traders learned various games while traveling in Arabic-speaking nations that involved the use of dice. "Al zahr" was commonly called out in Arabic as the dice were tossed. English speakers of the time adapted the sound "al zahr" to "hazard." As time passed, the term "hazard" came to first signify the dangers of playing dice games, since these games often also included the risks associated with losing money or goods while gambling. Over time, the term evolved to mean a general sense of danger. Another word that has taken a surprising detour from its original connotation is the term "nice." This word, which today means "kind" or "pleasant," once meant "foolish" or "ignorant." Through a diverse history of twists and turns, some of which are difficult to track, the definition evolved into its current meaning.

GLOSSARY

2. *dice*—two or more small blocks of wood, plastic, etc. usually with a different number of spots on each side, used in games

Directions:	Select the appropriate phrases from the answer choices and match them to the pairs of words to which they relate. TWO of the answer choices will not be used. **This question is worth 3 points** (3 points for 5 correct answers, 2 points for 4 correct answers, 1 point for 3 correct answers, and 0 points for 2, 1, or 0 correct answers).

graphology and autobiography	• •
escape and ballot	• •
hazard and nice	•

Answer Choices (choose 5 to complete the table):

(1) meanings are disconnected from the original definition of the words

(2) meanings were originally derived from the Romance languages

(3) meanings can be understood by knowing the meanings of prefixes, suffixes, and roots

(4) are not based on the literal meanings of the words

(5) meanings are based on word parts from Latin, Greek, or Germanic languages

(6) have origins that cannot be currently tracked in the English language

(7) meanings can be traced back to the traditional sense of the word

Paragraph

Carnivorous Plants

1▶   Unlike the majority of plants that create their nourishment from sunlight, such as the flowering hyacinth or the leafy coleus or the garden-variety dandelion, a limited number of plants are able to enhance their diet by fortifying it with insects and other small animals to supplement the food that they have produced from sunlight. These carnivorous plants can be categorized in two ways. The first category includes those with stationary traps that lure their intended victims and then trap them on a sticky surface or drown them in a pool of fluid. The other category includes those with active traps—moving parts that ensnare prey.

2▶   Each of the two categories can be broken down into subcategories. The stationary, or passive, trap category can be further divided by the types of passive traps individual carnivorous species use to lure in their prey. Two of the common types of these traps are passive pitfall and lobster-pot traps. Similarly, the species in the active trap category can also be broken down further based on the type of active trap they utilize, such as a snap or a flypaper trap.

3▶   Passive trap plants that use pitfall traps typically have a rolled or cuplike leaf structure that funnels the prey, primarily insects, down toward the digestive tract. Pitfall traps make use of water and digestive enzymes to both move the insect into the digestive area and to break down the insect and absorb its nutrients. Because of their structure and the tendency toward growing in areas with a high accumulation of rainfall, plants with pitfall traps can be in danger of drowning themselves if their traps become too full of water. Consequently, many varieties have evolved to include some kind of drainage mechanism that releases excess water and fluids from the traps. Plants referred to as pitcher plants, due to their capacity for collecting water, are a common type of pitfall trap plant.

4▶   Like pitfall trap plants, plants that have lobster-pot trap systems may take advantage of water flowing into the trap. However, unlike their passive counterparts, lobster-pot trap plants are more dependent on tiny bristles on their leaves that conduct the prey inescapably toward the digestive area of the plant. While lobster-pot plants are composed of chambers that insects find easy to enter, these same insects find it nearly impossible to emerge safely. The bristles, tiny hairs growing inside of the chambers, are positioned in such a manner that the insects are forced to move away from the exit, in the direction of the plant's "stomach." Some lobster-pot plants, such as corkscrew plants, use water flowing through the chambers to push the insect more rapidly along the bristles into the stomach to be digested.

5▶   A well-known category of active plant traps is the snap traps; an easily recognized example is the Venus flytrap. The Venus flytrap, the only known terrestrial snap trap, consists of leaves that are double-lobed and hinged in the middle. When the prey lands on one of the leaves, it triggers a signal through bristles on the surface, which causes the leaf to "snap" shut and enclose the victim inside. Further struggle from the prey results in tighter closure of the leaf and secretion of digestion enzymes that absorb the nutrients from the insect directly through the leaf. Once the prey is completely absorbed, a process that can take weeks, the leaf unhinges and opens again.

6▶   Flypaper traps are another common variety of active trap plants. Though not all flypaper traps are active, the majority do fall under this category. In an active flypaper trap, the leaves have virtually microscopic tentacles[1] that are coated in a sticky substance. Once an insect lands on a sticky area of the plant, the tentacles adhere to the insect. Not only do the tentacles stick to the prey, but they almost immediately begin to grow in reaction to discovering an edible substance. In a relatively short time, the insect is covered by the plant and the digestion process commences. The butterwort is a common example of a flypaper trap. As soon as the prey attaches to a butterwort leaf, a process is triggered that causes the leaf to expand until it is able to roll over and entirely enclose its victim.

GLOSSARY

1 *tentacles*—long thin parts of (usually) sea creatures that are used to capture food

Directions: Select the appropriate phrases from the answer choices, and match them to the type of carnivorous plant to which they relate. TWO of the answer choices will not be used. **This question is worth 3 points** (3 points for 5 correct answers, 2 points for 4 correct answers, 1 point for 3 correct answers, and 0 points for 2, 1, or 0 correct answers).

active traps	•
	•
passive traps	•
	•
	•

Answer Choices (choose 5 to complete the table):

(1) use a sticky substance to trap prey
(2) use water to aid in the entrapment of the insect
(3) direct the prey to move toward the digestive system
(4) use compartments lined with small hairs
(5) allow prey an easy chance to exit
(6) close shut when completely filled with liquid
(7) digest the prey directly on the leaf

PASSAGE FOUR (Question 4)

Paragraph

Hemingway and Faulkner

1▶ Despite writing in the same time period, enduring similar personal struggles as well as extraordinary triumphs, and being recognized as two of the most influential writers of the twentieth century, Ernest Hemingway and William Faulkner differed significantly in their styles and philosophies of writing. Both men were honored with multiple literary prizes, including the Pulitzer and Nobel prizes, perhaps the most coveted awards for any writer. Additionally, both men gained international fame for writing, and notoriety for their personal lives and the injuries they endured. But they did not share their literary styles. Hemingway wrote with precision and a minimalism that was drastically different from Faulkner's long, complex, and descriptive prose.

> Pay attention to the organization of ideas in the passage: chronological, cause/effect, comparison/contrast, problem/solution, and so on.

2▶ Ernest Hemingway was born shortly before the turn of the twentieth century, in a suburb of Chicago. He fought in World War I, where he met the first woman he intended to marry, a nurse with the Red Cross. Unfortunately, shortly after he returned to the States, the nurse wrote him and broke off the engagement. Hemingway began his writing career as a newspaper reporter. In 1920, Hemingway met and married his first wife, and they moved to Europe where Hemingway continued his work as a reporter while starting his writing career. Over the next few decades, Hemingway traveled the world, building his reputation as a novelist, while supporting himself at times with a variety of other types of writings, including a screenplay and play.

3▶ Hemingway wrote in a minimalist style. He concentrated purposely on framing his stories in sparse and simple language. Hemingway felt by telling one truth through simple action, dialogue, and "silence," he was in fact revealing a deeper truth that lay below the surface of the words he used. His style was concise, direct, and—literary critics would say—deceptively simple. Many believe this style was a result of his career as a reporter, where he learned to write factually and with clarity. However, beneath the simplicity, Hemingway's stories explore the themes of man's condition as much as by what is unsaid as what is said. Hemingway won the Pulitzer Prize in 1952, for his novel *The Old Man and the Sea*, a work he had completed in eight short weeks. He also achieved the honor of winning the Nobel Prize for Literature in 1954 for his contributions to the world of writing.

4▶ William Faulkner was also born at the end of the 1800s. Faulkner hoped to serve in the Army during World War I, though he was rejected for service because of his short stature. Faulkner's first love, Estelle Oldham, also married another man, leaving Faulkner heartbroken. Faulkner, like his literary contemporary, supported his dream of being a writer through various other means, including writing for journals, writing a play, and spending several years working on various screenplays.

5▶ In contrast to Hemingway's way of writing, Faulkner eschewed technique, once remarking that "The young writer would be a fool to follow a theory." His writing often derived from a "stream of consciousness" from which Faulkner allowed a variety of emotions and complexities to come into play in his stories. Faulkner's style was expressive. His emotionally charged and poetic stories contained lengthy, descriptive sentences that could at times be confusing to follow. Faulkner was the winner of two Pulitzer prizes, one in 1954 and one in 1962. He was also awarded the Nobel Prize in Literature in 1949.

6▶ Both authors experienced tragedy and pain in their lives. Both suffered an addiction to alcohol, and both suffered chronic pain from an accident. A few years before his death, while engaging in an activity he took up after he gained prosperity as a writer, Faulkner was seriously injured in a fall from a horse. Toward the end of Hemingway's life, he was injured in two consecutive plane crashes.

Directions:	Select the appropriate phrases from the answer choices, and match them to the writer to which they relate. TWO of the answer choices will not be used. **This question is worth 3 points** (3 points for 5 correct answers, 2 points for 4 correct answers, 1 point for 3 correct answers, and 0 points for 2, 1, or 0 correct answers).
Hemingway	• • •
Faulkner	• •

Answer Choices (choose 5 to complete the table):

(1) wrote complicated works filled with emotion
(2) lived a quiet and contented life
(3) wrote in a measured manner
(4) suffered severe injuries in plane accidents
(5) made his living only as a novelist
(6) wrote his Pulitzer-Prize winning novel in eight weeks
(7) won two Pulitzer Prizes

READING EXERCISE (Skills 9–10): Study the passage, and choose the best answers to the questions that follow.

Paragraph   **Species**

1▶ Millions of different species exist on the earth. These millions of species, which have evolved over billions of years, are the result of two distinct but simultaneously occurring processes: the processes of speciation and extinction. It is apparent that a balance between the two processes has been an important factor in the development and evolution of organisms. Even though the specific details of that balance are not yet clearly understood, scientists have come up with broad concepts of how each process works.

2▶ One of the processes that affects the number of species on earth is speciation, which results when one species diverges into two distinct species as a result of differences in natural selection in separate environments. Geographic isolation is one common mechanism that fosters speciation; speciation as a result of geographic isolation occurs when two populations of a species become separated for long periods of time into areas with different environmental conditions. After the two populations are separated, they evolve independently; if this divergence continues long enough, members of the two distinct populations eventually become so different genetically that they are two distinct species rather than one. The process of speciation may occur within hundreds of years for organisms that reproduce rapidly, but for most species the process of speciation can take thousands to millions of years. One example of speciation is the early fox, which over time evolved into two distinct species, the gray fox and the arctic fox. The early fox separated into populations which evolved differently in response to very different environments as the populations moved in different directions, one to colder northern climates and the other to warmer southern climates. The northern population adapted to cold weather by developing heavier fur, shorter ears, noses, and legs, and white fur to camouflage or hide itself in the snow. The southern population adapted to warmer weather by developing lighter fur and longer ears, noses, and legs, and keeping its darker fur for better camouflage protection.

3▶   Another of the processes that affects the number of species on earth is extinction, which refers to the situation in which a species ceases to exist. When environmental conditions change, a species needs to adapt to the new environmental conditions, or it may become extinct. Extinction of a species is not a rare occurrence but is instead a rather commonplace one: it has, in fact, been estimated that more than 99 percent of the species that have ever existed have become extinct. Extinction may occur when a species fails to adapt to evolving environmental conditions in a limited area, a process known as background extinction. In contrast, a broader and more abrupt extinction, known as mass extinction, may come about as a result of a catastrophic event or global climatic change. When such a disaster or global climatic change occurs, some species are able to adapt to the new environment, while those that are unable to adapt become extinct. From geological and fossil evidence, it appears that at least five great mass extinctions have occurred; the last mass extinction occurred approximately 65 million years ago, when the dinosaurs became extinct after 140 million years of existence on earth, marking the end of the Mesozoic Era and the beginning of the Cenozoic Era.

4▶   The fact that millions of species are in existence today is evidence that speciation has clearly kept well ahead of extinction. In spite of the fact that there have been numerous periods of mass extinction, there is clear evidence that periods of mass extinction have been followed by periods of dramatic increases in new species to fill the void created by the mass extinctions, though it may take 10 million years or more following a mass extinction for biological diversity to be rebuilt through speciation. When the dinosaurs disappeared 65 million years ago, for example, the evolution and speciation of mammals increased spectacularly over the millions of years that ensued. It is hard to imagine that this evolution and speciation could have occurred without the prior extinction of the dinosaurs, most of which would likely have threatened the existence of many of the subsequent mammal species.

1. Directions:	An introductory sentence for a brief summary of the passage is provided below. Complete the summary by selecting the THREE answer choices that express the most important ideas in the passage. Some sentences do not belong in the summary because they express ideas that are not presented in the passage or are minor ideas in the passage. **This question is worth 2 points** (2 points for 3 correct answers, 1 point for 2 correct answers, and 0 points for 1 or 0 correct answers).

The processes of speciation and extinction have affected species development on Earth.

-
-
-

Answer Choices (choose 3 to complete the chart):

(1) Though numerous species have become extinct, far more new species have developed than have been lost.
(2) Only 1 percent of the species that have existed have become extinct.
(3) A single species can develop into a distinct species through a process called speciation.
(4) The gray fox and the arctic fox separated into different species early in their development.
(5) Social isolation is a major factor that influences the degree of speciation.
(6) Numerous species become extinct when they fail to adapt to evolving conditions or fail to survive a catastrophic event.

2. Directions:	Select the appropriate phrases from the answer choices, and match them to the process to which they relate. TWO of the answer choices will not be used. **This question is worth 3 points** (3 points for 5 correct answers, 2 points for 4 correct answers, 1 point for 3 correct answers, and 0 points for 2, 1, or 0 correct answers).
speciation	• •
extinction	• • •

Answer Choices (choose 5 to complete the table):

(1) can result from failure to adapt to changing environments
(2) results in the creation of new species
(3) results in the merging of different species
(4) can result from failure to adjust to a catastrophic event
(5) can result from separation of populations
(6) can result from the commingling of different species
(7) results in the disappearance of a species

READING REVIEW EXERCISE (Skills 1–10): Read the passage and answer the questions that follow.

Paragraph

Decisions

1▶   In a theoretical model of decision making, a decision is defined as the process of selecting one option from among a group of options to carry out. **4A** Decisions are formed by a decision maker, the one who actually chooses the final option, in conjunction with a decision unit, all of those in the organization around the decision maker who take part in the process. **4B** In this theoretical model, the members of the decision unit react to an unidentified problem by studying the problem, determining the objectives of the organization, formulating options, evaluating the strengths and weaknesses of each of the options, and reaching a conclusion. **4C** Many different factors can have an effect on the decision, including the nature of the problem itself, external forces exerting an influence on the organization, the internal dynamics of the decision unit, and the personality of the decision maker. **4D**

2▶   During recent years, decision making has been studied systematically by drawing from such diverse areas of study as psychology, sociology, business, government, history, mathematics, and statistics. Analyses of decisions often emphasize one of three principal views, also called conceptual perspectives. Since none of the perspectives individually provides a complete illustration of the decision-making process, it is necessary to understand all three of them in order to gain a comprehensive picture of the process.

3▶   In the oldest of the three approaches, decisions are made by a rational actor, who makes a particular decision directly and purposefully in response to a specific threat from the external environment. It is assumed that this rational actor has clear objectives in mind, develops numerous reasonable options, considers the advantages and disadvantages of each option carefully, chooses the best option after careful analysis, and then proceeds to implement it fully. A variation of the rational actor model is a decision maker who is a satisfier, one who selects the first satisfactory option rather than continuing the decision-making process until the optimal decision has been reached.

4▶   A second perspective places an emphasis on the impact of routines on decisions within organizations. It demonstrates how organizational structures and routines such as standard operating procedures tend to limit the decision-making process in a variety of ways, perhaps by restricting the information available to the decision unit, by restricting the breadth of options among which the decision unit may choose, or by inhibiting the ability of the organization to implement the decision quickly and effectively once it has been taken. Preplanned routines and standard operating procedures are essential to coordinate the efforts of large numbers of people in massive organizations. However, these same routines and procedures can also have an inhibiting effect on the ability of the organization to arrive at optimal decisions and implement them efficiently. In this sort of decision-making process, organizations tend to take not the optimal decision but the decision that best fits within the permitted operating parameters outlined by the organization.

5▶   A third conceptual perspective emphasizes the internal dynamics of the decision unit and the extent to which decisions are based on political forces within the organization. This perspective demonstrates how bargaining among individuals who have different interests and motives and varying levels of power in the decision unit leads to eventual compromise that is not the preferred choice of any of the members of the decision unit. However, it is important to note that the most politically powerful members in the group do not always gain the most benefit from each of their individual decisions. Overall, the ultimate goal of each person in this type of unit tends to be maintaining or increasing their status and power in the group. Thus, people may sometimes concede their individual decisions in order to enhance their positions within the group.

6▶   Each of these three perspectives on the decision-making process demonstrates a different point of view on decision making, a different lens through which the decision-making process can be observed. It is safe to say that decision making in most organizations shows marked influences from each perspective; i.e., an organization strives to get as close as possible to the rational model in its decisions, yet the internal routines and dynamics of the organization come into play in the decision. Because of this, it is essential to be familiar with how each component can influence the decision-making process.

1. It can be inferred from the information in paragraph 1 that the theoretical decision-making process

  Ⓐ involves only the decision maker
  Ⓑ requires the contemplation of numerous options
  Ⓒ is made without the decision unit
  Ⓓ does not work in real situations

2. The phrase "in conjunction with" in paragraph 1 could best be replaced by

  Ⓐ along with
  Ⓑ tied to
  Ⓒ apart from
  Ⓓ connected to

3. All of the following are listed in paragraph 1 as having an effect on decisions EXCEPT

  Ⓐ evaluation of the problem
  Ⓑ focus on objectives
  Ⓒ generation of options
  Ⓓ open-ended discussions

4. Look at the four squares [■] that indicate where the following sentence could be added to the passage.

Additionally, when a decision must be made in a crisis situation, both stress and the speed at which events are progressing can have an effect, often a negative one, on the decision process.

Where will the sentence best fit? Click on a square [■] to add the sentence to the passage.

5. The phrase "drawing from" in paragraph 2 is closest in meaning to

  Ⓐ illustrating
  Ⓑ involving
  Ⓒ gathering
  Ⓓ attracting

6. It can be inferred from paragraph 3 that a "rational actor" would be least likely to
   - (A) deal with a specific threat
   - (B) work in a random fashion
   - (C) ponder various options
   - (D) consider disadvantages of options

7. The word "it" in paragraph 3 refers to
   - (A) each option
   - (B) the best option
   - (C) careful analysis
   - (D) variation

8. Why does the author mention "a satisfier, one who selects the first satisfactory option rather than continuing the decision-making process until the optimal decision has been reached" in paragraph 3?
   - (A) A satisfier shows contrasting behavior to a rational actor.
   - (B) A satisfier exhibits more common behavior than a rational actor.
   - (C) A satisfier is the predecessor of a rational actor.
   - (D) A satisfier shares some characteristics with a rational actor.

9. The word "places" in paragraph 4 could best be replaced by
   - (A) locates
   - (B) puts
   - (C) finds
   - (D) sets

10. Which of the sentences below best expresses the essential information in the highlighted sentence in paragraph 4? *Incorrect* choices change the meaning in important ways or leave out essential information.
    - (A) Set routines within organizations tend to constrain decisions.
    - (B) The restriction of information limits the number of options in a decision.
    - (C) Organizations need to set up strict procedures to maximize the effectiveness of decisions.
    - (D) Procedures are needed to ensure that decisions are implemented quickly and effectively.

11. The word "dynamics" in paragraph 5 is closest in meaning to
    - (A) explosions
    - (B) emotions
    - (C) philosophies
    - (D) interactions

12. According to paragraph 5, what is the end result of political bargaining within an organization?
    - (A) No decision is ever reached.
    - (B) Differing interests and motives are changed.
    - (C) No one is completely satisfied with the final outcome.
    - (D) The members of the decision unit leave the unit.

13. **Directions:** An introductory sentence for a brief summary of the passage is provided below. Complete the summary by selecting the THREE answer choices that express the most important ideas in the passage. Some sentences do not belong in the summary because they express ideas that are not presented in the passage or are minor ideas in the passage. **This question is worth 2 points** (2 points for 3 correct answers, 1 point for 2 correct answers, and 0 points for 1 or 0 correct answers).

Different perspectives on decision making must be considered in order to understand the process.

- •
- •
- •

Answer Choices (choose 3 to complete the chart):

(1) One model measures how satisfied all participants are after a given decision has been made.

(2) Decision making can be influenced by organizational structure and procedures and also limited by them.

(3) Another perspective considers how much a decision-making process has been manipulated and limited by factions within the organization.

(4) One model looks at how rational actors are able to work within organizational structures and routines to achieve optimal solutions.

(5) The decision-making process can differ in diverse areas such as psychology, sociology, business, government, history, mathematics, and statistics.

(6) How well a decision maker has analyzed a problem and possible solutions to achieve the optimal solution is the basis of one perspective.

READING POST-TEST

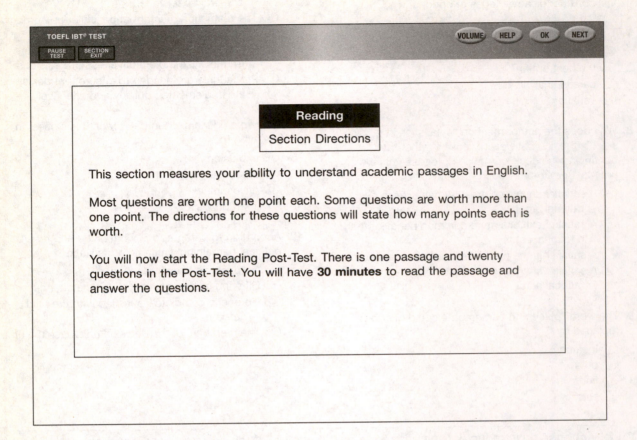

TOEFL IBT® TEST

PAUSE TEST   SECTION EXIT

VOLUME   HELP   OK   NEXT

Reading

Section Directions

This section measures your ability to understand academic passages in English.

Most questions are worth one point each. Some questions are worth more than one point. The directions for these questions will state how many points each is worth.

You will now start the Reading Post-Test. There is one passage and twenty questions in the Post-Test. You will have **30 minutes** to read the passage and answer the questions.

Read the passage and answer the questions that follow.

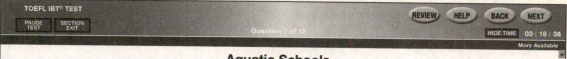

TOEFL IBT® TEST
PAUSE TEST   SECTION EXIT
Question 1 of 12
REVIEW   HELP   BACK   NEXT
HIDE TIME   00 : 18 : 38
More Available

Aquatic Schools

1▶ Many species of fish, particularly smaller fish, travel in schools, moving in tight formations often with the precision of the most highly disciplined military unit on parade. **5A** Some move in synchronized hordes, while others move in starkly geometric forms. **5B** In addition to the varieties of shapes of schools of fish, there are countless varieties of schooling behaviors. **5C** Some fish coalesce into schools and then spread out in random patterns, while others move into close formations at specific times, such as feeding times, but are more spread out at other times. **5D** Some move in schools composed of members of all age groups, while others move in schools predominantly when they are young but take up a more solitary existence as they mature. Though this behavior is quite a regular, familiar phenomenon, there is much that is not completely known about it, particularly the exact function that it serves and what mechanisms fish use to make it happen.

2▶ Numerous hypotheses have been proposed and tested concerning the purpose of schooling behavior in fish. Schooling certainly promotes the survival of the species, but questions arise as to the way the schooling enables fish to have a better chance of surviving. Certainly, the fact that fish congregate together in schools helps to ensure their survival in that schooling provides numerous types of protection for the members of the school. One form of protection derives from the sheer numbers in the school. When a predator attacks a school containing a huge number of fish, the predator will be able to consume only a small percentage of the school. Whereas some of the members of the school will be lost to the predator, the majority of the school will be able to survive. Another form of protection comes from the special coloration and markings of different types of fish. Certain types of coloration or markings such as stripes or patterns in vibrant and shiny colors create a visual effect when huge numbers of the fish are clustered together, making it more difficult for a potential predator to focus on specific members of the school. A final form of protection comes from a special sense that fish possess, a sense that is enhanced when fish swim in schools. This special sense is related to a set of lateral line organs that consist of rows of pores leading to fluid-filled canals. These organs are sensitive to minute vibrations in the water. The thousands of sets of those special organs in a school of fish together can prove very effective in warning the school about an approaching threat.

3▶ **15A** It is also unclear exactly how fish manage to maintain their tight formations. **15B** Sight seems to play a role in the ability of fish to move in schools, and some scientists believe that, at least in some species, sight may play the principal role. **15C** However, many experiments indicate that more than sight is involved. Some fish school quite well in the dark or in murky water where visibility is extremely limited. **15D** This indicates that senses other than eyesight must be involved in enabling the schooling behavior. The lateral line system most likely plays a significant role in the ability of fish to school. Because these lateral line organs are sensitive to the most minute vibrations and currents, this organ system may be used by fish to detect movements among members of their school even when eyesight is limited or unavailable. Some experts theorize that individual fish use the shifts they feel in the direction or intensity of the vibrations to signal when they need to move in closer, space out further apart, or even change direction.

4▶ One species of fish that schools in astoundingly large numbers is the herring. Smaller groups—that are still quite large—gather together in extraordinarily large populations during migratory periods. Trails of connected schools have been discovered that are over 60 miles (100 kilometers) in length. According to some experts, herring schools can accumulate up to about three billion fish in a single school. Interestingly, herring use their exceptional hearing to avoid predators while in the school and they create a specific formation for the same purpose. If observed from above, one can witness herring schools move into a "doughnut" formation around any obstacle they feel threatened by, thereby containing the threat in the inner hole of the doughnut.

READING

1. The author mentions "the most highly disciplined military unit on parade" in paragraph 1 in order to
   A describe the aggressive nature of a school of fish
   B provide an example of a way that military units travel
   C create a mental image of the movement of a school of fish
   D contrast the movement of a military unit with that of a school of fish

2. The word "hordes" in paragraph 1 is closest in meaning to
   A shapes
   B masses
   C pairs
   D patterns

3. All of the following are stated in paragraph 1 about schooling EXCEPT that
   A it is quite common
   B it can involve large numbers of fish
   C it can involve a number of different fish behaviors
   D it is fully understood

4. Which fish would be least likely to be in a school?
   A A large, older fish
   B A smaller, colorful fish
   C A young, hungry fish
   D A tiny, shiny fish

5. Look at the four squares [■] that indicate where the following sentence could be added to paragraph 1.

   These may take the shape, for example, of wedges, triangles, spheres, or ovals.

   Where would the sentence best fit? Click on a square [■] to add the sentence to the passage.

6. The word "it" in paragraph 1 refers to
   A existence
   B behavior
   C fish
   D function

7. Which of the sentences below best expresses the essential information in the first highlighted sentence in paragraph 2? *Incorrect* choices change the meaning in important ways or leave out essential information.
   A After an attack, the fish that survive tend to move into schools.
   B The survival of fish depends upon their ability to bring new members into the school.

C Many facts about the way that fish congregate in schools have been studied.
   D Fish travel in schools to protect themselves in various ways.

8. It can be inferred from information in paragraph 2 that when a predator attacks,
   A it cannot possibly consume all members of a school if the school is large enough
   B it rarely manages to catch any fish that are part of a school
   C it is usually successful in wiping out the entire school
   D it attacks only schools that lack sense organs

9. It is stated in paragraph 2 that
   A fish in schools rarely have distinct markings
   B schooling fish tend to have muted coloration
   C the effect of coloration is multiplied when fish are massed together
   D the bright coloration makes it easier for predators to spot fish

10. The word "minute" in paragraph 2 is closest in meaning to
    A timely
    B tiny
    C careful
    D instant

11. Which of the sentences below best expresses the essential information in the second highlighted sentence in paragraph 2? *Incorrect* choices change the meaning in important ways or leave out essential information.
    A There are thousands of ways that special organs warn fish about a predator.
    B When the fish in a school work together, they can use their sense organs to scare off any approaching threat.
    C The fish in a large school use their lateral line organs to send out warnings of the arrival of the school.
    D Because so many fish are in a school, all of their sense organs work well together to provide warnings.

12. The author begins paragraph 3 with "It is also unclear" in order to indicate that
    A contradictory information is about to be presented
    B it is necessary to clarify a previously made point
    C a second issue is about to be presented
    D it is unclear how a problem can be resolved

13. According to paragraph 3,
    Ⓐ fish cannot see well
    Ⓑ sight is the only sense used by fish to remain in schools
    Ⓒ not all fish use sight as their primary method to remain in schools
    Ⓓ fish can see quite well in the dark

14. The word "murky" in paragraph 3 is closest in meaning to
    Ⓐ cloudy
    Ⓑ warm
    Ⓒ clear
    Ⓓ deep

15. Look at the four squares [■] that indicate where the following sentence could be added to paragraph 3.

The purpose of schooling behavior is not the only aspect of schooling that is not fully understood.

Where would the sentence best fit? Click on a square [■] to add the sentence to the passage.

16. The word "This" in paragraph 3 refers to the ability of fish to
    Ⓐ see well in dark water
    Ⓑ stay in schools when they cannot see well
    Ⓒ swim in water where the visibility is low
    Ⓓ use their sight to stay in schools

17. According to paragraph 4, what makes schools of herring stand out from other schools?
    Ⓐ the extraordinary distances that they migrate
    Ⓑ the size of their schools
    Ⓒ their ability to use hearing to communicate with each other
    Ⓓ their formations as they travel

18. It is NOT stated in the passage that the lateral line system
    Ⓐ contains lines of pores
    Ⓑ can detect movement in the water
    Ⓒ quite possibly helps fish to remain in schools
    Ⓓ in fish is similar to sense organs in other animals

READING

19.
Directions: An introductory sentence for a brief summary of the passage is provided below. Complete the summary by selecting the THREE answer choices that express the most important ideas in the passage. Some sentences do not belong in the summary because they express ideas that are not presented in the passage or are minor ideas in the passage. **This question is worth 2 points** (2 points for 3 correct answers, 1 point for 2 correct answers, 0 points for 1 or 0 correct answers).

Although schooling behavior is common in many types of fish, there is still much to learn about the function and mechanisms of this phenomenon.

-
-
-

Answer Choices (choose 3 to complete the chart):
(1) Fish most likely move in schools in various types of water.
(2) Scholars are quite confident in their understanding of schooling behavior.
(3) Fish move in schools by using various senses.
(4) Fish may move in schools at various times of the day or night.
(5) Fish most likely move in schools in various ways.
(6) Much is not known about schooling behaviors.

20.

Directions: Select the appropriate phrases from the answer choices, and match them to the hypotheses to which they relate. TWO of the answer choices will not be used. **This question is worth 3 points** (3 points for 5 correct answers, 2 points for 4 correct answers, 1 point for 3 correct answers, and 0 points for 2, 1, or 0 correct answers).

hypotheses related to purpose	• • •
hypotheses related to manner	• •

Answer Choices (choose 5 to complete the table):

(1) Coloration provides protection.

(2) Lateral sense organs enable some fish to school.

(3) Sight provides protection.

(4) Coloration enables some fish to move.

(5) Large numbers provide protection.

(6) Sight enables some fish to school.

(7) Lateral sense organs provide protection.

Turn to pages 591–595 to diagnose your errors and *record* your results.

LISTENING

LISTENING DIAGNOSTIC PRE-TEST

L_DIR_A

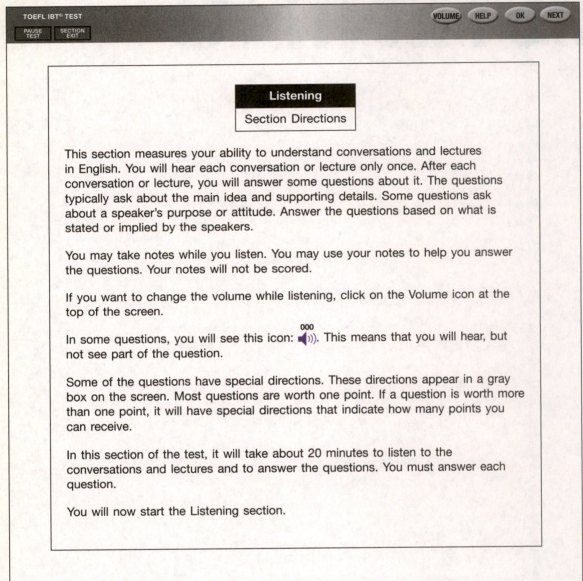

TOEFL IBT® TEST

PAUSE TEST | SECTION EXIT

VOLUME | HELP | OK | NEXT

Listening
Section Directions

This section measures your ability to understand conversations and lectures in English. You will hear each conversation or lecture only once. After each conversation or lecture, you will answer some questions about it. The questions typically ask about the main idea and supporting details. Some questions ask about a speaker's purpose or attitude. Answer the questions based on what is stated or implied by the speakers.

You may take notes while you listen. You may use your notes to help you answer the questions. Your notes will not be scored.

If you want to change the volume while listening, click on the Volume icon at the top of the screen.

In some questions, you will see this icon: 🔊))). This means that you will hear, but not see part of the question.

Some of the questions have special directions. These directions appear in a gray box on the screen. Most questions are worth one point. If a question is worth more than one point, it will have special directions that indicate how many points you can receive.

In this section of the test, it will take about 20 minutes to listen to the conversations and lectures and to answer the questions. You must answer each question.

You will now start the Listening section.

Questions 1–5

Listen to a conversation between an advisor and a student.

1. Why does the advisor want to talk with the student?
    - Ⓐ To discuss her phone call with the professor and what he said about the student
    - Ⓑ To help the student avoid failing a class by giving him advice about his studies
    - Ⓒ To find out more about the history professor's teaching style and exams
    - Ⓓ To explain what professors at the university require from their students

2. What problems does the student have?

Click on 2 answers.
- Ⓐ He is not doing well in several of his classes.
- Ⓑ He is not studying the textbook material carefully enough.
- Ⓒ He is not in class all the time.
- Ⓓ He is not sure about what is being tested.

3. What does the advisor imply about the history professor's exams?
    - Ⓐ They have a style that is familiar to most students.
    - Ⓑ They primarily test a specific approach discussed during lectures.
    - Ⓒ The teaching assistants can tell him which questions will be on the exams.
    - Ⓓ Many of the concepts they test cannot be found in the textbook.

4. Which of the following does the advisor recommend that the student do? **This question is worth 2 points** (2 points for 3 correct answers, 1 point for 2 correct answers, and 0 points for 1 or 0 correct answers).

Click on 3 answers.
- Ⓐ Ask to meet regularly with his history professor
- Ⓑ Find out what each professor expects of his or her students in every course
- Ⓒ Get up and go to his history class all the time
- Ⓓ Ask for help and clarification from teaching assistants in larger classes
- Ⓔ Take more careful notes on lectures and on textbook material

5. Listen again to part of the passage. Then answer the question.

What does the advisor mean when she says this:
    - Ⓐ She wants to meet the student next week to see how he is doing.
    - Ⓑ If the student goes to at least 50 percent of the lectures, he should do well.
    - Ⓒ The student must take responsibility for attending lecture sessions.
    - Ⓓ She is willing to show the student how to study for and pass his mid-semester exams.

LISTENING DIAGNOSTIC PRE-TEST   143

Questions 6–11 003

Listen to part of a lecture in a psychology class.

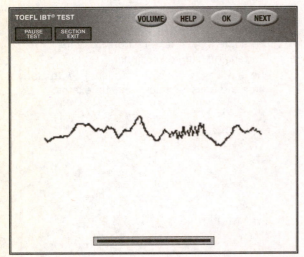

004
🔊))

6. What does the professor mainly want to get across in the discussion?
   - (A) How human sleep differs from the sleep of other animals
   - (B) What happens to the muscles of humans and other animals during sleep
   - (C) The types of brain-wave patterns that humans experience in sleep
   - (D) The characteristics of sleep in all types of living beings

7. What happens during human sleep?

Click on 2 answers.

- [A] Muscles become relaxed.
- [B] The rate of breathing increases.
- [C] The heart rate decreases.
- [D] Brain waves decrease throughout sleep.

8. Why does the professor mention sleepwalking?
   - (A) To differentiate between the sleep of humans and other mammals
   - (B) To give an example of how people sometimes act out their dreams while asleep
   - (C) To draw a contrast between muscle tone during REM sleep and during deep sleep
   - (D) To illustrate a sleep disorder that is common during REM sleep

9. Listen again to part of the passage. Then answer the question.

   Why does the professor say this: 🔊))
   - (A) To indicate that he is going to summarize part of the discussion
   - (B) To clarify that muscle tone is not an essential concept
   - (C) To change the topic of the discussion to something completely different
   - (D) To emphasize the relative importance of brain waves for the discussion

10. Which of these types of animals experience changes in brain waves during sleep? **This question is worth 2 points** (2 points for 4 correct answers, 1 point for 3 correct answers, and 0 points for 2, 1, or 0 correct answers).

Place a checkmark in the correct box.

	Experience changes in brain waves during sleep	Do not experience changes in brain waves
mammals	☐	☐
fish	☐	☐
birds	☐	☐
reptiles	☐	☐

11. What conclusion can be drawn from the discussion?
    - (A) Land animals dream, but marine animals do not.
    - (B) Only humans experience sleep with true dreaming periods.
    - (C) Most animals dream during sleep.
    - (D) Birds might dream of birds, but fish can't dream of fish.

Turn to pages 596–598 to *diagnose* your errors and record your results.

The second section on the TOEFL iBT® test is the Listening section. This section consists of six passages, each followed by five or six questions. You may take notes as you listen to the passages and use your notes as you answer the questions. Test takers are given 60 to 90 minutes to complete the Listening section.

- The **passages** are set in an academic environment. There are 2- to 4-minute conversations that take place outside of the classroom and 4- to 6-minute lectures that take place inside the classroom. The Listening section is divided into two parts, and each part of the Listening section contains one conversation and two lectures. Note: Sometimes on the actual TOEFL iBT® test there is a third part with an additional conversation and two lectures. In this case, three of the nine listening passages will not be scored, but you will not know which ones.* Therefore you should try to do your best to answer all of the questions for all of the passages.

- The **questions** may ask about main ideas and details, purpose, the function of what the speaker said or the speaker's stance, the organization of ideas, and inferences based on the passage.

Listening Section	Passage Type	Listening Length	Number of Questions
Part 1	1 conversation 2 lectures	2–4 minutes 4–6 minutes each	5 questions 6 questions each
Part 2	1 conversation 2 lectures	2–4 minutes 4–6 minutes each	5 questions 6 questions each
*Part 3	1 conversation 2 lectures	2–4 minutes 4–6 minutes each	5 questions 6 questions each

The following strategies can help you in the Listening section.

STRATEGIES FOR LISTENING

1. **Be familiar with the directions.** The directions on every test are the same, so it is not necessary to spend time reading the directions carefully when you take the test. You should be completely familiar with the directions before the day of the test.

2. **Do not worry if a listening passage is on a topic that is not familiar to you.** All of the information that you need to answer the questions is included in the passages. You do not need any special background knowledge to answer the questions.

3. **Listen carefully to the passage.** You will hear the passages one time only. You may not replay the audio passages during the test.

4. **Use the visuals to help you to understand the passages.** Each passage begins with a photograph showing the setting (such as a classroom in the case of lectures or a campus office in the case of conversations) and the person (such as a professor lecturing in the case of lectures) or people (such as two students or a professor/advisor and a student in the case of conversations) who are speaking. There may be other visuals (such as a diagram, a drawing, or a blackboard or whiteboard with important terminology) to help you to understand the content of the passage.

5. **Take quick notes as you listen to the spoken material.** You should focus on the main points and key supporting material. Do not try to write down everything you hear. Do not write down too many unnecessary details.

6. **Look at each question to determine what type of question it is.** The type of question tells you how to proceed to answer the question.

   - For *gist questions*, listen carefully to the beginning of the passage to develop an initial idea about the gist of the passage, or its purpose. Then, as you listen to the rest of the passage, adjust your idea about the main idea or general topic of the passage based on what the speakers are saying.

   - For *detail questions*, listen carefully to the details or facts in the passage. Then look for an answer that restates the information from the passage.

   - For *function questions*, listen carefully to what the speaker says in the part of the passage that is replayed. Then draw a conclusion about why the speaker says it.

   - For *stance questions*, listen carefully to what the speaker says in the part of the passage that is replayed. Then draw a conclusion about what the speaker feels.

   - For *organization questions*, listen carefully to each of the points in the passage, especially examples, and consider how these points are organized, how they relate to the main topic, or how different ideas are related to each other. In addition, some organization questions ask about the function of a speaker's statement such as introducing a topic or changing the topic. Then look for an answer that shows the organization of the points.

   - For *inference questions*, listen carefully to each of the points in the passage and consider how these points might be related in a way not specifically stated by the speakers. You may also be asked to put together details from the passage in order to draw a conclusion. Then choose answers that show the implied relationship among the points.

7. **Choose the best answer to each question.** You may be certain of a particular answer, but if not, you should eliminate any definitely incorrect answers and choose from among the remaining ones.

8. **Think carefully about a question before you answer it.** You may not return to a question later in the test. You have only one opportunity to answer a given question.

9. **Do not spend too much time on a question you are unsure of.** If you truly do not know the answer to a question, simply guess and go on.

10. **Monitor the time carefully on the title bar of the computer screen.** The title bar indicates the time remaining in the section, the total number of questions in the section, and the number of the question that you are working on. The clock does not run while you are listening to the passage or the questions.

11. **Guess to complete the section before time is up.** It can only increase your score to guess the answers to questions that you do not have time to complete. (Points are not subtracted for incorrect answers.)

The following skills will help you to implement these strategies in the Listening section of the TOEFL iBT® test.

BASIC COMPREHENSION

Basic comprehension questions are related to what is stated in the passage. These questions may ask about the overall **gist** (the main idea or overall topic), or they may ask about specific **details** in the passage.

Listening Skill 1: UNDERSTAND THE GIST

Gist questions are questions that ask about the overall ideas of a passage as a whole. They may ask about the *subject*, *topic*, or *main idea* of a passage. They may also ask what overall *purpose* the passage serves. It is important to understand that the gist of a passage may be directly stated in the passage, or you may have to synthesize (bring together) information from different parts of the passage to understand the overall gist.

Strategies to Answer Gist Questions

- Pay attention to the beginning of the conversation or lecture. Often, you can form an overall idea of the gist.

- Adjust your initial idea based upon what you hear through the remainder of the passage.

> Listen to any particular words that the speaker emphasizes or stresses (pronounces more loudly than other words). These emphasized words indicate important information.

Listen and look at an example of a part of a conversation. 005 🔊

Example 1

You see on the computer screen:

You hear:

(narrator) Listen to a conversation between an advisor and a student.

(student) I noticed that a comprehensive exam is required for my major, and I'm not exactly sure what that is.

(advisor) A comprehensive exam is given in the final quarter of your studies. Its purpose is to determine your overall competency.

(student) But how is it different from a final exam?

(advisor) Well, a final exam covers all the material taught in a specific course; a comprehensive exam, on the other hand, covers all of the materials taught in the entire program.

(student) And is it true that it's required for my major? I mean, it's not an option?

(advisor) (laughs) Sorry . . . it's not an option. It isn't required for all majors at this university, but it is required for yours.

After you listen to the conversation, the question and answer choices appear on the computer screen as the narrator states the question. This is a gist question that asks about the purpose of the passage.

You see on the computer screen:

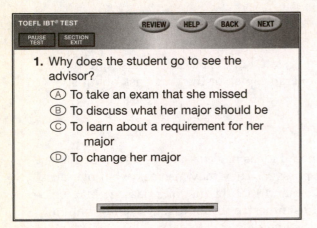

You hear: 006 🔊

(narrator)   Why does the student go to see the advisor?

The correct answer is the third answer choice. In the conversation, the student says *I noticed that a comprehensive exam is required for my major, and I'm not exactly sure what that is.* From this, it can be determined that the student goes to see her advisor in order *to learn about a requirement for her major*. The first answer choice is incorrect because she has not missed an exam. The second and fourth answer choices are incorrect because the student has already chosen her major and does not say she plans to change it.

Now listen and look at an example of another type of gist question. This gist question asks about the overall topic of the passage.

You see on the computer screen:

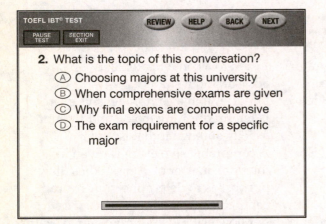

You hear: 006 🔊

(narrator)   What is the topic of this conversation?

The fourth answer choice is the correct response. In the conversation, the student says *I noticed that a comprehensive exam is required for my major, and I'm not exactly sure what that is,* and the professor says *a comprehensive exam isn't required for all majors at this university, but it is required for yours.* From this, it can be determined that the topic of the conversation is the exam requirement for a specific major. The first answer choice is incorrect because the student has already chosen her major. The second and third answer choices are incorrect because when and why comprehensive exams are given are only minor details in the conversation.

Now listen and look at an example of a lecture. 007 🔊

Example 2

You see on the computer screen:

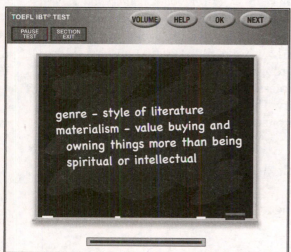

You hear:

(narrator)   Listen to part of a lecture in an American Literature class.

(Professor)   OK, so we're going to look at some examples of the style of American literature known as the Beat Generation . . . and, yes, it is spelled B-E-A-T. To understand the unconventional, experimental style of this genre of writing, you should know something about post-war USA in the 1940s and 1950s, uh . . . that's when the Beats surfaced. So, immediately following the end of World War II, the U.S. experienced an economic boom, and materialism ran rampant. That is, people had started to believe that buying and owning more and more things was much more valuable than developing themselves intellectually and spiritually. Uh . . . suburbs sprang up outside of urban areas; people chased the American Dream. Conventional literature . . . such as early twentieth-century Modernism, for example . . . was considered too carefully organized, even, well . . . a little too conservative. Now, as a reaction to the social materialism and formality of this writing style, a radical group of writers at Columbia University in New York began to create a form that broke with tradition, tearing apart or ignoring conventional literary structures and utilizing a bold, expressive style that was filled with raw feelings and language.

After you listen to the lecture, the question and answer choices appear on the computer screen as the narrator states the question. This is a gist question that asks about the *main idea* of the passage.

You see on the computer screen:

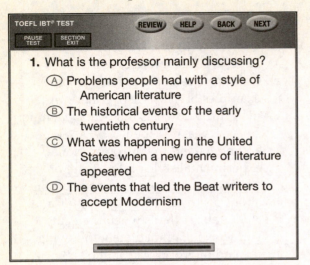

You hear: 008

(narrator)   What is the professor mainly
              discussing?

The correct answer is the third answer choice. In the conversation, the professor says, that *to understand the unconventional, experimental style of this genre of writing, you should know something about post-war USA in the 1940s and 1950s . . . when the Beats surfaced.* This means that the professor is speaking of the historical events that were happening when the genre or style of literature called the Beat Generation surfaced, or appeared. The first answer choice is incorrect because the passage does not mention problems people had with the literature. The second answer choice is incorrect because the professor is speaking of the mid-twentieth century (1940s–1950s), not the early twentieth century. The fourth answer choice is incorrect because, although Modernism was mentioned, the professor did not say that the Beat writers accepted it.

Now listen and look at an example of another type of gist question. 008

This gist question asks about the *purpose* of the passage.

You see on the computer screen:

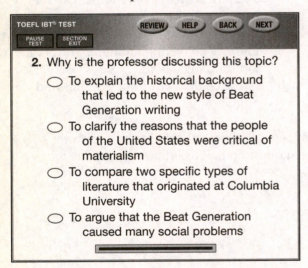

You hear:

(narrator)   Why is the professor discussing this
              topic?

The correct answer is the first answer choice. The professor says she is going to talk about a specific historical period in which the new Beat Generation writing *surfaced* or appeared so that the students will *understand the unconventional, experimental style, of this genre of writing*. The second answer choice is incorrect because the Beat Generation writers were critical of materialism, not the people of the United States who the professor indicates had become more materialistic. The third answer choice is incorrect because, while the style of Modernism (a type of literature) is briefly mentioned, there is no indication in the passage that it originated at Columbia University. The professor only states that there was a group of the Beat Generation writers at Columbia University. The fourth answer choice is incorrect because the passage does not say that the Beat Generation writers were the cause of social problems.

The following chart outlines the key points that you should remember about gist questions.

KEY POINTS FOR QUESTIONS ABOUT UNDERSTANDING THE GIST	
FREQUENCY OF QUESTION TYPE	There will usually be one gist question after every passage, and it is usually the first question after the passage. If there is a gist question, there will only be one per passage.
HOW TO IDENTIFY THE QUESTION	What is the subject of the passage? What is the topic of the discussion? What is the professor mainly discussing? What is the purpose of the talk? Why does the student go to see the advisor? Why . . . in the passage?
WHERE TO FIND THE ANSWER	Information to help you understand the gist may be directly stated at the beginning of the passage. It may also be necessary for you to draw a conclusion about the gist based upon information provided throughout the passage.
HOW TO ANSWER THE QUESTION	1. Listen carefully to the *beginning* of the passage to develop an initial idea about the gist of the passage. 2. Then, as you listen to the *rest of the passage*, adjust your idea of the gist of the passage as you consider what the speakers are saying.

In the exam, you may be able to eliminate incorrect answer choices by understanding what is wrong with them. For gist questions, incorrect answer choices may:
- be true, but be only a minor detail in the passage.
- mention some ideas or key words from the passage, but incorrectly state the relationship between ideas.
- incorrectly state the focus or viewpoint of the main idea.
- be untrue, but a logical conclusion if you only understand a few key words from the passage.

LISTENING EXERCISE 1: Listen to each passage and the questions that follow. Then choose the best answers to the questions.

PASSAGE ONE (Questions 1–2) 009

Listen to a conversation between a professor and a student.

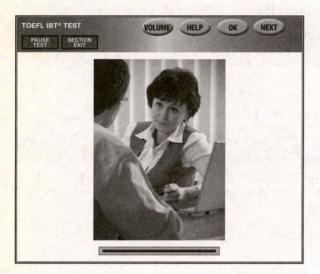

010

1. Why does the student go to see the professor?
   - Ⓐ To ask the professor for a form to change classes
   - Ⓑ To ask the professor's advice about a course
   - Ⓒ To get the professor's permission to take a higher-level course
   - Ⓓ To ask a question about some course material

2. What is the topic of the conversation?
   - Ⓐ The reasons the student wants to repeat a course
   - Ⓑ The reasons the student did not do well in the professor's course
   - Ⓒ The reasons the professor does not want to change his grade
   - Ⓓ The requirements and expectations of a course

PASSAGE TWO (Questions 3–4) 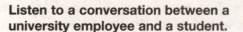 011

Listen to a conversation between a university employee and a student.

012

3. Why does the student go to the office?
   - Ⓐ To learn about a university policy
   - Ⓑ To solve a problem with a professor
   - Ⓒ To get help with the computer system
   - Ⓓ To find a missing report

4. What are the speakers mainly discussing?
   - Ⓐ The ways that the computer system works
   - Ⓑ The reason grades were not posted on the school server
   - Ⓒ The date when grades will finally be sent out to students
   - Ⓓ The reasons why the student missed an exam

PASSAGE THREE (Questions 5–6) 013

Listen to a student consulting a professor.

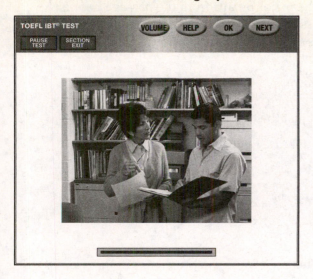

014

5. Why does the student go to see the professor?
   Ⓐ To ask the professor to clarify an assignment
   Ⓑ To present his research on three lakes
   Ⓒ To ask for details about the Caspian Sea
   Ⓓ To approach the professor about an incorrect assignment

6. Why are they discussing this material?
   Ⓐ The student has just seen a presentation about it.
   Ⓑ The student is preparing for an exam on it.
   Ⓒ The student must present it to his classmates.
   Ⓓ The student is writing a research paper.

Listen carefully to the information you hear after a speaker pauses or hedges. This information may provide an example, a definition, a repetition or restatement of an important idea, or a correction of a previously stated point.

PASSAGE FOUR (Questions 7–8) 015

Listen to part of a lecture in a meteorology class.

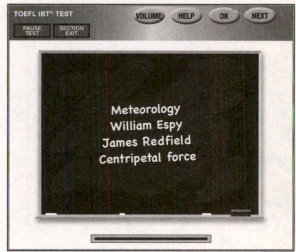

016

7. What is the topic of this discussion?
   Ⓐ The function of centripetal force in storms
   Ⓑ Two contrasting hypotheses on storms
   Ⓒ The history of meteorology
   Ⓓ Similar theories by two different scientists

8. Why is the professor discussing this topic?
   Ⓐ To explain how scientists can come up with an incorrect model of weather conditions
   Ⓑ To point out why observing something directly is more valuable than making a hypothetical prediction
   Ⓒ To illustrate how two scientists arrived at the truth through cooperation
   Ⓓ To make a point about how opposing models can both be correct in some way

Listening Skill 2: UNDERSTAND THE DETAILS

Detail questions ask you about specific pieces of information that are stated in a passage. As you listen to each passage, you should focus on the major details from the passage because questions about details always accompany the passages. Multiple-choice questions are used to test details, and these multiple-choice questions may have one correct answer or two correct answers.

Strategies to Answer Detail Questions

- Listen for the details that are discussed, not just the overall idea.

- Think about different ways to restate the details. Find the answer choice that accurately restates the information.

Listen and look at an example from part of a lecture. ◀)) ⁰¹⁷

Example 1

You see on the computer screen:

You hear:

(narrator)   Listen to part of a lecture in an astronomy class.

(professor) The *Giotto* spacecraft made a flyby of Halley's Comet in 1986, and this was important for what it revealed about the composition of the comet. Oh, and as a side note, one reason Halley's Comet is famous is that it's both visible to the naked eye, and it returns to pass by our planet every 76 years. That is, it has a period of return within a human lifetime, which gives many people the chance of seeing it. Anyway, back to the *Giotto* flyby. Enormous quantities of water were discovered within the comet, and this, along with further research, of course. . . this led many scientists to speculate that the Earth's water originally came mostly from collisions with comets. However, it was later discovered that the ratio of regular to heavy water—heavy water is regular water with an extra neutron . . . this ratio in the Earth's oceans is closer to that of the water in other outer-space objects—those orbiting rocks we call asteroids, and so actually doesn't correlate well with that of comets. So that discovery has ended up casting doubt on this original theory.

After you listen to the conversation, the first question and answer choices appear on the computer screen as the narrator states the question. This is a detail question with one correct answer.

You see on the computer screen:

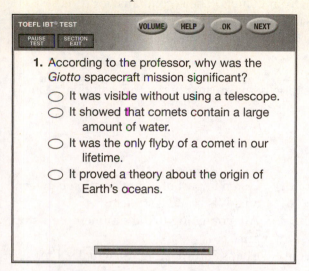

1. According to the professor, why was the *Giotto* spacecraft mission significant?
  - ○ It was visible without using a telescope.
  - ○ It showed that comets contain a large amount of water.
  - ○ It was the only flyby of a comet in our lifetime.
  - ○ It proved a theory about the origin of Earth's oceans.

You hear: 018 🔊))

(narrator)   According to the professor, why was the *Giotto* spacecraft mission significant?

Listen for contrast words, such as *however; on the other hand; but* or *in contrast.* The information following this type of word changes or alters the meaning of the information that came before it.

The correct answer is the second answer choice. In the lecture, the professor states that *the* Giotto *spacecraft made a flyby of Halley's Comet in 1986, and this was important for what it revealed about the composition of the comet,* which was that it contained *enormous quantities,* or a large amount, of water. The first answer choice is incorrect because it is not the reason the professor says the mission was important. The professor only mentions *as a side note* (not an important detail) that Halley's Comet is visible *to the naked eye* (without using a telescope). She does not say that the spacecraft mission was visible. The third answer is incorrect because the phrase *in a human lifetime* refers to the comet and not the mission. The fourth answer choice is incorrect because the presence of water did not prove a theory about Earth's oceans, but only helped with the formation of the theory.

Now listen and look at another example of a multiple-choice question about a direct detail. This question has two correct answers. 018 🔊))

You see on the computer screen:

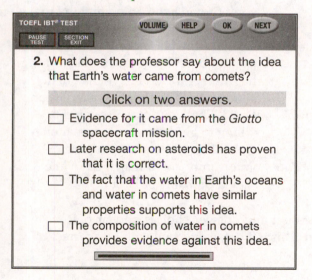

2. What does the professor say about the idea that Earth's water came from comets?

Click on two answers.

  - ☐ Evidence for it came from the *Giotto* spacecraft mission.
  - ☐ Later research on asteroids has proven that it is correct.
  - ☐ The fact that the water in Earth's oceans and water in comets have similar properties supports this idea.
  - ☐ The composition of water in comets provides evidence against this idea.

You hear:

(narrator)   What does the professor say about the idea that Earth's water came from comets?

The first and fourth answer choices are correct. The professor says that the discovery of water in comets *led many to speculate that the Earth's water originally came mostly from collisions with comets.* He also says that *it was later discovered that the ratio of regular to heavy water (composition of water) doesn't correlate well with that of comets. So that discovery has ended up casting doubt on this original theory.* This means that the composition of water in comets provides evidence against the idea that Earth's water came from comets. The second answer choice is incorrect because later research on asteroids has not supported the idea. The third answer choice is incorrect because, according to the professor, Earth's water and the water in comets do not have similar properties.

Now listen and look at an example from a conversation between an advisor and a student. 🔊))) ⁰¹⁹

Example 2

You see on the computer screen:

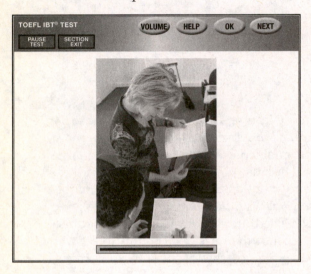

You hear:

(narrator) Listen to part of a conversation between an advisor and a student.

(advisor) Are you going to the summer internship fair?

(student) That's Saturday, right? Actually, I'm going to watch basketball over at friend's house. And besides, I already have a *job* lined up for the summer.

(advisor) Do you mean that construction job with your dad that you mentioned to me last time we talked?

(student) Yes, that's the one. There's no job search or application process needed to get it, and it pays much better than any internship.

(advisor) Yes, but you can get some incredibly important experience with internships. And I'm thinking that unless you're planning to do construction work after you graduate, that it's only cash. Uh, I don't mean it's a bad job, just that it won't provide you with anything that is especially great for your résumé.

(student) But that's my pocket money for the year. If I don't make any money during the summer, I won't have cash to do anything with during the school year.

(advisor) Well, I'll bet your parents would be willing to give you some more money if you showed them an amazing opportunity you'd managed to line up. They'd probably be proud.

After you listen to the conversation, the first question and answer choices appear on the computer screen as the narrator states the question. This is a detail question with two correct answers.

You see on the computer screen:

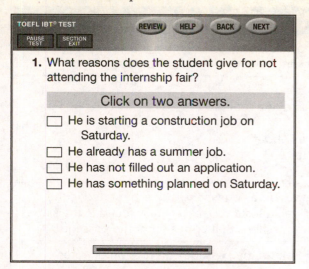

You hear:

(narrator) What reasons does the student give for not attending the internship fair?

The second and fourth answer choices are correct. The student says that he's going to watch basketball (his plans) on Saturday and that he already has a job lined up for the summer. The first answer choice is incorrect because his construction job starts in the summer, and not on Saturday. The third answer choice is incorrect because there is no mention of an application being required to attend the fair. The student only mentions that he does not have to go through an application process for the construction job.

Now listen and look at another question about the conversation. 020

You see on the computer screen:

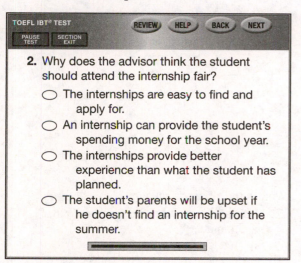

You hear:

(narrator) Why does the advisor think the student should attend the internship fair?

The third answer choice is correct. The advisor states that *you can get some really important experience with the internships and that the construction job won't provide you with anything that is especially great for your résumé.* Therefore, she believes the internships provide better experience than the job the student has planned. The first and second answer choices are incorrect because the student says that the construction job, not an internship, is easy and provides *pocket money*, or spending money. The fourth answer choice is incorrect because the advisor says that the student's parents will probably be *proud* if he finds a good opportunity, not that they will be upset if he does not.

The following chart outlines the key points you should remember about detail questions.

KEY POINTS FOR QUESTIONS ABOUT UNDERSTANDING THE DETAILS	
FREQUENCY	Detail questions are the most common question type. Every passage will have at least one, and they are quite common for lectures.
HOW TO IDENTIFY THE QUESTION	What is **stated** in the passage about . . .? What is **indicated** in the passage about . . . ? **According to** the speaker, . . . ? What does the professor **say about** . . . ? Why does the man **suggest** . . . ? How/When/Where did . . . ?
WHERE TO FIND THE ANSWER(S)	Information needed to answer detail questions is directly stated in the passage. The answers to detail questions are generally found in the same order in the passage as the questions that appear after the passage.
HOW TO ANSWER THE QUESTION	1. Listen carefully to the details in the passage and take quick notes on key terms. 2. Look for an answer that correctly restates the information from the passage. 3. Eliminate the definitely wrong answers and choose the best answers from the remaining choices.

Incorrect answer choices to detail questions may:
• be a logical choice that makes sense, but that is not mentioned in the passage.
• confuse the relationship between details that are mentioned in the passage.
• state a relationship between details that is opposite from the one stated in the passage.
• simply restate key words from the passage.

LISTENING EXERCISE 2: Listen to each passage and the questions that follow. Then choose the best answers to the questions.

PASSAGE ONE (Questions 1–5) 021

Listen to a conversation between an office worker and a student.

022

1. What is the student's situation?
   Ⓐ She wants to buy a parking sticker for her roommate.
   Ⓑ She needs to pay a parking ticket.
   Ⓒ She is trying to get her first parking sticker.
   Ⓓ She would like to get a discount on her first parking permit.

2. Why does the man suggest using the visitor parking lot?

- Ⓐ It costs less than the student will spend on gas for her roommate's car.
- Ⓑ She does not have to pay if she only uses it when she visits campus.
- Ⓒ It will be cheaper than buying a second parking sticker.
- Ⓓ She can pay for the parking lot now.

3. What does the man say about the parking sticker?

Click on two answers.

- Ⓐ It goes on the front window.
- Ⓑ It can be removed from the window.
- Ⓒ It must be put on the car by the man.
- Ⓓ It should be put on the left side of the window.

4. What is stated about parking on campus?

- Ⓐ Students may purchase half-day parking permits.
- Ⓑ Campus parking areas are distinguished by color.
- Ⓒ The visitor lot is free for people with a parking sticker.
- Ⓓ Parking stickers are marked with different colors.

5. Who parks in which areas?

Click on two answers.

- Ⓐ Students use yellow parking areas.
- Ⓑ Faculty and staff use blue parking areas.
- Ⓒ Students may use the blue visitor lot.
- Ⓓ Faculty and staff use yellow parking areas.

LISTENING

Listen to a discussion between a student and his professor.

8. What themes of the play are mentioned in the conversation?

> **Click on two answers.**

- A Complex scenery that symbolizes the cycles of life and death
- B The insignificance of daily life in comparison to birth and death
- C The lack of appreciation for the beauty of daily life
- D The simplicity of sets that allow more focus on characters

9. What does the professor say about Chuck and his classmates?

> **Click on two answers.**

- A Chuck has a lot of time to prepare his scene.
- B The classmates may answer discussion questions correctly without help from the performers.
- C The classmates' participation in the discussion is required.
- D Chuck will not have enough time to discuss all the themes of the play in ten minutes.

10. How will Chuck organize his time?

- A He will rehearse the scenes first, and then prepare the discussion.
- B He will ask students to prepare their lines, and then prepare the presentation.
- C He will make decisions and then write his presentation material.
- D He will write up a synopsis and questions, and then rehearse the scene.

6. What is Chuck's concern at the beginning of the discussion?

- A He is worried about memorizing his lines.
- B He doesn't know how to present the themes of the play to the class.
- C He is worried that it will be difficult to perform the scene.
- D He is uncomfortable with being a central character.

7. How will Chuck present the themes of the play to his classmates?

- A The class will discuss questions about the play and write a synopsis of the students' performance.
- B The class will divide into groups and write questions to discuss after the students' performance.
- C The class will discuss questions about both the students' performance and a summary of the play.
- D The class will read the play and then answer questions that the students will ask them.

Listen to part of a lecture in an education class. ⁰²⁵

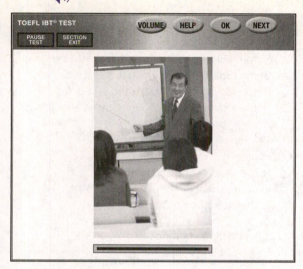

⁰²⁶

11. Who is listening to the lecture?
    - Ⓐ Experienced teachers
    - Ⓑ Students of American history
    - Ⓒ School administrators
    - Ⓓ Future teachers

12. What does the professor say about American schools before the late nineteenth century?
    - Ⓐ They did not concentrate very much on basic academic subjects.
    - Ⓑ They had not yet begun to encounter religious diversity.
    - Ⓒ They were not allowed to use the Bible as their textbook.
    - Ⓓ They did not question their responsibility for character education.

13. What is stated in the lecture about teachers in the early twentieth century?
    - Ⓐ Their behavior outside of class was unregulated.
    - Ⓑ They were expected to be of high moral character.
    - Ⓒ They were expected to avoid teaching morality to their students.
    - Ⓓ They were expected to be married.

14. What did the rules for teachers discussed in the lecture concern?

    Click on two answers.
    - Ⓐ How the teacher dressed
    - Ⓑ When the teacher was allowed to leave the classroom
    - Ⓒ Who the teacher could marry
    - Ⓓ Where the teacher could go

15. According to the lecture, what changes in education occurred in the second half of the twentieth century?

    Click on two answers.
    - Ⓐ Math and science received greater emphasis than before.
    - Ⓑ Teachers were required to have higher moral standards than before.
    - Ⓒ Educators recognized the diversity of values in American society.
    - Ⓓ Churches and families expected schools to take responsibility for character education.

16. What does the professor suggest parents will expect from teachers in the twenty-first century?

    Click on two answers.
    - Ⓐ To adhere to clear rules of behavior in and out of class
    - Ⓑ To confront a great diversity of values and beliefs
    - Ⓒ To instruct schoolchildren in the values of the dominant culture
    - Ⓓ To help develop the moral character of their students

> It is important to remember that the correct answers to detail questions will often use synonyms for words the speakers say in the passage. For example, if a speaker talks about an *author's perspective* on something, the correct answer may mention the *writer's view*.

LISTENING

PASSAGE FOUR (Questions 17-22)

Listen to part of a discussion in a geology class.

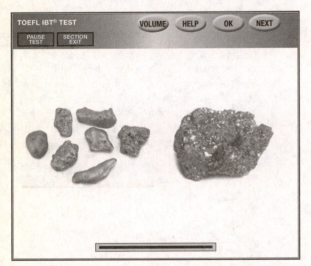

17. Why is iron pyrite called fool's gold?
    - (A) Some foolish people wasted time looking for it.
    - (B) Some foolish people thought that it was gold.
    - (C) Some foolish people preferred it to gold.
    - (D) Some foolish people thought it was an element.

18. In what way is iron pyrite similar to gold?
    - (A) In color
    - (B) In the shape of its crystals
    - (C) In composition
    - (D) In the size of it's cubes

19. What is iron pyrite composed of?

    ### Click on two answers.

    - [A] Gold
    - [B] Sulfur
    - [C] Pyrite
    - [D] Iron

20. According to the professor, which is true about iron pyrite?
    - (A) It flattens if it is struck.
    - (B) It is soft and can be scratched by other minerals.
    - (C) Its name comes from a Greek word meaning "fire."
    - (D) It is heavier than an equal volume of gold.

21. According to the professor, how does iron pyrite react to heat?

    ### Click on two answers.

    - [A] It creates smoke.
    - [B] It emits a bad smell.
    - [C] It produces sparks.
    - [D] It melts at high temperatures.

22. What will the professor have the students test in the lab?
    - (A) The similarities between gold and iron pyrite
    - (B) The reactions of sulfur compounds to heat
    - (C) The differences in characteristics of some other minerals
    - (D) The ability of iron pyrite to alter true gold

LISTENING EXERCISE (Skills 1–2): Listen to the passage and the questions that follow. Then choose the best answers to the questions.

Questions 1–7

Listen to a conversation between a professor and a student. 🔊 029

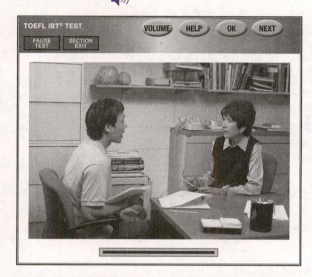

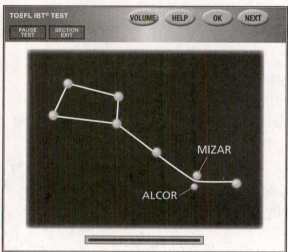

030 🔊

1. Why does the student go to see the professor?
   - Ⓐ To take a test he has missed
   - Ⓑ To get permission to write about a particular topic
   - Ⓒ To ask a question about material from the course text
   - Ⓓ To ask why certain material has been assigned

2. What is the topic of the paper he wants to write?
   - Ⓐ The use of stars in navigation
   - Ⓑ Various positions in the Roman military
   - Ⓒ The importance of astronomy in ancient Rome
   - Ⓓ A method of determining the roles for certain soldiers

3. Why were Roman soldiers asked to count the stars in the Big Dipper?
   - Ⓐ To determine if they could use the stars to navigate
   - Ⓑ To determine if they were knowledgeable about constellations
   - Ⓒ To determine if they could see well at long distances
   - Ⓓ To determine if they could count

4. What does the student say about stars?
   - Ⓐ The Big Dipper is part of a binary star.
   - Ⓑ Many people cannot see Mizar.
   - Ⓒ Alcor is part of a binary star.
   - Ⓓ The Big Dipper contains seven binary stars.

5. Which statements describe possible outcomes from the Roman eyesight test?

   Click on two answers.
   - Ⓐ A soldier would fight as an archer.
   - Ⓑ A soldier would fight on horseback.
   - Ⓒ A soldier would become an officer.
   - Ⓓ A soldier would fight on the front lines.

6. How does the term "survival of the fittest" relate to the test that the student describes?
   - Ⓐ The soldiers in the best physical shape tended to survive in battles.
   - Ⓑ The soldiers with better eyesight would fight from less dangerous positions.
   - Ⓒ The fittest Romans were not in the military and therefore tended to survive.
   - Ⓓ Those who could not see Alcor did not survive the Roman military tests.

7. What does the student say about the children of archers?

   Click on two answers.
   - Ⓐ They did not survive the battles on the front line.
   - Ⓑ They were less likely to have good eyesight than foot soldiers.
   - Ⓒ They developed an amazing ability to see stars.
   - Ⓓ They were likely to have the same eyesight as their fathers.

PRAGMATIC UNDERSTANDING

Pragmatic understanding questions ask about the more subtle understanding of spoken English than the main ideas and details that are part of basic comprehension. These questions may test the **function**, or purpose, of the speaker's words. They may also ask about the speaker's **stance**, or attitude, toward a particular subject.

Listening Skill 3: UNDERSTAND THE FUNCTION

In the Listening part of the test, you may be asked about the function, or purpose, of what a speaker says. This type of question asks you to understand not just *what* the speaker said but *why* the speaker said it. You may be asked, for example, to determine that a speaker said something in order to apologize, explain, clarify a point, change a topic, indicate a change of opinion, or suggest a new action. To answer this type of question, you must listen to what is said in a particular context and draw a conclusion about the speaker's purpose in saying it.

Strategies for Answering Function Questions

- Pay attention to the replayed part of the passage.

- Think about the context—the words and sentences surrounding the replayed part of the audio.

- Form an idea about *why* the speaker said what he or she did.

Listen and look at an example of a part of a listening passage. 🔊 031

Example 1

You see on the computer screen:

You hear:

(narrator)	Listen to a conversation between a professor and a student.
(student)	Professor Roberts, I have a question for you about the assignment.
(professor)	OK, if it's a short question.
(student)	It is. The assignment on the syllabus lists pages 101 through 120 in the text, and the last page of the assigned reading is a list of questions. I was wondering if we were supposed to read through the questions and just think about the answers or actually write out the answers.
(professor)	Well, you don't need to write out neat and formal answers, but you should be really familiar with them because we'll be talking about these questions during class, and I expect you to be prepared to answer them.
(student)	You mean we don't need to turn in our answers?
(professor)	That's right, but you might want to jot down notes on each so that you can refer to them during our discussion.

After you listen to the conversation, a function question asks about the speaker's purpose in saying something. To start this question, a part of the conversation is replayed.

You see on the computer screen:

You hear: **032** 🔊))

(narrator)   Listen again to part of the conversation. Then answer the question.

(student)   Professor Roberts, I have a question for you about the assignment.

(professor)   OK, if it's a short question.

The question and answer choices then appear on the computer screen as the narrator states the question.

You see on the computer screen:

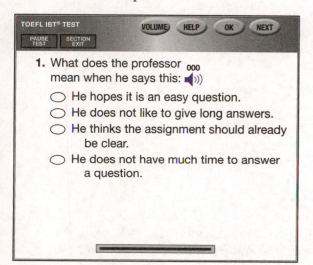

You hear: **032** 🔊))

(narrator)   What does the professor mean when he says this:

(professor)   OK, if it's a short question.

LISTENING

The fourth answer choice is correct. In the conversation, the student says, *Professor Roberts, I have a question for you* and the professor responds by saying, *OK, if it's a short question.* From this, it can be concluded that the professor means that he does not have much time to answer a question. The first answer choice is incorrect because the professor does not imply that the question should be easy. The second answer choice is incorrect because he does not imply that he does not like to give long answers in general. The third answer is incorrect because the professor does not imply that the assignment should already be clear to the student.

Now listen and look at an example of a question that asks about a different function. To start this question, a part of the conversation is replayed. **032** 🔊))

You see on the computer screen:

You hear:

(narrator) Listen again to part of the conversation. Then answer the question. 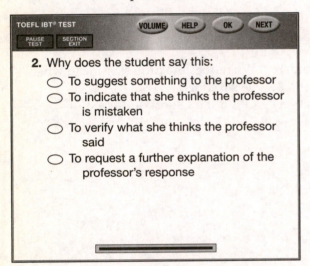⁰³²

(professor) Well, you don't need to write out neat and formal answers, but you should be really familiar with them because we'll be talking about these questions during class, and I expect you to be prepared to answer them.

(student) You mean we don't need to turn in our answers?

The question and answer choices then appear on the computer screen as the narrator states the question.

You see on the computer screen:

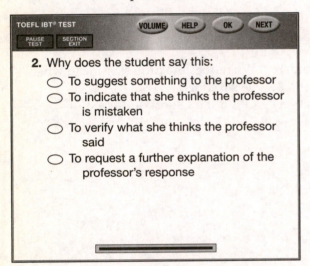

You hear:

(narrator) Why does the student say this:

(student) You mean we don't need to turn in our answers?

The third answer choice is correct. In the conversation, the professor says *well, you don't need to write out neat and formal answers, but you should be really familiar with them*, and the student responds by saying *you mean we don't need to turn in our answers?* From this, it can be concluded that the student said this to verify what she thinks the professor said. The first answer choice is incorrect because not turning in written answers is the professor's idea, not the student's suggestion. The second answer choice is incorrect because the student does not imply that the professor is mistaken. Finally, the fourth answer choice is incorrect because the student understands the professor and is verifying or confirming, not asking for further explanation.

Now listen and look at a part of a lecture. ⁰³³

Example 2

You see on the computer screen:

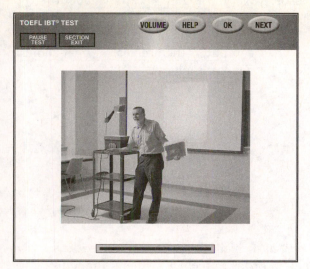

You hear:

(narrator) Listen to part of a lecture in a communications class. 033 🔊

(professor) So to get the ball rolling today, let me just say that as social media achieves its full potential, it'll come to be recognized as one of the greatest game changers in all of human history. Now, you may say, "What about Watson and Crick's DNA helix, or the invention of the Internet, or computers themselves, or what about nanotechnology?" And I admit that social media is not going to be of quite the same scale, necessarily, as every last one of these changes. Time will tell. But what I am saying is that I don't think I'm making something out of nothing. Social media is going to be more far-reaching than we can now imagine.

The function question that follows a conversation asks about the speaker's purpose in saying something. To introduce this question, a part of the conversation is replayed.

You see on the computer screen:

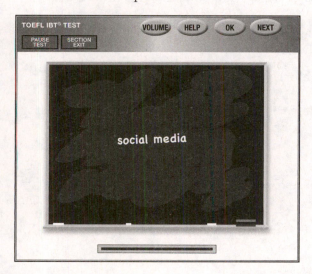

You hear:

(narrator) Listen again to part of the lecture. Then answer the question. 034 🔊

(professor) Let me just say that as social media achieves its full potential, it'll come to be recognized as one of the greatest game changers in all of human history. Now, you may say, "What about Watson and Crick's DNA helix, or the invention of the Internet, or computers themselves, or what about nanotechnology?" And I admit that social media is not going to be of quite the same scale, necessarily, as every last one of these changes. Time will tell.

The question and answer choices then appear on the computer screen as the narrator asks the question.

You see on the computer screen:

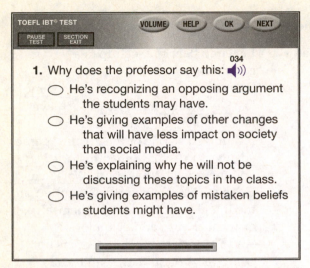

You hear:

(narrator) Why does the professor say this?
(professor) Now, <u>you may say,</u> "What about Watson and Crick's DNA helix, or the invention of the Internet, or computers themselves, or what about nanotechnology?"

The first answer choice is correct. He says, *you may say,* which serves to introduce ideas the students may have that oppose his own beliefs, in order to recognize them. Immediately afterward, he admits that social media may not be as important as all of the changes mentioned, but says it is a *game changer,* or something that brings great change. The second answer choice is incorrect because the professor says that *social media,* not the other examples of changes he just gave, may be less important, or *not . . . the same scale* as other changes. The third answer choice is incorrect because he does not give any reasons for why he is not discussing the topics in class. The fourth answer choice is incorrect because the topics are examples of important changes and not mistaken beliefs students have.

Now listen and look at an example of a question that asks about the function of an expression. 034

You see on the computer screen:

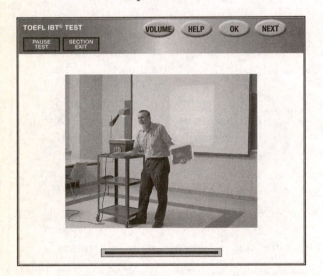

You hear:

(narrator) Listen again to part of the lecture. Then answer the question. 034
(professor) And I admit that social media is not going to be of quite the same scale, necessarily, as every last one of these changes. Time will tell. <u>But what I am saying is that I don't think I'm making something out of nothing. Social media is going to be more far-reaching than we can now imagine.</u>

The question and answer choices then appear on the computer screen as the narrator states the question.

You see on the computer screen:

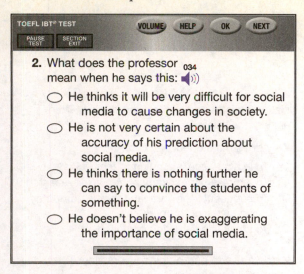

You hear:

(narrator)   What does the professor mean when he says this:

(professor)   I don't think I'm making something out of nothing.

> Although you may not know the meaning of the idiomatic expressions the speakers use, the context of the conversation and tone of the speakers' voices will often give clues to the meaning.

The fourth answer choice is correct. The expression *make something out of nothing* means to make an issue out of something that is not very important or to exaggerate the importance of something. The professor says he doesn't think he is doing that, so he doesn't believe he is exaggerating. The first answer choice is incorrect because the professor's statement does not imply that it will be difficult for social media to change the world; in fact, he believes the opposite to be true. The second answer choice is incorrect because the professor says social media *is going to be more far-reaching than we can now imagine,* which is a very certain statement. The third answer choice is incorrect because nothing in the lecture indicates that the professor thinks he can't convince the students; this answer choice confuses the expression *something out of nothing* with "nothing further."

The following chart outlines the key points that you should remember about function questions.

KEY POINTS FOR QUESTIONS ABOUT UNDERSTANDING THE FUNCTION	
FREQUENCY OF QUESTION TYPE	Questions about function are common, especially after conversations. There will usually be 0–2 questions about function per passage.
HOW TO IDENTIFY THE QUESTION	**Listen again** to part of the passage. **Why** does the speaker say this? *(replay)* **What** does the speaker **mean**? *(replay)* **What** does the speaker **imply**? *(replay)*
WHERE TO FIND THE ANSWER	The part of the passage that indicates the function of what the speaker says will be replayed for you.
HOW TO ANSWER THE QUESTION	1. Listen carefully to *what* the speaker says and the surrounding context in the part of the passage that is repeated. 2. Draw a conclusion about *why* the speaker says it.

The incorrect answer choices to function questions may:
- be a literal (word-by-word) interpretation of the words spoken, but not match the speaker's tone.
- give other possible meanings of the words the speaker uses, but not match the tone or fit into the context of the replayed passage.
- be a logical conclusion based on some of the words the speaker mentions.
- be an interpretation of words that sound similar to words the speaker uses.

LISTENING EXERCISE 3: Listen to each passage and the questions that follow. Then choose the best answers to the questions.

PASSAGE ONE (Questions 1–4) 035

Listen to a conversation between a librarian and a student.

036

1. Listen again to part of the conversation. Then answer the question.

   Why does the librarian say this: ◀))

   Ⓐ To indicate that the student has neglected something very basic
   Ⓑ To avoid offending the student while asking about something simple
   Ⓒ To imply that the student is wasting time on something very obvious
   Ⓓ To apologize for asking the student to repeat an explanation

2. Listen again to part of the conversation. Then answer the question.

   What does the librarian mean when he says this:

   Ⓐ Students may get angry when they do not understand their assignment.
   Ⓑ Students may not understand how the librarians can help them.
   Ⓒ Students often ask librarians to explain assignments when professors are not clear.
   Ⓓ Students often start researching without thoroughly reading and understanding the assignment

3. Listen again to part of the conversation. Then answer the question.

   Why does the student say this: ◀))

   Ⓐ To indicate she is starting to feel sick
   Ⓑ To express her excitement about the research
   Ⓒ To suggest to the librarian that the computer isn't working properly
   Ⓓ To imply she is getting confused

4. Listen again to part of the conversation. Then answer the question.

   What does the librarian mean when he says this: ◀))

   Ⓐ Only professors can use the library computers for research.
   Ⓑ The computers should not be used for personal concerns.
   Ⓒ The computers do not have video capabilities.
   Ⓓ The student will only be able to do her research at the library.

Listen to a conversation between an advisor and a student.

038

5. Listen again to part of the conversation. Then answer the question.

   What does the advisor mean when he says this: 🔊

   (A) The question is a difficult one to handle.
   (B) He can answer the question easily.
   (C) He knows how to apply for a scholarship.
   (D) He will take care of the transcript for her.

6. Listen again to part of the conversation. Then answer the question.

   What does the student mean when she says this: 🔊

   (A) It sounds difficult to do.
   (B) She does not think she can do it.
   (C) It sounds surprisingly easy.
   (D) She thinks the advisor is wrong.

7. Listen again to part of the conversation. Then answer the question.

   Why does the student say this: 🔊

   (A) She thinks the advisor is being impolite.
   (B) She realizes the news is not good for her.
   (C) She does not understand what the advisor is trying to tell her.
   (D) She wants the advisor to change the subject.

8. Listen again to part of the conversation. Then answer the question.

   Why does the advisor say this: 🔊

   (A) To suggest that it is not likely that the student will get what she wants
   (B) To show that he thinks the student will be lucky
   (C) To state that the student can always depend on him
   (D) To imply that it will not take longer than a week

9. Listen again to part of the conversation. Then answer the question.

   What does the advisor mean when he says this: 🔊

   (A) She should make her complaint about the price very brief.
   (B) She should be polite because the registrar is in a more powerful position than she is.
   (C) She should complain about the price because she does not have much money.
   (D) She should not complain because she hopes they make an exception for her.

Listen to part of a lecture in a zoology class.

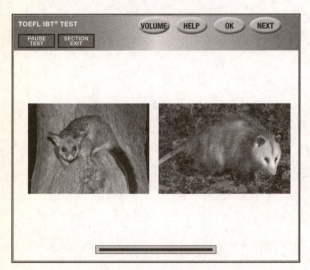

10. Listen again to part of the lecture. Then answer the question.

    Why does the professor say this:

    (A) She is irritated that the student would ask such a simple question.
    (B) She is surprised that the student has asked this question.
    (C) She has anticipated that a student would ask this question.
    (D) She is indicating to the student that now is not the time for questions.

11. Listen again to part of the lecture. Then answer the question.

    Why does the professor say this:

    (A) To explain why she will be using a name that students may be less familiar with
    (B) To indicate that students should try to inform other people about the mistaken name
    (C) To explain why she uses the common but incorrect name
    (D) To indicate that students should use the name *opossum* in class

12. Listen again to part of the lecture. Then answer the question.

    What does the professor mean when she says this:

    (A) "I'll answer questions in a little while, but not now."
    (B) "I prefer that you not interrupt my explanation with questions today."
    (C) "I'll explain clearly so there will not be any questions."
    (D) "I'll answer questions at the end of class."

13. Listen again to part of the lecture. Then answer the question.

    Why does the professor say this:

    (A) To make certain that the students understand what will be on the exam
    (B) To advise the students about something they should remember for later studies in the field
    (C) To encourage the students to continue studying animal behavior
    (D) To emphasize to the students the importance of attributing motives to animals

PASSAGE FOUR (Questions 14–19)

041

Listen to part of a lecture in an astronomy class.

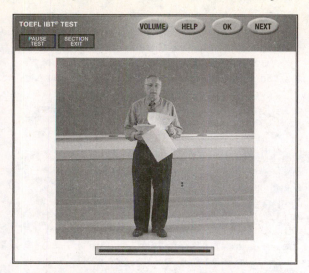

Giant Impact Theory
Theia

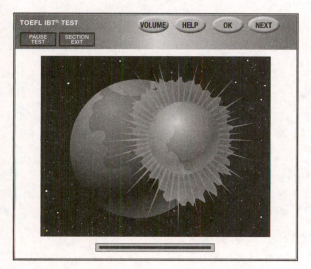

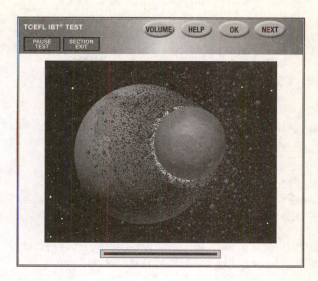

042

14. Listen again to part of the lecture. Then answer the question.

Why does the professor say this: 🔊)))

Ⓐ The students will agree with him that the name Theia is particularly fitting.

Ⓑ The students should remember the scientific name instead of the name Theia.

Ⓒ The students should be glad that the professor is pointing out what they should remember.

Ⓓ The students should be grateful that the name Theia is relatively easy to remember.

15. Listen again to part of the lecture. Then answer the question.

Why does the professor say this: 🔊))

Ⓐ He has changed his mind about when to show visual aids.

Ⓑ He is signaling that what he is about to say is important for understanding the lecture.

Ⓒ He is indicating that he is about to reveal some surprising information.

Ⓓ He has decided to completely change his plan for the lecture.

16. Listen again to part of the lecture. Then answer the question.

Why does the professor say this: 🔊))

Ⓐ He is presenting evidence that has not been explained by the model.

Ⓑ He is asking a question that he intends to answer.

Ⓒ He is going to describe a misunderstanding that many people have.

Ⓓ He is questioning the idea that the iron core of the Earth is important.

LISTENING

17. Listen again to part of the lecture. Then answer the question.

What does the professor mean when he says this: 🔊))

Ⓐ He is going to return to the main topic.

Ⓑ He is going to discuss something partially related to the main topic.

Ⓒ He is going to discuss something unusual.

Ⓓ He is going to talk about a new topic.

18. Listen again to part of the lecture. Then answer the question.

What does the professor mean when he says this: 🔊))

Ⓐ He is going to explain why the model is not true.

Ⓑ He is going to compare the model to another theory.

Ⓒ He is going to present problems with the model.

Ⓓ He is going to explain the model by using examples.

19. Listen again to part of the lecture. Then answer the question.

Why does the professor say this: 🔊))

Ⓐ To explain that the Giant Impact Model will always be questioned by science

Ⓑ To indicate that the Giant Impact Model might achieve the status of theory in the future

Ⓒ To argue that the Giant Impact Model will be proven true in the future

Ⓓ To state that he is not sure whether the Giant Impact Model qualifies as a theory

Speakers often use a rhetorical question, which is a question asked to make a statement rather than to get an answer. For example, *Why me?* and *Are you sure?* are questions in which an answer is not expected. *Why me?* is used to show that the speaker is upset, overwhelmed, etc. *Are you sure?* is used to tell someone that you don't believe the accuracy of the information just spoken.

Listening Skill 4: UNDERSTAND THE SPEAKER'S STANCE

This type of question asks about the speaker's stance, or attitude. This may be opinions, feelings, or degrees of certainty. The speaker may express likes, dislikes, or concerns. You may be asked, for example, to determine if the speaker feels impressed, enthusiastic, or bored about a particular topic. A speaker may also express how certain or doubtful he or she is about a topic, or about evidence or a theory. Generally, the speakers will not directly state the answers to these questions. You will have to infer the speakers' attitude from their tone of voice, choice of words, and the context of the conversation or lecture. Note that some stance questions will ask you to listen to a replayed portion of the passage; however, other types of stance questions do *not* have a replay portion.

Strategies to Answer Stance Questions

- Listen for tone of voice and word choice. If a part of the passage is repeated, pay careful attention to it.

- Form an idea about how the speaker feels, based on the tone of voice, word choice, and context.

Example 1 [043] 🔊))

You see on the computer screen:

You hear:

(narrator)   Listen to a conversation between an advisor and a student.

(advisor)   I'm sorry to hear that you are feeling a little lonely and miss your family. You know, it might help if you got involved in some campus activity where you could meet other people and make some friends. Are there any sports or other hobbies you enjoy doing?

(student)   Uh . . . I'm not really into sports, but I've been playing chess with my father since I was a kid.

(advisor)   Well then, you might think about joining the chess club. I belonged to it when I was a graduate student a few years ago, and I think you might really like it, too.

(student)   What did you do there?

(advisor)   We'd get together once a week for friendly competitions. Then each semester, the three best players from the club would compete in a tournament with players from other schools. I go to the tournaments regularly and this is still how it's organized.

(student)   The meetings once a week sound cool, but . . . uh . . . my chess playing just . . . uh . . . might not be quite up to the level of tournament play.

(advisor)   Uh, hang on a minute . . . just let me check the club schedule . . . OK, here it is; the meetings are on Wednesdays. So, why don't you go this Wednesday and check it out? You can go to the meetings for a while and then see if you're ready for a tournament in a few months.

After you listen to the conversation, the question and answer choices appear on the computer screen as the narrator states the question. This question is a stance question that asks about the speaker's attitude. To start this question, a part of the conversation is replayed.

You see on the computer screen:

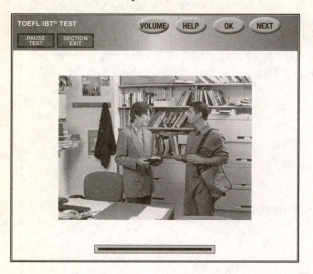

The question and answer choices then appear on the computer screen as the narrator states the question.

You see on the computer screen:

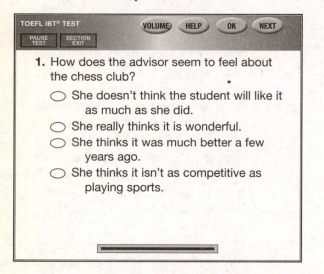

You hear: 🔊 044

(narrator) Listen again to part of the conversation. Then answer the question.

(student) Uh . . . I'm not really into sports, but I've been playing chess with my father since I was a kid.

(advisor) *Well* then, you might think about joining the chess club. I belonged to it when I was a graduate student a few years ago, and I think you might really like it, too.

You hear:

(narrator) How does the advisor seem to feel about the chess club?

The second answer choice is the best answer to this question. In the conversation, the advisor says, *Well then, you might think about joining the chess club. I belonged to it when I was a graduate student a few years ago, and I think you might really like it, too.* From this, it can be determined that she really thinks it is wonderful. The first answer choice is incorrect because the advisor says, *I think you might really like it, too.* The third answer choice is incorrect because although she mentions that she was a member a few years ago, the advisor does not compare the present and past clubs. The fourth answer choice is incorrect because the advisor doesn't say how she feels about the competitiveness of the club.

Now listen and look at an example of a different type of question that asks about the speaker's attitude. 🔊 044

You see on the computer screen:

You hear:

(narrator)   Listen again to part of the conversation. Then answer the question.

(student)   The meetings once a week sound cool, but . . . uh . . . my chess playing just . . . uh . . . might not be quite up to the level of tournament play.

The question and answer choices then appear on the computer screen as the narrator states the question.

You see on the computer screen:

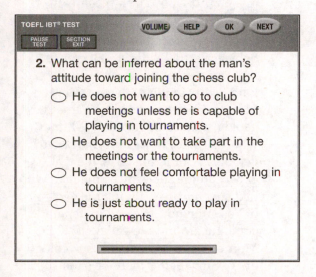

You hear:

(narrator)   Which sentence best expresses how the student feels?

The third answer choice is correct. In the conversation, the student says *the meetings once a week sound cool, but . . . uh . . . my chess playing just . . . uh . . . might not be quite up to the level of tournament play*. From this, it can be determined that he would most likely enjoy going to the meetings but would not feel comfortable playing in tournaments. The first and second answer choices misinterpret the student's attitude, and the fourth answer choice is a misinterpretation of the expression *not quite*, which <u>does not</u> mean *just about* in this context.

Now listen and look at an example from part of a lecture. **045** 🔊))

Example 2

You see on the computer screen:

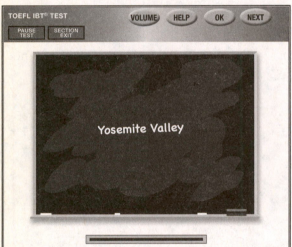

You hear:

(narrator)   Listen to part of a lecture in a geology class.

(professor)   Well, at the end of the nineteenth century, John Muir and the California state geologist at the time, Josiah Whitney, had very different theories on how the canyon in Yosemite National Park got its unusual box shape. For years, each man clung tenaciously to his theory, but the problem was that both of them lacked definitive proof. OK, so bit by bit, evidence began to mount in favor of Muir's theory that glacial action was responsible for the canyon's distinctive shape. But it wasn't until the twentieth century that all of the missing pieces of the puzzle were in place and Whitney should have conceded at that point. Um, I say "should have" because he never actually did so. Of course, this was a great upset, or, I guess kind of a triumph of the outsider for Muir because he was just an amateur geologist, in comparison to Whitney, who, as I said, was California's state geologist. But in this case, the real expert on the subject was the man who had spent years studying the geology of Yosemite up close and in person, climbing around the valley itself. So Muir came to understand the geology of Yosemite better than the state's official geologist.

After you listen to the lecture, the question and answer choices appear on the computer screen as the narrator states the question. This question asks about the speaker's attitude toward a theory. To start this question, a part of the conversation is replayed.

You see on the computer screen:

You hear: [046] 🔊))

(narrator)   Listen again to a part of the lecture. Then answer the question.

(professor)   Ok, so bit by bit evidence began to mount in favor of Muir's theory that glacial action was responsible for the canyon's distinctive shape. But it wasn't until the twentieth century that all of the missing pieces of the puzzle were in place and Whitney should have conceded at that point.

The question and answer choices then appear on the computer screen as the narrator states the question.

You see on the computer screen:

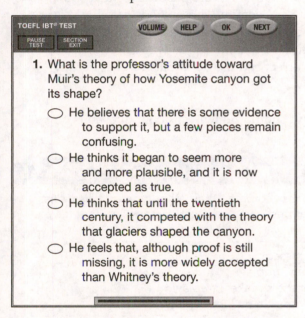

You hear:

(narrator)   What is the professor's attitude toward Muir's theory of how Yosemite canyon got its shape?

The second answer choice is correct. This question asks about how certain the professor is about the evidence for the theory. The professor says that *evidence began to mount*, meaning the theory began to seem more believable, or plausible, and that Whitney *should have conceded* because *the missing pieces were in place*. The professor implies that from the twentieth century forward, the question was settled and Muir's theory was accepted. The first answer choice is incorrect because the expression "the pieces are in place" means that nothing is missing or confusing. The third answer choice is incorrect because the theory about glaciers was Muir's theory. The fourth answer choice is incorrect because the professor's attitude is one of certainty that Muir's theory is correct, not that it has missing evidence.

The question and answer choices then appear on the computer screen as the narrator states the question. In this type of stance question, no part of the question is replayed.

You see on the computer screen:

You hear:

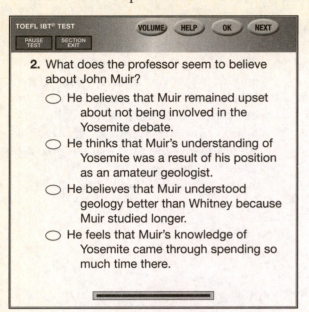

(narrator) What does the professor seem to believe about John Muir?

The fourth answer choice is correct. The professor says that *the real expert* [Muir] was the one who *had spent years . . . climbing around the valley itself*. Therefore, he believes that Muir gained his understanding by spending a long time in Yosemite. The first answer choice is incorrect because it misinterprets the meaning of "upset." The second answer choice is incorrect because the professor does not imply that Muir's amateur status was the reason he understood Yosemite. The third answer choice is incorrect because the professor does not say that Muir studied longer than Whitney.

The following chart outlines the key points that you should remember about questions on the speaker's stance.

KEY POINTS FOR QUESTIONS ABOUT UNDERSTANDING THE SPEAKER'S STANCE	
FREQUENCY OF QUESTION TYPE	Questions about stance are less common than other types of questions. There will usually be 0–1 per passage, and most passages will *not* have a question about stance.
HOW TO IDENTIFY THE QUESTION	Listen **again** to part of the passage. What does the speaker **mean**? *(replay)* What can be **inferred** about the speaker? *(replay)* What is the speaker's **attitude/opinion**? *(no replay)*
WHERE TO FIND THE ANSWER	The part of the passage that indicates what the speaker says will be replayed for you.
HOW TO ANSWER THE QUESTION	1. Listen carefully to *what* the speaker says and *how* the speaker says it in the part of the passage that is repeated. The tone of voice and choice of words will indicate the speaker's stance. 2. Draw a conclusion about *how* the speaker *feels*.

Incorrect answer choices may:
- be alternative meanings of words or expressions that do not match the context or speaker's tone.
- incorrectly summarize the speaker's certainty or feelings about a topic.
- repeat some of the words of the speaker, but change the meaning.
- express an opinion that contradicts other information in the passage.
- confuse one speaker's opinion with that of the other speaker or with another's.

LISTENING EXERCISE 4: Listen to each passage and the questions that follow. Then choose the best answers to the questions.

PASSAGE ONE (Questions 1–2) 047

Listen to a conversation between an advisor and a student.

048

1. Listen again to part of the discussion. Then answer the question.

   What is the advisor's attitude toward the student's original plan?

   Ⓐ He agrees that it will save her money in the end.
   Ⓑ He believes it will make it impossible for her to be admitted to graduate school.
   Ⓒ He thinks that there is a better way for her to achieve her goals.
   Ⓓ He doesn't feel that money should be a factor in her decision.

2. Listen again to part of the discussion. Then answer the question.

   What does the advisor seem to feel will be the impression the student will make on graduate schools if she follows his advice?

   Ⓐ He believes her low grades will not leave a bad impression if she does more research.
   Ⓑ He believes she will look like a better candidate if she gets a fellowship.
   Ⓒ He feels this plan will allow her to make a more favorable impression.
   Ⓓ He thinks getting good grades will be more impressive than taking part in research.

PASSAGE TWO (Questions 3–4) 049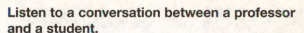

Listen to a conversation between a professor and a student.

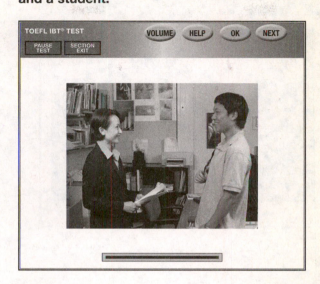

050

3. Listen again to part of the conversation. Then answer the question.

   How does the professor seem to feel about giving the surveys to students?

   Ⓐ She isn't sure the students will understand how to do it.
   Ⓑ She thinks it is unlikely to be the best strategy.
   Ⓒ She believes the student has enough time to do it.
   Ⓓ She is confident that it will be easy.

4. Listen again to part of the conversation. Then answer the question.

   What is the student's attitude about the professor's advice?

   Ⓐ He does not want to do it but will try to be positive.
   Ⓑ He thinks it will be better if his partner does it.
   Ⓒ He is very irritated because it will be too difficult.
   Ⓓ He finally agrees with the professor that it may be enjoyable.

PASSAGE THREE (Questions 5–6)

Listen to part of a lecture in a Native American Studies class.

5. How does the professor seem to feel about the design of the Iroquois village?

   Ⓐ It is too simple and primitive.
   Ⓑ Its design made it effective.
   Ⓒ It is special due to the complicated structures.
   Ⓓ It is superior to that of other Native American villages.

6. Listen again to part of the lecture. Then answer the question.

   What is the professor's attitude toward doing the assignment on the computer?

   Ⓐ It will be too easy for students to make copies of others' work.
   Ⓑ She prefers the perfection and elegance of the computer drawings.
   Ⓒ It will not convey the impression she wants as well as a hand-drawing will.
   Ⓓ It is an acceptable alternative if the student cannot draw well.

PASSAGE FOUR (Questions 7–8)

Listen to part of a lecture in a meteorology class.

hail
cumulonimbus clouds

7. Listen again to part of the discussion. Then answer the question.

   How does the professor feel about changing his ideas due to new evidence?

   Ⓐ He had difficulty with it in the past, but now he is used to it.
   Ⓑ He finds it frustrating if he has to do it constantly, but he usually enjoys it.
   Ⓒ He feels it makes his job as a researcher more difficult.
   Ⓓ He is excited by the process of modifying his understanding.

8. The professor's attitude toward hail prevention is that he believes

   Ⓐ that the evidence makes it impossible.
   Ⓑ that there will not be progress any time soon.
   Ⓒ that it is more exciting than predicting hail.
   Ⓓ that the current evidence is moderately promising.

Questions 1–6 055

Listen to part of a lecture in an American history class.

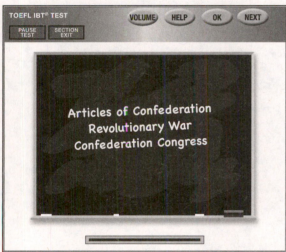

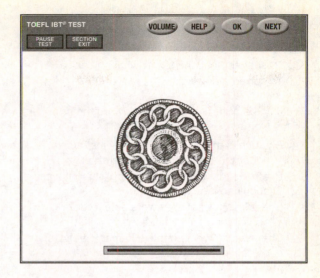

056

1. Listen again to part of the lecture. Then answer the question.

   Why does the professor say this:

   Ⓐ Because she wants the students to disagree with her
   Ⓑ Because she is trying to confuse the students
   Ⓒ Because she thinks that the students do not know the answer
   Ⓓ Because she believes that this information is correct

2. Listen again to part of the lecture. Then answer the question.

   What does the professor mean when she says this:

   Ⓐ "I'm happy you've done more than required."
   Ⓑ "I expect everyone else to do the recommended reading, too."
   Ⓒ "This will count as extra credit on your grade."
   Ⓓ "I am disappointed that other students have not read the textbook."

3. Listen again to part of the lecture. Then answer the question.

   What does the professor mean when she says this:

   Ⓐ She thinks that the answer the student gave is strange.
   Ⓑ She had by chance thought of the same idea earlier.
   Ⓒ She remembered the same joke as the student.
   Ⓓ She is surprised that the student's answer is correct.

LISTENING

4. Listen again to part of the lecture. Then answer the question.

Why does the professor say this: 🔊))

Ⓐ To show that she is uncertain

Ⓑ To change the subject

Ⓒ To suggest that she forgot what she said

Ⓓ To correct herself

5. What is the professor's attitude toward the members of the Confederation Congress?

Ⓐ She thinks they were completely ineffective under the Articles of Confederation

Ⓑ She feels that their only accomplishment was acquiring new territory.

Ⓒ She admires what they were able to do considering their limitations.

Ⓓ She felt they were effective in many areas, such as collecting taxes.

6. Listen again to part of the lecture. Then answer the question.

What is the professor's attitude toward the U.S. Constitution?

Ⓐ Currently, people mistakenly think everyone was in favor of it at the time it was written.

Ⓑ People today mistakenly believe that it was an unlawful seizure of power.

Ⓒ It wasn't necessary because the Articles of Confederation were enough to govern well.

Ⓓ Since its beginning, it has been praised by nearly everyone.

LISTENING REVIEW EXERCISE (Skills 1–4): Listen to the passage and the questions that follow. Then choose the best answers to the questions.

Questions 1–8 🔊 057

Listen to part of a lecture in a zoology class.

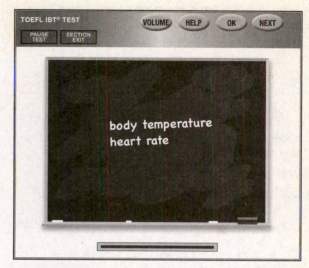

 058

1. What is the lecture mainly about?
   - Ⓐ Why the groundhog hibernates
   - Ⓑ Which folktales relate to hibernation
   - Ⓒ How various animals hibernate
   - Ⓓ How animals adapt to cold

2. What is mentioned by the professor as a way that various types of animals prepare for the cold weather?

   #### Click on two answers.

   - Ⓐ Some migrate to southern climates.
   - Ⓑ Some increase their activity.
   - Ⓒ Some hide food in or near their burrows.
   - Ⓓ Some eat more to prepare for hibernation.

3. Listen again to part of the lecture. Then answer the question.

What does the professor mean when he says this: 🔊

 Ⓐ It's not surprising that the groundhog is usually wrong.

 Ⓑ Surprisingly, the groundhog is generally correct.

 Ⓒ The groundhog's accuracy is not known.

 Ⓓ The groundhog is not particularly accurate.

4. Listen again to part of the lecture. Then answer the question.

Why does the professor say this: 🔊

 Ⓐ To indicate that Tom should have asked that question earlier

 Ⓑ To show that he should have defined hibernation earlier

 Ⓒ To state that the lecture should have been started earlier

 Ⓓ To indicate that the question had already been answered

5. Listen again to part of the lecture. Then answer the question.

How does the professor seem to feel about hibernation?

 Ⓐ It is the most efficient way to resist cold.

 Ⓑ Its causes remain mysterious.

 Ⓒ It is certainly not the best adaption to cold.

 Ⓓ It is more likely to be an adaption to food scarcity.

6. What happens to an animal during hibernation?

Click on two answers.

 Ⓐ Its body temperature increases.

 Ⓑ Its body temperature decreases.

 Ⓒ Its body stores more fat.

 Ⓓ Its heart rate decreases.

7. How does hibernation in a tree squirrel compare to other animals?

 Ⓐ Like bats, they only stop hibernating when disturbed.

 Ⓑ Like groundhogs, they sometimes come out during the winter.

 Ⓒ Like groundhogs, they hibernate throughout winter.

 Ⓓ Like bears, they do not fully hibernate.

8. What part of the bear most likely warms up first from hibernation?

 Ⓐ The head

 Ⓑ The paws

 Ⓒ The chest

 Ⓓ The tail

CONNECTING INFORMATION

Questions about connecting information involve a number of ideas rather than a single idea. These questions may ask about the **organization** of the ideas or about the **relationships** between or among ideas.

Listening Skill 5: UNDERSTAND THE ORGANIZATION

Organization questions are questions that ask about how the ideas in the passage are organized, or how they relate to the main topic or each other. They may ask specifically about how an example or idea relates to the main topic or other ideas, or they may ask you to fill out a chart that shows the organization. It is important to understand that this type of question is based on an understanding of the main points and how they are organized rather than on a single point.

Strategies to Answer Organization Questions

- Listen to the details and examples, and think about why they are discussed in relation to the overall passage.

- Look for organization of ideas such as comparison or contrast, cause and effect, etc.

Listen to and look at an example. **059**

Example 1

You see on the computer screen:

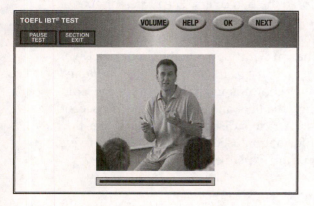

You hear:

(narrator) Listen to part of a lecture in a geography class.

(professor) All of the great rivers of the world have been around much longer than humanity, but what makes a river really old?

The Nile River in Africa, which is several hundred million years old, is believed to be the world's oldest river. It's also the longest, at 4,145 miles in length. As an old river, it doesn't change drastically in elevation for most of its length, and has a meandering path, a slow flow, and a wide flood plain. Now, let's discuss the young Colorado, which has deep, narrow valleys and a very rapid flow. I think you would appreciate the difference if you sailed down the two rivers. The wide riverboats used on the Nile wouldn't make it down the rolling and boiling white water of the Colorado. Let's also take a look at the Amazon River in South America. It's slightly shorter than the Nile at just over 4,000 miles in length, but it carries more water than any other river. And, although it is believed to be much younger than the Nile in absolute terms, we can observe in the Amazon many of the characteristics that put it into the same age class.

Again, by identifying another major river by age, the Columbia River in the Pacific Northwest—which has the greatest flow of any river in North America—we can see how, unlike the Amazon, it still displays its relative youth as it runs swiftly through high and spectacular mountain gorges.

After you listen to the lecture, the first question and answer choices appear on the computer screen as the narrator states the question. This is a multiple-choice question that asks about the organization of the information in the passage.

You see on the computer screen:

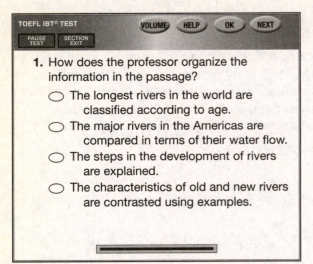

You hear: 060 🔊))

(narrator) How does the professor organize the information in the passage?

The fourth answer choice is correct. The professor first describes characteristics of the old Nile: *it doesn't change drastically in elevation for most of its length, and has a meandering path, a slow flow, and a wide flood plain.* He then contrasts the Nile River with the characteristics of the young Colorado[River], *which has deep, narrow valleys and a very rapid flow* and says, I think you would appreciate the difference if you sailed down the two rivers. The professor goes on to discuss another old river, the Amazon River: *although it is believed to be much younger than the Nile in absolute terms, we can observe in the Amazon many of the characteristics that put it into the same age class.* He then clearly contrasts the Amazon with the younger Columbia River: *we can see how, unlike the Amazon, it still displays its relative youth as it runs swiftly through high and spectacular mountain gorges.* The first answer choice is incorrect because the Colorado River is not one of the world's longest, although the Nile and Amazon are. The second answer choice is incorrect because the Nile River in Africa is discussed and the water flow of the rivers is mentioned, but is not the primary information used for contrasting the rivers. The third answer choice is incorrect because no steps are explained.

Now listen and look at an example of another type of organization question. This type of question is presented as a chart. You must demonstrate your understanding of how the information in the lecture is organized by clicking on the correct column to put each idea into the correct category.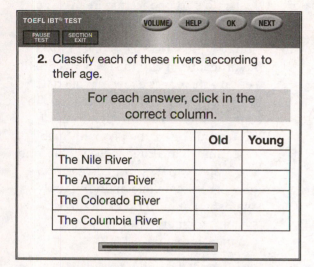

You see on the computer screen:

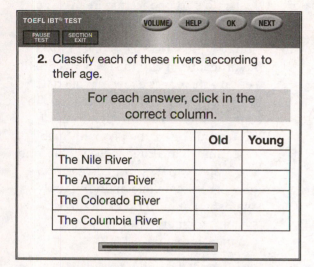

You hear:

(narrator)   Classify each of these rivers according to their age.

The correct answers are: Nile, old; Amazon, old; Colorado, young; Columbia, young. The professor says that the Nile is the world's oldest, that the Colorado is young, that the Amazon demonstrates characteristics that put it in the same age class (as the old Nile) and that the Columbia unlike the Amazon . . . still displays its relative youth. Charts with four categories are normally worth two points; you must categorize all answers correctly to get the points. Some charts may have fewer options and are worth less points. These charts will have special directions saying how many points they are worth.

Now listen to a lecture in an American history class. 🔊 061

Example 2

You see on the computer screen:

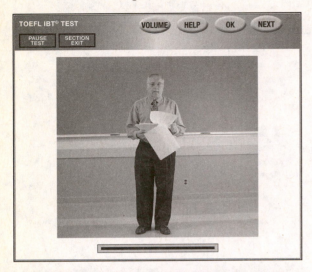

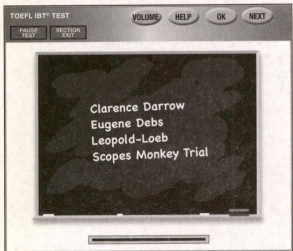

You hear:

Listen to part of a lecture in an American history class.

(professor) Today I'd like to discuss one of my favorite lawyers. In the early twentieth century there was a lawyer called Clarence Darrow who was special. To explain, let me run through three of his famous cases: the Leopold-Loeb case, um . . . the Eugene Debs case, and the Scopes Monkey Trial. In each case he worked to defend an individual against what he felt was an unjust system, sometimes for very little payment.

He defended a union president, Eugene Debs, who was being prosecuted by the federal government for leading a strike, for example. Also, in the Leopold-Loeb case he represented a pair of hated murderers. It was his most famous stand against capital punishment, which he felt was a biased institution anyway. And then there was the Scopes Monkey Trial, where Darrow defended a school teacher in the state of Tennessee for teaching evolution.

One of Darrow's greatest skills was that he was an amazing orator who could sometimes move his audience to tears. He would use poetry, make dramatic emotional appeals . . . you know, pull out all the stops to convince judges and jurors of his opinion. The emotional appeals often worked, and many times he won cases doing that.

Now listen and look at a question that asks you how a professor explains a concept. 🔊 062

You see on the computer screen:

You hear:

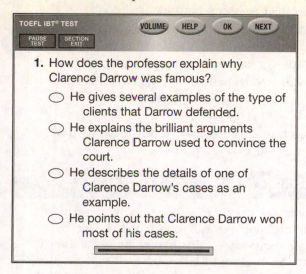

(narrator)   How does the professor explain why
Clarence Darrow was famous?

The first answer choice is correct. The professor says that *in each case* Clarence Darrow *worked to defend an individual against what he felt was an unjust system*, and then describes the clients in three different cases in which this was true. The second answer choice is incorrect because brilliant arguments were not mentioned. The third answer choice is incorrect because the professor does not describe one case in detail, but briefly mentions several cases. The fourth answer choice is incorrect because the professor did not mention whether Darrow won most of his cases.

Next, listen and look at an example of an organization question that asks you to identify the purpose of an example. This type of question tests your ability to understand how examples that speakers discuss fit into the organization of the passage and help illustrate the main points. ⁰⁶² ◀))

You see on the computer screen:

You hear:

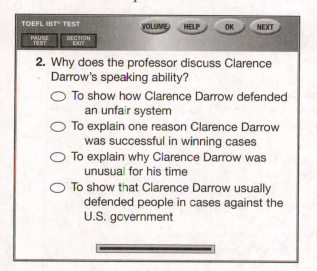

(narrator)   Why does the professor discuss
Clarence Darrow's speaking ability?

The second answer choice is correct. The professor says that oration was *one of Darrow's greatest skills,* and that *many times he won cases doing that* (making emotional appeals). The first answer choice is incorrect because the professor says that Darrow worked *against . . . an unfair system.* The third answer choice is incorrect because the professor does not imply that oratory skill was unusual in his time. The fourth answer choice is incorrect because some of the cases mentioned were not cases against the U.S. government; some were against state governments, such as the state of Tennessee.

The following chart outlines the key points you should remember about organization questions.

KEY POINTS FOR QUESTIONS ABOUT UNDERSTANDING THE ORGANIZATION	
FREQUENCY OF QUESTION TYPE	Questions that ask about organization are more likely to be asked after lectures than after conversations. Lectures will usually be followed by approximately 1–2 organization questions, but conversations will usually not be followed by organization questions (0–1). Questions that ask about the purpose of an example or how the passage is organized are generally the most common type of organization question while questions that ask you to arrange information in a chart are usually less common.
HOW TO IDENTIFY THE QUESTION	Why do the speakers **discuss/mention** . . .? **How** is the information **organized** . . .? **What** is **explained/illustrated** by the **example** of . . . **Click/Put a checkmark** in the correct **column/box** . . .
WHERE TO FIND THE ANSWER	Information to answer organization questions is generally not from one point in the passage, and may not be directly stated. It is necessary to understand all the main points, and how examples and details relate to each other and to the overall organization of the passage. Listen carefully to examples the speakers discuss, and draw a conclusion about how they relate to the main points in the passage.
HOW TO ANSWER THE QUESTION	1. Listen carefully to specific details and examples in the passage. 2. Consider why these ideas are discussed in relation to the overall passage. 3. Think about how the passage is organized: by comparison/contrast, cause/effect and so on. 4. Look for an answer that shows how the examples or details fit into the organization of the passage. 5. Eliminate the definitely wrong answers, and choose the best answer from the remaining choices.

Incorrect answer choices to organization questions may:
• be a logical reason to discuss the example, but have no relation to the main points in the passage.
• be a logical way to organize or introduce the information in the passage, but not what the professor actually uses.
• express a relationship among the main points in the passage that is not true.
• confuse details of an example to reach a conclusion that is not true.
• express an idea that is the opposite of what an example indicates.

LISTENING EXERCISE 5: Listen to each passage and the questions that follow. Then choose the best answers to the questions.

PASSAGE ONE (Questions 1–3)   063

Listen to a lecture in a biology class.

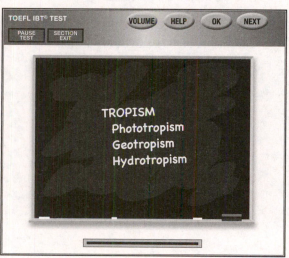

064

1. How does the professor illustrate the concept of phototropism?

  (A) He contrasts it with a description of how hydrotropism functions.
  (B) He uses pictures of pea plants to visually show the students.
  (C) He describes the growth of a houseplant near a window.
  (D) He describes how chemicals in leaves cause plant cells to move.

2. According to the professor, what is the significance of pea plants?

  (A) They are one of few species that demonstrate all kinds of tropism.
  (B) They have characteristics that make them common to use in research on tropism.
  (C) They are the easiest plants to perform experiments on.
  (D) They are the only plants that exhibit geotropism in space.

3. Indicate which parts of a plant exhibit each type of tropism, according to the discussion.

Put a checkmark in the correct column.

	Roots	Shoots
negative phototropism		
negative geotropism		
positive hydrotropism		

Listen to part of a lecture in an archaeology class.

Fossilization
Permineralization
Petrification

066

4. Why does the professor use the example of the fish and the lizard?

Ⓐ To explain why only animals that have bones will be fossilized

Ⓑ To illustrate how floods can quickly bury both land and sea animals

Ⓒ To contrast the process of petrification with that of permineralization

Ⓓ To explain how different factors affect the likelihood of creatures being preserved as fossils

5. Which of the following does the professor mention as being related to the process of fossilization?

Put a checkmark in the correct column.

	YES	NO
Physical characteristics of the organism's body		
The types of minerals within the sediments		
How widespread the species is on the planet		
Whether the organism lives on the land or in the sea		

6. Which of these steps occur as an animal becomes a fossil and becomes visible to humans?

Click on 3 answers.

A After an animal dies, its hard tissues decompose.

B Layers of sediment cover the remains of a dead animal.

C Minerals from the bones dissolve in groundwater.

D Hard tissue is replaced by minerals.

E Movements of the Earth cause the fossils to surface.

Listen to a lecture in a behavioral sciences class.

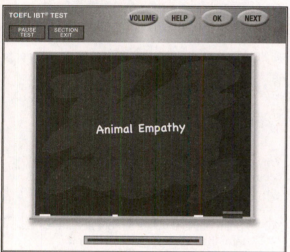

Animal Empathy

068

7. How does the professor introduce the topic of animal empathy?

   Ⓐ By discussing an early experiment with two different animals in Africa

   Ⓑ By comparing empathy in animals to empathy in humans

   Ⓒ By describing an example that is more ambiguous than it first appears

   Ⓓ By telling a personal anecdote to illustrate her point

8. How does the professor organize the lecture?

   Ⓐ She presents two studies whose conclusions do not provide definitive proof.

   Ⓑ She describes various studies in the order they were conducted.

   Ⓒ She proposes an argument and describes the studies that prove it to be true.

   Ⓓ She outlines various studies whose results seem to contradict each other.

9. How does the professor explain the conditions of the study on rats?

   Ⓐ By contrasting the conditions with the study on chimpanzees

   Ⓑ By focusing on the problems that made conclusions of the study inaccurate

   Ⓒ By showing the students a video of the experiment

   Ⓓ By describing a similar situation with humans

10. For which study did the professor suggest each alternative explanation of the animals' behavior?

For each explanation, put a checkmark in the correct column.		
	The study on chimpanzees	The study on rats
To relieve the subject's stress		
To satisfy a social function		
To reciprocate for past actions		

LISTENING

PASSAGE Four (Questions 11–14) 🔊⁰⁶⁹

Listen to part of a lecture in a physiology class.

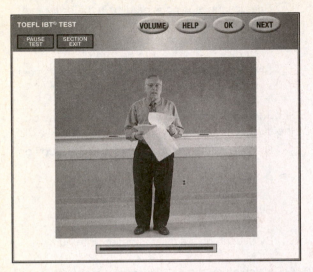

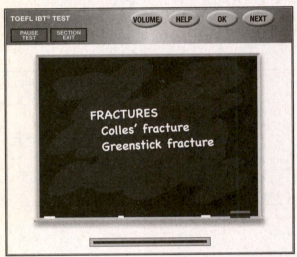

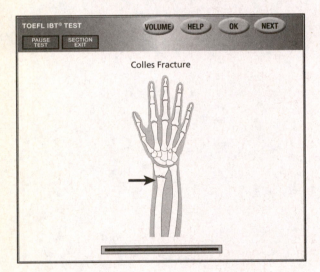

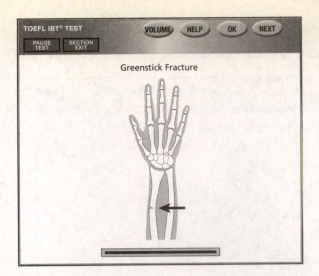

⁰⁷⁰ 🔊

11. How does the professor organize the information in the passage?
    - Ⓐ By presenting a selection of fractures from least to most serious
    - Ⓑ By presenting some specific fractures in order to introduce various treatments for them
    - Ⓒ By explaining one example from each general class of fractures
    - Ⓓ By introducing the healing processes for a variety of fractures

12. Why does the professor discuss the name "compound fracture?"
    - Ⓐ To define it as another name for a multiple fracture
    - Ⓑ To point out that this is a more accurate medical term than other names used for it
    - Ⓒ To remind students that this is just a casually used name and not a medical term
    - Ⓓ To clarify possible confusion around this common term

13. Why does the professor mention ways that people might fall?
    - Ⓐ To show how children get greenstick fractures
    - Ⓑ To indicate the seriousness of fractures that result from falling
    - Ⓒ To illustrate the cause of a very common fracture
    - Ⓓ To show why fractures are typically found in elderly people

14. According to the lecture, how serious are each of these types of fractures?

Put a checkmark in the correct box. This question is worth two points (2 points for 4 correct answers, 1 point for 3 correct answers, and 0 points for 2,1, or 0 correct answers).

	Very serious	May be serious or less serious	Less serious
open fracture	☐	☐	☐
greenstick fracture	☐	☐	☐
Colles' fracture	☐	☐	☐
simple fracture	☐	☐	☐

Listening Skill 6: UNDERSTAND RELATIONSHIPS: INFERENCES AND DRAWING CONCLUSIONS

This type of question asks you to recognize how different ideas or pieces of information in the passage are related. As you listen to a passage, you should listen to the different ideas that are presented and focus on how the ideas are interrelated. You may, for example, be asked to draw a conclusion, predict an outcome, make an inference, recognize a sequence, or determine the cause for a certain effect. It is important to understand that the answer to this type of question is based upon a number of ideas or pieces of information from the passage rather than on a single detail.

Strategies to Answer Relationship Questions

- Listen to how the different ideas in the passage are related.

- Listen to how the speakers react to each others' ideas.

- Draw a conclusion about the speakers' meaning.

Listen and look at an example. 🔊⁰⁷¹

EXAMPLE

You see on the computer screen:

You hear:

(narrator) Listen to a conversation between a tutor and a student.

(student) So, do you think you can help me with the new engineering problem set I e-mailed you yesterday?

(tutor) That depends. Are you serious about wanting to learn the material for this assignment? Because the last time you were here . . .

(student) Don't worry. I looked at it. I solved the easy ones, and I tried to do the confusing ones.

(tutor) Already? OK, so yes, I will meet you here at the peer tutoring center around 7:00 tomorrow night, and we'll go through the hard ones. This time, though, I don't blame you for needing help. This one took me longer than usual.

After you listen to the conversation, the question and answer choices appear on the computer screen as the narrator states the question. This is an inference question that asks you to draw a conclusion based on what the speaker means and the speaker's tone of voice.

You see on the computer screen:

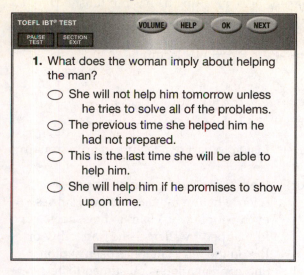

(narrator) Listen again to part of the conversation. Then answer the question.

(man) So, do you think you can help me with the new engineering problem set I e-mailed you yesterday?

(woman) That depends. Are you serious about wanting to learn the material for this assignment? Because the last time you were here . . .

(narrator) What does the woman imply about helping the man?

The second answer choice is correct. The woman implies that she will not help the man unless he is serious about wanting to learn the material for this assignment and implies that he was not serious the last time he was there. The man replies that he has already prepared by attempting the problem set. You can infer that the last time, he had not prepared before she helped him and she did not like it. The first answer choice is incorrect because she says she will help him because he has already tried to solve the problems. The third answer choice is incorrect because she is using last time to refer to when she helped him in the past, not that the present time will be <u>the</u> last or final time. The fourth answer choice is incorrect because the woman does not make any connection between helping him and his ability to be at the peer tutoring center on time.

Now listen and look at another question. 072

You see on the computer screen:

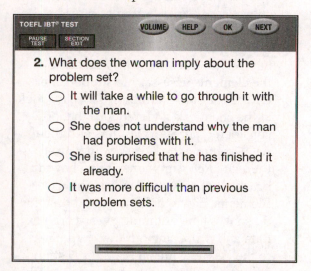

You hear:

(narrator) What does the woman imply about the problem set?

The fourth answer choice is correct. The woman says that she doesn't blame him for needing help, meaning she understands why he needs help. This statement, as well as when she says that this problem set *took . . . longer than usual,* implies that the problem set was harder than previous ones. The first answer choice is incorrect because she does not say or imply anything about how long it will take to help the man. The second answer choice is incorrect because she does understand why he needs help—it was difficult. The third answer choice is incorrect because the man says he *tried to do the confusing ones*, meaning he has not finished. The woman does seem surprised that he has already prepared, however.

Now listen and look at how this type of question applies to a part of a lecture. 🔊 073

Example 2

You see on the computer screen:

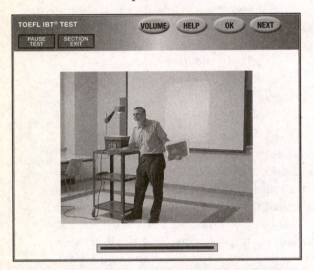

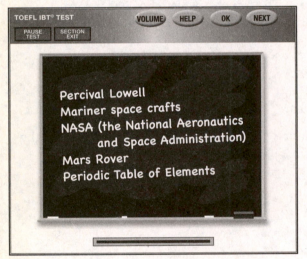

You hear:

(narrator) Listen to part of a lecture in an astronomy class.

(professor) Well, certainly in popular culture— science fiction movies, fictional stories, even people who claim to have been kidnapped by aliens—the possibility of life on the red planet has been explored and confirmation is presumed to be within our grasp. But, no matter what we might imagine or believe, the fact remains that there has never been any verifiable proof of life on Mars. Now . . . scientific investigations have been ongoing for decades, including telescopic observations in the late 1800s by Percival Lowell, and the orbiting *Mariner* spacecrafts of the 1960s and 1970s. But only in the twenty-first century—I know as a young student, this would have been beyond my wildest dreams— umm . . . NASA and the Mars Science Laboratory, or MSL, have been able to collect geochemical samples directly from the surface of Mars. And what have they found? No, not little gray or green beings, however, they did find some of the elements necessary to support life. OK, so for our next unit, we'll take a look at the chemicals and minerals that are considered necessary for life, and then we'll examine the latest findings from the Mars *Rover* missions. If you haven't brushed up on your Periodic Table of Elements, now would be a good time to do so. We'll be examining very complex data and proposing our own hypotheses to the "Is there life on Mars?" question, and you will be expected to move quickly through our research. Don't let a lack of basic chemistry knowledge slow us down.

After you listen to the lecture the question appears on the computer screen as the narrator reads it, followed by answer choices. This is an inference question that asks you to draw a conclusion based on information that is not directly stated by the professor.

You see on the computer screen:

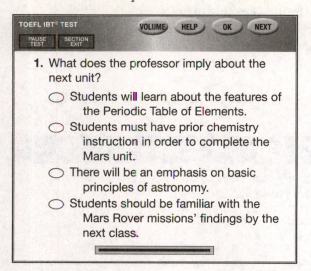

You hear: 🔊 074

(narrator) What does the professor imply about the next unit?

The second answer choice is correct. The professor says that *If you haven't brushed up on your Periodic Table of Elements, now would be a good time to do so*, meaning they should review (brush up on) information they have already learned. The first answer choice is incorrect because the professor says that students should *brush up on the table*, which means they learned it sometime in the past, not that they are going to start learning it. The third answer choice is incorrect because the professor implies that the material is not basic by describing the material to be examined as *complex data*, and stating that *a lack of basic chemistry knowledge* would slow them down. The fourth answer choice is incorrect because the Mars Rover findings are what they will be examining.

Now listen and look at a question that asks you to make a prediction based on conclusions you can draw from the lecture. 🔊 074

You see on the computer screen:

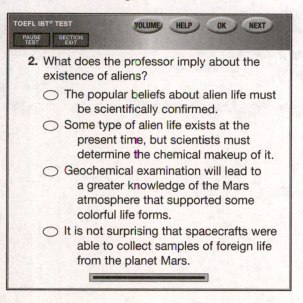

You hear:

(narrator) What does the professor imply about the existence of aliens?

LISTENING

The first answer choice is correct. The professor states that *confirmation is presumed to be within our grasp. But . . . the fact remains that there has never been any verifiable* (clearly demonstrated) *proof of life on Mars.* The second answer choice is incorrect because there has not been *any verifiable proof of life on Mars.* The third answer choice is incorrect because, while it is true that there was a geochemical examination, there is no mention that it led to knowledge about *colorful life forms; no gray or green beings* were found. The fourth answer choice is incorrect because the professor implies that he is surprised at the ability to collect samples from Mars by saying *I know as a young student, this would have been beyond my wildest dreams* and no *foreign life* samples were taken.

The following chart outlines the key points you should remember about relationship questions.

KEY POINTS FOR QUESTIONS ABOUT RELATIONSHIPS	
FREQUENCY OF QUESTION TYPE	Questions that ask about inferences and conclusions are less common. There will usually be 0–1 per passage.
HOW TO IDENTIFY THE QUESTION	What will the speaker **probably/most likely** do next? What does the speaker **imply** . . . ? *(replay)* What can be **inferred** . . . ?
WHERE TO FIND THE ANSWER	Information to answer relationship questions is *not* directly stated in the passage. It is necessary to understand the main points and draw a conclusion based on the main points to answer the question.
HOW TO ANSWER THE QUESTION	1. Listen carefully to each of the points in the passage and how speakers react to each others' ideas. 2. Based on the overall conversation, draw a conclusion about the speaker's meaning. 3. Look for an answer that expresses a relationship that can be inferred from information in the talk. 4. Eliminate the definitely wrong answers, and choose the best answer from the remaining choices.

Correct answers generally do not repeat the exact same vocabulary that was used in the passage.
Incorrect answer choices for inference questions may:
• confuse details of the passage, leading to an incorrect conclusion.
• describe another type or category mentioned in the talk, but not the one the question is asking about.
• be a logical conclusion that does not connect with other information in the passage.
• express a conclusion or inference that is the opposite of what is expressed in the passage.
• be partially correct except for one detail in the answer.

LISTENING EXERCISE 6: Listen to each passage and the questions that follow. Then choose the best answers to the questions.

PASSAGE ONE (Questions 1–2)

Listen to conversation between an advisor and a student.

1. What is implied about the math placement test?
   Ⓐ It is longer and more difficult than the English placement test.
   Ⓑ It is required for all students who register for classes at the university.
   Ⓒ Students usually fail it if they do not study.
   Ⓓ Not passing it will delay the student's entrance into science classes.

2. What is the student most likely going to do?
   Ⓐ Take the English test today and the math test next week
   Ⓑ Take the English, math, and Spanish placement tests next week
   Ⓒ Study a little for the math test and take it next week along with the English test
   Ⓓ Skip the math and Spanish placement tests but take the English test next week

PASSAGE TWO (Questions 3–4)

Listen to a conversation between a professor and a student.

3. What does the professor imply about the research paper?
   Ⓐ Students should choose topics for it that are not politically controversial.
   Ⓑ She does not recommend supporting an argument in the paper that would present a legal challenge.
   Ⓒ Students should not use sources from the Internet for their papers.
   Ⓓ Deadlines are planned to permit major revisions of the paper.

4. What will the student probably do?
   Ⓐ Get some instructions at the library on how to sort his information and use its database
   Ⓑ Choose another topic for his paper and start over again
   Ⓒ Spend more time at the library looking for studies online using the library's computer system
   Ⓓ Make minor adjustments to his outline and resource list to include scientific studies

Listen to part of a lecture in a psychology class.

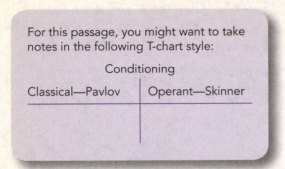

For this passage, you might want to take notes in the following T-chart style:

Conditioning

Classical—Pavlov	Operant—Skinner

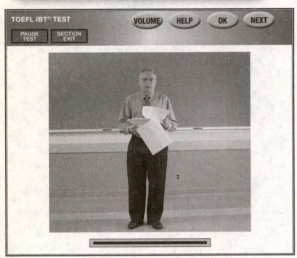

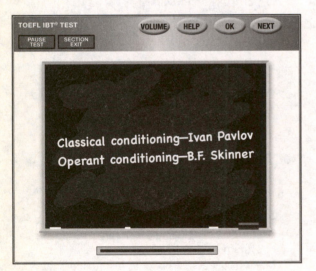

Classical conditioning—Ivan Pavlov
Operant conditioning—B.F. Skinner

5. What does the professor imply about operant conditioning?

Ⓐ It has very few characteristics in common with classical conditioning.

Ⓑ It is actually a more complex form of classical conditioning.

Ⓒ It involves consciously or unconsciously learning the consequences of actions.

Ⓓ It works more easily on animal subjects than human subjects.

6. Which of the following represents a case of classical conditioning?

Ⓐ A child avoids arguing with his sister so his parents will let him watch TV after a few nights of losing the privilege for fighting with her.

Ⓑ A student gives a pigeon a food pellet after it pecks a lever until the pigeon immediately pecks the lever when it is hungry.

Ⓒ A rat avoids going into an area of its cage after receiving shocks in that area.

Ⓓ A researcher sounds an alarm whenever a little boy sees a rabbit until the boy demonstrates a fear of rabbits.

PASSAGE FOUR (Questions 7–9) 081 🔊

Listen to part of a lecture in an economics class.

082

7. What does the professor imply about rent controls?

Ⓐ They prove the economic theory the professor is explaining because they result in lower overall demand for rental units.

Ⓑ They represent an economic theory that can be observed locally.

Ⓒ They are based on an effective economic theory that provides encouragement for investors.

Ⓓ They do not illustrate a logical economic theory because people react to them in unexpected and irrational ways.

8. Which topic would satisfy the professor's requirements?

Ⓐ An in-depth analysis of the theoretical model of diminishing returns

Ⓑ A detailed comparison of the theoretical model of diminishing returns and a theoretical model of diminishing marginal utility

Ⓒ An analysis of the recent failure of National Bank based on the theoretical model of diminishing returns

Ⓓ A detailed comparison of the U.S. stock market crashes of 1929 and 1987

9. Which of the following ways of completing the assignment would satisfy the professor's requirement?

Ⓐ Giving a six-minute presentation and asking at least one question after each student's presentation

Ⓑ Giving a brief presentation followed by five minutes of asking the audience questions

Ⓒ Giving a concise, rehearsed presentation and asking a question after a few other presentations

Ⓓ Giving a presentation similar to the professor's demonstration and asking some questions about other students' presentations

LISTENING

LISTENING EXERCISE (Skills 5–6): Listen to the passage and the questions that follow. Then choose the best answers to the questions.

Listen to part of a lecture in a United States history course.

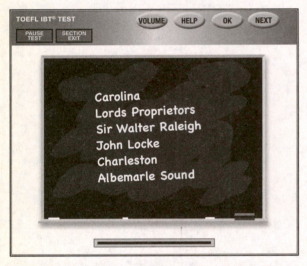

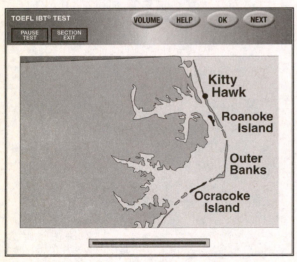

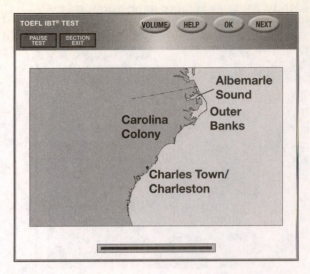

084

1. How does the professor introduce the topic?
   Ⓐ She describes the challenges faced by the first permanent British settlement in North America.
   Ⓑ She explains the reasons that the colony of Virginia was not settled until after Carolina.
   Ⓒ She describes the first attempt at a permanent English colony in North America.
   Ⓓ She lists some examples of the bravery of the first British settlers in North America.

2. Listen again to part of the lecture. Then answer the question.

   What does the speaker imply when she says this:
   Ⓐ The British had already conquered the Virginians in order to establish a colony in Carolina.
   Ⓑ The earlier settlers from Virginia had established residence and would oppose the British rule of law.
   Ⓒ Carolina was composed of multiple colonies acting as one with the Lord Proprietors.
   Ⓓ The proprietors would not meet with any resistance from the Virginians.

3. Why does the professor mention the colonies of Virginia, Massachusetts Bay, and Pennsylvania?
   Ⓐ To contrast successful colonization with the unsuccessful settlement in Roanoke Island
   Ⓑ To establish the geographic proximity of the British settlements
   Ⓒ To illustrate that the result of colonization of Carolina was not unique
   Ⓓ To provide examples of existing settlements in Carolina by 1670

4. Which of the following are aspects of the government drawn up by John Locke for Carolina?

Click on 3 answers

Ⓐ It allowed some colonists to vote for a governing council.

Ⓑ It put control of the colony in the hands of the eight Lords Proprietors.

Ⓒ It provided colonists with a democratic form of government.

Ⓓ It abolished all of the social classes separating the colonists.

Ⓔ It provided some degree of religious tolerance.

5. Why does the professor describe the details of John Locke's plan for government?

Ⓐ To show how it influenced later governments in Carolina

Ⓑ To demonstrate how it was completely modern and advanced

Ⓒ To show why colonists in Carolina thought it was not religious enough

Ⓓ To illustrate its mix of both progressive and old-fashioned elements

6. What does the professor imply about the plan for government drawn up by Locke?

Ⓐ The colonists first welcomed the plan, and then later rejected it.

Ⓑ The people of Charleston disliked it from the beginning.

Ⓒ It was more popular in North Carolina than in South Carolina.

Ⓓ It was a style of government with which the colonists were familiar.

7. Which of the following statements are true of the settlements at Charleston and Albemarle Sound?

Put a checkmark in the correct column.

	Charleston	Albermarle Sound
Governed by Lords Proprietors until 1729		
The capital of the colony of Carolina		
Rebelled against the Lords Proprietors		

LISTENING REVIEW EXERCISE (Skills 1–6): Listen to the passage and the questions that follow. Then choose the best answers to the questions.

Questions 1–6

Listen to a lecture in a botany class.

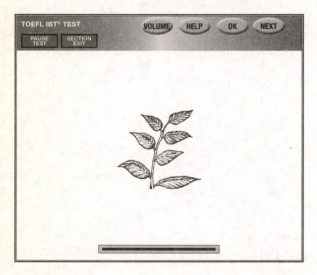

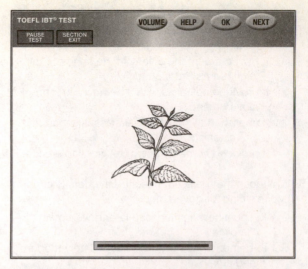

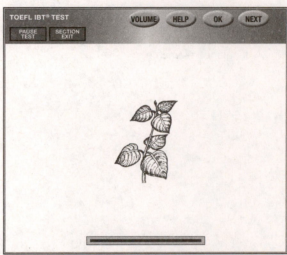

086

1. Why is the professor discussing leaf arrangements with the students?

   Ⓐ To prepare them for an assignment
   Ⓑ To prepare them for an exam
   Ⓒ To review a completed assignment
   Ⓓ To review an exam that was given

2. What points does the professor want to make about leaf arrangements on plants?

   Click on 2 answers.

   Ａ Leaves always appear in even-numbered patterns.
   Ｂ Leaf arrangements are generally quite orderly.
   Ｃ Leaves tend to be arranged far away from nodes.
   Ｄ Leaves tend to be arranged in ways that maximize the light that reaches them.

3. Drag the appropriate description of each type of leaf arrangement to the box below the name of the leaf arrangement. This question is worth 2 points (2 points for 3 correct answers, 1 point for 2 correct answers, and 0 points for 1 or 0 correct answers).

> Click on a phrase. Then drag it to the space where it belongs. Each answer will be used one time only.

Has one leaf per node	Has two leaves per node	Has three leaves per node
Opposite	Alternate	Whorled

4. Drag the appropriate description of leaf arrangement occurrences to the box below the name of the leaf arrangement. This question is worth 2 points (2 points for 3 correct answers, 1 point for 2 correct answers, and 0 points for 1 or 0 correct answers).

> Click on a phrase. Then drag it to the space where it belongs. Each answer will be used one time only.

Is the least common	Is neither the most nor the least common	Is the most common
Opposite	Alternate	Whorled

5. What does the professor say about the botanical garden?

> Click on 2 answers.

A It belongs to the university.
B It has quite a limited number of plants.
C The plants in it are not labeled.
D It has examples of all three leaf structures.

6. Listen again to part of the lecture. Then answer the question.

What does the professor mean when he says this: ◀))

Ⓐ "Class is not over yet."
Ⓑ "I have something more to say."
Ⓒ "You need to be careful."
Ⓓ "Please help me out with this."

LISTENING POST-TEST

L_DIR_A

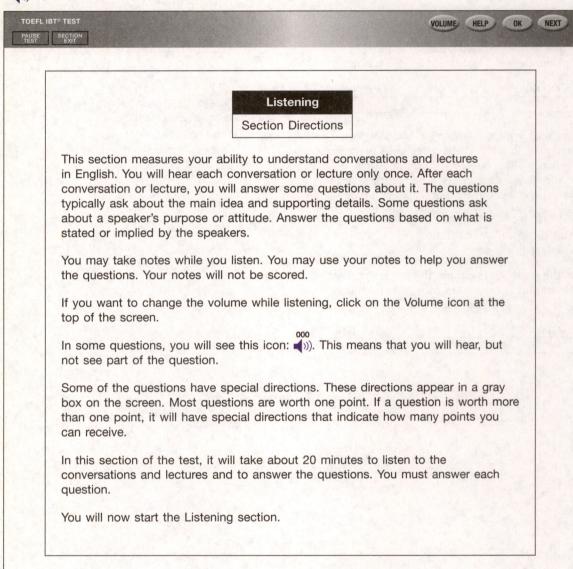

TOEFL IBT® TEST   VOLUME   HELP   OK   NEXT

PAUSE TEST   SECTION EXIT

Listening
Section Directions

This section measures your ability to understand conversations and lectures in English. You will hear each conversation or lecture only once. After each conversation or lecture, you will answer some questions about it. The questions typically ask about the main idea and supporting details. Some questions ask about a speaker's purpose or attitude. Answer the questions based on what is stated or implied by the speakers.

You may take notes while you listen. You may use your notes to help you answer the questions. Your notes will not be scored.

If you want to change the volume while listening, click on the Volume icon at the top of the screen.

In some questions, you will see this icon: 🔊))). This means that you will hear, but not see part of the question.

Some of the questions have special directions. These directions appear in a gray box on the screen. Most questions are worth one point. If a question is worth more than one point, it will have special directions that indicate how many points you can receive.

In this section of the test, it will take about 20 minutes to listen to the conversations and lectures and to answer the questions. You must answer each question.

You will now start the Listening section.

Listen as a student consults with a professor.

088

1. Why is the student talking with the professor?

   Ⓐ To ask the professor to explain an assignment from a class she missed

   Ⓑ To clarify part of an assignment the professor had already described in class

   Ⓒ To get further information about a composer whose music they heard in class

   Ⓓ To ask for permission to research a composer who was not covered in class

2. Listen again to part of the passage. Then answer the question.

   What does the professor mean when he says this:

   Ⓐ The student can choose a composer not covered in class, but it will be more work.

   Ⓑ The professor does not recommend that students choose a composer not previously discussed in class.

   Ⓒ The student should choose a composer not covered in class to show her passion for music.

   Ⓓ The student can choose a composer covered in class, but she will still need to do extra research.

3. Which of these must the students do to complete the project? **This question is worth 2 points** (2 points for 3 correct answers, 1 point for 2 correct answers, and 0 points for 1 or 0 correct answers).

   Click on 3 answers.

   Ⓐ Develop their own original musical style

   Ⓑ Research a composer they choose themselves

   Ⓒ Study the writing style of a composer

   Ⓓ Perform a composition written by a composer

   Ⓔ Write a piece of music in the style of a composer

4. Why does the professor bring up the music of Schubert?

   Ⓐ To give the student an idea for a composer she could choose for her project

   Ⓑ To test whether the student was in class and paying attention all week

   Ⓒ To determine if his music course will be too difficult for the student to complete

   Ⓓ To give an example of another student's project and to give the woman confidence

5. How does the professor seem to feel about the student's ability to complete the assignment?

   Ⓐ He thinks she will probably not be able to write a good piece of music.

   Ⓑ He thinks she will find it easy to complete after she starts.

   Ⓒ He thinks she may find it difficult, but she will enjoy it.

   Ⓓ He thinks she can be successful if she gets a lot of extra help.

LISTENING

Listen to a disscussion in a geography class.

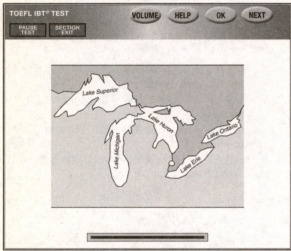

090

6. What is the instructor's main point?

Ⓐ That there are reasons to support the idea that Lake Superior is not the largest of the Great Lakes

Ⓑ That certain arguments support traditional ideas about the Great Lakes

Ⓒ That there are reasons to support the idea that Lake Michigan and Lake Huron are acting as two distinct lakes

Ⓓ That scientific data demonstrate that the Great Lakes are actually one large lake

7. Listen again to part of the passage. Then answer the question.

Why does the instructor say this: 🔊

Ⓐ To confirm that the answer the students believe is really correct

Ⓑ To trick the students into thinking that it is a really easy question

Ⓒ To encourage the students to answer quickly

Ⓓ To show that the answer the students believe is correct is not

8. What does the professor say about the Great Lakes?

Ⓐ A river separates Lake Huron from Lake Michigan.

Ⓑ Features of Mackinac strait point to it being considered the sixth Great Lake.

Ⓒ Several features of the Great Lakes have been misidentified by geographers.

Ⓓ Lakes Huron and Michigan are in a constant state of disequilibrium.

9. Listen again to part of the passage. Then answer the question.

How does the professor seem to feel about the student's response?

Ⓐ It needs further explanation.

Ⓑ Nothing was correct in it.

Ⓒ It was exceptional.

Ⓓ He hopes the other students can do better.

10. Which of the following facts provides evidence for the idea that Lakes Huron and Michigan are acting as one lake? **This question is worth 2 points** (2 points for 3 correct answers, 1 point for 2 correct answers, and 0 points for 1 or 0 correct answers).

For each statement, place a checkmark in the correct column.

	Provide evidence	Does not provide evidence
The elevation of both lakes is the same.		
The flow of water between the two lakes can go back and forth.		
Together Lakes Michigan and Huron are larger than Lake Superior.		

11. What can be inferred from the discussion?

(A) Large lakes are more likely to act as one than smaller lakes.

(B) For two lakes to act as one, they must be at the same overall elevation.

(C) In the future, scientists could find that other Great Lakes also act as one.

(D) For two lakes to act as one, they must be connected by river systems.

Turn to pages 596–598 to diagnose your errors and record your results.

SPEAKING

S_DIR_B

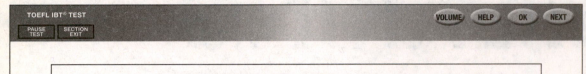

| TOEFL IBT® TEST | VOLUME HELP OK NEXT |

PAUSE TEST | SECTION EXIT

Speaking

Section Directions

In this section of the test, you will be able to demonstrate your ability to speak about a variety of topics. You will answer six questions by speaking into the microphone. Answer each of the questions as completely as possible.

In some questions, you will speak about familiar topics. Your response will be scored on your ability to speak clearly and coherently about the topics.

In other questions, you will first read a short text. Then, the text will go away and you will listen to a talk on the same topic. You will then be asked a question about what you have read and heard. You will need to combine appropriate information from the text and the talk to provide a complete answer. Your response will be scored on your ability to speak clearly and coherently and on your ability to accurately convey information.

In the final questions, you will listen to part of a conversation or lecture. You will then be asked a question about what you have heard. Your response will be scored on your ability to accurately convey information and speak clearly and coherently.

You may take notes while you read and while you listen to the conversations and lectures. You may use your notes to help prepare your response. Listen carefully to the directions for each question. The directions will not be written on the screen.

For each question you will be given a short time to prepare your response. A clock will show how much preparation time is remaining. When the preparation time is up, you will be told to begin your response. A clock will show how much response time is remaining. A message will appear on the screen when the response time has ended.

Question 1

Read the question. You have 15 seconds to plan a response and 45 seconds to give your spoken response.

Who is someone living that you admire? Describe this person and explain why you admire him or her. Use specific reasons and examples to support your opinion.

Question 2

Read the question. You have 15 seconds to plan a response and 45 seconds to give your spoken response.

Some people take vacations that are very relaxing and are not filled with many activities. Other people take very exciting vacations where they do many new things. Which do you think is a better way to spend a vacation and why? Use specific examples and details to support your answer.

Question 3

Read the notice from the Humanities Department about a new policy. You have 45 seconds to read the notice.

Notice from the Humanities Department

Because so many students have been registering for classes in the Humanities Department for which they have not fulfilled the prerequisites, the faculty committee of the Humanities Department has decided that a new policy will go into effect for the coming semester. This new policy, which was instituted by a unanimous vote of the faculty committee of the Humanities Department, is that all students who want to register for courses other than introductory courses in the Humanities Department must obtain signatures from their advisors before registering for these courses. It is the responsibility of advisors to determine if students have completed appropriate prerequisites before authorizing enrollment in courses.

Now listen to two students as they discuss the notice. **091** 🔊

Now answer the following question: **092** 🔊

The woman expresses her opinion of the notice from the Humanities Department. State her opinion and the reasons she gives for holding that opinion.

You have 30 seconds to prepare an answer. After the 30 seconds, you have 60 seconds to respond to the question.

SPEAKING

Question 4

Read the passage about nonverbal communication. You have 45 seconds to read the passage.

> Nonverbal communication is any kind of communication that takes place without the use of words. It can refer to facial expressions such as smiling or frowning; it can refer to movements of the head such as nodding the head to show agreement or shaking it to show disagreement; it can refer to hand gestures such as offering the hand to shake in greeting or waving the hand to say "hello" or "good-bye." Nonverbal communication can also refer to a whole host of other ways of communicating without words inasmuch as nonverbal communication is limited only by exclusion: it is any type of communication *without* words. Communication is verbal if words are used; it is nonverbal if words are not used.

Listen to a passage on the same topic in a psychology class. ⁰⁹³

Now answer the following question: ⁰⁹⁴

Explain how the examples of nonverbal communication given by the professor illustrate limitations of this type of communication.

You have 30 seconds to prepare an answer. After the 30 seconds, you have 60 seconds to respond to the question.

Question 5

Listen to a conversation between two students. ⁰⁹⁵

Now answer the following question: ⁰⁹⁶

The students discuss two possible solutions to the woman's problem. Describe the problem. Then explain which of the two solutions you prefer and explain why.

Question 6

Now listen to part of a lecture in a biology class. ⁰⁹⁷ 🔊))

Now answer the following question: ⁰⁹⁸ 🔊))

Using points and examples from the lecture, explain how it was proven that bats use echolocation.

Turn to pages 599–609 to *assess* the skills used in the test, *score* the test
using the Speaking Scoring Criteria, and *record* your results.

SPEAKING OVERVIEW

The third section on the TOEFL iBT® test is the Speaking section. It takes approximately 20 minutes to complete this section of the test, and you will be asked to respond to six questions. You will speak into a microphone and your response will be recorded and sent to specially trained raters to be scored. Each question will be graded on a scale of 0 to 4, and then the total score will be scaled to a score of 30 so that the Speaking section is worth the same total points as the Reading, Listening, and Writing sections (see **Scoring** for details).

Each of the speaking questions is different and you will use different strategies for each question. There are six questions: two independent questions and four integrated questions. Two of the integrated questions combine reading and listening with speaking, and the other two integrated questions combine listening with speaking.

- The two **independent** questions each consist of a question to be answered using ideas from your personal experience rather than from material that is given to you.

Speaking Question	Usual Expectations For A Response	Preparation Time	Response Time
Question 1: Free-choice Response	Form your own answer based on the question and explain why you chose it, using examples from your personal experience.	15 seconds	45 seconds
Question 2: Paired-choice Response	Choose one answer from two possible actions, situations, or opinions presented in the question and explain the reasons for your choice, using examples from your personal experience.	15 seconds	45 seconds

- The two **reading, listening, and speaking integrated** questions each consist of a reading passage, a listening passage, and a question that asks how the ideas in the two passages are related.

Speaking Question	Usual Expectations For A Response	Reading Time	Listening Time	Preparation Time	Response Time
Question 3: Campus-based Announcement —Opinion	Describe the opinion of one of the speakers concerning a campus announcement and explain the reasons the speaker gives for the opinion.	45–50 seconds	60–90 seconds	30 seconds	60 seconds
Question 4: Academic Setting— Concept/ Example (General/ Specific)	Explain how specific examples concerning two or three points made by the lecturer illustrate a general concept described in a short academic reading passage.	45–50 seconds	60–90 seconds	30 seconds	60 seconds

- The two **listening and speaking integrated** questions each consist of a longer listening passage and a question that asks you to summarize the key point.

Speaking Question	Usual Expectations For A Response	Listening Time	Preparation Time	Response Time
Question 5: Campus-based Problem/ Recommendation (Solution)	Explain the problem described by one or both of the speakers in the conversation. Choose one solution or recommendation from the two or more that are discussed and give reasons or examples to support your choice.	60–90 seconds	20 seconds	60 seconds
Question 6: Academic Setting— Summary	Summarize the main points of a short lecture on an academic subject, using supporting details or examples from the lecture to illustrate the main points.	1½–2 minutes	20 seconds	60 seconds

Scoring the Speaking Section

On the TOEFL iBT® test, all of your responses for the Speaking section will be recorded and sent to trained raters for scoring. Each response will be scored from 0 to 4. Then the total scores for each question will be added together and scaled to give you a score for the Speaking section from 0 to 30, as is done with each of the other three sections on the TOEFL iBT® test.

Each response you record will be scored holistically, meaning that the overall effectiveness of your response will be evaluated. The raters will be evaluating your response in three areas: fluency, language, and development.

Fluency:
The raters will evaluate how smoothly and clearly you give your response. A good response will have a steady, natural flow of speech, without long pauses and with natural pacing. The pronunciation will be understandable, with intonation, rhythm, and sounds that are natural in English. There may be an accent, but it will not interfere with the comprehensibility of the response. On the other hand, a fair or poor response may have long pauses or pronunciation that is not natural in English. In addition, there will not be a good flow of ideas, or the response may be hard to understand because of incorrect intonation and unclear articulation.

Language:
How well you use English to convey ideas will be evaluated. This includes using correct grammar and appropriate vocabulary. A good response will accurately use a variety of language structures, from basic to complex, and grammar to clearly express ideas, whether personal ideas or ideas paraphrased from the reading and listening passages. It will use vocabulary that is appropriate to the topic and to spoken, academic English. There may be a few small grammar or vocabulary usage errors, but these will not make it hard to understand the

response. On the other hand, a fair or poor response will occasionally or often have grammar or vocabulary mistakes that make it difficult to understand the ideas in the response.

Development:

Development means how well you organize your ideas into a coherent answer. It is evaluated differently in the independent questions, where you give your own ideas, and the integrated questions, where you relate ideas from the reading and listening passages. In both cases, however, it includes the organization of your response. A good response is organized in a way that makes it easy to understand the ideas and how they connect to each other. It uses transitional language that shows, for example, whether the ideas expressed are examples, reasons, or new ideas. On the other hand, a fair or poor response sounds somewhat or very disorganized and ideas are disconnected from each other.

In the independent responses (Questions 1 and 2), the clarity of your supporting ideas is evaluated as part of development. A good answer will be organized and coherent, but it will also use examples and reasons that help the listener understand why you have chosen a particular response. On the other hand, a fair or poorly developed response might sound repetitive, give only lists of reasons without connections or transitions, or otherwise fail to use supporting ideas to explain why you have chosen a specific response.

In the integrated responses (Questions 3 to 6), the accuracy of the information you relate is evaluated as part of development. A response that earns a good score will accurately summarize the important information from the passages to clearly answer the question in the time allowed. On the other hand, a fair or poor response will present ideas from the passages in a way that does not clearly and accurately show how the ideas are connected, or it may leave out information that is important to fully answer the question.

If your response accurately answers the question and is easy to understand, it will receive a better score. If there are occasional places where the listener gets confused because of accent, language mistakes, or disorganization, or if the information you convey has slight inaccuracies or small omissions, your response will be rated as fair. On the other hand, if there are major problems in any of these areas, your response will be rated as poor.

To score well in the Speaking section, find activities and exercises that will help you practice all of the three aspects on which you will be evaluated. Speak, read, and listen to academic and everyday English regularly to improve overall fluency, grammar, and vocabulary. Practice summarizing and paraphrasing conversations and academic passages to improve your ability to use English to clearly communicate ideas in an organized way. Study and practice the grammar, language structures, and pronunciation points presented in this chapter to improve your use of language and accent. Familiarize yourself with the expectations for the different questions so that you can concentrate on giving clear, accurate, organized responses on the day of the exam.

There are various strategies and tips that can help you get a high score on the speaking responses. Some strategies, such as using transitional language and English rhythm patterns should be practiced thoroughly before you plan to take the TOEFL iBT® test. Trying to use new strategies for the first time on the test could result in mistakes in responses, which are not clear to the raters. Other strategies, such as answering the question directly in your first introductory statement, can immediately improve your response. You should practice all of the skills presented in this book before you take the test in order to ensure that you record your best answers on the day of the test. Finally, as always, the best way to improve fluency and evaluate the clarity of your speaking is to find opportunities to talk with native English speakers.

Because each of the speaking questions is different, there are different strategies for each one.

The following strategies can help you on the Independent questions in the Speaking section.

STRATEGIES FOR AN INDEPENDENT SPEAKING QUESTION (QUESTION 1 AND QUESTION 2)

1. **Be familiar with the directions.** The directions on every test are the same, so it is not necessary to spend time reading the directions carefully when you take the test. You should be completely familiar with the directions before the day of the test. You can use the time given for the directions to prepare charts for taking notes and organizing your responses, or you can click on Continue to dismiss the directions.

2. **Read the question carefully, and answer the question exactly as it is asked.** The question will ask your opinion on a familiar subject and ask for reasons and examples that support your opinion or choice. Quickly select a response and think of reasons and examples that explain your opinion or choice.

3. **Organize your response.** Use the preparation time to quickly write down a few reasons and examples using abbreviations and symbols. These will help you remember your ideas and will guide the organization of your response. Prepare an introductory sentence that directly answers the question.

4. **Support your opinion with specific examples.** Avoid giving lists of reasons or long descriptions. Concentrate on giving specific examples from your personal experience that show why you have chosen a particular opinion.

5. **Use useful language and transitions to make your response cohesive.** Your response will be easier to understand if you show how the ideas in your response are related using transitions.

6. **Use vocabulary, sentence structures, and grammatical points that you know and are comfortable with.** Although using advanced grammar and vocabulary correctly will help raise your score, it is equally important that your answer be clear and fluent. Using language you are not comfortable with can result in pauses or mistakes that interfere with your natural expression of ideas.

7. **Speak clearly and use natural, English-language rhythm patterns.** It is better to speak clearly so that you can be understood than to race through your response so that you will be able to say more. Use appropriate pauses, intonation, and stress to highlight important points and transitions.

8. **Monitor the time carefully on the title bar of the computer screen.** The title bar indicates how much time you have to prepare and complete your response. Adjust your response, to make it shorter or longer, based on how much time remains.

The following strategies can help you on the reading, listening, and speaking integrated questions in the Speaking section.

STRATEGIES FOR AN INTEGRATED SPEAKING QUESTION (QUESTION 3 AND QUESTION 4: READING, LISTENING, AND SPEAKING)

1. **Be familiar with the directions.** The directions on every test are the same, so it is not necessary to spend time reading the directions carefully when you take the test. You can use the time given for the directions to prepare charts for taking notes and organizing your responses, or you can click on Continue to dismiss the directions.

2. **Do not worry if the material in the integrated question is on a topic that is not familiar to you.** All of the information that you need to plan your response is included in the passages. You do not need any special background knowledge to answer the questions.

3. **Read the passage carefully.** The text will disappear after 45 seconds, and you cannot read it again. It will provide background information for the listening passage that follows.

4. **Take abbreviated notes on the reading passage.** As you are reading the passages, briefly write down a few key words, reasons, or characteristics. Use abbreviations and symbols, and do not try to write down every detail.

5. **Listen carefully to the passage.** You will hear the passage one time only. Listen for two or three main points and try to determine how the listening passage connects to what you have just read.

6. **Take abbreviated notes as you listen to the spoken material.** The speaker(s) will address two or sometimes three major points and give reasons or examples to illustrate these points. Try to note key information to help you organize your response. Do not try to write down everything you hear.

7. **Read and listen to the question carefully.** Even if you are familiar with the question type, read the question carefully to make sure you understand what the question is asking you to do. You must address all parts of the question to receive a high score.

8. **Use the preparation time wisely to organize your response.** You will have 30 seconds to look at your notes and make connections between points made in the reading and listening passages. Decide the order in which you will discuss the major points and how much time you have for each one. If you find it useful, mark your notes with lines and numbers to guide your response.

9. **Deliver your response in a concise and organized manner.** Your introductory statement should address the question asked. Follow your plan to discuss all of the points that the question is asking. Do not give too many details. Give only enough detail so that someone who had not listened to or read the passages would understand your response.

10. **Use useful language and transitions to make your response cohesive.** Your response is easier to understand if you use useful language correctly and show how the ideas in your response are related by using transitions.

11. **Use vocabulary, sentence structures, and grammatical points that you know and are comfortable with.** Although using advanced grammar and vocabulary correctly will help your score, it is equally important that your answer be clear and fluent. Using language you are not comfortable with can result in pauses or mistakes that interfere with your natural expression of ideas.

12. **Speak clearly and steadily with natural English language intonation and stress patterns.** If you speak too quickly, the raters may have difficulty understanding your response. On the other hand, if you pause often and for long periods of time, your answer will sound less fluent. Practice English stress patterns and intonation before you take the test and use them to make your response easier to understand.

13. **Monitor the time carefully on the title bar of the computer screen.** Adjust your response in order to be able to discuss all of the points that the question asks in the time remaining.

The following strategies can help you on the listening and speaking integrated questions in the Speaking section.

STRATEGIES FOR AN INTEGRATED SPEAKING QUESTION (QUESTION 5 AND QUESTION 6: LISTENING AND SPEAKING)

1. **Be familiar with the directions.** The directions on every test are the same, so it is not necessary to spend time reading the directions carefully when you take the test. You can dismiss the directions by clicking on Continue.

2. **Do not worry if the material in the integrated question is on a topic that is not familiar to you.** All of the information that you need to plan your response is included in the listening passages. Preparing for the exam by reading and listening to a variety of English materials may help you understand the passage; however, you will not need any special background knowledge in order to give your response.

3. **Listen carefully to the passage.** You will hear the passage one time only. Be familiar with the question types and the likely organization of the conversation or lecture you will hear. Listen for two or three main ideas and examples or reasons that support the main ideas.

4. **Take organized abbreviated notes as you listen to the spoken material.** Take brief notes on the main points using a chart or organized outline based on the question you are answering. For Question 5 you will be noting suggestions or opinions and reasons, but for Question 6 you will be noting the topic, main ideas, and supporting examples.

5. **Read and listen to the question carefully.** You should be familiar with the type of question that will probably be asked, but the question may be slightly different from what you expect. Make sure you understand the question and exactly what points you must address to fully answer it.

6. **Use the preparation time to organize your response.** You have 20 seconds to decide which points you must make in your response and how much time to spend on each point. If you find it helpful, number the points in your notes to help guide your response.

7. **Deliver your response in a concise and organized manner.** Using your notes as a guide, address all of the main points asked by the question. Give only enough details so that someone who had not listened to the conversation or lecture would understand your response. You will receive a higher score for a simple, organized answer that addresses everything that the question asks than for a response with many unnecessary details that does not fully answer the question.

8. **Use transitions and intonation to make your response cohesive.** Use transitional phrases to show how the ideas in your response are related. Practicing English pronunciation, rhythm, and intonation can help make your answer more understandable to the raters.

9. **Use vocabulary, sentence structures, and grammatical points that you know and are comfortable with.** Although using advanced grammar and vocabulary <u>correctly</u> will help your score, it is equally important that your answer be clear and fluent. Using language you are not comfortable with can result in pauses or mistakes that interfere with your natural expression of ideas.

10. **Speak clearly and steadily.** You should be familiar with the speed at which you can speak steadily and still be understood. Adjust the amount of detail in your responses based on a speaking pace that is comfortable for you.

11. **Monitor the time carefully on the title bar of the computer screen.** Adjust your response in order to be able to address all of the major points that the question requires in the time remaining.

SPEAKING SKILLS

The following skills will help you to implement these strategies in the Speaking section of the TOEFL iBT® test.

SPEAKING QUESTIONS 1 AND 2: INDEPENDENT SPEAKING QUESTIONS

There are two independent speaking questions. Both questions will be about general topics, and they will ask you to express your opinion. They will also ask you to give reasons and examples from your personal experience to support your choice. You will have 15 seconds to think of reasons and examples and to plan your response. You will then have 45 seconds to record your response. A clock on the screen will count down the 15 seconds of preparation time and another will count down the response time. You must answer the question clearly and give examples that support your ideas in order to receive a high score.

SPEAKING QUESTION 1: FREE-CHOICE RESPONSE

The first of these two independent speaking questions is the free-choice response. This question will generally ask about a person, place, event, or object that is familiar to you. There is no single right answer to this question—you should choose an answer that you can support with reasons and examples from your own life. You must choose an answer and quickly think of examples during the 15 seconds of preparation time. Then you should give a fluent, organized response in 45 seconds.

Speaking Question	Usual Expectations For A Response	Preparation Time	Response Time
Question 1: Free-choice Response	Form your own answer based on the question and explain why you chose it, using examples from your personal experience.	15 seconds	45 seconds

Speaking Skill 1: USE YOUR NOTES TO PLAN THE FREE-CHOICE RESPONSE TO SPEAKING QUESTION 1

In this question you will hear and see a question. Then a clock labeled "Preparation Time" will appear on the screen and count down from 15 seconds.

The first step in Speaking Question 1 is to understand the question. You must determine what the question is asking you to do, so you can plan your response. The question may be phrased in different ways. It may ask you what you enjoy or think is important, or it may ask about something you do *not* enjoy. It may ask you what advice you would give a friend about a specific problem or issue, or it may ask you to choose from several options. Nevertheless, the question will always ask for your opinion and for reasons or examples to support that opinion.

Study the following question.

Example Question 1A
What is the most important quality in a good neighbor? Give specific reasons and examples to support your ideas.

As you read this question, you should quickly determine that you must choose one important quality you think a good neighbor should have. Then you should give reasons or examples to explain *why* you think this quality is important. Quickly write down a few ideas as notes. You will have 15 seconds before you speak to plan your ideas.

Study the following notes for planning the response to the question, which include symbols and abbreviations.

NOTES (Example Question 1A):

ANS (answer):	consideration
R (reason):	respect
EX (example):	mom's neighbrs
	usual quiet
	when party, tell—X (not) upset
	nice—shovel snow 4 mom

PLAN (Example Question 1A):

In order to plan the response using your notes, find the information that states your answer to the question, reasons that support your answer, and specific examples that support your answer.

1. Find the information that states your answer to the question from the notes.

   ANS: consideration

   Use this information to give an introductory sentence that will directly answer the question by stating that the most important quality of a good neighbor is consideration.

2. Find the information that states the reason(s) that supports your answer.

   R: respect

   After you have stated the answer to the question, use the reason for choosing it from your notes, that it is a way to show respect, to support your answer and form the next part of the response.

3. Find the specific examples in your notes that support the answer you chose.

   EX: mom's neighbrs usual quiet   when party, tell—X upset
           nice—shovel snow 4 mom

   These notes will help you form the rest of your response to the question by supporting your answer with examples from your own personal experience.

Look at another example that asks you to choose from several options something you would <u>not</u> enjoy.

Example Question 1B
Which of the following activities would you probably NOT enjoy spending most of the day doing: shopping at a mall, hiking in the mountains, playing video games with friends, or relaxing at home alone? Use reasons and details to support your response.

> Notice that abbreviations (shortened words) and symbols are used so that the speaker does not have to write down a lot in the notes. You are the only one who has to understand your notes, so write only enough to help you remember the points you want to make when giving your response. See the note taking section on pp. xxii–xxv.

When you read this question, you should understand that you have to describe something you do *NOT* enjoy.
You are given four different activities to choose from and you must give reasons and details to explain why you would not enjoy doing one of these activities for a day.

Study the following notes for planning the response below.

NOTES (Example Question 1B):

ANS: X home alone

R: like ppl (people) (w/friends)

EX: 1st TV, later bored, want 2 talk
        like 2 get out, interact
        home = lonely, restlss

PLAN (Example Question 1B):

In order to plan the response using your notes, find the information that states your answer to the question, reasons that support your answer, and specific examples that support your answer:

1. Find the information that states your answer to the question from the notes (remember it's a negative question about something you would *not* enjoy doing).

   ANS: home alone

   Use this information to give an introductory sentence that will directly answer the question by stating which of the activities you would not enjoy; spending the day at home alone.

2. Find the information that states the reason(s) that supports your answer.

   R: like ppl (people) (w/friends)

   After you have stated the answer to the question, use the reason for choosing it from your notes, that you like people and being with friends, to support your answer and form the next part of the response.

3. Find the specific examples in your notes that support the answer you chose.

   EX: 1st TV, later bored, want 2 talk
          like 2 get out, interact
          home = lonely, restlss

   These notes will help you form the rest of your response to the question by supporting your answer with examples from your own personal experience (e.g., when home alone, you get bored just watching television and want to talk and interact with others so you aren't lonely or restless).

Quickly thinking of reasons and examples to support your opinion can be challenging for some students, so you should practice coming up with examples quickly while you are preparing for the test. Think of your favorite places, people you like, or memorable events, for example. You should ask yourself why you think a specific way about something, and what you have experienced that influences how you feel about it. For instance, if you admire your uncle because he is patient, then give an example of when he demonstrated this patience. If you would not enjoy a vacation on a cruise ship, think of the activities on a ship you would not like and why they would make you feel unhappy. If your favorite place to go is the beach because your friends are there, describe what you do and how you feel when you are there. In order to come up with good support, think of examples that will clearly show the raters what you mean.

The following chart outlines the key information for using the 15 seconds allowed to plan your response for Speaking Question 1.

KEY POINTS FOR USING YOUR NOTES TO PLAN THE FREE-CHOICE RESPONSE	
UNDERSTAND THE QUESTION	Read each question carefully and decide what you must do to fully answer it.
CHOOSE A RESPONSE	Quickly choose a response you can support with reasons or examples from your own experience.
GIVE REASONS AND SPECIFIC EXAMPLES	Base the number of points you will include in your response on how fast you can deliver your answer. If you can speak fluently and clearly, you can give more than one reason or example. If you speak slowly, give one reason and support it with one or two specific examples.

SPEAKING EXERCISE 1: For each of the following questions, prepare a plan that shows the reasons and examples that you will include in your response. On the actual TOEFL iBT® test, you have only 15 seconds to write ideas and plan your response. While doing these practice exercises, time yourself and try to increase the speed at which you can think of reasons and examples.

The first question has a plan to show you an example of a question type that asks you to give advice to a friend about a problem or a specific issue. The notes (underlined) use many symbols and abbreviated words because the speaker does not have much time to write many words. He has written only enough to remind himself of the ideas he wants to use when he gives the response. The notes are explained in parentheses so that you can understand what they mean. When you write your notes, they should look similar to what is underlined. Use them to remind yourself of ideas and to help you organize your response.

1. Imagine that a friend asks you for advice on how to learn English. Indicate what advice you would give to your friend and explain the reasons you would give this advice.

> ANS: practice (The best way to learn English is to practice it.)
>
> R: pt = commun (The point of learning a language is to communicate.)
>
> EX: speak ↑ fluency (By practicing speaking, you increase fluency.)
> —spoke w/Ss, Eng club (When I was learning English, I spoke with other students; went to an English club.)
>
> listen, read (You should also practice listening and reading.)
> —TV = ev-day Eng ↑ (Watching TV programs helped me learn everyday English to communicate better. On TV, I often heard . . .)
> —read Eng news = ↑vocab, cult (Reading the news in English improved my vocabulary and helped me understand the culture.)

2. Who has helped you the most to get where you are today, and how has that person helped you? Use specific examples to support your response.

> ANS:
>
> R:
>
> EX:

3. What is a place you go to often and that you enjoy? Describe the place and explain why you like it. Use specific reasons and examples to support your answer.

> ANS:
>
> R:
>
> EX:

4. Describe an activity that you have to do regularly but do NOT enjoy doing. Explain the reasons the activity is not enjoyable for you, using examples and details to support your response.

> ANS:
>
> R:
>
> EX:

5. What is your favorite day of the year? Describe it and explain why it is your favorite day. Use examples and details to support your response.

> ANS:
>
> R:
>
> EX:

6. What kind of movie do you NOT enjoy watching: an action movie, a horror movie, a science-fiction movie, a drama or art film, for example? Explain why you do not enjoy this type of movie using reasons and examples from your personal experience.

> ANS:
>
> R:
>
> EX:

7. What advice would you give someone who is moving to your city from another country? What do you think are the most important things for this person to know and why? Use specific examples to support your response.

> ANS:
>
> R:
>
> EX:

8. Describe a time in your life when you made an important decision. Explain the decision and the reasons you believe it was important. Give reasons and details to support your response.

> ANS:
>
> R:
>
> EX:

9. Think of a purchase you regret making. (A purchase is a thing or a service that you buy.) Describe the purchase and explain why you think it was a bad idea.

> ANS:
>
> R:
>
> EX:

10. If you were going to rent an apartment in a good location, would you place the most importance on the qualities of the building (for example, an elevator, a place to exercise, or a pool), on the apartment (for example, lots of light, wood floors, or carpeting), or simply on price and size? Use reasons and examples to support your response.

> ANS:
>
> R:
>
> EX:

Speaking Skill 2: USE YOUR PLAN TO MAKE THE FREE-CHOICE RESPONSE TO SPEAKING QUESTION 1

After you have planned your response, you need to record it into the microphone. In order for the raters to understand your response, you should speak clearly and steadily. Do not pause for long periods, and do not speak too quickly, or the raters may not be able to understand you. While you are giving your response, watch the time. You can add more examples if there is time, but it is probably better not to include a planned example rather than to try to speak very quickly to add more information. Speaking too quickly can cause you to make more pronunciation and grammar mistakes. In summary, adjust your plan and the number of points you give to the speed at which you are comfortable speaking, not the reverse.

When you are delivering your response for Speaking Question 1, you should keep several strategies in mind:

- Start with an introductory statement first, which directly answers the question.

- Give a reason for your answer, using your notes and your plan as a guide.

- Support your answer with specific examples from your personal experience.

- Keep track of the time and adjust your answer accordingly to add or omit information.

- Use transitions, appropriate intonation, and pauses to make your answer cohesive and easier to understand.

Look at the plan based on the notes for the response to Example Question 1A. Then, look at and listen to a sample response based on the plan.

Example Question 1A

What is the most important quality in a good neighbor? Give specific reasons and examples to support your ideas.

PLAN (Example Question 1A):

Answer: Use this part of the plan to form an introductory statement for the response that states your answer.

consideration

Reason: State the reason for the answer.

respect

Examples: Use this part of plan to form the rest of your response to the question by giving examples from your personal experience to support your answer.

mom's neighbors usual quiet   when party, tell—X upset

nice—shovel snow 4 mom

SAMPLE RESPONSE (Example Question 1A): 🔊 **099**

For me, the most important quality a good neighbor can have is consideration. Consideration means doing nice things for your neighbor and not doing annoying things. The reason being considerate is so important is that it's the way to show respect for your neighbor. I think that's the most important thing for helping people get along with each other. For example, my mom's neighbors are really considerate. They're usually quiet, but if they do have parties, they always tell my mom before they do. That way she doesn't get upset because she knows it'll be noisy. They also do nice things for her, like shovel the snow away from the front of her house. And if she goes out of town, they watch her house for her.

You should notice that the first statement in the response answers the question. The reason that the speaker chose consideration is given, and it is illustrated with specific examples from the speaker's experience. The speaker follows her plan, but decides to add another example in the response (*And if she goes out of town, they watch her house for her.*). This response does not have a concluding sentence; a concluding sentence is not necessary for a high score. It is better to spend time on a good example or explanation than on a concluding sentence. Transitions and useful language (highlighted) are used to show how the points in the response are related to each other and to the main idea.

Now look at the plan based on the notes for the response to Example Question 1B. Then, look at and listen to a sample response based on the plan.

Example Question 1B

Which of the following activities would you probably NOT enjoy spending most of the day doing: shopping at a mall, hiking in the mountains, playing video games with friends, or relaxing at home alone? Use reasons and details to support your response.

PLAN (Example Question 1B):

> **Answer:** Use this part of the plan to form an introductory statement for the response that states your answer.
>
> X home alone
>
> **Reason:** State the reason for the answer.
>
> like ppl (w/friends)
>
> **Examples:** Use this part of plan to form the rest of your response to the question by giving examples from your personal experience to support your answer.
>
> 1st TV, later bored, want 2 talk
>
> like 2 get out, interact
>
> home = lonely, restlss

SAMPLE RESPONSE (Example Question 1B): 🔊 ¹⁰⁰

> Of all these activities, I would not enjoy spending a day at home alone. That's because I like being with other people. I like doing things with friends, but a whole day at home alone would not be fun. I could watch TV for a while, but I get bored after a few hours alone, and I want someone to talk to. Plus, I like to get out of my house. I like to walk around and have contact with other people. On the other hand, if I'm home alone all day, I feel lonely and restless, not happy.

This response answers the question in an introductory statement. It gives the reason and then examples of how the speaker feels when he is at home alone, following his plan for the response. The response includes useful language and transitions (highlighted) to show how ideas in the response are connected. This response has a concluding sentence that summarizes how the speaker feels about being home alone. Although it is not necessary to have a conclusion, if you have a few seconds left and no more examples, you might consider adding one sentence that summarizes the response.

While you practice before taking the TOEFL iBT® test, time and evaluate your own responses. If possible, record yourself. Practice giving opinions, reasons, and examples using transitions, and practice features of natural English pronunciation. This will help you to build fluency and become familiar with how many points you can include in the response time given.

The following chart outlines the key information for using the 45 seconds allowed to make your response for Speaking Question 1.

KEY POINTS FOR USING YOUR PLAN TO MAKE THE FREE-CHOICE RESPONSE	
START WITH AN INTRODUCTION	Start your response with an introduction that directly answers the question.
GIVE REASONS FROM YOUR PLAN	Give reasons that you can support with specific examples. Use your plan to help guide your response, but consider adjusting your response if you think of new examples.
USE EXAMPLES FROM YOUR EXPERIENCE	You should give specific examples from your personal experience to show why you chose your answer. Do not give lists or long descriptions. Concentrate on using brief, but relevant examples to illustrate one or two reasons.
BE AWARE OF TIMING	As you speak, you should keep track of the time and adjust your response to make sure you fully answer the question. A concluding sentence is not necessary, but you might consider adding one if you have some time remaining.

The useful language and pronunciation tips below can help you make your response easier to understand. Practice this language and these tips in the weeks before you take the TOEFL iBT® test.

USEFUL LANGUAGE AND TRANSITIONAL PHRASES
Practice using key structures in the weeks before you take the TOEFL iBT® test until you are comfortable and fluent with them. This way you can use them naturally when you give your spoken answers on the test. Although you should use more formal transitions in your writing, the language given in these boxes is what will sound natural in a spoken response.
To give reasons: *The reason (that)* + subject + verb . . . + *is that* . . . *That's because* *First of all/For one thing,* The reason the kitchen is my favorite room is that it's . . . I hate dusting furniture. That's because it's boring. My favorite food is sushi. First of all/For one thing, it's healthy.
To add more points: *Another reason/example . . . is/was . . .* *Plus . . .* *In addition . . .* *Subject + (auxiliary/be verb) + also + verb* Another example of when speaking Spanish was useful was . . . My uncle encouraged me to study. Plus he read to me a lot. You can also ask questions more easily. They also have more . . .
To give examples: *For example, For instance* *(noun/noun phrase), like/such as + noun(s)* *Like . . .* (informal) OR *What I mean is . . .* We saw a lot of beautiful places. For example, we visited . . . There are a lot of sports I enjoy playing like soccer, tennis, or biking. He was consistent. Like he made everyone obey the same rules. He was consistent. What I mean is he made everyone obey the same rules.

MAKING YOUR RESPONSE EASIER TO UNDERSTAND:
Using pauses and intonation to mark transitions.

Some features of English pronunciation can greatly affect how well a listener will understand your response. These suggestions will introduce some of these features and give tips on how to make your speaking sound more natural to an English speaker. You can find more information and practice for these pronunciation features on the Internet.

HOW ENGLISH PRONUNCIATION FUNCTIONS	Pauses can indicate changes in ideas. New ideas generally have a higher pitch and volume.	. . . for helping people get along with each other. (pause) For EXAMPLE, (short pause) my MOM'S NEIGHBORS are . . .
YOUR RESPONSE	You should pause briefly after you finish a point, and raise your voice slightly as you begin the next point. Doing this can immediately make it easier to understand your response because the listener will understand when you are changing to a new idea.	

SPEAKING EXERCISE 2: Create responses for the independent speaking questions that you have been working on in Speaking Skills 1–2. You have 45 seconds to make your response. Follow your plan and time yourself. Adjust your plan and repeat your response until you can fit it into 45 seconds.

SPEAKING REVIEW EXERCISE (SKILLS 1–2): Read each question. On a separate piece of paper, try to use only 15 seconds to take notes on the main points of each response. Use abbreviations and symbols (see note taking on pp. xxii–xxv). Then respond to each question in 45 seconds.

1. Describe a job that is interesting to you and explain why it is interesting. Use specific examples to support your response.

2. What do you believe is a good age to get married? Explain the reasons for your opinion using specific examples to support your response.

3. A city can invest money in improving safety, for example, by increasing law enforcement and the number of police, or by improving infrastructure, such as roads or water-delivery systems. Or cities might invest in attractions such as parks or sports stadiums. What do you think is the best way for a city to invest its resources and why? Use specific details and examples in your response.

4. Which type of class, mathematics, art, language, or history would you NOT enjoy taking? Explain why you would not like to take this type of class using examples and details to support your response.

5. Describe the most important thing that you own. It might be important for practical, professional, or personal reasons. Explain why this object is important to you using examples and details to support your response.

SPEAKING QUESTION 2: THE PAIRED-CHOICE RESPONSE

The second speaking question is similar to the first question. The timing for preparation and for a response is the same, and you will be asked a question that will be based on your personal experience. In addition, you will also be required to give reasons and specific examples to explain your choice. The difference between the two questions is that in the second question, you will be asked to choose between two options and give reasons for your choice. It does not matter which choice you select; there is no "correct" answer. Both choices can be supported, so you should choose whichever response you can most fully explain with personal reasons and examples.

Speaking Question	Usual Expectations For A Response	Preparation Time	Response Time
Question 2: Paired-choice Response	Choose one answer from two possible actions, situations, or opinions presented in the question and explain the reasons for your choice, using examples from your personal experience.	15 seconds	45 seconds

Speaking Skill 3: USE YOUR NOTES TO PLAN THE PAIRED-CHOICE RESPONSE TO SPEAKING QUESTION 2

A question will appear on the screen and a narrator will read it. Then a clock labeled "Preparation Time" will appear and count down from 15 seconds.

The first step in Speaking Question 2 is to understand the question. You must determine what two options the question is asking you to choose from and who the question is asking about. The question may ask about something that is a personal preference, for example, what is best for you, or the question may ask which of two options you think is better for a group of people or an organization, such as students, a business, or young people. Whether you are answering for yourself or another group, you should think of reasons and examples from your own experience to support your choice.

Study the following question.

Example Question 2A
Do you like to try new kinds of food or eat the same kind of food all the time? Explain your choice using reasons and examples to support your response.

You should notice that the question is asking about you personally, and whether *you like to try new kinds of food* or to *eat the same kind of food*. You must state your choice and then explain why you chose it with reasons and examples from your experience. Quickly write down a few ideas as notes. You will have 15 seconds before you speak to plan your ideas.

Study the following notes for planning a response to the question.

NOTES (Example Question 2A):

> ANS: *pref eat same food, X (not) new food*
>
> IDEA 1: *Pref same food*
>
> R: <u>*X like new food*</u>, *new ingred = scary, I'm picky*
>
> EX: <u>*fancy restrnt*</u>—*weird ingred, fruit w/meat X (not) taste good*

PLAN (Example Question 2A):

In order to plan the response using your notes, find the option you chose (your answer), reasons that support your choice, and the examples that support your choice:

> 1. Find the option or preference you chose to answer the question from the notes. Find any additional ideas that expand your answer.
>
>   ANS: *pref eat same food*
>
>   IDEA 1: *pref eat same food, X (not) new food*
>
>   This information will help you form an introductory statement that states which option you prefer.
>
> 2. Find the reasons in the notes that support the choice you made.
>
>   R: *new ingred=scary*
>
>   *I'm picky*
>
>   This information will help you form the next part of your response, which states the reasons for your choice.
>
> 3. Find the specific examples in your notes that support the option you chose.
>
>   EX: <u>*fancy restrnt*</u>—*weird ingred, fruit w/meat X (not) taste good*
>
>   These notes will help you form the rest of your response to the question by supporting your choice with examples from your own personal experience.

The introductory statement indicates which of the two options the speaker prefers by saying that the speaker prefers to eat food she knows, but does not like new food. After this, the plan indicates that the speaker will give two reasons why she does not like new food: new ingredients are scary to her, and she is picky about food. Then the speaker will describe a specific example from her own experience: a visit to a fancy restaurant, which served food with weird ingredients and where nothing tasted good.

Look at another question that asks you to choose which of the two options you think is better for other people.

Example Question 2B

Some universities are large and have thousands of students who are provided with many resources. Others are much smaller, with fewer students who may receive more personal attention. Which do you think is better for students and why? Use specific reasons and examples to support your answer.

The question asks you to choose between *large universities* and *small universities*, and say why you believe your choice is better *for students*. You may support your choice with examples from what you know about the situation generally, from your personal experience, or both.

Study the notes for planning the response below.

NOTES (Example Question 2B):

```
ANS:    lrg univ

R1:     >opport 4 Ss
        + profs + facil

EX:     friend schl big
        chem prof famous, imprt research
        + lab equip

R2:     more fun + act w/1000's Ss

EX:
```

PLAN (Example Question 2B):

In order to plan the response using your notes, find the option you chose (your answer), reasons that support your choice, and the examples that support your choice:

1. Find the option or preference you chose to answer the question from the notes.

   ANS: lrg univ

   This information will help you form an introductory statement that states which option you prefer.

2. Find the first reason in the notes that supports the choice you made and the example that supports the first reason.

   R1: >opport 4 Ss, + profs + facil

   EX: <u>friend schl big</u>=chem prof famous, imprt research

   + lab equip

   This information will help you form the next part of your response, which states the reasons for your choice and provides an example from your personal experience to support the first reason.

3. Find the second reason in the notes that supports the choice you made and the example that supports the first reason.

   R2: more fun+ act w/1000's Ss

   These notes will help you form the rest of your response to the question by adding another reason from your own personal experience.

You can see in this plan that the speaker has chosen large universities, and gives a general reason to support this: there are more opportunities for students. The reasons he offers to support this choice are better professors and more facilities, and they are illustrated with an example from the speaker's experience, his friend's school. The plan gives examples of advantages his friend's school has. A second reason is then planned, which is that big universities are more fun because there are more students and activities, but the speaker has not written examples for this reason yet. This plan is easy to adjust while the speaker is recording his response. If there is time, and he thinks of examples, the second reason can be included. On the other hand, if time is running out, the second reason can be omitted. The first reason, with its examples, provides enough information to answer the question.

It is almost always possible to think of situations and reasons for <u>both</u> choices. However, it is not recommended that you try to support both sides. Your response will probably sound disorganized and poorly supported since you will be trying to include too many ideas. Choosing one option and supporting the choice with reasons and examples usually results in a clearer response and a higher score. You may also choose to say something about why you do not like the other choice, as an alternative to a conclusion.

When giving examples from their personal experience, most students find it easier to give truthful examples. In addition, the truth usually sounds more convincing to the raters. Nevertheless, if you can make it sound believable, it may be better to give an invented, made-up example than no example at all.

The following chart outlines the key information for using the 15 seconds allowed to plan your response for Speaking Question 2.

KEY POINTS FOR USING YOUR NOTES TO PLAN THE PAIRED-CHOICE RESPONSE	
UNDERSTAND THE QUESTION	Read each question carefully. Make sure that you are clear about what choice you are being asked to make, and who it is being asked about.
CHOOSE A RESPONSE	Quickly choose a response you can support with reasons or examples.
GIVE REASONS AND EXAMPLES	Briefly note reasons and examples from your experience that support your choice.
BE AWARE OF TIMING	Base the number of points you will include in your response on how fast you can deliver your answer. If you can speak fluently and clearly, you can give more than one reason or example. If you speak slowly, give one reason and support it with one or two specific examples.

SPEAKING EXERCISE 3: For each of the following questions, prepare a plan that shows the type of information you will include in your response. On the actual TOEFL iBT® test, you have only 15 seconds to do this. While doing these practice exercises, time yourself and try to increase the speed at which you can think of reasons and examples. Sample notes for the first question have been provided for you.

Remember to refer to the note taking section on pages xxii–xxv for meanings of common abbreviations and symbols.

1. Some universities require undergraduate students to live on campus in dormitories their first year. Other universities allow freshmen to live wherever they want. Which do you think is better for students and why?

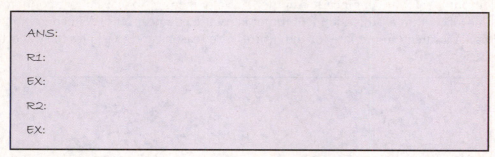

ANS: in dorm

RS 1:   meet >ppl

EX: 1styr @ college, met doz Ss

R 2:   get help

EX: 1styr, X (not) know campus, classes, places, etc. ↑ppl 2 get ideas fr

2. Some people prefer to buy their own food and cook it at home. Others find that frequently eating out at restaurants is better suited to their lives. Which option is better for your current lifestyle and why? Use details to support your response.

ANS:

R1:

EX:

R2:

EX:

3. Some people believe that sixteen- and seventeen-year-olds should be allowed to drive. Others believe that people should not drive until they are eighteen or older. Which option do you support and why? Give examples and details to support your response.

ANS:

R1:

EX:

R2:

EX:

4. Is it better to have a career that pays a lot of money, but requires long hours and limits your time with your family, or a career that does not pay so much, but has shorter hours and allows you more time with your family? Use reasons and examples to support your choice.

ANS:

R1:

EX:

R2:

EX:

SPEAKING

5. Some people believe that children should begin studying math and writing at a very young age. Others believe that young children should spend their time playing. Which do you believe is better for children and why? Use examples and details to support your response.

ANS:

R1:

EX:

R2:

EX:

6. One way to prepare for the future job market is to try to learn something about a lot of different jobs within a professional field such as mechanical engineers, civil engineers, or computer software engineers. Another strategy is to try to learn a lot about only one specific job within a profession (computer software engineer only). Which do you think is a better strategy to prepare for the future? Use reasons and examples to support your response.

ANS:

R1:

EX:

R2:

EX:

7. Some students study alone, while others study with friends. Which do you think is better for students and why? Use details and examples to support your response.

ANS:

R1:

EX:

R2:

EX:

8. Some people prefer to learn a new skill by watching someone else do it first. Others prefer to learn a new skill by trying to do it by themselves. Which method of learning do you prefer and why? Use specific examples to support your response.

ANS:

R1:

EX:

R2:

EX:

9. If your school was given a large amount of money, would you prefer that it be used to build new classrooms or for buying new computers? Use reasons and details to support your response.

> ANS:
>
> R1:
>
> EX:
>
> R2:
>
> EX:

10. Some people make decisions quickly based on their past experience. Others carefully consider all options and make decisions slowly. Which option do you believe results in better decisions? Use reasons and details to support your response.

> ANS:
>
> R1:
>
> EX:
>
> R2:
>
> EX:

Speaking Skill 4: USE YOUR PLAN TO MAKE THE PAIRED-CHOICE RESPONSE TO SPEAKING QUESTION 2

When you are delivering your response for Speaking Question 2, you should keep several strategies in mind:

- Start with an introductory statement that directly answers the question and states which option you prefer.

- Give a reason for your choice, using your notes and your plan as a guide.

- Support your choice with specific examples from your personal experience.

- Keep track of the time and adjust your answer accordingly to add or omit information.

- Use transitions, appropriate intonation, and pauses to make your answer cohesive and easier to understand.

Look at the plan based on the notes for the response to Example Question 2A. Then, look at and listen to a sample response based on the plan.

SPEAKING

Example Question 2A

Do you like to try new kinds of food or eat the same kind of food all the time? Explain your choice using reasons and examples to support your response.

PLAN (Example Question 2A):

Answer: Use this part of the plan to form an introductory statement for the response that states your answer by indicating which option you prefer.

Pref eat same food

x (not) new food

Reasons: State the reasons for the option you prefer.

new ingred = scary

I'm picky

Examples: Use this part of plan to form the rest of your response to the question by giving examples from your personal experience to support your answer.

fancy restrnt—weird ingred, fruit w/meat X taste good

SAMPLE RESPONSE (Example Question 2A): 🔊 **101**

> I prefer to eat the food I know rather than new food. I just don't like eating new things. I usually think new ingredients are kind of scary. Also, it turns out that I'm picky about food and don't like a lot of things. One example is the last time I went to a nice restaurant with friends. Everything on the menu had weird ingredients, like fruit with meat. It all sounded awful, so I ordered a nice, reliable steak. Then when everyone got their meals, we all tried everything. Everyone else's food tasted as strange as I'd imagined it would.

This response answers the question in the first statement. The speaker then uses the transition *also* to introduce the reasons why she does not like new food. Two specific reasons are given, and then the speaker illustrates those reasons with a specific example from her experience. Transitions (highlighted) are used to connect ideas. The response is good, but it is long and the supporting example comes at the end of the response. You can plan a creative response like this one if you are confident and have a very high level of fluency, but if you run out of time without completely answering the question, your score may be lowered.

Look at the plan based on the notes for the response to Example Question 2B. Then, look at and listen to a sample response based on the plan.

Example Question 2B

Some universities are large and have thousands of students who are provided with many resources. Others are much smaller, with fewer students who may receive more personal attention. Which do you think is better for students and why? Use specific reasons and examples to support your answer.

PLAN (Example Question 2B):

> **Answer:** Use this part of the plan to form an introductory statement for the response that states your answer by indicating which option you prefer.
>
> lrg univ
>
> **Reason 1 and Example:** State the first reason for the option you prefer and the example that supports this reason.
>
> >opport 4 Ss
>
> + profs + facil
>
> friend schl big
>
> chem prof famous, imprt research
>
> + lab equip
>
> **Reason 2:** State the second reason for the option you prefer.
>
> more fun+ act w/1000's Ss

SAMPLE RESPONSE (Example Question 2B): 🔊 ¹⁰²

> I think a large university with thousands of students is better than a smaller university because it offers more opportunities to the students. For example, a big university has a lot more money to hire world-famous professors and pay for better facilities. A friend of mine goes to a big university, and he has a lot of opportunities. For example, he works with a famous chemistry professor who is doing important research. So my friend can be a part of it. And the school also has great laboratory equipment. A little school wouldn't have enough money to hire such important professors, and they couldn't afford the best equipment.

This response has an introductory statement that gives the speaker's preference and the reason he has for the preference. Next, the speaker gives two general examples, better professors and facilities. After that, the speaker gives the specific example of his friend's school, describing a famous professor and great laboratory equipment. Then, instead of following his plan, the speaker omits the second example and instead contrasts the examples he gave for the large university with a small school. The speaker decided to say something about why he did not prefer the other choice, as an alternative to his conclusion. The response is more cohesive than the original plan. In the response, the speaker chose to explain the examples a little more fully instead of adding another reason for which he may not have had enough support.

Before taking the TOEFL iBT® test, be familiar with which planning strategies work for you and with the grammar of useful language. If you are comfortable with the organization and language for your response, you can concentrate on making your pronunciation clear and fluent as you speak.

The following chart outlines the key information for using the 45 seconds allowed to make your response for Speaking Question 2.

KEY POINTS FOR USING YOUR PLAN TO MAKE THE RESPONSE	
START WITH AN INTRODUCTION	Start your response with an introductory statement that directly states which of the choices you prefer.
GIVE REASONS FROM YOUR PLAN	Give reasons that you can support with specific examples. Use your plan to help guide your response, but consider adjusting your response if you think of new examples.
USE EXAMPLES FROM YOUR EXPERIENCE	You should give specific examples from your personal experience to show why you chose your answer. Do not give lists or long descriptions. Concentrate on using brief, but relevant examples to illustrate one or two reasons.
BE AWARE OF TIMING	As you speak, you should keep track of the time and adjust your response to make sure you fully answer the question. A concluding sentence is not necessary, but you might consider adding one if you have some time remaining.

The useful language and pronunciation tips below can help you make your response easier to understand. Practice this language and these tips in the weeks before you take the TOEFL iBT® test.

USEFUL LANGUAGE AND TRANSITIONAL PHRASES
To give your opinion: *In my opinion,* *I think/believe* *For me,* In my opinion, freshmen should live on campus. I believe it's better to take time for important decisions. For me, small classes are better than larger ones.
To give a preference: *I prefer + noun + rather than/to + noun* *I prefer + verb + -ing + rather than/instead of + verb + -ing* *I'd (I would) rather + base verb + than + base verb* I prefer the city rather than the country. I prefer eating in restaurants instead of cooking. I'd rather play sports than watch them.
To give results/reasons: *. . . , so . . .* *That way . . .* *That's why . . .* She got married early, so she could start a family young. I take time to decide. That way I make fewer mistakes. I need a quiet place to study. That's why I prefer to study alone.

MAKING YOUR RESPONSE EASIER TO UNDERSTAND: Using correct sentence stress.		
HOW ENGLISH PRONUNCIATION FUNCTIONS	Stressed syllables in content words, such as nouns, verbs, and negatives have a higher pitch and volume. The syllables are also longer. Structure words, such as prepositions, pronouns, and auxiliary verbs have lower pitch and volume, and syllables are shorter.	*. . . suchimPORtant proFESsors, and they COULDn'tafFORD the BEST eQUIPment.*
YOUR RESPONSE	You should lengthen and put more emphasis on stressed syllables in content words like nouns, adjectives, verbs, negatives, and adverbs. Doing this will make it easier for the raters to hear important information and make your English sound more natural.	

SPEAKING EXERCISE 4: Create responses for the independent speaking questions that you have been working on in Speaking Skills 3–4. Use the plans you have made and time yourself as you give your response. You have 45 seconds to make the response. Adjust your plan and repeat your response until you can fit it into the 45-second response time.

SPEAKING REVIEW EXERCISE (SKILLS 3–4): Read each question. On a separate piece of paper, try to use only 15 seconds to take notes on the main points of each response. Use abbreviations and symbols. (See note taking on pp. xxii–xxv.) Then respond to each question in 45 seconds.

1. If your teacher makes a mistake, is it better to correct the teacher or ignore the mistake? Use reasons and examples to support your response.

2. Some people say that a person has to take chances in life to be successful. Others believe that careful planning is a safer and better way to succeed. Which opinion do you believe? Give reasons and examples in your response.

3. Some professors give essay exams for which students must write long answers in their own words. Other professors give multiple choice exams, for which students must choose correct answers to questions from several answer choices provided. Which type of exam do you think better tests students' knowledge and why do you think so? Use specific details and examples to support your response.

4. Some people believe that the main purpose of art, including music and movies, is entertainment or enjoyment. Others say that the purpose of art is to express important ideas and make people think. Which one do you believe is the primary purpose of art and why? Use details and examples in your response.

5. In general, is it better for a business to spend its money on hiring fewer employees with more experience, or more employees with less experience? Support your choice with reasons and examples.

SPEAKING QUESTIONS 3 AND 4: INTEGRATED QUESTIONS (READING, LISTENING, AND SPEAKING)

There are two integrated questions that integrate speaking with reading and listening. In these questions you will have 45 seconds to read a short passage, which will then disappear. You will then listen to a short passage in which a professor is lecturing on a topic related to the reading passage or some students are discussing ideas from the reading passage. After that, you will hear and see a question that asks you to answer a question about the listening passage using information from both the listening and reading passage. You have 30 seconds to prepare your response and then 60 seconds to record your response. A clock on the screen will show you how much time you have left to read, another will count down the 30 seconds of preparation time, and another will count down the 60 seconds of response time.

SPEAKING QUESTION 3: CAMPUS-BASED INTEGRATED READING, LISTENING, AND SPEAKING

Speaking Question 3 presents a topic of interest to students on a college campus. The reading passage is usually some type of announcement or proposal, and the listening passage is a conversation between two students who are discussing the topic of the reading passage. One or both of the students express their opinion and the reasons they have for the opinion. The question typically asks you to summarize one student's opinion and explain the reasons the student holds that opinion. **You should NOT give your personal opinion for Speaking Question 3, only the opinions of the student(s).**

Speaking Question	Usual Expectations For A Response	Reading Time	Listening Time	Preparation Time	Response Time
Question 3: Campus-based Announcement —Opinion	Describe the opinion of one of the speakers concerning a campus announcement and explain the reasons the speaker gives for the opinion.	45–50 seconds	60–90 seconds	30 seconds	60 seconds

Speaking Skill 5: NOTE THE MAIN POINTS AS YOU READ FOR SPEAKING QUESTION 3

In integrated Speaking Question 3, you will be asked to read a short passage. This may be an announcement, a bulletin, a letter, or an article on a topic of interest to university students, such as housing, parking, new construction, or campus events or policies. The passage will describe a policy, proposal or event and usually give reasons for or against the proposal in the announcement. It is important for you to be able to read the passage of 75–100 words and take notes on the main points in 45 seconds. When the time for reading is over, the passage will disappear from your screen and you will not be able to see it again. Therefore, you should take notes on what the topic of the announcement is, the main points related to the topic or the reasons given for the announcement.

Look at the following example of a reading passage for the integrated Speaking Question 3.

Example Question 3 Reading Passage A

> ### A notice from the Office of the University President
> Effective Monday, November 11th, no pets will be allowed on the university campus. This applies to all university professors, administrators, students, and visitors alike. This policy is being put in place for the comfort and safety of everyone on campus and because buildings on campus are not built to accommodate pets. The only exception to this rule is animals such as Seeing Eye® dogs that are trained for use in assisting persons with disabilities. Any other pets, no matter how large or small, are unequivocally not allowed. Anyone who fails to follow this policy will face immediate action by the university.

While you read the text, you should take notes on the topic and main points of the reading passage. Look at these notes on the topic and main points of the reading passage. Notice that the notes about the reading passage are on the left side, with space on the right side for notes about the listening passage which you will hear directly after the reading passage.

Reading Passage (Read):	Listening Passage (Listen):
Top (topic): X pets on campus!	
MPs (main points):	
—4 comf/safe, bldg X accom	
—excp disabil	
—X follow = immed act by univ	

These notes include the main point of the notice: no pets allowed on campus except animals to help the disabled, and the notice sounds very serious (!). The reasons given for this policy are the comfort and safety of every one on campus and the fact that the campus buildings don't accommodate pets. The notes say that if the new policy is not followed, the university will take some sort of negative action against anyone who breaks the rules. Abbreviations and symbols are used so that the note-taker can write down the important ideas in a short amount of time.

Now look at the example and the notes for another reading passage.

Example Question 3 Reading Passage B

> ### A notice from the Office of Student Housing
> Because the increase in the number of students has exceeded the residential capacity of campus housing, the university has been forced to withdraw the guarantee of four years of on-campus housing for undergraduate students. Students will still be guaranteed three years of access to university housing, but there will be a lottery system in place for any remaining residential spots for those who wish to stay a fourth year in on-campus housing. There is also an off-campus housing board where students may search postings for housing near the campus.

Reading Passage (Read):	Listening Passage (Listen):
Top (topic): ↑↑ Ss = X guar 4 yrs camp hous	
MPs (main points):	
—3 yrs hous only	
—lottery syst 4 remain hous	
—board 4 off-camp hous	

The notes indicate the topic: there is no longer a guarantee of four years of housing on campus, only three. It also notes the reason and the two points the announcement makes. There are too many students to allow all of them to have on-campus housing, so there is a lottery system for any remaining places, and there is a board with postings for off-campus housing.

Make sure you take notes as you are reading the passage. It is important to have information in your notes about what the subject of the announcement is so you can understand the listening passage that follows. A few, brief notes about what is being announced and the reasons for the announcement can make planning your answer easier.

The following chart outlines the key information for dealing with the reading passage for integrated Speaking Question 3.

KEY INFORMATION FOR NOTING THE MAIN POINTS IN THE READING PASSAGE	
READ THE ENTIRE PASSAGE	Read the entire passage carefully as you are taking notes in order to completely understand the topic of the announcement and reasons for it.
TAKE NOTES ON THE MAIN POINTS	Focus on and write abbreviated notes on the main points, including the topic, key words, reasons for the announcement, and suggestions or requirements the announcement gives. Leave a blank column on the opposite side of your reading notes for the listening notes you will need to take when you hear the conversation.

SPEAKING EXERCISE 5: Read each of the following passages, and note the *topic* and the reasons, implications, or other *main points* that are used to support the topic. On the actual TOEFL iBT® test, you will have 45 seconds to read the passage and take notes. Time yourself and try to improve your reading and note-taking speed as you complete the exercises below. (Notice that the notes about the reading passage are on the left side of the paper, with space on the right side for notes about the related listening passage which you will hear later in this unit.)

1. Read the passage. Take notes on the main points of the reading passage. You have 45 seconds to read the passage.

> *A notice from campus administration*
> This campus has a serious problem with bicycles: too many students are parking their bicycles in unauthorized places. This creates safety issues with bikes blocking walkways as well as accidents and collisions. Beginning on Monday, November 1, any bicycles left in unauthorized places will be ticketed. Please note that there is authorized parking for bicycles along the east and west sides of campus. Parking of bicycles is permitted only in places where signs are posted indicating this.

Read: Listen:

Top (topic):

MPs (main points):

2. Read the passage. Take notes on the main points of the reading passage. You have 45 seconds to read the passage.

> *An announcement from the campus bookstore*
> At the end of the semester, most textbooks in good condition can be sold back to the bookstore for a rebate of 30 percent of the original price. This program allows students to buy used copies of textbooks from the bookstore at a discounted price. The bookstore is announcing that it will no longer be buying editions of some textbooks. If the textbook will be replaced by a new edition of the same book the following semester, then the old edition of the textbook will not be eligible for buyback. This has become necessary due to problems students and professors have had using old editions of textbooks.

Read: Listen:

Top:

MPs:

3. Read the passage. Take notes on the main points of the reading passage. You have 45 seconds to read the passage.

> **An announcement from a professor**
>
> This semester I am instituting a new policy concerning late assignments. For reasons of fairness to all my students and Teaching Assistants, I will not accept any late assignments; no excuses will be accepted, not even serious illness or injury. On the date that an assignment is due, it is your responsibility to get it in on time or receive a grade of zero. To compensate for the strictness of this policy, we will drop your lowest assignment grade should you fail to turn in an assignment on time, and it will not be averaged into your final grade. Nevertheless, I strongly recommend getting your assignments done early so that you can meet the deadlines even if something serious comes up.

Read: Listen:

TOP:

MPs:

Speaking Skill 6: NOTE THE MAIN POINTS AS YOU LISTEN FOR SPEAKING QUESTION 3

In Speaking Question 3, the Campus-based Announcement – Opinion question, you will also be asked to listen to a man and a woman discussing the announcement you have just read. One or both speakers will express their opinion of the announcement and the reasons they have for the opinion. You should listen carefully for these opinions and reasons, and you should take abbreviated notes on the opinions of the speakers and reasons for their opinions. You can take notes on the side of your paper opposite your notes on the reading passage. This will make it easier to draw connections between the reading passage and the listening passage during the preparation time.

Now read and listen to two students discussing the notice from the Office of the University President that you read above.

(narrator)	Now listen to two students as they discuss the notice.
(man)	What's the deal with the new policy on pets?
(woman)	Oh, you saw that? I guess one of the professors has a pet snake that got loose and ended up in the president's office. I heard the president kind of freaked out.
(man)	What? Just because of one incident? It's not fair for the president to penalize everyone just because one professor was careless.
(woman)	Yeah, it's a pretty harsh reaction.
(man)	I think it's too strict. You know, a lot of local people, not students, who live off campus use the paths on the campus to walk their dogs. It's not a safety issue because they control their dogs. If the university makes them stop, it'll cut down the interaction between people on campus and off.
(woman)	I guess I do see a lot of people walking their dogs, and they are pretty considerate about it.
(man)	Exactly. I've talked with a few of them and they've actually been really interesting people. It sort of helps the university be part of the neighborhood.
(woman)	It does seem kind of pointless to drive them away from the campus.
(man)	I'll bet the president hasn't really thought this through.

As you listen to the passage, you should take notes on the opinions of the speakers and the reasons they hold their opinions. Look at these notes on the listening passage. Notice that only one speaker expresses a strong opinion about the notice, and that his reasons for the opinion are a response to one reason given in the reading passage: safety.

Now look at the combined reading and listening notes.

Read:	Listen:
Top: X pets on campus!	Op (opinion): M—X like policy X pets
MPs:	
—4 comf/safe, bldg X accom	[W—reas = prof's snake in pres offc]
—excep disabil	R4 (reasons for opinion):
—X follow = immed act by univ	M: X fair, pres punish all, ++strict
	—ppl off camp walk dogs, control, safe
	—↓ interact btw camp & neigh

These notes indicate that the man doesn't like the policy against pets. The notes also indicate, according to the woman, the president issued the policy because there was a professor's snake in his office. The notes include the information that the man does not think it is fair for the president to penalize or punish everyone and that the president's policy is too strict. According to the notes, another reason that the man does not like the policy is that people, who live off campus and who use paths on campus to walk their dogs, control the animals and so, they are not a safety issue. He also believes that the policy will decrease interaction between students on campus and people in the neighborhood.

Now listen to two students discussing the notice from the Office of Student Housing that you read. Notice that in this conversation both speakers express opinions, and these opinions directly address the reason and suggestions made in the announcement.

Example Question 3 Listening Passage B 🔊 104

(narrator)   Now listen to two students as they discuss the notice.

(man)   I can't believe they're taking away the guarantee of four years of housing. That means I'll have to look for a place to live off campus my senior year.

(woman)   Yeah. It's because of all the new students. I guess they have to get more tuition money to pay for all the new laboratories and athletic facilities.

(man)   I think they should just stop taking any more new students until they finish building enough dorms and residences for everyone.

(woman)   No way. If they took fewer students, they'd have to hike the tuition up for the rest of us. So, I'd prefer lower tuition and more students.

(man)   I guess you have a point. But it's going to be a pain to have to find a place to live off campus my last year.

(woman)   I don't think it will be that hard, Dave. You can rent one of those off-campus houses that are posted on the board. I think they're not so expensive if you share with a couple of other guys.

(man)   Maybe. But I'd have to figure out another way to get around if I lived very far . . . buy a car or something.

(woman)   You know what, though? I talked to a woman in the housing office the other day. She said that even after everyone uses their three years of guaranteed housing, there are still going to be a lot of places left over.

(man)   Oh, really? She said that?

(woman)   Yeah. She said that most people who want to stay on campus a fourth year should be able to get housing in the lottery. It's not going to be so competitive.

(man)   Well, that makes me feel better. If it's not going to be a huge, long process to find a place to live, then I guess I can live without a guarantee.

Now look at the combined reading and listening notes.

<table>
<tr><td>

Read:

Top: ↑↑ Ss = X guar 4 yrs camp hous
MPs:
—3 yrs hous only

—lottery syst 4 remain hous
—board 4 off-camp hous

</td><td>

Listen:

Op:
M—diff 2 find hous sr yr
M—X new Ss until build ++ dorm $ residence

R4:
M—need car 4 far fr camp hous
Op:
W—↑ Ss pay 4 new labs, athl facil
W—pref>Ss, ↓$
R4:
W—lottery X compete, EZ get hous 4ᵗʰyr
W—off-camp board, share, rent ↓$

</td></tr>
</table>

The notes for the listening section are divided between what the man says and the woman says. The notes indicate that the woman thinks that the university is enrolling more students in order to pay for new laboratories and athletic buildings, that she prefers to have more students rather than higher tuition, that the man can use the off-campus housing board to find a house to share inexpensively, and that the lottery for remaining housing spots is not going to be competitive so it will be easy for students to get housing during their senior year. The notes indicate that the man thinks that the university should not enroll more students until housing for them has been built, that it will be difficult to find housing his senior year, and that he may need to get a car if he lives very far off campus.

This style of notes makes it clear what each speaker says and could be used for a question that asks about either the man's or the woman's opinion. Because you do not know which person the question will ask about, you should take notes on the opinions of both speakers. In many cases, however, only one of the speakers will have a strong opinion about the announcement.

In Speaking Question 3, the Campus-based Announcement-Opinion question, the announcement will usually give reasons for the announcement or change, and in the conversation the speakers will often directly address those reasons. Focusing on the reasons given in the announcement and the conversation, and briefly noting them, will help you organize your answer during the planning time given before you speak.

The following chart outlines the key information for dealing with the listening passage in integrated Speaking Question 3.

KEY POINTS FOR NOTING THE MAIN POINTS IN THE LISTENING PASSAGE	
LISTEN FOR OPINIONS AND REASONS	Listen carefully for the opinions of the speakers concerning the announcement and the reasons they have these opinions.
TAKE NOTES ON THE OPINIONS AND REASONS	On the opposite side of your notes for the reading passage, take abbreviated notes on the opinions of the speakers and the reasons they give for holding those opinions.

SPEAKING EXERCISE 6: Listen to each of the following passages, and take notes on the *opinions of the speakers* and the *reasons* that are used to support their opinions. Before you listen, copy your notes for the reading passages from Speaking Exercise 5 on pp. 250–252 in the space provided below. Or take notes on the listening passage next to the notes you already took for Speaking Exercise 5.

1. Listen to two students as they discuss the notice. 🔊 105

A notice from campus administration

Read:

Top (topic):

MPs (main points):

Listen:

OP (opinion):

R4 (reasons for the opinion):

---

2. Listen to two students as they discuss the announcement. 🔊 106

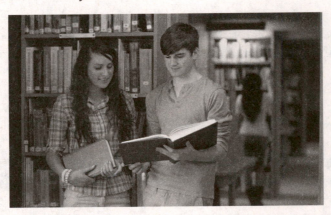

An announcement from the campus bookstore

Read:

Top:

MPs:

Listen:

OP:

R4:

---

3. Listen to two students as they discuss a professor's announcement. ¹⁰⁷ 🔊))

An announcement from a professor

Read: Listen:

TOP: OP:

MPS: R4:

Speaking Skill 7: USE YOUR NOTES TO PLAN THE RESPONSE FOR SPEAKING QUESTION 3

After you have taken notes on the main points of both the reading passage and the listening passage in Speaking Question 3, you will read a question and plan your response. The question will appear on the screen and the narrator will read it. You will then have 30 seconds to plan a response to the question. A clock on the screen will count down the preparation time. At the end of the 30 seconds, a narrator will tell you to begin speaking.

The question will most likely ask you to state the opinion of one of the speakers concerning the announcement and ask you to say why the speaker holds this opinion. You should read the question carefully to be sure that you know what information your response must include. Decide what points you need to answer the question, mark them, and decide how much time you will spend making each point.

Look at Example Question 3A below for the first reading passage in Skill 5 and the first listening passage in Skill 6.

Example Question 3A
The man gives his opinion of the notice from the Office of the University President concerning pets. State his opinion and explain the reasons he gives for holding that opinion.

In order to completely answer this question, you should briefly describe what the notice is about, you must state what the man's opinion of the notice is, and say why he has this opinion. Notice that the question does not ask about the woman's opinion. Although you can include some of the woman's comments in your response, you must focus on what the man believes. You should *not* give your personal opinion in your response to this question. The question does not ask for your opinion and you may receive a lower score if you add your own personal opinion. Although the question for Speaking Question 3 usually asks for the opinion and reasons given by one speaker, you should always read and listen to the question carefully so you know what information to include in your response.

After you understand the question, you should prepare a plan for your response. Look at the notes you have taken on the reading passage and the listening passage. Focus on what is being announced, the reasons or main points given, and how the speakers respond to these reasons or main points when they give their opinions.

Remember: You should NOT give your personal opinion for Speaking Question 3, only the opinions of the student(s).

Look at the notes and the plan for Example Question 3A.

NOTES (Example Question 3A):

Read:	Listen:
Top: X pets on campus!	Op: M—X like policy X pets
MPs:	
—4 comf/safe, bldg X accom —excep disabil —X follow = immed act by univ	W—reas = prof's snake in pres offc R4: M—X fair, pres punish all, ++strict —people off camp walk dogs, control, safe —↓ interact btw camp & neigh

PLAN (Example Question 3A):

In order to plan the response using your notes, find the topic of the notice and the main points related to it, the opinion of the person (man or woman) about whom the question is asking, and the reason that person has for holding the opinion:

1. Find what the notice is about from the reading notes and find the man's <u>opinion</u> of it from the listening notes.

   OP: M—X like policy X pets excp disabil // M: X fair, pres punish all, ++strict

   These notes will help you answer the first part of the question that asks you to state the man's opinion and this should be the first thing you record for your response. You will need to use the notes from the reading to explain the policy about which the man is expressing his opinion.

2. Find the man's <u>reasons</u> from the listening passage notes for his opinion, and find the notes in the reading passage about details in the policy with which he is disagreeing.

   —4 comf/safe, bldg X accom (reason for policy from the reading)

   R4: M: people off camp walk dogs, control, safe

   ↓ interact btw camp & neigh (man's reason for disagreeing from the listening)

   These notes will help you answer the second part of the question that asks you to explain the man's reasons for his opinion.

   Note: If time allows, you could mention what the woman says the reason for the policy is: [W—*reas= prof's snake in pres offc*]. However, this is not completely necessary as you are only being asked about the man's opinion and his reasons for this opinion.

Now look at Example Question 3B.

Example Question 3B

The woman expresses her opinion of the change announced in the notice. Explain her opinion and the reasons she gives for that opinion.

The question asks you to explain only the opinion of the woman concerning the notice. A good response to this question should concentrate on the woman's opinion and her reasons.

Look at the notes and the plan for Example Question 3B.

NOTES (Example Question 3B):

Read:	Listen:
Top: ↑↑ Ss = X guar 4 yrs camp hous	Op:
MPs:	M—diff 2 find hous sr yr
—3 yrs hous only	M—X new Ss until build ++ dorm $ residence
—lottery syst 4 remain hous	R4:
—board 4 off-camp hous	M—need car 4 far fr camp hous
	Op:
	W—↑ Ss pay 4 new labs, athl facil
	W—pref>Ss, ↓$
	R4:
	W—lottery X compete, EZ get hous 4thyr
	W—off-camp board, share, rent ↓$

PLAN (Example Question 3B):

In order to plan the response using your notes, find the topic of the notice and the main points related to it, the opinion of the person (man or woman) about whom the question is asking, and the reason that person has for holding the opinion:

> 1. Find what the notice is about from the reading notes and find the woman's *opinion* of it from the listening notes.
>
>   Top: ↑↑ Ss = X guar 4 yrs camp hous
>
>   —3 yrs hous only
>
>   OP: W: ↑Ss pay 4 new labs, athl facil
>
>   W—pref>Ss, ↓$
>
>   These notes will help you answer the first part of the question that asks you to state the woman's opinion and this should be the first thing you record for your response. You will need to use the notes from the reading to explain the policy about which the woman is expressing her opinion.
>
> 2. Find the woman's *reasons* from the listening passage notes for her opinion, and find the notes in the reading passage about details in the policy with which she is disagreeing.
>
>   Top: (from the reading)
>
>   —lottery syst 4 remain hous
>
>   —board 4 off-camp hous
>
>   R4: (woman's reason for agreeing from the listening)
>
>   W—lottery X compete, EZ get hous 4th yr
>
>   W—off-camp board, share, rent ↓$
>
>   These notes will help you answer the second part of the question that asks you to explain the woman's reasons for his opinion.
>
> Note: The question is asking only about the woman's opinion, so you are not required to discuss the man's opinion in order to answer the question. In the case of this conversation, addressing the woman's opinion and reasons for it would most likely use all of the time allotted.

Be realistic about how many points you can address from the reading and listening passages based on how fast you know you can speak and still be easily understood. If each point normally takes you 10–12 seconds, you cannot cover more than 2 or 3 points; you will have to decide which points to discuss and which to omit.

The following chart outlines the key information for using the 30 seconds allowed to plan your response for the integrated Speaking Question 3.

KEY POINTS FOR USING YOUR NOTES TO PLAN YOUR RESPONSE	
UNDERSTAND THE QUESTION	Read the question carefully. Be sure you know who the question is asking about (the man or the woman), what information you must include in your response, and which points you do not have to mention.
FIND THE INFORMATION	Look at your notes to find the information that will answer the question asked. Add any extra information that you remember, but that you did not have time to write down before.
PLAN THE RESPONSE	Mark your notes to help you organize the points you will make in your response and the order in which you will make each point. Use your plan to determine the order in which you will make each point.

SPEAKING EXERCISE 7: Read the questions below for each of the reading and listening passages you have worked on in Speaking Exercises 5 and 6, pp. 250–252 and pp. 256–257. Then look at the notes you took for those exercises. Find the information to answer the questions in your notes, and mark the notes to plan an organized response to the question. You will have 30 seconds to plan your response on the actual TOEFL iBT® test. Time yourself, trying to take only 30 seconds to plan your response.

1. The man gives his opinion on the policy concerning bicycle parking on campus. State his opinion and the reasons he gives for having that opinion.

2. Describe the man's opinion of the announcement from the campus bookstore. Explain his opinion and the reasons that he has this opinion.

3. The woman expresses her opinion of the policy for late assignments given in the class syllabus. State her opinion and the reasons she gives for holding that opinion.

Speaking Skill 8: USE YOUR PLAN TO MAKE THE RESPONSE FOR SPEAKING QUESTION 3

After you have planned your response, you need to make your response. You will have 60 seconds to record the response to Speaking Question 3. A clock on the screen will count down the response time as you record your response. At the end of 60 seconds, the clock will disappear, the computer will stop recording your answer, and the screen will indicate that the response time has ended.

While you are making your response, you should think about the following strategies:

- Start with a topic statement.
- Explain the speaker's opinion and reasons for that opinion, following your plan.
- Give only the most relevant details from the listening and reading passages.
- Use useful language to show attribution (man or woman) and the connections between ideas.
- Speak clearly using the English pronunciation points you have practiced to make your response sound more natural.

Look at the plan for responding to Example Question 3A from Speaking Skills 5 and 6. Then, look at and listen to a sample response based on the plan.

SPEAKING SKILL 8 / QUESTION 3   261

PLAN (Example Question 3A):

Opinion: Use this part of the plan to state the man's opinion about the policy in the notice in your response. This will form your introductory statement.

OP: M—X like policy X pets excp disabil // M: X fair, pres punish all, ++strict

Reasons for the opinion: State the reasons, based on the policy, the man gives for his opinion.

—4 comf/safe, bldg X accom (reason for policy from the reading)

M: people off camp walk dogs, control, safe

↓ interact btw camp & neigh

Additional information: If time allows, you could mention what the woman says is the reason for the policy

[W—reas= prof's snake in pres offc]

SAMPLE RESPONSE (Example Question 3A): 🔊 108

The man doesn't agree with the policy on pets. The policy states that no pets are allowed on campus, except for animals to help disabled people. The woman tells him that the president changed the policy because he found a pet snake in his office, but the man thinks that the president is reacting too strongly, and that it's not fair to punish everyone. The man also says that people from the neighborhood walk their dogs on campus. According to the notice, animals aren't going to be allowed on campus for safety reasons, but the man disagrees and says that the dogs are safe because people control them. Finally, the man believes that if people can't walk their dogs, there will be less friendly interaction between students on campus and the people in the neighborhood.

You should notice that this response begins with an introductory statement that gives the man's opinion on the policy. Then the response briefly explains the policy and goes on to explain the reasons the man gives for his opinion. The response gives only enough details about the policy for the listener to understand. For example, the response does not talk about consequences (*immediate action by the university*) for not following the policy because it is not relevant for answering the question. However, the pet snake found in the president's office is mentioned because it is relevant to one of the man's reasons: he thinks the president is reacting too strongly to one event. The response uses useful language and transitions (highlighted) to show how ideas are related and to show whether the ideas came from the man, the woman, or the notice.

Now look at the plan for responding to Example Question 3B from Speaking Skills 5 and 6. Then, look at and listen to a sample response based on the plan.

PLAN (Example Question 3B):

> **Opinion:** Use this part of the plan to state the man's opinion about the policy in the notice in your response. This will form your introductory statement.
>
> ↑↑ Ss = X guar 4 yrs camp hous
>
> —3 yrs hous only
>
> W: ↑ Ss pay 4 new labs, athl facil
>
> W—pref > Ss, ↓$
>
> **Reasons for the opinion:** State the reasons, based on the policy, the woman gives for her opinion.
>
> —lottery syst 4 remain hous
>
> —board 4 off-camp hous
>
> W—lottery X compete, EZ get hous 4th yr
>
> W—off-camp board, share, rent ↓$

SAMPLE RESPONSE (Example Question 3B): 🔊 **109**

> The students are discussing a notice that says that students will only have three years of guaranteed housing instead of four. The woman is in favor of the notice, and she gives a few reasons. She says that the university needs more students so it can pay for things like new labs. She thinks that it's better to have more students than to pay higher tuition. Another reason is that she believes it will be easy to find housing during the last year of their studies. The notice says that there is a lottery system for housing, and she tells the man that there will probably be spaces for people who want to live on campus their senior year. She also tells the man that students can use the off-campus housing board to find cheap places that they can share.

This response begins with an introductory statement that explains the policy stated in the notice. The response then explains the woman's opinion of the policy. It goes on to give the reasons for the woman's opinion. It follows the plan to completely answer the question and does not include any details that are not relevant to the woman's opinion or reasons. The response does not mention what the man thinks because the question is not asking about his opinion, only the woman's. Notice that the student giving this response does not offer a personal opinion; remember that you are not being asked to give your own opinion. The response uses transitions and key phrases (highlighted) to make it clear where the information comes from and how the ideas are related.

Practice using useful language and English intonation and stress patterns when you state your summary aloud. Remember that your response will be evaluated on the basis of how fluent you are. Following your plan can help you speak at a steady pace and avoid long pauses as you try to remember important points. Check the clock and do not spend too much time on any one point. However, do not try to speak very quickly and discuss too many points from the passages; this will probably make your response harder to understand. Practice this speaking question before the date you are planning to take the TOEFL iBT®

> Practice the skills you need for Speaking Question 3 by listening to television or movies in English and summarizing what was said and the reasons for any opinions or reasons for the results of actions you hear expressed.

test so you are familiar with how many different points you are able to discuss fluently; use this knowledge when planning and making your response during the test.

The following chart outlines the key information for using the 60 seconds allowed to make your response for integrated Speaking Question 3.

KEY POINTS FOR USING YOUR PLAN TO MAKE THE RESPONSE	
START WITH AN INTRODUCTORY STATEMENT	Start your response with a *topic statement* that states the opinion of the man or woman, briefly describes the policy, or includes both the topic and the opinion.
EXPLAIN THE OPINION AND REASONS	Following the plan you have made with your notes, explain the opinion of the speaker that the question asks about and the reasons the speaker holds this opinion.
INCLUDE ONLY RELEVANT DETAILS	Include details from the reading passage and listening passage only if they are relevant to the question asked. You do not need to include details that do not relate to the speaker's opinion or reasons.
CONNECT IDEAS USING USEFUL LANGUAGE	Practice using useful language in the weeks before you take the test. When you give your response, use language structures and transitions you are comfortable with to show how ideas are connected with each other. Use attribution signals to show who said these ideas or where they came from.

The useful language and pronunciation tips below can help you make your response easier to understand. Practice this language and these tips in the weeks before you take the TOEFL iBT® test.

USEFUL LANGUAGE AND TRANSITIONAL PHRASES
To report who said something or where information came from (attribution signals):   *According to* + noun,   Subject + *says/thinks/believes* + (*that*)   Subject + *tells* + object + (*that*)   According to the policy, students need a parking sticker . . .   The man says that the policy is unfair.   The woman tells him that she likes the idea.
To show agreement: Subject + *agrees* + (*with* + noun)/(*that* + subject + verb)   Subject + *is in favor of* + noun/verb + *-ing*   Subject + *likes/supports the idea/policy/proposal*   The student agrees with the reasons given in the policy.   The woman is in favor of having more students.   The man supports the idea of building a new stadium.
To express disagreement: Subject + *doesn't agree/disagrees* + (*with* + noun)/(*that* + subject + verb)   Subject + *is against* + noun/verb + *-ing*   Subject + *doesn't like/opposes* . . .   The man doesn't agree that pets are unsafe.   The students are against the proposal.   The woman opposes the policy.

MAKING YOUR RESPONSE EASIER TO UNDERSTAND: Practicing difficult sounds.

HOW ENGLISH PRONUNCIATION FUNCTIONS	English has some sounds that other languages do not have. These can be difficult for students to pronounce. You may have difficulty pronouncing some English vowels or consonants. They may be the same sounds with which other speakers of your native language have problems.	theory /θ/ the, but /ə/
YOUR RESPONSE	You should try to determine which English sounds are typically difficult for you and for the people who speak your native language. Study and practice these difficult vowels and consonants in the time before you take the TOEFL iBT® test, so that you can pronounce them more clearly. Even a small improvement can make your English easier to understand and raise the score for the fluency of your response.	

SPEAKING EXERCISE 8: Create responses for the integrated reading, listening, and speaking questions that you have been working on in Speaking Skills 5–8. You have 60 seconds to give your response. Time yourself and repeat your response until you can finish it within the 60-second response time.

SPEAKING REVIEW EXERCISE (SKILLS 5–8): Read the proposal from the Office of Student Activities. You will have 45 seconds to read the passage.

The Office of Student Activities

Currently, there are two fitness rooms on campus for students and faculty—the facilities at the new Washington Recreation Center, and the weight room at the old Franklin Street Center. Many students have complained that the equipment in the Franklin Street Center weight room is old and few students use it, while the Washington Recreation Center lacks sufficient aerobic machines. Since the Franklin Street Center is due for renovation in two years, and there will be no improvements to the facilities until that time, it has been proposed to close the Franklin Street Center weight room and use the money usually spent on its maintenance to buy new aerobic machines for the Washington Recreation Center.

SPEAKING

Now listen to two students as they discuss the proposal.  🔊¹¹⁰

Now answer the following question. You have 30 seconds to prepare and then 60 seconds to deliver your answer. 🔊¹¹¹

> The man gives his opinion of the proposal. State his opinion and the reasons he gives for holding it.

SPEAKING QUESTION 4: ACADEMIC SETTING INTEGRATED READING, LISTENING, AND SPEAKING

For Speaking Question 4, you will be asked to read a passage on an academic topic and listen to a lecture on the same topic. You will then answer a question that requires you to relate information from both the reading passage and the lecture. It will generally ask you to explain how the specific examples from the listening illustrate the general concept from the reading passage. The question and your response will mainly focus on the listening passage, but you will be required to integrate information from the reading passage in order to answer the question fully. You will not need to have any prior knowledge of the subject; all the information you need to answer the question will be contained in the reading passage and the listening passage that follows it.

Speaking Question 4 is considered challenging by many test takers. Before you take the TOEFL iBT® test, practice listening to and reading a variety of academic subjects in English. This will improve your understanding of academic concepts and vocabulary, enabling you to better understand the academic reading and listening passages on the TOEFL iBT® test.

Speaking Question	Usual Expectations For A Response	Reading Time	Listening Time	Preparation Time	Response Time
Question 4: Academic Setting— Concept / Example (General / Specific)	Explain how specific examples concerning two or three points made by the lecturer illustrate a general concept described in a short academic reading passage.	45–50 seconds	60–90 seconds	30 seconds	60 seconds

Speaking Skill 9: NOTE THE MAIN POINTS AS YOU READ FOR SPEAKING QUESTION 4

In Speaking Question 4, you will read a passage on an academic subject. The passage will typically introduce a general concept from an introductory academic course and define, describe, or give characteristics of the concept. The reading may also describe a problem. It is important for you to be able to read an academic passage of 75–100 words in the time allowed and take notes on the main points of the passage. You have 45 seconds to read the passage and a clock on the screen will count down the reading time. When the time for reading is over, the passage will disappear from your screen and you will not be able to see it again. Therefore, you should take notes on the topic of the passage, a short definition of the concept, if it is given, and major details concerning the concept.

Look at the following example of a reading passage for the integrated Speaking Question 4.

Example Question 4 Reading Passage A

> *Photoreceptor cells*
>
> Our eyes contain two kinds of cells, known as photoreceptors, which are sensitive to light. These two types of cells are called rods and cones. The rods are more sensitive to light than the cones; in other words, they can detect fainter light than cones. However, rods are not sensitive to color. Cones, on the other hand, are sensitive to colors, but cannot detect faint light. Cones are concentrated in the center of our field of vision, where we focus our eyes. Rods, in contrast, are distributed throughout the periphery; just outside the center of our field of vision.

As you read the passage and understand the main points, you should take notes on the topic and main points of the reading passage. Writing down a few main ideas from the passage will help you organize your answer during the 45-second preparation time.

Look at these notes on the topic and main points of the reading passage. The notes leave space on the right side for taking notes on the listening passage that follows.

Read:	Listen:
Top: <u>photoreceptor cells</u> = sens 2 light	
MPs:	
2 kind:	
—rods: ↑ sens 2 light	
X color /	
outside ctr <u>field of vision</u>	
—cones: ↓ sens 2 light	
sens 2 color	
in ctr field of vision	

The notes include the topic, photoreceptor cells, and a description of what they are. As the notes indicate, the reading passage compares two types of these cells. The notes are divided into these two types, and characteristics of each type are listed next to their names. Abbreviations and symbols are used, and key words that either indicate the topic ("photoreceptor cells") or indicate important terms ("field of vision") are underlined.

Now look at another example from a business class.

Example Question 4 Reading Passage B

> *Equity Theory*
> The equity theory of employee satisfaction in business focuses on comparisons between employees; the basis of this theory is that workers in an organization evaluate their treatment by the organization by comparing their treatment to the treatment of other workers in the organization. According to this theory, workers evaluate their return for contribution, what they contribute to the company and what they receive in return for it, and compare their return for contribution to what other employees contribute and receive in return. A worker who receives a return for contribution that is equal to or greater than the return for contribution of other employees will be content, while a worker whose return for contribution is less will not be content.

Read: Listen:

Top: <u>equity theory</u> = how employees eval treatmnt
by company

MPs:
—<u>return 4 contribution</u> (r4c) (compare what put in vs.
   what get out)
   —r4c> others, employee happy
   —r4c< others, X happy

The notes define equity theory. The term *return for contribution* is underlined and explained in parentheses. It means that employees compare the contributions they put into a company to what they receive in return or get out of the company. Only a few words are used to remind the note-taker of this idea.

As you read the passage, you will probably not have time to write very much. Often only a few words or symbols is enough to remind you of a main point, however, and having even a few simple notes can help you listen for key information in the lecture that follows the reading passage and organize your response.

The following chart outlines the key information for dealing with the reading passage in integrated Speaking Question 4.

KEY POINTS FOR NOTING THE MAIN POINTS IN THE READING PASSAGE	
READ AND UNDERSTAND THE PASSAGE	Read the passage carefully and be sure you understand what the general concept and the main points of the passage are. After 45 seconds, the passage will disappear, and you will not see it again.
TAKE NOTES ON THE PASSAGE	Take abbreviated notes on the main points of the text as you are reading. Try to write down the topic, a short definition of it, and characteristics or other main ideas. Mark any key terms you may want to use in your response. Leave a blank column on the opposite side of your reading notes for the listening notes you will need to take when you hear the conversation.

SPEAKING EXERCISE 9: Read each of the following passages, and take notes that include the *topic* and a definition of it, characteristics, or other *main points* that are used to support the topic. On the actual TOEFL iBT® test you will have 45 seconds to read the passage and take notes. Time yourself and try to improve your reading and note-taking speed as you complete the exercises below. (Notice that the notes about the reading passage are on the left side of the paper, with space on the right side for notes about the related listening passage, which you will hear later in this unit.)

1. Read the passage. Take notes on the topic and the main points of the reading passage. You have 45 seconds to read the passage.

Hotspots

As the enormous pieces of the Earth's outer crust move in a process called plate tectonics, they come into contact with each other and sink under and rise above one another. Most of the world's volcanoes and earthquakes occur where these plates meet or at what is referred to as the plate boundary. Nevertheless, volcanic activity may occur in the middle of large plates because of hotspots. Currents of molten rock from deep within the Earth can rise up in the middle of a continent or ocean and create a hotspot not far below the surface crust. These hotspots can cause volcanoes and other geothermal activity far from plate boundaries.

Read: Listen:

Top:

MPs:

2. Read the passage. Take notes on the topic and the main points of the reading passage. You have 45 seconds to read the passage.

Election Polling

Election polling is a type of survey that is used to find out how certain people feel about an issue or about a candidate for a government position or office in an election. After the polling information is collected, the results are then tallied up. Because it is not feasible to contact every individual in a large population, a representative sample of people can be polled and generalized to the population as a whole using statistical analysis. Getting a sample large enough to be reliably generalized to the whole population can be problematic, but sample bias is often a bigger problem. Sample bias occurs when the people polled do not truly represent a typical cross-section of the population as a whole.

Read: Listen:

Top:

MPs:

---

3. Read the passage. Take notes on the topic and the main points of the reading passage. You have 45 seconds to read the passage.

Long-term memory

Two different types of long-term memories, or memories that we store for days, months, or years, are implicit and explicit memories. Implicit memories are often motor memories of how to make our bodies do something, such as how to swim or say a particular word, whereas explicit memories are things such as events in our lives, personal experiences, and specific facts. These two types of memories are moved from short-term memory to long-term memory in different ways. Explicit memories are stored by means of a structure in the brain called the hippocampus; in contrast, implicit memories are stored by a different pathway.

Read: Listen:

Top:

MPs:

Speaking Skill 10: NOTE THE MAIN POINTS AS YOU LISTEN FOR SPEAKING QUESTION 4

For Speaking Question 4, the Academic Setting—Concept/Example or General/Specific question, you will also be asked to listen to an academic passage as part of the question. The listening passage usually lasts from 60–90 seconds, and it will give specific examples that illustrate the general concept described in the reading passage. The lecturer will usually make two or three major points, describing a few examples that show how the general concept outlined in the reading passage works or can be further explained. Sometimes the listening passage will explain how a solution to the problem discussed in the reading was approached.

As you listen to the passage, you should focus on how the examples in the lecture illustrate the concept described in the reading passage. For instance, the lecture may give specific examples of a concept that is described generally in the reading passage. The listening passage may describe the work of one scientist who made important discoveries concerning the theory introduced in the reading passage. The lecture may describe the work of a specific artist that reflects an artistic style defined in the text. Using the reading as general background, listen for specific examples that illustrate the concept.

Now listen to the lecture that is part of the integrated Speaking Question 4 on photoreceptor cells that is related to the previous reading passage on the same topic.

Example Question 4 Listening Passage A 🔊 112

(narrator)   Now listen to a lecture on this topic in a physiology class.

(professor)   OK now I'm going to give you a few examples of how the different distribution and light sensitivities of these two types of photoreceptors affect visual perception. You've probably observed these effects, but you may not have known the explanation before.

Because only the rod cells are sensitive to very low light, say at night or . . . or a room lit by candlelight, you don't see colors in these situations. Think about it. At night, the cones don't function due to the faint light, only the rods. But, because only the cones allow us to see in color, everything is black and white. It's only when there's more light, um . . . like under a streetlamp at night, or uh when someone turns on the main lights in a dark room that things suddenly acquire color.

You can also see effects of the sensitivity and distribution of the rods in action if you look at a very dim star in the sky. You might have noticed before that a star such as this can be seen if you look a little to the left or right of the star. But if you look directly at the star, uh . . . I mean, center it in your field of vision, the star disappears. Move your focus a little away from the star and it suddenly reappears. This is because of the concentration of the very sensitive rods outside the center of your field of vision, a little to the left or the right, and the lower light sensitivity of the cone cells at the center of your field of vision.

As you listen to the passage, you should take notes on the specific examples in the lecture. Now look at the combined reading and listening notes.

Read:	Listen:
Top: <u>photoreceptor cells</u> = sens 2 light	EX: effects of 2 types
MPs:	—↓lght (@ night/candles), everything blk&wht
2 kind:	b/c rods only, cones X in low lght
—rods: ↑ sens 2 light	↑ lght (strtlamp) cones → color
X color	—see <u>dim</u> star only 2 lft/rght side of ctr
outside ctr <u>field of vision</u>	look direct = disappear b/c
—cones: ↓ sens 2 light	rods—2 side of ctr field of vision
sens 2 color	cones—X lght sens in ctr field of vision
inctr field of vision	

The notes from the lecture include examples of the effects of the differences between the two types of rod and cone cells. Two examples are noted after a dash (—) and then a few major points are included under each example, including reasons that the lecturer gives for each. Using these example notes as a model, do not try to write everything—only enough detail to remember the main examples and reasons. Notice that some key terms are underlined to indicate that they were stressed by the lecturer and therefore, are important.

Now listen to the lecture about equity theory that is related to the previous reading passage on the same topic.

Example Question 4 Listening Passage B 🔊 113

(narrator)   Now listen to a lecture on this topic in a business class.
(professor)   Let's look at a couple of cases to see the equity theory in action. We'll talk about this theory in terms of an imaginary employee. Let's call him Bill. In the first case,

a coworker of Bill's, named Sally, has the same job title as Bill and does the same amount of work. She makes a little less money, but she has more flexible hours. She can leave work earlier or come in later if she needs to, whereas Bill is paid a little extra to be available during certain set hours. He can't come and go like Sally can. Oh, and they have similar offices. In this situation, Bill will feel satisfied with his job if he values the extra money more than the flexibility of work hours. That's because, in his opinion, he receives equal or better return for his contribution than Sally does. According to the equity theory, Sally will also feel satisfied if she values the flexible hours more than the extra money. Even though she does the same amount of work as Bill, or makes the same contribution, she knows that her schedule is much more flexible than Bill's. Sally is satisfied because the return for her contribution is more valuable to her than her coworker, Bill's would be.

The second case is different. In the second case, a coworker of Bill's, named Tom, has the same job title and set hours and does the same amount of work as Bill. But Tom makes less money, and has a smaller office than Bill. So, in this case, Tom will not feel satisfied because he receives a lower return for his contribution than his coworker, Bill, does.

Read:	Listen:
Top: <u>equity theory</u> = how employees eval treatmnt by company	EX: equity theory—Bill: = wrk (work), title, office > \$ but < flex (flexibility)
	—Sally: = Bill wrk title, office < \$ but > flex sched
MPs:	B happy if \$ > import than flex-time
—<u>return 4 contribution</u> (r4c) (compare what put in vs. what get out)	S happy if flex > \$
—r4c> others, employee happy	for both B & S r4c ≥ <u>cowrker</u>—Tom:
—r4c< others, X happy	= B's work, title, flex but < \$, ↓ offc.

The notes for the listening include examples of the equity theory that was explained in the reading passage. The three example employees are indicated by first initials, and some details are noted to explain how each employee's case illustrates the equity theory. Symbols, like greater than/more (>) and less than (<) are used to avoid writing a lot of words. Key words are underlined and marked to indicate that they were stressed by the lecturer and therefore, are important.

At first, some students find it hard to take notes as they listen. Start by writing only a few key words about the main points as you hear each example described. As you practice taking notes while you listen, you will get more skilled at distinguishing important points and more comfortable writing them in a shortened form that you can use to organize and give your response. Start slowly and build your note-taking skills.

Another important skill for responses that involves academic topics, as Speaking Questions 4 and 6 do, is writing down key terms and indicating important words and terms that were stressed by the lecturer. When you recognize key terms in the reading or listening passage that you need to use in your response, you should try to write them down. If the terms come from the reading passage, you should listen to how the lecturer pronounces them in the listening passage. If the term comes from the listening passage, don't worry about spelling; just try to write down something that is close to what you hear.

The following chart outlines the key information for dealing with the listening passage in integrated Speaking Question 4.

KEY INFORMATION FOR NOTING THE MAIN POINTS IN THE LISTENING PASSAGE	
LISTEN FOR EXAMPLES	Using the information from the reading passage as background information, listen for examples that illustrate more specifically the general concept from the reading passage.
NOTE EXAMPLES AND MAIN POINTS	Write abbreviated, organized notes as you understand the examples. Use your own words and write only enough detail to remember the main points for your response. Mark key terms and any words that are stressed by the lecturer.

SPEAKING EXERCISE 10: Listen carefully to each of the following passages, focusing on how the specific main points from the lecture illustrate the general concept from the reading passage. Note the *main examples* or *points* and a few details to explain the main points. Before you listen, copy your notes for the reading passage on the same topic in the space provided below. Or take notes about the listening next to your notes for the reading passage on the previous pages.

1. Now listen to a lecture on this topic in a geology class. ◀))) 114

Read:	Listen:

2. Now listen to a lecture on this topic in a political science class.  ⁣115 🔊))

Read:
Listen:

3. Now listen to a lecture on this topic in a psychology class. ⁣116 🔊))

Read:
Listen:

Speaking Skill 11: USE YOUR NOTES TO PLAN THE RESPONSE FOR SPEAKING QUESTION 4

After you have read the passage and listened to the lecture in Speaking Question 4, you will see and hear a question. You will then have 30 seconds to prepare a response to the question. A clock on the screen will count down the preparation time. At the end of the 30 seconds, a narrator will tell you to begin speaking.

The question will ask about how the specific information from the listening passage illustrates the general concept described in the reading passage. The language of the question can vary based on the relationship between the reading and the listening passage, so it is important to read the question carefully to be sure that you know what information your answer must contain.

Look at the question below for reading passage A in Skill 9 and listening passage A in Skill 10.

Example Question 4A

The professor discusses some examples of visual perception. Explain how the examples demonstrate the differences in the two types of photoreceptor cells.

The question asks you to concentrate on the examples given in the lecture and to describe how they can be explained by differences between the types of photoreceptor cells. The response should be organized to include all of the examples discussed by the professor. The examples should be explained using the information from both the reading and the listening passage about the differences between the two types of cells.

To prepare a plan for your response, you should look at the notes you have taken on both the reading passage and the listening passage and focus on how the ideas in the reading and listening passages are related. Find the information (specific examples in this case) in your notes that answers the question asked. Mark your notes if you want, with numbers, lines, or other devices to help you organize your response.

Look at the notes for reading passage A in Skill 9 and listening passage A in Skill 10.

NOTES (Example Question 4A):

Read:	Listen:
Top: <u>photoreceptor cells</u> = sens 2 light	EX: effects of 2 types
MPs:	—↓lght (@ night/candles), everything blk&wht
2 kind:	b/c rods only, cones X in low lght
—rods: ↑ sens 2 light	↑ lght (strtlamp), cones → color
X color	—see <u>dim</u> star only 2 lft/rght side of ctr
outside ctr <u>field of vision</u>	look direct = disappear b/c
—cones: ↓ sens 2 light	rods—2 side of ctr field of vision
sens 2 color	cones—X lght sens in ctr field of vision
in ctr field of vision	

PLAN (Example Question 4A): In order to plan the response using your notes, discuss the examples in the lecture and relate them to the topics and main points from the reading passage.

1. Find the topic from the listening notes and use information from the reading notes to further define it.

   EX: *effects of 2 types* (topic of listening passage)

   Top: *photoreceptor cells = sens 2 light* (definition of the topic from the reading)

   These notes will help you form an introductory statement for the response.

2. Find the two examples of the effects of photoreceptor cells from the listening passage notes and find the notes in the reading passage, which further define the two types of photoreceptor cells, the rods and cones:

   EX—*↓ lght (@ night/candles), everything blk & wht b/c rods only, cones X in low lght; ↑ lght (strtlamp), cones → color* (first example from the listening)

   MP—*rods: ↑ sens 2 light, X color; —cones: ↓ sens 2 light, sens 2 color* (information from the reading, which defines rods and cones)

   EX—*see dim star only 2 lft/rght side of ctr; look direct = disappear b/c rods —2 side of ctr field of vision; cones—X lght sens in ctr field of vision* (second example from the listening)

   MP—*rods: outside ctr field of vision; —cones: in ctr field of vision* (information from the reading, which defines rods and cones)

   These notes will help you form the rest of your response to the question by connecting the specific information from the examples in the listening notes to the general information about rods and cones in the reading passage.

   In your response, note that you should discuss both of the examples of visual perception in the same order as the lecturer discussed them.

Now look at the question below for reading passage B in Skill 9 and listening passage B in Skill 10.

Example Question 4B
Explain how the examples of different employees illustrate the equity theory.

A response that completely answers the question will discuss the specific examples from the lecture and make it clear how these examples demonstrate the theory introduced in the reading passage. The focus of the question is on the examples from the lecture, so a good response will focus on the information from the listening passage and use some information from the reading passage to explain the connection between the examples and the theory.

Look at the notes for the reading and listening passages for Example Question 4B above.

NOTES (Example Question 4B):

Read:	Listen:
Top: equity theory = how employees eval treatmnt by company	EX: equity theory
MPs:	—Bill: = wrk, title, office > $ but < flex
—return 4 contribution (r4c) (compare what put in vs. what get out)	—Sally: =Bill wrk title, office < $ but > flex sched
—r4c > others, employee happy	—B happy if $ > import than flex-time
—r4c < others, X happy	—S happy if flex > $
	—for both B & S r4c ≥ cowrker—Tom
	T = B's work, title, flex but < $, ↓ offc
	T = X happy b/c r4c < B's r4c

PLAN (Example Question 4B): In order to plan the response using your notes, discuss the examples in the lecture and relate them to the topics and main points from the reading passage.

1. Find the topic from the listening notes and use information from the reading notes to further define it.

   EX: equity theory—Bill: = wrk, title, office > $ but < flex (topic of the listening passage)

   Top: equity theory = how employees eval treatmnt by company —return 4 contribution (r4c) (compare what put in vs. what get out) (definition of the topic from the reading)

   These notes will help you form an introductory statement for the response.

2. Find the two examples that illustrate the equity theory from the listening passage notes and find the notes in the reading passage, which define equity theory as it relates to each example:

   EX: Sally = Bill wrk title, office < $ but > flex sched; B happy if $ > import than flex-time; S happy if flex > $ (first example from the listening, comparing Sally and Bill)

   MP—r4c > others, employee happy (information from the reading that relates to this example)

   EX: for both B & S r4c ≥ cowrker Tom; T = B's work, title, flex but < $, ↓ offc; T = X happy b/c r4c < B's (second example from the listening, comparing Bill (and Sally) to Tom)

   MP—r4c < others, X happy (information from the reading that relates to this example)

   These notes will help you form the rest of your response to the question by connecting the specific information from the examples in the listening notes to the general information about equity theory in the reading passage.

Note that this plan gives the speaker less than 10 seconds to make each point.

For Speaking Question 4, you should look at your notes and make a plan that can help you focus and organize your ideas as you give your response. Mark the points that will answer the question and put them in a logical order. Consider your speaking fluency and how many points you will be able to make and still be easily understood.

The following chart outlines the key information for using the 30 seconds allowed to plan your response for integrated Speaking Question 4.

KEY POINTS FOR USING YOUR NOTES TO PLAN THE RESPONSE	
UNDERSTAND THE QUESTION	Read the question carefully. Be sure you know what information you must include in your response and which points you do not have to mention.
FIND THE INFORMATION	Look at your notes to find the information that will answer the question asked. Look for connections between ideas from the reading and the listening.
PLAN THE RESPONSE	Mark your notes to help you organize the points you will make in your response and the order in which you will make each point

SPEAKING EXERCISE 11: Look at the notes that you took for the reading passages in Speaking Exercise 9 (pages 269–270) and the listening passages in Speaking Exercise 10 (pages 274–275). Read the question. Then, using your notes, prepare a plan for your response. Decide which points you need to include to completely and accurately answer the question, the order in which you will speak about each point, and approximately how much time you will spend on each point. You have 30 seconds to plan each response. Time yourself to get used to answering the question in the response time allowed.

1. The professor describes the formation of the Hawaiian Islands and Yellowstone National Park. Describe how their formation can be explained by the existence of hotspots.

2. Explain how the examples given by the professor illustrate various problems that have occurred with telephone election polls.

3. Using the examples discussed by the professor about the patient H.M., explain how they illustrate the different ways that implicit and explicit memories are stored.

Speaking Skill 12: USE YOUR PLAN TO MAKE THE RESPONSE FOR SPEAKING QUESTION 4

After the 30 seconds of planning time ends, the narrator will tell you to begin speaking. You will have 60 seconds to record your response, and a clock on the screen will count down the time. At the end of 60 seconds, the clock will disappear, the computer will stop recording your response, and the narrator will tell you to stop speaking.

As you record your response, you should think about the following strategies:

- Start with a topic statement.
- Explain the main points of the lecture, following your plan.
- Give only the most relevant details from the listening and reading passages.
- Use useful language to show attribution (where the information is drawn from; either the listening passage or the reading passage) and the connections between ideas.
- Speak clearly using the English pronunciation points you have practiced to make your response sound more natural.

Look at the plan for responding to Question 4A from Speaking Skill 10. Then, look at and listen to a sample response based on the plan.

The professor discusses some examples of visual perception. Explain how the examples demonstrate the differences in the two types of photoreceptor cells.

PLAN (Example Question 4A):

> **Topic:** Use this part of the plan to form a topic statement for the response.
>
> <u>photoreceptor cells</u> = sens 2 light effects of 2 types
>
> **Examples and definitions:** Use this part of the plan to form the rest of your response for discussing specific examples from the lecture of the topic and definitions from the reading.
>
> —rods: ↑ sens 2 light, X color; — cones: ↓ sens 2 light, sens 2 color
>
> ↓lght (@ night/candles), everything blk&wht b/c rods only, cones X in low lght, ↑ lght (strtlamp), cones → color
>
> —rods: outside ctr <u>field of vision</u>, —cones: in ctr field of vision
>
> see <u>dim</u> star only 2 lft/rght side of ctr look direct = disappear b/c rods—2 side of ctr field of vision cones—X lghtsens in ctr field of vision

SAMPLE RESPONSE [Example Question 4A]: 🔊 **117**

> The lecturer gives two examples of how we see things. These examples show the differences between two different photoreceptor cells in our eyes that capture light and color, called rods and cones. The first example is that when there isn't much light, such as candlelight, everything looks black and white. This is because the rods are the only kinds of cells that are sensitive in dim light, but they can't capture color. Cones sense color, but they can't detect dim light, like the low light at night. Next, the professor says that if we look directly at a star that isn't bright, it can disappear. But if we look to either side of the star, we can see it. He goes on to say that this is because the center of our vision has fewer rods that sense dim light. Instead, they are more concentrated to the left or right of the center of the field of vision.

You should notice that this response begins with a topic statement that directly addresses the question asked. Then the speaker explains each of the examples given in the lecture, as the questions ask her to do. The response gives a few relevant details from the reading passage and listening passage to explain how differences between the two types of light sensitive cells (the rods and cones) are illustrated in the examples given by the lecturer. The response is organized to completely and accurately answer the question, concentrating on the examples given in the listening passage. Unnecessary details are not included, and all of the information comes from the reading and listening passages, <u>not</u> from the speaker's own knowledge of the subject. Useful language and transitions (highlighted) are used to show the connection between ideas.

Now, look at the plan for responding to Example Question 4B from Speaking Skill 10. Then, look at and listen to a sample response based on the plan.

Example Question 4B

Explain how the examples of different employees illustrate the equity theory.

PLAN (Example Question 4B):

Topic: Use this part of the plan to form a topic statement for the response.

equity theory = how employees eval treatmnt by company—
return 4 contribution (r4c) (compare what put in vs. what get out)
Bill: = wrk, title, office > $ but <flex

Examples and definitions: Use this part of the plan to form the rest of your response for discussing specific examples from the lecture of the topic and definitions from the reading.

r4c> others, employee happy
Sally: = Bill wrk title, office < $ but > flex sched
B happy if $ > import than flex-time; S happy if flex > $

r4c < others, X happy
for both B & S r4c ≥ cowrker—Tom; T = B's work, title, flex but < $, ↓ offc;
T = X happy b/c r4c < B's

SAMPLE RESPONSE (Example Question 4B): 🔊 118

The examples given in the lecture describe the pay and benefits of some employees and describe what equity theory says about their job satisfaction. Equity theory says that people compare what they get out of the company to what they put in, and this is called return for contribution. The professor talks about two employees that get equal work and offices, but one, Bill, gets more pay and less flexibility in his schedule. And the other, Sally, gets the opposite. Equity theory says that if Bill likes money more than flexibility, he'll be happy, and if Sally likes flexibility more, she'll be happy, too. They will both feel that they get the same or better returns for contribution than the other one. Then the professor contrasts this with another employee, Tom, who does the same work but for less money and in a worse office. The theory says that Tom will be unsatisfied because he gets less return for contribution than the other employees.

This response begins with a topic statement that answers the question directly. The response briefly defines the theory in the speaker's own words, and then describes the examples. Not many details are given from the reading passage because the question does not primarily ask about it. Instead, the response ties the professor's examples to the definition from the reading to completely and accurately answer the question. Useful language is used to attribute (say where information came from), give definitions, and connect ideas.

Many students find integrated Speaking Question 4 to be the most challenging of the speaking questions. Students may find it difficult to understand the academic concepts presented in the reading and listening, to discuss all of the main points in 60 seconds, or both. Before you plan to take the test, practice listening to and reading a variety of academic subjects in English. Your understanding of academic concepts, vocabulary, and discussions will improve, and you will be more likely to understand the academic reading and listening passages on the test (as well as at a university later). Practice taking notes and verbally summarize these notes with a partner to build your fluency of expression.

During the TOEFL iBT®test, use your knowledge of what Speaking Question 4 typically asks in order to focus on the specific examples in the listening passage and to connect them to the general concept in the reading passage. If you plan your response and follow this plan as you speak, you will probably find it easier to cover all or most of the important points in 60 seconds.

The following chart outlines the key information for using the 60 seconds allowed to make your response for integrated Speaking Question 4.

KEY POINTS FOR USING YOUR PLAN TO MAKE THE RESPONSE	
START WITH A TOPIC STATEMENT	Start your response with a *topic statement* that fully addresses the question that is being asked. State the topic of the reading and listening passage and the relationship between the two.
EXPLAIN EXAMPLES	Following the plan you have made with your notes, explain the examples or major points of the lecture. Include all of the information the question is asking for.
USE DETAILS TO MAKE IDEAS	Include details from the reading passage and listening passage to help make the examples you are explaining clear. Include only enough details from the listening and reading passages so the listener can understand how the specific examples from the lecture illustrate the general concept from the reading.
CONNECT IDEAS USING USEFUL LANGUAGE	Practice using useful language before you take the test. When you give your response, use language structures and transitions you are comfortable with to show how ideas are connected with each other. Use attribution signals to show where the ideas came from; either the listening passage or the reading passage.

The useful language and pronunciation tips below can help you make your response easier to understand. Practice this language and these tips in the weeks before you take the TOEFL iBT® test.

USEFUL LANGUAGE AND TRANSITIONAL PHRASES
To report where information comes from: *As is stated in the listening/reading passage, . . .* *. . . as indicated in the reading/lecture* *The professor/reading says/states that . . .* *As is stated in the reading passage, the employee will be unhappy . . .* Rods detect colors, as indicated in the lecture. The professor says that the plate moves southwest . . .
To give a definition: name of term, *which is/means* + definition definition, *called/named/known as* + name of term definition, *which is called/named/known as* + name . . . explicit memory, which is the memory of facts and experiences. . . . the movement of earth's plates, known as plate tectonics. . . . surveys of people's opinions, which are called polls.
To report more of what someone says: Subject + *goes on to say that* Subject + *add(s)* + noun/(that) + subject + verb *another/a further* + noun She goes on to say that there is a new volcano rising. He adds that she was a feminist. She adds another example. The professor gives a further example of the theory.

MAKING YOUR RESPONSE EASIER TO UNDERSTAND: Using correct word stress		
HOW ENGLISH PRONUNCIATION FUNCTIONS	Each word has a stressed syllable, which means that syllable is said louder, with a higher pitch, and extended for a longer period of time than other syllables. This also applies to some combinations of words, such as phrasal verbs and compound nouns.	. . . deSCRIBE what EQuityTHEORy says aBOUT their JOBsatisFACtion. The second syllables of *describe* and *about* are stressed. The capitalized syllables are stressed the most in *equity theory* and *job satisfaction*.
YOUR RESPONSE	As you study new vocabulary before you take the TOEFL iBT® test, note which syllable in a word is stressed the most and practice stressing it. There are rules that you can study to learn the correct stress of word combinations, such as compound nouns and adjectives, adjective-noun combinations, and phrasal verbs. Practice marking the stressed syllable(s) of key words you hear while listening to the exercises in this book so that you can pronounce them correctly in your response.	

SPEAKING EXERCISE 12: Create responses for the integrated reading, listening, and speaking questions that you have been working on in Speaking Exercises 9–11 (pp. 269–270, 274–275, and 279). You have 60 seconds to give your response. Time yourself and practice giving the response until you can speak clearly, but still get the necessary information into the 60-second response time.

SPEAKING REVIEW EXERCISE (SKILLS 9–12): Read the passage below and take notes on the main points. You have 45 seconds to read it. Then, listen to a lecture on the same subject and take notes. Next, read the question. You have 30 seconds to prepare a response using the notes you have taken on the reading and listening passages. Give your response. You have 60 seconds to give a fluent, organized response that completely and accurately answers the question.

Transcendentalism

Transcendentalism is a philosophical, religious, social, and artistic movement that reached its peak in the mid-nineteenth century. Established in the northeastern United States, the movement was reacting to other philosophical and religious currents that were dominant at the time, as well as trying to establish a singularly American style of artistic expression, distinct from European influence. Transcendentalism emphasizes the inherent goodness of man and the ability of each individual to achieve moral and spiritual self-improvement by, among other things, experiencing nature and using the senses and intuition to arrive at understanding. Transcendentalism's emphasis on individual freedom and responsibility led its proponents to support the causes of social justice and equality.

Now listen to a lecture on the same subject in an American Literature class. 🔊 **119**

Now answer the following question. You have 30 seconds to prepare, and 60 seconds to speak. 🔊 **120**

How do the books written by Emerson and Fuller illustrate some of the main principles of Transcendentalism?

QUESTIONS 5 AND 6: INTEGRATED QUESTIONS (LISTENING AND SPEAKING)

There are two speaking questions that integrate speaking with listening. For both of these questions you will listen to passages that are slightly longer than the listening passages in Questions 3 and 4. For Question 5, you will listen to a conversation between a man and a woman, often students, concerning a campus topic. For Question 6, you will listen to a single professor giving an academic lecture. For both questions, when you have finished listening to the passage, a narrator will read a question that will appear on the screen. Both Speaking Questions 5 and 6 will ask you to summarize the main points of the listening passage. In Speaking Question 5, you will also be asked to give your opinion. You have 20 seconds to prepare, and 60 seconds to record a response. A clock on the screen will show you how much time you have left to prepare, and another will count down the 60 seconds of response time when you begin recording.

SPEAKING QUESTION 5: CAMPUS-BASED INTEGRATED LISTENING AND SPEAKING

The listening passage for Speaking Question 5 generally involves a problem that is a typical one students would have on a college campus. The speakers might be discussing a problem with a class, a roommate, schedules, or transportation. The problem often involves only one speaker, but it may be a problem that concerns both speakers. The speakers will discuss at least two solutions to the problem, and respond to any solutions that are given. The passage will usually last from 60–90 seconds. After you hear the passage, you will hear and see a question. Typically the question asks you to summarize the problem and say which of the two solutions you prefer and why. This is the only question that

> Improving your listening comprehension takes a lot of practice. In addition to practicing conversations in English, listen to television and movies in English, which will help to improve your understanding.

integrates speaking with listening where you must give your personal opinion. You will then have 20 seconds to prepare and 60 seconds to speak.

Speaking Question	Usual Expectations For A Response	Listening Time	Preparation Time	Response Time
Question 5: Problem / Recommendation (Solution)	Explain the problem described by one or both of the speakers in the conversation. Choose one solution or recommnedation from the two or more that are discussed and give reasons or examples to support your choice.	60–90 seconds	20 seconds	60 seconds

Speaking Skill 13: NOTE THE MAIN POINTS AS YOU LISTEN FOR SPEAKING QUESTION 5

As you listen to the passage, you should focus on the problem that the speakers describe, the suggestions or solutions that are offered, and any reasons given for the suggestions or the speakers' reactions to them.

You should take notes on the passage and try to practice note-taking as much as you can before you take the TOEFL iBT® test.

Now, look at and listen to the following example of a listening passage for integrated Speaking Question 5.

Example Question 5 Listening Passage A ◀)) [121]

(narrator)	Listen to a conversation between two students.
(woman)	Hi, Brett.
(man)	Hi, Karen.
(woman)	You don't look too happy, Brett. Is anything the matter?
(man)	Well, I'm having trouble in my economics class, and I just talked to the professor. She didn't seem too sympathetic.
(woman)	She didn't? What's the problem?

(man)	Well, it's that I'm on the baseball team, and the away games are all on the weekend. I mean, usually when we're traveling to another school for a weekend game, we leave around noon on Friday.
(woman)	And?
(man)	The thing is that the discussion section for my economics class meets on Friday at 1:15. I've missed three of the last four Fridays, and part of my total grade is going to be based on participation.
(woman)	Did you explain to your professor why you've been missing class?
(man)	Yeah, but she was not happy about it at all.
(woman)	I suppose if they're grading participation in the discussion you kind of have to be there, right? Listen, have you thought about switching to a different section of the class? I think there's another discussion section on Tuesdays in the early evening.
(man)	Hmm . . . I hadn't thought about that . . . I guess I could check, but then I'd have to ask to leave the Tuesday baseball practice a little early.
(woman)	Or you could drop the class and take it over next semester.
(man)	Well, then I wouldn't get credit for the class. And I'd be behind schedule to graduate on time.
(woman)	Why not just take more classes next semester? You don't have to pay by the class, and the economics class won't be as much work because you'll already have done part of it this semester.
(man)	Yeah, I suppose next semester I won't be playing baseball, so I'll have a lot more time to study for an extra class.

Now look at the notes for the listening passage. Notice that the notes include only the problem and the solutions given for the problems. In addition, the notes indicate which speaker, the man or the woman, gave the information. This style of taking notes creates an outline of the major points, which can be used to form a plan for the response to Speaking Question 5. A space is left for giving your own opinion about which of the two solutions you prefer.

NOTES (Example Question 5A):

P (problem): M—miss econ clss discuss sect Fri b/c bsebll game
grade = particip discuss sect, prof X happy

S1 (Solution 1): W—change discuss sect 2 Tues
        (M—leave bsebll pract early?)

S2 (Solution 2): W—drop clss, take next semes
        (M—X cred & behind grad sched)
        M—No bsebll next semes, > time,
        EZ b/c repeat material X pay class

OP (my opinion):

These notes include the problem described in the listening passage, which is that the man is missing the discussion section for his economics class on Fridays because of out-of-town baseball games he needs to go to, that the grade for that economics class is based on participation in the discussion section, and that the professor is not happy about the man missing the discussions. The first solution proposed by the woman is to change to another section of the class on Tuesday, and the man's reaction is noted in parentheses. The second solution from the woman is noted, again with the man's reaction in parentheses. Some reasons the speakers discuss for the second suggestion are noted under this suggestion: the man will not have baseball next semester and thus will have more time, the class will be easy because he will be repeating a lot of the material, and he does not pay for his studies by class. The last line, *OP*, will be filled in during the 20 seconds of planning time allowed for Speaking Question 5.

For this style of note-taking, you only have to write down the major points and note who is saying what, and your response is already organized for you.

Now look at and listen to another conversation and then, look at the notes which follow it.

Example Question 5 Listening Passage B 🔊 122

(narrator)	Listen to a conversation between two students.
(man)	Hey, Karen, are you taking organic chemistry next trimester? I was thinking we might study together again.
(woman)	Actually, I'm going to wait until the spring trimester to take it. The class next trimester is accelerated, and it's supposed to be really hard. You're not taking that one are you?
(man)	I was going to because Dr. Alvaro is teaching the psychology class I want to take in the spring, and it's at the same time as the chemistry class.
(woman)	I don't know about you taking that kind of chemistry class next trimester. I mean, you'll have to do the same amount work as a regular class in a much shorter time, Brad and. . .uh, you're not doing that great in chemistry this trimester.
(man)	Dr. Alvaro's class is supposed to be fantastic, and he only teaches it once a year.
(woman)	You should wait until next year to take his class. You have to take chemistry this year, and if you take the accelerated chemistry class next trimester, you might not be able to handle it.
(man)	Well, I guess I could join a study group for the class and get a tutor if I need to. If I start off right, I know I can do better than I did in chemistry this trimester. But, if I wait a year for Dr. Alvaro's class, I might not be able to work it into my schedule. Or he might leave, which he does sometimes.
(woman)	I suppose, but I think you're taking a big chance that you'll fall behind and have to drop it.

NOTES (Example Question 5B):

> P: M —chem clss nxt trimstr
>
> S1: W—X clss b/c accel clss= hard, take in spring trimstr
>
> P w/ S1 (problem with solution 1):
> M—nxt trimstr b/c clss conflict in spring = wants psych clss @ same time chem clss
> (W—accel clss = 2 much 2 learn in shrt time &
> man X good @ chem.)
>
> S2: W—take psych clss nxt yr ,chem clss spring
> P w/ S2: M—psych prof good, 1x/yr only
> M—study grp, tutor4 chem clss next trimstr,
> if spring class miss psych class, but nxt yr psych
> clss maybe probs w/ sched or prof leave
> (W—big risk b/c fall behind/drop clss)
>
> OP (my opinion):

These notes summarize the key points that the man and woman each make, in the order they make them. The woman's reactions are noted in parentheses. In addition, the problems that the man has with each of the woman's suggested solutions are noted. The note-taker used abbreviations and symbols to record information, but did not try to write everything the speakers said. These notes contain more detail than might be needed for the response. For example, there may not be enough time to include everything the woman said, but some details can be omitted when the response is given. The positive aspect of this note-taking style is that, again, your response is already organized.

While you are practicing for the TOEFL iBT® test, try different styles of note-taking to see which works best for you.

The following chart outlines the key information for dealing with the listening passage in integrated Speaking Question 5.

KEY INFORMATION FOR NOTING THE MAIN POINTS IN THE LISTENING PASSAGE	
LISTEN FOR KEY POINTS	Focus on listening for the problem and the suggested solutions on how to solve the problem. Listen for reasons the speakers give for each solution they suggest.
TAKE NOTES ON KEY IDEAS	Use the style of note-taking that is most helpful for you. Use abbreviations and symbols to write down the problem, the suggestions made or the solutions offered, and important reasons for or against the suggested solutions.

SPEAKING EXERCISE 13: Listen to each of the conversations and take notes on the problem discussed, solutions offered, and reactions of the speakers to the solutions.

1. Listen to a conversation between two students. 🔊)) **123**

2. Listen to a conversation between two students. 🔊)) **124**

3. Listen to a conversation between two students. 🔊)) **125**

Speaking Skill 14: USE YOUR NOTES TO PLAN THE RESPONSE FOR SPEAKING QUESTION 5

After you have listened to the conversation, a question will appear on your screen and a narrator will read the question. You will then have 20 seconds to prepare a response. A clock labeled "Preparation Time" will appear on the screen and count down the 20 seconds. At the end of the 20 seconds, a narrator will tell you to begin speaking.

The question will ask you to describe one speaker's problem and then choose one of the solutions the speakers discussed that you think is better and explain why. Read the question carefully to see what you must include in your response, but it is not always necessary to describe both solutions that were discussed. However, you must give your personal opinion on how the speaker(s) should resolve the problem and reasons you have for holding this opinion. You can support your opinion with reasons the speakers give in the conversation, your own personal experience in similar situations, or both.

Look at this question about the man's problem with his economics class from Listening Passage 5A in Skill 13.

Example Question 5A

The students discuss two possible solutions to the man's problem. Describe the problem. Then state which of the two solutions you prefer and explain why.

To answer this question, you have to include three things: a description of the problem, your opinion on which solution is better, and reasons that you think the solution you prefer is better.

To prepare a plan for your response, you should look at the notes you have taken on the listening passage and find the key information you need to answer the question. You will need to find details about the problem and the solution you prefer, to explain the problem clearly and support your choice. Then you should use the information you found in your notes to plan a response.

Look at the notes and the plan for a response to Example Question 5A.

NOTES (Example Question 5A):

> P: M—miss econ clss discuss sect Fri b/c bsebll game
> grade = particip discuss sect, prof X happy
>
> S1: W—change discuss sect 2 Tues
> (M—leave bsebll pract early?)
>
> S2: W—drop clss, take next semes
> (M—X cred & behind grad sched)
> M—No bsebll next semes, > time, EZ b/c repeat material X
> pay class
>
> OP: change sect, EZ (if can leave bsebll pract early)
> drop class = waste time & lose cred; U never
> know future sched

PLAN (Example Question 5A):

In order to plan the response using your notes, find the key information about the problem, your opinion, and reasons that support your opinion:

1. Find the problem from the listening notes.

   P: M—miss econ clss discuss sect Fri b/c bsebll game

   grade = particip discuss sect, prof X happy

   These two major details from the notes will help you form an introductory statement for the response, which states the problem.

2. Form your opinion based on one of the solutions given from the listening notes.

   S1: W—change discuss sect 2 Tues (one solution offered by the woman)

   change sect, EZ (if can leave bsebll pract early) (opinion chosen based on the woman's first solution)

   Your opinion from the notes should be stated after the problem is defined.

3. Find the reasons in the notes to support your opinion and, if there is time to cover it in the response, find the solution not chosen and give reasons from the notes for not choosing that solution. Include your own reasons based on your personal experience from the notes:

   M—No bsebll next semes, > time, EZ b/c repeat material X pay class (reasons for supporting the opinion)

   S2: W—drop clss, (M—X cred & behind grad sched) (reason for not supporting the other solution)

   U never know future sched (reason based on personal experience)

   These notes will help you form the rest of your response to the question by supporting your opinion (and giving reasons for not supporting the other solution offered).

Now look at the question about the man's problem with the chemistry class for Listening Passage 5B in Skill 13.

Example Question 5B

The students discuss two possible solutions to the man's problem. Explain the problem. Then state which of the solutions to the problem you think is better and why.

You can see that the question is very similar to Example Question 5A. It asks you to give the same information in the response: an explanation of the problem, which solution you prefer, and reasons you prefer it.

Look at the notes and the plan for a response to Example Question 5B.

SPEAKING

NOTES (Example Question 5B):

> P: M —chem clss nxt trimstr
> S1: W—X clss b/c accel clss = hard, take in spring
> trimstr
>
> P w/ S1 (problem with solution 1):
> M—nxt trimstr b/c clss conflict in spring =
> wants psych clss @ same time chem clss)
> (W—accel clss = 2 much 2 learn in shrt time & man X good @ chem.)
>
> S2: W—take psych clss nxt yr ,chem clss spring
> P w/ S2: M—psych prof good, 1x/yr only
> M—study grp, tutor 4 chem clss next trimstr, if spring class miss psych
> class, but nxt yr psych clss maybe probs w/ sched or prof leave
> (W—big risk b/c fall behind/drop clss)
>
> Op: M—take chem clss next trimstr b/c study grp &
> tutor nxt yr 4 psych clss X good b/c something change
> take hard clss = test limits & handle hard clss in future

PLAN (Example Question 5B):

In order to plan the response using your notes, find the key information about the problem, your opinion, and reasons that support your opinion:

1. Find the problem from the listening notes.

   P: M—chem clss nxt trimstr // W—X clss b/c accel clss // M—nxt trimstr b/c clss conflict in spring = wants psych clss @ same time chem clss

   These two major details from the notes will help you form an introductory statement for the response, which states the problem.

2. Form your opinion based on one of the solutions given and find the reasons to support it in the listening notes. If there is time to cover it in the response, find the solution *not* chosen and give reasons from the notes for *not* choosing that solution. Include your own reasons based on your personal experience from the notes:

   M—take chem clss next trimstr b/c study grp & tutor (opinion and first reason)

   nxt yr 4 psych clss X good b/c something change (other solution and reason for not choosing it)

   take hard clss = test limits & hndle hard clss in future (two reasons based on personal experience)

This plan summarizes the problem using information from several parts of the conversation. Then, the response will give the speaker's opinion and three reasons to support the opinion. The speaker's opinion and the last two reasons based on personal experience have been added to the notes during the planning time. The plan indicates that the response should summarize the problem in less than half of the response time allowed and that the reasons for the opinion will use the majority of the remaining 60 seconds. Note that the response only briefly mentions the other solution. The plan can be adjusted during the response; for instance, if there isn't enough time, one or two of the reasons can be dropped.

As the plans demonstrate, you can give reasons for your choice, or against the other choice. You can use the same reasons as the speakers do in the conversation, or you can use reasons that come from your personal experience. The most important thing to remember is that you must plan to allow enough time to give your opinion and reasons in order to fully answer the question and receive a top score.

Even if you do not have time to take detailed notes like those above, you should try to write down a few ideas to help you remember the information you need to include in your response. It is important that you write down a few words to remind you to give your opinion and to help you remember one or two reasons that support your opinion. Concentrate on planning a response that answers the question without giving unnecessary details.

If you speak fluently, you can include more details or reasons. However, you should concentrate on the points that answer the question and avoid giving more details than are necessary. You do not need to describe all of the suggestions and reasons the speakers give—only who and what the question asks about.

The following chart outlines the key information for using the 20 seconds allowed to plan your response for integrated Speaking Question 5.

KEY POINTS FOR USING YOUR NOTES TO PLAN THE RESPONSE	
UNDERSTAND THE QUESTION	Read the question carefully to be sure that you understand what information you must include in your response.
FIND OR ADD THE INFORMATION	Find the information to answer the question in your notes, including the problem, whose problem it is (man or woman), the solutions offered, reasons for or against the solutions, and your opinion based on these reasons. Add any information that you feel is appropriate for your response, such as your own opinion and reasons.
PLAN THE RESPONSE	Plan the number of points you will discuss, the order in which you will discuss them, and how much time you will spend on each one. Adjust the number of reasons and details you will discuss based on how fast or slowly you can speak naturally and clearly.

SPEAKING EXERCISE 14: Look at the notes that you took for the listening passages in Speaking Exercise 13 (p. 289). Read the question. Then, using your notes, prepare a plan for your response. Decide which points you need to include to completely and accurately answer the question, the order in which you will speak about each point, and approximately how much time you will spend on each point. You have 20 seconds to plan a response. Time yourself to get used to answering the question in the response time allowed.

1. The students discuss two possible solutions to a problem. Describe the students' problem. Then state which of the two solutions you think is better and why.

2. The students discuss two possible solutions to the man's problem. Describe the man's problem. Then state which of the two solutions you prefer and why.

3. The students discuss two possible solutions to the man's problem. Describe the man's problem. Then state which of the two solutions you think is better and why.

SPEAKING EXERCISE 14   293

Speaking Skill 15: USE YOUR PLAN TO MAKE THE RESPONSE FOR SPEAKING QUESTION 5

After the 20 seconds of planning time has finished, the narrator will tell you to begin speaking. You will have 60 seconds to record your response, and a clock on the screen will count down the time. At the end of 60 seconds, the clock will disappear, the computer will stop recording your response, and the narrator will tell you to stop speaking. As you record your response, you should think about the following strategies:

- Start with a topic statement that summarizes the problem and indicate whose problem it is (man or woman).

- State which solution you think is better and give the reasons for your opinion, following your plan.

- Give only the most relevant details from the listening passage.

- Use useful language to report the solutions and show connections between the solutions and the reasons for them.

- Speak clearly using the English pronunciation points you have practiced to make your response sound more natural.

Look at the plan for responding to Example Question 5A from Speaking Skill 14. Then, look at and listen to a sample response based on the plan.

Example Question 5A
The students discuss two possible solutions to the man's problem. Describe the the problem. Then state which of the two solutions you prefer and why.

PLAN (Example Question 5A):

Problem: Use this part of the plan to form an introductory statement for the response.

M—miss econ clss discuss sect Fri b/c bsebll game

grade = particip discuss sect, prof X happy

Your Opinion: State your opinion based on one of the solutions after the problem is explained.

Solution 1: W—change discuss sect 2 Tues

change sect, EZ (if can leave bsebll pract early)

Reasons to Support Your Opinion / Not Support Other Solution: Use this part of the plan to form the rest of your response to the question by supporting your opinion with specific reasons (and giving reasons for not supporting the other solution offered if you have enough time).

M—No bsebll next semes, > time, EZ b/c repeat material X pay class

(reasons for supporting the opinion)

Solution 2: W—drop clss, (M—X cred & behind grad sched)

(reason for not supporting the other solution)

U never know future sched

(reason based on personal experience)

SAMPLE RESPONSE (Example Question 5A): 🔊

> The man's problem is that he misses the discussion section for his economics class on Fridays because he plays baseball and has to go to games at other schools. His grade is based on participation, so he's not doing well at all. The woman recommends trying to switch to the Tuesday discussion section for the class, and I think that's a better idea. If he can leave his baseball practice early on Tuesday, that sounds easier than dropping a class and losing credit for it. Besides, it's a waste of time to take the same class twice. If he's not having problems in his other classes, he shouldn't drop economics. Finally, you never know what your future schedule will be like. Like the man said, it might be hard for him to make up the credits later and graduate on time.

You should notice that this response summarizes the problem in the first two sentences. The response gives only enough details so that the problem is clear to the listener. Then the response states the solution that the speaker prefers. The rest of the response gives three reasons why the speaker thinks changing to another discussion section is a better idea. Notice that the reasons may be from the conversation (it might be hard to graduate on time) or from the speaker's personal experience (taking the same class twice is a waste of time). Useful language and transitions (highlighted) are used to connect ideas and report what the speakers say in the conversation.

Now look at the plan for Example Question 5B. Then, look at and listen to the sample response based on the plan.

Example Question 5B
The students discuss two possible solutions to the man's problem. Explain the problem. Then state which of the solutions to the problem you think is better and why.

PLAN (Example Question 5B):

> **Problem:** Use this part of the plan to form an introductory statement for the response.
>
> M—chem clss nxt trimstr // W—X clss b/c accel clss // M—nxt trimstr b/c clss conflict in spring = wants psych clss @ same time chem clss
>
> **Your Opinion and Reasons to Support Your Opinion / Not Support Other Solution:** State your opinion based on one of the solutions after the problem is explained. Use this part of the plan to form the rest of your response to the question by supporting your opinion with specific reasons (and giving reasons for not supporting the other solution offered if you have enough time).
>
> M—take chem clss next trimstr b/c study grp & tutor
>
> (opinion and first reason)
>
> nxt yr 4 psych clss X good b/c something change
>
> (other solution and reason for not choosing it)
>
> take hard clss = test limits & hndle hard clss in future
>
> (two reasons based on personal experience)

> The problem the man has is that he has to take chemistry this year, and the easier class in the spring conflicts with a psychology class he wants to take. The woman advises him not to take the chemistry class the next trimester because it's accelerated and really difficult. If I were the man, I would take the harder class the next trimester. If he is serious about joining a study group and getting a tutor, he should be able to keep up and not fall behind in the accelerated class. And he's right that if he waits a year to take the psychology class he wants, something else may come up. But most of all, if he takes a hard class, he can test his limits. He can find out if he'll be able to handle really hard classes in the future.

This response begins by explaining the problem in two sentences. It follows the plan to summarize the problem clearly in a short amount of time. Then the response states which solution the speaker prefers. This plan leaves most of the response time for explaining the reasons for the opinion. Finally the response gives three reasons why the man should take the harder class, and one reason that the man should not choose the other solution of waiting a year. Two of the reasons are from the conversation, and the last two come from the speaker's personal experience. This response gives four reasons, but if the response time is running out, one or two reasons for the opinion would be enough. Useful language and transitions (highlighted) are used to summarize and report what the speakers say, and to connect ideas.

One problem students often have is not being able to give their opinion and reasons for the opinion before the response time runs out. In order to have enough time to say which solution you prefer and why, you should combine key points into one or two sentences to briefly summarize the problem. This will also leave you enough time to give your opinion and fully describe the reasons for preferring one solution.

If you tend to speak slowly, then concentrate on explaining the problem in less than 20 seconds, explaining the solution you prefer in 20 seconds or less, and spending the rest of the time on one or two reasons to support your opinion. Plan your response with the minimum number of points that will still fully answer the question. On the other hand, if you can speak more fluently, instead of giving more details about the problem or other solutions, it may be better to try to think of a few reasons, based on your own experience, for preferring one solution. You can add examples to illustrate those reasons, spending a little more of the response time discussing your personal experience. You will probably earn a higher score for a response that quickly summarizes the problem and the best solution, and discusses the reasons that support your opinion than you will for a response that gives too many details from the conversation.

The following chart outlines the key information for using the 60 seconds allowed to make your response for integrated Speaking Question 5.

KEY POINTS FOR USING YOUR PLAN TO MAKE THE RESPONSE

EXPLAIN THE PROBLEM	Start your response with one or two sentences that clearly, but briefly, explain the problem. Do not give more details than are necessary.
EXPLAIN THE SOLUTION YOU PREFER AND GIVE REASONS TO SUPPORT IT	Explain which solution you prefer, giving only enough details so that the listener understands the solution. Then explain why you would choose this solution, using reasons from the conversation, your personal experience, or both. If you have enough time, you can also explain why you do not prefer the other solution.
TIMING	Watch the time as you are summarizing the problem and the solution you prefer. Leave enough time to give your opinion and reasons to support it.
USE USEFUL LANGUAGE TO REPORT AND CONNECT IDEAS	Practice using useful language to explain solutions and give reasons for your opinion before you take the test. When you give your response, use language structures and transitions you are comfortable with to make your response easier to understand.

The useful language and pronunciation tips below can help you make your response easier to understand. Practice this language and these tips in the weeks before you take the TOEFL iBT®test.

USEFUL LANGUAGE AND TRANSITIONAL PHRASES

To report suggestions and advice (solutions):
Subject + *recommends/suggests* + *that* + subject + base verb
Subject + *recommends/suggests* + verb + *-ing*
Subject + *advises/tells/encourages* + object + (*not*) *to* + verb
He suggests that she take a quick nap between classes.
She recommends wearing a mask when he sleeps.
The man tells her not to wait to register for the class.

To give more reasons:
Besides/Also/What's more + positive statement + *too* OR negative statement + *either.*
(*But*) *Most of all/Most importantly,*
Organizing notes saves time. Besides, it's a way to study.
He'll have more money, too. She won't waste time either.
But most of all, she'll learn a lot from the experience.

To agree/disagree with what someone says:
Subject + *is right/wrong that* (or *right/wrong about* + noun, *but is right/wrong about*)
Subject + *has/makes a good point that*
It's true/not true that
He's right that tea is healthy, but he's wrong about cake.
She makes a good point that he isn't doing well in class.
It's not true that taking the bus is easier than driving.

MAKING YOUR RESPONSE EASIER TO UNDERSTAND: Linking words

HOW ENGLISH PRONUNCIATION FUNCTIONS	English speakers link the endings of words to the beginnings of the following words. Ending consonants link with beginning vowels and beginning consonants, and this may change the sounds of the consonants.	The problem the man has is that he has to take chemistry this year. The word *has* links with *is* and sounds like /haziz/. *Take* links with *chemistry*, and there is only one /k/ sound: /teikemistri/. *This* links with *year* and sounds like "sh" /s/: /thisier/
YOUR RESPONSE	Listen for and imitate the way English speakers link words together. Practice this before you take the TOEFL iBT® test when you speak, read aloud, or repeat after listening. When you give your response, try to link words together in the way you have practiced. Do not pronounce each word separately. Linking words will make your response more fluid and natural sounding.	

SPEAKING EXERCISE 15: Create responses for the integrated Speaking questions that you have been working on in Speaking Exercises 13–14 (pp. 289 and 293). You have 60 seconds to give your response. Time yourself and repeat your response until you can get the necessary information into the 60-second response time.

SPEAKING REVIEW EXERCISE (Skills 13–15): Listen to the conversation and take notes on the problem, the solutions proposed, and the reasons or reactions of the speakers. ◀))) ^128

Now answer the following question. You have 20 seconds to plan your response and 60 seconds to speak. ◀))) ^129

Question 5
The students discuss two possible solutions to the woman's problem. Explain the problem. Then state which of the solutions to the problem you think is better and why.

SPEAKING QUESTION 6: ACADEMIC INTEGRATED LISTENING AND SPEAKING

In the second listening and speaking integrated question, Speaking Question 6, you will be asked to listen to an academic passage. In this passage a professor will introduce an academic topic and then discuss examples, implications, reasons, or some other aspects of the topic. Normally the professor will discuss two major points related to the topic and explain each of these points more fully. You will then be asked a question about the passage that will ask you to summarize the main ideas of the topic using points from the lecture. The time for the preparation and for giving the response is the same as for Speaking Question 5.

Speaking Question	Usual Expectations For A Response	Listening Time	Preparation Time	Response Time
Question 6: Academic Setting— Summary	Summarize the main points of a short lecture on an academic subject, using supporting details or examples from the lecture to illustrate the main points.	60–90 seconds	20 seconds	60 seconds

Speaking Skill 16: NOTE THE MAIN POINTS AS YOU LISTEN FOR SPEAKING QUESTION 6

In Speaking Question 6, a professor will give a lecture on an academic topic and usually make two major points about the topic of the lecture using specific details to explain the points. For example, the professor may introduce a theory, and then give two examples of how the theory is applied in real life. The professor may also describe a historical event or a scientific phenomenon, process, concept, or method and give two major reasons to explain how or why it happened or developed. The professor may describe evidence for, or subcategories, of the topic. The information generally comes from introductory university courses, and you do not need to have previous knowledge of the topic to understand the lecture. All the information you need to answer the question will be contained in the listening passage. The passage is usually 60 to 90 seconds long.

As you listen to the lecture, you should take notes on the topic, the major points the professor makes, and a few details that will help you explain the points when you make your response. Listen for pauses and expressions like, "The next point I'd like to make . . ." ; "Let's move on to . . ." or "So now, let's discuss . . ." that signal that the professor is going to discuss new point.

Now listen to and look at a lecture for integrated Speaking Example Question 6A and then, look at the notes for the lecture below.

Example Question 6 Listening Passage A 130 ◀))

(narrator) Listen to part of a lecture in a Western civilization class.
(professor) The Persian Empire of the fifth and sixth century BCE was the first that brought the Greek world into direct contact with an empire that included Egypt, Mesopotamia, and extended even as far as India. For the first time, with part of the Greek lands under Persian control, ideas and trade goods could spread more freely from the lands of the Near East to the Greek city-states. And these city-states would become very influential in the formation of Western culture. Now, how the Persians managed to increase the speed at which goods and ideas moved can be traced to several policies that facilitated communication and trade throughout their empire.

So, as far as trade goes, the Persians were one of the first cultures to use stamped coins as money. They also partially put into place standard weights and measures, so people could use the same type of money and units of measurement in many different areas of the Persian Empire. Having these standard units helped make trade a lot easier. It makes sense, right? Because this standardization made it possible for merchants to understand what the different quantities and prices were in each of the different places where they were trading. And the Persians also built roads. Although they were originally built to help move military troops quickly, the roads also made travel and trade easier throughout the empire.

And, related to my second point, the roads also made communication easier. You see, news could travel much faster along the roads, and so, the Persian king had a constant stream of messengers bringing information to and from the capital and the outer edges of the empire. Communication was also facilitated by the eventual dominance of one language as the primary language of the empire. The diverse people within the empire spoke their own languages, of course, but many also knew and used the primary language. With the same language spoken and understood across such a large territory, it made the spread of ideas much faster.

NOTES (Example Question 6A):

TOPIC: how Persian Empire move goods & ideas fast, Persian Empire ↑ influ Greece → devel west civ	
Main Ideas: trade ↑	**Supporting Details:** —stamped coins 4 $$ —standrd weight & meas = ++ EZ 4 merchants b/c understand dif quant & price evrywhr go —roads = travl & trade ++ EZ 4 merchants
communication ↑	—roads = news travl fast & king's messenger syst 2 & fr capitl & edge emp — 1 main lang= ↑ spread ideas b/c many spoke same lang

These notes include the topic of the lecture and some information about the topic (the Persian Empire influenced Greece, which, in turn, led to the formation of Western civilization). Next, the notes are divided into two main ideas related to the topic, on the left, and supporting details for the two main ideas on the right. The supporting details for *trade* (how the Persian Empire moved goods) are *coins, standardized weights and measures, and roads*, all of which made it *easier for merchants* to trade goods more quickly. The supporting details for *communication* are *roads* and *one main language*. The student did not try to write down notes for everything but only included enough details to help remember and plan the response.

Now listen to and look at another lecture and then look at the notes for the lecture below.

Example Question 6 Listening Passage B 🔊¹³¹

(narrator)   Listen to part of a lecture in a psychology class.
(professor)   While we're on the subject of depression, I'd like to discuss a condition called Seasonal Affective Disorder, or S-A-D . . . um . . . that spells "sad," and as you'll see, it's a very appropriate term for the condition. It generally occurs in the fall and winter, but then it tends to disappear when spring comes. It can be relatively mild, or severe enough that the sufferer becomes dangerously depressed. The cause seems to be a lack of light during the late fall and winter months. The evidence for this is that SAD occurs during the darker months of the year, and it is more common at higher latitudes like Alaska or Norway—it's almost unknown in sunny tropical climates. And, the final piece of evidence is the effectiveness of phototherapy as a treatment, which I'll get to in a moment.

SPEAKING

SPEAKING SKILL 16 / QUESTION 6   301

So, OK, it's believed that light suppresses—uh, holds down the production of a specific chemical in our bodies. On the other hand, this naturally occurring chemical increases during the times of year when there is less light, which is what triggers the symptoms of depression in SAD. We don't know the exact mechanism, but some treatments can often greatly reduce the symptoms. One treatment, called phototherapy, is to use a special kind of a light box in your home . . . now, the light in this box is 10 to 20 times brighter than a regular lamp . . . and you keep the light turned on and pointed at you while sitting in front of it for a specific period of time. For most people, there are no side effects, but you may have to spend up to 2 hours a day in the light. Some studies indicate that certain medications can be just as effective as light therapy, but of course the side effects of some of these are often serious. And so you can see that we have established a cause for this type of depression and some rather effective ways to treat it. However, we are not so clear on the exact mechanisms that result in individual variations in the symptoms and in the responses to the treatments.

NOTES (Example Question 6B):

TOPIC: SAD, kind of depression
—Appear fall, ↑ winter, disappear spring

Main Ideas:

cause

treatments

Supporting Details:

— ↓ light, late fall & winter
— evid: ↑latitude = ↑SAD ppl
— ↑light → ↓spec body chem
— ↓light →↑spec chem → depress (X know why)

— phototherapy: light box in home, sit frt 4 spec time
— meds (↑ side efx)

These notes include the topic of the lecture and a brief definition of it. Some details about SAD are included below the topic. Next, the notes are divided into two main ideas on the left side of the notes: the cause and the treatments. Supporting details are included about the cause on the right side of the notes. The symbols and abbreviations mean that more (↑) light causes a specific chemical in the body to decrease (↓) while lower (↓) light in winter causes the chemical to increase (↑), which causes SAD and its symptoms of depression. The evidence is included that in higher latitudes (further north) there are more people (*ppl*) with SAD. Two treatments are noted with details: *phototherapy* and *medications*.

One of the best ways to prepare for listening to lectures on the TOEFL iBT® test is to practice well before you take the test. There are many websites online that have lectures on numerous academic topics. Try listening to a few lectures on subjects you find interesting or useful, and take notes on the main ideas and supporting details in the lectures. You will improve your listening comprehension and your academic vocabulary, and you may learn new information about specific topics that could help you more easily understand the topics on the TOEFL iBT® test.

The following chart outlines the key information for dealing with the listening passage in integrated Speaking Question 6.

KEY INFORMATION FOR NOTING THE MAIN POINTS IN THE LISTENING PASSAGE

LISTEN FOR THE TOPIC, MAIN IDEAS, AND SUPPORTING DETAILS	Listen for the topic of the lecture and the two or three main ideas related to the topic, such as the examples, reasons, or categories that the professor discusses. Listen for supporting details that explain or illustrate the main ideas.
TAKE NOTES ON THE TOPIC, MAIN IDEAS, AND SUPPORTING DETAILS	Using symbols and abbreviations, note the topic and main ideas the professor discusses. Write down a few words about supporting details that will help you remember them so you can plan your response. Use a style of note-taking that allows you to distinguish between main ideas and important supporting details such as dividing your notes into a left-hand column for main ideas and a right-hand column for supporting details.

SPEAKING EXERCISE 16: Listen to each of the following lectures, and note the *topic,* the *main ideas,* and *supporting details.*

1. Listen to the lecture and take notes in the space provided for you below. ¹³² ◀))

TOPIC:

Main Ideas   Supporting Details

2. Listen to the lecture and take notes in the space provided for you below. 🔊 **133**

TOPIC:

Main Ideas   Supporting Details

3. Listen to the lecture and take notes in the space provided for you below. 🔊 **134**

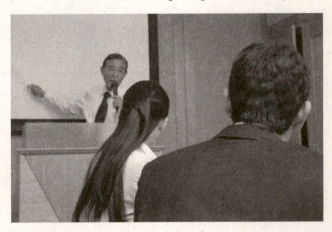

TOPIC:

Main Ideas   Supporting Details

Speaking Skill 17: USE YOUR NOTES TO PLAN THE RESPONSE FOR SPEAKING QUESTION 6

After you have listened to the lecture, you will see and hear a question about it. You will then have 20 seconds to prepare a response to the question. A clock will appear on the screen and count down the 20 seconds of preparation time.

The question for each listening passage will be different, but it will always ask you to use points from the lecture to summarize the main ideas that the professor discusses. You should read the question carefully to determine exactly what information you must include in your response. You should respond to the question using only the information provided in the lecture. If you have previous knowledge about the topic of the lecture, you should not use that knowledge in your response.

To prepare a plan for your response, look at the notes you have taken on the lecture and focus on the main points and the specific details that support the main points. Once you have decided which points to discuss, put them in the order you want to discuss them.

Look at the question below for Example Question 6 Listening Passage A, about the Persian Empire in Skill 16.

Example Question 6A

Using points and examples from the lecture, explain how the Persian Empire made the rapid movement of goods and ideas possible throughout their empire.

Note that the question is asking about the two main ideas from the lecture, trade (*goods*) and communication (*ideas*), and is asking you to use details from the lecture that support the main ideas.

Look at the notes and the plan for a response to Example Question 6A.

NOTES (Example Question 6A):

TOPIC: how Persian Empire move goods & ideas fast
Persian Empire ↑ influ Greece → dev west civ

Main Ideas:	Supporting Details:
trade↑	—stamped coins 4 $$
	—standrd weight & meas = ++ EZ 4 merchants b/c understnd dif quant & price evrywre go
	—roads = travl& trade ++ EZ 4 merchants
communication↑	—roads = news travl fast & king's messengr syst 2 & fr capital & edge emp
	—one main language = ↑ spread ideas b/c many spoke same language

---

PLAN (Example Question 6A):

In order to plan the response using your notes, find the topic, the main ideas, and the details that support the main ideas:

1. Find the topic from the listening notes:

   how Persian Empire move goods & ideas fast

   The topic from the notes will help you form an introductory statement for the response, which explains very briefly what the lecture is about.

2. Find the first main idea and the two supporting details for this main idea:

   trade↑

   —stamped coins 4 $$—standrd weight & meas

   = ++ EZ 4 merchants b/c understnd dif quant & price everywhere go

   The first main idea and the supporting details for it will form the first part of your response.

3. Find the second main idea and the two supporting details for this main idea:

   communication↑

   —roads = news travl fast & king's messengr syst 2 & fr capital & edge emp

   —one main language = ↑ spread ideas b/c many spoke same language

   The second main idea and the supporting details for it will form the second part of your response.

The plan starts with the topic of the lecture first. Then the plan includes the first main idea (*trade*) and the supporting details that explain it. The plan indicates that two related details will be discussed as one point. The reason (= . . . *b/c*) that the details support the main idea is included. The plan also includes the second main idea (*communication*) and the supporting details for it. The reasons (= . . . *b/c*) that the details support the main idea is included. This plan for the response includes all of the information that the question asks for in an organized way. On the other hand, some details, such as that Persia influenced Greece, the country that led to the beginning of Western civilization (*Persian Empire ↑ influ Greece → west civ*) are not included in the plan because they are not relevant to the question. With six points to discuss, the speaker will have about 10 seconds to make each point during the 60 seconds of response time.

Now look at the notes and the plan for a response to Example Question 6B, about SAD from Skill 16.

Example Question 6B
Using points and examples from the lecture, explain the cause of Seasonal Affective Disorder (SAD) and the treatments for it.

Note that the question is asking you to explain the (one) cause and (the more than one) treatments of Seasonal Affective Disorder (SAD). These are the two main points from the lecture.

NOTES (Example Question 6B):

```
TOPIC: SAD, kind of depression
—Appear fall, ↑ winter, disappear spring

Main Ideas:              Supporting Details:

cause                    — ↓ light, late fall & winter
                         — evid: ↑latitude = ↑SAD ppl
                         — ↑light → ↑spec chem → depress (X know why)

treatments               — phototherapy: light box in home, sit frt 4 spec time
                         — meds (↑ side efx)
```

PLAN (Example Question 6B):

In order to plan the response using your notes, find the topic, the main ideas, and the details that support the main ideas:

1. Find the topic from the listening notes:

   SAD, kind of depression

   — Appear fall, ↑ winter, disappear spring

   The topic from the notes will help you form an introductory statement for the response, which explains very briefly what the lecture is about and provides a short definition.

2. Find the first main idea and the supporting details for this main idea:

   cause

   — ↓ light, late fall & winter

   — ↓light → ↑spec chem → depress (X know why)

   The first main idea and the supporting details for it will form the first part of your response.

3. Find the second main idea and the two supporting details for this main idea:

   treatments

   — phototherapy: light box in home, sit frt 4 spec time

   — meds (↑ side efx)

   The second main idea and the supporting details for it will form the second part of your response.

The plan starts with the topic and a short definition of it. Then the plan includes the first main idea, the *cause*, and some supporting details that the professor mentions about the cause. Note that not all of the detailed information about the cause is included in the plan because it is not needed to answer the question for the response. The plan also includes the second main idea of two *treatments* for SAD, and then provides supporting details for each one. According to this plan, about half the response time of 30 seconds will be used for defining SAD and explaining the cause, and the other half, the remaining 30 seconds, will be spent on describing the two treatments for SAD.

Organize your notes in a way that will help you to include all of the information necessary to fully answer the question, but avoid repeating ideas or including unnecessary details. You can express several main ideas and supporting details in one or two sentences by using transitions and adjective clauses and phrases to effectively connect them.

The following chart outlines the key information for using the 20 seconds allowed to plan your response for the integrated Speaking Question 6.

KEY POINTS FOR USING YOUR NOTES TO PLAN THE RESPONSE	
UNDERSTAND THE QUESTION	Read the question carefully to be sure that you understand what information you must include. Expect that the question will ask you to explain the main ideas of the listening passage using points from the lecture.
FIND THE INFORMATION	Find the information to answer the question in your notes. Decide which supporting details you must include in your response to clearly explain the main ideas.
PLAN THE RESPONSE	Plan the number of points you will discuss, the order in which you will discuss them, and how much time you will spend on each one. Adjust the number of details you will discuss based on how fast or slowly you can speak naturally and clearly.

SPEAKING EXERCISE 17: Look at the notes that you prepared for the listening passages in Speaking Exercise 16 (pp. 303–304). Read the question. Then prepare a plan for your response. You have 20 seconds to plan a response.

1. Using points and examples from the lecture, explain the advantages and disadvantages of the two approaches for controlling pollution.

2. Using points and examples from the lecture, explain the characteristics of creative problem solving.

3. Using points and examples from the lecture, explain the "Lapita Only" theory of Polynesian migration and how the evidence the professor describes both supports and contradicts it.

Speaking Skill 18: USE YOUR PLAN TO MAKE THE RESPONSE FOR SPEAKING QUESTION 6

After the 20 seconds of planning time has finished, the narrator will tell you to begin speaking. You will have 60 seconds to record your response, and a clock on the screen will count down the time. At the end of 60 seconds, the clock will disappear, the computer will stop recording your response, and the narrator will tell you to stop speaking. As you record your response, you should think about the following strategies:

- Start with an introductory statement that states the topic and provides any necessary definition of it.

- Explain the two or three main ideas, following your plan.

- Give only the most relevant supporting details from the lecture that help make the main ideas clear.

- Use useful language and transitions to show connections between the topic, main ideas, and supporting details.

- Speak clearly using the English pronunciation points you have practiced to make your response sound more natural.

Look at the plan for responding to Example Question 6A from Speaking Skill 17. Then, look at and listen to a sample response based on the plan.

Example Question 6A

Using points and examples from the lecture, explain how the Persian Empire made the rapid movement of goods and ideas possible throughout their empire.

PLAN (Example Question 6A):

TOPIC: Use this part of the plan to form an introductory statement for the response, which explains very briefly what the lecture is about.

how Persian Empire move goods & ideas fast

FIRST MAIN IDEA: Use the first main idea and the two supporting details for this main idea to form the next part of your response.

trade↑

—stamped coins 4 $$ —standrd weight & meas

= ++ EZ 4 merchants b/c understnd dif quant & price everywhere go

SECOND MAIN IDEA: Use the second main idea and the two supporting details for this main idea to form the next part of your response.

communication↑

—roads = news travl fast & king's messengr syst 2 & fr capital & edge emp

—one main language = ↑ spread ideas b/c many spoke same language

---

> The lecture explains how the Persian Empire moved goods and ideas throughout the empire very quickly. The professor first points out that the empire had standardized coins and weights and measures. This made it easy for merchants to understand the different prices and amounts of goods in many different places, which led to an increased speed in trade. The professor also mentions that roads helped improve trade. She says that roads made travel and trade faster. As for movement of ideas, the roads also made communication faster and easier. According to the lecture, the king of the Persian Empire had a message system between the capital and the edges of the empire, which also improved communication. Finally, the professor indicates that many people spoke a common language, which also helped to speed up the spread of ideas.

The response begins by summarizing the topic of the lecture and responding directly to the information in the question. Each main idea is described accurately in the speaker's own words, and a few supporting details are used to make it clear how these details support the main ideas. Useful language and transitions (highlighted) are used to show the relationships between the main ideas, and causes and results or to indicate new points, and to report what the professor said.

Now look at the plan for Example Question 6B from Speaking Skill 17. Then, look at and listen to the sample response based on the plan.

Example Question 6B
Using points and examples from the lecture, explain the cause of Seasonal Affective Disorder (SAD) and the treatments for it.

PLAN (Example Question 6B):

TOPIC: Use this part of the plan to form an introductory statement for the response, which explains very briefly what the lecture is about and provides a short definition.

SAD, kind of depression

— Appear fall, ↑ winter, disappear spring

FIRST MAIN IDEA: Use the first main idea and the two supporting details for this main idea to form the next part of your response.

cause

— ↓ light, late fall & winter

— ↓ light → ↑spec chem → depress (X know why)

SECOND MAIN IDEA: Use the second main idea and the two supporting details for this main idea to form the next part of your response.

treatments

—phototherapy: light box in home, sit frt 4 spec time

—meds (↑ side efx)

> The lecture is about SAD, which is a kind of depression that appears in the fall, gets worse in the winter, and then goes away in the spring. The professor describes the cause and two treatments for this depression. First, the professor says that SAD comes from the lower amount of sunlight in winter. He explains that less light leads to more of a certain chemical in our bodies, which then results in depression for the people who suffer from SAD. After that he discusses two effective treatments. The first is phototherapy, where the patient puts a light box in his or her house and then turns it on and sits in front of it for a while every day. The other treatment described is medications, but the professor points out that these can have bad side effects.

The response begins by summarizing the topic of the lecture and giving a brief definition of it. Then, the two main ideas are summarized, which directly address the question. Next, the response discusses the cause of SAD, including only enough detail so that the raters can clearly understand it. After that, the two treatments are described, again with only a few brief details. The response uses useful language and transitions (highlighted) to connect information, to report what the professor says, and to clearly indicate the causes and effects of SAD.

To get a high score on this question, you must clearly convey the information from the lecture in an understandable, organized way. Following a plan for your response and making sure you accurately cover the topic and two or three main ideas will help you do well on the *organization* element of the scoring. Practicing useful language and using English daily to listen, read, and speak will help you on the *grammar and vocabulary* elements of the scoring.

To do well on the *fluency* element of the scoring, you should practice speaking English as much as possible every day. Become comfortable with paraphrasing and summarizing academic ideas and the topics of casual conversations in as few words as possible. Develop your academic and everyday vocabulary, comprehension, and verbal fluency. Practice using useful language and transitions, and English pronunciation before you take the TOEFL iBT® test so that you are comfortable with them on the day of the test.

The chart on the following page outlines the key information for using the 60 seconds allowed to make your response for integrated Speaking Question 6.

KEY POINTS FOR USING YOUR PLAN TO MAKE THE RESPONSE

STATE THE TOPIC	Start your response with a brief explanation of the lecture topic and a short definition of it if necessary. Make sure that you are responding directly to the information in the question.
RELATE THE MAIN IDEAS TO THE QUESTION	Using your plan, explain how the main ideas from the lecture answer the question you are asked. You should discuss two or three main points.
INCLUDE RELEVANT SUPPORTING DETAILS	Include only the relevant supporting details about each main idea to make your explanation clear. Do not try to include all of the details from the lecture.
USE USEFUL LANGUAGE AND TRANSITIONS TO REPORT AND CONNECT IDEAS	Before you plan to take the TOEFL iBT® test, practice using the useful language in the chart below. When you give your response, use this language to report and connect the topic, the main ideas, and the supporting details and to clarify the relationship among these points in the response.

USEFUL LANGUAGE AND TRANSITIONAL PHRASES

To report main ideas, supporting details, and other key points:
proves/demonstrates/shows/supports the idea + *that* + subject + verb
points out/indicates/says/mentions/explains + *that* + subject + verb
gives an example(s)/points out/mentions/discusses + noun
This proves that low light results in increased melatonin.
The professor indicates that they used coins and mentions that they. . .
He gives an example and points out the reasons . . .

To give more information about a subject*:
person, *who/that* + verb or *thing, that/which* + verb statement, *which* + verb
statement or noun, verb + *-ing*/past participle
Polynesians who sailed east left pottery that was later found by archaeologists.
They connect to the Internet, which makes them more useful.
Polynesians, sailing east left pottery later found by archaeologists.

To give causes and effects/results:
leads to/causes/results in or *ends up* + verb + *-ing*
is caused by/results from/comes from/stems from
Setting pollution limits ends up preventing further reductions.
Similar words result from having a common ancestral language.
The tax is too high. And that means companies go out of business.

*These structures are called relative or adjective clauses and reduced adjective clauses. There are various rules for using them, but learning to use them correctly will allow you to put much more information into shorter statements.

MAKING YOUR RESPONSE EASIER TO UNDERSTAND: Weakening common structure words

HOW ENGLISH PRONUNCIATION FUNCTIONS	Many very short words are not fully pronounced and are instead "weakened." That means they are pronounced with a lower pitch, with a short vowel (often /ə/), and may lose consonant sounds. This is common with prepositions (*to, for*), pronouns (*him, her, them*), conjunctions (*and, but*), and auxiliary verbs (*have*).	*This made it easy for merchants to understand prices and amounts of goods . . .* All of the highlighted words are weakened—pronounced with a lower pitch and shortened. it /ət/ for /fər/ to/tə/ and /ən/ of /əv/ or even /ə/
YOUR RESPONSE	Listen for and imitate the way English speakers weaken small structure words. Practice this before you take the TOEFL iBT® test when you speak, read aloud, or repeat after listening. When you give your response, pronounce these little words at a lower pitch and shorten them more than the important content words. The raters will find it easier to hear the important words and understand your response better overall if you do this rather than pronouncing small words too strongly.	

SPEAKING EXERCISE 18: Create responses for the integrated speaking questions that you have been working on in Speaking Exercises 16 and 17 (pp. 303–304 and p. 308). You have 60 seconds to give your response. Follow the plan you have made from your notes. Time yourself and repeat your response until you can get the necessary information into the 60-second response time.

SPEAKING REVIEW EXERCISE (SKILLS 16–18): Listen to the lecture and take notes on the topic, the main ideas, and the supporting details. ¹³⁷🔊))

Now answer the following question. You have 20 seconds to plan your response and 60 seconds to speak. ¹³⁸🔊))

Question 6

Using points and examples from the lecture, describe the primary and secondary amino acid structure of proteins.

SPEAKING POST-TEST

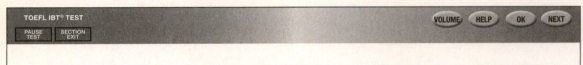

Speaking

Section Directions

In this section of the test, you will be able to demonstrate your ability to speak about a variety of topics. You will answer six questions by speaking into the microphone. Answer each of the questions as completely as possible.

In some questions, you will speak about familiar topics. Your response will be scored on your ability to speak clearly and coherently about the topics.

In other questions, you will first read a short text. Then, the text will go away and you will listen to a talk on the same topic. You will then be asked a question about what you have read and heard. You will need to combine appropriate information from the text and the talk to provide a complete answer. Your response will be scored on your ability to speak clearly and coherently and on your ability to accurately convey information.

In the final questions, you will listen to part of a conversation or lecture. You will then be asked a question about what you have heard. Your response will be scored on your ability to accurately convey information and speak clearly and coherently.

You may take notes while you read and while you listen to the conversations and lectures. You may use your notes to help prepare your response.

Listen carefully to the directions for each question. The directions will not be written on the screen.

For each question you will be given a short time to prepare your response. A clock will show how much preparation time is remaining. When the preparation time is up, you will be told to begin your response. A clock will show how much response time is remaining. A message will appear on the screen when the response time has ended.

Question 1

Read the question. You have 15 seconds to write down brief notes for a response on a separate piece of paper. You then have 45 seconds to respond to the question.

Imagine that you are trying to choose a neighborhood in which to live. What do you think is the most important characteristic that the neighborhood you are choosing should have and why do you think so? Use examples and details in your response.

Question 2

Read the question. You have 15 seconds to write down brief notes for a response on a separate piece of paper. You then have 45 seconds to respond to the question.

The Internet has made it possible for people to choose the news they watch or read instead of being limited to reading the same news stories in printed newspapers or listening to the same television news reports. Some people believe that this is having a positive effect on society, while others believe the effect is negative. Which opinion do you support, and why? Use examples and details to support your choice.

Question 3

Read the notice. On a separate piece of paper, take brief notes on the main points of the notice. You have 45 seconds to read the notice.

Notice from University Food Services
University Food Services is notifying students that the King Cafeteria will be closed from May 1st through the summer for much needed repairs and modernization. The cafeteria will open again for the fall semester with an expanded menu and will be operating much more efficiently according to the university's goal of reducing waste. Students with meal cards who usually use the King Cafeteria will be able to use their meal cards at the other three student cafeterias. Until the end of the semester, students may also use their cards at the four additional cafés on campus.

Now listen to two students as they discuss the notice. 139 🔊))

Now answer the following question. You have 30 seconds to plan a response and 60 seconds to deliver the response. 🔊 140

The man expresses his opinion of the notice. State his opinion and the reasons he gives for holding that opinion.

Question 4

Read the passage. On a separate piece of paper, take brief notes on the main points of the reading passage. You have 45 seconds to read the passage.

Social Learning Environments

It is important for an effective teacher to recognize that various types of social environments can be established in the classroom based upon the goals that are to be met. Three of the major types of social environments that can be established are a cooperative environment, a competitive environment, and an individualistic environment. In a cooperative classroom environment, the students work together to complete questions. In a competitive social environment, students try to complete questions or come up with better answers more quickly than other students. In an individualistic environment, students work by themselves to complete work. In American school systems, students are expected to be able to operate, depending on specific purposes, in all three types of social learning environments.

Now listen to part of a lecture on the same topic in an education class. 🔊 141

Now answer the following question. You have 30 seconds to plan a response and 60 seconds to deliver the response 🔊 142

Explain how the two examples given by the professor illustrate ways of establishing social learning environments.

Question 5

Listen to a conversation between two students. 🔊 143

Now answer the following question. You have 20 seconds to plan a response, and 60 seconds to deliver the response. 🔊 144

The students discuss two possible solutions to the woman's problem. Briefly summarize the problem. Then state which of the two solutions you think is better and why.

Question 6

Listen to part of a lecture in an astronomy class. 🔊 145

Now answer the following question. You have 20 seconds to plan a response, and 60 seconds to deliver your response. 🔊 146

Using points and examples from the lecture, explain the conditions that could make life possible on planets and moons outside the habitable zone.

Turn to pages 599–609 to *assess* the skills used in the test, *score* the test using the Speaking Scoring Criteria, and *record* your results.

SPEAKING

WRITING

WRITING DIAGNOSTIC PRE-TEST

TOEFL IBT® TEST	VOLUME HELP OK NEXT
PAUSE TEST SECTION EXIT	

Writing
Section Directions

This section measures your ability to communicate in writing in an academic environment. There will be two writing tasks.

For the first writing task, you will read a passage and listen to a lecture about an academic topic. Then you will write a response to a question that asks you about the relationship between the lecture and the reading passage.

For the second task, you will demonstrate your ability to write an essay in response to a question that asks you to express and support your opinion about a topic or issue.

Now listen to the directions for the first writing task.

Integrated Writing Directions

For this task, you will first have three minutes to read a passage about an academic topic. You may take notes on the passage if you wish. The passage will then be removed and you will listen to a lecture about the same topic. While you listen, you may also take notes.

Then you will have 20 minutes to write a response to a question that asks you about the relationship between the lecture you heard and the reading passage. Try to answer the question as completely as possible using information from the reading passage and the lecture. The question does not ask you to express your personal opinion. You will be able to see the reading passage again when it is time for you to write. You may use your notes to help you answer the question.

Typically, an effective response will be 150 to 225 words long. Your response will be judged on the quality of your writing and on the completeness and accuracy of the content. If you finish your response before time is up, you may click on Next to go on to the second writing task.

Independent Writing Directions

For this task, you will write an essay in response to a question that asks you to state, explain, and support your opinion on an issue. You will have 30 minutes to plan, write, and revise your essay.

Typically, an effective essay will contain a minimum of 300 words. Your essay will be judged on the quality of your writing. This includes the development of your ideas, the organization of your essay, and the quality and accuracy of the language you use to express your ideas.

If you finish your essay before time is up, you may click on Next to end this section. When you are ready to continue, click on the Dismiss Directions icon.

Question 1

Read the passage.

Reading Time: 3 minutes

Deforestation has been opposed in many countries and on several continents, due to the rapid disappearance of rainforests. Yet, deforestation is likely to continue because, for some, the benefits outweigh the drawbacks. One benefit is that deforestation provides specific regions with opportunities for economic growth. With the world population continuing to grow ever larger, more food is needed. Rainforests can be cut down and the cleared land can then be used to expand commercial farming, which not only helps feed the increasing population, but provides economic sustainability for both farmers and governments.

In addition, deforestation provides much-needed space for living. Many countries, in which rainforests are located, are over-crowded and their people are living in only a small section of the country. Deforestation provides the chance for smaller, local tribes to be moved to the newly cleared land. As a result of these tribes relocating, there is a better balance of population density and better living conditions for the greatest number of people.

Finally, although environmentalists will certainly disagree, deforestation actually helps the environment. As it stands now, the United States is proposing that 25 billion dollars be spent on protecting the world's rainforests. The proposal offers carbon credits. What this means is that for every dollar that a country invests in saving the rainforests, it is permitted to emit one ton of carbon dioxide. Therefore, banning deforestation may be counterproductive. Countries that do reduce deforestation will cause carbon prices to decrease. This would make global warming worse instead of better.

Listen to the passage. 🔊⁾⁾⁾ ^147

Now answer the following question: 🔊⁾⁾⁾ ^148

Summarize the points made in the lecture, being sure to explain how they challenge specific arguments raised in the reading.

Response Time: 20 minutes

Read the question. Then write your response.

What recent news story has affected you the most? In what ways has it affected you? Use specific reasons and examples to support your answer.

Response Time: 30 minutes

Turn to pages 610–616 to *assess* the skills used in the test, *score* the test, using the Writing Scoring Criteria, and *record* your results.

WRITING OVERVIEW

The last section on the TOEFL iBT® test is the Writing section. This section consists of two tasks, one integrated task and one independent task. You will type your responses to these two tasks directly on the computer.

- The **integrated** task consists of a 250 to 300 word reading passage and a 1 to 2 minute lecture on the same academic topic. The information in the reading passage and the information in the listening passage are related, but the listening passage does not simply repeat what is in the reading passage. You should take notes on the information in each of the passages, and then you must write a 150 to 225 word response about how the information in the two passages is related. You have 20 minutes to both plan and type your response to the question on the computer screen.

- The **independent** task consists of an essay topic. You must write an essay of approximately 300 words on the topic that is given. The ideas in your essay come from your personal experience rather than from material that is given to you. You have 30 minutes to both plan and type your essay response on the computer screen.

> Remember to use a general statement and supporting information in your response. Here's an example: *The best way to research topics for class assignments is by using the Internet. The Internet provides more sources than a library. For example, you can find information from other researchers, from journals, from various colleges, and from videos available online. Information can be accessed from remote places, such as your dorm room or apartment.*

Writing Question	Usual Expectations For A Response	Reading Time	Listening Time	Response Length	Combined Preparation and Response Time
Question 1: Integrated Writing— Academic Reading, Listening, Writing	Write about the relationship between an academic reading passage and a listening passage. Explain how information in the listening passage casts doubt on, opposes, or challenges points in the reading. (You may occasionally be asked to explain how the information in the listening passage adds to or answers information from the reading passage.)	3 minutes	1–2 minutes	150–225 words	20 minutes
Question 2: Independent Writing— Experience and Knowledge	Write about your opinion on a specific issue, using your experience and knowledge to provide reasons and examples to support your opinion.	none	none	300 words	30 minutes

Because these tasks are different, there are different strategies for each task. The following strategies can help you on the integrated task in the Writing section.

STRATEGIES FOR THE INTEGRATED WRITING TASK

1. **Be familiar with the directions.** The directions on every test are the same, so it is not necessary to spend time reading the directions carefully when you take the test. You should be completely familiar with the directions before the day of the test. You can use the time given for the directions to prepare charts for taking notes or you can click on `Continue` to dismiss the directions and use your time on the passages and questions.

2. **Do not worry if the material in the integrated task is on a topic that is not familiar to you.** All of the information that you need to write your response is included in the passage. You do not need any special background knowledge to answer the questions.

3. **Read the reading passage carefully.** You will have only a limited amount of time to read the passage.

4. **Take brief notes as you read the passage.** You should focus on the three main points and key supporting material. Do not try to write down everything you read. Do not write down too many unnecessary details.

5. **Listen carefully to the passage.** You will hear the passage one time only. You are not allowed to hear the passage again.

6. **Take brief notes as you listen to the lecture.** You should focus on the three main points and key supporting material. Do not try to write down everything you hear. Do not write down too many unnecessary details.

7. **Organize your response very clearly.** You should have an overall topic statement that shows the relationship between the reading passage and the listening passage. You should also have paragraphs that address how each point from the listening passage relates to each point of the reading passage.

8. **Use transitions to make your response cohesive.** Your essay is easier to read and understand if you show how the ideas in your response are related.

9. **Use only vocabulary, sentence structures, and grammatical points that you know and are comfortable with.** This is not the best time to try out new words, structures, or grammar points.

10. **Monitor the time carefully on the title bar of the computer screen.** The title bar indicates how much time you have to complete your response.

11. **Finish writing your response a few minutes early so that you have time to edit what you wrote.** You should spend the last three to five minutes checking your response for problems in sentence structure and grammatical errors.

The following strategies can help you on the independent task in the Writing section.

STRATEGIES FOR THE INDEPENDENT WRITING TASK

1. **Be familiar with the directions.** The directions on every test are the same, so it is not necessary to spend time reading the directions carefully when you take the test. You should be completely familiar with the directions before the day of the test. You can use the time given for the directions to prepare charts for taking notes or you can click on `Continue` to dismiss the directions and use your time on the passages and questions.

2. **Read the question carefully, and answer the question exactly as it is asked.** Take some time at the beginning of the task to be sure that you understand the question and what the question is asking you to do.

3. **Organize your response very clearly.** You should think of having an introduction, body paragraphs that develop the introduction, and a conclusion to end your essay.

4. **Use transitions to make your essay cohesive.** Your essay is easier to read and understand if you show how the ideas in your essay are related.

5. **Whenever you make a general statement, be sure to support that statement.** You can use examples, reasons, facts, or personal information to support any general statement.

6. **Use only vocabulary, sentence structures, and grammatical points that you know and are comfortable with.** This is not the best time to try out new words, structures, or grammar points.

7. **Monitor the time carefully on the title bar of the computer screen.** The title bar indicates how much time you have to complete your essay.

8. **Finish writing your essay a few minutes early so that you have time to edit what you wrote.** You should spend the last three to five minutes checking your essay for problems in sentence structure and grammatical errors.

The following skills will help you to implement these strategies in the Writing section of the TOEFL iBT® test.

WRITING QUESTION 1: INTEGRATED TASK

Writing Skill 1: NOTE THE MAIN POINTS AS YOU READ

In the integrated task in the Writing section of the TOEFL iBT® test, you will have to read an academic passage as part of the task. It is important for you to be able to read an academic passage of around 300 words in a short period of time. Look at an example of a reading passage that is part of an integrated writing task on fracking.

Example Reading Passage 1A

Hydraulic fracturing, known as "fracking," is a relatively new drilling technology for extracting natural gas from shale rock deep underground. The process involves injecting a mix of sand, chemicals, and water into a well at high pressure in order to break up underground shale rock to release natural gas. This promising innovation, which has led to a shale gas boom, has yielded economic benefits, been proved safe, and contributed to a bright energy future for the United States, with its vast supplies of shale.

The economic gains from fracking are already clear. Increased domestic production has caused the price of natural gas to decline by nearly 50 percent and kept prices low for American consumers, who get 24 percent of their electricity from natural gas. The natural gas boom also delivers enormous economic opportunities to states in the form of jobs and large infusions of dollars into the economy.

Fortunately, the fracking process is perfectly safe. Studies show that shale from the large Marcellus formation in Pennsylvania does not negatively affect private water wells or increase radioactivity in rivers. Neither do the chemicals used in fracking affect the groundwater, so the water remains safe to drink. The air around several drilling sites was tested, with no major health threats reported. Moreover, since fracking produces half the carbon dioxide and under a third of the nitrogen oxides of coal, it is safe for the environment.

While wind, solar and other energies generate much excitement, they generate very little energy. Wind accounts for only 2 percent and solar 0.03 percent of the power Americans use, with 49 percent coming from coal, the "dirtiest" energy source. The power generated from the Marcellus Shale alone is equivalent to over 60,000 wind turbines or 25 coal-fired power plants. Fracking is the wave of the future.

As you read the passage, you should take notes on the topic and main points of the reading passage. Look at these notes on the topic and main points of the reading passage on fracking. Notice that the notes for the reading passage are on the left side, with space on the right side for notes on the listening passage, which you will hear directly after the reading passage.

> You can type your notes directly on the answer screen for the integrated writing task and then, fill them in as you type your answer.

NOTES:

Reading (Read):	Listening (Listen):

Top: Fracking- get nat'gas +++
 	
MPs
— + econ +
   ↑ natr'l gas prod'n →↓ prces
   ↑ jobs & ↑ $ to states
— Safe:
   X affect drinking H_2O or rivers
   ≤ CO_2 cmpd to coal—cleaner for env't
— Lots of pw'r (cmpd to wind/solar) →the future	

These notes show that the topic of the reading passage is the benefits of *fracking*, which is defined as a method of getting natural gas from under the ground. The main points about fracking are that it has yielded economic gains, that it is a safe technology, and that it provides a lot of power.

Now look at another example of a reading passage that is part of an integrated writing task on emotions.

Example Reading Passage 1B

Scientists have reached a broad consensus that emotions are genetically hardwired into all human beings. In the 1870s, renowned biologist Charles Darwin theorized that emotions are a product of natural selection. According to Darwin, our ancestors developed emotions as an evolutionary tool to respond to challenges to the species. Since then, research in the field of affective science has enhanced our understanding of both emotional experience and the recognition of emotion. Researchers in affective science, the interdisciplinary field that includes the behavioral, biological, and social sciences have corroborated Darwin's hypothesis. They have concluded that emotions are a species-wide evolutionary adaptation and that they are innate rather than learned.

Despite tremendous cultural variation, individuals from every corner of the world seem to share the same core emotions. Researchers in affective science have found that numerous basic emotions, such as happiness, anger, fear and sadness, are shared by all humans, regardless of geography or cultural diversity. Many affective scientists also consider embarrassment, guilt, love, pride, and other emotions to be universal. This universality is one factor that has led to the conclusion that emotions must be innate.

Not only do people all around the world share the same emotions, but they use the same facial expressions to show these emotions, and they can recognize this expression in other people from widely divergent cultures. Even the vocalization, or sound, of emotions seems to be global. Researchers from the University of London studied people from Britain and from remote traditional villages of northern Namibia in Africa. Participants from these very dissimilar cultures could easily identify the other group's emotions when they listened to the sounds of their laughter and crying. It is likely that specific facial muscle structures have evolved to allow individuals to produce universally recognizable emotional expressions.

As you read the passage, you should take notes on the topic and main points of the reading passage. Look at the notes on the following page on the topic and main points of the reading passage about emotions.

NOTES:

Read:	Listen:
Top: emotions (Es) MPs:	Top: MPs:
—Es = univs'l/innate (Darwin & resrch by Aff. Sci-tists)	—
—Same Es-all cultures in wrld →	—
—Same way to exprss Es all over (fac'l exp'n & vocaliz'n) Rsrch: Pple frm Brit & Afr. undstnd laugh/cry	—

These notes show that the topic of the reading passage is emotions. The main points about the topic are that emotions are universal and innate, according to Darwin and research by affective scientists; that the same emotions exist in all cultures worldwide; and that people all over use the same ways to express emotions, such as facial expressions and vocalizations. A supporting detail for the last main point is that research shows that people from Great Britain and Africa could understand each other's emotions through their laughter and crying.

The following chart outlines the key information for dealing with the reading passage in the integrated writing task.

NOTE THE TOPIC AND MAIN POINTS IN THE READING PASSAGE	
TOPIC	Listen carefully and make sure that you understand and take notes on the *topic* of the reading passage. Note the key words and general ideas that define the topic.
MAIN POINTS	Then focus on the *three main points* that are used to support the topic of the reading passage. Take brief notes using symbols and abbreviations. Don't worry about writing down small details or examples. Leave a blank column on the opposite side of your reading notes for the listening notes you will need to take when you hear the listening passage.

WRITING EXERCISE 1: Read each of the passages, and note the *topic* and the *main points* that are used to support each topic.

1. Read the passage. Take notes on the topic and main points of the reading passage.

Homeschooling is becoming more and more popular in the United States and the number of students being homeschooled is higher than ever before. However, this move toward homeschooling does not seem to be best for the children involved. For one thing, children in homeschools will not learn as much as children in traditional schools. This is because traditional schools demand that students learn a huge amount of material to pass from grade to grade. Homeschools are generally not set up in such a way that they can demand that students master a certain amount of material before they pass on to a new level. For another, children in homeschools do not have much social interaction with other children; they do not have a classroom full of students to interact with, as children in traditional schools most certainly do. Furthermore, these children generally have only a parent and perhaps a few siblings to interact with on a regular basis. This can hinder their social development and make it difficult for them to interact with their peers in other settings. Finally, traditional schools offer a wide variety of subjects, more subjects than it is possible to offer in a homeschool, including special classes like music, art, and physical education. Therefore, homeschooled children will not have the established and wide-ranging curriculum that is available in traditional schools. In the end, homeschooling may leave many children with future disadvantages when they must compete for jobs and interact in work environments with others who have received a traditional education and long exposure to various social settings.

Read:	Listen:
Top:	Top:
MPs:	MPs:
—	—
—	—
—	—

2. Read the passage. Take notes on the topic and main points of the reading passage.

More and more schools are eliminating mandatory physical education, and this trend should continue due to the validity of parental oppositions. Every year, a growing number of parents become upset that their children are being required to participate in physical education classes at school. They feel that children should not be forced to take a physical education class if they do not want to. Many feel their children are individuals who should be able to make their own decisions about their bodies and not be required by school officials or a curriculum to engage in physical activities. They feel children should make their own decisions, because, for example, some want to avoid uncomfortable situations if they are self-conscious about their bodies or suffer from stress because they are nervous about physical performance. Those who oppose the physical education requirement also think it distracts from other, more purely educational pursuits, such as math, science, or literature. It is argued that students often know from a young age, what kind of job they want later, and therefore, if children take classes in their chosen area of interest, it is more beneficial than compelling them to take a physical education class. Lastly, these parents feel that required physical education courses expose their children to unnecessary and potentially expensive injuries that may result in long-term or permanent damage.

Read:	Listen:
Top:	Top:
MPs:	MPs:
—	—
—	—
—	—

3. Read the passage. Take notes on the topic and main points of the reading passage.

With the rise of Internet blogs and 24-hour news cycles, the traditional, printed newspaper is becoming obsolete. People, especially younger generations, prefer to access information on a need-to-know basis instead of consuming the news that a company has decided to include in its daily edition. Today's consumers obtain the news topics that they desire from multiple online sources. For example, a reader may visit a financial site for the latest stock market numbers and then go to a local site for information about their town's budget meeting. In addition, due to the immediacy of accessing information, newspapers can no longer keep up with the latest details of a story. They are often out-dated by the time they are published. Finally, as the readership shifts from print to online information sources, so does the advertising revenue. Instead of advertisers buying large ad spaces in the paper, they use social media promotions and targeted sites to attract customers. This has resulted in a major decline in revenue for newspapers. Consequently, many papers in smaller markets have already folded, and many papers in larger markets have decreased to approximately half the size they were in their heyday.

Read:	Listen:
Top:	Top:
MPs:	MPs:
—	—
—	—
—	—

Writing Skill 2: NOTE THE MAIN POINTS AS YOU LISTEN

For the integrated task in the Writing section of the TOEFL iBT® test, you will have to listen to an academic passage as part of the task. In this part of the integrated task, it is important for you to be able to listen to an academic passage of approximately 2 minutes and take notes on the main points of the listening passage as you listen.

Look at and listen to the following example of a listening passage that is part of the integrated writing task on fracking.

Example Listening Passage 1A [149]))

(professor) Fracking sounds like the greatest innovation since the Internet, doesn't it!? Well, I'm afraid the reading is rather one-sided. Fracking is extremely controversial, and justifiably so.

It has many negative aspects. The economic benefits have certainly been enjoyed by the fracking industry, but the states . . . well, they've paid a tremendous price. Floods of new workers have poured into states with shale sites. This has caused housing prices to skyrocket, so average young families can no longer afford homes in their own communities. Local governments have had to spend more on services, like police, trash collection, and schools. And the burden of treating health problems associated with fracking also falls to the states, which . . . umm . . . leads to the safety issue.

The industry has spent many millions of dollars trying to persuade people that fracking is safe. But the process is inherently unsafe. The liquid injected into the ground contains many known cancer-causing substances, such as uranium, radium, and methane. These *toxins* leach out, contaminating groundwater. Methane levels tested at some sites were *17 times higher* than elsewhere. Also, the waste fluid left in pits to evaporate contaminates the air. There have been thousands of cases of *respiratory illness and other health problems* . . . and we haven't even begun to see the long-term effects. Scientists also say that the increased earthquake activity around drilling sites is due to fracking.

While it's true that natural gas now provides significantly more power than alternative energies, remember: wind and solar are still very "young." Naturally, at this stage, they are less efficient. If the government invested as much money in them as it has in natural gas, solar and wind could compete fairly. There may be no choice; scientists now believe that America's natural gas reserves were greatly overestimated. They warn that there may be only 23 years' worth of gas left nationwide. Clean and safe renewable energies represent the best hope for the long term.

Look at these notes on the topic and main points of the listening passage on fracking.

NOTES:

Read:	Listen:
Top: Fracking - get nat'gas +++	F: - X benfcl, negtv

MPs
— + econ +
  ↑ natr'l gas prod'n → ↓ prces
  ↑ jobs & ↑ $ to states
	MPs
	—X econ bens
	Only indstr benfts: X states
	  ↑ Lots wrkrs to sts→hsg prices ↑ X affrd
	Loc'l govts: ↑ $: police, schls , trsh, hlth probs

— Safe:
  X affect drinking H_2O or rivers
  ≤ CO_2 cmpd to coal-cleaner for env't
	—X safe:
	Liq: cncr-csing toxins (uran'm,meth,rad'm) →
	grndH_2O & evaps into air→illness. Future? Long-term?
	↑ Erthqks

— Lots of pw'r (cmpd to wind/solar)→the future	—nat'l gs ≥ pwr than sol/wnd. B/c new. Govt: shld invest = $—>fair comp'n X lots resrces—only enuf for 23 yrs? Renw'ble enrg for future +++

These notes show that the topic of the listening passage is that fracking is not beneficial and is *controversial* and negative. The main points about fracking are that it has not yielded economic gains to states, only to the industry; that it is not a safe technology; and that although natural gas provides more power at the present time, it is only because solar and wind power are new. Also, the supply is depleting and renewable energy is necessary for the future.

Now look at and listen to another example of a listening passage that is part of the integrated writing task on emotions.

(*professor*)   I'm afraid that the reading exaggerates the so-called **consensus** that emotions are an evolutionary adaptation and therefore innate. Many affective scientists support a different perspective—that emotions are socially constructed and vary in important ways across cultural boundaries.

Substantial evidence exists that many basic emotions are culturally specific. Let's consider two emotions represented by the Japanese words *oime,* a feeling of indebtedness and *fureai,* which refers to a feeling of connectedness to others. These emotions of interdependency and connectedness felt by Japanese people do not have parallels in the west. This makes sense, though. Since Japanese culture strongly values the collective, or group, individuals raised in the culture feel—and need words for—the emotions *oime* and *fureai.* Since Western cultures tend to focus more on the individual, they do not name or experience these emotions in the same way.

Finally, let's consider the claim that people, no matter how diverse their cultures may be, use the same facial expressions and vocalizations to express emotions. The problem was that the study described in the reading was too narrow. Researchers looked only at happiness and sadness. But . . . what about other emotions, such as guilt and love? These emotions have not been studied . . . and for good reason: they have no clear outward facial expression or vocalization. Without any identifiable expression, these emotions cannot be studied, so the claim of universality cannot be proved. Finally, even emotions that are thought to be both universal and observable actually differ from culture to culture. Take, for example, anger. The Inuit or Eskimo people of the Arctic almost never show outward signs of anger. An aggressive response would be too risky in this small culture living closely together in harsh conditions.

Look at these notes on the topic and main points of the listening passage on emotions.

NOTES:

Read:	Listen:
Top: emotions (Es) MPs: —Es = univs'l/innate (Darwin & resrch by Aff. Sci-tists) —Same Es—all cultures in wrld → —Same way to exprss Es all over (fac'l exp'n & vocaliz'n) Rsrch: Pple frm Brit & Afr. undstnd laugh/cry	Top: Es X innate MPs: — Consensus exag'd Other persp've:E's soc'ly constructed--vary across cult's —X! Ex: Japan: wrds/feelings—interdepce/connctdnss, but not in West b/c dif values: J=collctv v. W=indvdl — Prob w/study--incl'd only 2 Es Other Es. e.g., guilt/love—no outward fac'l exprs'ns→can't study→can't prove unvs'l Anger— Esk pple-X show b/c small cult/live close/harsh cond'ns

These notes indicate that the topic of the listening passage is emotions are not innate. The main points challenge the main points in the reading passage. First, the *broad consensus* of scientists believing that emotions are innate is *exaggerated, and* there are aspects of emotion that are socially constructed and vary across cultures; Second, emotions are not expressed the same in all cultures. Japan's emotions of interdependence and connectedness have no parallels in the west. Third, there are problems with the study that found *facial expressions and vocalizations* universal. Only two emotions were investigated, and without other emotions such as guilt and love, the study's conclusion *cannot be proven*.

The following chart outlines the key information for dealing with the listening passage in the integrated writing task.

NOTE THE TOPIC AND MAIN POINTS IN THE LISTENING PASSAGE	
TOPIC	Listen carefully and make sure that you understand and take notes on the *topic* of the listening passage. Note the key words and general ideas that define the topic.
MAIN POINTS	On the opposite side of your notes for the reading passage, take abbreviated notes on the *three main points* that are used to support the topic of the listening passage. Make sure to notice important ideas that support the topic. You don't need to focus on the small examples and details.

WRITING EXERCISE 2: Listen to each of the following passages, and note the *topic* and the *main points* that are used to support the topic.

1. Listen to the passage. Take notes on the topic and main points of the listening passage. Before you listen, copy your notes for the reading passage on the same topic in the space provided below. Or take notes about the listening next to your notes for the reading passage on the previous pages.

Homeschooling 🔊)) [151]

Read:	Listen:
	TOP:
	MPS:

2. Listen to the passage. Take notes on the topic and main points of the listening passage. Before you listen, copy your notes for the reading passage on the same topic in the space provided below. Or take notes about the listening next to your notes for the reading passage on the previous pages.

Physical Education 🔊)) [152]

Read:	Listen:
	TOP:
	MPS:

3. Listen to the passage. Take notes on the topic and main points of the listening passage. Before you listen, copy your notes for the reading passage on the same topic in the space provided below. Or take notes about the listening next to your notes for the reading passage on the previous pages.

Newspapers

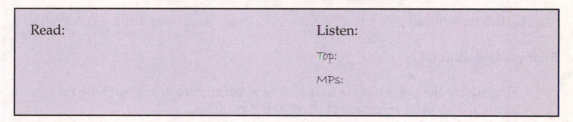

Read:	Listen:
	Top:
	MPs:

Writing Skill 3: PLAN A POINT-BY-POINT RESPONSE USING YOUR NOTES

After you have noted the topic and main points of both the reading and the listening passages in the integrated writing task, you need to read the question carefully and then, plan your response within the 20 minutes allowed for both planning and typing your response.

The question will ask about the relationship between the main points of the reading passage and the main points of the listening passage. The question will most likely ask how the information in the listening passage *answers problems raised in the reading, casts doubt on, opposes, or challenges points in the reading,* or *supports or strengthens points in the reading.* A listening passage may cast doubt on the reading passage by providing arguments against the information in the reading. On the other hand, occasionally, a listening passage may strengthen a point by providing additional examples.

An efficient way to plan your response is to use an outline format that you can fill in using your notes. Or, if you have already typed your notes on the computer answer screen, you can simply organize them into an outline by cutting and pasting. The following page shows what one possible outline for a point-by-point essay might look like.

GENERAL OUTLINE:

   I. **Topic Statement:** Point out that the lecture in the listening passage challenges, casts doubt on, or opposes points in the reading passage. In some cases, you might have to mention that the lecture adds to or supports the reading passage.

  II. **Paragraph 1:** Discuss the first main point from the listening lecture and how it relates to the first main point from the reading passage.

 III. **Paragraph 2:** Explain how the second main point from the listening lecture relates to the second main point from the reading passage.

 IV. **Paragraph 3:** Show how the third main point from the listening lecture relates to the third main point from the reading passage.

  V. **Conclusion:** If time allows, summarize the essay. (See Writing Skill 6, p. 346 for more information on writing a conclusion.)

Now look at the following example of a question in the integrated writing task on fracking.

Example Question 1A

> **Summarize the points made in the lecture, being sure to explain how they challenge specific arguments raised in the reading.**

You can see that the question is asking you to show how the information in the listening passage challenges the arguments raised in the reading passage.

To prepare a plan for your response, you should look at the notes you have taken on the reading and the listening passages. You should then think about how the ideas in the two passages are related. Look at the notes and plan for the response on fracking.

NOTES (Example Question 1A):

Read:	Listen:
Top: Fracking- get nat'gas +++	F: X benfcl, negtv
MPs	MPs
— + econ +	—X econ bnfts
↑ natrl gas prodctn →→ prces	Only indstr bnfts: X states
↑ jobs & ↑ $ to states	↑ Lots wrkrs to sts→hsng prices ↑X affrd
	Locl govts: ↑ $: police, schls, trsh, hlth probs
— Safe:	—X safe:
X affect drinking H_2O or rivers	Liq: cncr-csing toxins (uranm, methn, radm)
≤ CO_2 cmpd to coal-clnr for envrmt	→ grnd H_2O & evaps into air→illnes, future? long-term?
	↑ Erthqks
— Lots of pwr (cmpd to wind/solar)→the future	—natl gs≥pwr than sol/wnd. B/c new. Govt: shld invest =$—>fair comp'n
	X lots resrces—only enuf for 23 yrs?
	Renwbl enrg for future +++

PLAN (Example Question 1A):

Topic: Reading—Fracking - get natl gas +++
        Listening—X benfcl, negtv

Use this part of your notes to state how the information in the listening passage challenges or opposes the topic in the reading passage, including a definition of the topic from the reading.

Paragraph 1: Listening—X econ bnfts
                Only indstr bnfts: X states
                ↑ Lots wrkrs to sts→hsng prics ↑ X affrd
                Locl govts: ↑ $: police, schls, trsh, hlth probs
            Reading—+ econ +
                ↑ natrl gas prodctn → ↑prics
                ↑ jobs & ↑ $ to states

Use this part of your notes to begin the body of your answer by relating the first main point in the listening passage to the first main point in the reading passage.

Paragraph 2: Listening—X safe
                Liq: cncr-csing toxins (uranm, methn, radm) → grnd H_2O & evaps into air→illness,future? long-term?
                ↑ Erthqks
            Reading—Safe
                X affect drinking H_2O or rivers
                ≤ CO_2 cmpd to coal-clnr for envt

Use this part of your notes to continue the body of your answer by relating the second main point in the listening passage to the second main point in the reading passage.

Paragraph 3: Listening—natl gs≥ pwr than sol/wnd B/c new
                Govt: shld invest =$—> fair comp'n
                X lots resrcs—only enuf for 23 yrs?
                Renwbl enrg for future +++
            Reading—Lots of pwr (cmpd to wind/solar)→the future

Use this part of your notes to end the body of your answer by relating the third main point in the listening passage to the third main point in the reading passage, including the conclusion indicated in the listening passage.

From this plan, you can see that the ideas in the reading passage and the ideas in the listening passage are related. The plan shows that the reading passage describes a technique (fracking) used to acquire natural gas, and the benefits of using this method. The listening passage challenges the ideas in the reading passage by opposing the use of fracking and providing negative aspects of the technique.

Now look at another example of a question in the integrated writing task on emotions. In the example on the following page, the information in the listening passage casts doubt on the information in the reading passage.

Example Question 1B

> **Summarize the points made in the lecture, being sure to explain how they cast doubt on specific points made in the reading.**

You can see that the question is asking you to show how the information in the listening passage helps to show that the information in the reading passage is not accurate.

To prepare a plan for your response, you should look at the notes you have taken on the reading passage and the notes you have taken on the listening passage. You should then look at how the ideas in the two passages are related.

Now look at the notes and plan for the response on emotions.

NOTES (Example Question 1B):

Read:	Listen:
Top: emotions (Es) innate MPs: —Es = univs'l/innate accrd 2 Darwin & rsrch by Aff. Scintsts) —Same Es – all cultures in wrld → —Same way to exprss Es all over (fac'l exp'n & vocaliz'n) Rsrch: Pple frm Brit & Afr. undstnd laugh/cry	Top: Es X innate MPs: — Consensus exag'd Other persp've: E's soc'ly constructed--vary across cult's —X! Ex: Japan:wrds/feelings—interdepce/connctdnss, but not in West b/c dif values: J=collctv v. W=indvdl — Prob w/study--incl'd only 2 Es Other Es. e.g., guilt/love—no outward fac'l exprs'ns→can't study→can't prove unvs'l Anger—Esk pple-X show b/c small cult/live close/harsh cond'ns

PLAN (Example Question 1B):

> Topic: **Reading**—emotions (Es) innate
> . **Listening**—Es X innate
>
> Use this part of your notes to state how the information in the listening passage addresses the problems of topic in the reading passage, including a definition of the topic from the reading.
>
> **Paragraph 1:** **Listening**—Consensus exag'd
> Other persp've: E's soc'ly constructed--vary across
> **Reading**—Es = univs'l/innate accrd 2 Darwin & rsrch by Aff. Scintsts)
>
> Use this part of your notes to begin the body of your answer by relating the first main point in the listening passage to the first main point in the reading passage.
>
> **Paragraph 2:** **Listening**—X same Es – all cultures in wrld! (Ex: Japan:wrds/feelings—intrdpndnc/ connctdnss, but X in West. b/c dif values: J=collctv v. W=indvdl)
>
> **Reading**—Same Es – all cultures in wrld →
>
> Use this part of your notes to continue the body of your answer by relating the second main point in the listening passage to the second main point in the reading passage.
>
> **Paragraph 3:** **Listening**—Prob w/study--incl'd only 2 Es
> Other Es. e.g., guilt/love—no outward fac'l exprs'ns → can't study → can't prove unvs'l
> Anger---Esk pple-X showb/c small cult/live close/harsh cond'n
> **Reading**—Same way to exprss Es all over (fac'l exp'n & vocaliz'n) Rsrch: Pple frm Brit & Afr. undstnd laugh/cry
>
> Use this part of your notes to end the body of your answer by relating the third main point in the listening passage to the third main point in the reading passage, including the conclusion indicated in the listening passage.

From this plan, you can see that the ideas in the reading passage and the ideas in the listening passage are related. The plan shows that the reading passage describes similarities in emotions from culture to culture and the listening passage describes situations when emotions differ from culture to culture. The listening passage casts doubt on the conclusion in the reading passage by showing that emotions are not innate or universal.

The chart on the following page outlines the key information you should use for creating a plan from your notes before you write your response to the integrated writing task.

PLAN A POINT-BY-POINT RESPONSE

CHALLENGING, OPPOSING, OR CASTING DOUBT ON THE READING PASSAGE	The question may ask how the listening passage shows that the reading passage may not be accurate. This type of question may be worded in the following ways: Summarize the points made in the lecture, being sure to specifically explain how they **cast doubt on** specific points made in the reading passage. Summarize the points made in the lecture, being sure to specifically explain how they **challenge/oppose** specific claims/arguments made in the reading passage.
DISCUSSING PROBLEMS IN THE READING PASSAGE	The question may ask how the listening passage solves, addresses, or answers the problems in the reading passage. This type of question may be worded in the following way: Summarize the points made in the lecture, being sure to specifically explain how they **answer** the specific problems presented/raised in the reading passage.
SUPPORTING OR STRENGTHENING THE READING PASSAGE	The question may ask what the listening passage strengthens or supports in the reading passage. This type of question is less common than the other types of questions. It may be worded in the following ways: Summarize the points made in the lecture, being sure to specifically explain how they **support** the explanations in the reading passage. Summarize the points made in the lecture, being sure to specifically explain how they **strengthen** specific points made in the reading passage.

WRITING EXERCISE 3: Look at the notes that you prepared for the reading passages in Writing Exercise 1 (pp. 328–330) and the listening passages in Writing Exercise 2 (pp. 334–335). Read the question for each task. Then, on a separate piece of paper, prepare a plan for your response.

1. **Homeschooling:** Summarize the points made in the lecture, being sure to specifically explain how they challenge specific arguments made in the reading passage.

2. **Physical Education:** Summarize the points made in the lecture, being sure to specifically explain how they oppose the points presented in the reading passage.

3. **Newspapers:** Summarize the points made in the lecture, being sure to specifically explain how they cast doubt on specific points made in the reading passage.

Writing Skill 4: WRITE A POINT-BY-POINT RESPONSE USING YOUR PLAN

After you have planned your response, you should begin writing your response using the point-by-point structure. Your response should begin with an overall topic statement that shows how the information in the reading passage and the information in the listening passage are related. The essay will also contain three body paragraphs, each focusing on one main point from the listening passage and one main point from the reading passage and explaining how they are related. Look at the parts of the plan from the integrated writing task on fracking (Example Question 1A) and then, how they are used to write a sample topic statement and three sample body paragraphs.

Example Question 1A

Plan Topic Statement (see Writing Skill 6, p. 346): Fracking - get natl gas +++; X benfcl, negtv

Sample Topic Statement: The reading passage describes fracking and discusses several benefits, whereas the lecture challenges these benefits and opposes this practice.

Plan Paragraph 1: Listening = X econ bnfts
Only indstr bnfts: X states
Lots ↑ Wrkrs to sts→hsng prics ↑ X affrd
Locl govts:↑ $: police, schls, trsh, hlth probs

Reading = + econ +
↑ natrl gas prodctn →↓ prics
↑ jobs & ↑ $ to states

Sample Paragraph 1: While the gas industry has benefited economically from fracking, according to the speaker, the states have not. Because the industry has attracted so many new workers, housing prices have risen so sharply that people can't afford to buy homes. Moreover, local governments have to shoulder the cost of the additional law enforcement, education and other services needed, as well as the cost of treating fracking-related illnesses. This information contradicts the reading's assertion that fracking has benefited local economies.

Plan Paragraph 2: Listening = X safe
Liq: cncr-csing toxins (uranm,methn,radm) → grnd H_2O &
evaps into air→illness,future? long-term?
↑ Erthqks

Reading = Safe
X affect drinking H_2O or rivers
≤ CO_2 cmpd to coal-clnr for envt

Sample Paragraph 2: The reading's claim about safety is also refuted by the lecturer, who mentions the cancer-causing substances contained in the fracking liquid injected into the ground. These toxins can escape into the groundwater and evaporate into the air. As a result, people have become ill, and she worries about the potential long-term effects.

Plan Paragraph 3: Listening = natl gs≥pwr than sol/wnd B/c new
Govt: shld invest =$-->fair comp'n
X lots resrcs—only enuf for23 yrs?
Renwbl enrg for future +++

Reading = Lots of pwr (cmpd to wind/solar)→the future

Sample Paragraph 3: The speaker acknowledges that the U.S. produces far more power from natural gas than from solar or wind. However, she thinks that this is only because these alternative energies are still new and that if the government invested as heavily in them as it has in the gas industry, they would be competitive. Because of all the drawbacks of fracking and because natural gas resources are not as abundant as once thought, the speaker believes that renewable energies are the best option.

Now look at the parts of the plan from the integrated writing task on emotions (Example Question 1B). As you study this information, you should think about writing three body paragraphs. Each of the three paragraphs should focus on the information in the reading passage about how cultures are similar and the ways they are different as discussed in the lecture. Each main point in the listening notes should be a paragraph in the essay.

Example Question 1B

Plan Topic Statement (see Writing Skill 6, p. 346): emotions (Es) innate; Es X innate

Sample Topic Statement: The reading explains that humans all over the world are biologically programmed to experience and express emotions the same way because emotions are universal and innate. However, the lecture casts doubt on this view.

Plan Paragraph 1: Listening = Consensus exag'd

Reading = Es = univs'l/innate accrd 2 Darwin & rsrch by Aff. Scintsts)

Sample Paragraph 1: The speaker says that the reading overstates its position that "a broad consensus" of scientists agree emotions are innate and universal. He states that many affective scientists have a very different perspective; they believe that emotions are learned, and that they vary from culture to culture.

Plan Paragraph 2: Listening = X same Es – all cultures in wrld! (Ex: Japan:wrds/feelings— intrdpndnc/connctdnss, but X in West. b/c dif values: J=collctv v. W=indvdl)

Reading = Same Es –all cultures in wrld

Sample Paragraph 2: The lecturer also refutes the reading's claim that people worldwide feel the same emotions. He gives the example of Japanese words for feeling indebted to and connected to others. These emotions, both related to interdependence, exist in Japan because the culture prizes the group. They do not exist in western cultures, which focus more on the individual.

Plan Paragraph 3: Listening = — Prob w/study--incl'd only 2 Es
Other Es. e.g., guilt/love—no outward fac'l exprs'ns→can't study→ can't prove unvs'l
Anger---Esk pple-X show b/c small cult/live close/harsh cond'n

Reading =Same way to exprss Es all over (fac'l exp'n & vocaliz'n) Rsrch: Pple frm Brit & Afr. undstnd laugh/cry

Sample Paragraph 3: Finally, the speaker is not convinced that people in different cultures show emotion in the same way. He questions the findings of the Britain-Namibia study because it looked only at happiness and sadness. Emotions like guilt or love have not been studied because they are not outwardly visible. Therefore, there is no proof that these emotions are expressed the same globally. The lecturer discusses the Eskimo people, who do not even show anger, much less in the same way that other cultures do.

You should notice again that each paragraph contains one main point from the reading and one main point from the listening and shows how the points are related. Each includes terminology from Example Question 1B.

The following chart outlines key information you should remember about planning before you write a point-by-point essay.

WRITE A POINT-BY-POINT ESSAY USING YOUR PLAN	
OUTLINE	There are five paragraphs in an outline for a point-by-point essay: a short topic statement paragraph, three paragraphs each detailing a main point from the lecture and its related point from the reading, and a short conclusion paragraph.
TERMINOLOGY	Be sure to include the terminology, *casts doubt on, challenges, opposes, addresses, supports, strengthens, answers,* or *solves* from the question in the body of your essay.

WRITING EXERCISE 4: Look at the notes and plan that you prepared for the integrated writing tasks in Writing Exercise 3. Then, on a separate piece of paper, write three body paragraphs for each of the topics from page 340.

1. Homeschooling

    Paragraph 1

    Paragraph 2

    Paragraph 3

2. Physical Education

    Paragraph 1

    Paragraph 2

    Paragraph 3

3. Newspapers

    Paragraph 1

    Paragraph 2

    Paragraph 3

Writing Skill 5: USE AN ALTERNATIVE METHOD TO WRITE YOUR RESPONSE: BLOCK METHOD

Another method you can choose for planning your response to the integrated writing task is the block method. Instead of using the point-by-point method of combining a main point from the listening passage with the related main point from the reading passage in the same paragraph, the block method uses one paragraph for the main points from the listening and then, a new paragraph following it for the related points from the reading passage. Although the previous point-by-point method is the preferred method, the block method is a good way for you to practice and improve your comprehension if you are not yet at a high enough level to use the point-by-point method comfortably.

A possible outline for a block method essay might look like this:

GENERAL OUTLINE:

I. **Topic Statement:** Include information about the topics of each of the passages and about how the two passages are related.

II. **Paragraph 1:** Briefly discuss the three main points from the reading passage.

III. **Paragraph 2:** Discuss the three main points from the listening lecture, and how they address or answer the points in the reading passage.

IV. **Conclusion:** If time allows, summarize the essay. (See Writing Skill 6, p. 346 for more information on writing a conclusion.)

Look at the notes for the integrated writing task on emotions (Example Question 1B). As you study this information, you should think about how the two passages are related.

NOTES (Example Question 1B):

Read:	Listen:
Top: emotions (Es) innate MPs: -Es = univsl/innate accrd 2 Darwin & rsrch by Affctv Scintsts) -Same Es – all cultures in wrld → -Same way to exprss Es all over (facl expn & vocliztn) Rsrch: Pple frm Brit & Afr. undstnd laugh/cry	Top: Es X innate MPs: -- Consensus exagrtd Other prspctv: Es socly cnstrctd--vary acrss cults --X! Ex: Japan:wrds/feelngs—interdpndnc/connctdnss, but not in West b/c dif vals: J=collctv v. W=indvdl -- Prob w/study--incld only 2 Es Other Es, ex guilt/love—no outwrd facl exprsns→ can't study→can't prove unvsl Anger---Esk pple-X show b/c small cult/live close/harsh cndns

The notes show that the reading passage describes similarities in emotions from culture to culture that lead to the conclusion that emotions are universal and innate, and the listening passage describes situations when emotions differ from culture to culture. The listening passage casts doubt on the conclusion in the reading passage by showing that emotions are not always similar from culture to culture, and therefore are learned, not innate.

Now look at a possible plan for the integrated writing Example Question 1B using the block method.

PLAN (Example Question 1B):

Plan Topic Statement (see Writing Skill 6, p. 346): emotions (Es) innate; Es X innate

Sample Topic Statement: The reading explains that humans all over the world are biologically programmed to experience and express emotions the same way because emotions are universal and innate. However, the lecture casts doubt on this view.

Plan Paragraph 1: Reading = Es = univsl/innate accrd 2 Darwin & rsrch by Affctv Scintsts; same Es –all cultures in wrld ; same way to exprss Es all over (facl expn & vocliztn); Rsrch: Pple frm Brit & Afr. undstnd laugh/cry

Sample Paragraph 1: In the reading passage, the author discusses the idea that emotions are universal and innate, according to the research of Charles Darwin and affective scientists. The reading points out that numerous emotions are shared by many cultures throughout the world. Because cultures have the same emotions, they are expressed in the same way, through facial expressions and vocalizations. For example, people from Great Britain and from remote areas of Africa both understand each other's vocalizations for crying and laughter. From these facts, the author draws the conclusion that emotions are innate, rather than learned.

Plan Paragraph 2: Listening = Consensus exagrtd; other prspctv: Es socly cnstrctd--vary acrss cults; prob w/study--incld only 2 Es; other Es, ex guilt/love—no outwrd facl exprsns→can't study→can't prove unvsl; Anger---Esk pple-X show b/c small cult/live close/harsh cndns

Sample Paragraph 2: The listening passage casts doubt on the conclusion in the reading passage by stating that the consensus in the reading was greatly exaggerated. The lecturer explains that many other affective scientists believe that emotions are learned. The lecturer also refutes the reading's claim that people worldwide feel the same emotions. He gives the example of Japanese words for feeling indebted to and connected to others. These emotions, both related to interdependence, exist in Japan because the culture prizes the group. They do not exist in western cultures, which focus more on the individual. The lecturer points out that the study of British and African emotions was flawed, because it tested only two emotions. He cites research about certain Eskimo cultures and how they do not express anger, due to living in close and harsh conditions. These facts lead to the conclusion that emotions are learned and not intrinsic.

The following chart outlines the key information you should remember about using the block method to write your response.

USE AN ALTERNATIVE METHOD TO WRITE YOUR RESPONSE: BLOCK METHOD	
OUTLINE	There are three or four paragraphs in an outline for a block method essay: a short topic statement paragraph, one paragraph that briefly states the main points from the reading, one paragraph that details main points from the lecture and how they answer the points from the reading, and a short conclusion if time permits.
TERMINOLOGY	Include the terminology, *casts doubt on*, *challenges*, *opposes*, *supports*, *strengthens*, *addresses*, *answers*, or *solves* from the question in the body of your essay.

WRITING EXERCISE 5: Look at the notes that you prepared for the reading passages in Writing Exercise 1 (pp. 328–330) and the listening passages in Writing Exercise 2 (pp. 334–335). Read the question for each task (p. 340). Then, on a separate piece of paper, write block method paragraphs for the reading and lecture for each of the integrated writing tasks that you worked on in Writing Exercises 1–4.

1. **Homeschooling**
   - A. paragraph on reading
   - B. paragraph on listening

2. **Physical Education**
   - A. paragraph on reading
   - B. paragraph on listening

3. **Newspapers**
   - A. paragraph on reading
   - B. paragraph on listening

Writing Skill 6: WRITE A TOPIC STATEMENT AND CONCLUSION

TOPIC STATEMENT

After you have planned your response, you should begin writing your response with an overall topic statement. Your topic statement should show how the information in the reading passage and the information in the listening passage are related. Include the terminology from the question such as *casts doubt on, challenges, opposes, supports, strengthens, addresses, answers,* or *solves.*

Look at the question and the information from the notes for the integrated writing task on fracking in Writing Skill 2.

Example Question 1A

> **Summarize the points made in the lecture, being sure to explain how they challenge specific arguments raised in the reading.**

> TOPIC OF READING PASSAGE: Fracking — get natl gas +++;
>
> TOPIC OF LISTENING PASSAGE: Fracking X benfcl

As you study this information, you should think about the question and about writing an overall topic statement that includes information about the topics of each of the passages and about how the listening passage addresses the points discussed in the reading passage.

Look at a possible topic statement for the integrated writing task on fracking in Writing Skill 2.

> Topic Statement
>
> The reading passage describes fracking and discusses several benefits, whereas the lecture challenges these benefits and opposes this practice.

You should notice again that this topic statement does not include all the details about the topic and instead simply gives the overall idea. It also includes the terminology *challenges* from the question.

Now look at the question and the information from the integrated writing task on emotions in Writing Skill 2.

Example Question 1B

> **Summarize the points made in the lecture, being sure to explain how they cast doubt on specific points made in the reading.**

TOPIC OF READING PASSAGE: emotions (Es) innate

TOPIC OF LISTENING PASSAGE: Es X innate

As you study this information, you should think about the question and about writing an overall topic statement that includes information about the topics of each of the passages and about how the listening passage casts doubt on the main points made in the reading passage.

Look at a possible topic statement for the integrated writing task on emotions.

Topic Statement

The reading explains that humans all over the world are biologically programmed to experience and express emotions the same way because emotions are universal and innate. However, the lecture casts doubt on this view.

You should notice again that this topic statement does not include all the details about the topic and instead simply gives the overall idea.

The following chart outlines the key information you should use for planning your topic statement before you write your response for the integrated writing task.

WRITE A TOPIC STATEMENT	
STATE THE RELATIONSHIP BETWEEN THE LISTENING PASSAGE AND THE READING PASSAGE	The topic statement should come at the beginning of your response. It should include a brief definition of the topic that is being discussed by both the listening passage and the reading passage. This topic statement should show how the topic of the reading passage and the topic of the listening passage are related.
USE TERMINOLOGY TO INDICATE THE RELATIONSHIP BETWEEN THE PASSAGES	Be sure to indicate the type of relationship between the ideas in the listening and reading. Mention whether the listening passage is casting doubt on, opposing, challenging points in the reading passage or answering problems in it or if the listening passage is supporting or strengthening the reading passage.

CONCLUSION

A conclusion is not necessary, but if time permits, you can include a short conclusion to summarize what you wrote. Make sure to keep track of your time. If you do not have time, do not write a conclusion.

However, if you do have time to write a conclusion, consider briefly summarizing the main points or paraphrasing (putting into different words) the topic statement.

Look at the final points from the notes for the integrated writing task on fracking in Writing Skill 2.

> Lots of pw'r (cmpd to wind/solar) →the future;
>
> But nat'l gs ≥pwr than sol/wnd. B/c new govt: shld invest =$—>fair comp'n
>
> X lots resrces—only enuf for 23 yrs?
>
> Renw'ble enrg for future +++

You can see that combining this information will provide a simple conclusion.

Look at a possible conclusion for the integrated writing task on fracking.

> Conclusion
>
> Because of all the drawbacks of fracking and because natural gas resources are not as abundant as once thought, the speaker believes that renewable energies are the best option.

Now look at the topic statement from the example for the integrated writing task on emotions in Writing Skill 2.

> The reading explains that humans all over the world are biologically programmed to experience and express emotions the same way because emotions are universal and innate. However, the lecture casts doubt on this view.

You can see that the topic statement indicates that the lecturer believes emotions are learned while the reading passage presents the idea that they are natural.

Look at a possible conclusion for the integrated writing task on emotions.

> Conclusion
>
> In short, the speaker provides arguments and evidence to support the perspective that emotions are not genetically hardwired, but rather learned and culturally specific.

In this conclusion, the topic statement has been paraphrased, using slightly different language.

WRITING EXERCISE 6: Look at the plans that you prepared for the integrated writing tasks in Writing Exercise 3. Then write a topic statement for each task that addresses the question.

1. **Homeschooling:** Summarize the points made in the lecture, being sure to specifically explain how they challenge specific arguments made in the reading passage.

   The lecturer states that _____

   _____

   _____.

   The lecturer's opinion is quite different from the opinion expressed in the reading passage, which is _____

   _____

   _____.

2. **Physical Education:** Summarize the points made in the lecture, being sure to specifically explain how they oppose the points presented in the reading passage.

   According to the lecture, _____

   _____

   _____

   The information in the lecture opposes _____

   _____

   _____

3. **Newspapers:** Summarize the points made in the lecture, being sure to specifically explain how they cast doubt on specific points made in the reading passage.

   The lecture discusses _____

   _____

   _____

   The information in the lecture casts doubt on what is stated in the reading passage about

   _____

   _____

   _____.

Writing Skill 7: REVIEW SENTENCE STRUCTURE

After you have written your response, it is important for you to save some time at the end if possible to review the sentence structure in your response. You should check the sentence structure of simple sentences, compound sentences, and complex sentences.

NOTE: For a review of sentence structure, see APPENDIX.

Look at the following sentences from a response about the development of a new theory.

Since a new <u>theory</u> <u>was developed</u> within the last decade.
           S   V

The <u>reading passage</u> <u>explains</u> a theory, the <u>listening passage</u>
       S   V   S

<u>discusses</u> the historical background of the theory.
    V

One <u>issue</u> that the lecturer points out <u>it</u> <u>is</u> that the main facts
     S   S V

contradict the theory.

The sentence structure of each of these sentences is not correct. The first sentence is an incorrect simple sentence. In this sentence, the subordinate connector *Since* in front of the subject and verb *theory was developed* makes the sentence incomplete. The second sentence is an incorrect compound sentence. In this sentence, the main clauses *reading passage explains . . .* and *listening passage discusses . . .* are connected with a comma (,), and a comma cannot be used to connect two main clauses. The third sentence is an incorrect complex sentence. In this sentence, the main subject is *issue* and the verb is *is*; there is an extra subject *it*, which makes the sentence incorrect.

The following chart outlines the key information you should use for reviewing sentence structure.

REVIEW SENTENCE STRUCTURE	
SENTENCE STRUCTURE	Check for errors in sentence structure in your response. Be sure to check for errors in simple sentences, compound sentences, and complex sentences.

WRITING EXERCISE 7: Correct the errors in sentence structure in the following passages. (The number in parentheses at the end of each paragraph indicates the number of errors in the paragraph.)

1.   (A) The lecturer discusses the benefits of a particular style management, which opposes another style of management supported by the reading passage. Both of the management styles they were proposed by Douglas McGregor. *(2)*

       (B) The listening passage discusses the theory Y management style, which is an participative style. In this type of management, the manager believes it is that employees work for enjoyment. This directly opposes the theory X management style discussed in the reading. In which the manager believes that employees that employees don't do not like to work. *(4)*

       (C) The listening passage explains that the theory Y manager does not need force employees to work by using threats and punishment, which it is the method of getting employees to work in the theory X style. This is because the theory Y employees they work for enjoyment. Instead, the role of the theory Y manager is set objectives and then to reward employees. As they meet these objectives. *(5)*

2.
   (A) The reading discusses why choosing to attend a trade or vocational school is preferable to pursuing a four-year college degree, the lecturer casts doubt on this by discussing the reasons to attending a traditional college. *(2)*

   (B) The reading introduces the obvious cost benefit of attending a trade school. In difficult economic times, spending less on education it is often necessary in order for people to support themselves while pursuing training. The listening passage refutes this by explaining that the trade school, while costing significantly less than a traditional college, it does not provide the diversity and comprehensive options are available in a university. *(3)*

   (C) In addition. While the vocational school it provides targeted education towards a specific career, the lecturer explains that a wide range of experiences they are gained in college. And this allows students to be more flexible and apply their knowledge to multiple fields. *(4)*

Writing Skill 8: REVIEW GRAMMAR

After you have written your response, it is important for you to review the grammar in your response.

NOTE: For a review of grammar, see APPENDIX.

Look at the following sentence from a response on a scientific phenomenon.

> **Though scientists are quite sure that this phenomenon exist, it's causes are not so clear.**

In this sentence, the verb *exist* does not agree with the singular subject *phenomenon;* to correct this error, you can change *exist* to *exists.* The contracted subject and verb *it's* in front of the noun *causes* should be changed to a possessive adjective; to correct this error, you can change *it's* to *its.*

The following chart outlines the key information you should use for reviewing grammar.

REVIEW GRAMMAR	
GRAMMAR	Check for errors in grammar in your response. Be sure to check for errors with nouns and pronouns, verbs, adjectives and adverbs, articles, and agreement.

WRITING EXERCISE 8: Correct the errors in grammar in the following passages. (The number in parentheses at the end of each paragraph indicates the number of errors in the paragraph.)

1.
   (A) The reading passage discusses attempt to deal with the problem of spelling in much words in American English; the listening passage explained why this attempt was not a successfully one. *(4)*

   (B) The reading passage explains that there is a problem in spelling a number of word in English where the spelling and pronunciation does not match; it then goes on to explain that philanthropist Andrew Carnegie made an efforts to resolve this. He gave an huge amount of dollars to establish a board calling the Simplified Spelling Board. As the name of a board indicates, its' purpose was to simplify the spellings of a words that are difficult to spell in English. Because of all of work that the board did, spellings like <u>ax</u> (instead of <u>axe</u>) and <u>program</u> (instead of <u>programme</u>) had become acceptable in American English. *(11)*

   (C) The listening passage explain why the work of the Simplified Spelling Board does not last. According to the listening passage, the main reason for the board's problems were that it went too far. They tried to establish spellings like <u>yu</u> (instead of <u>you</u>) and <u>tuff</u> (instead of <u>tough</u>). There was a real negative reaction to the attempt to change spelling too much, and eventually the board was dissolving. *(5)*

2.   (A) The reading passage describes type of learning, and the listening passage challenged the ideas about this types of learning. *(3)*

(B) The reading passage discusses aversive conditioning, which is defined as learning involving an unpleasant stimulus. In this type of learning, an unpleasant stimulus is applied every times that a certain behavior occur, in an attempt to stop the behavior. The listening passage explains how the unpleasant stimulus could being harmful to the subject. The stimulus can be so unpleasant that the subject stops participate in the conditioning altogether. The reading explains that a learner can behaves in two different ways in response to the knowledge that something unpleasant will soon occur. Avoidance behavior is change in behavior before the stimulus is applied to avoid the unpleasant stimulus, while escape behavior is the opposite, a change in behavior after the application of the stimulus to cause them to stop. The lecturer points out that avoidance can extend to the learner not participating at all after escaping the first application of the stimulus. *(8)*

(C) The reading passage also provides long example of aversive conditioning. This extended example is about the alarm in much cars that buzzed if the driver's seat belt is not fastened. In this example, the method of aversive conditioning that is applied to drivers are that every time a driver tries to drive with the seat belt unfastened, the buzzer went off. The driver exhibits avoidance behavior if he or she has fasten the seat belt before driving to avoid hearing the buzzer. The driver exhibits escape behavior if he or she attach the seat belt after the alarm had started to buzz, to stop the buzzing. The listening raises the question of another type of response to the example, such as the learner fastening the seat belt without actually wearing it. *(8)*

WRITING REVIEW EXERCISE (Skills 1–8): Read the passage. Take notes on the topic and main points of the reading passage.

The mysterious and much studied Stonehenge is an enormous, prehistoric structure located on the Salisbury Plain in the south of England. Its main structure consists of 30 upright stones, weighing 26 tons each, arranged in a circle, with 30 additional 6-ton stones sitting on top of the upright stones. There is a second circle of stones inside the main circle that is remarkably similar to the outer circle since its stones are also upright with additional stones perched atop them. One of the most commonly held theories about the construction of Stonehenge is that it was built by the Druids. These high priests of the Celtic culture in England are believed by many to have had the structure at Stonehenge constructed in order to hold their religious ceremonies in that location. This idea was first proposed by John Aubrey (1626–1697).

Dr. William Stukeley (1687–1765), another antiquarian and scholar, being aware of Aubrey's previous claims from a century earlier, also developed a keen interest in the people who had been involved in the building of Stonehenge. Stukeley became interested in the study of a possible relationship between the massive structure and the Druids, and he came to strongly hold the same belief as Aubrey had. Stukeley wrote the scholarly work *Stonehenge, A Temple Restored to the British Druids* (1740) to publicize his opinion that the Druids were unquestionably responsible for Stonehenge, and that they used this site for religious worship and other ceremonies.

The exact year of its construction was unknown, but since the prevailing belief was that the monument was erected by the Druids, it was assumed it was constructed during the age of Druids.

Listen to the passage. On a piece of paper, take notes on the topic and main points of the listening passage. [154] 🔊

Now answer the following question. You have 20 minutes to plan and write your response: [155] 🔊

Summarize the points made in the lecture, being sure to specifically explain how they cast doubt on specific points made in the reading passage.

WRITING QUESTION 2: INDEPENDENT TASK

Writing Skill 9: DECODE THE ESSAY PROMPTS

You will have 30 minutes to plan and complete the independent writing task. In order to achieve a good score, your essay should be about 300 words in length.

The first and most important step in the independent task in the Writing section of the TOEFL iBT® Test is to decode the essay topic to determine how to write your outline. Writing topics generally give very clear clues about how your answer should be constructed. It is important to follow the clear clues that are given in the topic when you are planning your answer. You will probably not be given too much credit for a response that does not cover the topic in the way that is intended. Study the following essay topic.

Example Essay Topic Question 2
Do you agree or disagree with the following statement?

> **Smartphones and online social networks have destroyed communication between friends and family.**

Use specific reasons and examples to support your opinion.

Each topic in the independent task shows you exactly *what* you should discuss and *how* you should organize your response. You must decode the topic carefully to determine the intended way of organizing your response, and you must include an introduction and a conclusion.

This means you need to determine what the prompt is asking you to write. In this example, it is asking for your opinion and asking for specific reasons and examples that support your opinion.

Read the prompt carefully. Look for key words to make sure you understand the topic. In this case, *smartphones, social networks, destroyed, communication,* and *friends and family* are important.

Then notice the verb being used. For this topic, the verb is *agree* or *disagree*. This lets you know exactly what you need to do; you need to decide if you agree or disagree with the statement and then plan your response accordingly.

Support your essay with the kinds of support that the essay topic asks for (such as *reasons, details,* or *examples*), and try to *personalize* your essay as much as possible by using your own experience. The more support you have, the better your essay will be.

The following chart outlines the types of essay questions that you should look for when decoding the prompt.

DECODE THE ESSAY PROMPTS		
Types	**Explanation**	**Examples and *Key Words***
OPINION	This prompt is asking for your opinion. State your opinion and then support it with details and examples. Be sure to clearly state your opinion at the beginning of your answer.	Do you **agree or disagree** with the following statement? Cell phones should be prohibited in restaurants? **Use specific reasons and examples** to support your opinion. **What is the most important** key to success on the TOEFL iBT® test? **Why** is it important? Use reasons and specific details to support your answer. **In your opinion**, what is the **best way** to make new friends? Use reasons and examples to explain your answer. Some people believe that teachers should be evaluated by their students. **Do you think** that they should be? Use reasons and specific details to support your answer.
PREFERENCE	This prompt is asking you to choose your favorite item or which of several items you prefer. State your preference directly and then give reasons for your choice.	Movies affect people in different ways. Explain what **your favorite** movie is and **why** it affected you. Use reasons and examples to support your answer. **Some** students **prefer** to study alone. **Others prefer** to study with another person or in a group. **Which way do you prefer?** Use reasons and examples to support your answer. When you attend a university, **would you prefer** to live on campus **or** off campus? Use reasons and examples to support your answer. In your country, **is there** a need for **more** agricultural development **or** is there **more** need for industrial development? Use reasons and specific details to support your answer.

HYPOTHETICAL (imagined situation)	This prompt may contain an "if question." Answer by stating what you would do in that particular situation and explain why. Use examples from your personal experience or from the experience of others that you know about.	*Imagine that* you have been given the chance to travel anywhere in the world. You can choose a friend to go with you. Who would you take with you on the trip and why? Use reasons and specific details to support your answer. *If you could* meet a famous actor, who would that be, and *why*? Use specific reasons and examples to support your answer.
EXPLAIN/ DESCRIBE	This prompt is asking you to answer a general question and then give specific reasons and examples for your answer. This type of question will definitely require you to think before you write.	Technology will continue to change the world in many ways. *Discuss* the ways you think technology will change people's lives in the future. Use examples and details in your answer. What are some of the qualities of a good friend? Use specific details and examples to *explain* your answer.
COMPARE/ CONTRAST/ ADVANTAGES/ DISADVANTAGES	This prompt asks you to compare items or explain the advantages of items. Like the other prompts, you will need to provide specific reasons and examples. If time allows, you may also want to discuss how the items contrast or the disadvantages of the items.	Some people believe that children should be taught a specific skill, such as how to play chess or piano at a very early age. Others believe children should be outdoors playing when they are young. *Compare these two views. Which* do you agree with and *why*? Use specific reasons and examples to support your answer. Some people think it is better to have a job they like than to make a lot of money. Others believe that making money is the most important part of a job. *Compare the advantages* of these two attitudes. Which attitude do you agree with? Support your choice with specific details.

WRITING EXERCISE 9: For each of the following writing topics, list the verb and key vocabulary. Decide which type the prompt is. The first one has been done for you.

1. People have various ways of relieving stress. What do you think are some of the most effective ways that people can relieve stress? Use specific reasons and examples to support your response.

> VERB: think
>
> KEY WORDS: most effective ways
>
> TYPE: opinion

2. What famous place would you like to visit? Use details and reasons to explain your response.

```
VERB:

KEY WORDS:

TYPE:
```

3. Do you agree or disagree with the following statement?

   Actions speak louder than words.

   Use specific reasons and examples to support your response.

```
VERB:

KEY WORDS:

TYPE:
```

4. Compare yourself today and yourself five years ago. In what ways are you the same or different? Use specific examples to support your response.

```
VERB:

KEY WORDS:

TYPE:
```

5. Some people prefer to play team sports, while others prefer to play individual sports. Discuss the advantages of each. Then indicate which you prefer and why. Use specific reasons and examples to support your response.

```
VERB:

KEY WORDS:

TYPE:
```

6. If you could change one thing about your school, what would you change? Use reasons and specific examples to support your answer.

```
VERB:

KEY WORDS:

TYPE:
```

7. Many people believe that the best teachers have specific characteristics. Discuss the characteristics that you think make a good teacher. Use reasons and examples to support your response.

> VERB:
>
> KEY WORDS:
>
> TYPE:

8. Do you agree or disagree with the following statement?

   Travel is important for personal development.

   Use specific reasons and examples to support your response.

> VERB:
>
> KEY WORDS:
>
> TYPE:

9. It can be quite difficult to learn a new language. What do you think are the most difficult aspects of learning a new language? Give reasons and examples to support your response.

> VERB:
>
> KEY WORDS:
>
> TYPE:

10. Do you agree or disagree with the following statement?

    The TOEFL iBT® test is a wonderful test!

    Use reasons and examples to support your response.

> VERB:
>
> KEY WORDS:
>
> TYPE:

Writing Skill 10: PLAN BEFORE YOU WRITE: OUTLINING

A good thing to do before writing is to create a plan. Writing a brief outline before writing the essay can lead to a better score because the essay is likely to be better organized and contain all the required parts. Developing a brief outline does not take much time. You should limit your outlining time to 5 minutes. By doing so, you allow yourself 25 minutes to write and check the essay. Remember that your essay needs to be 300 words.

Each prompt type has an outline type that can be used for it. Notice that each outline has a section for an introduction and a conclusion. Fill those in last. More information about introductions and conclusions will be covered in Skill 13 (p. 367). The general format for outlines is very similar.

Note that you don't have to provide three supporting points and examples if it is not possible for you to do so. The length of your essay is important, but it is more important that you respond directly to the topic and provide effective examples and support using good grammar, vocabulary, and structure.

The following chart outlines the types of outlines that you could use for the different prompts.

Category	Outline

OPINION (OR AGREE/DISAGREE)	I. Introduction (state your opinion)
	II. Give Reason 1
	   a. Offer support and examples
	III. Give Reason 2
	   a. Offer support and examples
	IV. Give Reason 3
	   a. Offer support and examples
	V. Conclusion

PREFERENCE	I. Introduction (state your preference)
	II. Give Reason 1
	   a. Offer support and examples
	III. Give Reason 2
	   a. Offer support and examples
	IV. Give Reason 3
	   a. Offer support and examples
	V. Conclusion

HYPOTHETICAL	I. Introduction (state what you would do)
	II. Give Reason 1
	   a. Offer support and examples
	III. Give Reason 2
	   a. Offer support and examples
	IV. Give Reason 3
	   a. Offer support and examples
	V. Conclusion

EXPLAIN/ DESCRIBE	I. Introduction (state your idea)
	II. Give Reason 1
	   a. Offer support and examples
	III. Give Reason 2
	   a. Offer support and examples
	IV. Give Reason 3
	   a. Offer support and examples
	V. Conclusion

COMPARE/ CONTRAST/ ADVANTAGES/ DISADVANTAGES	I. Introduction (state how the items are similar or different; what is good or not good about the items)
	II. Give Comparison/Contrast 1 OR Advantage/Disadvantage 1
	   a. Offer support and examples
	III. Give Comparison/Contrast 2 OR Advantage/Disadvantage 2
	   a. Offer support and examples
	IV. Give Comparison/Contrast 3 OR Advantage/Disadvantage 3
	   a. Offer support and examples
	V. Conclusion

Look at this sample outline for an essay answering the question about smartphones. Note the use of symbols and abbreviations to save time.

> I. *Your opinion*—x destroy comm b/w frnds & family ppl comm wrldwd w/ ++ frequency
>
> II. *Reason 1*—locate lost frnds &distant family quick & get info re
> *support/example* a. big storm (elec & phone X, but genrl post online w/battery-powr laptop comput)
> Ex: info re my uncle
>
> III. *Reason 2*—shy ppl comm better online
> *support/example* a. ex introvert stdnt help fr peer 4 assgnmnt
>
> IV. *Reason 3*—ppl actually talk ++ than b4
> *support/example* a. easier ≥writ lttrs &wait 4 mail
>
> V. *Conclusion*—modern tech improve comm

WRITING EXERCISE 10: For each of the following writing prompts, on a separate piece of paper, create a brief outline for a response.

1. People have various ways of relieving stress. What do you think are some of the most effective ways that people can relieve stress? Use specific reasons and examples to support your response.

2. What famous place would you like to visit? Use details and reasons to explain your response.

3. Do you agree or disagree with the following statement?

   Actions speak louder than words.

   Use specific reasons and examples to support your response.

4. Compare yourself today and yourself five years ago. In what ways are you the same or different? Use specific examples to support your response.

5. Some people prefer to play team sports, while others prefer to play individual sports. Discuss the advantages of each. Then indicate which you prefer and why. Use specific reasons and examples to support your response.

6. If you could change one thing about your school, what would you change? Use reasons and specific examples to support your answer.

7. Many people believe that the best teachers have specific characteristics. Discuss the characteristics that you think make a good teacher. Use reasons and examples to support your response.

8. Do you agree or disagree with the following statement?

   Travel is important for personal development.

   Use specific reasons and examples to support your response.

9. It can be quite difficult to learn a new language. What do you think are the most difficult aspects of learning a new language? Give reasons and examples to support your response.

10. Do you agree or disagree with the following statement?

   The TOEFL iBT® test is a wonderful test!

   Use reasons and examples to support your response.

Writing Skill 11: WRITE UNIFIED SUPPORTING PARAGRAPHS

A good way to begin writing effective supporting paragraphs for an independent writing task is to prepare, using your notes and outline carefully, but quickly, before you begin to write. Then, as you write, you should think about introducing the main idea of each paragraph, supporting the main idea with adequate details, and connecting the ideas together in a unified paragraph. You should use cohesive techniques such as repeated key words, rephrased key ideas, pronouns and determiners for reference, and transition expressions to unify each paragraph.

> Transition expressions help the reader understand the relationship between supporting ideas in your essay. See the chart on page 363 for useful transition expressions.

NOTE: For further work on cohesion, see APPENDIX.

Look at the question and the outline for the first supporting paragraph of the essay from Writing Skills 9 and 10 and the supporting paragraph that is based on the outline.

Example Essay Topic Question 2

Do you agree or disagree with the following statement?

Smartphones and online social networks have destroyed communication between friends and family.

Use specific reasons and examples to support your opinion.

II. locate lost frnds & distant family quick & get info re
   a. big storm (elec & phone X, but post online w/battery-powr laptop comput)
   Ex: info re my uncle

The first point I would like to make is that smartphones and social networking can help people locate lost friends and distant family quickly. This technology allows us to get information about how they are doing. For example, during a big storm in my area, the electricity was out and phone lines in the hardest hit places weren't working. However, when I put a general posting online, using my battery-powered laptop computer, asking for anyone with information to help locate my elderly uncle, I got a lot of responses. I was able to find out he was OK.

As you read the first supporting paragraph in the essay, you should note that the first sentence of the paragraph is a topic sentence that indicates that the first supporting paragraph is the first reason (*the first point I would like to make . . .*) you have to support your opinion. The remaining sentences in the paragraph are details and a specific, personal example. You should also note the techniques that have been used to make the paragraph cohesive. The phrase *this technology* is a rephrasing of the key ideas *smartphones* and *social networking*, the phrase *for example* and the word *however* are transition expressions. Pronouns are also used throughout to connect sentences.

Look at the notes on the second supporting paragraph of the essay and the supporting paragraph that is based on the outline.

III. shy ppl comm better online
   a. ex introvert stdnt help fr peer 4 assgnmnt

Another point I'd like to make is that smartphones and online social networks help shy people communicate better. Let me illustrate this with one of my friends who is very introverted. It was hard for her to make friends when she first started classes at her university. Her grades were not good because she was too shy to talk to her classmates when she needed their help. However, by using text messaging, e-mail, and social networking, she was able to communicate with her classmates about assignments. Finally, she was able to talk to them in person.

As you read the second supporting paragraph in the essay on smartphones and online social networks, you should note that the first sentence of the paragraph is a topic sentence (*Another point I'd like to make . . .*) that indicates that the second supporting paragraph is about how the technology helps shy people communicate, and the rest of the sentences are details from an example about a person whom the writer knows. Notice the techniques that have been used to make the paragraph cohesive. The phrase *very introverted* is a rephrasing of the topic sentence idea involving *shy people*. The phrase *Let me illustrate this with* is used to introduce an example and the words *however* and *finally* are transition expressions. Pronouns are also used throughout to connect sentences.

The following chart outlines the key information you should use when writing unified supporting paragraphs.

WRITE UNIFIED SUPPORTING PARAGRAPHS	
ORGANIZATION	Each supporting paragraph should include a sentence with the main idea of the paragraph, the topic sentence, and several sentences with supporting ideas, examples, or details.
COHESION	To make a supporting paragraph cohesive, you should use a variety of techniques, such as repeated and rephrased key ideas, pronouns and determiners, and transition expressions.

WRITING EXERCISE 11: Read the question and the paragraph that responds to it (on the following page). Then answer the questions that follow.

> It can be quite difficult to learn a new language. What do you think are the most difficult aspects of learning a new language? Give reasons and examples to support your response.

English is not an easy language to learn. Of all the possible problems that I have experienced when trying to learn this language, the most difficult problem that I have encountered is that English does not seem to be spoken by Americans in the same way that **it** was presented in my textbooks. For instance, the first time that I asked an American a question, I got a **strange response**. The man who answered my question said something that sounded like "**Dunno.**" I was sure that I had never studied this expression in my textbooks, and I could not find anything like it in my textbooks, and I could not find anything like it in my dictionary. I was **surprised** to learn later from a friend that this mysterious-sounding answer was really nothing more than a shortened version of "I do not know." Not too long after that I had an even more interesting example of my most difficult problem in learning English. One evening, I was unable to do some chemistry homework problems, so the next morning I asked a classmate if she had been able to do **them.** I was amazed when **she** gave the rather bizarre answer that the assignment had been a "piece of cake." I was not quite sure what a piece of cake had to do with the chemistry assignment, so I responded that I was not quite sure that the assignment really was a piece of cake. I have learned by now that she meant that the assignment was quite easy. Overall, I'm sure it is clear from these two examples what I find so difficult about the English language.

Repeated and rephrased key ideas
1. How many times does the key word "difficult" appear in the passage?
2. How many times does the key word "problem(s)" appear in the passage?
3. How is the phrase "**strange response**" rephrased in the passage?
4. How is the expression "**Dunno**" rephrased in the passage?
5. How is the word "**surprised**" rephrased in the passage?

Pronouns and determiners
6. What noun does the pronoun "**it**" refer to?
7. What noun does the pronoun "**them**" refer to?
8. What noun does the pronoun "**she**" refer to?
9. How many times is the determiner "this" used to refer back to a previous idea?
10. How many times is the determiner "these" used to refer back to a previous idea?

Transition expressions
11. Which transition expression shows that the first example will follow?
12. Which transition expression shows that the second example will follow?
13. Which transition expression shows that the summary of the main point follows?

Now write unified supporting paragraphs for the independent writing tasks that you worked on in Writing Exercises 9–10.

Writing Skill 12: CONNECT THE SUPPORTING PARAGRAPHS

To make sure your essay is as cohesive as possible, you should clearly show how the ideas in the supporting paragraphs in your essay are related. This can be accomplished (1) with a transition expression such as *the first, the most important,* or *a final way,* or (2) with a transition sentence that includes the idea of the previous paragraph and the idea of the current paragraph. It is best to use a combination of these two types of transitions. The following example illustrates how transitions can be used to show the relationships between the supporting paragraphs in an essay.

Refer to the following chart to make sure you include transitions in your essays.

Purpose	Transition Expressions
ADDING INFORMATION	*also, additionally, moreover, furthermore, in addition, another*
COMPARING AND CONTRASTING	*similarly, likewise, however, on the other hand, but, in contrast, unlike*
GIVING EXAMPLES	*for example, for instance, to illustrate*
SEQUENCING	*first/second/third, before/during/after, next, finally, eventually, later, then*
EXPLAINING OR DESCRIBING	*in fact, specifically, actually, particularly*
CONCLUDING	*to summarize, in conclusion*

Look at this example of an outline and supporting paragraphs for the following question. Notice the use of transition expressions in the supporting paragraphs, which are organized point-by-point.

Some people prefer to work in groups on projects. Other people prefer to work alone. Compare the advantages of working in groups with the advantages of working alone. Which would you prefer? Use details and examples to support your response.

Essay Outline

INTRODUCTION: advantages—wrk in grps & individ

SUPPORTING PARAGRAPH 1: advantg 1—wrk in grps = opportun 2 wrk w/othrs advantg 1 wrk individ = past success & enjoy wrk when & how want

SUPPORTING PARAGRAPH 2: advantg 2—wrk in grps = lss wrk 4 individ advantg 2 wrk individ = wrk own way & X rely othrs 4 good grade

CONCLUSION: better 4 me wrk individ

Transitions

(to introduce SP1): The first point I would like to make is that there are strong advantages to working in groups. The main one that it offers is the opportunity to work with others. Although this is a strong advantage to working in groups, there are some even more compelling advantages for me to work by myself. An important one is that I have had previous success working this way, so I know it works for me. Another advantage of working by myself is that I get the enjoyment of doing work when and how I want.

(to introduce SP2): In addition to learning to work with others, working in a group usually means that there is less work for individual members. However, in comparison, I find that working alone is preferable because I can do the work my own way and I don't have to rely on others to get their work done so I can get a good grade.

The first supporting paragraph is introduced with the transition expression *The first point* to show that this is one of the first of the points that you are going to discuss in your essay about the advantages of working in groups. Then, this first point is compared to the second point of working individually by using *although . . . more compelling advantage for me to work by myself* for contrast. This supporting paragraph goes on to discuss the advantages of working individually by using the phrases *An important one* and *another advantage*.

The second supporting paragraph is introduced with a transition sentence that shows how this paragraph is related to the previous paragraph; *In addition to learning to work with others,* (first point from the first supporting paragraph) *. . . there is less work for individual members* (new, second point for the second supporting paragraph). Again, this second point about the advantages of working in groups is compared to the advantages of working alone by using the transition expressions *However* and *in comparison*.

The following chart outlines the key information that you should use for connecting the supporting paragraphs in your essay.

CONNECT THE SUPPORTING PARAGRAPHS	
TRANSITION EXPRESSIONS	You can use transition expressions such as *the first, the next, in addition, another, finally* to connect the supporting paragraphs.
TRANSITION SENTENCES	You can use a transition sentence that relates the topic of the previous paragraph to the topic of the current paragraph.

WRITING EXERCISE 12: For each outline of an essay, write sentences to introduce each of the supporting paragraphs. You should use a combination of transition expressions and transition sentences. Look at the chart of transition expressions on page 363 to help you.

Question 1:
Some people think that owning a car in a big city has many advantages. Others feel that owning a car in a big city has many disadvantages. Discuss the advantages and disadvantages of owning a car in a big city. Which do you think is better? Give specific reasons to support your answer.

1. INTRO: difficult decision about whether or not to own a car in a big city
    SP1:   • the advantages of owning a car in a big city
    SP2:   • the disadvantages of owning a car in a big city

    SP1:   _The advantages of having a car in a big city are numerous._

    SP2:   _There may be numerous advantages to owning a car in a big city; however, there are also_

    distinct disadvantages.

Question 2:

Many people read for fun and in order to relax. What do you think are the most relaxing types of reading? Use specific details and examples to support your opinion.

2. INTRO: three types of reading that I enjoy and that help me relax
   SP1:   • science fiction
   SP2:   • romances
   SP3:   • sports magazines

   SP1:   _____
           _____

   SP2:   _____
           _____

   SP3:   _____
           _____

Question 3:

Some people prefer to travel alone. Others like to travel in groups. Which do you think is the best way to travel? Use specific reasons and examples to explain your choice.

3. INTRO: prefer to travel in groups
   SP1:   • benefit 1 of traveling in groups
   SP2:   • benefit 2 of traveling in groups

   SP1:   _____
           _____

   SP2:   _____
           _____

Question 4:

What characteristics do you think are most important for becoming a successful student? Use specific details and examples to support your answer.

4. INTRO: most important characteristics leading to success as a student
   SP1:   • self-motivation
   SP2:   • desire to succeed
   SP3:   • joy in learning

   SP1:   _____
           _____

   SP2:   _____
           _____

   SP3:   _____
           _____

Question 5:

Do you agree or disagree with the following statement?

Living for today is better than living for tomorrow.

Use specific reasons and examples to support your answer.

5. INTRO: living for tomorrow is better than living just for today
    SP1:   • reason 1 for believing living for tomorrow is a better philosophy; compare to living for today
    SP2:   • reason 2 for believing living for tomorrow is a better philosophy; compare to living for today

    SP1:   _____

              _____

    SP2:   _____

              _____

Question 6:

Some students feel that grades help motivate students to learn. Others feel that grades can discourage students from learning. Discuss the advantages and disadvantages of grading students. Which do you think it true? Use specific reasons and details to support your opinion.

6. INTRO: grades are important to encourage students to learn; advantages and disadvantages
    SP1:   • disadvantage 1 of grades; advantage 1 of grades
    SP2:   • disadvantage 2 of grades; advantage 2 of grades

    SP1:   _____

              _____

    SP2:   _____

              _____

Question 7:

Imagine that a person you know is trying to learn a new language. What advice would you give to this person about the best ways to learn a new language? Use specific details and examples to support your answer.

7. INTRO: three pieces of advice to someone trying to learn a new language
    SP1:   • listen to videos, television programs, radio programs in the new language
    SP2:   • talk with native speakers of the language every chance you get
    SP3:   • read newspapers, magazines, books in the new language

    SP1:   _____

              _____

    SP2:   _____

              _____

    SP3:   _____

              _____

Question 8:

Today many people are concerned about the destruction of the Earth's environment. In your opinion, what steps should the government take to protect the Earth from further harm? Use specific reasons and details to explain your answer.

8. INTRO: three steps the government should take to protect the Earth's environment
    SP1:   • educate people about the causes and effects of environmental damage
    SP2:   • create and enforce laws that penalize those who damage the environment
    SP3:   • reward those who are environmentally conscious with tax cuts

    SP1:   _____

             _____

    SP2:   _____

             _____

    SP3:   _____

             _____

Writing Skill 13: WRITE THE INTRODUCTION AND CONCLUSION

INTRODUCTION

The purpose of the introduction is to:

- First, interest the reader in your topic.

- Then explain clearly to the reader what (the topic) you are going to discuss.

- Finally, explain how you are going to organize the discussion.

Study the following essay topic.

Essay Topic

> **Some people prefer to work in groups on projects, while other people prefer to work alone. What are the advantages of each, and which do you prefer? Use details and examples to support your response.**

The following example shows one possible introduction to an essay on this topic.

INTRODUCTION

The school where I have been a student for the last 16 years has a system that places a higher value on individual achievement than it does on group achievement. Because I was a rather successful student in this school for most of my life, I know a lot about the advantages of working individually on projects. However, I can only imagine the advantages of working on projects in groups.

In the first part of the introduction, the writer provides background information that he or she has been a successful student in an educational system that is based on a lot of individual work, to interest the reader in the topic. By the end of the introduction, the reader also understands that the writer intends to discuss the advantages of individual work, based on personal experience, and then to discuss the advantages of working in groups from her or his imagination.

The following chart outlines the key information that you should use for writing an introduction.

WRITE THE INTRODUCTION	
INTEREST	You should begin your introduction with information that will *interest* the reader in your topic.
TOPIC	You should state the *topic* directly in the middle of the introduction.
ORGANIZATION	You should end the introduction with a statement that shows the *organization* of the discussion of the topic.

CONCLUSION

The purpose of the conclusion is to:

- Close your essay by summarizing the main points of your discussion.

- Make sure that the reader clearly understands your exact ideas on the topic.

- Make sure the reader clearly understands the reasons you feel the way that you do about the topic.

The ideas in your conclusion should be clearly related to the ideas that you began in the introduction. You should indicate what you intend to discuss in the essay in the introduction, and you should indicate the outcome or results of the discussion in the conclusion.

Essay Topic

> **Some people prefer to work in groups on projects, while other people prefer to work alone. What are the advantages of each, and which do you prefer? Use details and examples to support your response.**

The following example shows a possible conclusion to an essay on this topic.

> CONCLUSION
>
> I have worked individually throughout my education, and I have been successful working in this way because this style of work is a good match with my personality. I can imagine that, for some people, the cooperative benefits that come from working in groups might be a good thing. However, I prefer to continue to work alone. I hope that the success that I have had up to now by working in this way will continue to make me successful in the future.

Here the writer refers back to the personal information that was mentioned in the introduction, saying *I have worked individually throughout my education, and I have been successful working in this way. . . .* The writer also briefly summarizes the advantages of each style of work by mentioning that working individually is *a good match with my personality* and that working in groups has *cooperative benefits*. Finally, the writer clearly states a preference for working individually because of the success that this style of work has brought *up to now.*

The following chart outlines the key information that you should use for writing a conclusion.

WRITE THE CONCLUSION	
OVERALL IDEA	You should make sure that your *overall idea* is very clear.
MAIN POINTS	You should summarize the *main points* that you used to arrive at this overall idea.
INTEREST	You should refer back to the information that you used to *interest* the reader in the introduction.

WRITING EXERCISE 13: For each of the following writing topics, on a separate piece of paper, write introductions that include material to *interest* the reader in the topic, a statement of the specific *topic,* and a statement showing the *organization* of the discussion of the topic. Then write conclusions that restate the main idea, summarize the main points, and refer back to the information that you used to interest the reader in the introduction. The first one has been done for you.

1. Some people prefer to work in one company for their entire career. Others think it is better to move from company to company. Discuss the advantages of each position. Which do you think is better and why? Use specific reasons and examples to support your response.

> INTRODUCTION: In my family, we have experience both in staying with one company for a long time and in moving from one company to another. For me personally, moving from company to company is better. However, each of these ways of working has its own advantages.
>
> CONCLUSION: From this, I think you can understand why I prefer to better my career by moving from company to company. I do understand that there are advantages in staying with one company for a long time; I certainly hear about these advantages from my family over and over. However, I have come to the conclusion that something different is better for me.

2. What famous place would you like to visit? Use details and reasons to explain your response.

3. Do you agree or disagree with the following statement?

    Actions speak louder than words.

    Use specific reasons and examples to support your response.

4. Compare yourself today and yourself five years ago. In what ways are you the same or different? Use specific examples to support your response.

5. Some people prefer to play team sports, while others prefer to play individual sports. Discuss the advantages of each. Then indicate which you prefer and why. Use specific reasons and examples to support your response.

6. If you could change one thing about your school, what would you change? Use reasons and specific examples to support your answer.

7. Many people believe that the best teachers have specific characteristics. Discuss the characteristics that you think make a good teacher. Use reasons and examples to support your response.

8. Do you agree or disagree with the following statement?

   Travel is important for personal development.

   Use specific reasons and examples to support your response.

9. It can be quite difficult to learn a new language. What do you think are the most difficult aspects of learning a new language? Give reasons and examples to support your response.

10. Do you agree or disagree with the following statement?

    The TOEFL iBT® Test is a wonderful test!

    Use reasons and examples to support your response.

Writing Skill 14: REVIEW SENTENCE STRUCTURE

After you have written your essay, it is important for you to save some time at the end if possible to review the sentence structure in your essay. You should check the sentence structure of simple sentences, compound sentences, and complex sentences.

NOTE: For a review of sentence structure, see APPENDIX.

Look at the following sentences from an essay about a test.

Because the <u>test</u> in history class <u>was</u> extremely difficult.
    s v

I finally <u>passed</u> the test, otherwise I <u>would have had</u> to take it over.
s   v   s   v

The <u>grade</u> that I intended to get <u>it</u> <u>was</u> much higher.
    s   s v

The sentence structure of each of these sentences is not correct. The first sentence is an incorrect simple sentence. In this sentence, the subordinate connector *Because* in front of the subject and verb *test . . . was* makes the sentence incomplete. The second sentence is an incorrect compound sentence. In this sentence, the main clauses *I . . . passed . . .* and *I would have had . . .* are connected with a comma (,), and a comma cannot be used to connect two main clauses. The third sentence is an incorrect complex sentence. In this sentence, the main subject is *grade* and the verb is *was*; there is an extra subject *it,* which makes the sentence incorrect.

The following chart outlines the key information you should use for reviewing sentence structure.

REVIEW SENTENCE STRUCTURE	
SENTENCE STRUCTURE	Check for errors in sentence structure in your response. Be sure to check for errors in simple sentences, compound sentences, and complex sentences.

WRITING EXERCISE 14: Correct the errors in sentence structure in the following passages. (The number in parentheses at the end of each paragraph indicates the number of errors in the paragraph.)

(A) I definitely believe that taking part in organized team sports is beneficial. However, is beneficial for much more than the obvious reasons. Everyone recognizes, of course, that participation in sports provides obvious physical benefits. It leading to improved physical fitness, it also provides a release from the stresses of life. I spent my youth taking part in a number of organized sports, including football, basketball, and volleyball, as a result of this experience I understand that the benefits of participation much greater than the physical benefits. *(5)*

(B) One very valuable benefit that children get from taking part in sports it is that it teaches participants teamwork. What any player in a team sport needs to learn it is that individual team members must put the team ahead of individual achievement. Individuals on one team who are working for individual glory rather than the good of the team they often end up working against each other. A team made up of individuals unable to work together often not a very successful team, it is usually a complete failure. *(5)*

(C) What also makes participation in team sports valuable it is that it teaches participants to work to achieve goals. Playing sports it involves setting goals and working toward them, examples of such goals are running faster, kicking harder, throwing straighter, or jumping higher. Athletes learn that can set goals and work toward them until the goals accomplished. Is through hard work that goals can be met. *(6)*

(D) By taking part in sports, can learn the truly valuable skills of working together on teams and working to accomplish specific goals. These goals not just beneficial in sports, more importantly, the skills that are developed through sports they are the basis of success in many other aspects of life. Mastering these skills leading to success not only on the playing field but also in the wider arena of life. *(5)*

Writing Skill 15: REVIEW GRAMMAR

After you have written your essay, it is important for you to review the grammar in your response.

NOTE: For a review of grammar, see APPENDIX.

Look at the following sentence from an essay on the effects of television.

Television certainly *has changing* society in *very* big way.

In this sentence, the past participle rather than the present participle *changing* should be used after the helping verb *has*; to correct this error, you can change *changing* to *changed*. The article *a* also needs to be added because the countable singular noun *way* requires an article; to correct this error, you can change *very* to *a very*.

The following chart outlines the key information you should remember about reviewing grammar.

REVIEW GRAMMAR	
GRAMMAR	Check for errors in grammar in your response. Be sure to check for errors with nouns and pronouns, verbs, adjectives and adverbs, articles, and agreement.

WRITING EXERCISE 15: Correct the errors in grammar in the following passages. (The number in parentheses at the end of each paragraph indicates the number of errors in the paragraph.)

(A) In my first semester at the university, I was overwhelm by the differences between university studies and high school studies. In high school, I had easily be able to finish the number of work that was assigned, and if on certain occasion I did not complete an assignment, the teacher quickly tells me to make up the work. The situation in my university classes were not at all like the situation in high school. *(6)*

(B) I was tremendously surprising at the volume of work assigned in the university. Unlike high school courses, which perhaps covered a chapter in two week, university courses regular covered two or three chapters in one week and two or three other chapters in the next week. I have been able to keep up with the workload in high school, but it was difficult for me to finish all the reading in mine university classes even though I tried real hard to finish all of them. *(7)*

(C) The role that the teacher took in motivating students to get work done were also very different in my university. In high school, if an assignment was unfinishing on a date that it was due, my teacher would immediate let me know that I had made really a mistake and needed to finish an assignment right away. In my university classes, however, professors did not inform regularly students to make sure that we were get work done on schedule. It was really easy to put off studying in the beginning of each semesters and really have to work hard later in the semester to catch up on my assignments. (9)

(D) During my first year in the university, I had to set firm goal to get things done by myself instead of relying on others to watch over me and make sure that I have done what I was supposed to do. With so much assignments, this was quite a task difficult, but I now regular try to do my best because I dislike being very far behind. It seems that I have turn into quite a motivating student. *(7)*

WRITING REVIEW EXERCISE (Skills 9–15):

Read the question. On a piece of paper, take notes on the topic and main points for a response. Then write your response.

> **Some people show their emotions, while other people work hard to keep their emotions from showing. What are the advantages of each type of behavior? Which behavior do you prefer? Use specific reasons and details to support your response.**

Response Time: 20 minutes

WRITING POST-TEST

Writing
Section Directions

This section measures your ability to communicate in writing in an academic environment. There will be two writing tasks.

For the first writing task, you will read a passage and listen to a lecture about an academic topic. Then you will write a response to a question that asks you about the relationship between the lecture and the reading passage.

For the second task, you will demonstrate your ability to write an essay in response to a question that asks you to express and support your opinion about a topic or issue.

Now listen to the directions for the first writing task.

Integrated Writing Directions

For this task, you will first have three minutes to read a passage about an academic topic. You may take notes on the passage if you wish. The passage will then be removed and you will listen to a lecture about the same topic. While you listen, you may also take notes.

Then you will have 20 minutes to write a response to a question that asks you about the relationship between the lecture you heard and the reading passage. Try to answer the question as completely as possible using information from the reading passage and the lecture. The question does not ask you to express your personal opinion. You will be able to see the reading passage again when it is time for you to write. You may use your notes to help you answer the question.

Typically, an effective response will be 150 to 225 words long. Your response will be judged on the quality of your writing and on the completeness and accuracy of the content. If you finish your response before time is up, you may click on Next to go on to the second writing task.

Independent Writing Directions

For this task, you will write an essay in response to a question that asks you to state, explain, and support your opinion on an issue. You will have 30 minutes to plan, write, and revise your essay.

Typically, an effective essay will contain a minimum of 300 words. Your essay will be judged on the quality of your writing. This includes the development of your ideas, the organization of your essay, and the quality and accuracy of the language you use to express your ideas.

If you finish your essay before time is up, you may click on Next to end this section. When you are ready to continue, click on the Dismiss Directions icon.

Question 1

Read the passage. On a piece of paper, take notes on the topic and main points of the reading passage.

Historically, astrology, which is a belief in a relation between astronomical phenomena and actual events, was considered an academic practice worthy of respect. It was accepted as a reliable source of predictions for a person's life and for future world events. Ancient cultures from the Mayans to early Chinese developed astrological systems to predict world events. Astrologers during the Renaissance used the money they raised by predicting the future to pay for their scholarly and artistic pursuits. World leaders consulted astrologers to gain insight into the movement of enemy troops or assist them in critical decision making. Literature and music of past centuries is filled with mentions of astrology, including Chaucer's *The Canterbury Tales* from the fourteenth century.

Western astrology was based on the location and movement of constellations in the sky throughout the year. It involves horoscopes based on a study of date of birth in relation to signs of the zodiac. People born under a particular sign are believed to possess specific qualities unique to that sign, and their horoscopes predict upcoming events and times of wealth, sickness, love, etc. In many countries today, there is a long-standing tradition of consulting astrologers for insights into daily life. In fact, the belief in astrological accuracy has resulted in changes to society. Even one recent U.S. president, Ronald Reagan, was known to consult his horoscope on a regular basis.

Listen to the passage. On a piece of paper, take notes on the topic and main points of the listening passage. 156 🔊

Now answer the following question: 157 🔊

Summarize the points made in the lecture, being sure to specifically explain how they oppose specific points made in the reading passage.

Question 2

Read the question. On a piece of paper, take notes on the topic and main points for a response. Then write your response.

Do you agree or disagree with the following statement?

It is better to be safe than sorry.

Use reasons and examples to support your response.

Turn to pages 610–616 to *assess* the skills used in the test, *score* the test, using the Writing Scoring Criteria, and *record* your results.

MINI-TEST 1

READING

20 minutes

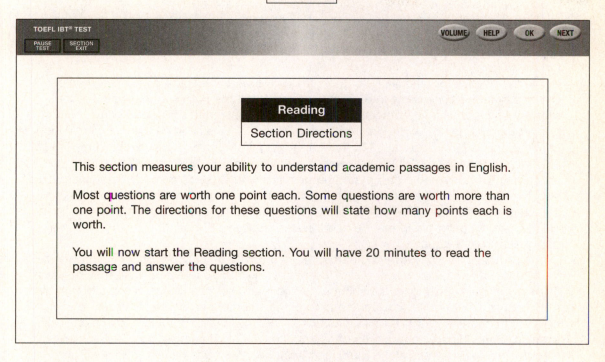

TOEFL IBT® TEST

PAUSE TEST | SECTION EXIT

VOLUME | HELP | OK | NEXT

Reading

Section Directions

This section measures your ability to understand academic passages in English.

Most questions are worth one point each. Some questions are worth more than one point. The directions for these questions will state how many points each is worth.

You will now start the Reading section. You will have 20 minutes to read the passage and answer the questions.

Read the passage and answer the questions that follow.

The Lost Gold

1► Most people are familiar with a battle known as the Battle of the Little Bighorn, or Custer's Last Stand. The basics of this familiar event are that five companies of the Seventh Cavalry, a total of 248 men, were led into battle in the valley of the Little Big Horn River in Montana by a thirty-six year old major-general named George Armstrong Custer; on June 24, 1876, these five companies were completely overwhelmed and decimated by a huge coalition of Sioux and Cheyenne. A footnote to this historical event that has been lost among all the drama and significance of the battle itself is the story of a missing fortune in gold.

2► In the days before the Battle of the Little Big Horn, two separate bands of men on two separate missions came into contact and initiated the events that have led to the mystery of today. The first of these bands of men consisted of driver Gil Longworth and two armed guards on a mule-drawn freight wagon that was heading east carrying a load of miners' gold from Bozeman, Montana, to a freight company in Bismarck, North Dakota. The second of these bands of men was on a military supply boat that was heading north on the Big Horn River to a designated rendezvous with Custer's commanding officer. This supply boat was under the command of a Captain Marsh, who was unfamiliar with this stretch of the Big Horn River and overshot the meeting location. By the time he realized his mistake, he determined that he had traveled between 15 and 20 miles north of the designated meeting place.

3► On June 26, the day after the battle, the two bands of men met up. Longworth and the guards were anxious to get out of the area as quickly as they could, so they begged the army officer to take over the shipment of gold and see that it was eventually delivered to Bismarck. Captain Marsh agreed and took the shipment on board his vessel, and Longworth and the guards retreated as quickly as possible back toward Bozeman. That evening, when Marsh realized how dangerous the situation actually was, he decided to hide the gold somewhere along the river. Marsh debarked and headed for shore, taking two of his most trusted officers and the gold with him; the trio returned to the boat some three and a half hours later without their valuable cargo.

4► **8A** Marsh left the dangerous area with his men and was not able to return for around three years. **8B** At that point, he made an attempt to notify the freight company in Bismarck about the hidden shipment of gold, but by that time the company had gone out of business. **8C** Marsh left the military and lived the kind of working class life one might expect as the captain of a riverboat. **8D** The two officers who had helped Marsh hide the gold continued working on the supply boat until they retired some sixteen years later.

5► Though what happened to the gold is not known today, what is stated above is known with a fair amount of well-researched certainty. There are historical records showing that Longworth did leave Bozeman on a mule-train accompanied by two guards and that they were heading for Bismarck with a load of gold; there are records showing that the gold was transferred to the military supply boat under the command of Captain Marsh; there are records showing that the three men from the supply boat did indeed leave their vessel with the gold for a period of only a few hours and then returned empty-handed; there are records showing that these three lived out their lives without any indication that either they or their descendants had obtained a huge fortune in gold. What is not known is the fate of the gold. Perhaps a future fortune hunter might wish to spend time examining records from the period in detail in the hope of finding a missed clue or, instead simply head to the banks of the Big Horn River.

1. It is stated in paragraph 1 that the story of the lost gold
   A. contradicts the historical account of the Battle of the Little Bighorn
   B. has more importance than the Battle of the Little Bighorn
   C. is only one tiny part of the events surrounding the Battle of the Little Bighorn
   D. is one of the most dramatic events of the Battle of the Little Bighorn

2. The word coalition in paragraph 1 is closest in meaning to
   A. alliance
   B. society
   C. collapse
   D. ambush

3. The word that in paragraph 1 refers to
   A. a huge coalition
   B. a footnote
   C. this historical event
   D. the drama

4. What is NOT mentioned in the passage about the two bands of men?
   A. how Longworth and his men were traveling
   B. what Longworth and his men were carrying
   C. how Marsh and his men were traveling
   D. what Marsh and his men were carrying

5. The word stretch in paragraph 2 could best be replaced by
   A. section
   B. diameter
   C. string
   D. extension

6. Which of the sentences below best expresses the essential information in the highlighted sentence in paragraph 3? Incorrect choices change the meaning in important ways or leave out essential information.
   A. The men left the boat to look for the gold but returned without it.
   B. Marsh gave the gold to two of his officers, and the officers disappeared with the gold.
   C. The men left the boat with the gold and returned fairly soon without it.
   D. It took only a few hours for the men to carry the gold to the boat.

7. What inference can be drawn from the way the men who hid the gold lived?
   A. They never benefited financially from the gold.
   B. Their lives were changed considerably because of the gold.
   C. They most likely really found the gold.
   D. They most likely wished they had never found the gold.

8. Look at the four squares [■] that indicate where the following sentence could be added to the passage.

   Numerous lost shipments had forced the company to cease operations.

   Where would the sentence best fit? Click on a square to add the sentence to the passage.

9. The phrase empty-handed in paragraph 5 is closest in meaning to
   A. on time
   B. as planned
   C. with nothing
   D. without gloves

10. The purpose of the last paragraph of the passage is to
    A. introduce an alternate theory about the lost gold
    B. contradict the information in the previous paragraphs
    C. provide further information about the Battle of Little Bighorn
    D. summarize points that were presented in previous paragraphs

11. **Directions:** Select the appropriate answer choices about three men involved in a historical event, and match them to the correct category. This question is worth 4 points.

Answer Choices	Custer
Was hired to deliver a shipment of gold over land	
Was commanding a military supply ship	
Led a number of cavalry companies	**Marsh**
Won the Battle of Little Bighorn	
Hid a treasure in gold	
Turned his shipment over to a military officer	
Lost a famous battle	**Longworth**
Attempted to contact the freight office	
Eventually found the buried treasure	

Turn to pages 591–594 to *diagnose* your errors and *record* your results.

MINI-TEST 1

LISTENING

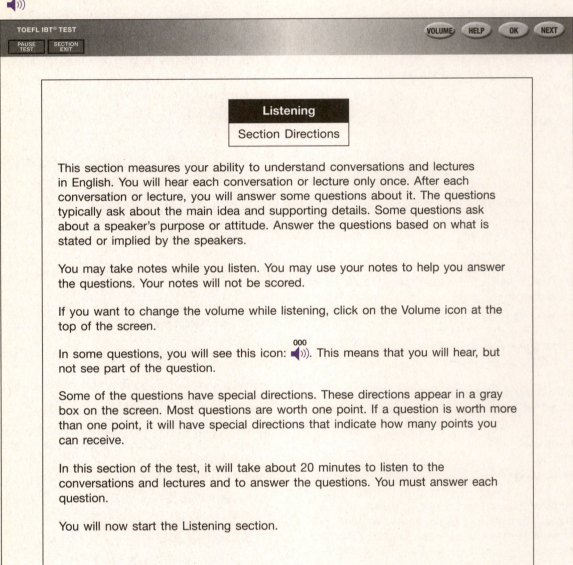

TOEFL IBT® TEST

PAUSE TEST | SECTION EXIT

VOLUME | HELP | OK | NEXT

Listening
Section Directions

This section measures your ability to understand conversations and lectures in English. You will hear each conversation or lecture only once. After each conversation or lecture, you will answer some questions about it. The questions typically ask about the main idea and supporting details. Some questions ask about a speaker's purpose or attitude. Answer the questions based on what is stated or implied by the speakers.

You may take notes while you listen. You may use your notes to help you answer the questions. Your notes will not be scored.

If you want to change the volume while listening, click on the Volume icon at the top of the screen.

In some questions, you will see this icon: 🔊)). This means that you will hear, but not see part of the question.

Some of the questions have special directions. These directions appear in a gray box on the screen. Most questions are worth one point. If a question is worth more than one point, it will have special directions that indicate how many points you can receive.

In this section of the test, it will take about 20 minutes to listen to the conversations and lectures and to answer the questions. You must answer each question.

You will now start the Listening section.

Listen as a student consults with a lab assistant.

159

1. Why does the student go to see the lab assistant?
   - (A) To discuss two issues related to the science lab
   - (B) To discuss why he did not do a good job on his first lab assignment
   - (C) To find out what he must do to complete his lab report
   - (D) To talk about the members of his science lab group

2. Listen again to part of the passage. Then answer the question.

   Why does the lab assistant answer the student's question with this question:
   - (A) She has not understood what the student has asked.
   - (B) She is not sure who is in the student's group.
   - (C) She would like to know if the student has really done any work with his group.
   - (D) She has made an assumption about the group from the student's questions.

3. What does the lab assistant suggest that the group should try?
   - (A) Completing the lab session without talking
   - (B) Spending more time talking during the lab session
   - (C) Meeting before the lab session to have a discussion
   - (D) Working individually in the science lab

4. Listen again to part of the passage. Then answer the question.

   How does the student seem to feel about his group?
   - (A) He thinks his group does work very deliberately.
   - (B) He feels that the group is not able to get things done effectively.
   - (C) He is not sure when or where the group is meeting.
   - (D) He is afraid that his group does not have enough time to do a good job.

5. What does the lab assistant say about the lab report?
   - (A) It must be completed by the group.
   - (B) Each member may decide how to prepare the report.
   - (C) Each individual must write a part of the report.
   - (D) The report must be prepared in a very specific way.

Listen to a lecture in an American literature class.

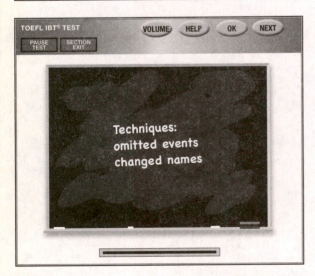

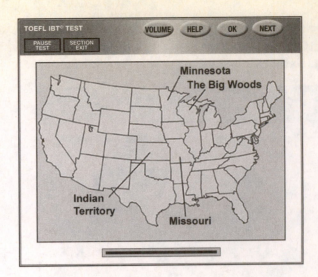

161

6. Listen again to part of the passage. Then answer the question.

   Why does the professor begin the lecture in this way?
   - (A) To show how the coming lecture is related to a previous lecture
   - (B) To outline the various topics that will be covered in the course
   - (C) To indicate that the topic will be covered not today, but in a future lecture
   - (D) To emphasize the importance of the lecture topic

7. How is the information in the lecture presented?
   - (A) Two different genres are contrasted using examples.
   - (B) Various examples of one genre are compared.
   - (C) Various characteristics of a genre are described using an example.
   - (D) Events in the life of the author are outlined chronologically.

8. How is the *Little House* series classified?
   - (A) As historical non-fiction
   - (B) As autobiography
   - (C) As historical fiction
   - (D) As altered history

9. What three statements are true about Laura Wilder's *Little House* series? **This question is worth 2 points** (2 points for 3 correct answers, 1 point for 2 correct answers, and 0 points for 1 or 0 correct answers).

Click on 3 answers.

   - (A) Laura made up many of the events.
   - (B) Laura wrote the books during her childhood.
   - (C) Every event in the books happened.
   - (D) Not every event in Laura's life was recorded.
   - (E) Names of some negatively portrayed people were changed.

10. What event did Laura omit from her books?

    Ⓐ A move to the Indian Territory
    Ⓑ A problem she had with Nellie Olsen
    Ⓒ Her father's storytelling sessions
    Ⓓ The birth and death of her brother

11. Can these conclusions be drawn from the lecture?
This question is worth 2 points (2 points for 4 correct answers, 1 point for 3 correct answers, and 0 points for 2, 1, or 0 correct answers).

For each answer, click in the YES or NO column.	YES	NO
Historical fiction is not always accurate.		
Historical fiction is usually autobiographical.		
Wilder's fiction was more pleasant than her actual life.		
Most of Wilder's life was too unpleasant for a children's story.		

Turn to pages 595–598 to *diagnose* your errors and *record* your results.

MINI-TEST 1

SPEAKING

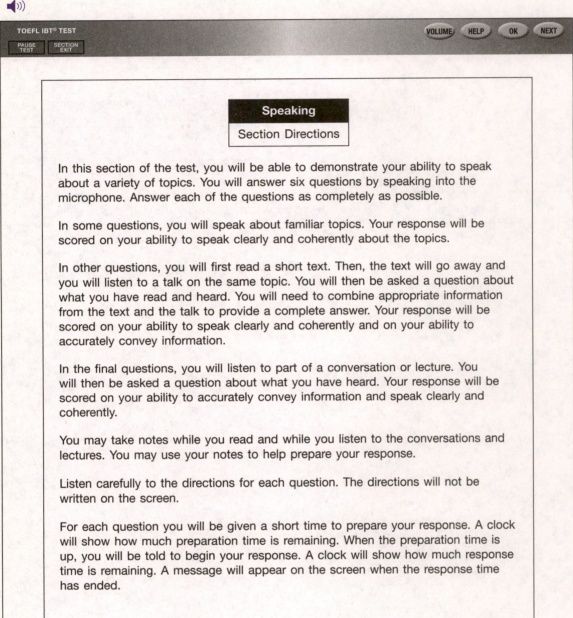

TOEFL IBT® TEST VOLUME HELP OK NEXT

PAUSE TEST SECTION EXIT

Speaking
Section Directions

In this section of the test, you will be able to demonstrate your ability to speak about a variety of topics. You will answer six questions by speaking into the microphone. Answer each of the questions as completely as possible.

In some questions, you will speak about familiar topics. Your response will be scored on your ability to speak clearly and coherently about the topics.

In other questions, you will first read a short text. Then, the text will go away and you will listen to a talk on the same topic. You will then be asked a question about what you have read and heard. You will need to combine appropriate information from the text and the talk to provide a complete answer. Your response will be scored on your ability to speak clearly and coherently and on your ability to accurately convey information.

In the final questions, you will listen to part of a conversation or lecture. You will then be asked a question about what you have heard. Your response will be scored on your ability to accurately convey information and speak clearly and coherently.

You may take notes while you read and while you listen to the conversations and lectures. You may use your notes to help prepare your response.

Listen carefully to the directions for each question. The directions will not be written on the screen.

For each question you will be given a short time to prepare your response. A clock will show how much preparation time is remaining. When the preparation time is up, you will be told to begin your response. A clock will show how much response time is remaining. A message will appear on the screen when the response time has ended.

Question 1

Read the question. You have 15 seconds to plan an answer and 45 seconds to give your spoken response.

> **If you were the leader of your country, would you most want to help the people be richer, healthier, or better-educated?**

> Preparation Time: 15 seconds
> Response Time: 45 seconds

Question 2

Read the part of a syllabus. You have 45 seconds to read the passage.

> Reading Time: 45 seconds

Part of the syllabus in a history class

Part of the grade for this class includes watching films on the themes of the course. This semester we are making a change in the way we evaluate this. In the past, students checked out films from the library reserves and then submitted reports on them. The result, however, was that films were unavailable at the end of the course as many students typically procrastinated in watching the films. In addition, the reports did not encourage deep analysis. So this semester you will sign up each week to watch one of the films on the list and then join a discussion session, led by a teaching assistant, on that film during that week. The grade for the discussion sessions will be pass/fail based on participation in the discussion.

Now listen to the conversation. 🔊 ⁱⁿ¹⁶²

Now answer the following question. You have 30 seconds to prepare an answer and 60 seconds to give your spoken response. 🔊)) [163]

The man gives his opinion of the change in the grading policy. State his opinion and the reasons he gives for holding it.

Preparation Time: 30 seconds
Response Time: 60 seconds

Question 3
Listen to the passage. Then respond to the question. 🔊)) [164]

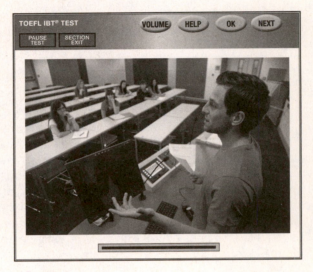

Now answer the following question. You have 20 seconds to prepare an answer and 60 seconds to give your spoken response. 🔊)) [165]

Using points from the lecture, explain how glaciers form.

Preparation Time: 20 seconds
Response Time: 60 seconds

Turn to pages 599–608 to *assess* the skills used in the test, *score* the test using the Speaking Scoring Criteria, and *record* your results.

MINI-TEST 1

WRITING

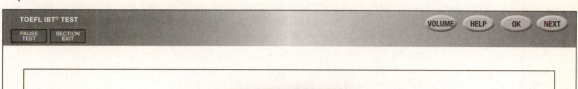

Writing
Section Directions

This section measures your ability to communicate in writing in an academic environment. There will be two writing tasks.

For the first writing task, you will read a passage and listen to a lecture about an academic topic. Then you will write a response to a question that asks you about the relationship between the lecture and the reading passage.

For the second task, you will demonstrate your ability to write an essay in response to a question that asks you to express and support your opinion about a topic or issue.

Now listen to the directions for the first writing task.

Integrated Writing Directions

For this task, you will first have three minutes to read a passage about an academic topic. You may take notes on the passage if you wish. The passage will then be removed and you will listen to a lecture about the same topic. While you listen, you may also take notes.

Then you will have 20 minutes to write a response to a question that asks you about the relationship between the lecture you heard and the reading passage. Try to answer the question as completely as possible using information from the reading passage and the lecture. The question does not ask you to express your personal opinion. You will be able to see the reading passage again when it is time for you to write. You may use your notes to help you answer the question.

Typically, an effective response will be 150 to 225 words long. Your response will be judged on the quality of your writing and on the completeness and accuracy of the content. If you finish your response before time is up, you may click on Next to go on to the second writing task.

Independent Writing Directions

For this task, you will write an essay in response to a question that asks you to state, explain, and support your opinion on an issue. You will have 30 minutes to plan, write, and revise your essay.

Typically, an effective essay will contain a minimum of 300 words. Your essay will be judged on the quality of your writing. This includes the development of your ideas, the organization of your essay, and the quality and accuracy of the language you use to express your ideas.

If you finish your essay before time is up, you may click on Next to end this section. When you are ready to continue, click on the Dismiss Directions icon.

Many new businesses have trouble finding ways to attract customers. Since their brands or products are not known to the general public, it is often challenging for new firms to get the word out unless the companies are willing to invest in a large marketing campaign. By offering steep discounts (often at a profit loss), new businesses can generate a lot of interest in their brands without having to spend too much on advertising.

Everyone loves a discount. New companies can offer their products on "daily deals" web sites. These web sites specialize in offering deals of the day for a short period of time. They often have a large following and the people who visit them usually post about exceptional deals found on other related web sites. This type of organic traffic will lead to attracting new customers. Once these new customers see the quality of the product, they will return and be more willing to pay full price.

The more people see the discounted prices, the more the brand will be recognized. Many studies have shown that companies that advertise online have better brand recognition than those that do not. If the discount is good enough, more and more people will want to share it with their friends via social media and this leads to more people recognizing the brand in the future, whether it is offered at a discount or not.

Finally, when a new company offers their products at a lowered price, it will garner the attention of the media and web sites that report on consumer products and spending. This type of publicity is free and greatly increases brand awareness. Once the brand has been reported on and talked about by journalists, it becomes part of the consumer's conscience and it most likely will be considered as an option when it comes time for the consumer to make a purchase.

Listen to the passage. Then answer the question. **166** ◀))

Now answer the following question: **167** ◀))

How does the information in the listening passage cast doubt on the information presented in the reading passage?

Response Time: 20 minutes

Turn to pages 609–614 to *assess* the skills used in the test, *score* the test using the Writing Scoring Criteria, and *record* your results.

MINI-TEST 2

READING

20 minutes

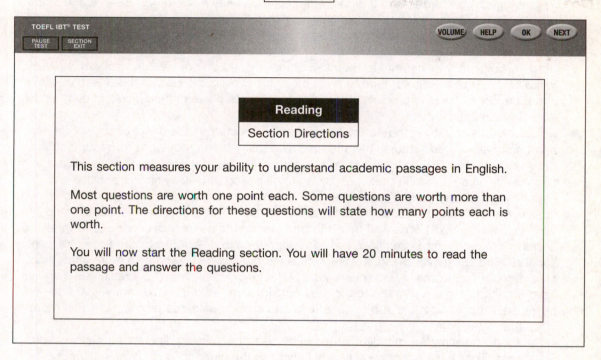

Read the passage and answer the questions that follow.

Birth Order

1▶   A considerable body of research has demonstrated a correlation between birth order and aspects such as temperament and behavior, and some psychologists believe that the order in which we are born significantly affects the development of our personality. Psychologist Alfred Adler was a pioneer in this field. A key point in his research and in the hypothesis that he developed based on it was that it was not the actual numerical birth position that affected personality; instead, it was the similar responses in large numbers of families to children in specific birth order positions that had an effect. For example, first-borns, who have their parents to themselves initially and do not have to deal with siblings in the first part of their lives, tend to have their first socialization experiences with adults and therefore to find the process of learning to relate to peers more difficult, in contrast to later-born children.

2▶   Numerous studies since Adler's have been conducted on the effect of birth order and personality. These studies have tended to classify birth order types into four different categories: first-born, second-born and/or middle, last, and only child. Studies have consistently shown that first-born children are disposed to display similar positive and negative personality traits. First-borns have consistently been linked with academic achievement in various studies; in one study, the number of National Merit scholarship winners who are first-borns was found to be equal to the number of second- and third-borns combined. First-borns have been found to be more responsible and assertive than second/middle/last-borns and are likely to rise to positions of leadership more often than others; more first-borns have served in the U.S. Congress and as U.S. presidents than have those born in other birth-order positions. However, studies have shown that first-borns are liable to be more subject to stress and were considered problem children more often than later-borns.

3▶   Second-born and/or middle children demonstrate markedly different tendencies from first-borns. They have a tendency to feel inferior to the older child or children because it is difficult for them to comprehend that their lower level of accomplishment is a function of age rather than ability, and they often try to succeed in areas other than those in which their older sibling or siblings excel. **7A** They are inclined to be more trusting, accepting, and focused on others than the more self-centered first-borns, and they usually have a comparatively higher level of success in team sports than do first-borns or only children, who more often excel in individual sports. **7B** This sense of cooperation and desire to make others happy is also why so many second-born/middle children have a disposition toward being the family mediator or peacekeeper. **7C** It is not uncommon for these types of children to later have successful careers in fields such as international relations, litigation, and social work, to name a few. **7D**

4▶   The last-born child is the one who is likely to be the eternal baby of the family and thus often demonstrates a strong sense of security. Last-borns collectively attain the highest degree of social success and show the highest levels of self-esteem of all the birth-order positions. They often display less competitiveness than older brothers and sisters and are more apt to take part in less competitive group games or in social organizations such as sororities and fraternities.

5▶   Only children have a propensity to exhibit some of the main characteristics of first-borns and some of the traits of last-borns. Only children are liable to exhibit the strong sense of security and self-esteem demonstrated by last-borns while, like first-borns, they are more achievement oriented and more likely than middle- or last-borns to have academic success. However, only children are inclined to have the most problems establishing close relationships and display a lower need for affiliation than other children. Thus, only children tend more than any other birth position to have fewer friends and intimate relationships throughout their lives, though they do have a tendency to maintain their relationships for longer periods of time.

1. The word "correlation" in paragraph 1 could best be replaced by
   Ⓐ interaction
   Ⓑ parallel
   Ⓒ connection
   Ⓓ consequence

2. What is stated in paragraph 1 about Adler?
   Ⓐ He was one of the first to study the link between birth order and behavior.
   Ⓑ He believed that it was the actual birth order that affected personality.
   Ⓒ He had found that the responses by family members had little to do with temperament.
   Ⓓ He was the only scientist to study this phenomenon.

3. According to paragraph 1, what can be inferred about later-born children?
   Ⓐ They relate better to their parents than their siblings.
   Ⓑ They typically interact well with peers.
   Ⓒ They are usually withdrawn and timid.
   Ⓓ They do not know their parents well.

4. According to paragraph 2, what is NOT mentioned of first-borns?
   Ⓐ They tend to do better in school.
   Ⓑ They are liable to become leaders.
   Ⓒ They behave better than younger siblings.
   Ⓓ They are more disciplined and confident.

5. Which of the sentences below best expresses the essential information in the highlighted sentence in paragraph 2? *Incorrect* choices change the meaning in important ways or leave out essential information.
   Ⓐ In spite of certain characteristics that first-borns possess, many of them become leaders.
   Ⓑ An interesting fact that is difficult to explain is that many first-borns have served in high government positions.
   Ⓒ Because first-borns tend to be very assertive, they are uncomfortable serving in government positions.
   Ⓓ Several examples support the idea that first-borns have characteristics that make them leaders.

6. The word "markedly" in paragraph 3 is closest in meaning to
   Ⓐ noticeably
   Ⓑ slightly
   Ⓒ vaguely
   Ⓓ objectively

7. Look at the four squares [■] that indicate where the following sentence could be added to paragraph 3.

   Though this tendency usually only pertains to their siblings, it may extend to parental relations as well.

   Where would the sentence best fit? Click on a square [■] to add the sentence to the passage

8. According to the passage, why do second-born/middle children feel like they cannot measure up to their older sibling(s)?
   Ⓐ First-borns tend to do better in individual sports than their younger siblings.
   Ⓑ They do not understand that their inabilities are due to the fact that they are younger.
   Ⓒ Middle children tend to have a lower level of accomplishment than first-borns.
   Ⓓ They are constantly trying to make everyone else in the family happy, not themselves.

9. According to paragraph 4, what does the author imply about sororities and fraternities?
   Ⓐ They appeal to last-borns because they are typically not competitive organizations.
   Ⓑ Only last-borns participate in them.
   Ⓒ They are difficult to get into because they are very competitive organizations.
   Ⓓ They are popular with last-borns because they foster their self-esteem.

10. Which word below is closest in meaning to the word "propensity" in paragraph 5?
    Ⓐ weakness
    Ⓑ predisposition
    Ⓒ habit
    Ⓓ longing

11. What does the author say about only children?
    Ⓐ They get a strong sense of security from younger children/last-borns.
    Ⓑ They are more likely to do better academically than first-born children.
    Ⓒ They tend to have friendships that do not outlast those that other children have.
    Ⓓ They may have fewer close friends than children in other birth positions.

12. The word "they" in paragraph 5 refers to
    Ⓐ other children
    Ⓑ relationships
    Ⓒ only children
    Ⓓ friends

13.

Directions: An introductory sentence for a brief summary of the passage is provided below. Complete the summary by selecting the THREE answer choices that express the most important ideas in the passage. Some sentences do not belong in the summary because they express ideas that are not presented in the passage or are minor ideas in the passage. **This question is worth 2 points** (2 points for 3 correct answers, 1 point for 2 correct answers, and 0 points for 1 or 0 correct answers).

It has been discovered that birth order can dramatically impact personality development.

-
-
-

Answer Choices (choose 3 to complete the chart):

(1) Birth order types have been classified into four distinct categories.
(2) Similar responses in large families to children in specific birth order determines personality.
(3) Only children and first-borns are inclined to be much more achievement oriented.
(4) Last-borns and only children both demonstrate a strong sense of security.
(5) The actual numerical birth position strongly affects personality development.
(6) The way members of a family respond to children in specific birth positions affects their personality.

Turn to pages 591–594 to *diagnose* your errors and *record* your results.

MINI-TEST 2

LISTENING

L_DIR_A

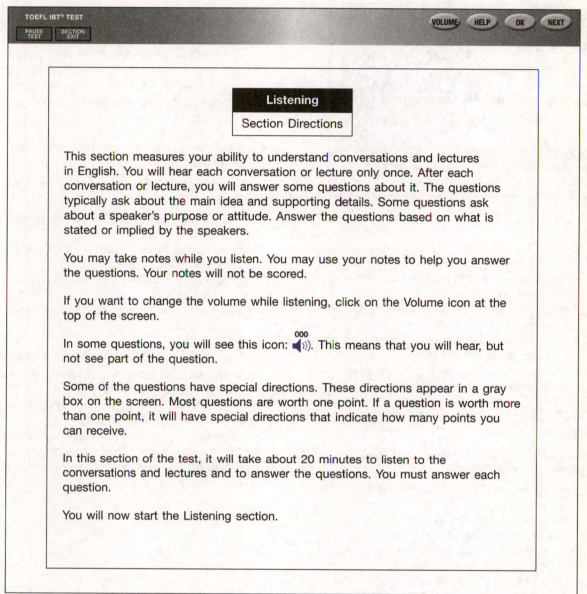

Listening

Section Directions

This section measures your ability to understand conversations and lectures in English. You will hear each conversation or lecture only once. After each conversation or lecture, you will answer some questions about it. The questions typically ask about the main idea and supporting details. Some questions ask about a speaker's purpose or attitude. Answer the questions based on what is stated or implied by the speakers.

You may take notes while you listen. You may use your notes to help you answer the questions. Your notes will not be scored.

If you want to change the volume while listening, click on the Volume icon at the top of the screen.

In some questions, you will see this icon: 🔊))). This means that you will hear, but not see part of the question.

Some of the questions have special directions. These directions appear in a gray box on the screen. Most questions are worth one point. If a question is worth more than one point, it will have special directions that indicate how many points you can receive.

In this section of the test, it will take about 20 minutes to listen to the conversations and lectures and to answer the questions. You must answer each question.

You will now start the Listening section.

Listen as a student consults with a professor.

169
))

1. Why does the student go to see the professor?
   Ⓐ The professor asked students with problems to come see him.
   Ⓑ All of the students in the class are meeting the professor to discuss their outlines.
   Ⓒ She made an appointment to discuss problems she is having with her outline.
   Ⓓ A classmate advised her to get help from the professor during office hours.

2. Listen again to part of the conversation. Then answer the question.

   How does the professor seem to feel about the Haymarket Affair?
   Ⓐ He agrees that it was important and had important effects.
   Ⓑ He believes its effects were much more important outside of the United States.
   Ⓒ He thinks it was important but not relevant to the argument of her paper.
   Ⓓ He thinks that she is overestimating its importance.

3. What problems does the professor have with the student's outline? **This question is worth 2 points** (2 points for 3 correct answers, 1 point for 2 correct answers, and 0 points for 1 or 0 correct answers).

   Click on 3 answers.
   Ⓐ It concentrates too much on narrating one incident.
   Ⓑ It does not address any of the important causes of the lack of support for socialism in the United States.
   Ⓒ It needs less description and more analysis.
   Ⓓ It lacks enough historical background on the Haymarket Affair.
   Ⓔ It does not equally develop the various supporting ideas.

4. Listen again to part of the conversation. Then answer the question.

   What does the professor mean when he says this:))
   Ⓐ Her outline has a good balance of general and specific ideas.
   Ⓑ Her outline is not perfect, but it is good enough to write her paper.
   Ⓒ Her outline should be focused on only one argument.
   Ⓓ Her outline is a good mix of narration and analysis.

5. What conclusion can be drawn about the student?
   Ⓐ She will change her thesis to something more focused and do more research.
   Ⓑ She will keep her original thesis and do more research on different causes.
   Ⓒ She will concentrate on describing the events of the Haymarket Affair in more detail.
   Ⓓ She will eliminate most of the material about the Haymarket Affair.

Listen to a discussion in an archaeology class.

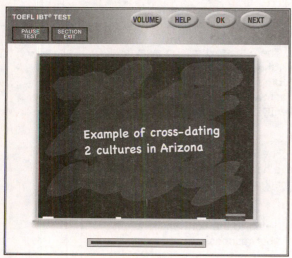

Example of cross-dating
2 cultures in Arizona

6. What is the main topic of this discussion?

Ⓐ A way of comparing the culture of two different archaeological sites

Ⓑ A method of determining the age of an ancient civilization

Ⓒ The method of counting tree rings to date cultures

Ⓓ The dates that various cultures existed in Arizona

7. How is the information in the discussion presented?

Ⓐ Various cultures are contrasted.

Ⓑ A series of cultures are presented in chronological order.

Ⓒ The reasons why a certain technique works are listed.

Ⓓ A concept is explained through an extended example.

8. What do archaeologists compare when using cross-dating?

Ⓐ Two cultures, each with unknown dates

Ⓑ Two methods of dating cultures

Ⓒ One culture with known and one culture with unknown dates

Ⓓ The known dates of two cultures

9. What is true about tree-ring dating, according to the discussion?

Ⓐ It compares a sample with a pattern of tree rings that is already known.

Ⓑ It can be used to date all types of areas.

Ⓒ It was used effectively to date the southern culture.

Ⓓ It relies on archaeological sites being undisturbed by digging.

10. Is each of these true about the areas discussed in the lecture? **This question is worth 2 points** (2 points for 4 correct answers, 1 point for 3 correct answers, and 0 points for 2, 1, or 0 correct answers).

For each answer, click in the YES or NO column.		
	YES	NO
The dates of the northern culture were determined from tree-ring dating.		
Pieces of southern pottery were found in the northern area.		
The dates of the southern culture were determined from cross-dating.		
Pieces of northern pottery were found in the southern area.		

11. Listen again to part of the conversation. Then answer the question.

How does the professor seem to feel about the student's question?

Ⓐ She believes that the student is asking an obvious question only to gain attention.

Ⓑ She thinks that students shouldn't interrupt with such obvious questions.

Ⓒ She feels that the answer should be obvious to the student if he thinks about it.

Ⓓ She believes that it is an obvious question, but an important one to ask.

Turn to pages 595–598 to *diagnose* your errors and *record* your results.

MINI-TEST 2

SPEAKING

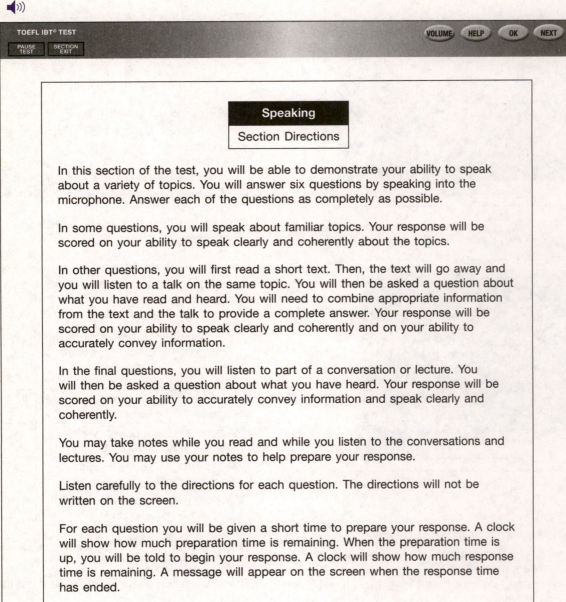

TOEFL IBT® TEST

PAUSE TEST | SECTION EXIT

VOLUME | HELP | OK | NEXT

Speaking
Section Directions

In this section of the test, you will be able to demonstrate your ability to speak about a variety of topics. You will answer six questions by speaking into the microphone. Answer each of the questions as completely as possible.

In some questions, you will speak about familiar topics. Your response will be scored on your ability to speak clearly and coherently about the topics.

In other questions, you will first read a short text. Then, the text will go away and you will listen to a talk on the same topic. You will then be asked a question about what you have read and heard. You will need to combine appropriate information from the text and the talk to provide a complete answer. Your response will be scored on your ability to speak clearly and coherently and on your ability to accurately convey information.

In the final questions, you will listen to part of a conversation or lecture. You will then be asked a question about what you have heard. Your response will be scored on your ability to accurately convey information and speak clearly and coherently.

You may take notes while you read and while you listen to the conversations and lectures. You may use your notes to help prepare your response.

Listen carefully to the directions for each question. The directions will not be written on the screen.

For each question you will be given a short time to prepare your response. A clock will show how much preparation time is remaining. When the preparation time is up, you will be told to begin your response. A clock will show how much response time is remaining. A message will appear on the screen when the response time has ended.

Question 1

Read the question. You have 15 seconds to plan an answer and 45 seconds to give your spoken response.

Some people believe that getting a full-night's sleep and then staying awake all day allows them to be more productive. Others believe that sleeping less at night and taking short naps during the day allows them to get more done. Which approach to sleep works best for you? Use reasons and examples to support your opinion.

> Preparation Time: 15 seconds
> Response Time: 45 seconds

Question 2

Read the passage on leadership roles. You have 45 seconds to read the passage.

> Reading Time: 45 seconds

> ### Leadership Roles
> Have you ever considered the various roles that a group leader might take on? There can be many different kinds of leadership roles in groups; two of the many possible kinds of leadership roles are instrumental leadership and expressive leadership. Instrumental leadership is group leadership that emphasizes the completion of tasks by the group. Instrumental leadership is focused on getting the task done. Expressive leadership is different from instrumental leadership in that it is concerned with the well-being of the group; expressive leadership is concerned with ensuring that all members of the group are comfortable working together.

Now listen to the passage. 🔊 172

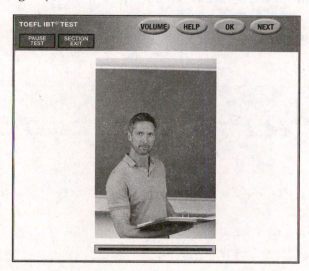

Now answer the following question. You have 30 seconds to prepare an answer and 60 seconds to give your spoken response. ◀))) 173

The speaker gives two examples of different types of leaders. Explain how the actions of the leaders correspond to the types of leadership described in the text.

> Preparation Time: 30 seconds
> Response Time: 60 seconds

Question 3
Listen to the conversation. ◀))) 174

Now answer the following question. You will have 20 seconds to prepare an answer and 60 seconds to give your spoken response. ◀))) 175

The students are discussing a problem the man has. Describe his problem and say which of the proposed solutions you prefer.

> Preparation Time: 20 seconds
> Response Time: 60 seconds

Turn to pages 599–608 to *assess* the skills used in the test, *score* the test using the Speaking Scoring Criteria, and *record* your results.

MINI-TEST 2

WRITING

W_DIR_C

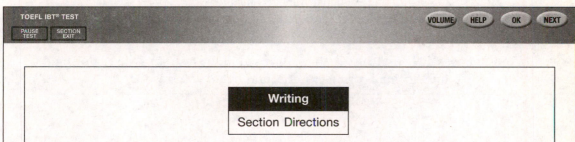

Writing

Section Directions

This section measures your ability to communicate in writing in an academic environment. There will be two writing tasks.

For the first writing task, you will read a passage and listen to a lecture about an academic topic. Then you will write a response to a question that asks you about the relationship between the lecture and the reading passage.

For the second task, you will demonstrate your ability to write an essay in response to a question that asks you to express and support your opinion about a topic or issue.

Now listen to the directions for the first writing task.

Integrated Writing Directions

For this task, you will first have three minutes to read a passage about an academic topic. You may take notes on the passage if you wish. The passage will then be removed and you will listen to a lecture about the same topic. While you listen, you may also take notes.

Then you will have 20 minutes to write a response to a question that asks you about the relationship between the lecture you heard and the reading passage. Try to answer the question as completely as possible using information from the reading passage and the lecture. The question does not ask you to express your personal opinion. You will be able to see the reading passage again when it is time for you to write. You may use your notes to help you answer the question.

Typically, an effective response will be 150 to 225 words long. Your response will be judged on the quality of your writing and on the completeness and accuracy of the content. If you finish your response before time is up, you may click on Next to go on to the second writing task.

Independent Writing Directions

For this task, you will write an essay in response to a question that asks you to state, explain, and support your opinion on an issue. You will have 30 minutes to plan, write, and revise your essay.

Typically, an effective essay will contain a minimum of 300 words. Your essay will be judged on the quality of your writing. This includes the development of your ideas, the organization of your essay, and the quality and accuracy of the language you use to express your ideas.

If you finish your essay before time is up, you may click on Next to end this section. When you are ready to continue, click on the Dismiss Directions icon.

Question

Read the question. On a piece of paper, take notes on the main points of a response. Then write your response.

What historical event in your country has had a major effect on your country? Give reasons and examples to support your response.

Response Time: 30 minutes

Turn to pages 609–614 to *assess* the skills used in the test, *score* the test using the Writing Scoring Criteria, and *record* your results.

MINI-TEST 3

READING

20 minutes

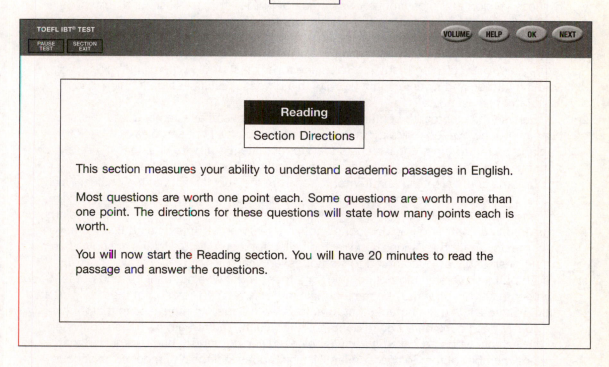

PAUSE TEST   SECTION EXIT

VOLUME   HELP   OK   NEXT

Reading

Section Directions

This section measures your ability to understand academic passages in English.

Most questions are worth one point each. Some questions are worth more than one point. The directions for these questions will state how many points each is worth.

You will now start the Reading section. You will have 20 minutes to read the passage and answer the questions.

Read the passage and answer the questions that follow.

Ketchup

1▶ The sauce that is today called ketchup (or catsup) in Western cultures is a tomato-based condiment that is quite distinct from the Eastern ancestors of this product. A sauce called *ke-tiap* was in use in China at least as early as the seventeenth century, but the Chinese version of the concoction was made of pickled fish, shellfish, and spices. Its popularity spread to Singapore and Malaysia, where it was called *kechap*. The Indonesian *ketjab* derives its name from the same source as the Malaysian sauce but is made from very different ingredients. The Indonesian *ketjab* is made by cooking black soy beans, fermenting them, placing them in a salt brine for at least a week, cooking the resulting solution further, and sweetening it heavily; this process results in a dark, thick, and sweet variation of soy sauce.

2▶ Early in the eighteenth century, sailors from the British navy came across this exotic condiment on voyages to Malaysia and Singapore and brought samples of it back to England on return trips. English chefs tried to recreate it but were unable to do so exactly and thus ended up substituting original ingredients for locally grown items such as mushrooms and walnuts in an attempt to recreate the special taste of the original Asian sauce. Variations of it became quite the rage in eighteenth-century England, including some that utilized fruit such as apples, blackberries, and even peaches. These versions appeared in a number of recipe books and were featured as an exotic addition to savory pies, meats, and other sauces. One recipe called for ingredients such as anchovies and strong beer, and was guaranteed to last for seven years.

3▶ The English version did not contain tomatoes, and it was not until the end of the eighteenth century that they became a main ingredient in the ketchup of the newly created United States. It is quite notable that tomatoes were added to the sauce in that they had previously been considered quite dangerous to health. The tomato had been cultivated by the Aztecs, who had called it *tomatl*; however, early botanists had recognized that it was a member of the *Solanacaea* family, which does include a number of poisonous plants. Many believed the tomato to be deadly, and we now know that the leaves of the tomato plant are poisonous, though the fruit, of course, is not. To the disappointment of many botanists, the U.S. Department of Agriculture to this day labels the tomato as a vegetable rather than as a fruit. This is due to the fact that the related tariff laws define a product based on its use, not on its botanical or any other definition. Because tomatoes are, culinarily speaking, used as vegetables instead of as fruit, this is how they have been officially labeled.

4▶ **10A** Thomas Jefferson, who cultivated the tomato in his gardens at Monticello and served dishes containing tomatoes at lavish feasts, often receives credit for changing the reputation of this now ubiquitous item. **10B** Soon after Jefferson had introduced the tomato to American society, recipes combining the newly fashionable tomato with the equally trendy and exotic sauce known as *ketchap* began to appear. **10C** By the middle of the nineteenth century, both the tomato and tomato ketchup were staples of the American kitchen. **10D**

5▶ Tomato ketchup, popular though it was, was quite time-consuming to prepare. But a long cooking time would have eliminated any danger of being poisoned. In 1876, the first mass-produced tomato ketchup, a product of German-American Henry Heinz, went on sale and achieved immediate success. Heinz even spearheaded the now famous bottle that his concoction came in. From tomato ketchup, Heinz branched out into a number of other products, including various sauces, pickles, and relishes. By 1890, his company had expanded to include sixty-five different products but was in need of a marketing slogan. Heinz settled on the slogan "57 Varieties" because he liked the way that the digits 5 and 7 looked in print, in spite of the fact that this slogan understated the number of products that he had at the time.

1. What does paragraph 1 say about the origins of the sauce now known as ketchup?
   Ⓐ It is not clear where ketchup first originated.
   Ⓑ Ketchup has had many variations throughout Asian countries.
   Ⓒ Ketchup's popularity caused it to spread throughout Asia.
   Ⓓ The origins of ketchup are less important than its ingredients.

2. The word "variation" in paragraph 1 could best be replaced by
   Ⓐ alteration
   Ⓑ version
   Ⓒ difference
   Ⓓ modification

3. It can be inferred from paragraph 2 that English chefs were unsuccessful at recreating the sauce because
   Ⓐ certain key ingredients were unavailable
   Ⓑ mushrooms and walnuts were not obtainable
   Ⓒ the Asian sauce was too special to recreate
   Ⓓ poor quality samples were brought back

4. The word "rage" in paragraph 2 could best be replaced by
   Ⓐ anger
   Ⓑ distinction
   Ⓒ misunderstanding
   Ⓓ fashion

5. What is true of ketchup in eighteenth-century England?
   Ⓐ It was difficult to find in England.
   Ⓑ It was quite like the original Asian recipe.
   Ⓒ It was mainly composed of fresh fruit.
   Ⓓ In all of its forms, it was very popular.

6. According to the passage, what can be inferred about tomatoes being added to ketchup?
   Ⓐ It took many years for this to happen.
   Ⓑ Americans were not worried about the potential for poisoning by tomatoes.
   Ⓒ Tomatoes were added after discovering that they were eaten by the Aztecs.
   Ⓓ Adding tomatoes was done very carefully.

7. The author mentions "To the disappointment of many botanists" in paragraph 3 in order to
   Ⓐ show that the U.S. Department of Agriculture is insensitive
   Ⓑ explain that the information may not be scientifically accurate
   Ⓒ give an example of a conflict between botanists and the USDA
   Ⓓ provide an example of a falsely labeled product

8. According to paragraph 3, the tomato plant
   Ⓐ is related to some poisonous plants
   Ⓑ was considered poisonous by the Aztecs
   Ⓒ has leaves that are considered edible
   Ⓓ has fruit that is sometimes quite poisonous

9. The word "they" in paragraph 3 refers to
   Ⓐ tariff laws
   Ⓑ fruit
   Ⓒ vegetables
   Ⓓ tomatoes

10. Look at the four squares [■] that indicate where the following sentence could be added to paragraph 4.

    It turned from very bad to exceedingly good.

    Where would the sentence best fit? Click on a square [■] to add the sentence to the passage.

11. According to paragraphs 4 and 5, what is NOT mentioned about the popularity of ketchup in the United States?
    Ⓐ Ketchup's popularity was in part due to Thomas Jefferson.
    Ⓑ The addition of the tomato boosted ketchup's popularity.
    Ⓒ It would have been more popular if it had been easier to prepare.
    Ⓓ Henry Heinz helped make ketchup a household staple.

12. Which of the sentences below best expresses the essential information in the highlighted sentence in paragraph 5? *Incorrect* choices change the meaning in important ways or leave out essential information.
    Ⓐ Heinz selected a certain slogan even though it was inaccurate because he liked the look of it.
    Ⓑ Heinz was eventually able to settle a dispute about which slogan would be the best for his company.
    Ⓒ Heinz was unable to print out the actual number of varieties, so he printed out a different number.
    Ⓓ Heinz's company actually had far fewer products than the slogan indicated that it did.

13.

Directions: An introductory sentence for a brief summary of the passage is provided below. Complete the summary by selecting the THREE answer choices that express the most important ideas in the passage. Some sentences do not belong in the summary because they express ideas that are not presented in the passage or are minor ideas in the passage. **This question is worth 2 points** (2 points for 3 correct answers, 1 point for 2 correct answers, and 0 points for 1 or 0 correct answers).

The sauce known as ketchup has gone through many variations and has become one of the world's most commonly used condiments.

-
-
-

Answer Choices (choose 3 to complete the chart):

(1) An English version of the sauce became popular after sailors returned home with samples.

(2) A plant called the *tomatl* is known to have been cultivated by the Aztecs.

(3) Ketchup was produced in a time-consuming way by German immigrants.

(4) The sauce was first developed in Asia, and contained a variety of exotic ingredients.

(5) The sauce known as *ketjab* was a variation of the Chinese sauce that contained tomatoes.

(6) Americans added the tomato to the sauce and later mass produced it.

Turn to pages 591–594 to *diagnose* your errors and *record* your results.

MINI-TEST 3

LISTENING

L_DIR_A

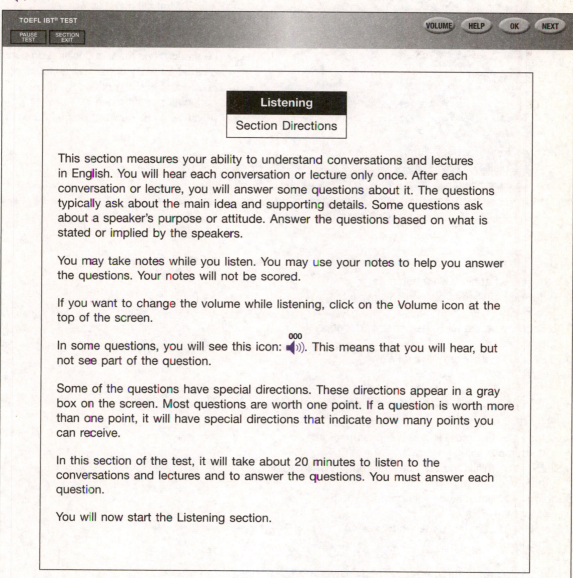

TOEFL IBT® TEST

PAUSE TEST | SECTION EXIT

VOLUME | HELP | OK | NEXT

Listening
Section Directions

This section measures your ability to understand conversations and lectures in English. You will hear each conversation or lecture only once. After each conversation or lecture, you will answer some questions about it. The questions typically ask about the main idea and supporting details. Some questions ask about a speaker's purpose or attitude. Answer the questions based on what is stated or implied by the speakers.

You may take notes while you listen. You may use your notes to help you answer the questions. Your notes will not be scored.

If you want to change the volume while listening, click on the Volume icon at the top of the screen.

In some questions, you will see this icon: 🔊))). This means that you will hear, but not see part of the question.

Some of the questions have special directions. These directions appear in a gray box on the screen. Most questions are worth one point. If a question is worth more than one point, it will have special directions that indicate how many points you can receive.

In this section of the test, it will take about 20 minutes to listen to the conversations and lectures and to answer the questions. You must answer each question.

You will now start the Listening section.

Listen as a student consults with an advisor.

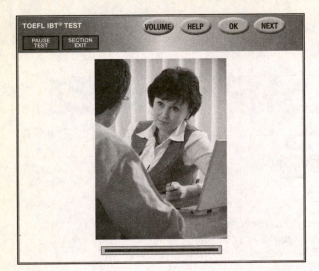

177

1. Why does the student go to see the advisor?
   Ⓐ To decide what his major should be
   Ⓑ To decide between two seemingly similar courses
   Ⓒ To decide when to fulfill the general education requirement
   Ⓓ To decide whether or not to take an introductory-level course

2. What differentiates Biology 101 from the other course?
   Ⓐ Biology 101 has more lectures and is therefore worth more units.
   Ⓑ Biology 101 fulfills the science requirement while the other course does not.
   Ⓒ Biology 101 has a laboratory component and more math.
   Ⓓ Biology 101 can only be taken by science majors.

3. Listen again to part of the passage. Then answer the question.

   What does the advisor mean when she says this:
   Ⓐ "That's not completely correct, but you'll understand later."
   Ⓑ "That's more or less accurate."
   Ⓒ "We have different opinions on this."
   Ⓓ "That's an impolite way to summarize the differences."

4. What decision does the advisor seem to think that the student should make fairly soon?
   Ⓐ Whether his major will be within the sciences or not
   Ⓑ How he should fulfill the general education requirements
   Ⓒ Whether or not to study biology
   Ⓓ Exactly what his major is

5. What can be concluded from the conversation?
   Ⓐ The student has made a decision on a major.
   Ⓑ The student really does not like science.
   Ⓒ The student has completed his general education requirements.
   Ⓓ The student has decided which course to take.

Questions 6–11 178 🔊))

Listen to a lecture in a gemology class.

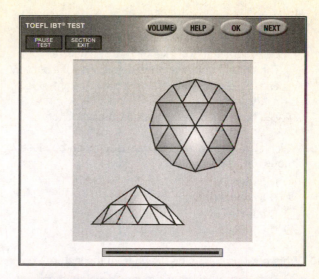

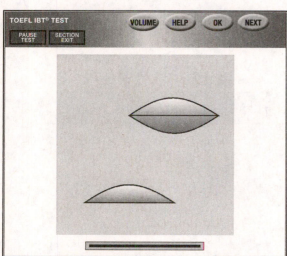

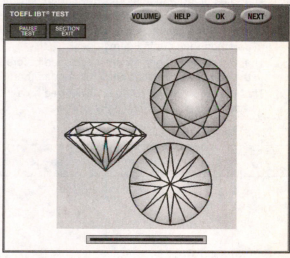

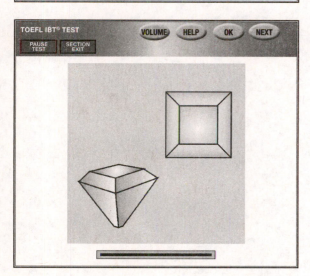

179
🔊))

6. How does the professor present the different styles of gems?

- Ⓐ From the least common to the most common
- Ⓑ From the simplest to the most complex
- Ⓒ From the oldest to the most recently developed
- Ⓓ From the least expensive to the most expensive

7. What does the professor say about faceting?

| Click on 2 answers. |

- Ⓐ There is no evidence that it was done earlier than the fifteenth century.
- Ⓑ It may have been done earlier than the fifteenth century.
- Ⓒ Europe was most likely the first place it was done.
- Ⓓ It was definitely done in the fifteenth century in Europe.

8. According to the lecture, which is true about the different styles of finishing gems?
   Ⓐ The cabochon is challenging to set in jewelry.
   Ⓑ The brilliant cut developed before the rose cut.
   Ⓒ The brilliant cut begins with a natural eight-sided crystal shape.
   Ⓓ The table cut developed after the cabochon.

9. Which style of gem is no longer used much because it does not reflect light well?
   Ⓐ The rose cut
   Ⓑ The cabochon
   Ⓒ The table cut
   Ⓓ The brilliant cut

10. What conclusion can be drawn from the lecture?
    Ⓐ That the cutting of gemstones developed earlier than the polishing of gemstones
    Ⓑ That polishing gemstones has become more common than cutting gemstones
    Ⓒ That the cutting of gemstones developed before the principles of optics were fully understood
    Ⓓ That the cutting of gemstones developed as a result of the understanding of optics

11. In the talk, the professor explains how each of these styles of gems was finished. Check whether each style was cut or polished to its final shape, according to the passage. **This question is worth 3 points** (3 points for 4 correct answers, 2 points for 3 correct answers, 1 point for 2 correct answers, and 0 points for 1 or 0 correct answers).

For each answer, click in the POLISHED or CUT column.		
	POLISHED	**CUT**
Brilliant		
Cabochon		
Rose		
Table		

Turn to pages 595–598 to *diagnose* your errors and *record* your results.

MINI-TEST 3

SPEAKING

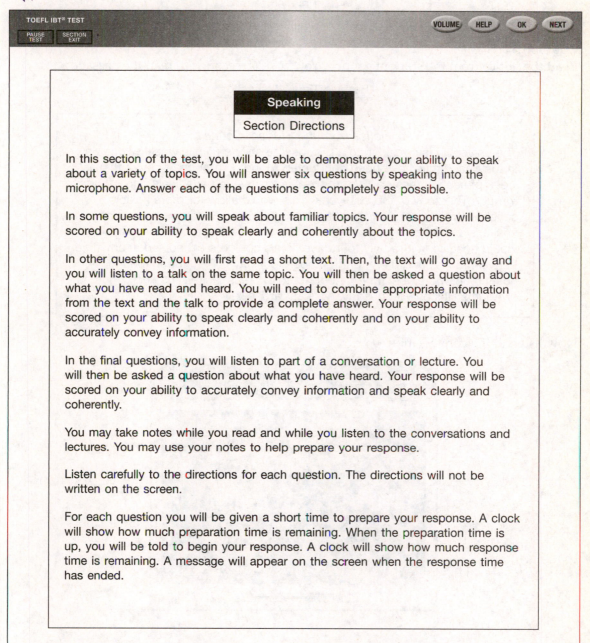

TOEFL IBT® TEST   VOLUME   HELP   OK   NEXT

PAUSE TEST   SECTION EXIT

Speaking

Section Directions

In this section of the test, you will be able to demonstrate your ability to speak about a variety of topics. You will answer six questions by speaking into the microphone. Answer each of the questions as completely as possible.

In some questions, you will speak about familiar topics. Your response will be scored on your ability to speak clearly and coherently about the topics.

In other questions, you will first read a short text. Then, the text will go away and you will listen to a talk on the same topic. You will then be asked a question about what you have read and heard. You will need to combine appropriate information from the text and the talk to provide a complete answer. Your response will be scored on your ability to speak clearly and coherently and on your ability to accurately convey information.

In the final questions, you will listen to part of a conversation or lecture. You will then be asked a question about what you have heard. Your response will be scored on your ability to accurately convey information and speak clearly and coherently.

You may take notes while you read and while you listen to the conversations and lectures. You may use your notes to help prepare your response.

Listen carefully to the directions for each question. The directions will not be written on the screen.

For each question you will be given a short time to prepare your response. A clock will show how much preparation time is remaining. When the preparation time is up, you will be told to begin your response. A clock will show how much response time is remaining. A message will appear on the screen when the response time has ended.

Question 1
Read the question. You have 15 seconds to plan an answer and 45 seconds to give your spoken response.

Which place in your hometown would you like to take visitors to see?

> Preparation Time: 15 seconds
> Response Time: 45 seconds

Question 2
Read the notice from the student council. You have 45 seconds to read the passage.

> Reading Time: 45 seconds

Notice from the Student Council

The university is considering a proposal to shorten finals week by one day. In the past, finals have been conducted Monday through Friday of the last week of each semester. The proposal is to instead have finals only Monday through Thursday of the last week. This would allow for more flexible scheduling of travel plans and leave the following Friday for submitting final assignments. Because this would mean the same number of finals would need to fit into only four days, finals could be scheduled at any time between 8 A.M. and 8 P.M. during those four days. The student council is hosting an open meeting for students to express their views and concerns at Adams Hall on Wednesday, April 5th at 7 P.M.

Now listen to the conversation. 🔊 ⁽¹⁸⁰⁾

Now answer the following question. You have 30 seconds to prepare an answer and 60 seconds to give your spoken response. 181 🔊

The woman gives her opinion of the proposed change to the finals schedule. State her opinion and the reasons she gives for her opinion.

> Preparation Time: 30 seconds
> Response Time: 60 seconds

Question 3

Listen to the passage. Then respond to the question. 182 🔊

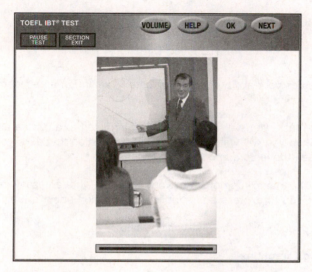

Now answer the following question. You have 20 seconds to prepare an answer and 60 seconds to give your spoken response. 183 🔊

Using points and examples from the lecture, explain how neoclassicism influenced the rules of grammar in English.

> Preparation Time: 20 seconds
> Response Time: 60 seconds

Turn to pages 599–608 to *assess* the skills used in the test, *score* the test using the Speaking Scoring Criteria, and *record* your results.

MINI-TEST 3

WRITING

TOEFL IBT® TEST   VOLUME   HELP   OK   NEXT

PAUSE TEST   SECTION EXIT

Writing

Section Directions

This section measures your ability to communicate in writing in an academic environment. There will be two writing tasks.

For the first writing task, you will read a passage and listen to a lecture about an academic topic. Then you will write a response to a question that asks you about the relationship between the lecture and the reading passage.

For the second task, you will demonstrate your ability to write an essay in response to a question that asks you to express and support your opinion about a topic or issue.

Now listen to the directions for the first writing task.

Integrated Writing Directions

For this task, you will first have three minutes to read a passage about an academic topic. You may take notes on the passage if you wish. The passage will then be removed and you will listen to a lecture about the same topic. While you listen, you may also take notes.

Then you will have 20 minutes to write a response to a question that asks you about the relationship between the lecture you heard and the reading passage. Try to answer the question as completely as possible using information from the reading passage and the lecture. The question does not ask you to express your personal opinion. You will be able to see the reading passage again when it is time for you to write. You may use your notes to help you answer the question.

Typically, an effective response will be 150 to 225 words long. Your response will be judged on the quality of your writing and on the completeness and accuracy of the content. If you finish your response before time is up, you may click on Next to go on to the second writing task.

Independent Writing Directions

For this task, you will write an essay in response to a question that asks you to state, explain, and support your opinion on an issue. You will have 30 minutes to plan, write, and revise your essay.

Typically, an effective essay will contain a minimum of 300 words. Your essay will be judged on the quality of your writing. This includes the development of your ideas, the organization of your essay, and the quality and accuracy of the language you use to express your ideas.

If you finish your essay before time is up, you may click on Next to end this section. When you are ready to continue, click on the Dismiss Directions icon.

Read the passage. On a piece of paper, take notes on the main points of the reading passage.

Reading Time: 3 minutes

Frederick Winslow Taylor, author of *The Principles of Scientific Management* (1911), was a leading proponent of the scientific management movement in the early twentieth century, a philosophy dedicated to improving the speed and efficiency of workers on factory floors.

In order to institute the principles of this philosophy in factories, managers would first conduct thorough time-and-motion studies in which they sent out time-and-motion inspectors to workstations with stopwatches and rulers to time and measure the movements each factory worker was making in doing his or her job. The purpose of these studies was to identify wasted motion and energy in order to improve efficacy[1] and thereby improve productivity and factory profits.

According to Taylor's principles, scientific managers could use the results of extensive time-and-motion studies to institute changes in their factories in order to make the factories more productive. One major type of change that could be instituted was that the jobs of lower-skilled workers could be reorganized. These workers could also be instructed in the most efficient way of doing their jobs, taught how to stand and where to look, and how to move their bodies.

Another major type of change was that higher-skilled and more highly paid workers could be replaced with lower-skilled, lower-paid workers. If the jobs of the more highly skilled workers could be broken down into more manageable tasks, then employees with less specialized skills could more easily be brought in to replace various components of a higher-skilled worker's job. Factory management hoped that, by instituting these kinds of changes as a result of scientific time-and-motion studies, there could be greatly improved productivity and lower costs, and therefore much greater profits, in the factories.

GLOSSARY

1. *efficacy*—how effectively the desired result is produced

Listen to the passage. On a piece of paper, take notes on the main points of the listening passage. 184 ◀))

Now answer the following question: 185 ◀))

How do the ideas in the listening passage cast doubt on the ideas in the reading passage?

Response Time: 20 minutes

Turn to pages 609–614 to *assess* the skills used in the test, *score* the test using the Writing Scoring Criteria, and *record* your results.

MINI-TEST 4

READING

20 minutes

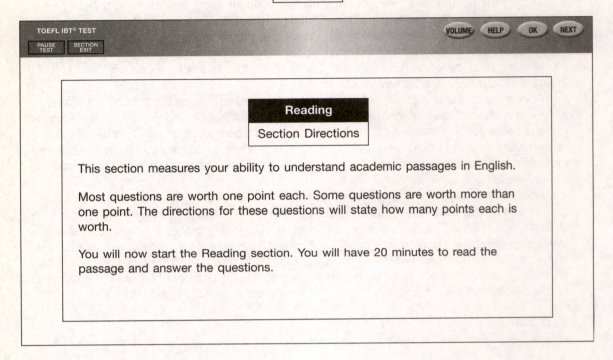

Read the passage and answer the questions that follow.

Estuaries

1▶ Fresh water from land enters the ocean through rivers, streams, and groundwater flowing through valleys. These valleys that channel fresh water from land to the salty ocean, and that range from extremely narrow stream-cut channels to remarkably broad lagoons behind long barrier islands, are called estuaries.

2▶ A number of types of estuaries are commercially vital. Many estuaries important for trade are the mouths of major rivers. The powerful flow of water in these rivers maintains channels that are deep enough for navigation by ocean-bound vessels, and the rivers themselves provide transportation of goods to points farther inland. In addition, estuaries formed as a result of tectonic or glacial activity are sometimes sufficiently deep to provide ports for oceangoing vessels. The types of estuaries that are not viable as ports of call for ocean commerce are those that are not wide enough, too shallow, and not powerful enough to prevent the buildup of sediment.

3▶ Estuary systems, which vary to reflect the geology of the coasts where they are found, can be broadly categorized as one of two different types. One type of estuary system is the type that is found in flooded coastal plains, the broad land areas that extend out to the continental shelves, on the Atlantic coasts of North and South America, Europe, and Africa, for example. On the other end of the spectrum is an estuary system that encompasses the mountainous coasts, with their rugged topography, such as those found along the Pacific coasts of North and South America.

4▶ Today, much of the eastern coast of the United States is a flooded coastal plain. During the last Ice Age, much of what is today the submerged continental shelf was exposed as an extended part of the continent. Intricate river systems composed of main rivers and their tributaries cut valleys across the plains to the edge of the shelf, where they released the fresh water that they carried into the ocean. Then, as the ice melted at the end of the Ice Age, rising waters reached inland over the lower areas, creating today's broad drowned river valleys. On today's flooded coastal plains, the water is comparatively shallow and huge amounts of sand and sediment are dumped. **9A** These conditions foster the growth of extensive long and narrow offshore deposits, many of which are exposed above the water as sand spits or barrier islands. **9B** These deposits are constantly being reshaped, sometimes extremely slowly and sometimes quite rapidly, by the forces of water and wind. **9C** It is common along flooded coastal plains for drowned river valleys to empty into lagoons that have been created behind the sandspits and barrier islands rather than emptying directly into the ocean. **9D** These lagoons support vigorous biological activity inasmuch as they are shallow, which causes them to heat up quickly, and they are fed by a constant inflow of nutrient-rich sediments.

5▶ Unlike the flooded coastal plains, the mountainous coasts have a more rough and irregular landscape with deeper coastal waters. There is less sand and sediment. In addition, external systems of barrier islands are not as pervasive as they are on flooded coastal plains because the mountainous topography blocks the flow of sediments to the coast and because the deeper ocean water inhibits the growth of barrier islands. Without the protection of barrier beaches, mountainous coasts are more exposed to direct attack by the erosive forces of waves. Different geological processes contribute to the uneven geographical features along mountainous coasts. The tectonic activity that creates them can cause large blocks of the Earth's crust to fall below sea level; San Francisco Bay in California and the Strait of Juan de Fuca in northern Washington formed in this way. In the northern latitudes, coastal fjords were created as glaciers cut impressive u-shaped valleys through mountains and now carry fresh water from the land to the ocean.

1. What is true of estuaries?
   - (A) They are always important to local commerce.
   - (B) They are mainly composed of fresh water.
   - (C) They are extremely narrow channels made by streams.
   - (D) They connect fresh water sources with the ocean.

2. According to paragraph 2, what is an important quality of a commercially viable estuary?
   - (A) That its mouth be farther inland
   - (B) That it be deep enough for cargo ships
   - (C) That it not be too powerful or shallow
   - (D) That it be located near a large city

3. What can be inferred about estuaries formed by tectonic or glacial activity?
   - (A) They are rarely utilized as ports of call.
   - (B) Ocean vessels cannot always port in them.
   - (C) They are not powerful or wide enough.
   - (D) Sediment tends to build in them.

4. Why does the author mention "On the other end of the spectrum" in paragraph 3?
   - (A) To introduce information about estuaries.
   - (B) To provide an example of mountains.
   - (C) To introduce contradicting information.
   - (D) To explain the spectrum of estuaries.

5. The word "those" in paragraph 3 refers to
   - (A) topography
   - (B) estuary system
   - (C) mountainous coasts
   - (D) Pacific coasts

6. The word "encompasses" in paragraph 3 is closest in meaning to
   - (A) surrounds
   - (B) encircles
   - (C) includes
   - (D) borders

7. According to the passage, what is implied about the last Ice Age?
   - (A) The continental shelf submerged the ice.
   - (B) Sea levels were much lower at that time.
   - (C) Deep valleys were cut along the coasts.
   - (D) There was a long period of drought.

8. Which of the words below is closest in meaning to "Intricate" in paragraph 4?
   - (A) convoluted
   - (B) tangled
   - (C) confusing
   - (D) complex

9. Look at the four squares [■] that indicate where the following sentence could be added to paragraph 4.

   Some changes to the deposits can take place gradually over decades, while others can be quite radical in a period of only a few hours as the result of major storm activity.

   Where would the sentence best fit? Click on a square [■] to add the sentence to the passage.

10. The word "foster" in paragraph 4 could best be replaced by
    - (A) promote
    - (B) back
    - (C) suppress
    - (D) enrich

11. Which of the sentences below best expresses the essential information in the highlighted sentence in paragraph 4? *Incorrect* choices change the meaning in important ways or leave out essential information.
    - (A) Biological activity contributes to the formation of lagoons by heating them up and providing a source of food.
    - (B) Lagoons become more and more shallow as they heat up and flow into the ocean.
    - (C) A lot of life exists in lagoons due to the fact that the water level is low and there is a steady source of fertile residue.
    - (D) The flow of sediments into lagoons causes biological activity, which in turn causes the lagoons to heat up.

12. According to paragraph 5, why are mountainous coasts more vulnerable to erosion?
    - (A) The rough landscape makes it easy for waves to erode mountainous coasts.
    - (B) Mountainous coasts are unprotected by coastal plains.
    - (C) Barrier beaches are not present to prevent waves from eroding mountainous coasts.
    - (D) The deeper, colder waters of mountainous coasts cause more erosion.

13.

Directions: An introductory sentence for a brief summary of the passage is provided below. Complete the summary by selecting the THREE answer choices that express the most important ideas in the passage. Some sentences do not belong in the summary because they express ideas that are not presented in the passage or are minor ideas in the passage. **This question is worth 2 points** (2 points for 3 correct answers, 1 point for 2 correct answers, and 0 points for 1 or 0 correct answers).

Estuaries, of which there are two main types, are vital geological features along the Atlantic and Pacific.

-
-
-

Answer Choices (choose 3 to complete the table):

(1) The most viable estuaries for commercial use are those that formed as a product of tectonic or glacial activity.

(2) Flooded coastal plains and mountainous coasts display similar characteristics which reflect their unique geology.

(3) Flooded coastal plains, found primarily along the Atlantic Ocean, were formed at the end of the last Ice Age.

(4) Lagoons, located behind barrier islands or sand spits, are commonly filled up by flooded coastal plains.

(5) Many estuaries, on both the Atlantic and Pacific coasts, serve as important commercial ports.

(6) Mountainous coasts are much more vulnerable to the erosive forces of water, which is evidenced in their topography.

Turn to pages 591–594 to *diagnose* your errors and *record* your results.

MINI-TEST 4

LISTENING

L_DIR_A

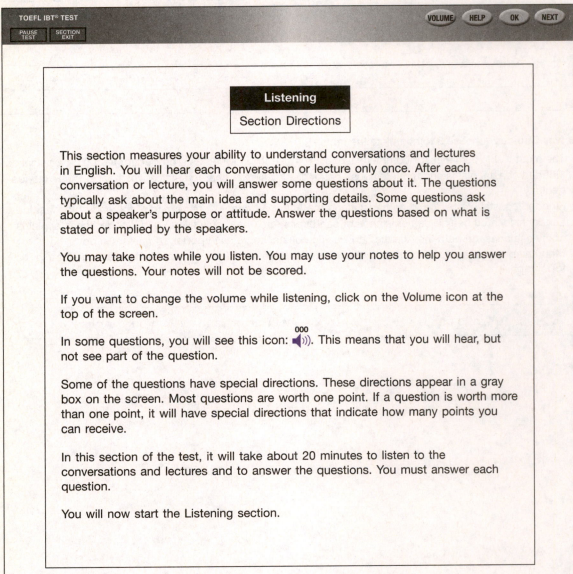

Listen as a student consults with a professor.

187

1. Why does the student go to see the professor?
   - Ⓐ To retake an exam at the professor's request
   - Ⓑ To explain to the professor why her grade was so low
   - Ⓒ To make up an exam that she missed
   - Ⓓ To look for a solution to the problem of a bad grade

2. Listen again to part of the passage. Then answer the question.

   Why does the professor say this: 🔊
   - Ⓐ To revert to an earlier topic
   - Ⓑ To reinforce what he just said
   - Ⓒ To clarify what the student's question was
   - Ⓓ To ask the student a question

3. What are the professor's grades based on?

   Click on 2 answers.
   - Ⓐ A unit exam
   - Ⓑ Unit exams
   - Ⓒ A cumulative exam
   - Ⓓ Homework assignments

4. What is a cumulative exam?
   - Ⓐ An exam that covers only the last topics of a course
   - Ⓑ An exam that covers all the units in the course
   - Ⓒ The first exam given in the course
   - Ⓓ The exam with the highest grade

5. What solution does the professor offer to the student?
   - Ⓐ Forget about the material on the last exam and concentrate on the new material
   - Ⓑ Retake the exam during office hours
   - Ⓒ Ask another student to help her take better notes
   - Ⓓ Look over her failed exam and bring questions to him

Questions 6–11

Listen to a lecture in a geography class.

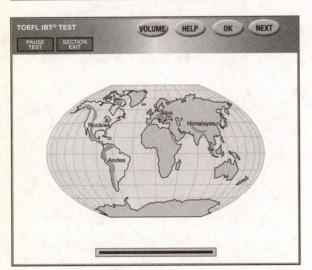

6. What is the topic of this lecture?
- Ⓐ A comparison of the world's oldest and newest mountain ranges
- Ⓑ An explanation of the formation of today's tall mountain ranges
- Ⓒ Examples of the four different stages of mountain-building
- Ⓓ Methods of proving which mountains are still rising

7. According to the lecture, is each of these statements true about the Alps and the Himalayas? **This question is worth 2 points** (2 points for 4 correct answers, 1 point for 3 correct answers, and 0 points for 2, 1, or 0 correct answers).

For each answer, click in the YES or NO column.

	YES	NO
The Alps and the Himalayas can be considered parts of the same mountain range.		
Both mountain ranges were formed when the Eurasian plate collided with the southern plate.		
Both mountain ranges continue to rise and get taller.		
Both mountain ranges are older than the Andes.		

8. According to the lecture, which statements are true about the Rocky Mountains? **This question is worth 2 points** (2 points for 3 correct answers, 1 point for 2 correct answers, and 0 points for 1 or 0 correct answers).

Click on 3 answers.
- Ⓐ They are older than any of the other ranges discussed.
- Ⓑ They were created when one tectonic plate slid on top of another.
- Ⓒ They were created by volcanic action.
- Ⓓ They are part of the same range as the Andes.
- Ⓔ They are no longer rising, but instead are losing height.

9. What does the professor explain by using the example of a doormat?
- Ⓐ Why the Rockies are far from the coast
- Ⓑ How the Himalayas began to form
- Ⓒ Why the Alps and Himalayas can be thought of as one range
- Ⓓ Why the Rockies are older than the Alps and Himalayas

10. According to the lecture, what is subduction?

Ⓐ When one tectonic plate slides under another, generally resulting in the formation of volcano chains

Ⓑ When one tectonic plate collides with another, crushing up and forming mountains

Ⓒ When one tectonic plate pushes into another, causing both plates to lift and form mountains

Ⓓ When two tectonic plates pull apart, resulting in the formation of chains of volcanoes as magma comes up

11. What aspect of the formation of the Andes does the professor emphasize?

Click on 2 answers

Ⓐ They began forming many millions of years before the Himalayas and the Alps.

Ⓑ They continue to grow higher and higher.

Ⓒ Under the Andes, one tectonic plate sits atop another.

Ⓓ Volcanic action was important in their formation.

Turn to pages 595–598 to *diagnose* your errors and *record* your results.

MINI-TEST 4

SPEAKING

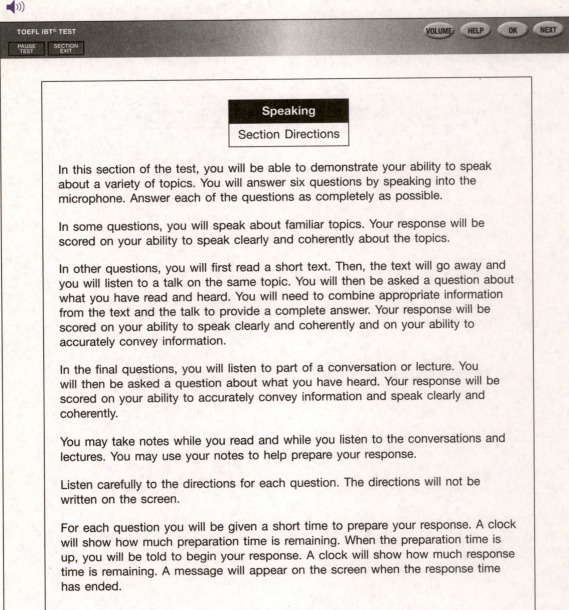

TOEFL IBT® TEST

VOLUME   HELP   OK   NEXT

PAUSE TEST   SECTION EXIT

Speaking

Section Directions

In this section of the test, you will be able to demonstrate your ability to speak about a variety of topics. You will answer six questions by speaking into the microphone. Answer each of the questions as completely as possible.

In some questions, you will speak about familiar topics. Your response will be scored on your ability to speak clearly and coherently about the topics.

In other questions, you will first read a short text. Then, the text will go away and you will listen to a talk on the same topic. You will then be asked a question about what you have read and heard. You will need to combine appropriate information from the text and the talk to provide a complete answer. Your response will be scored on your ability to speak clearly and coherently and on your ability to accurately convey information.

In the final questions, you will listen to part of a conversation or lecture. You will then be asked a question about what you have heard. Your response will be scored on your ability to accurately convey information and speak clearly and coherently.

You may take notes while you read and while you listen to the conversations and lectures. You may use your notes to help prepare your response.

Listen carefully to the directions for each question. The directions will not be written on the screen.

For each question you will be given a short time to prepare your response. A clock will show how much preparation time is remaining. When the preparation time is up, you will be told to begin your response. A clock will show how much response time is remaining. A message will appear on the screen when the response time has ended.

Question 1

Read the question. You have 15 seconds to plan an answer and 45 seconds to give your spoken response.

When they take a vacation in a place where they don't know anyone, some people prefer to find out about the best places to go and things to do using guidebooks and the Internet. Others say that the best way to find out about a place you don't know is by speaking to local people. When you go to a new place, which do you prefer and why?

> Preparation Time: 15 seconds
> Response Time: 45 seconds

Question 2

Read the passage about nullification. You have 45 seconds to read the passage.

> Reading Time: 45 seconds

Nullification

The issue of nullification was one that was faced by the United States early in the history of the country. As the country was becoming established, there was a lack of clarification as to the balance of power between the states and the federal government. Nullification was a doctrine by which states believed they could nullify, or refuse to accept, laws passed by the federal government of the United States. In other words, states that believed in their right to nullification believed that they had the authority to reject laws passed by the federal government; the federal government, of course, believed that the states did not have the right to reject federal laws.

Now listen to the passage. ◀)) 190

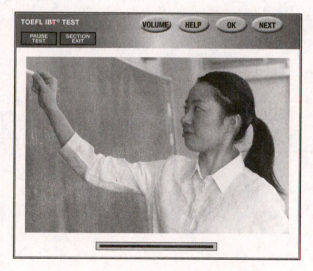

Now answer the following question. You have 30 seconds to prepare an answer and 60 seconds to give your spoken response. 191 ◀))

The reading and listening passages both discuss the issue of nullification. Explain what nullification is and how the examples the professor gives illustrate the concept.

> Preparation Time: 30 seconds
> Response Time: 60 seconds

Question 3
Listen to the passage. Then respond to the question. 192 ◀))

Now answer the following question: 193 ◀))

The students are discussing a problem the man has. Describe the problem. Then say which of the solutions you think is better and why.

> Preparation Time: 20 seconds
> Response Time: 60 seconds

Turn to pages 599–608 to *assess* the skills used in the test, *score* the test using the Speaking Scoring Criteria, and *record* your results.

MINI-TEST 4

WRITING

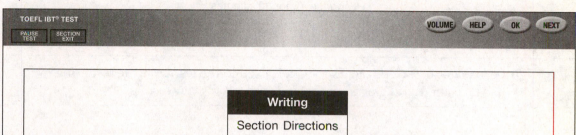

Writing

Section Directions

This section measures your ability to communicate in writing in an academic environment. There will be two writing tasks.

For the first writing task, you will read a passage and listen to a lecture about an academic topic. Then you will write a response to a question that asks you about the relationship between the lecture and the reading passage.

For the second task, you will demonstrate your ability to write an essay in response to a question that asks you to express and support your opinion about a topic or issue.

Now listen to the directions for the first writing task.

Integrated Writing Directions

For this task, you will first have three minutes to read a passage about an academic topic. You may take notes on the passage if you wish. The passage will then be removed and you will listen to a lecture about the same topic. While you listen, you may also take notes.

Then you will have 20 minutes to write a response to a question that asks you about the relationship between the lecture you heard and the reading passage. Try to answer the question as completely as possible using information from the reading passage and the lecture. The question does not ask you to express your personal opinion. You will be able to see the reading passage again when it is time for you to write. You may use your notes to help you answer the question.

Typically, an effective response will be 150 to 225 words long. Your response will be judged on the quality of your writing and on the completeness and accuracy of the content. If you finish your response before time is up, you may click on Next to go on to the second writing task.

Independent Writing Directions

For this task, you will write an essay in response to a question that asks you to state, explain, and support your opinion on an issue. You will have 30 minutes to plan, write, and revise your essay.

Typically, an effective essay will contain a minimum of 300 words. Your essay will be judged on the quality of your writing. This includes the development of your ideas, the organization of your essay, and the quality and accuracy of the language you use to express your ideas.

If you finish your essay before time is up, you may click on Next to end this section. When you are ready to continue, click on the Dismiss Directions icon.

Read the question. On a piece of paper, take notes on the main points of a response. Then write your response.

> **Some people prefer to take a position in a company and work for the company. Other people think it is better to go into business for themselves. Which do you think is better? Give reasons and examples to support your response.**

Response Time: 30 minutes

Turn to pages 609–614 to *assess* the skills used in the test, *score* the test using the Writing Scoring Criteria, and *record* your results.

MINI-TEST 5

READING

20 minutes

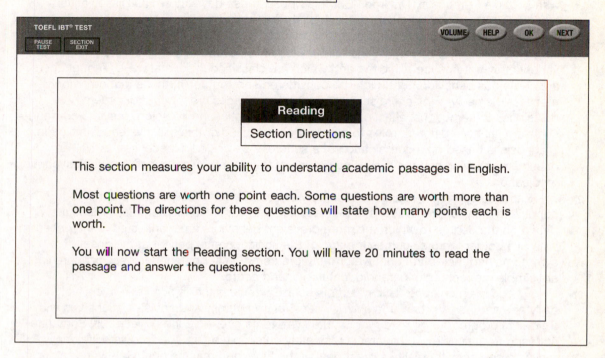

Read the passage and answer the questions that follow.

Schizophrenia

1▶   Schizophrenia, from the Greek *"skhizein,"* meaning "split" and *"phren,"* meaning "mind," affects approximately 0.3 percent to 0.7 percent of the global population, typically young adults. Among the general public, schizophrenia is often confused with Multiple Personality Disorder. But this illness, these days known as Dissociative Identity Disorder, is not the same as schizophrenia in that the latter has to do with the "splitting" of mental functions, rather than the individual's identity. Rather than being a single disease, schizophrenia is in reality a cluster of psychological disorders in which a variety of symptoms are exhibited and which are classified in several ways. Though there are numerous behaviors that might be considered schizophrenic, those that commonly manifest themselves in severe schizophrenic disturbances are thought disorders, delusions, and emotional afflictions. The fields of genetics, neurobiology, psychology, and sociology all have different roles to play in the unraveling of this still mysterious affliction. Diagnosis is based on a combination of a sufferer's perceived experiences as well as observed behavior, and the prevailing course of treatment mainly consists of antipsychotic medication.

2▶   Because schizophrenia is not a solitary illness but is in reality a group of related conditions, schizophrenics tend to be classified into various subcategories. These are based on the degree to which the more prevalent behaviors are manifested in the patient as well as other factors such as the age of the schizophrenic patient at the onset of symptoms and their duration. Five of the more common subcategories of schizophrenia are simple, hebephrenic, paranoid, catatonic, and acute.

3▶   **6A** The main characteristic of simple schizophrenia is that it begins at a relatively early age and reveals itself in a slow withdrawal from family and social relationships with a gradual progression toward more acute symptoms over a period of years. **6B** Someone suffering from simple schizophrenia may early on simply be apathetic toward life, may maintain contact with reality a great deal of the time, and may be out in the world rather than hospitalized. **6C** Over time, however, the symptoms, particularly thought and emotional disorders, increase in severity. **6D**

4▶   Hebephrenic schizophrenia is a relatively serious form of the disease that is characterized by intensely disturbed thought processes as well as highly emotional and bizarre behavior. Those suffering from this type of schizophrenia have hallucinations and delusions and appear quite incoherent; their behavior is often extreme and rather inappropriate to the situation, perhaps full of unwarranted laughter, or tears, or obscenities that seem unrelated to the moment. This kind of schizophrenia represents a rather critical and ongoing disintegration of personality that makes this type of schizophrenic unable to play a role in society.

5▶   Paranoid schizophrenia is different from other forms of the disease in that the outward behavior of the sufferer often seems quite appropriate; this type of schizophrenic is frequently able to get along in society for long periods of time. However, a paranoid schizophrenic is afflicted with extreme delusions of persecution, often accompanied by delusions of grandeur. While this type of schizophrenic has strange delusions and unusual thought processes, his or her outward behavior is not as incoherent or unusual as a hebephrenic's behavior. A person living with this version of schizophrenia can appear alert and intelligent much of the time but can also turn suddenly hostile and violent in response to imagined threats.

6▶   Another type of schizophrenia is the catatonic variety, which is typified by alternating periods of extreme excitement and stupor. There are abrupt changes in behavior, from frenzied intervals of elation and animation to stuporous periods of withdrawn behavior. During the former, the catatonic schizophrenic may exhibit excessive and sometimes violent behavior; during the latter, this person may remain mute and unresponsive to the environment.

7▶   A final type of schizophrenia is acute schizophrenia, which is marked by a sudden onset of schizophrenic symptoms such as confusion, excitement, emotionality, depression, and irrational fear. The acute schizophrenic, unlike the simple schizophrenic, shows a sudden appearance of the disease rather than a slow progression from one stage of it to the other. Additionally, the sufferer exhibits various types of schizophrenic behaviors during different episodes, sometimes displaying the characteristics of hebephrenic, catatonic, or even paranoid schizophrenia. In this type of schizophrenia, the patient's personality seems to have completely broken down.

1. The passage states that schizophrenia
   Ⓐ originated in ancient Greece
   Ⓑ is generally confusing to people
   Ⓒ is often mistaken for another disease
   Ⓓ splits one's identity into sections

2. According to paragraph 1, what is NOT true of schizophrenia?
   Ⓐ It encompasses many symptoms.
   Ⓑ It primarily afflicts young people.
   Ⓒ Many disciplines research schizophrenia.
   Ⓓ Treatments from several fields are available.

3. What can be inferred about the different types of schizophrenia?
   Ⓐ They are common at certain ages.
   Ⓑ There are more than five classifications.
   Ⓒ They are each a single illness.
   Ⓓ They all last roughly the same amount of time.

4. Which of the sentences below best expresses the essential information in the highlighted sentence in paragraph 3? *Incorrect* choices change the meaning in important ways or leave out essential information.
   Ⓐ Simple schizophrenia generally starts at an early age and slowly worsens.
   Ⓑ All types of schizophrenics withdraw from their families as their disease progresses.
   Ⓒ Those suffering from simple schizophrenia tend to move more and more slowly over the years.
   Ⓓ It is common for simple schizophrenia to start at an early age and remain less severe than other types of schizophrenia.

5. The word "apathetic" in paragraph 3 could best be replaced by
   Ⓐ halfhearted
   Ⓑ indifferent
   Ⓒ lazy
   Ⓓ pitiful

6. Look at the four squares [■] that indicate where the following sentence could be added to paragraph 3.

   So, a person with this type of schizophrenia would not, at least initially, display any visible warning signs of the disease.

   Where would the sentence best fit? Click on a square [■] to add the sentence to the passage.

7. The phrase "unwarranted" in paragraph 4 could best be replaced by
   Ⓐ unforgiveable
   Ⓑ gratuitous
   Ⓒ inappropriate
   Ⓓ justified

8. According to paragraph 5, it is stated that paranoid schizophrenics
   Ⓐ have difficulty assimilating into society
   Ⓑ are often very important people
   Ⓒ on the surface, behave inappropriately
   Ⓓ often feel they are victims of evil plots

9. The phrase "get along" in paragraph 5 is closest in meaning to
   Ⓐ be friendly
   Ⓑ be compatible
   Ⓒ circulate
   Ⓓ cope

10. The author uses the word "while" in paragraph 5 in order to show that paranoid schizophrenics
    Ⓐ think in a way that is materially different from the way that they act
    Ⓑ have strange delusions at the same time that they have unusual thought patterns
    Ⓒ can think clearly in spite of their strange behavior
    Ⓓ exhibit strange behaviors as they think unusual thoughts

11. The phrase "the former" in paragraph 6 refers to
    Ⓐ abrupt changes
    Ⓑ intervals of elation and animation
    Ⓒ stuporous periods of withdrawn behavior
    Ⓓ the catatonic variety

12. According to the passage, acute schizophrenia is unique in that
    Ⓐ the patient tends to have a gradual onset of symptoms
    Ⓑ the sufferer experiences excitement and fear exclusively
    Ⓒ symptoms from other subcategories of schizophrenia are present
    Ⓓ the patient breaks down their other personalities

13.

Directions: An introductory sentence for a brief summary of the passage is provided below. Complete the summary by selecting the THREE answer choices that express the most important ideas in the passage. Some sentences do not belong in the summary because they express ideas that are not presented in the passage or are minor ideas in the passage. **This question is worth 2 points** (2 points for 3 correct answers, 1 point for 2 correct answers, and 0 points for 1 or 0 correct answers).

Schizophrenia can be classified into several types, each composed of a variety of symptoms and behaviors.

-
-
-

Answer Choices (choose 3 to complete the chart):

(1) Among other factors, the extent to which certain symptoms are displayed leads to diagnosis of one or another particular type of schizophrenia.

(2) Some varieties of schizophrenia allow the sufferer to be an active member of society, at least for part of their lives.

(3) Schizophrenics of all classifications experience periods of withdrawal and stupor.

(4) Many people who would like to be in positions of power and leadership are diagnosed with paranoid schizophrenia.

(5) Several types of schizophrenia bar the patient from playing a role in society due to the severity and variety of symptoms.

(6) Hebephrenic schizophrenia is, perhaps more than any other type of the disease, characterized by extreme behavior and hallucinations.

Turn to pages 591–594 to *diagnose* your errors and *record* your results.

MINI-TEST 5

LISTENING

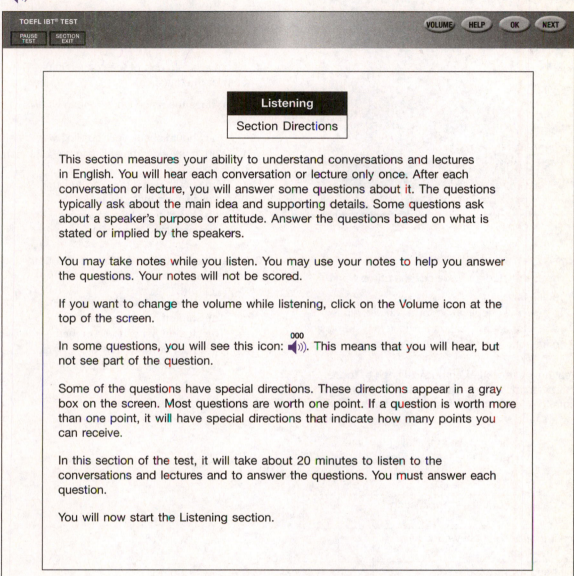

TOEFL IBT® TEST

PAUSE TEST   SECTION EXIT

VOLUME   HELP   OK   NEXT

Listening
Section Directions

This section measures your ability to understand conversations and lectures in English. You will hear each conversation or lecture only once. After each conversation or lecture, you will answer some questions about it. The questions typically ask about the main idea and supporting details. Some questions ask about a speaker's purpose or attitude. Answer the questions based on what is stated or implied by the speakers.

You may take notes while you listen. You may use your notes to help you answer the questions. Your notes will not be scored.

If you want to change the volume while listening, click on the Volume icon at the top of the screen.

In some questions, you will see this icon: 🔊. This means that you will hear, but not see part of the question.

Some of the questions have special directions. These directions appear in a gray box on the screen. Most questions are worth one point. If a question is worth more than one point, it will have special directions that indicate how many points you can receive.

In this section of the test, it will take about 20 minutes to listen to the conversations and lectures and to answer the questions. You must answer each question.

You will now start the Listening section.

Listen as a student consults with a worker in a university office.

 195

1. Why does the student go to see the office worker?

   Ⓐ To ask for a letter of reference

   Ⓑ To turn in an application for a scholarship

   Ⓒ To ask for an application for university admission

   Ⓓ To find out how to apply for a particular program

2. Does the office worker emphasize each of these requirements? **This question is worth 2 points** (2 points for 4 correct answers, 1 point for 3 correct answers, and 0 points for 2, 1, or 0 correct answers).

For each answer, click in the YES or NO column.

	YES	NO
The date the completed application is due		
The importance of answering all of the questions		
The need to write four essays		
The information to be included in the reference letters		

3. Why does the student ask about the question on high school ranking?

   Ⓐ It is an example of a question he finds difficult to answer.

   Ⓑ It seems like a question that would take too much time to answer.

   Ⓒ He thinks that his high school ranking might be too low.

   Ⓓ He thinks it will take too long to get the information.

4. Listen again to part of the conversation. Then answer the question.

What does the office worker mean when she says this?

   Ⓐ You should check your spelling very carefully.

   Ⓑ You must show the ability to pay attention to details.

   Ⓒ You should use formal, polite language when answering the questions.

   Ⓓ You should try to use academic words and complicated vocabulary.

5. What does the office worker say about the letters of reference?

Click on 2 answers.

   Ⓐ The student needs two of them.

   Ⓑ The student needs three of them.

   Ⓒ Two must be written by professors.

   Ⓓ Only one can be written by a professor.

Listen to a discussion in an oceanography class.

197 🔊))

6. What is this discussion mainly about?
   Ⓐ Why oceanic volcanoes occur
   Ⓑ How certain coral structures are formed
   Ⓒ Where atolls are most likely to occur
   Ⓓ How lagoons get their color

7. What is an atoll?
   Ⓐ A circle of coral and algae around a submerged volcanic island
   Ⓑ A circle of coral and magma surrounding a tropical volcanic island
   Ⓒ An island formed from coral and volcanic rock in warm water
   Ⓓ A submerged island of coral surrounded by a ring of volcanic rocks and sand

8. What does the professor explain by describing the movement of a bubble in honey?
   Ⓐ How the volcano explodes and releases its pressure
   Ⓑ Why the volcanic island sinks below the surface of the water
   Ⓒ How the sea floor rises until the atoll breaks the surface of the water
   Ⓓ Why the coral forms in a circular shape

9. Which of these steps occur as part of the process of atoll formation? **This question is worth 2 points** (2 points for 4 correct answers, 1 point for 3 or 2 correct answers, and 0 points for 1 or 0 correct answers).

For each answer, click in the YES or NO column.	YES	NO
A volcanic island forms in the tropical ocean.		
Rocks from the eroding volcano form an atoll ring.		
Coral grows in a circle around the volcanic island.		
The volcano disappears below the water because it erodes and sinks.		

10. What is true about a lagoon?

Click on 2 answers.

Ⓐ It may be a different color than the surrounding ocean.

Ⓑ It is composed of living coral.

Ⓒ It gets smaller and smaller as time passes.

Ⓓ It becomes less healthy for coral with time.

11. Listen again to part of the discussion. Then answer the question.

What can be inferred about the professor's lectures?

Ⓐ They usually start with a simplified explanation of a complex topic.

Ⓑ They usually start with a simple story about the topic.

Ⓒ They usually start with a simple topic that he finds particularly interesting.

Ⓓ They usually start with pictures of the topic the professor will discuss.

Turn to pages 595–598 to *diagnose* your errors and *record* your results.

MINI-TEST 5

SPEAKING

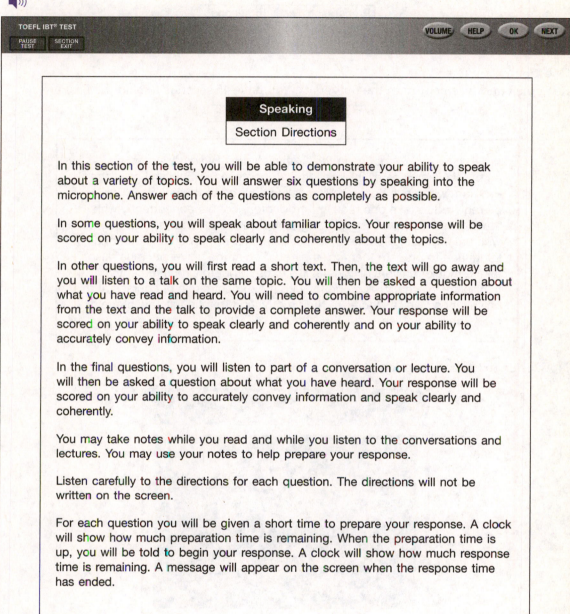

TOEFL IBT® TEST

PAUSE TEST   SECTION EXIT

VOLUME   HELP   OK   NEXT

Speaking

Section Directions

In this section of the test, you will be able to demonstrate your ability to speak about a variety of topics. You will answer six questions by speaking into the microphone. Answer each of the questions as completely as possible.

In some questions, you will speak about familiar topics. Your response will be scored on your ability to speak clearly and coherently about the topics.

In other questions, you will first read a short text. Then, the text will go away and you will listen to a talk on the same topic. You will then be asked a question about what you have read and heard. You will need to combine appropriate information from the text and the talk to provide a complete answer. Your response will be scored on your ability to speak clearly and coherently and on your ability to accurately convey information.

In the final questions, you will listen to part of a conversation or lecture. You will then be asked a question about what you have heard. Your response will be scored on your ability to accurately convey information and speak clearly and coherently.

You may take notes while you read and while you listen to the conversations and lectures. You may use your notes to help prepare your response.

Listen carefully to the directions for each question. The directions will not be written on the screen.

For each question you will be given a short time to prepare your response. A clock will show how much preparation time is remaining. When the preparation time is up, you will be told to begin your response. A clock will show how much response time is remaining. A message will appear on the screen when the response time has ended.

Question 1

Read the question. You have 15 seconds to plan an answer and 45 seconds to give your spoken response.

Do you believe that working hard, being lucky, or knowing the right people is the most important factor for success in life?

| Preparation Time: 15 seconds |
| Response Time: 45 seconds |

Question 2

Read the announcement from the university. You have 45 seconds to read the passage.

| Reading Time: 45 seconds |

A notice in the Administration Building

As of this semester, all international students in the English Language Program who have been provisionally admitted to the university will be required to take one regular introductory course concurrently with their last semester of English language instruction. That is, all students who are expecting to take their last semester of English as a Second Language to prepare them for their studies at the university must also take a regular university course. We expect that this requirement will familiarize international students with the expectations of courses at this university as well as increase their motivation to take full advantage of their English studies.

Now listen to the conversation. [198]

Now answer the following question. You have 30 seconds to prepare an answer and 60 seconds to give your spoken response. 🔊))) 199

The man gives his opinion of the new policy. State his opinion and the reasons he gives for having that opinion.

Preparation Time: 30 seconds
Response Time: 60 seconds

Question 3
Listen to the passage. Then respond to the question. 🔊))) 200

Now answer the following question:

Using points and examples from the passage, explain how the concept of zero-sum games is related to the study of economic systems. 🔊))) 201

Preparation Time: 20 seconds
Response Time: 60 seconds

Turn to pages 599–608 to *assess* the skills used in the test, *score* the test using the Speaking Scoring Criteria, and *record* your results.

MINI-TEST 5

WRITING

TOEFL IBT® TEST		VOLUME	HELP	OK	NEXT
PAUSE TEST	SECTION EXIT				

Writing
Section Directions

This section measures your ability to communicate in writing in an academic environment. There will be two writing tasks.

For the first writing task, you will read a passage and listen to a lecture about an academic topic. Then you will write a response to a question that asks you about the relationship between the lecture and the reading passage.

For the second task, you will demonstrate your ability to write an essay in response to a question that asks you to express and support your opinion about a topic or issue.

Now listen to the directions for the first writing task.

Integrated Writing Directions

For this task, you will first have three minutes to read a passage about an academic topic. You may take notes on the passage if you wish. The passage will then be removed and you will listen to a lecture about the same topic. While you listen, you may also take notes.

Then you will have 20 minutes to write a response to a question that asks you about the relationship between the lecture you heard and the reading passage. Try to answer the question as completely as possible using information from the reading passage and the lecture. The question does not ask you to express your personal opinion. You will be able to see the reading passage again when it is time for you to write. You may use your notes to help you answer the question.

Typically, an effective response will be 150 to 225 words long. Your response will be judged on the quality of your writing and on the completeness and accuracy of the content. If you finish your response before time is up, you may click on Next to go on to the second writing task.

Independent Writing Directions

For this task, you will write an essay in response to a question that asks you to state, explain, and support your opinion on an issue. You will have 30 minutes to plan, write, and revise your essay.

Typically, an effective essay will contain a minimum of 300 words. Your essay will be judged on the quality of your writing. This includes the development of your ideas, the organization of your essay, and the quality and accuracy of the language you use to express your ideas.

If you finish your essay before time is up, you may click on Next to end this section. When you are ready to continue, click on the Dismiss Directions icon.

Read the passage. On a piece of paper, take notes on the main points of the reading passage.

Reading Time: 3 minutes

In recent years, there has been a surge in the number of families that feel that the conventional way of teaching, that is in a school, whether it be public or private, is not meeting the needs of their children. As a result, many parents have taken on the role of school instructor on top of the many other responsibilities that they have. There are many convincing arguments that can be made to support this new trend in education.

Firstly, many parents feel that the curriculum that has been developed and put forward in most schools is either inappropriate, or not challenging enough for their children, and in the end, is harmful to them. They believe that many of the courses taught in school are either presenting children with information that is morally wrong, or that some subjects or activities do not stimulate their child's intellect the way that school should, which means that their children will have fewer opportunities to attend a top university or to be competitive in the job market.

Secondly, many parents who have made the transition into homeschooling feel a great sense of gratification and accomplishment while watching their children learn and grow. Most parents only get to spend a few precious hours a day with their children, often times much less, but this has to be done while getting household chores finished, and dinner ready, so it can hardly be described as "quality time." When children are homeschooled, the bond that they have with their parents becomes very strong, and the relationship benefits until the child leaves home as a young adult. In contrast, children who attend school outside of the home tend to spend a great deal of time alone, without any parental supervision, and this can lead to a host of problems later in life.

Finally, a strong argument that many parents have for taking their children out of regular school and educating them at home is that a great number of children do not feel safe when they are in school. Many students are the victims of bullying and harassment by other children, sometimes leading to violence, and this can severely traumatize a child and therefore seriously hinder their ability to feel safe and secure enough to learn while at school. The home is the safest possible environment for a child to learn in, and the student will inevitably be more academically successful than his or her peers, who are distracted by the stresses of school life.

Listen to the passage. On a piece of paper, take notes on the main points of the listening passage. **202** ◀))

Now answer the following question: ◀》) ²⁰³

How does the information in the listening passage add to the ideas presented in the reading passage?

Response Time: 20 minutes

Turn to pages 609–614 to *assess* the skills used in the test, *score* the test using the Writing Scoring Criteria, and *record* your results.

MINI-TEST 6

READING

20 minutes

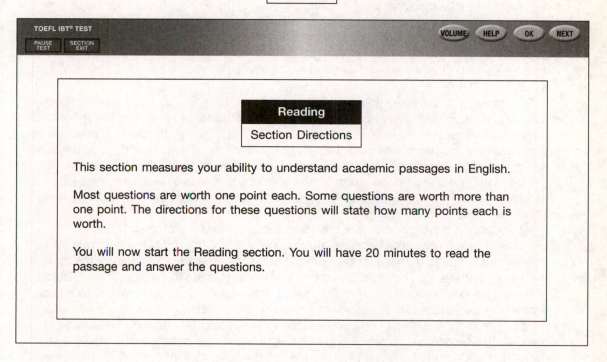

Read the passage and answer the questions that follow.

Exxon Valdez

1▶   Crude oil from the North Slope fields near Prudhoe Bay on the north coast of Alaska is carried by pipeline to the port of Valdez on the southern coast and from there is shipped by tanker to the West Coast. At approximately midnight, on March 24, 1989, one of the worst environmental disasters in U.S. history involving the *Exxon Valdez* took place. For reasons that remain unclear, the tanker, tasked with transporting oil from southern Alaska to Los Angeles, California, ran aground on Bligh Reef, about 25 miles south of the Port of Valdez. A staggering 10.8 million gallons of unrefined oil, nearly one-fifth of the ship's total cargo, was dumped into the frigid waters of a 16-kilometer-wide channel of Prince William Sound.

2▶   The damage that ensued was almost too severe to assess. The huge oil slick spread rapidly and coated more than 14,000 kilometers (9,000 miles) of shoreline. Though actual numbers can never be known, it is believed that at least a half million birds, thousands of seals and otters, quite a few whales, and an untold number of fish were killed as a result, not to mention the hundreds of miles of rocky beaches coated with the thick, sticky oil. To make matters worse, a large storm hit the area of the spill two days after the fact, and turned much of the oil into tarballs, or in many places, into a frothy mousse, making cleanup that much more prolonged.

3▶   **7A** Decades before this disaster, environmentalists had predicted just such an enormous oil spill in this area because of the treacherous nature of the waters due to the reefs and icebergs that lie just beneath the surface of the water, as well as the many violent storms there. **7B** They had urged that oil be transported to the continental United States by land-based pipeline rather than by oil tanker or by undersea pipeline to reduce the potential damage to the environment posed by the threat of an oil spill. **7C** Alyeska, a consortium of the seven oil companies working in Alaska's North Slope fields, argued against such a land-based pipeline on the basis of the length of time that it would take to construct and on the belief, or perhaps wishful thinking, that the probability of a tanker spill in the area was extremely low. **7D**

4▶   Government agencies such as the Environmental Protection Agency (EPA) were assured by Alyeska and Exxon that such a pipeline was unnecessary because appropriate protective measures had been taken; that within five hours of any accident there would be enough equipment and trained workers to clean up any spill before it managed to cause much damage. However, when the *Exxon Valdez* spill actually occurred, Exxon and Alyeska were unprepared, in terms of both equipment and personnel, to deal with the spill. As a result, thousands of untrained workers, who had little to no experience operating the specialized machinery used in the aftermath of an oil spill, had to be hired to help with the cleanup effort. This meant that replacing equipment such as the booms used to contain the oil and channel it to disposal vessels became a regular occurence. Though it was a massive spill, appropriate personnel and equipment available in a timely fashion could have reduced the damage considerably. Exxon ended up spending billions of dollars on the cleanup itself, which consisted of not only the workers and the equipment, but also the transportation, food, lodging, logistical support and supervision necessary to ensure that the job was done right. Estimates put the daily cost to Exxon at around a thousand dollars per worker per day. With over 10,000 workers on the payroll, the cost was a heavy one. In addition, the company spent further billions in fines and damages to the state of Alaska, the federal government, commercial fishermen, property owners, and others harmed by the disaster. The total cost to Exxon was more than $8 billion.

5▶   A step that could possibly have prevented this accident even though the tanker did run into submerged rocks would have been a double hull on the tanker. Today, almost all merchant ships have double hulls, but only a small percentage of oil tankers do. Legislation passed since the spill requires all new tankers to be built with double hulls. Many older tankers have received dispensations to avoid the $25 million cost per tanker to convert a single hulled tanker to one with a double hull, but compared with the $8.5 billion cost of the Exxon Valdez catastrophe, it is a comparatively paltry sum.

1. What is stated in paragraph 1 about the *Exxon Valdez*?
   - (A) It was carrying oil from Los Angeles to Prudhoe Bay, Alaska.
   - (B) It hit the reef at approximately 25 minutes past midnight.
   - (C) It lost a significant part of its payload as a result of the spill.
   - (D) It ran aground 25 miles from Prince William Sound.

2. According to paragraph 2, what can be inferred about the damage caused by the oil spill?
   - (A) It was extremely severe and widespread.
   - (B) It led to untold numbers of killed animals.
   - (C) It was exceedingly difficult to measure.
   - (D) It was much worse along the shoreline.

3. The word "coated" in paragraph 2 could best be replaced by
   - (A) covered
   - (B) warmed
   - (C) filled
   - (D) blackened

4. The phrase "the fact" in paragraph 2 refers to
   - (A) a large storm
   - (B) the spill
   - (C) the area
   - (D) two days

5. According to the passage, what is true of environmentalists?
   - (A) They knew that there were many reasons to fear that a large disaster would occur.
   - (B) They thought that though there were many dangers, tankers were the best alternative.
   - (C) They believed that an undersea pipeline was too costly and dangerous.
   - (D) They did not believe that oil should be drilled in or transported from Alaska.

6. In paragraph 3, "treacherous" is most likely
   - (A) unreliable
   - (B) deceptive
   - (C) perilous
   - (D) protected

7. Look at the four squares [■] that indicate where the following sentence could be added to paragraph 3.

   Unfortunately, this line of reasoning proved incorrect, with disastrous results.

   Where would the sentence best fit? Click on a square [■] to add the sentence to the passage.

8. The author uses the expression "wishful thinking" in paragraph 3 in order to
   - (A) emphasize the idea that the belief was misguided
   - (B) explain the desire for the pipeline to be built
   - (C) describe the hope that an oil spill could be cleaned up quickly
   - (D) emphasize the wish that a lot of oil would be discovered

9. The word "measures" in paragraph 4 could best be replaced by
   - (A) laws
   - (B) steps
   - (C) maneuvers
   - (D) quantities

10. What is NOT mentioned in the passage as a factor that made the spill so costly?
    - (A) Inadequate numbers of workers were available on short notice.
    - (B) Fines to many parties who suffered damages as a result of the spill had to be paid.
    - (C) Support networks were necessary to ensure the clean up was done correctly.
    - (D) Equipment was of poor quality and needed to be replaced.

11. What does the author imply about the booms used to contain the oil?
    - (A) They needed to be replaced because they were poorly constructed.
    - (B) They broke because of overuse, due to the magnitude of the spill.
    - (C) They had to be replaced because untrained workers did not use them correctly.
    - (D) Only a few were replaced because of their prohibitive cost.

12. Which of the sentences below best expresses the essential information in the highlighted sentence in paragraph 5? *Incorrect* choices change the meaning in important ways or leave out essential information.
    - (A) It is not expensive to build double-hulled tankers, so all tankers have them, so as to avoid the cost of an oil spill.
    - (B) Although new tankers are legally required to have double hulls, not all older tankers have them because it is too expensive.
    - (C) Laws have been passed requiring all tankers, both old and new, to have double hulls, but only a few ships have this feature, so oil spills are more common.
    - (D) In spite of legislation, many ship owners have avoided installing double hulls, even though this is less costly than an oil spill.

13.

Directions: An introductory sentence for a brief summary of the passage is provided below. Complete the summary by selecting the THREE answer choices that express the most important ideas in the passage. Some sentences do not belong in the summary because they express ideas that are not presented in the passage or are minor ideas in the passage. **This question is worth 2 points** (2 points for 3 correct answers, 1 point for 2 correct answers, and 0 points for 1 or 0 correct answers).

The *Exxon Valdez* oil spill is a tragedy that could have been less severe or prevented altogether.

-
-
-

Answer Choices (choose 3 to complete the chart):

(1) Half a million birds and thousands of seals lost their lives as a result of the spill.

(2) Alyeska and Exxon knew that the likelihood of a large oil spill was very small.

(3) Environmentalists had warned that oil spills were a possibility, and recommended actions be taken.

(4) Appropriate numbers of response staff and equipment would have lessened the extent of the disaster.

(5) New legislation enacted since the spill will force new ships to be constructed with double hulls.

(6) By transporting the crude oil via an undersea pipeline, such a catastrophe may have been averted.

Turn to pages 591–594 to *diagnose* your errors and *record* your results.

MINI-TEST 6

LISTENING

L_DIR_A

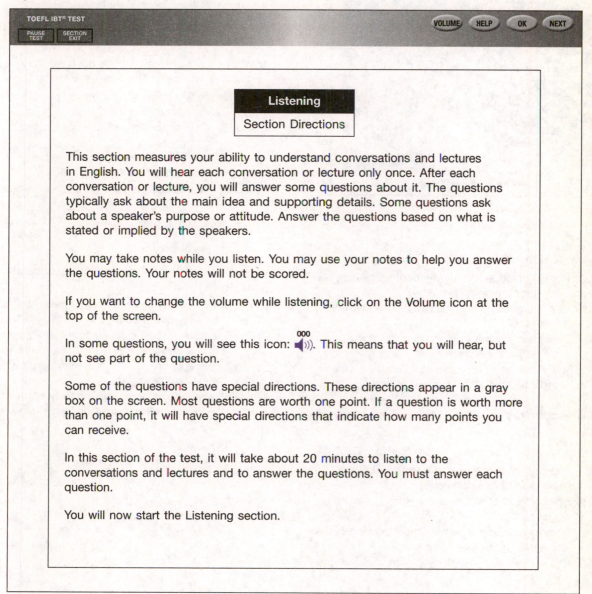

Listening

Section Directions

This section measures your ability to understand conversations and lectures in English. You will hear each conversation or lecture only once. After each conversation or lecture, you will answer some questions about it. The questions typically ask about the main idea and supporting details. Some questions ask about a speaker's purpose or attitude. Answer the questions based on what is stated or implied by the speakers.

You may take notes while you listen. You may use your notes to help you answer the questions. Your notes will not be scored.

If you want to change the volume while listening, click on the Volume icon at the top of the screen.

In some questions, you will see this icon: ◀))). This means that you will hear, but not see part of the question.

Some of the questions have special directions. These directions appear in a gray box on the screen. Most questions are worth one point. If a question is worth more than one point, it will have special directions that indicate how many points you can receive.

In this section of the test, it will take about 20 minutes to listen to the conversations and lectures and to answer the questions. You must answer each question.

You will now start the Listening section.

Listen as a student consults with his professor.

²⁰⁵

1. Why does the student go to see the professor?
   Ⓐ To get guidance on writing about something the professor may not like
   Ⓑ To ask for advice about a situation with another professor
   Ⓒ To explain why he wants to contradict the professor in his paper
   Ⓓ To talk about a problem he is having with the topic he has been assigned

2. Listen again to part of the passage. Then answer the question.

   What can be inferred about the professor?
   Ⓐ She previously expressed a strong dislike of Hemingway's writing style.
   Ⓑ She prefers not to talk about Hemingway in class.
   Ⓒ She does not usually express her opinion of the authors they study to the class.
   Ⓓ She expressed a negative opinion of Hemingway in class.

3. What does the professor tell the student about challenging his professors?
   Ⓐ He should do so if he has strong arguments based on thorough research.
   Ⓑ He should never challenge professors' strongest beliefs directly.
   Ⓒ He should find opportunities to challenge professors to earn their respect.
   Ⓓ He can be sure that the professors will be objective and fair about his challenges.

4. What aspect of Hemingway's book will the student probably write about?
   Ⓐ He will write about the relationship between the main characters.
   Ⓑ He will describe the scientific aspects of Hemingway's writing.
   Ⓒ He will show how Hemingway's writing demonstrated his tolerant attitude.
   Ⓓ He will write about points in the book where Hemingway removed portions.

5. Listen again to part of the conversation. Then answer the question.

   How does the professor seem to feel about the student's topic?
   Ⓐ She is looking forward to him challenging her beliefs about Hemingway.
   Ⓑ She doesn't like his focus on the characters, but is somewhat interested.
   Ⓒ It concerns one aspect of Hemingway's writing she finds interesting.
   Ⓓ She is happy that he is going to work on an author she likes more than Hemingway.

Listen to a lecture in a zoology class.

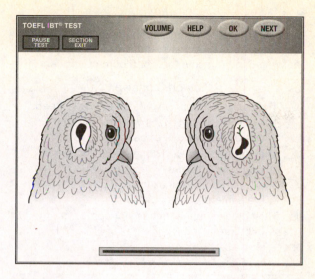

207

6. How is the information in the lecture organized?
   A The professor explains reasons why the barn owl's hearing is better than other animals.
   B The professor outlines physical adaptations that allow barn owls to hunt in darkness.
   C The professor describes the results of a series of experiments on one animal species.
   D The hearing of various animals is compared to that of humans.

7. Listen again to part of the passage. Then answer the question.

   What does the professor mean?
   A The professor does not like the sound the barn owl makes.
   B Many people think the sound of the barn owl is unpleasant.
   C Many people consider the call of the barn owl to be somewhat agreeable.
   D The barn owls in this area have a different call from those in other places.

8. According to the professor, what is true about the barn owl's specialized hearing?

   Click on 2 answers.
   A It allows the owl to hunt in total darkness.
   B It has been studied more than human hearing.
   C It allows the owl to locate other owls by hearing their calls.
   D It allows the owl to form a mental map.

9. According to the professor, what is the purpose of the heart-shaped feather pattern on the barn owl's face?
   A to funnel light into the owl's eyes
   B to amplify and direct sound
   C to determine the direction of prey
   D to allow the owl to fly silently

10. According to the lecture, what is true about the barn owl's ears? **This question is worth 2 points** (2 points for 3 correct answers, 1 point for 2 correct answers, and 0 points for 1 or 0 correct answers).

Click on 3 answers.

Ⓐ They sit at different heights on the owl's head.

Ⓑ They allow the owl to tell whether a sound comes from above or below.

Ⓒ They point downward so they don't interfere with sound waves.

Ⓓ They create differences in sound that the owl's brain interprets as position.

Ⓔ They block sounds that do not come from the owl's prey.

11. Which of the following are adaptations that help the barn owl hear and locate prey? **This question is worth 2 points** (2 points for 3 correct answers, 1 point for 2 correct answers, and 0 points for 1 or 0 correct answers).

For each answer, click in the YES or NO column.

	YES	NO
The pattern of the feathers of its face		
The asymmetrical height of its ears		
The specialized feathers of its wings		
The shape and position of its beak		

Turn to pages 595–598 to *diagnose* your errors and *record* your results.

MINI-TEST 6

SPEAKING

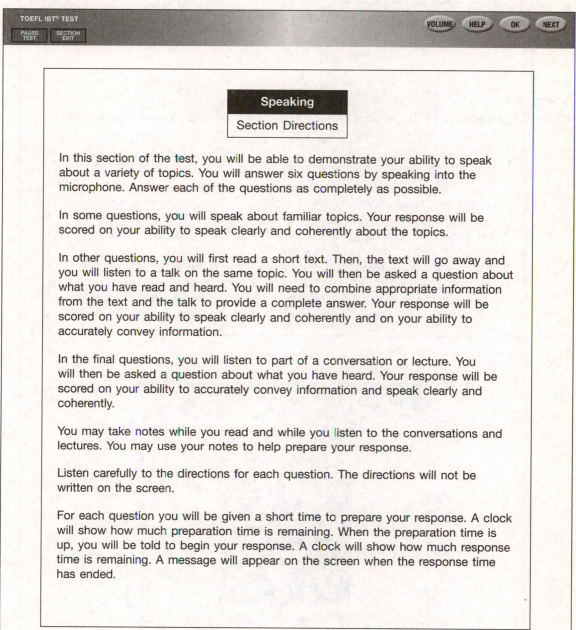

TOEFL IBT® TEST

PAUSE TEST   SECTION EXIT

VOLUME   HELP   OK   NEXT

Speaking

Section Directions

In this section of the test, you will be able to demonstrate your ability to speak about a variety of topics. You will answer six questions by speaking into the microphone. Answer each of the questions as completely as possible.

In some questions, you will speak about familiar topics. Your response will be scored on your ability to speak clearly and coherently about the topics.

In other questions, you will first read a short text. Then, the text will go away and you will listen to a talk on the same topic. You will then be asked a question about what you have read and heard. You will need to combine appropriate information from the text and the talk to provide a complete answer. Your response will be scored on your ability to speak clearly and coherently and on your ability to accurately convey information.

In the final questions, you will listen to part of a conversation or lecture. You will then be asked a question about what you have heard. Your response will be scored on your ability to accurately convey information and speak clearly and coherently.

You may take notes while you read and while you listen to the conversations and lectures. You may use your notes to help prepare your response.

Listen carefully to the directions for each question. The directions will not be written on the screen.

For each question you will be given a short time to prepare your response. A clock will show how much preparation time is remaining. When the preparation time is up, you will be told to begin your response. A clock will show how much response time is remaining. A message will appear on the screen when the response time has ended.

Question 1

Read the question. You have 15 seconds to plan an answer and 45 seconds to give your spoken response.

> **Some people feel that the most important thing leaders can do is stand by their principles, convincing others to believe what they do. Other people say that good leaders must be flexible and change their views or compromise with others. Which characteristic is more important in good leaders?**

> Preparation Time: 15 seconds
> Response Time: 45 seconds

Question 2

Read the passage about the solar system. You have 45 seconds to read the passage.

> Reading Time: 45 seconds

Formation of the Solar System

Around 5 billion years ago, what is today our Solar System was most likely a spinning cloud of gas and dust. The vast majority of gas and dust in this cloud began clumping together to form our Sun, and some of the rest of the material began forming clumps that became the planets in our Solar System, including our Earth. As our planet came together, it formed into a globe with a layered structure. The way that this layered structure ended up was with the heavier material in the middle of the globe and the lighter material on the outside surrounding the heavier material.

Now listen to the passage. ◀)) 208

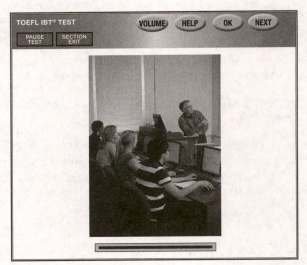

Now answer the following question. You have 30 seconds to prepare an answer and 60 seconds to give your spoken response. 🔊 209

The reading and listening passage discuss the formation of the layered structure of the Earth. Explain the two original theories and the process that is believed to have taken place.

> Preparation Time: 30 seconds
> Response Time: 60 seconds

Question 3
Listen to the conversation. 🔊 210

Now answer the following question. You will have 20 seconds to prepare an answer and 60 seconds to give your spoken response. 🔊 211

The students discuss the woman's problem. Describe her problem and say which solution you prefer and why.

> Preparation Time: 20 seconds
> Response Time: 60 seconds

> Turn to pages 599–608 to *assess* the skills used in the test, *score* the test using the Speaking Scoring Criteria, and *record* your results.

MINI-TEST 6

WRITING

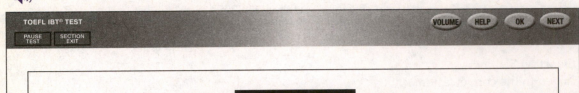

Writing
Section Directions

This section measures your ability to communicate in writing in an academic environment. There will be two writing tasks.

For the first writing task, you will read a passage and listen to a lecture about an academic topic. Then you will write a response to a question that asks you about the relationship between the lecture and the reading passage.

For the second task, you will demonstrate your ability to write an essay in response to a question that asks you to express and support your opinion about a topic or issue.

Now listen to the directions for the first writing task.

Integrated Writing Directions

For this task, you will first have three minutes to read a passage about an academic topic. You may take notes on the passage if you wish. The passage will then be removed and you will listen to a lecture about the same topic. While you listen, you may also take notes.

Then you will have 20 minutes to write a response to a question that asks you about the relationship between the lecture you heard and the reading passage. Try to answer the question as completely as possible using information from the reading passage and the lecture. The question does not ask you to express your personal opinion. You will be able to see the reading passage again when it is time for you to write. You may use your notes to help you answer the question.

Typically, an effective response will be 150 to 225 words long. Your response will be judged on the quality of your writing and on the completeness and accuracy of the content. If you finish your response before time is up, you may click on Next to go on to the second writing task.

Independent Writing Directions

For this task, you will write an essay in response to a question that asks you to state, explain, and support your opinion on an issue. You will have 30 minutes to plan, write, and revise your essay.

Typically, an effective essay will contain a minimum of 300 words. Your essay will be judged on the quality of your writing. This includes the development of your ideas, the organization of your essay, and the quality and accuracy of the language you use to express your ideas.

If you finish your essay before time is up, you may click on Next to end this section. When you are ready to continue, click on the Dismiss Directions icon.

Read the question. On a piece of paper, take notes on the topic and main points for a response. Then write your response.

Traveling to a different country can be both exciting and frustrating at the same time. What are the most important pieces of advice that you would give visitors coming to your country? Give reasons and details to support your response.

Response Time: 30 minutes

Turn to pages 609–614 to *assess* the skills used in the test, *score* the test using the Writing Scoring Criteria, and *record* your results.

MINI-TEST 7

READING

20 minutes

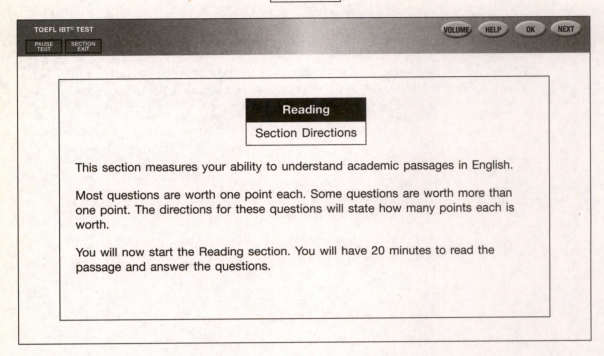

TOEFL IBT® TEST

PAUSE TEST   SECTION EXIT

VOLUME   HELP   OK   NEXT

Reading

Section Directions

This section measures your ability to understand academic passages in English.

Most questions are worth one point each. Some questions are worth more than one point. The directions for these questions will state how many points each is worth.

You will now start the Reading section. You will have 20 minutes to read the passage and answer the questions.

Read the passage and answer the questions that follow.

Plate Tectonics

1▶   The upper portion of the Earth's lithosphere, which contains the heavier oceanic and the lighter continental crusts, consists of a series of rigid plates that are in constant motion. The theory of plate tectonics provides a cohesive model to explain the integrated actions of continental drift, seafloor spreading, and mountain formation, as well as volcanic islands and ocean trenches.

2▶   The Earth's plates vary considerably in size, as some are estimated to be continental or even hemispheric in size, while others are believed to be much smaller. Though the actual boundaries and sizes and shapes of the plates are not known for sure, it has been postulated that there are six major plates and somewhere around the same number of smaller ones. Most of the plates consist of both *sial* (continental) and *sima* (oceanic) crust. They are in continuous movement, though at an extremely slow pace, and this shifting causes frequent interactions between plates.

3▶   For the time being, scientists have identified three different types of boundaries between plates. At a divergent boundary, plates are moving away from each other. This type of boundary usually occurs at an underwater mountain range, or mid-ocean ridge, where new material is being added to the seafloor—known as seafloor spreading—from deeper within the Earth. Volcanic islands are the result of this type of plate boundary, as the gap that the diverging plates leave behind can be filled with molten lava, which rises from the Earth's mantle. Eventually, the lava builds to such an extent that it breaches the surface of the water. Shallow earthquakes and underwater volcanoes are also associated with this type of plate activity.

4▶   At a convergent boundary, plates are moving toward each other and collide, causing vast folding and crumpling along the edges of the plates, or in many cases, one of the plates may slowly tuck under the other. In the first kind of convergent boundary, the two plates that crash into each other are both composed of continental, or sial crust. This is where large mountain ranges, such as the Himalayas, form. Other convergent boundaries occur when an oceanic plate collides with either a continental plate or another oceanic plate. In both cases, one crust will be forced under the other (usually it is the oceanic crust that does this). **7A** Though this subduction is slow, it can nonetheless be quite catastrophic as the crustal material of the submerging plate gradually melts into the fiery hot depths below. **7B** The surrounding crust is usually relatively unstable and is characterized by numerous deep earthquakes and a significant amount of volcanic activity. **7C** The boundaries between convergent plates are generally found around the edges of ocean basins and are sometimes associated with deep ocean trenches. **7D**

5▶   A third type of boundary is a transform boundary, or transform fault, which involves two plates sliding past each other laterally,[1] without the folding and crumpling that occurs at a convergent boundary. Transform boundaries are also known as conservative boundaries because the lithosphere[2] is neither created nor destroyed. This boundary is thought to be far less common than the other two types of boundaries. It can usually be found on the ocean floor, but one well-known exception of this is the San Andreas Fault, in California, which has been responsible for many devastating earthquakes in the region.

6▶   The concept of plate tectonics provides an understanding of the massive rearrangement of the Earth's crust that has apparently taken place. It is now generally accepted that the single supercontinent known as Pangaea indeed existed, that it subsequently broke apart into two giant pieces, Gondwanaland in the south and Laurasia in the north, and that the continents attached to the various crustal plates separated and drifted in various directions. The landmass that is today known as India was originally part of Gondwanaland in the Southern Hemisphere, but it broke off approximately 200 million years ago and drifted north to collide with part of Laurasia, to create the world's tallest mountains.

GLOSSARY

1. *laterally*—toward the side
2. *lithosphere*—the rocky outer layer of the Earth

1. The word "cohesive" in paragraph 1 is closest in meaning to
   (A) unified
   (B) detailed
   (C) limited
   (D) lengthy

2. According to paragraph 2, it is certain that the Earth's plates
   (A) are much smaller than previously believed
   (B) are all the size of the hemispheres
   (C) have well known boundaries and shapes
   (D) often come in contact with one another

3. The word "postulated" in paragraph 2 is closest in meaning to
   (A) recommended
   (B) hypothesized
   (C) proven
   (D) assumed

4. The author uses the expression "For the time being" at the beginning of paragraph 3 in order to indicate that
   (A) more types of boundaries might be found in the future
   (B) interactions are currently occurring between plates
   (C) all possible types of boundaries have been discovered
   (D) the major plates are all currently moving away from each other

5. According to the passage, how do volcanic islands form?
   (A) as a result of seafloor spreading
   (B) as a reaction of diverging plates
   (C) as a result of lava accumulation
   (D) as a by-product of underwater mountains

6. It is implied in the passage that mountain ranges
   (A) are the result of volcanic islands forming
   (B) only form when sial crusts converge
   (C) are never found on the ocean floor
   (D) can get tucked under a continental plate

7. Look at the four squares [■] that indicate where the following sentence could be added to paragraph 4.

   Mariana Trench, at over 6 miles (10.9 km) deep at the southern tip, is the deepest part of the world's oceans, and is a result of the subduction of the Pacific plate underneath the Mariana plate.

   Where would the sentence best fit? Click on a square [■] to add the sentence to the passage.

8. All of the following are mentioned about subduction EXCEPT
   (A) It is usually the result of an oceanic plate that is forced to submerge.
   (B) It can happen quite abruptly, causing cataclysmic natural disasters.
   (C) Severe earthquakes and volcanic eruptions are common effects of subduction.
   (D) Trenches in the depths of the ocean are sometimes located in subduction zones.

9. Which of the sentences below best expresses the essential information in the highlighted sentence in paragraph 5? *Incorrect* choices change the meaning in important ways or leave out essential information.
   (A) The San Andreas Fault is known to scientists as a transform boundary because of the damage it inflicts to the ocean floor.
   (B) The San Andreas Fault is found, like other transform boundaries, on the ocean floor and is the cause of earthquakes.
   (C) The San Andreas Fault, unlike most transform boundaries, is not located on the ocean floor, and is the source of strong earthquakes.
   (D) Most transform boundaries are located on the ocean floor and do not cause much damage, like the San Andreas Fault in California.

10. What can be inferred about the supercontinent Pangaea?
    (A) This theory was not always regarded as true.
    (B) It eventually split off into many pieces.
    (C) It ended up in many different places.
    (D) It collided with the Northern Hemisphere.

11. The word "it" in paragraph 6 refers to
    (A) landmass
    (B) India
    (C) Gondwanaland
    (D) Southern Hemisphere

12.

Directions: The answer choices below are each used to describe one of the types of boundaries. Complete the table by matching appropriate answer choices to the boundaries they are used to describe. TWO of the answer choices will not be used. **This question is worth 3 points** (3 points for 5 correct answers, 2 points for 4 correct answers, 1 point for 3 correct answers, and 0 points for 2, 1, or 0 correct answers).

Divergent boundary	•
	•
Convergent boundary	•
	•
Transform boundary	•

Answer Choices (choose 5 to complete the table):

(1) Occurs when two plates remain stationary in relation to each other.
(2) Resulting lava flows may cause the formation of volcanic islands.
(3) Mountain chains can often be found at these boundary sites.
(4) Relatively little damage is caused, with some notable exceptions.
(5) The seafloor spreads as a consequence of molten mantle material.
(6) Continuous continental shifting is the result of this boundary type.
(7) A precarious crust causes frequent earthquakes and volcanic eruptions.

Turn to pages 591–594 to *diagnose* your errors and *record* your results.

MINI-TEST 7

LISTENING

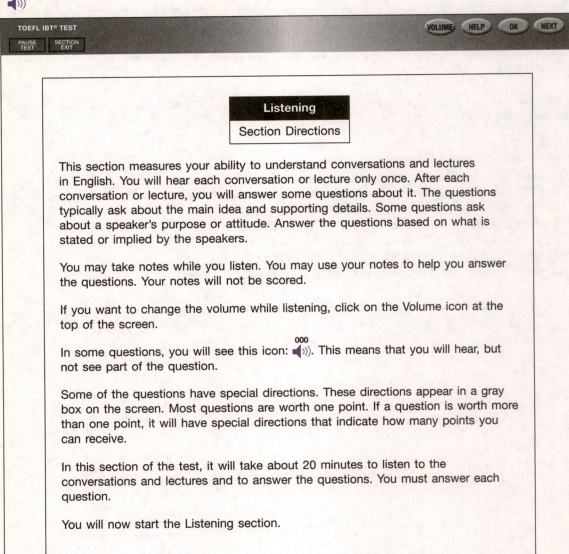

TOEFL IBT® TEST   VOLUME HELP OK NEXT

PAUSE TEST   SECTION EXIT

Listening
Section Directions

This section measures your ability to understand conversations and lectures in English. You will hear each conversation or lecture only once. After each conversation or lecture, you will answer some questions about it. The questions typically ask about the main idea and supporting details. Some questions ask about a speaker's purpose or attitude. Answer the questions based on what is stated or implied by the speakers.

You may take notes while you listen. You may use your notes to help you answer the questions. Your notes will not be scored.

If you want to change the volume while listening, click on the Volume icon at the top of the screen.

In some questions, you will see this icon: 🔊. This means that you will hear, but not see part of the question.

Some of the questions have special directions. These directions appear in a gray box on the screen. Most questions are worth one point. If a question is worth more than one point, it will have special directions that indicate how many points you can receive.

In this section of the test, it will take about 20 minutes to listen to the conversations and lectures and to answer the questions. You must answer each question.

You will now start the Listening section.

Listen as a student consults with a professor.

213

1. Why does the student go to talk with the professor?

   Ⓐ To find out which part of the presentation the professor wants each group member to do

   Ⓑ To discuss how to resolve a problem his group is having organizing the presentation

   Ⓒ To set up a meeting with his group and the professor to discuss their presentation

   Ⓓ To discuss the issues his group has developed for their presentation

2. Listen again to part of the passage. Then answer the question.

   What does the professor mean when she says this:

   Ⓐ "I'm not the right person to answer your question."

   Ⓑ "Can you please specify what your presentation is about?"

   Ⓒ "Your question is a really good one, so it's complicated to answer."

   Ⓓ "I can't answer until I understand better what your question is."

3. What does the professor think the students have done wrong?

   Ⓐ They are concentrating on dividing up topics too early.

   Ⓑ They have come up with too many issues.

   Ⓒ They need to determine more than one issue.

   Ⓓ They have determined the problems but not the solutions.

4. What does the professor imply about the students' presentation?

   Ⓐ They should first decide who will present problems and who will present solutions.

   Ⓑ Deciding how to organize the presentation will be the most difficult part.

   Ⓒ She expects all four of the group members to speak during the presentation.

   Ⓓ They should choose one of the three ways the professor suggested to present the material.

5. Listen again to part of the passage. Then answer the question.

   Why does the professor say this:

   Ⓐ To emphasize the need for the group members to think of creative solutions

   Ⓑ To reassure the student that possible solutions will be provided in the case study

   Ⓒ To warn the student against using solutions that are not provided in the case study

   Ⓓ To remind the student that she will discuss solutions in class

Questions 6–11 🔊²¹⁴

Listen to a lecture in a music class.

🔊²¹⁵

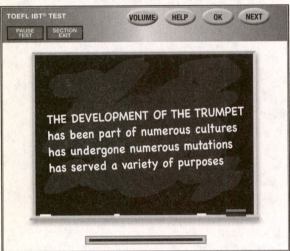

THE DEVELOPMENT OF THE TRUMPET
has been part of numerous cultures
has undergone numerous mutations
has served a variety of purposes

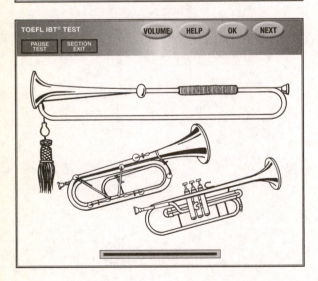

6. What is the lecture mainly about?

Ⓐ A chronological examination of major improvements that have led to the modern trumpet

Ⓑ The various uses and forms of the trumpet through history

Ⓒ A comparison of the characteristics of a trumpet used for music versus one used for simple communication

Ⓓ The reasons why the trumpet was not traditionally used for music

7. Which of these points does the professor make about the development of the trumpet? **This question is worth 2 points** (2 points for 4 correct answers, 1 point for 3 correct answers, and 0 points for 2, 1, or 0 correct answers).

For each answer, click in the YES or NO column.		
	YES	**NO**
The culture where the earliest trumpet developed is known.		
Today's trumpet is much like the earliest trumpet.		
The trumpet has been used in many different ways.		
Many different types of music have been written for the trumpet.		

8. Which of the following facts were mentioned by the lecturer about the trumpet? **This question is worth 2 points** (2 points for 3 correct answers, 1 point for 2 correct answers, and 0 points for 1 or 0 correct answers).

Click on 3 answers

Ⓐ It has been used in ceremonies to announce the arrival of someone important.

Ⓑ The most intricate trumpets were carved from stone.

Ⓒ It has been used on the top of mountains to communicate long distances.

Ⓓ It was made of metal only in the last few centuries.

Ⓔ The tubing was bent to make the trumpet easier to handle.

9. When did different parts of the trumpet develop?

Click on 2 answers.

Ⓐ The trumpet's tubing was initially straight and later the tubing became looped.

Ⓑ Valves were added to the trumpet before a bell was added.

© The tubing on the trumpet was looped before a bell was added.

Ⓓ A bell was added to an early trumpet that was a long straight tube.

10. Listen again to part of the passage. Then answer the question.

Why does the professor say this?

Ⓐ To indicate that his third point is not as important as the other two

Ⓑ To inform the students that he will speak more about the second point after he talks about the third

© To inform the students that he prefers that they wait until he finishes the third point to ask any questions

Ⓓ To indicate that he has already spent too much time speaking about his second point

11. Why does the professor say that not much music was written for the trumpet until the last two centuries?

Ⓐ Few people achieved true mastery of the instrument until the eighteenth century.

Ⓑ Before then, few people realized it could be used for anything besides communication.

© Until the eighteenth century, trumpets were physically difficult to maneuver and play.

Ⓓ Before then the trumpet could not easily play all the notes in classical scales.

Turn to pages 595–598 to *diagnose* your errors and *record* your results.

MINI-TEST 7

SPEAKING

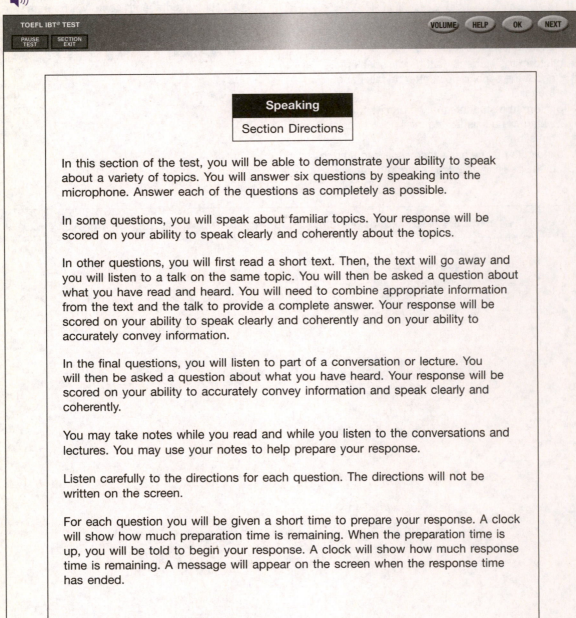

TOEFL IBT® TEST

PAUSE TEST   SECTION EXIT   VOLUME   HELP   OK   NEXT

Speaking

Section Directions

In this section of the test, you will be able to demonstrate your ability to speak about a variety of topics. You will answer six questions by speaking into the microphone. Answer each of the questions as completely as possible.

In some questions, you will speak about familiar topics. Your response will be scored on your ability to speak clearly and coherently about the topics.

In other questions, you will first read a short text. Then, the text will go away and you will listen to a talk on the same topic. You will then be asked a question about what you have read and heard. You will need to combine appropriate information from the text and the talk to provide a complete answer. Your response will be scored on your ability to speak clearly and coherently and on your ability to accurately convey information.

In the final questions, you will listen to part of a conversation or lecture. You will then be asked a question about what you have heard. Your response will be scored on your ability to accurately convey information and speak clearly and coherently.

You may take notes while you read and while you listen to the conversations and lectures. You may use your notes to help prepare your response.

Listen carefully to the directions for each question. The directions will not be written on the screen.

For each question you will be given a short time to prepare your response. A clock will show how much preparation time is remaining. When the preparation time is up, you will be told to begin your response. A clock will show how much response time is remaining. A message will appear on the screen when the response time has ended.

Question 1

Read the question. You have 15 seconds to plan an answer and 45 seconds to give your spoken response.

Some people feel that English pronunciation is difficult, others cite the amount of vocabulary, and other people say the number of exceptions to grammar rules is the most difficult aspect of learning English. What do you believe is the most difficult aspect of learning English? Use reasons and specific details to support your answer.

> Preparation Time: 15 seconds
> Response Time: 45 seconds

Question 2

Read the notice about the garage. You have 45 seconds to read the passage.

> Reading Time: 45 seconds

Notice on Parking Garage Construction

On June 4th, the South Parking Garage will be demolished to make way for a new parking structure. The new garage is to be completed by mid-October and will quadruple the parking capacity of the current structure. It is expected that this increased capacity will alleviate the lack of parking spaces for students as well as providing some public parking for the stores and restaurants on Dallas Street. Students will have to pay a nominal fee, subsidized by revenues from public parking, to obtain a parking pass each semester that will allow them to use the new parking structure.

Now listen to the conversation. 216 🔊

Now answer the following question. You have 30 seconds to prepare an answer and 60 seconds to give your spoken response. ²¹⁷ 🔊))

> **The woman gives her opinion of the announcement concerning the South Parking Garage. State her opinion and the reasons she gives for holding that opinion.**

> Preparation Time: 30 seconds
> Response Time: 60 seconds

Question 3
Listen to the passage. Then respond to the question. ²¹⁸ 🔊))

Now answer the following question. You have 20 seconds to prepare an answer and 60 seconds to give your spoken response. ²¹⁹ 🔊))

> **Using points and examples from the lecture, describe the NIMBY response and the views of fairness involved in the response.**

> Preparation Time: 20 seconds
> Response Time: 60 seconds

Turn to pages 599–608 to *assess* the skills used in the test, *score* the test using the Speaking Scoring Criteria, and *record* your results.

MINI-TEST 7

WRITING

W_DIR_C

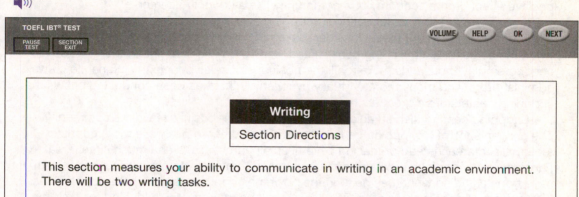

Writing

Section Directions

This section measures your ability to communicate in writing in an academic environment. There will be two writing tasks.

For the first writing task, you will read a passage and listen to a lecture about an academic topic. Then you will write a response to a question that asks you about the relationship between the lecture and the reading passage.

For the second task, you will demonstrate your ability to write an essay in response to a question that asks you to express and support your opinion about a topic or issue.

Now listen to the directions for the first writing task.

Integrated Writing Directions

For this task, you will first have three minutes to read a passage about an academic topic. You may take notes on the passage if you wish. The passage will then be removed and you will listen to a lecture about the same topic. While you listen, you may also take notes.

Then you will have 20 minutes to write a response to a question that asks you about the relationship between the lecture you heard and the reading passage. Try to answer the question as completely as possible using information from the reading passage and the lecture. The question does not ask you to express your personal opinion. You will be able to see the reading passage again when it is time for you to write. You may use your notes to help you answer the question.

Typically, an effective response will be 150 to 225 words long. Your response will be judged on the quality of your writing and on the completeness and accuracy of the content. If you finish your response before time is up, you may click on Next to go on to the second writing task.

Independent Writing Directions

For this task, you will write an essay in response to a question that asks you to state, explain, and support your opinion on an issue. You will have 30 minutes to plan, write, and revise your essay.

Typically, an effective essay will contain a minimum of 300 words. Your essay will be judged on the quality of your writing. This includes the development of your ideas, the organization of your essay, and the quality and accuracy of the language you use to express your ideas.

If you finish your essay before time is up, you may click on Next to end this section. When you are ready to continue, click on the Dismiss Directions icon.

Read the passage. On a piece of paper, take notes on the main points of the reading passage.

Reading Time: 3 minutes

How to stimulate an economy has always been widely debated, but one thing that many economists agree on is that large-scale construction projects have a unique ability to stimulate local economies. And no other type of construction project can have a lasting positive effect on the economy of a community like a shopping center.

It is undeniable that constructing a shopping center will create a great deal of jobs for those people living in the area. Considerable employment opportunities will be created when the actual project is being constructed, and when it is completed, there will be a need to employ thousands more to fill the positions of sales people, maintenance crews, administrators, and many more. Virtually every study that has been conducted shows that shopping centers are a great source of job creation.

Shopping centers also stimulate the growth of other businesses in the community. The convenience of a shopping center allows a consumer to purchase more goods in a centralized area instead of making several small purchases over a much larger area. Furthermore, shopping centers attract consumers from other communities since they might have trouble finding what they need in their own neighborhoods. This behavior provides a great economic stimulus to the area where the shopping center is located for both the businesses in the shopping center and those around it.

Because of the greater number of stores, shopping centers offer substantial diversity, which often encourages consumer spending. A buyer can find any item or product that they seek while visiting a shopping center. It has been shown that when a consumer is presented with more shopping choices, they tend to spend more. This is a win-win situation for both consumers and local businesses. Consumers get what they want, and businesses make more profit.

Listen to the passage. On a piece of paper, take notes on the main points of the listening passage. ²²⁰ 🔊))

Now answer the following question: ²²¹ 🔊))

How does the information in the reading passage contrast with the information in the listening passage?

Response Time: 20 minutes

Turn to pages 609–614 to *assess* the skills used in the test, *score* the test using the Writing Scoring Criteria, and *record* your results.

MINI-TEST 8

READING

20 minutes

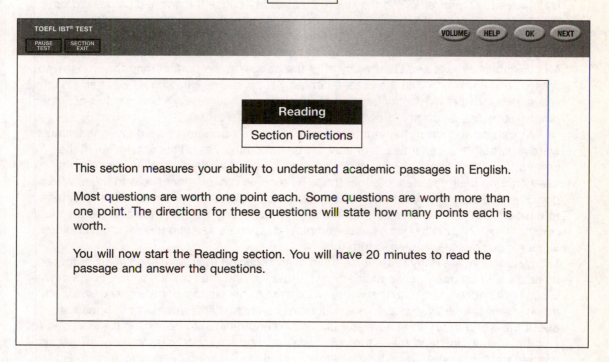

Reading

Section Directions

This section measures your ability to understand academic passages in English.

Most questions are worth one point each. Some questions are worth more than one point. The directions for these questions will state how many points each is worth.

You will now start the Reading section. You will have 20 minutes to read the passage and answer the questions.

Read the passage and answer the questions that follow.

Limners

1▶ The earliest known American painters, who were active in the latter part of the seventeenth century and the early part of the eighteenth century, were described in documents, journals, and letters of the time as *limners.* Most of the paintings created by limners were portraits, and they were unsigned because the finished pieces did not belong to the limners who created them but were instead the possessions of the subjects in the portraits. These works today are named after the subjects portrayed in them, and a particular artist is known only as the creator of a particular portrait; thus a piece is named *Mrs. Elizabeth Freake and Baby Mary* after the people in the portrait, and the limner who created it is known only as the Freake Limner. Art historians who specialize in art from this era have been able to identify clusters of portraits painted by each of a number of limners but, in many cases, do not know the name of the actual artist.

2▶ As can be seen from the fact that portraits created by limners went unsigned, limners were regarded more as artisans or skilled tradesmen than as artists and as such, they earned their living like many did at the time: as itinerant workers moving from town to town offering their services to either those who could pay or, more likely, to those who had goods or services to offer in return. They were able to paint portraits for those desiring to have a tangible representation of a family member for posterity; they also did a variety of other types of painting jobs to stay employed, such as painting the walls of buildings, signs for businesses, and even furniture.

3▶ **9A** Some of the early portraitists most likely received their education in art or trained as artisans in Europe prior to their arrival in America and then trained others in the new world in their craft; because they were working in undeveloped or minimally developed colonial areas, their lives were quite difficult. **9B** They had little access to information about the world of art and supplies were limited and difficult to obtain, so they needed to mix their own paints and make their own brushes and stretched canvasses. **9C** They also needed to be prepared to take on whatever painting jobs were needed to survive. **9D**

4▶ There seem to be two broad categories of painting styles used by the portraitists, the style of the New England limners and the style of the New York limners. The former used a decorative style with flat characters, ones that seemed to lack mass and volume. This is not because the New England limners had no knowledge of painting techniques but was instead because they were using the style of Tudor painting that became popular during the reign of Queen Elizabeth I, a method that included subjects with a two-dimensional woodenness, yet with the numerous highly decorative touches and frills popular in the English court.

5▶ The New York limners had a rather different approach from their New England cousins, and this was because New York had a different background from the rest of New England. Much of New England had been colonized by the English, and thus the basis for the style of the New England limners was that which was popular among the English monarchy and nobility. However, the Dutch had settled the colony of New Amsterdam, and though it became an English colony in 1664 and was renamed New York, the Dutch character and influence was strongly in place during the era of the limners. The New York limners, as a result, were influenced by the Dutch artists of the time rather than the Tudor artists. Dutch art, unlike the more flowery Tudor art, was considerably more sober. In addition, the New York limners lacked the flat portrayals of characters like those from the New England variety, and instead made use of light and shade to create more lifelike portraits.

1. According to the passage, a limner was
   Ⓐ someone who wrote in many documents
   Ⓑ someone who was not respected by the elite
   Ⓒ a portrait artist in the colonial United States
   Ⓓ an artist who refused to sign a work of art

2. Which of the sentences below best expresses the essential information in the highlighted sentence in paragraph 1? *Incorrect* choices change the meaning in important ways or leave out essential information.
   Ⓐ Art historians have been able to identify characteristics in paintings indicating that the paintings were created by limners.
   Ⓑ Artists from the era of limners painted clusters of portraits without knowing whom they were painting.
   Ⓒ People studying art have been able to identify clusters of artists who had painted portraits of the same subjects.
   Ⓓ Certain groups of portraits are known to have been painted by the same limner, though the limner's name is often not known.

3. The word "itinerant" in paragraph 2 is closest in meaning to
   Ⓐ successful
   Ⓑ uneducated
   Ⓒ wandering
   Ⓓ touring

4. What can be inferred about the way that limners earned their living?
   Ⓐ They often did things that were distasteful in order to survive.
   Ⓑ They worked as artisans and skilled tradesmen rather than as artists.
   Ⓒ They could only survive by painting portraits of wealthy families.
   Ⓓ They usually bartered their art in exchange for things they needed to live.

5. The word "posterity" in paragraph 2 is closest in meaning to
   Ⓐ prominent display
   Ⓑ future generations
   Ⓒ social acceptance
   Ⓓ delayed gratification

6. What is true about the living conditions of limners in America?
   Ⓐ A severe lack of resources made becoming a successful limner a challenge.
   Ⓑ Because life was hard, their art could not be very good.
   Ⓒ Working on other jobs to stay alive kept most limners from their art.
   Ⓓ Limners were forced to paint the underdeveloped colonies where they lived.

7. It can be inferred from paragraph 3 that some limners originally from Europe
   Ⓐ would not possibly have had any formal preparation
   Ⓑ were quite knowledgeable about the world of art
   Ⓒ were held in high esteem by the population
   Ⓓ were all formally trained as art instructors

8. The phrase "take on" in paragraph 3 could best be replaced by
   Ⓐ accept
   Ⓑ grab
   Ⓒ allow
   Ⓓ negotiate

9. Look at the four squares [■] that indicate where the following sentence could be added to paragraph 3.

   A formal training in the art of portraiture was not a guarantee for most limners.

   Where would the sentence best fit? Click on a square [■] to add the sentence to the passage.

10. The phrase "the former" in paragraph 4 refers to
    Ⓐ portraitists
    Ⓑ The New England limners
    Ⓒ The New York limners
    Ⓓ two broad categories

11. Why does the author state, "However, the Dutch had settled the colony of New Amsterdam"?
    Ⓐ to provide background information about the New England limners.
    Ⓑ to indicate why the Tudor style of painting was possible.
    Ⓒ to give a reason for the highly flowery Dutch paintings.
    Ⓓ to explain why the style of the New England limner was different.

12.

Directions: The answer choices below are each used to describe one of the groups of limners. Complete the table by matching appropriate answer choices to the groups of limners they are used to describe. TWO of the answer choices will not be used. **This question is worth 3 points** (3 points for 5 correct answers, 2 points for 4 correct answers, 1 point for 3 correct answers, and 0 points for 2, 1, or 0 correct answers).

Only the New York limners	•
	•
Only the New England limners	•
	•
Both the New York and New England limners	•

Answer Choices (choose 5 to complete the table):

(1) Used a style of painting typical at the English court at the time
(2) Painted portraits of Queen Elizabeth I and her courtiers
(3) Were influenced by the Dutch style of painting more than the English
(4) Signed portraits with the name of the subject in them followed by word "limner"
(5) Portraits were two-dimensional and contained many ostentatious adornments
(6) Depicted scenes of the difficult life in the colonial United States of the 17th century
(7) Had a more lifelike representation of its subjects and little to no decorative touches

Turn to pages 591–594 to *diagnose* your errors and *record* your results.

MINI-TEST 8

LISTENING

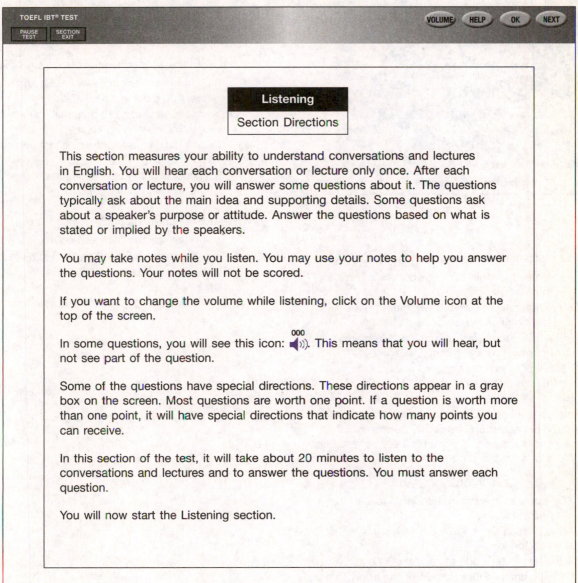

Listening

Section Directions

This section measures your ability to understand conversations and lectures in English. You will hear each conversation or lecture only once. After each conversation or lecture, you will answer some questions about it. The questions typically ask about the main idea and supporting details. Some questions ask about a speaker's purpose or attitude. Answer the questions based on what is stated or implied by the speakers.

You may take notes while you listen. You may use your notes to help you answer the questions. Your notes will not be scored.

If you want to change the volume while listening, click on the Volume icon at the top of the screen.

In some questions, you will see this icon: This means that you will hear, but not see part of the question.

Some of the questions have special directions. These directions appear in a gray box on the screen. Most questions are worth one point. If a question is worth more than one point, it will have special directions that indicate how many points you can receive.

In this section of the test, it will take about 20 minutes to listen to the conversations and lectures and to answer the questions. You must answer each question.

You will now start the Listening section.

Listen as a student consults with an advisor.

223

1. What problem does the student have?
   Ⓐ She has been taking more courses in business than in sociology.
   Ⓑ She has not yet decided whether to declare sociology as her major field of study.
   Ⓒ She has not fulfilled as many requirements for her major as she thought she had.
   Ⓓ She has failed two classes in her major and must repeat them.

2. What is stated about the courses the student has taken? **This question is worth 2 points** (2 points for 3 correct answers, 1 point for 2 correct answers, and 0 points for 1 or 0 correct answers).

   Click on 3 answers.
   Ⓐ One course she thought counted toward her major does not.
   Ⓑ She passed one course but with a grade that was too low.
   Ⓒ She has to take one of her courses again.
   Ⓓ The business course she took can apply to her sociology major.
   Ⓔ There was no way for the student to know that one course was misleadingly labeled.

3. Listen again to part of the passage. Then answer the question.

   What does the advisor mean when he says this:
   Ⓐ "I'm afraid this will be painful for you."
   Ⓑ "I am beginning to lose patience with you."
   Ⓒ "I'm trying to be diplomatic."
   Ⓓ "I'm going to say this directly."

4. Listen again to part of the conversation. Then answer the question.

   What does the advisor mean when he says this:
   Ⓐ "I'm going to check in a few weeks and make sure you're doing what I said."
   Ⓑ "You need to take more personal responsibility for completing your major."
   Ⓒ "I won't have time to see you again to discuss your major."
   Ⓓ "It's important that we trust each other so I can help you with your plan."

5. What is the woman probably going to do?
   Ⓐ Take more elective business courses
   Ⓑ Take the class she failed again next semester
   Ⓒ Wait until later in her studies to retake Research Methods
   Ⓓ Concentrate on the requirements for her major

Listen to a lecture in a chemistry class.

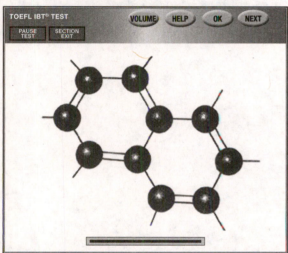

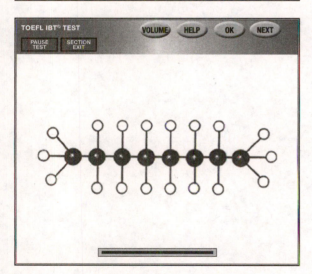

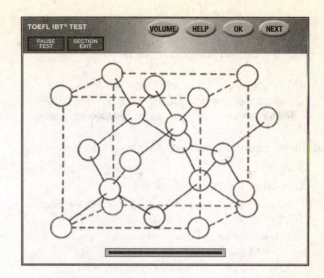

225

6. What is unusual about carbon?
   - Ⓐ The number of compounds it forms
   - Ⓑ The metallic state of the compounds it forms
   - Ⓒ The simplicity of how it forms life
   - Ⓓ The hardness of all the compounds it forms

7. Is each of the statements true about the structure of substances containing carbon? **This question is worth 2 points** (2 points for 4 correct answers, 1 point for 3 correct answers, and 0 points for 2, 1, or 0 correct answers).

For each answer, click in the YES or NO column.		
	YES	**NO**
Graphite has a complex pattern of carbon atoms.		
Soap has a chain of 15–17 atoms.		
Octane has a chain of 8 carbon atoms.		
Diamond has rings of 6 carbon atoms each.		

8. Which two molecules do NOT contain only carbon atoms?

   Click on 2 answers.

   - Ⓐ A graphite molecule
   - Ⓑ An octane molecule
   - Ⓒ A soap molecule
   - Ⓓ A diamond molecule

9. What is NOT true about the uses of molecules containing carbon?

Ⓐ One carbon compound can be used to make soap.

Ⓑ Graphite can be used in pencils.

Ⓒ Octane is the only type of gasoline molecule.

Ⓓ Diamond can be used to cut other substances.

10. Listen again to part of the passage. Then answer the question.

Why does the professor say this: 🔈&#9))

Ⓐ To demonstrate that what he said was wrong

Ⓑ To explain that he needs to leave

Ⓒ To let the class know that he had a good reason for what he said

Ⓓ To indicate that he had previously said something incorrect

11. What overall conclusion can be drawn from the discussion?

Ⓐ Carbon atoms can be part of many extremely different molecules.

Ⓑ Carbon can form molecules only with other carbon atoms.

Ⓒ Carbon must have other substances with it to form molecules.

Ⓓ Carbon atoms attach easily to all other kinds of atoms.

Turn to pages 595–598 to *diagnose* your errors and *record* your results.

MINI-TEST 8

SPEAKING

S_DIR_B

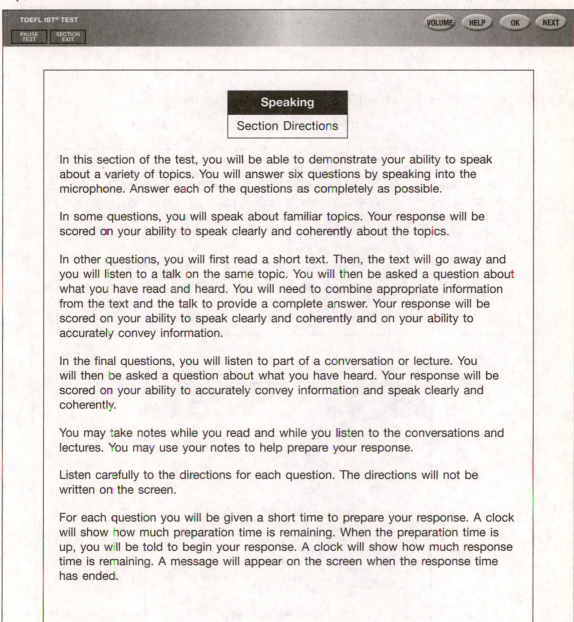

TOEFL IBT® TEST

PAUSE TEST | SECTION EXIT

VOLUME | HELP | OK | NEXT

Speaking
Section Directions

In this section of the test, you will be able to demonstrate your ability to speak about a variety of topics. You will answer six questions by speaking into the microphone. Answer each of the questions as completely as possible.

In some questions, you will speak about familiar topics. Your response will be scored on your ability to speak clearly and coherently about the topics.

In other questions, you will first read a short text. Then, the text will go away and you will listen to a talk on the same topic. You will then be asked a question about what you have read and heard. You will need to combine appropriate information from the text and the talk to provide a complete answer. Your response will be scored on your ability to speak clearly and coherently and on your ability to accurately convey information.

In the final questions, you will listen to part of a conversation or lecture. You will then be asked a question about what you have heard. Your response will be scored on your ability to accurately convey information and speak clearly and coherently.

You may take notes while you read and while you listen to the conversations and lectures. You may use your notes to help prepare your response.

Listen carefully to the directions for each question. The directions will not be written on the screen.

For each question you will be given a short time to prepare your response. A clock will show how much preparation time is remaining. When the preparation time is up, you will be told to begin your response. A clock will show how much response time is remaining. A message will appear on the screen when the response time has ended.

Question 1

Read the question. You have 15 seconds to plan a response and 45 seconds to give your spoken response.

Would you prefer to go to a big party with a lot of people, many of whom you don't know, or a small gathering with only close friends? Use specific reasons and details to support your response.

> Preparation Time: 15 seconds
> Response Time: 45 seconds

Question 2

Read the passage about Freud. You have 45 seconds to read the passage.

> Reading Time: 45 seconds

Freud and Dreams

The psychologist Sigmund Freud felt that dreams came from the pressures of the repressed desires of our deepest subconscious. He felt that as we were awake our social conditioning kept control of our animalistic desires. These desires came out in dreams, but not directly since in their natural forms they were so shocking that they were unacceptable to our conscious minds. Thus for Freud, our dreams represented our minds living out shocking thoughts and murderous fantasies, thus releasing emotional pressure, while expressing them in an indirect and less threatening way.

Now listen to the passage. 🔊)) ²²⁶

Now answer the following question. You have 30 seconds to prepare an answer and 60 seconds to give your spoken response. **227** ◀))

> **Using points from the listening passage, describe the evidence against Freud's theory on the origin of dreams.**

> | |
> |---|
> | Preparation Time: 30 seconds |
> | Response Time: 60 seconds |

Question 3

Listen to the conversation. **228** ◀))

Now answer the following question. You will have 20 seconds to prepare an answer and 60 seconds to give your spoken response. **229** ◀))

> **The students are discussing the man's problem. Describe the problem. Then say which of the solutions you prefer and why.**

> | |
> |---|
> | Preparation Time: 20 seconds |
> | Response Time: 60 seconds |

> Turn to pages 599–608 to *assess* the skills used in the test, *score* the test using the Speaking Scoring Criteria, and *record* your results.

MINI-TEST 8

WRITING

TOEFL IBT® TEST

PAUSE TEST   SECTION EXIT   VOLUME   HELP   OK   NEXT

Writing

Section Directions

This section measures your ability to communicate in writing in an academic environment. There will be two writing tasks.

For the first writing task, you will read a passage and listen to a lecture about an academic topic. Then you will write a response to a question that asks you about the relationship between the lecture and the reading passage.

For the second task, you will demonstrate your ability to write an essay in response to a question that asks you to express and support your opinion about a topic or issue.

Now listen to the directions for the first writing task.

Integrated Writing Directions

For this task, you will first have three minutes to read a passage about an academic topic. You may take notes on the passage if you wish. The passage will then be removed and you will listen to a lecture about the same topic. While you listen, you may also take notes.

Then you will have 20 minutes to write a response to a question that asks you about the relationship between the lecture you heard and the reading passage. Try to answer the question as completely as possible using information from the reading passage and the lecture. The question does not ask you to express your personal opinion. You will be able to see the reading passage again when it is time for you to write. You may use your notes to help you answer the question.

Typically, an effective response will be 150 to 225 words long. Your response will be judged on the quality of your writing and on the completeness and accuracy of the content. If you finish your response before time is up, you may click on Next to go on to the second writing task.

Independent Writing Directions

For this task, you will write an essay in response to a question that asks you to state, explain, and support your opinion on an issue. You will have 30 minutes to plan, write, and revise your essay.

Typically, an effective essay will contain a minimum of 300 words. Your essay will be judged on the quality of your writing. This includes the development of your ideas, the organization of your essay, and the quality and accuracy of the language you use to express your ideas.

If you finish your essay before time is up, you may click on Next to end this section. When you are ready to continue, click on the Dismiss Directions icon.

Read the question. On a piece of paper, take notes on the main points of a response. Then write your response.

Do you agree or disagree with the following statement?
I think there is too much violence in movies.

Give specific reasons and examples to support your response.

| Response Time: 30 minutes |

Turn to pages 609–614 to *assess* the skills used in the test, *score* the test using the Writing Scoring Criteria, and *record* your results.

COMPLETE TEST 1

READING

60 minutes

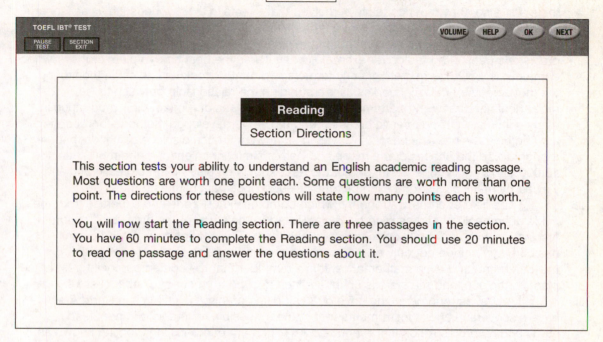

Read the passage and answer the questions that follow.

Paragraph

Prehistoric Astronomers

1▶   Prehistoric peoples most certainly noted with interest the recurring patterns of movements in the sky of such celestial bodies as the sun, the moon, the planets, and the stars. Also, they most certainly perceived that events in their world, such as seasonal fluctuations in weather, which in turn affected the lives of the plants and animals in their world, often related to the movements of the celestial bodies. Because it was important for prehistoric people to predict, for example, when it was the best time to plant crops or when game herds would be migrating, early farmers and hunters took an interest in monitoring the movements of celestial bodies. Understanding the relationship between these movements and recurring patterns of events on Earth was of fundamental importance in many cultures; thus, cultures in areas around the world developed methods for recording astronomical events. The Lascaux Caves in southwest France disclose paintings that are thought to be the phases of the moon and perhaps a lunar calendar dated more than 15,000 years ago. Stonehenge, one of the best-known prehistoric structures in England, is viewed by many as just one example of a celestial observation infrastructure.[1]

2▶   **7A** The field of archeoastronomy, which combines knowledge and expertise from the fields of archeology and astronomy, is dedicated to the study of the prehistoric cultures' fascination with and focus on the skies above them. This field of interrelated specialties has come to include not only seasons and calendars, but also modes of navigation, measurement, and even mathematics. It is a reminder that the contemporary interest in the planets, the sun, and the stars is an inheritance derived from our ancient ancestors.

3▶   **7B** Archeoastronomers who have been studying prehistoric cultures in North America have discovered various instruments that made it possible for prehistoric people to study and record astronomical events. **7C** An alignment of stones in Wyoming known as the Bighorn Medicine Wheel, the remnants of a circular-shaped structure created with wooden posts at Cahoki in Illinois, and specially designed windows in structures of the southwestern United States that allowed the rays of the sun to hit designated marks on inside walls are all believed to be early technologies for monitoring and measuring astronomical events. **7D**

4▶   One particular construction, located in the Chaco Canyon area of New Mexico, has been the subject of considerable attention and discussion among archeologists and astronomers. This mechanism, which is at least 700 years old, consists of large slabs of rock located on top of the flat surface of a high butte[2] that seem to form a place for observation of sorts. What makes it appear to experts to be an observatory is that the slabs of rock are positioned so that shafts of sunlight fall between them and hit spiral markings carved into the side of a rock wall. As the sun changes positions with the progression of the seasons, the shafts of light fall in different places on the markings in the face of the rock wall. Using this system, it must have been possible for early inhabitants of the area to predict upcoming seasonal changes and the events that were based on those changes.

5▶   If the alignment of rocks and rock wall was indeed purposeful, how did the arrangement come to be? A question that has been the focus of considerable discussion is whether the stones were actually placed in their current location by early inhabitants of the region or whether the forces of nature created the arrangement that the inhabitants then used. While some scientists argue that the stones could not have fallen in the current arrangement by mere happenstance and must have been purposefully positioned, others find it hard to believe that the huge stones could have been moved. It is easier to believe that the marks on the rock wall were placed to identify the positions where sunlight shone through the slabs that had fallen naturally. Whether or not these large rocks were positioned by the local population, the structure correlating the positions of the slabs and the markings on the cliff wall represents a remarkably inventive method of registering astronomical events.

GLOSSARY
1. *infrastructure*—building, road, or facility
2. *butte*—a tall hill with steep vertical sides and often a flat top

1. The phrase "related to" in paragraph 1 could best be replaced by
   Ⓐ had the same cause as
   Ⓑ coordinated with
   Ⓒ were caused by
   Ⓓ described

2. It is NOT mentioned in paragraph 1 that prehistoric peoples were interested in
   Ⓐ the movements of the stars
   Ⓑ changes in the weather
   Ⓒ migration patterns of certain animals
   Ⓓ mythology or religion

3. The word "fundamental" in paragraph 1 could best be replaced by
   Ⓐ some
   Ⓑ dependable
   Ⓒ supreme
   Ⓓ intrinsic

4. Which of the following would an archeoastronomer be most likely to study?
   Ⓐ Plans to send a spacecraft to Mars
   Ⓑ Potential remnants of an early civilization's lunar calendar
   Ⓒ Tools used by a prehistoric tribe to grow food
   Ⓓ Geological formations on the Moon

5. The phrase "derived from" in paragraph 2 could best be replaced by
   Ⓐ taken from
   Ⓑ started by
   Ⓒ shared with
   Ⓓ stolen from

6. The author mentions "An alignment of stones in Wyoming," "a circular-shaped structure . . . at Cahoki," and "specially designed windows in structures of the southwestern U.S." in paragraph 3 in order to
   Ⓐ provide proof that archeoastronomers have been studying prehistoric cultures
   Ⓑ provide support for the idea that North American cultures built creative structures
   Ⓒ provide evidence that certain astronomical events have not changed over time
   Ⓓ provide examples of ways that prehistoric peoples monitored occurrences in the sky

7. Look at the four squares [■] that indicate where the following sentence could be added to paragraphs 3 or 4.

   This apparent understanding of certain aspects of astronomy by many prehistoric cultures is of great academic interest today.

   Where would the sentence best fit? Click on a square [■] to add the sentence to the passage.

8. What is stated in paragraph 4 about the construction in Chaco Canyon?
   Ⓐ It was created from a single piece of stone.
   Ⓑ It prevents sunlight from entering the area.
   Ⓒ It was built before the fourteenth century.
   Ⓓ It is located in a canyon.

9. The phrase "of sorts" in paragraph 4 is closest in meaning to
   Ⓐ of opportunity
   Ⓑ of some kind
   Ⓒ of the past
   Ⓓ of fate

10. The word "them" in paragraph 4 refers to
    Ⓐ experts
    Ⓑ slabs
    Ⓒ shafts
    Ⓓ markings

11. Which of the sentences below best expresses the essential information in the highlighted sentence in paragraph 5? *Incorrect* choices change the meaning in important ways or leave out essential information.
    Ⓐ One issue is whether the stones were positioned by nature or by people.
    Ⓑ Early inhabitants often discussed where the stones should be placed.
    Ⓒ The current location of the stones was chosen because it provides the most natural setting.
    Ⓓ There is much discussion about how often early inhabitants moved the stones.

12. The word "happenstance" in paragraph 5 is closest in meaning to
    Ⓐ standing
    Ⓑ event
    Ⓒ order
    Ⓓ chance

13.

This passage discusses the study of astronomy as it refers to prehistoric cultures in North America.

-
-
-

Answer Choices (choose 3 to complete the chart):

(1) The structure at Chaco Canyon was most likely used for something other than astronomy.

(2) Prehistoric cultures in North America were not as advanced in their study of astronomy as were cultures in other parts of the world.

(3) One structure used by one prehistoric culture to monitor astronomical events was either discovered or created by the culture.

(4) Prehistoric cultures in North America created devices to monitor astronomical events.

(5) The Bighorn Medicine Wheel was constructed with stones.

(6) Prehistoric cultures in North America probably understood the relationship between astronomy and their daily lives.

READING 2

Read the passage and answer the questions that follow.

Paragraph

Truman and the Railroads

1▶   The period following World War II was filled with a succession of crises as the United States focused on the difficulty of postwar conversion to a peacetime economy. A threatened railroad strike in 1946 was one of many crises that led to increased attention to the conflicting relationships between government interests, business interests, and organized labor interests.

2▶   Organized labor, which had fared well during the war years of 1939–1945, now faced severe problems because of the swift demobilization and discharge from military service of 13 million service personnel following the war. Demobilization provided a sudden influx of new people looking for jobs. In addition, the industrial conversions from wartime to peacetime production were destabilizing to the economy and the success of economic recovery was at best worrisome. During late 1945 and early 1946, a record wave of labor disputes and strikes hit the United States. At the height of the conflicts, more than 500 strikes were under way, some of them in industries highly critical to the overall U.S. economy, including coal, steel, cars, and oil. And additional strikes and disputes were expected. When a national strike was threatened by railroad workers in the spring of 1946, the government moved in to resolve the issues, believing that the U.S. economic recovery would be threatened were a railroad strike to take place.

3▶   President Harry S. Truman had dealt patiently with the labor problems until the spring of 1946. Throughout his political career, Truman had been a friend of organized labor and his party had been strongly supported by labor in national elections. When the railroad strike was first threatened, he called for a 60-day mediation period while the differences, particularly the main issue of a wage hike for railroad workers, were negotiated between railroad management and labor. By April, 18 of the 20 unions related to the railroads had arrived at an agreement. However, the remaining unions, the Brotherhood of Railroad Trainmen and the Brotherhood of Locomotive Engineers, which together controlled 280,000 workers and were essential to the operation of the railroads, were dissatisfied and set a date to strike.

4▶   The day before the strike deadline, Truman's patience wore thin, and he signed an executive order authorizing government seizure of the railroads. **21A** Under threat of having the government take over operation of the railroads, the two unions in question agreed to a five-day delay before striking. **21B** Truman also suggested an 18.5-cent per hour pay raise for railroad workers. **21C** The suggestion was rejected by the unions. **21D** As the strike deadline approached, negotiations remained unsuccessful. The strike began as scheduled and had an immediate impact; of the country's 200,000 trains, only a few hundred remained in operation. Infuriated, Truman took to the radio waves and delivered a burning speech to the public; two days later, he delivered a speech to Congress blasting the striking workers and urging Congress to take unprecedented steps to break the strike, including a request for approval to draft striking workers into military service. As Truman was delivering the speech, he was handed a note stating that the strike had been settled.

5▶   Even though the conflict was resolved, deep issues had been raised over the role government should play in disputes between businesses and organized labor. Truman's proposal to use the federal government to draft strikers into the armed forces brought this question to the fore. Although management was pleased with the toughness that Truman had shown and many citizens were pleased that disruption of the economy had been avoided, many expressed concern about the constitutionality of Congress taking such a step. The draft provision was eventually removed from Truman's proposal.

6▶   The Labor Management Relations Act (also known as the Taft-Hartley Act) was enacted in the year following the strike to restrict the activities and power of labor unions. The results of the act, however, were ambiguous. Railroad and steel strikes occurred again in 1950, near the end of Truman's presidency. Truman's intervention at that time was significant, as the president had just ordered American troops into a war. Truman ordered an emergency board to negotiate a settlement, but the unions again rejected the recommendations. The president resolved to have the U.S. Army seize the nation's railroads. Not until 1952 did the unions accept the administration's terms and go back to work and return the railroads to their owners.

14. The phrase "fared well" in paragraph 2 is closest in meaning to
   Ⓐ recovered from illness
   Ⓑ won battles
   Ⓒ made good wages
   Ⓓ benefitted

15. According to paragraph 2, in late 1945 and early 1946
   Ⓐ there were labor problems because too many workers were in the military
   Ⓑ too many people were leaving the military and entering the workforce
   Ⓒ there were 500 strikes in the railroad industry
   Ⓓ there was a very high number of strikes in critical industries

16. The phrase "critical to" in paragraph 2 is closest in meaning to
   Ⓐ unwelcomed in
   Ⓑ important for
   Ⓒ unhappy with
   Ⓓ angered by

17. According to paragraph 3, it is NOT true that all the railroad workers
   Ⓐ were in favor of the strike
   Ⓑ were interested in higher pay
   Ⓒ in two unions set a strike date
   Ⓓ turned down Truman's offer of a pay raise

18. Why does the author mention "280,000 workers" in paragraph 3?
   Ⓐ to indicate how many workers were opposed to the strike
   Ⓑ to demonstrate that the railroads were not really a critical industry
   Ⓒ to illustrate the total number of U.S. railroad workers
   Ⓓ to reinforce the seriousness of the strike threat that remained

19. The phrase "wore thin" in paragraph 4 is closest in meaning to
   Ⓐ was extended
   Ⓑ decreased
   Ⓒ increased
   Ⓓ lost weight

20. What was the most important stated reason for Truman's actions to keep the railroads operating?
   Ⓐ Many people rode the trains to and from work.
   Ⓑ Commercial airlines and a national highway system did not yet exist.
   Ⓒ He didn't like unions and organized labor deciding government policy.
   Ⓓ A railroad stoppage would create problems for the American economy.

21. Look at the four squares [■] that indicate where the following sentence could be added to paragraph 4.

   This was an offer that was considerably more generous than previous offers.

   Where would the sentence best fit? Click on a square [■] to add the sentence to the passage.

22. The word "steps" in paragraph 4 could best be replaced by
   Ⓐ paces
   Ⓑ measures
   Ⓒ stairs
   Ⓓ suggestions

23. It can be inferred from paragraph 4 that
   Ⓐ Truman actually drafted striking workers into the military
   Ⓑ Congress passed a law allowing the drafting of striking workers
   Ⓒ it was the threat of drafting strikers that ended the strike
   Ⓓ Truman was actually opposed to drafting workers into the military

24. Which of the sentences below best expresses the essential information in the highlighted sentence in paragraph 5? *Incorrect* choices change the meaning in important ways or leave out essential information.
   Ⓐ Though some were pleased that Truman had kept the economy going, there was concern about how he had done it.
   Ⓑ During the 1946 strike, the economy was disrupted, and Congress was forced to take steps to fix it.
   Ⓒ Because of the effects of the 1946 strike on the citizens of the country, it was necessary for Congress to make changes to the Constitution.
   Ⓓ Management took tough actions during the strike; as a result, Congress expressed concern about the steps that management had taken.

25. Which of the sentences below best expresses the essential information in the highlighted sentence in paragraph 6? *Incorrect* choices change the meaning in important ways or leave out essential information.

  (A) The strike situation lasted two years.
  (B) The strike situation began again two years later.
  (C) Truman ended a strike in 1950, but it took two years to get the railroads operating normally again.
  (D) Truman did not want to give the railroads back to the owners until after the war.

26.

Directions: An introductory sentence for a brief summary of the passage is provided below. Complete the summary by selecting the THREE answer choices that express the most important ideas in the passage. Some sentences do not belong in the summary because they express ideas that are not presented in the passage or are minor ideas in the passage. **This question is worth 2 points** (2 points for 3 correct answers, 1 point for 2 correct answers, and 0 points for 1 or 0 correct answers).

This passage discusses harsh steps Truman took with the railroads.

-
-
-

Answer Choices (choose 3 to complete the chart):

(1) He made himself president of the railroad.
(2) He enabled the government to take control of the railroads.
(3) He brought wartime veterans in to work for the railroads.
(4) He suggested putting striking workers into the military.
(5) He passed a law making strikes by railroad workers illegal.
(6) He made strong speeches arguing against a railroad strike.

Read the passage and answer the questions that follow.

Paragraph
Mathematical Bases

1▶   The system of numeration that is now most widely used is a base-10 system with the following characteristics: each number from 1 to 10 as well as the powers of 10 (such as 100 or 1,000) has a distinctive name, and the names of the other numbers tend to be combinations of the names of the numbers from 1 to 10 and the powers of 10.

2▶   In most Indo-European, Semitic, and Mongolian languages, the numerical systems have a decimal base and conform at least approximately to this theoretical model. The almost universal adoption of the base-10 numerical system was undoubtedly influenced by the fact that humans have ten digits on their hands (fingers), since people most likely first learned to count on their fingers. Though these numerical systems are convenient for reasons of anatomy (body structure), they are sometimes not as mathematically practical; computers, for example, use a base-2 system. Some mathematicians suggest a base-11 or base-12 might be better since 11 is a prime number (only divisible by 1 and 11) and 12 is divisible by more numbers than 10.

3▶   Base-10 numerical systems were not the only systems based on anatomical parts: there were also systems based on 5 and 20. While it is difficult to find a number system that is a purely base-5, or quinary system, it is possible to find number systems that have traces of groupings by fives, and these systems are most likely what remains of older systems that developed from counting the fingers on one hand. In a quinary system, there are distinct units for numbers 1 through 5, but the words for numbers 6 through 9 are compounds of five-and-one, five-and-two, five-and-three, and so on. Remnants of quinary systems can be found today only in historical records of ancient languages, such as that of the early Sumerians.

4▶   Examples of base-20, or vigesimal, systems, most likely developed from counting by making use of all the digits, are more common than are those of base-5 systems. A number of early cultures, including the Mayans, the Aztecs, and the Celts, developed numerical systems that involved counting by 20s. The Mayan calendar had 20 months of 20 days each, and the Mayans counted years in terms of 20-year periods rather than decades; study of the Aztec numbers for 1 through 20 shows that the names of the first five numbers are related to the fingers of one hand, the names of the next five numbers are related to the fingers of the other hand, the names of the numbers 11 through 16 are related to the toes on one foot, and the names of numbers 16 through 20 are related to the toes on the other foot. In Celtic languages, counting is also done by 20s, and a number of other European languages maintain remnants of this characteristic. In French and Latin, the words for 20 are clearly remnants of a vigesimal system in that they are distinct words not derived from words for "two-tens," which would occur in a purely base-10 system, and the way of expressing the number 80 is by counting by 20s and saying "four-twenties." In English, the way of counting by 20s was to use the word "score"; this method of counting was commonly used by Shakespeare and was still in use at the time of Abraham Lincoln, who opened his famous address at Gettysburg by saying: "Four score and seven years ago. . . ."

5▶   Some cultures had systems based upon 60, a system with a major drawback in that it requires 60 distinct words for numbers 1 through 60. **35A** In Sumerian, Babylonian, Greek, and Arab cultures, for example, the sexagesimal system was a scholarly numerical system. **35B** Sexagesimal systems were obviously not developed based on body parts, and numerous theories have been raised to explain how such systems came about, but it is not known conclusively which of these theories is correct. **35C** One hypothesis is that 60 was chosen as the base because it is the lowest number with a great many divisors (1, 2, 3, 4, 5, 6, 10, 12, 15, 20, 30, 60). **35D** Another theory provides a more natural explanation for the use of 60 as a base: the approximate number of days in a year is 360, which supposedly led to the use of 360 degrees in a circle and was reduced to the more manageable 60, which is one-sixth of 360.

6▶ Computer technology has brought about a new base, the binary system with the base-2. But because this system developed from an electrical switch which can be "on" or "off," the numerals used are 0 and 1. This is about the only system where "0" represents both a value and the absence of a value. In other words, the absence of a value (0 or "off") is as an important a piece of information as a value (1 or "on"). But in the world outside the computer chip, binary systems are extremely difficult to use as every number would have to consist only of 0s and 1s.

27. Which of the sentences below best expresses the essential information in the highlighted sentence in paragraph 2? *Incorrect* choices change the meaning in important ways or leave out essential information.

(A) Different bases are required for systems without body parts.

(B) Computers cannot count to 10 easily.

(C) Mathematicians agree that a numerical system based on a number with the most divisors would be the best system.

(D) Either base-11 or base-12 might be preferable, but for opposite reasons, and even a base-2 system is useful.

28. The author begins paragraph 3 by mentioning "Base-10 numerical systems" in order to

(A) introduce a new topic in paragraph 3

(B) indicate that base-10 systems are based on anatomy, while other systems are not

(C) emphasize that base-10 systems were less common than other systems

(D) relate the topic of paragraph 3 to the topic of paragraph 2

29. The word "traces" in paragraph 3 could best be replaced by

(A) remnants

(B) tracks

(C) results

(D) processes

30. The word "digits" in paragraph 4 could best be replaced by

(A) hands

(B) numbers

(C) fingers and toes

(D) measurements

31. The phrase "this characteristic" in paragraph 4 refers to

(A) using Celtic words

(B) counting by 20s

(C) relating the names of numbers to the toes

(D) counting on the toes of one foot

32. The passage indicates that all of the following languages show characteristics of a vigesimal system EXCEPT

(A) Latin

(B) Celtic

(C) English

(D) Greek

33. It can be determined from paragraph 4 that four score and seven is equal to

(A) 47

(B) 87

(C) 327

(D) 749

34. The word "drawback" in paragraph 5 is closest in meaning to

(A) disadvantage

(B) attraction

(C) reversal

(D) interest

35. Look at the four squares [■] that indicate where the following sentence could be added to paragraph 5.

It was one that was used mainly for scientific study and analysis.

Where would the sentence best fit? Click on a square [■] to add the sentence to the passage.

36. The word "natural explanation" in paragraph 5 is closest in meaning to

(A) expected meaning

(B) popular description

(C) logical conclusion

(D) based on the physical world

37. The number *25* would most likely be

(A) a distinct number in a quinary system

(B) a variation of "five-fives" in a decimal system

(C) a variation of "twenty-plus-five" in a vigesimal system

(D) a variation of "two-tens-plus-five" in a sexagesimal system

38.

Directions: Select the appropriate phrases from the answer choices, and match them to the numerical systems to which they relate. TWO of the answer choices will not be used. **This question is worth 3 points** (3 points for 5 correct answers, 2 points for 4 correct answers, 1 point for 3 correct answers, and 0 points for 2, 1, or 0 correct answers).	
decimal system	• •
vigesimal system	•
sexagesimal system	• •

Answer Choices (choose 5 to complete the table):

(1) Most likely based on the fingers of one hand
(2) The most commonly used system
(3) Most likely based on the fingers and toes
(4) Most likely not based on the fingers and toes
(5) Most likely based on the toes on both feet
(6) Not known to have been used by the masses in any culture
(7) Most likely based on the fingers on both hands

Turn to pages 591–594 to *diagnose* your errors and *record* your results.

COMPLETE TEST 1

LISTENING

60 minutes

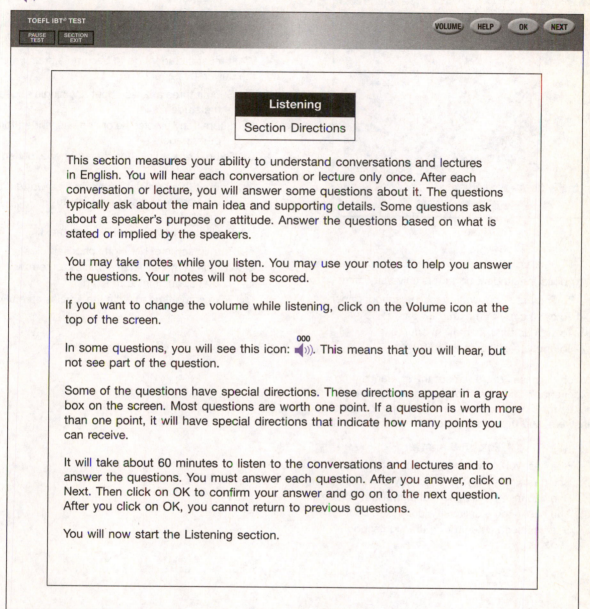

TOEFL IBT® TEST

PAUSE TEST | SECTION EXIT

VOLUME | HELP | OK | NEXT

Listening

Section Directions

This section measures your ability to understand conversations and lectures in English. You will hear each conversation or lecture only once. After each conversation or lecture, you will answer some questions about it. The questions typically ask about the main idea and supporting details. Some questions ask about a speaker's purpose or attitude. Answer the questions based on what is stated or implied by the speakers.

You may take notes while you listen. You may use your notes to help you answer the questions. Your notes will not be scored.

If you want to change the volume while listening, click on the Volume icon at the top of the screen.

In some questions, you will see this icon: 🔊))). This means that you will hear, but not see part of the question.

Some of the questions have special directions. These directions appear in a gray box on the screen. Most questions are worth one point. If a question is worth more than one point, it will have special directions that indicate how many points you can receive.

It will take about 60 minutes to listen to the conversations and lectures and to answer the questions. You must answer each question. After you answer, click on Next. Then click on OK to confirm your answer and go on to the next question. After you click on OK, you cannot return to previous questions.

You will now start the Listening section.

Questions 1–5 230

Listen as a student consults with a university office worker.

231

1. Why does the student go to this university office?
   - (A) To find out about writing for the school paper
   - (B) To get a copy of the student paper
   - (C) To sign up for a journalism course
   - (D) To apply for a job as an editor

2. Which of these are true about the student's experience? **This question is worth 2 points** (2 points for 3 correct answers, 1 point for 2 correct answers, and 0 points for 1 or 0 correct answers).

   ### Click on 3 answers.
   - (A) She has worked on the high school paper.
   - (B) She has worked on the university school paper.
   - (C) She has taken a high school journalism course.
   - (D) She has taken a university journalism course.
   - (E) She has been an editor on the high school paper.

3. Listen again to part of the passage. Then answer the question.

   Why does the office worker say this:
   - (A) To try to convince the student to change her mind
   - (B) To verify that he understood the student accurately
   - (C) To encourage the student
   - (D) To correct something he just said

4. What must a student do to become a staff writer on the university paper?
   - (A) Submit three articles about any single aspect of the student's life
   - (B) Submit any articles he or she has written for other papers
   - (C) Submit one article about his or her experience as a writer
   - (D) Submit three articles he or she has written about different aspects of student life

5. What will the student most likely do next?
   - (A) Turn in some of her high school articles
   - (B) Turn in some university articles tomorrow
   - (C) Forget about joining the paper
   - (D) Take some time to write the articles carefully

Listen to a discussion from a geography class.

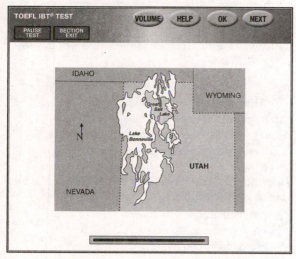

²³³

6. What is the instructor trying to accomplish?

   Ⓐ She is outlining the history of a particular area.

   Ⓑ She is describing how different types of lakes function.

   Ⓒ She is comparing and contrasting two related lakes.

   Ⓓ She is explaining how two different lakes developed distinctly.

7. When did Lake Bonneville come into existence?

   Ⓐ 10,000 years ago

   Ⓑ 100,000 years ago

   Ⓒ 1,000,000 years ago

   Ⓓ 10,000,000 years ago

8. Listen again to part of the passage. Then answer the question.

   What does the instructor mean when she says this: ◀))

   Ⓐ "Take more time to answer if you want."

   Ⓑ "I think your answer is not correct."

   Ⓒ "I didn't hear you. Can you repeat, please?"

   Ⓓ "I think you're not very sure about your answer."

9. Is each of these true according to the lecture? **This question is worth 2 points** (2 points for 4 correct answers, 1 point for 3 correct answers, and 0 points for 2, 1, or 0 correct answers).

For each answer, click in the YES or NO column.	YES	NO
Lake Bonneville is a 20,000 square-mile lake.		
The Great Salt Lake is a freshwater lake.		
Lake Bonneville is older than the Great Salt Lake.		
The Great Salt Lake has no outlet.		

10. What is stated about the Weber, the Bear, and the Jordan Rivers?

   Click on 2 answers.

   Ⓐ They feed into the Great Salt Lake.

   Ⓑ They carry deposits out of the Great Salt Lake.

   Ⓒ They are saltier than the Great Salt Lake.

   Ⓓ They deposit a million tons of minerals and salts into the Great Salt Lake each year.

11. How much salt has built up in the Great Salt Lake?

   Ⓐ 6 tons

   Ⓑ 600 tons

   Ⓒ 6 million tons

   Ⓓ 6 billion tons

Questions 12–17 ²³⁴

Listen to a discussion by a group of students taking a business class.

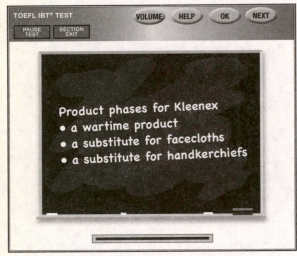

²³⁵

12. Why are the students meeting?
- Ⓐ They are reviewing class lecture notes.
- Ⓑ They are preparing for a presentation.
- Ⓒ They are working on a paper.
- Ⓓ They are preparing for an exam.

13. Listen again to part of the discussion. Then answer the question.

Why does the man say this:
- Ⓐ He thinks the marketing of the products is not as important as the history.
- Ⓑ He is afraid the other students do not know what course they are taking.

- Ⓒ He is concerned that the presentation does not have the correct focus.
- Ⓓ He would like to remind the others that they are taking two different courses.

14. Drag the appropriate explanation of the period of time that each product was associated with to the box below the product. **This question is worth 2 points** (2 points for 3 correct answers, 1 point for 2 correct answers, and 0 points for 1 or 0 correct answers).

> Click on a phrase. Then drag it to the space where it belongs. Each answer will be used one time only.

Were associated with the period before 1920	Were associated with the period in the 1920s	Were associated with the period in the 1930s
Facecloths	**Bandages**	**Handkerchiefs**

15. What was the situation at Kimberly-Clark at the end of World War I?

> Click on 2 answers.

- Ⓐ It had a surplus of its product.
- Ⓑ It needed to develop a new product.
- Ⓒ It no longer needed to market its product.
- Ⓓ It needed to begin marketing its product.

16. How did Kimberly-Clark learn that its product had a use as a handkerchief?
- Ⓐ From customer letters
- Ⓑ From research scientists
- Ⓒ From marketing experts
- Ⓓ From famous actresses

17. Drag the appropriate description of each marketing strategy to the box below the product that it was associated with. **This question is worth 2 points** (2 points for 3 correct answers, 1 point for 2 correct answers, and 0 points for 1 or 0 correct answers).

> Click on a phrase. Then drag it to the space where it belongs. Each answer will be used one time only.

Were associated with consumer testing	Were associated with no market strategy	Were associated with famous actresses
Facecloths	**Bandages**	**Handkerchiefs**

Questions 18–22 ²³⁶

Listen as a student consults with a professor.

237

18. Why does the student go to see the professor?
    - Ⓐ To talk about how to prepare for a coming exam
    - Ⓑ To figure out why she did not do well on an exam
    - Ⓒ To discuss the answer to an exam question
    - Ⓓ To find out how the professor wants her to evaluate information

19. How did the student most likely prepare for the exam?
    - Ⓐ She did not study at all.
    - Ⓑ She studied only a little.
    - Ⓒ She spent a lot of time memorizing information.
    - Ⓓ She never learned how to study.

20. What problem did the student have with the question about steps in the process?
    - Ⓐ She did not know what the process was.
    - Ⓑ She did not know what the steps in the process were.
    - Ⓒ She did not list all of the steps in the process.
    - Ⓓ She failed to show the strengths and weaknesses of the steps in the process.

21. What problem did the student have with the question about theories?
    - Ⓐ She did not know what the theories were.
    - Ⓑ She did not clearly show the similarities and differences in the theories.
    - Ⓒ She stated incorrect information about the theories.
    - Ⓓ She clearly described both of the theories.

22. Which exam question would this professor most likely use?
    - Ⓐ What are the key points of a policy?
    - Ⓑ Who supports a policy and who does not?
    - Ⓒ What are the strengths and weaknesses of a policy?
    - Ⓓ When was a policy developed and put into practice?

Questions 23–28

Listen to a lecture in an American history class.

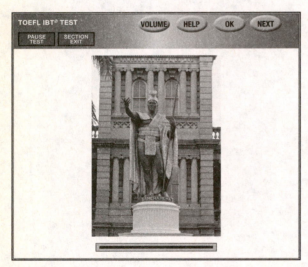

239

23. What does the lecturer mainly discuss?
    - (A) The role of Captain Cook in the history of Hawaii
    - (B) How the monarchy in Hawaii came to be
    - (C) Events leading up to the end of the Hawaiian monarchy
    - (D) The queen who built up the Hawaiian monarchy

24. Why does the lecturer most likely mention King Kamehameha and Captain Cook?
    - (A) They played important roles in the history of Hawaii leading up to Liliuokalani.
    - (B) They succeeded in convincing Liliuokalani to change what she was doing.
    - (C) They were both instrumental in causing the monarchy of Hawaii to fall.
    - (D) They were both in Hawaii at the same time that the monarchy was established there.

25. What does the professor say about James Cook?
    - (A) He was the Earl of Sandwich.
    - (B) He fought to unite the islands under one king.
    - (C) He served as one of the kings of Hawaii.
    - (D) He named the islands after a British nobleman.

26. What did Liliuokalani believe, according to the professor?
    - (A) That the monarchy should end
    - (B) That the monarch's power should be limited
    - (C) That someone else should be the monarch
    - (D) That the monarch should have complete authority to rule

27. Which of the following did NOT happen to Liliuokalani?

Ⓐ She became queen in 1891.
Ⓑ She ruled Hawaii until the end of her life.
Ⓒ She received a pension from the government.
Ⓓ She was removed from power.

28. In the talk, the professor discusses a series of events in the history of Hawaii. Summarize the sequence by putting the events in the correct order. **This question is worth 2 points** (2 points for 4 correct answers, 1 point for 3 or 2 correct answers, and 0 points for 1 or 0 correct answers).

> Click on a sentence. Then drag it to the space where it belongs. Use each sentence only once.

The monarchy disappeared.
Kamehameha became king.
The islands had different monarchs.
Liliuokalani became queen.

1. _____
2. _____
3. _____
4. _____

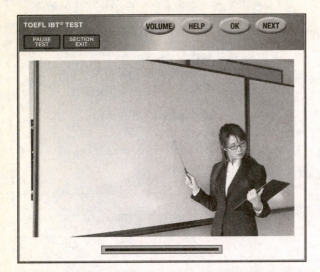

Listen to a lecture in a science class.

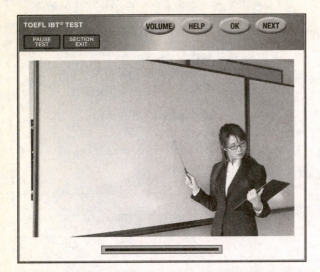

241
🔊))

29. What is the main topic of the lecture?
   Ⓐ The causes of an accident
   Ⓑ The history of a nuclear power plant
   Ⓒ An accident and its effects
   Ⓓ The construction of the reactors at Three-Mile Island

30. How many pressurized water reactors are there at Three-Mile Island?
   Ⓐ One
   Ⓑ Two
   Ⓒ Three
   Ⓓ Four

31. What does the lecturer say about the PWRs during the accident?
   Ⓐ There were no problems with the PWRs.
   Ⓑ There was a problem with only one of the PWRs.
   Ⓒ There were problems with one PWR after another.
   Ⓓ There were problems with more than one PWR.

32. Did each of these contribute to the accident discussed in the lecture? **This question is worth 2 points** (2 points for 4 correct answers, 1 point for 3 correct answers, and 0 points for 2, 1, or 0 correct answers).

For each answer, click in the YES or NO column.		
	YES	NO
A cooling valve was stuck closed.		
Instruments were misread.		
The emergency cooling was turned on.		
A partial meltdown occurred.		

33. What is stated in the lecture about a complete meltdown?
   Ⓐ One occurred at Three-Mile Island.
   Ⓑ One occurs if uranium begins to melt.
   Ⓒ It requires the emergency water cooling system to be turned on.
   Ⓓ It involves the total meltdown of the uranium in the fuel core.

34. How does the lecturer seem to feel about the accident at Three-Mile Island?
   Ⓐ It was not at all serious.
   Ⓑ Its seriousness was extremely exaggerated.
   Ⓒ It was not as serious as it could have been.
   Ⓓ It was quite catastrophic.

Turn to pages 595–598 to *diagnose* your errors and *record* your results.

COMPLETE TEST 1

SPEAKING

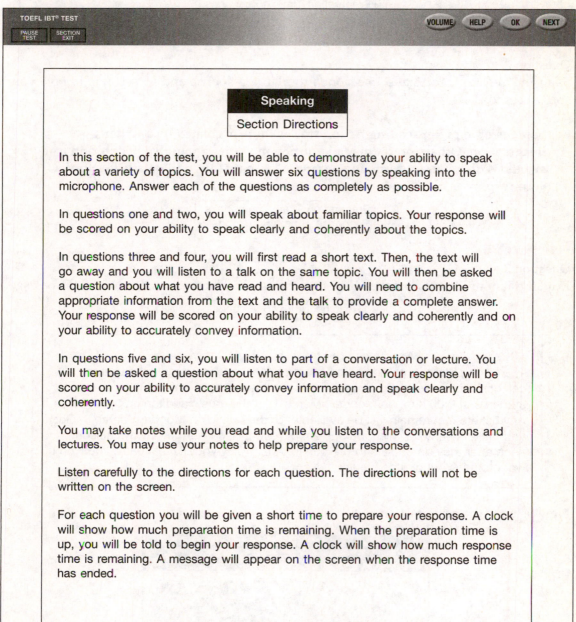

TOEFL IBT® TEST

PAUSE TEST   SECTION EXIT

VOLUME   HELP   OK   NEXT

Speaking

Section Directions

In this section of the test, you will be able to demonstrate your ability to speak about a variety of topics. You will answer six questions by speaking into the microphone. Answer each of the questions as completely as possible.

In questions one and two, you will speak about familiar topics. Your response will be scored on your ability to speak clearly and coherently about the topics.

In questions three and four, you will first read a short text. Then, the text will go away and you will listen to a talk on the same topic. You will then be asked a question about what you have read and heard. You will need to combine appropriate information from the text and the talk to provide a complete answer. Your response will be scored on your ability to speak clearly and coherently and on your ability to accurately convey information.

In questions five and six, you will listen to part of a conversation or lecture. You will then be asked a question about what you have heard. Your response will be scored on your ability to accurately convey information and speak clearly and coherently.

You may take notes while you read and while you listen to the conversations and lectures. You may use your notes to help prepare your response.

Listen carefully to the directions for each question. The directions will not be written on the screen.

For each question you will be given a short time to prepare your response. A clock will show how much preparation time is remaining. When the preparation time is up, you will be told to begin your response. A clock will show how much response time is remaining. A message will appear on the screen when the response time has ended.

Question 1
Read the question. You have 15 seconds to plan an answer and 45 seconds to give your spoken response.

What is the most important quality or character feature a person should exhibit? Use reasons and details to support your response.

> Preparation Time: 15 seconds
> Response Time: 45 seconds

Question 2
Read the question. You have 15 seconds to plan a response and 45 seconds to give your spoken response.

Some people prefer reading fiction stories that are created by a writer's imagination. Others prefer to read nonfiction stories about real people and true events. Which literary form do you prefer? Use reasons and details to support your response.

> Preparation Time: 15 seconds
> Response Time: 45 seconds

Question 3
Read the announcement from the Music Department. You have 45 seconds to read the passage.

> Reading Time: 45 seconds

> ### *Announcement from the Music Department*
> The Spring Show is an annual program of vocal and instrumental music to celebrate the season of spring. Tickets for this fantastic event will go on sale for students at 9:00 a.m. on Monday, March 1, at the music auditorium ticket office. Any tickets that remain will be available for the public on Monday, March 8. Get your tickets early for this fabulous annual event because they always sell out soon after they go on sale to the public. Again, buy your tickets early. You won't want to miss out on this fabulous event.

Now listen to the conversation. 🔊 242

Now answer the following question. You have 30 seconds to prepare an answer and 60 seconds to give your spoken response. ²⁴³ 🔊))

> Preparation Time: 30 seconds
> Response Time: 60 seconds

The man expresses his opinion about purchasing tickets to the show announced in the notice. Explain his opinion and the reasons he gives for that opinion.

Question 4

Read the passage about communication. You have 45 seconds to read the passage.

> Reading Time: 45 seconds

Great Ape Communication

Quite a few scientific studies have been conducted on communication by the great apes, a group of primates composed of gorillas, chimpanzees, and orangutans. What has been concluded in these studies is that the great apes communicate in a variety of ways that include, but are not limited to, facial expressions, gestures with their appendages, and a variety of calls. The large primates use this wide variety of methods for communication to express a broad range of awareness to other members of their group, such as anger, fear, approaching danger, dominance over the group, or even acceptance of members into that group.

Now listen to the passage. ²⁴⁴ 🔊))

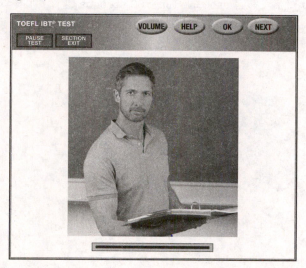

Now answer the following question. You have 30 seconds to prepare an answer and 60 seconds to give your spoken response. ²⁴⁵ 🔊))

How does the information in the listening passage add to what is explained in the reading passage?

> Preparation Time: 30 seconds
> Response Time: 60 seconds

Question 5
Listen to the conversation. ²⁴⁶ 🔊

Now answer the following question. You will have 20 seconds to prepare an answer and 60 seconds to give your spoken response. ²⁴⁷ 🔊

The students discuss several possible solutions to the woman's problem. Explain the problem. Then state which of the solutions to the problem you think is best and why.

Preparation Time: 20 seconds
Response Time: 60 seconds

Question 6

Listen to the passage. Then respond to the question. **248**))

Now answer the following question. You have 20 seconds to prepare an answer and 60 seconds to give your spoken response. **249**))

Using points and examples from the lecture, explain the economic policy of mercantilism.

> Preparation Time: 20 seconds
> Response Time: 60 seconds

> Turn to pages 599–608 to *assess* the skills used in the test, *score* the test using the Speaking Scoring Criteria, and *record* your results.

COMPLETE TEST 1

WRITING

W_DIR_F

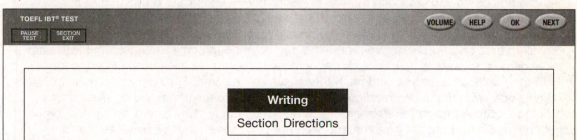

Writing

Section Directions

This section measures your ability to communicate in writing in an academic environment. There will be two writing tasks.

For the first writing task, you will read a passage and listen to a lecture about an academic topic. Then you will write a response to a question that asks you about the relationship between the lecture and the reading passage.

For the second task, you will demonstrate your ability to write an essay in response to a question that asks you to express and support your opinion about a topic or issue.

Now listen to the directions for the first writing task.

Integrated Writing Directions

For this task, you will first have three minutes to read a passage about an academic topic. You may take notes on the passage if you wish. The passage will then be removed and you will listen to a lecture about the same topic. While you listen, you may also take notes.

Then you will have 20 minutes to write a response to a question that asks you about the relationship between the lecture you heard and the reading passage. Try to answer the question as completely as possible using information from the reading passage and the lecture. The question does not ask you to express your personal opinion. You will be able to see the reading passage again when it is time for you to write. You may use your notes to help you answer the question.

Typically, an effective response will be 150 to 225 words long. Your response will be judged on the quality of your writing and on the completeness and accuracy of the content. If you finish your response before time is up, you may click on Next to go on to the second writing task.

Independent Writing Directions

For this task, you will write an essay in response to a question that asks you to state, explain, and support your opinion on an issue. You will have 30 minutes to plan, write, and revise your essay.

Typically, an effective essay will contain a minimum of 300 words. Your essay will be judged on the quality of your writing. This includes the development of your ideas, the organization of your essay, and the quality and accuracy of the language you use to express your ideas.

If you finish your essay before time is up, you may click on Next to end this section. When you are ready to continue, click on the Dismiss Directions icon.

Question 1

Read the passage. On a piece of paper, take notes on the main points of the reading passage.

Reading Time: 3 minutes

Ruling and governing boards, as well as communities, states, and countries, are facing decisions on how to deal with the use of performance enhancing drugs (PEDs) in sports. The decision should be an easy one: PEDs should not be banned from sports. PEDs are another way for athletes to achieve greatness, much like the use of special swimming suits shaved time off of professional swimmers' races. Although critics suggest that PEDs are dangerous, the fact is that athletes frequently endanger their lives by trying to go further, do more difficult activities, and push themselves to the limit. They decide to participate knowingly, with the understanding that there are risks to their health and physical well-being. Football players, skateboarders, surfers, etc., know they face brain injuries, broken limbs, and more, but the government does not ban these activities because they are dangerous. Using performance enhancing drugs is just one more way in which athletes could be harmed. In addition, using PEDs in athletics is simply a matter of free choice. If athletes want to improve their performance by using these substances, they should be allowed to make this choice. No one else is being harmed by the decision, and so it should not be one determined by governments, but rather a personal decision. Finally, a ban on these substances will actually promote an unfair advantage to wealthier athletes or teams. This is due to the fact that the wealthy players can invest greater money into research on developing undetectable products or better methods to prevent detection. But allowing the substances would put them under closer scrutiny in which they can be regulated by the sporting associations.

Listen to the passage. On a piece of paper, take notes on the main points of the listening passage. 250 🔊

Now answer the following question: 251 🔊

How does the information in the listening passage cast doubt on the information presented in the reading passage?

Response Time: 20 minutes

Question 2

Read the question. On a piece of paper, take notes on the main points of your response. Then write your response.

Many families have important traditions that all or most family members share. What is one of your family traditions and what makes this particular tradition important? Use specific reasons and details to support your response.

Response Time: 30 minutes

Turn to pages 609–614 to *assess* the skills used in the test, *score* the test using the Writing Scoring Criteria, and *record* your results.

COMPLETE TEST 2

READING

$$\boxed{\text{60 minutes}}$$

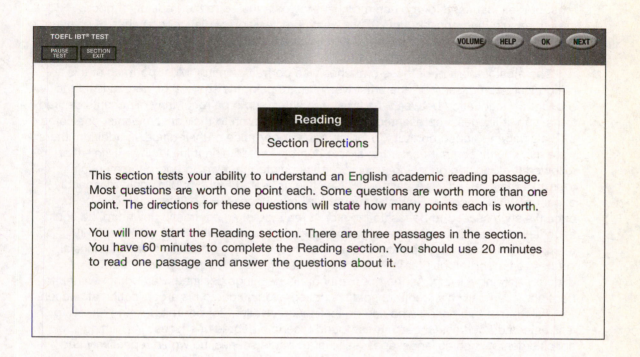

READING 1

Read the passage and answer the questions that follow.

Paragraph

Seventeenth-Century Dutch Painting

1▶   The seventeenth century is generally acknowledged as the golden age of Dutch painting. At this time the Netherlands was the most prosperous nation in Europe, leading the continent in commerce, scientific advancements, and the arts. In the Netherlands, most of the inhabitants of the rich merchant towns adhered to the tradition of good craftsmanship, and consequently there was a proliferation of distinct branches of painting. The majority of painters of this period had to concentrate on a certain branch of painting, constituting the bulk of their artistic output.

2▶   The most important of these branches was portrait painting. Most portraits of this period were commissioned (the artist was hired to paint the subject) or were at least the product of negotiation between the artist, the sitter, and a patron. Many merchants desired to have their likeness represented in a painting to pass on to their descendants, or elected officials commissioned portraits to indicate the importance of their office. In addition, there were many local committees or governing boards—so dominant in Dutch civil life—that followed the tradition of having group portraits painted that would adorn the meeting rooms of the companies. A painter whose style appealed to the public could reasonably expect a steady income. However, no matter how successful a painter may have been, once his style ceased to be fashionable or in the face of an economic downturn, he could experience severe financial hardship. For example, Rembrandt van Rijn (1606–1669), the most renowned Dutch painter of the seventeenth century, had his greatest financial success as a portrait painter in Amsterdam, but in his later years had considerable difficulty earning a living. As the popularity of his paintings declined, Rembrandt went into debt and eventually his creditors sold his house and liquidated his art collection at auction.

3▶   Painters of this period who had no inclination or talent for portrait painting turned to less esteemed genres. Once an artist found a certain degree of success in painting in a specific genre, such as landscapes, still life, or battle scenes, he would repetitively and without originality, stick with that genre. **8A** Unlike portrait painters, the genre painters had to paint their pictures first, and then try to find prospective buyers for their works. **8B** To some degree many of these artists were happy to be relieved of the burden of having to please a patron, who often dictated what the artist was to create. **8C** However, once freed from the patronage system, the genre painter was at the mercy of the changeable tastes of the buying public. **8D** These painters had to either go into the market places and sell directly to their customers, or rely on middlemen who would buy paintings in bulk from an artist at a reduced price and then later sell the paintings at a considerable mark-up.

4▶   Moreover, competition among genre painters was intense. It has been estimated that approximately 1.3 million paintings were produced over a 20-year period. Because of the sheer volume of production, the price of paintings was relatively low with the exception of the most fashionable painters of the times, whose works could sell for considerable sums of money. These factors often forced less-skilled painters into a restrictive degree of specialization, producing essentially the same painting repeatedly to ensure a stable but meager income.

5▶   Landscape painting was one of the most mass produced genres of the seventeenth century. The tradition of landscape painting in the Netherlands began in the previous century. These earlier landscapes, however, lacked a sense of realism due to the fact that a semi-aerial viewpoint, rather than a frontal viewpoint, was used in order to add more detail to the composition. Often these paintings were created in the artist's studio, not out in nature, requiring the artist to paint these scenes from memory or partially from imagination. However, landscape paintings in the seventeenth century were in a more realistic style based on drawings made outdoors, and employing a ground-level viewpoint. The ground-level point of view allowed for lower horizons in the compositions, which made it possible for the artists to paint impressive cloud formations that are a hallmark of Dutch landscape paintings of this period. Favorite subjects in landscape paintings were coastal sand dunes, winter scenes with frozen canals and streams, and rivers with broad adjoining meadows where cattle grazed. Landscapes with cattle in the foreground also became a popular subgenre at the time, capitalizing on the fact that cows were a symbol of prosperity to the Dutch.

1. According to paragraph 1, most of the Dutch artists of the seventeenth century
   Ⓐ had experience in the fields of business and science
   Ⓑ produced most of their work in a specific genre
   Ⓒ created works in traditional branches of painting
   Ⓓ were unaware of the adherence to traditional craftsmanship

2. The word "prosperous" in paragraph 1 is closest in meaning to
   Ⓐ affluent
   Ⓑ populous
   Ⓒ sophisticated
   Ⓓ prestigious

3. The word "proliferation" in paragraph 1 is closest in meaning to
   Ⓐ standardization
   Ⓑ alteration
   Ⓒ increase
   Ⓓ improvement

4. According to paragraph 2, all of the following were reasons for people to commission portraits EXCEPT
   Ⓐ to decorate their offices with the portraits
   Ⓑ to hand down the portraits to later generations of their family
   Ⓒ to give the portraits as gifts during business negotiations
   Ⓓ to indicate the level of their political power

5. According to paragraph 2, even the most successful artists could experience
   Ⓐ restrictions on the number of patrons they were allowed to have
   Ⓑ being prohibited from serving on local committees or governing boards
   Ⓒ their art not being included in prestigious collections
   Ⓓ financial setbacks due to changes in the public's taste

6. The word "inclination" in paragraph 3 is closest in meaning to
   Ⓐ incentive
   Ⓑ preference
   Ⓒ example
   Ⓓ experience

7. In paragraph 3, it can be inferred that portrait painters
   Ⓐ had arranged for their payment before they started a painting
   Ⓑ were more likely to paint in different genres than less skilled painters
   Ⓒ were not overly concerned about pleasing their patrons
   Ⓓ painted their works in order to satisfy prospective customers

8. Look at the four squares [■] that indicate where the following sentence could be added to paragraph 3.

   An artist who painted in these less prestigious branches of painting could not depend on commissions.

   Where would the sentence best fit? Click on a square [■] to add the sentence to the passage.

9. Which of the sentences below best expresses the essential information in the highlighted sentence in paragraph 3? *Incorrect* choices change the meaning in important ways or leave out essential information.
   Ⓐ Artists lowered their prices in order to sell directly to customers who wanted to avoid the high markups associated with middlemen.
   Ⓑ Customers depended on middlemen to find the best paintings in the market despite their huge markups.
   Ⓒ Artists depended on middlemen to sell large quantities of their paintings or they had to find individual buyers themselves.
   Ⓓ Considerable markups encouraged artists to sell the bulk of their paintings directly to customers rather than middlemen in the market places.

10. According to paragraph 4, because of the high volume of paintings being produced in the seventeenth century

(A) Artists were freed from having to paint the same kind of paintings repeatedly.

(B) The financial survival of artists depended on their specialization in a narrow range of paintings.

(C) Most artists were forced out of financial necessity to produce more fashionable paintings.

(D) Most artists could receive considerable sums of money from the sale of their paintings.

11. According to paragraph 5, landscape paintings prior to the seventeenth century

(A) used a frontal viewpoint which allowed for more detail in the paintings

(B) had certain characteristics that made them less realistic than later landscapes

(C) had a high level of realism because they were based on outdoor sketches

(D) lacked detail because the semi-aerial viewpoint was employed in landscapes of this period

12. In paragraph 5, why does the author discuss cloud formations?

(A) to introduce some of the most favorite subjects seen in landscape paintings

(B) to discuss why horizons are a common feature of landscapes

(C) to discuss a benefit of the frontal viewpoint

(D) to explain the importance of basing landscapes on drawings produced outdoors

13.

Directions: An introductory sentence for a brief summary of the passage is provided below. Complete the summary by selecting the THREE answer choices that express the most important ideas in the passage. Some sentences do not belong in the summary because they express ideas that are not presented in the passage or are minor ideas in the passage. **This question is worth 2 points** (2 points for 3 correct answers, 1 point for 2 correct answers, and 0 points for 1 or 0 correct answers).

The seventeenth century witnessed the highpoint of Dutch painting.

-
-
-

Answer Choices (choose 3 to complete the chart):

(1) Many painters had to directly market their paintings and overproduction reduced the overall income of painting professionals.

(2) Landscapes with cattle in the foreground became the most popular subgenre during the seventeenth century.

(3) Battle scenes appealed to the Dutch public because they capitalized on the Netherlands' successful military history.

(4) Despite the predominance of portraiture, portrait painters often faced financial adversity.

(5) In his later years, Rembrandt, who once was the most renowned painter of the era, lost his popularity.

(6) In the seventeenth century, landscapes were a popular genre that possessed a greater sense of realism.

Read the passage and answer the questions that follow.

Paragraph   **The Neanderthals**

1▶   Relatively recent archeological finds have brought about a considerable alteration in perception about the Neanderthals. Neanderthals had previously been characterized more as primitive beasts than as intelligent and compassionate human ancestors. However, evidence suggests that they may have been more sophisticated than previously thought.

2▶   A Neanderthal skeleton was first discovered in 1829 near Enis, Belgium. Workers uncovered an incomplete skeleton consisting of a skull cap, two femur bones, three bones from the right arm and two from the left arm, fragments of the shoulder blades, and ribs. The workers thought that these remains were of a bear and turned them over to a local, amateur naturalist. But it would not be until 1856 that Neanderthals would be identified as being a distinct species of hominid by Johann Karl Fuhlrott. **18A** Although it is debated exactly how and when Neanderthals went extinct, it is conservatively accepted that Neanderthals lived during a period that extended from at least 40,000 to 100,000 years ago in a variety of environments ranging from relatively warm and arid to extremely frigid areas. **18B** Neanderthals are thought to have died out from competition with Homo sapiens, although some scientists have suggested they were wiped out by climate change. **18C** The Neanderthals can be distinguished from modern man in that they had a more robust skeleton and stronger facial structure with a more protruding brow, a broader nose, and larger teeth. **18D** Casts made of Neanderthal skulls by archeologists indicate that Neanderthal cranial capacity was as large as modern humans, suggesting little difference in brain size.

3▶   It has been known for some time that Neanderthals were rather skilled stone artisans. They are best known for their production of stone tools, which included a large number of scrapers and pointed implements such as blades used for big-game hunting. The techniques that the Neanderthals used to prepare these tools demonstrated a clear and important technological advance over their predecessors. Edges of their stone tools have been recently studied under microscopes and this has shed new light on their function. Many of the tools seem to have been for working with wood, both for hacking at large branches and for doing more detailed work on smaller pieces; other tools were clearly for food preparation, both meat and vegetables; still others, which resemble many of today's suede and leather tools, were employed to work with animal hides.

4▶   A clearer picture of Neanderthals has come about recently as archeologists have determined that, in addition to the known ability to develop and use tools in a rather skilled way, Neanderthals also exhibited evidence of beliefs and social rituals, aspects of life that were newly introduced by Neanderthals and that provide evidence of humanlike thoughts and feelings. Neanderthal cemeteries have been discovered in numerous places and the remains in these cemeteries have provided proof of social organization and ritual among the Neanderthals. One skeleton of a Neanderthal was found with a crushed skull; the blow on the top of the head, perhaps from a falling boulder, had quite obviously been the cause of death. What was interesting was that study of the skeleton showed that while he had been alive this man had been seriously handicapped with a defect that had limited use of the upper right side of his body, and that he was blind in one eye. The fact that he had survived well into old age was a strong indication that others had been helping to care for him and to provide him with food rather than allowing him to die because he was no longer physically fit. Other skeletal remains of Neanderthals indicate the practice of burial rituals. Another skeleton of a grown male was found surrounded by pollen from eight different flowers, including ancestors of today's hyacinth, bachelor's button, and hollyhock; experts are convinced that the flowers could not have been growing in the cave where they were found and that the pollen had been deliberately arranged around the body.

5▶   Previously all prehistoric cave art has been attributed solely to Homo sapiens, with the oldest works dating from 32,000 to 37,000 years old in the Chauvet Cave in southern France. However startling new research has revealed that several paintings of a red sphere, handprints, and seals found in a cave in southern Spain are considerably older than the paintings from Chauvet and are the first and only known artistic images created by Neanderthals. Researchers analyzed organic residue on the paintings and they were dated at being between 43,500 and 42,300 years old. Neanderthals, who were known to hunt seals, lived in the caves before becoming extinct about 30,000 years ago. The dating of the Spanish cave paintings is noteworthy because it's around the time when Homo sapiens were first coming into Europe from Africa.

14. According to paragraph 1, recent archeological discoveries have suggested that Neanderthals were

   A less intelligent than other predecessors of modern human beings

   B more complex creatures than they were traditionally believed to be

   C more skillful hunters of big game animals than previously assumed

   D lacking the compassion that later humans possessed

15. The word "distinct" in paragraph 2 is closest in meaning to

   A isolated

   B separate

   C successful

   D extinct

16. In paragraph 2, it can be inferred that the first discovery of Neanderthal bones were not identified as a distinct species of hominid because

   A they were misidentified as animal remains

   B the skeleton was missing several important bones

   C the exact date of the Neanderthals' extinction was being debated at the time

   D there was no existing technology that could accurately date the remains

17. According to paragraph 2, all of the following are characteristics that distinguish Neanderthals from modern humans EXCEPT

   A a brow that sticks out

   B a smaller brain

   C a wider nose

   D a stronger skeleton

18. Look at the four squares [■] that indicate where the following sentence could be added to paragraph 2.

   Neanderthals have been found in areas as diverse as desert-like regions of the Middle East and glacial areas of northern Europe.

   Where would the sentence best fit? Click on a square [■] to add the sentence to the passage.

19. According to paragraph 3, Neanderthal tools were used for all of the following tasks EXCEPT

   A chopping wood

   B harvesting vegetables

   C cooking meals

   D processing animal skins

20. The word "employed" in paragraph 3 is closest in meaning to

   A utilized

   B enhanced

   C refined

   D recycled

21. In paragraph 4, the author discusses "Neanderthal cemeteries" in order to

   A indicate that Neanderthals buried their dead in the same manner as their predecessors did

   B illustrate the ways that Neanderthals' thoughts about death were evolving

   C contrast Neanderthals' burial rituals with their predecessors' burial rituals

   D introduce an example of a social ritual practiced by Neanderthals

22. According to paragraph 4, the fact that the skeleton with the crushed skull was from a person who lived well into old age suggests that

   A his handicap did not limit his mobility

   B the limited use of the right side of his body did not prevent him from providing himself with food

   C he was assisted by others because he was physically unable to take care of himself.

   D the falling boulder was not the cause of his death.

23. Which of the sentences below best expresses the essential information in the highlighted sentence in paragraph 4? *Incorrect* choices change the meaning in important ways or leave out essential information.

Ⓐ Because the pollen is from flowers that still exist today and it is arranged in a specific pattern, experts believe that the flowers were not wild but cultivated by the Neanderthals.

Ⓑ Since the pollen came from flowers not grown in the cave where it was discovered, it indicates that the burial ceremony could not have taken place in the cave.

Ⓒ Since the pollen seems to be arranged in an intentional way and the plants were grown in a different place, it suggests the pollen has some ceremonial purpose.

Ⓓ Because the pollen was arranged in a specific way around the skeleton, it indicates that the skeleton is male and not female.

24. The word "attributed" in paragraph 5 is closest in meaning to

Ⓐ restricted
Ⓑ credited
Ⓒ adopted
Ⓓ rejected

25. The word "startling" in paragraph 5 is closest in meaning to

Ⓐ astonishing
Ⓑ accurate
Ⓒ complex
Ⓓ positive

26.

Directions: An introductory sentence for a brief summary of the passage is provided below. Complete the summary by selecting the THREE answer choices that express the most important ideas in the passage. Some sentences do not belong in the summary because they express ideas that are not presented in the passage or are minor ideas in the passage. **This question is worth 2 points** (2 points for 3 correct answers, 1 point for 2 correct answers, and 0 points for 1 or 0 correct answers).

Recent archeological discoveries have shed new light on our understanding of Neanderthals.

-
-
-

Answer Choices (choose 3 to complete the chart):

(1) Recent fossil evidence shows that Neanderthals lived in a much more limited area than previous believed.

(2) Close examination of Neanderthal tools show that they were used for a variety of tasks.

(3) Although the exact reasons why the Neanderthals went extinct and when it happened are not clear, it has been acknowledged that Neanderthals created the oldest known cave painting.

(4) The first discovery of a Neanderthal skeleton was in 1829 near Enis, Belgium by workers who uncovered an incomplete skeleton.

(5) Evidence of Neanderthal social ritual suggests the Neanderthals were linguistically more advanced than their predecessors were.

(6) The remains found in several Neanderthal cemeteries provide evidence that suggests that Neanderthals were compassionate beings and possessed social customs.

READING 3

Read the passage and answer the questions that follow.

Paragraph

The Silent Era

1▶ The first thirty-five years of motion picture history are called "the silent era," even though films were accompanied by music or live narration—from the Japanese *benshi* (narrators) crafting multi-voiced dialogue narratives, and original musical compositions performed by pianists or organists, to symphony-size orchestras—because there was no mechanical means for recording and playing back recorded dialogue or music in synchronization[1] with the reel of film. Films of this era progressed from very rudimentary to much more elaborate in the years that bookended the era of silent films,1894 to 1928.

2▶ The silent era of motion pictures began when the Kinetograph and the Kinetoscope, inventions created in Thomas Edison's New Jersey laboratory in 1892 to film and to view short sequences respectively, were used to create and present 30-second films of novelty acts to American and European audiences in 1894.The Kinetoscope was a cabinet that was designed for a single viewer; the viewer would look through an eyepiece in the cabinet and watch a short series of moving pictures. Edison's decision not to pursue international patents on his devices led to many improvements by European inventors on Edison's initial ideas. One such improvement is the Cinématographe, which was developed by the French brothers Auguste and Louis Lumière. The Cinématographe was a three-in-one device that could record, develop, and most notably, project motion pictures for a large audience, and it was this machine that turned the motion picture into a worldwide phenomenon. The Lumières held the first public screening of their motion pictures at the Grand Café in Paris in 1895. **31A** Their debut was received enthusiastically and had a significant impact on popular culture at that time. **31B** For the next few years, the films created were rather brief and often cited as the first primitive documentaries: each film consisted of a single shot from a lone stationary viewpoint. **31C** By 1897 the initial enthusiasm for the Lumière films faded as audiences desired something more entertaining. **31D**

3▶ A transitional period from 1908 to 1917 was an era in which motion pictures changed from a primitive documentary medium to a more expressive art form. Actors developed their ability to convey ideas without words and creative inter-titles provided written commentary between sections of the moving images. Filming techniques were developed, with the introduction of such stylistic devices as alternating closeups and long shots. Films became longer, and the range of genres expanded considerably from the earlier documentaries. The French filmmaker Georges Méliès, whose uncanny ability for creating imaginary worlds in his films, pioneered the emerging genre of science fiction.

4▶ By 1917, a major shift in the film industry had occurred. France had been the world's leading exporter of films prior to World War I, but the destructive effects of the war had decimated the film industry in France. By 1917, the United States had assumed leadership in the motion-picture industry, and the sleepy town of Hollywood, California, which had been used as a winter shooting site for filmmakers from the east coast of the United States as early as 1907, had become the center of the filmmaking industry. D.W. Griffith's film, *The Birth of a Nation* (1915), was a milestone during this period of both technical advancement in cinematography and inventive narrative technique. Griffith's *The Birth of a Nation* is considered by many not only to be the motion picture industry's first blockbuster, breaking all previous box office records, but also the first feature-length movie (having a running time of over an hour), and paved the way for the eventual dominance of the feature-length movie in subsequent years.

5▶ However, by the end of the 1920s, the era of silent films ended rather abruptly. Edison and other inventors had introduced technology for creating motion pictures with sound at various times throughout the early decades of the twentieth century, but those early devices could not ensure good enough sound quality and amplification[2] to induce studios to try any of them out. Finally, Warner Brothers took a chance with the 1927 film, *The*

GLOSSARY

1. *synchronization*—coordinated; at the same time
2. *amplification*—an increase in the loudness of sound

Jazz Singer, which starred popular recording artist Al Jolson and featured both singing and talking. When *The Jazz Singer* became a tremendous hit, Warner Brothers and Fox immediately converted to producing motion pictures with sound; the other large studios, believing that talking pictures might be only a flash in the pan, continued making silent pictures for one more year. When it became clear that talking pictures were the future of film rather than merely a passing fad, the remaining studios converted to the exclusive production of talking films a year later; by 1929, all of the films produced in Hollywood studios were talking pictures, and the era of silent films was over.

27. According to paragraph 1, despite the fact that there was no mechanical means of playing back recordings synchronized to movies,
    Ⓐ early silent movies continued to become more complex
    Ⓑ efforts were made to add sound to silent movies by other means
    Ⓒ narratives became more important than the music that accompanied some silent movies
    Ⓓ compositions performed by pianists or organists became increasingly elaborate

28. The word "rudimentary" in paragraph 1 is closest in meaning to
    Ⓐ professional
    Ⓑ practical
    Ⓒ difficult
    Ⓓ primitive

29. According to paragraph 2, in what way was the Cinématographe an improvement on the Kinetoscope?
    Ⓐ The Cinématographe weighed less and was therefore more portable.
    Ⓑ The Cinématographe was presented to the general public before the Kinetoscope was.
    Ⓒ The Cinématographe allowed a larger audience to view a motion picture at one time.
    Ⓓ The Cinématographe was received more enthusiastically than the Kinetoscope was.

30. The word "stationary" in paragraph 2 is closest in meaning to
    Ⓐ fixed
    Ⓑ varying
    Ⓒ distant
    Ⓓ dominant

31. Look at the four squares [■] that indicate where the following sentence could be added to the passage.

    They depicted short everyday scenes of people taking part in outdoor activities, laborers working at a construction site, and travelers scurrying through a train station.

    Where would the sentence best fit? Click on a square [■] to add the sentence to the passage.

32. According to paragraph 3, all of the following are characteristics of the transitional period from 1908 to 1917 EXCEPT
    Ⓐ a greater number of documentaries about scientific topics
    Ⓑ new camera techniques
    Ⓒ more expressive acting
    Ⓓ a greater variety of types of movies being made

33. In paragraph 4, it can be inferred that the film industry in the United States
    Ⓐ was not the most internationally dominant film industry before World War I
    Ⓑ was adversely affected by World War I
    Ⓒ was not affected by competition with the French film industry before World War I
    Ⓓ tried to destroy the French film industry during World War I

34. In paragraph 4, all of the following make the film *The Birth of a Nation* notable EXCEPT
    Ⓐ It received critical acclaim.
    Ⓑ It had a relatively long running time.
    Ⓒ It employed innovative camera techniques.
    Ⓓ It was a great financial success.

35. According to paragraph 5, why did other movie studios not immediately change to producing motion pictures with sound after Warner Brothers' success with *The Jazz Singer*?
    Ⓐ Many movie studios had contracts that stipulated that they exclusively produce silent movies.
    Ⓑ It was thought that motion pictures starring popular recording artists were technically difficult to make.
    Ⓒ They thought that the popularity of motion pictures with sound would be short-lived.
    Ⓓ Movie studios were not aware that Edison and other inventors had improved sound technology.

36. The word "induce" in paragraph 5 is closest in meaning to

(A) increase

(B) extend

(C) delay

(D) motivate

37. The word "them" in paragraph 5 refers to

(A) Edison and other inventors

(B) early devices

(C) sound quality and amplification

(D) studios

38. Which of the sentences below best expresses the essential information in the highlighted sentence in paragraph 5? *Incorrect* choices change the meaning in important ways or leave out essential information.

(A) Once the movie studios were certain that pictures with sound were going to be successful, they converted to talking pictures relatively quickly.

(B) The future of film was presented in a series of talking films that were produced in Hollywood and released in 1929.

(C) The era of silent films ended when the exclusive production for making talking pictures was required by movie studios.

(D) By 1929, it was clear to movie studios that talking pictures were only a fad, so they decided not to produce them until sometime in the future.

39. **Directions:** An introductory sentence for a brief summary of the passage is provided below. Complete the summary by selecting the THREE answer choices that express the most important ideas in the passage. Some sentences do not belong in the summary because they express ideas that are not presented in the passage or are minor ideas in the passage. **This question is worth 2 points** (2 points for 3 correct answers, 1 point for 2 correct answers, and 0 points for 1 or 0 correct answers).

In the history of motion pictures, the years from 1894 to 1928 are known as the silent era.

-
-
-

Answer Choices (choose 3 to complete the chart):

(1) Despite the success of the first movie with sound, many movie studios continued to make silent movies for a few years, but eventually movies with sound replaced silent movies.

(2) Warner Brothers was the first movie studio to commercially release a movie with sound, *The Jazz Singer,* which starred popular recording artist Al Jolson.

(3) The early science-fiction movies of Georges Méliès helped the French film industry to remain competitive after World War I.

(4) The first attempts to synchronize recorded sound with motion pictures took place in Japan at the end of the nineteenth century.

(5) The first two decades of the twentieth century were times of transformation in motion pictures in which technical and artistic improvements were made, and the American companies led the film industry.

(6) Edison's devices were the first to introduce moving pictures to the general public, but it was the development of later inventors that made it a more widespread phenomena.

Turn to pages 591–594 to *diagnose* your errors and *record* your results.

COMPLETE TEST 2

LISTENING

L_DIR_D

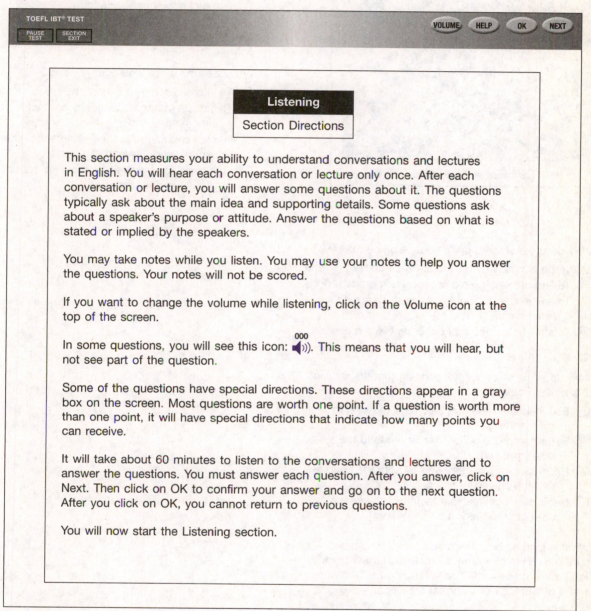

Listening
Section Directions

This section measures your ability to understand conversations and lectures in English. You will hear each conversation or lecture only once. After each conversation or lecture, you will answer some questions about it. The questions typically ask about the main idea and supporting details. Some questions ask about a speaker's purpose or attitude. Answer the questions based on what is stated or implied by the speakers.

You may take notes while you listen. You may use your notes to help you answer the questions. Your notes will not be scored.

If you want to change the volume while listening, click on the Volume icon at the top of the screen.

In some questions, you will see this icon: ◀))). This means that you will hear, but not see part of the question.

Some of the questions have special directions. These directions appear in a gray box on the screen. Most questions are worth one point. If a question is worth more than one point, it will have special directions that indicate how many points you can receive.

It will take about 60 minutes to listen to the conversations and lectures and to answer the questions. You must answer each question. After you answer, click on Next. Then click on OK to confirm your answer and go on to the next question. After you click on OK, you cannot return to previous questions.

You will now start the Listening section.

Listen as a student consults with a university office worker.

 253

1. Why does the student go to see the office worker?
   Ⓐ To determine why his grades were so low
   Ⓑ To find out why he did not receive a grade report
   Ⓒ To ask where he could find the student with the same name
   Ⓓ To replace an incorrect document with a correct one

2. Why does the office worker suggest that the student talk to his professors?
   Ⓐ Because she feels that they took too long to submit the grades
   Ⓑ Because she does not fully understand the man's problem
   Ⓒ Because they are more familiar with the courses that the university offers
   Ⓓ Because she thinks that they might have the correct grade report

3. What is stated about the grade report the student received? **This question is worth 2 points** (2 points for 3 correct answers, 1 point for 2 correct answers, and 0 points for 1 or 0 correct answers).

Click on 3 answers.

   Ⓐ It was sent to his current residence.
   Ⓑ It was sent to his dorm.
   Ⓒ It listed the wrong grade for Latin American history.
   Ⓓ It listed grades for mathematics and physics classes.
   Ⓔ It had his correct name and address on it.

4. According to the office worker, what caused the student's problem?
   Ⓐ The student made a mistake on the change of address form.
   Ⓑ The office did not receive the student's change of address form.
   Ⓒ The student's professor did not send out a corrected grade report.
   Ⓓ One of the office workers incorrectly processed the change of address form.

5. Listen again to part of the conversation. Then answer the question.

   Why does the office worker say this:
   Ⓐ To express confusion about the similar names
   Ⓑ To explain that this situation is not that uncommon
   Ⓒ To explain that this is the first time that she experienced this kind of situation
   Ⓓ To explain the university is too small for this situation to happen

Listen to a lecture in a government class.

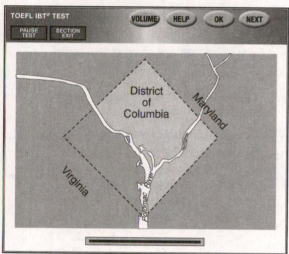

255
🔊

6. What is the lecture mainly about?
   Ⓐ How Pierre Charles L'Enfant designed the city of Washington, D.C.
   Ⓑ How the location of Washington, D.C. was decided
   Ⓒ How Washington, D.C. was governed before direct elections
   Ⓓ Factors that make Washington, D.C. a distinctive city

7. According to the lecture, why did politicians from the southern states not want New York City to be the capital city?
   Ⓐ They thought it was too far from the southern states.
   Ⓑ They thought the weather was too hot and humid in summer.
   Ⓒ They did not like the European inspired design of the city
   Ⓓ They did not like the idea of the capital city not being a part of any state.

8. According to the lecture, how was the local government chosen when Washington, D.C. was first established?
   Ⓐ People voted in a nationwide election.
   Ⓑ Congress appointed a mayor.
   Ⓒ The president chose the local government.
   Ⓓ The local government was run by the military.

9. According to the lecture, what two points make Washington, D.C. different from other U.S. cities?

   Click on 2 answers.

   Ⓐ It was named after a famous president.
   Ⓑ It is not part of any state.
   Ⓒ It has streets radiating from the center of the city.
   Ⓓ It became self-governing only recently.

10. Is each of these true according to the lecture? **This question is worth 2 points** (2 points for 4 correct answers, 1 point for 3 correct answers, and 0 points for 2, 1, or 0 correct answers).

For each answer, click in the YES or NO column.	YES	NO
Part of the original state of Virginia was used to create Washington, D.C.		
Washington, D.C. used to be part of the state of Virginia.		
Part of Washington, D.C. was returned to the state of Virginia.		
Today, Washington, D.C. is part of the state of Virginia.		

11. What is stated in the lecture about the capitol building?
   Ⓐ It is located on a street that runs north and south.
   Ⓑ It is located on the highest point in the city.
   Ⓒ It was not finished when the government officially moved to Washington, D.C.
   Ⓓ George Washington lived there during his first term as president.

Questions 12–17 256

Listen to a discussion in a history class.

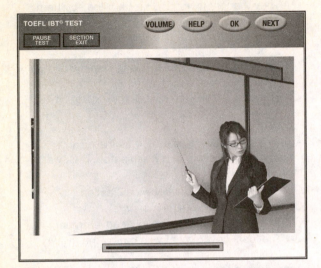

parchment
palimpsest

257

12. What is the lecture mainly about?
    Ⓐ Why parchment is superior to paper
    Ⓑ How the invention of the printing press affected the production of palimpsests
    Ⓒ How new technology is aiding in the research of palimpsests
    Ⓓ How a writing material was produced and recycled

13. According to the lecture what made paper a more attractive material than parchment?
    Ⓐ Paper has a smoother surface.
    Ⓑ Paper was less expensive.
    Ⓒ Paper production was less labor intensive.
    Ⓓ Paper is stronger and lasts longer.

14. According to the professor, why was parchment cut up into rectangular pieces?
    Ⓐ so that not much parchment was wasted
    Ⓑ to make it easier to write on the parchment
    Ⓒ because that was the easiest shape to cut
    Ⓓ because it made it easier to bind the parchment together

15. According to the lecture, what was the hair removal solution made of?
    Ⓐ fruit juice
    Ⓑ decaying vegetables
    Ⓒ animal blood
    Ⓓ alcohol

16. According to the lecture, why are palimpsests beneficial to our understanding of earlier periods?
    Ⓐ Some ancient books or manuscripts only exist in palimpsests.
    Ⓑ They give researchers insight into the technology available before the Middle Ages.
    Ⓒ They are more accurate and reliable than books produced in the late Middle Ages.
    Ⓓ Most palimpsests were produced before the beginning of the Middle Ages.

17. Listen again to part of the lecture. Then answer the question.

    Why does the professor say this: 🔊

    Ⓐ To make a comparison
    Ⓑ To clarify a previous point
    Ⓒ To provide a concrete example
    Ⓓ To introduce a new point

Listen to a conversation between a student and a professor.

259

18. Why does the student go to see the professor?

Ⓐ To discuss something about an assigned reading

Ⓑ To get some clarification about a point from a previous lecture

Ⓒ To get some information about a homework assignment

Ⓓ To discuss some recent research she read about

19. What information in the article did the student find surprising?

Ⓐ The fact that almost two-thirds of all squid species are bioluminescent

Ⓑ The claim that the squid used the flash of light to disorient its prey

Ⓒ The suggestion that the flashes of light made by the squid might be a way of measuring distance

Ⓓ The suggestion that the particular species of squid is a lazy swimmer

20. According to the professor, why did some marine biologists assume that the particular species of squid discussed in the conversation was an inactive swimmer?

Ⓐ Because the squid was eaten by relatively slow moving sperm whales

Ⓑ Because the remains of the squid suggested that they lacked adequate muscles

Ⓒ Because the remains of the squid were not fully digested

Ⓓ Because it is well known that sperm whales only prey on slow moving creatures

21. What conclusions can be drawn about the student's textbook? **This question is worth 2 points** (2 points for 3 correct answers, 1 point for 2 correct answers, and 0 points for 1 or 0 correct answers).

Click on 3 answers.

ⒶAⒷ It was written prior to the research about giant squids mentioned in the journal article.

ⒶBⒷ It does not refer students to the video of the squids' bright flashes.

ⒶCⒷ It contains details about the relatively fast swimming speed of giant squid in deep water.

ⒶDⒷ A new edition of the textbook should include information about studies done off the coast of Japan.

ⒶEⒷ It was written by the same authors of the journal article.

22. Listen again to part of the conversation. Then answer the question.

Why does the professor say this?

Ⓐ To indicate that he disagrees with the student's opinion

Ⓑ To add support to a point that he is trying to make

Ⓒ To emphasize how slow the speed is

Ⓓ To introduce some additional research

Questions 23–28 260

Listen to a lecture in a geology class.

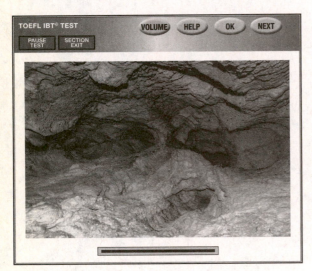

261

23. What is the lecture mainly about?

Ⓐ New research about how solution caves are formed
Ⓑ Why caves are named after the process by which they were formed
Ⓒ The differences between sea caves and lava caves
Ⓓ Characteristics that are associated with a particular kind of cave

24. According to the lecture, sea caves are most often found in what kind of area?

Ⓐ Along sandy coastlines
Ⓑ In areas where the rock is soft
Ⓒ In areas where the ocean is calm
Ⓓ In areas where cracks have been made in hard rock

25. According to the lecture, lava caves form when

Ⓐ the edges of a lava channel start to harden and form a tube

Ⓑ a lava channel reaches the deepest point of a fast moving river

Ⓒ lava channels remain underwater

Ⓓ a tube becomes so clogged with lava that no more lava can flow through the tube

26. According to the lecture, what are two factors necessary for the formation of a solution cave? **This question is worth 2 points** (2 points for 3 correct answers, 1 point for 2 correct answers, and 0 points for 1 or 0 correct answers).

Click on 3 answers.

Ａ Rock consisting of less than 80% calcium carbonate

Ｂ Rock that is fairly close to the surface

Ｃ A moderate amount of precipitation

Ｄ Rock that is smooth and unbroken

Ｅ An adequate amount of plant life.

27. According to the lecture, what makes it possible for rings of limestone to begin forming on the ceilings of solution caves?

Ⓐ Water in a solution cave is losing carbon which slows down the flow of water entering the cave.

Ⓑ Water in a solution cave has a higher concentration of carbon dioxide than surface water.

Ⓒ Water in a solution cave is less able to retain limestone because it is losing carbon dioxide.

Ⓓ Hollow soda straws become clogged with accumulating limestone deposits.

28. Listen again to part of the lecture. Then answer the question.

Why does the professor say this: 🔊

Ⓐ To indicate that the point is obvious

Ⓑ To introduce a new point

Ⓒ To refer back to a previous point

Ⓓ To try to clarify a point

Listen to a discussion in a biology class.

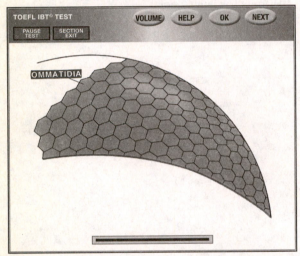

263
🔊

29. What is the lecture mainly about?

Ⓐ How butterflies use polarized light in finding a mate

Ⓑ The similarities and differences of several types of compound eyes

Ⓒ The structures and capabilities of a particular type of compound eye

Ⓓ How the ommatidium evolved in butterflies

30. What is stated in the lecture about ommatidia?

Click on 2 answers.

Ⓐ There are thousands of ommatidia on a compound eye.

Ⓑ The ommatidia each have thousands of sides.

Ⓒ The ommatidia cover the surface of a compound eye.

Ⓓ The ommatidia all point in the same direction.

31. What can be inferred from the lecture about butterfly migration?

Ⓐ Most species begin their migration at the same time.

Ⓑ It is more difficult to navigate on a cloudy day.

Ⓒ Birds are better at navigating over long distances than butterflies.

Ⓓ Butterflies are only able to perceive a limited range of light.

32. Are these statements true about the compound eye? **This question is worth 3 points** (3 points for 4 correct answers, 2 points for 3 correct answers, 1 point for 2 correct answers, and 0 points for 1 or 0 correct answers).

For each answer, click in the YES or NO column.		
	YES	**NO**
A compound eye can easily detect tiny movements.		
A compound eye can focus extremely well.		
It is currently believed that a compound eye can see compound pictures.		
It is currently believed that a compound eye can see a single detailed image.		

33. According to the lecture how does the ability to see polarized light help butterflies find a mate?

Ⓐ It helps the males to differentiate between different species of butterflies that live in the rain forest.

Ⓑ The polarized light prevents the females from blending in too much with the background foliage.

Ⓒ It helps the females to avoid detection by predators during the mating season.

Ⓓ It helps the males send signals to females about mating.

34. Listen again to part of the lecture. Then answer the question.

Why does the professor say this: 🔊

Ⓐ To illustrate a previous point

Ⓑ To contrast the actions of two insects

Ⓒ To include a bit of humor into the lecture

Ⓓ To suggest something for the students to try

Turn to pages 595–598 to *diagnose* your errors and *record* your results.

COMPLETE TEST 2

SPEAKING

S_DIR_E

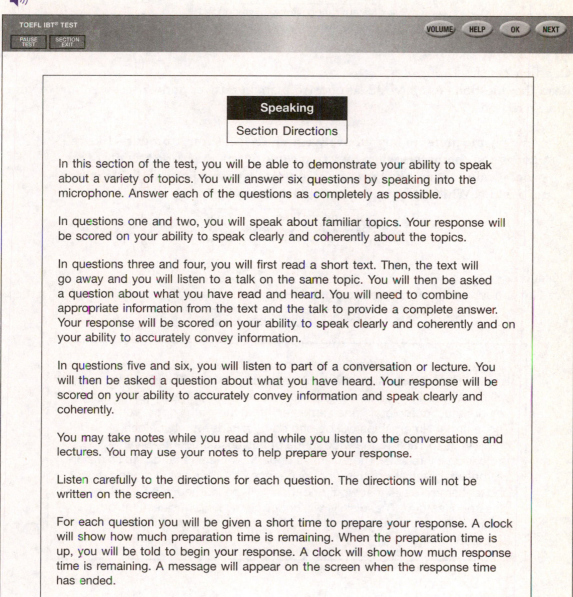

TOEFL IBT® TEST

PAUSE TEST   SECTION EXIT

VOLUME   HELP   OK   NEXT

Speaking

Section Directions

In this section of the test, you will be able to demonstrate your ability to speak about a variety of topics. You will answer six questions by speaking into the microphone. Answer each of the questions as completely as possible.

In questions one and two, you will speak about familiar topics. Your response will be scored on your ability to speak clearly and coherently about the topics.

In questions three and four, you will first read a short text. Then, the text will go away and you will listen to a talk on the same topic. You will then be asked a question about what you have read and heard. You will need to combine appropriate information from the text and the talk to provide a complete answer. Your response will be scored on your ability to speak clearly and coherently and on your ability to accurately convey information.

In questions five and six, you will listen to part of a conversation or lecture. You will then be asked a question about what you have heard. Your response will be scored on your ability to accurately convey information and speak clearly and coherently.

You may take notes while you read and while you listen to the conversations and lectures. You may use your notes to help prepare your response.

Listen carefully to the directions for each question. The directions will not be written on the screen.

For each question you will be given a short time to prepare your response. A clock will show how much preparation time is remaining. When the preparation time is up, you will be told to begin your response. A clock will show how much response time is remaining. A message will appear on the screen when the response time has ended.

Question 1
Read the question. You have 15 seconds to plan an answer and 45 seconds to give your spoken response.

Parents are responsible for making sure that their children lead healthy lives. What can parents do to ensure that their children have healthy lifestyles?

Preparation Time: 15 seconds
Response Time: 45 seconds

Question 2
Read the question. You have 15 seconds to plan an answer and 45 seconds to give your spoken response.

Some people prefer to buy innovative high-tech electronic products like cell phones and computers when they first come out on the market, while other people would rather buy these devices after they have been available in stores for a while. Which way do you prefer? Explain why.

Preparation Time: 15 seconds
Response Time: 45 seconds

Question 3
Read an announcement from the campus newspaper. You have 45 seconds to read the notice.

Reading Time: 45 seconds

New Requirement for Business Students
Beginning next semester, all business majors enrolled in their senior year will be required to participate in a work experience program. Graduating seniors must complete a one semester internship with a local company. These unpaid internships will be offered by a wide variety of local companies to cater to the wide range of business students' diverse professional interests. The business department feels that business majors will benefit greatly from this work experience by developing organizational and leadership skills that would not normally be learned in a formal classroom setting. These skills will undoubtedly help business majors to secure permanent employment once they have completed the program and graduated.

Now listen to the conversation.

Now answer the following question. You have 30 seconds to prepare an answer and 60 seconds to give your spoken response. 265

The woman expresses her opinion of the business department's new policy. State her opinion and explain the reasons she gives for holding that opinion.

Preparation Time: 30 seconds
Response Time: 60 seconds

Question 4

Read a passage from a psychology textbook. You have 45 seconds to read the passage.

Reading Time: 45 seconds

Need for Affiliation

By our very nature human beings are highly social creatures and we find ourselves in a variety of social groups in the course of our lives. People have a deep-seated need to identify with and belong to a group that is called the "need for affiliation." We have an intense desire to be a member of a successful social group because it signifies our own success and positive self-worth. This strong desire to be accepted by a group can be a strong motivational force and affect our behavior and the choices that we make in our lives. Conversely, the notion of not being accepted by a social group and the feeling of embarrassment associated with not belonging to a social group may also be a determining factor in both important and inconsequential decisions that we make.

Now listen to part of a lecture. [266] ◀))

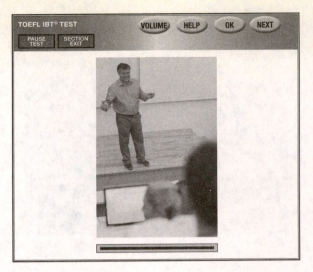

Now answer the following question. You have 30 seconds to prepare an answer and 60 seconds to give your spoken response. [267] ◀))

Describe what the Need for Affiliation is and explain how the advertisement discussed by the professor relates to this concept.

Preparation Time: 30 seconds
Response Time: 60 seconds

Question 5
Listen to the conversation. [268] ◀))

Now answer the following question. You will have 20 seconds to prepare an answer and 60 seconds to give your spoken response. [269] ◀))

Briefly summarize the woman's problem. Then state which solution you would recommend. Explain the reasons for your recommendation.

Preparation Time: 20 seconds
Response Time: 60 seconds

Question 6

Listen to part of a lecture. Then respond to the question. 🔊 270

Now answer the following question. You have 20 seconds to prepare an answer and 60 seconds to give your spoken response. 🔊 271

> **Using the examples of wolves and ants from the lecture, explain how living in groups can help animals acquire food.**

> Preparation Time: 20 seconds
> Response Time: 60 seconds

> Turn to pages 599–608 to *assess* the skills used in the test, *score* the test using the Speaking Scoring Criteria, and *record* your results.

COMPLETE TEST 2

WRITING

W_DIR_F

TOEFL IBT® TEST   VOLUME   HELP   OK   NEXT

PAUSE TEST   SECTION EXIT

Writing
Section Directions

This section measures your ability to communicate in writing in an academic environment. There will be two writing tasks.

For the first writing task, you will read a passage and listen to a lecture about an academic topic. Then you will write a response to a question that asks you about the relationship between the lecture and the reading passage.

For the second task, you will demonstrate your ability to write an essay in response to a question that asks you to express and support your opinion about a topic or issue.

Now listen to the directions for the first writing task.

Integrated Writing Directions

For this task, you will first have three minutes to read a passage about an academic topic. You may take notes on the passage if you wish. The passage will then be removed and you will listen to a lecture about the same topic. While you listen, you may also take notes.

Then you will have 20 minutes to write a response to a question that asks you about the relationship between the lecture you heard and the reading passage. Try to answer the question as completely as possible using information from the reading passage and the lecture. The question does not ask you to express your personal opinion. You will be able to see the reading passage again when it is time for you to write. You may use your notes to help you answer the question.

Typically, an effective response will be 150 to 225 words long. Your response will be judged on the quality of your writing and on the completeness and accuracy of the content. If you finish your response before time is up, you may click on Next to go on to the second writing task.

Independent Writing Directions

For this task, you will write an essay in response to a question that asks you to state, explain, and support your opinion on an issue. You will have 30 minutes to plan, write, and revise your essay.

Typically, an effective essay will contain a minimum of 300 words. Your essay will be judged on the quality of your writing. This includes the development of your ideas, the organization of your essay, and the quality and accuracy of the language you use to express your ideas.

If you finish your essay before time is up, you may click on Next to end this section. When you are ready to continue, click on the Dismiss Directions icon.

Questions 1–2

Question 1

Read the passage. On a piece of paper, take notes on the main points of the reading passage.

Reading Time: 3 minutes

Marco Polo

In his book, *Marco Polo,* an Italian merchant claimed to have traveled through China and met the Mongol ruler of China, <u>Kublai Khan</u> during the thirteenth century. However, many historians suggest that Polo's accounts of his travels in China were fabricated with the help of Arab and Persian merchants who had visited China, and that Polo never set foot in China. There are several reasons why the credibility of Marco Polo's accounts of his travels to China in the thirteenth century has been called into question.

In his book Polo claimed that he was a trusted advisor to Kublai Khan, participating in military actions and even serving as a governor for three years. However, there is no mention of Polo in any Chinese records. This is highly unusual because the Chinese were meticulous record keepers and one would assume that if Polo was so politically well connected there should be some written record about him.

It is extremely puzzling that Polo never mentioned tea, which was popular in China. The Chinese were the first culture to cultivate tea plants and develop the custom of drinking tea. Chinese records indicate that the use of tea dates as far back as the first millennium B.C. Tea drinking was widespread as a beverage that was consumed for pleasure on social occasions during the period that Polo was traveling around China and writing his journals. Given the uniqueness of this custom, it seems that this would have been of great interest to Polo if he had actually been to China.

Throughout Polo's accounts of China, he paid great attention to and reported in great detail about the architecture of the buildings he saw in China. However, not even once did Polo mention perhaps the most famous structure in China, the Great Wall. The Great Wall, a massive defensive structure, was built many decades before Polo supposedly traveled to China. It was built to prevent the Mongol people, who ruled China during the period that Polo claimed to have been in China, from conquering China. If Polo truly spent several years exploring China, we would definitely expect that there would be some reference to the Great Wall in his journals.

Listen to the passage. On a piece of paper, take notes on the main points of the listening passage. 🔊 272

Now answer the following question: 273

Summarize the points made in the lecture, being sure to explain how they challenge the specific points made in the reading passage.

Response Time: 20 minutes

Question 2

Read the question. On a piece of paper, take notes for the main points of your response. Then write your response.

Do you agree or disagree with the following statement?

Professional athletes, such as football and basketball players, should not be paid the high salaries that they receive from their teams.

Response Time: 30 minutes

Turn to pages 609–614 to *assess* the skills used in the test, *score* the test using the Writing Scoring Criteria, and *record* your results.

APPENDIX

COHESION

It is important when you are producing material on the TOEFL iBT® test that you use a variety of methods to create **cohesion**.[1] Be sure you know how to use repeated and rephrased key ideas, pronouns and determiners, and transition expressions to create cohesion.

Appendix A1: Use Repeated and Rephrased Key Ideas

One way to make your written and spoken English more cohesive is to use repeated and rephrased key ideas. Look at the following example of repeated and rephrased key ideas used for cohesion.

> I think that the most important characteristic in a friend is honesty. If someone is a friend, then he or she must be *honest*. I can trust someone only if he or she is truthful. If a friend of mine does not tell me the *truth*, then he or she can no longer be considered a friend.

In this example, the key idea *honesty* is repeated as *honest* and rephrased as *truthful* and *truth* to make the passage cohesive.

The following list provides the key information that you should remember about using repeated key ideas to make your written and spoken English more cohesive.

Using Repeated and Rephrased Key Ideas for Cohesion
1. Use repeated key ideas.
2. Use rephrased key ideas.
3. Use a variety of ways to make your English cohesive.

---

[1] **Cohesion** is a characteristic of language in which ideas flow or attach together smoothly.

Appendix Exercise A1: Fill in the blanks in each pair of sentences with one of the words from the box above the pairs of sentences to make the sentences cohesive. You should use each answer one time only.

chance	competitor	energy	outcome	pleases	shocked	speaks

1. I am happy you have the opportunity to go there. It _____ me that you have been given such a _____.

2. Jan is quite a dynamic speaker. She always _____ with a great amount of _____.

3. The results of the competition were entirely unexpected. The _____ was _____ by the _____.

acts	brief	determined	positive	problems	remarks	resolved

4. The lawyer made a short statement. His _____ were quite _____.

5. The problems are not insurmountable. The _____ can be _____.

6. If you look at his actions in a negative way, you might say that he is stubborn. Conversely, if you look at the way he _____ in a _____ way, you might say that he is _____.

answers	complex	eventually	explanation	finish	indicated	succinct

7. Laura said that she would get it done sometime. She _____ that she would _____ it _____.

8. I do not want you to ramble on and on in your responses. Your _____ should be _____.

9. You have explained this in an overly simplistic way. You really need a more _____ _____.

animated	appreciates	concept	discussions	episode	involved	novel	reasons

10. Your idea is quite innovative. It is a _____ _____.

11. This professor seems to welcome lively debate. He _____ _____ _____.

12. Can you explain why you took part in this incident? Can you give me your _____ for being _____ in this _____?

Appendix A2: Use Pronouns and Determiners

A second way to make your written and spoken English more cohesive is to use **pronouns**[2] and **determiners**[3] to refer back to previous ideas. Some pronouns and determiners that can be used for cohesion are in the following table.

		Pronouns			Determiners	
Subject	**Object**	**Possessive**	**Reflexive**	**Demonstrative**	**Possessive**	**Demonstrative**
I	me	mine	myself	this	my	this
you	you	yours	yourself	that	your	that
he	him	his	himself	these	his	these
she	her	hers	herself	those	her	those
it	it		itself		its	
we	us	ours	ourselves		our	
you	you	yours	yourselves		your	
they	them	theirs	themselves		their	

Look at the following example showing pronouns and determiners used for cohesion.

> Ben worked very hard on a project. *He* did all of the work on *it* by *himself*, and *his* professor was very pleased with *this* assignment.

In this example, the pronoun *He* refers to the noun *Ben*, the pronoun *it* refers to the noun *project*, the pronoun *himself* refers to the noun *Ben*, the determiner *his* refers to the noun *Ben*, and the determiner *this* refers to the noun *assignment*. These pronouns and determiners help to make the passage cohesive.

The following list provides the key information that you should remember about using pronouns and determiners to make your written and spoken English more cohesive.

Using Pronouns and Determiners for Cohesion

1. Use pronouns to refer back to previous ideas.
2. Use determiners to refer back to previous ideas.
3. Use a variety of ways to make your English cohesive.

---

[2] **Pronouns** are words that take the place of nouns.
[3] **Determiners** are words that accompany nouns to identify the nouns.

Appendix Exercise A2: Fill in each blank with one of the pronouns or determiners from the box above the passage to make the passage cohesive. You should use each answer one time only.

her	herself	she	them	this	this

1. A researcher has been conducting a study on the causes of cancer. She has been
   conducting _____ study by _____. Up to now,
   _____ has determined several possible causes of cancer and
   has decided to focus on the most promising of _____. Though
   _____ research has not yet yielded a conclusive result, the researcher
   hopes _____ will occur soon.

it	mine	our	our	ourselves	ourselves	this	we	your

2. You and I have _____ work cut out for _____. You have to
   finish _____ part of the project, and I have to finish _____.
   Then when we have each finished _____ own parts of the project,
   _____ can get together to finish _____. We have to take it
   upon _____ to get _____ project done.

their	them	themselves	themselves	these	they	they

3. Some students have a huge writing assignment to complete by Friday. However,
   _____ students have procrastinated for quite some time, and now
   _____ are in a bind, so _____ only hope of finishing the
   assignment on time is for _____ to stay up all night for the next two
   nights to get it done. The students have gotten _____ into this situation,
   and now _____ will have to work very hard to get _____
   out of it.

he	he	he	him	himself	his	his	it	this

4. David is regretting that he signed up for the advanced history course. Unfortunately,
   _____ signed up for _____ course because
   _____ thought that _____ could be quite interesting. It did
   not take long for _____ to figure out that _____ reasoning
   had been rather faulty. He told _____ that _____ needed
   to be more careful in _____ decision-making in the future.

Appendix A3: Use Transition Expressions

A third way to make your written and spoken English more cohesive is to use transition expressions to indicate how ideas are related. Some transition expressions that can be used for cohesion are listed in the following table.

Transition Expressions			
Expression	**Meaning**	**Expression**	**Meaning**
therefore	result follows	in addition	more information follows
as a result	result follows	moreover	more information follows
thus	result follows	furthermore	more information follows
consequently	result follows		
		in contrast	opposite information follows
for example	example follows	on the other hand	opposite information follows
for instance	example follows	nevertheless	unexpected information follows
		nonetheless	unexpected information follows
in conclusion	conclusion follows	however	opposite or unexpected information follows
in summary	conclusion follows		
in fact	emphasis follows	fortunately	something lucky follows
indeed	emphasis follows	surprisingly	something unexpected follows
		interestingly	something unexpected follows

Look at the following example showing transition expressions used for cohesion.

> A group of students really wanted an environmental science program to be added to the university curriculum. The students presented their request to the university; *in addition*, they got hundreds of signatures on a petition. *Nonetheless*, their request was denied.

In this example, the transitions *in addition* and *Nonetheless* are used to make the passage cohesive.

The following list provides the key information that you should remember about using transition expressions to make your written and spoken English more cohesive.

Using Transition Expressions for Cohesion
1. Use transition expressions to show how ideas are related.
2. Use a variety of ways to make your English cohesive.

Appendix Exercise A3: Fill in each blank with one of the transition expressions from the box above the passage to make the passage cohesive. You should use each answer one time only.

For instance	Fortunately	Furthermore	However	In fact

1. I certainly thought Juan would do a good job. _____, he failed miserably.

2. There are many ways to make a good impression on your boss. _____, one way is to come to work on time.

3. You should always show up for work on time. _____, you should never leave work early.

4. I can argue that you need to spend more time on this job. _____, you should spend several hours on it.

5. He tried recently to get that job. _____, that job is now his.

in contrast	in summary	moreover	nonetheless	therefore

6. Freshmen are taking the introductory course; juniors, _____, are taking the advanced course.

7. Freshmen have already studied biology; _____, they must still take the introductory biology course.

8. A basic math course is required for freshmen; all freshmen, _____, must take the course.

9. Freshmen must take three lecture courses; _____, they must take one laboratory course.

10. Juniors must take three lecture courses and three laboratory courses; _____, they will be very busy.

as a result	for example	in conclusion	on the other hand	surprisingly

11. Marie studied really hard for the exam; _____, she failed the exam.

12. A few students did quite well on the exam; the rest, _____, did quite poorly.

13. There were a few high grades on the exam. Miko, _____, had 99% correct.

14. Some students did not prepare for the exam; _____, they did not do so well.

15. The students who studied hard did well on the exam, and those who did not study hard did poorly; _____, one can say that the exam grades depended on preparation.

| consequently | in addition | indeed | interestingly | nevertheless |

16. Tickets are required for the concert; _____, anyone who wants to go to the concert must purchase a ticket.

17. A sonata will be performed at the concert; _____, a concerto will be performed.

18. Luisa does not like classical music; _____, her friends have talked her into going.

19. There will be a guest performer at the concert; _____, the guest performer is someone quite famous.

20. The audience truly appreciated the performance; _____, the audience thought the performance was wonderful.

Appendix Review Exercise (A1–A3): Circle the cohesive devices in the following passages. Label each as R/R (a repeated or rephrased key idea), P/D (a pronoun or determiner), or T (a transition expression).

_P/D_ 1. Lee gave an explanation for his unusual behavior. It was that he had been afraid. His fear had caused him to act this way.

_____ 2. The board has indicated that it is now in accord on the key point of the bill. However, agreement on this main point was not easy for the board to reach.

_____ 3. The professor discussed several important concepts in the lecture. The focus of her lecture was the development of these concepts.

_____ 4. One member of the group was opposed to the plan. He objected vociferously. Nonetheless, the plan was implemented immediately.

_____ 5. Assignments must be turned in on time. Absolutely no late assignments will be accepted. In fact, any assignment that is not submitted on time will receive a grade of zero.

_____ 6. An account of the incident appeared in the newspaper. Unfortunately, many of the details in this account were not accurate. The newspaper needs to print a retraction to correct these inaccuracies.

_____ 7. You must decide whether to write a thesis or to take a comprehensive exam, and you must make this decision yourself. Choosing between a thesis and a comprehensive exam is a major decision.

_____ 8. Even in the beginning, all the members of the group worked very hard on the project. Indeed, from the outset, a huge amount of effort was invested in the project. Not surprisingly, their effort was not wasted; they were rewarded with a high grade on the project.

_____ 9. Dr. Singer gave an assignment in class today. However, the students are confused about what the assignment actually is. The professor spoke for quite some time about the assignment, but he said a number of contradictory things. These contradictory things are what caused the students to be confused.

_____ 10. A number of major corporations are sending representatives to campus this week to interview students who are seeking jobs in these corporations. Any students wishing to have interviews should sign up in the campus placement office. The corporate representatives will be on campus for only a brief time, and the number of interviews is limited. Thus, it is important to sign up for interviews immediately.

SENTENCE STRUCTURE

It is important when you are producing material on the TOEFL iBT® test that you use a variety of correct sentence structures. You should be sure that you know how to use simple sentences, compound sentences, and complex sentences.

Appendix A4: Use Correct Simple Sentences

A simple sentence has only one **clause**.[4] Two types of sentence structure errors are common in sentences with only one clause: (1) the clause can be missing a subject or a verb, and (2) the clause can be introduced by a subordinate adverb clause connector.

The first type of incorrect simple sentence is a sentence that is missing a subject or a verb.

        Incorrect: Generally, <u>is</u> important to fill out the form completely.
                              VERB

        Correct: Generally, it is important to fill out the form completely.

        Incorrect: The <u>ideas</u> on how to construct the project.
                       SUBJECT

        Correct: The ideas on how to construct the project are good.

The first sentence is incorrect because it has the verb *is* but is missing a subject. The second sentence is incorrect because it has a subject *ideas* but is missing a verb.

Another type of incorrect simple sentence is one that includes a subordinate adverb clause connector in front of the subject and the verb. The following chart lists common subordinate adverb clause connectors.

Subordinate Adverb Clause Connectors							
Time		**Cause**	**Condition**	**Contrast**	**Manner**	**Place**	
after	once	as	if	although	as	where	
as	since	because	in case	even	in that	wherever	
as long as	until	inasmuch	provided	though			
as soon as	when	as	providing	though			
before	whenever	now that	unless	while			
by the time	while	since	whether	whereas			

Look at the following examples of incomplete sentences.

        Incorrect: *Because* the <u>manager</u> of the company <u>instructed</u> me to do it.
                           SUBJECT   VERB

        Correct: The manager of the company instructed me to do it.

        Incorrect: *Even though* the <u>contest</u> <u>was run</u> in an unfair manner.
                                 SUBJECT   VERB

        Correct: The contest was run in an unfair manner.

---

[4] A **clause** is a group of words that has both a subject and a verb.

The first sentence is incorrect because the subordinate adverb clause connector *Because* is in front of the subject *manager* and the verb *instructed*. The second sentence is incorrect because the subordinate adverb clause connector *Even though* is in front of the subject *contest* and the verb *was run*.

The following list provides the key information that you should remember about using correct simple sentences.

Using Correct Simple Sentences

1. A simple sentence is a sentence with one clause.
2. A simple sentence must have both a subject and a verb.
3. A simple sentence may not be introduced by a subordinate adverb clause connector.

Appendix Exercise A4: Underline the subjects once and the verbs twice. Circle the subordinate clause connectors. Then indicate if the sentences are correct (C) or incorrect (I).

_____ 1. The obvious reasons for the selection of the candidate.

_____ 2. When everyone in the room decided to leave.

_____ 3. I found the ideas rather unsettling.

_____ 4. Often discusses the advantages of the situation.

_____ 5. A preference for movies with lots of action.

_____ 6. Fortunately, the piece of paper with the crucial information was found.

_____ 7. As soon as the article appears in the newspaper.

_____ 8. Definitely is not proper to make that suggestion.

_____ 9. His agreement with me about the important issues.

_____ 10. It happened that way.

_____ 11. As no one else in the world would have made the same decision.

_____ 12. Without any hesitation made a decision not to return.

_____ 13. An agreement as to the amount to be paid has been reached.

_____ 14. A poem written on a piece of faded parchment.

_____ 15. Now that you have told me about your childhood.

_____ 16. We forgot.

_____ 17. To take the medicine at the right time to be the most effective.

_____ 18. If you think about the problem just a little more.

_____ 19. Unfortunately, the manager already made the decision.

_____ 20. Even though you gave me a gift for my birthday.

Appendix A5: Use Correct Compound Sentences

A compound sentence has more than one **main clause**.[5] The main clauses in a compound sentence can be connected correctly with a coordinate conjunction (*and, but, or, so, yet*) and a comma (,) or with a semi-colon (;). Look at the following examples.

> Jack studies hard. He gets high grades.
>
> Jack studies hard, so he gets high grades.
>
> Jack studies hard; he gets high grades.

In the first example, the two main clauses *Jack studies hard* and *He gets high grades* are not combined into a compound sentence. In the second example, the two main clauses are combined into a compound sentence with the coordinate conjunction *so* and a comma. In the third example, the same two main clauses are combined into a compound sentence with a semi-colon.

It is possible to use adverb transitions in compound sentences. (See Appendix A3 for a list of transition expressions.) It is important to note that adverb transitions are not conjunctions, so either a semi-colon or a coordinate conjunction with a comma is needed.

Look at the following examples of sentences with adverb transitions.

> Jack studies hard. As a result, he gets high grades.
>
> Jack studies hard, and, as a result, he gets high grades.
>
> Jack studies hard; as a result, he gets high grades.

In the first example, the two main clauses *Jack studies hard* and *he gets high grades* are not combined into a compound sentence even though the adverb transition *As a result* is used. In the second example, the two main clauses are combined into a compound sentence with the coordinate conjunction *and* and a comma; the adverb transition *as a result* is included after the coordinate conjunction. In the third example, the same two main clauses are combined into a compound sentence with a semi-colon, and the adverb transition is set off from the second main clause with a comma.

The following list provides the key information that you should remember about using correct compound sentences.

Using Correct Compound Sentences

1. A compound sentence is a sentence with more than one main clause.
2. The main clauses in a compound sentence may be joined with either a semi-colon (;) or a coordinate conjunction (*and, but, or, so, yet*) and a comma (,).
3. An adverb transition can be used in a compound sentence, but either a semi-colon or a coordinate conjunction and a comma is still needed.

---

[5] A **main clause** is an independent clause that has both a subject and a verb and is not introduced by a subordinate clause connector.

Appendix Exercise A5: Underline the subjects once and the verbs twice in the main clauses. Circle the punctuation, transitions, and connectors that join the main clauses. Then indicate if the sentences are correct (C) or incorrect (I).

____ 1. The <u>matter</u> <u><u>was</u></u> really important, I <u><u>could to decide</u></u> too quickly.

____ 2. The children broke the rules, but their parents did not find out.

____ 3. She expected to graduate in the spring, however she did not graduate until fall.

____ 4. My family moved a lot during my youth; as a result, I always had to make new friends.

____ 5. I made a firm promise to my friend and I vowed to keep it.

____ 6. Sam did not sign in prior to work, so he signed in afterwards.

____ 7. The students waited in a long line to register. Finally, they got to the front of the line.

____ 8. His parents advised him to think about it some more he did not take their advice.

____ 9. My first job in the company was as a part-time worker, later I was given a full-time job.

____ 10. Tom really wanted to be successful, yet he did not know how to accomplish this.

____ 11. We must return the books to the library today, otherwise we will have to pay a fine.

____ 12. She always tries not to get too angry. However, she sometimes loses her temper.

____ 13. Therefore she has gotten a job, she can pay all of her bills.

____ 14. She had the surgery recommended by her doctor; as a result, she is doing better now.

____ 15. They left the money in a savings account, it began to collect some interest.

____ 16. I wanted to get a high-paying job last summer; unfortunately, this was impossible.

____ 17. I will have to study harder, or I will not be able to get a scholarship.

____ 18. An accident occurred at the corner, afterwards, the police came and wrote a report.

____ 19. The plan has a number of advantages it also has a number of disadvantages.

____ 20. The directions must be followed exactly; otherwise, the outcome will be very bad.

Appendix A6: Use Correct Complex Sentences

A complex sentence has one main clause and at least one **subordinate clause**.[6] Noun, adjective, and adverb clauses are all types of subordinate clauses. Each of the following sentences is a complex sentence because it contains a subordinate clause.

> I cannot believe <u>what he did</u>.
> NOUN CLAUSE

> The runner <u>who finishes first</u> wins the trophy.
> ADJECTIVE CLAUSE

> I will return to the task <u>when I am able</u>.
> ADVERB CLAUSE

The first complex sentence contains the subordinate noun clause *what he did*. The second complex sentence contains the subordinate adjective clause *who finishes first*. The final complex sentence contains the subordinate adverb clause *when I am able*.

A variety of errors with complex structures can occur in student writing, but two errors that occur with great frequency are (1) repeated subjects after adjective clauses, and (2) repeated subjects after noun clauses as subjects. To understand these two problems, you must recognize adjective and noun clauses. The following chart lists connectors that introduce adjective and noun clauses.

Subordinate Adjective and Noun Clause Connectors				
Adjective Clause Connectors	**Noun Clause Connectors**			
who	who	when	whichever	if
whom	whoever	whenever	why	that
which	what	where	how	
that	whatever	which	whether	

Look at the following examples of errors with adjective and noun clauses.

> Incorrect: A good <u>friend</u> **who lives down the street** <u>she</u> <u>did</u> me a favor.
>   SUBJECT   SUBJECT VERB

> Correct: A good friend who lives down the street did me a favor.

> Incorrect: **What my advisor told me yesterday** <u>it</u> <u>was</u> very helpful.
>   NOUN CLAUSE   SUBJECT VERB

> Correct: What my advisor told me yesterday was very helpful.

The first sentence is incorrect because it contains an extra subject. The correct subject *friend* comes before the adjective clause *who lives down the street*, and an extra subject *she* comes after the adjective clause. To correct this sentence, you should omit the extra subject *she*. The second sentence is also incorrect because it contains an extra subject. *What my advisor told me yesterday* is a noun clause subject, and this noun clause subject is followed by the extra subject *it*. To correct this sentence, you should omit the extra subject *it*.

---

[6] A **subordinate clause** is a dependent clause that has both a subject and a verb and is introduced by a subordinate clause connector.

The following list provides the key information that you should remember about using correct complex sentences.

> ## Using Correct Complex Sentences
>
> 1. A complex sentence is a sentence with one main clause and one or more subordinate clauses.
> 2. Noun clauses, adjective clauses, and adverb clauses are subordinate clauses.
> 3. When a subject comes before an adjective clause, you should not add an extra subject after the adjective clause.
> 4. When a noun clause is used as a subject, you should not add an extra subject after the noun clause.

Appendix Exercise A6: Underline the subjects once and the verbs twice in the main clauses. Circle the subordinate noun and adjective clauses. Then indicate if the sentences are correct (C) or incorrect (I).

_____ I 1. The reason (that) he took the money it was to pay the bills.

_____ 2. Why the man did something so terrible will never be known.

_____ 3. The ticket that I need to get onto the plane was not included in the packet.

_____ 4. What the lifeguard did it was quite heroic.

_____ 5. The day when I found out the news it was a good day.

_____ 6. The teacher whose advice I remember to this day was my sixth grade teacher.

_____ 7. Where we went on vacation it was such a gorgeous place.

_____ 8. That Deko really said those words it could not be refuted.

_____ 9. The man who helped me the most in my life he was my high school coach.

_____ 10. How the paper got finished on time remains unclear to me.

_____ 11. What caused the accident on the freeway it is still unknown.

_____ 12. The plans that we made for our trip were not carefully thought out.

_____ 13. The process by which the decisions were made it was very slow.

_____ 14. Whatever she gets is what she deserves.

_____ 15. The employee who has the information that you need is out of the office.

_____ 16. What Min wrote in the letter it could not be taken back.

_____ 17. The officer who stopped me on the highway he gave me a ticket for speeding.

_____ 18. How he could believe something that is so incredible is beyond me.

_____ 19. The reason that I applied to the public school was that the tuition was lower.

_____ 20. Why they said what they said to the man who tried to assist them it was not clear.

Appendix Review Exercise (A4–A6): Correct the errors in the following passages.

1. I have two very personal reasons for coming to this conclusion. One of the reasons is related to my family relationships, the other is related to my finances.

2. A decision has been reached but the decision has not yet been announced. We must wait until four o'clock, that is when the decision will be announced.

3. What just happened this morning it was a complete shock to me. My math professor announced in class this morning that the exam that was scheduled for next Friday it would be given this morning. Unfortunately, I was not prepared for the exam this morning because did not expect the exam to be given then.

4. The department has announced that only two scholarships will be awarded and that more than a hundred applications for the scholarships have already been received. Nonetheless, I am still going to submit my application.

5. My family never really wanted to make so many moves, it had to do so. Because it was necessary for my father's career, so we moved almost every year.

6. I expect your papers to be very clearly organized; thus, you are required to turn in an outline before you complete your papers. Your outline should be turned in within two weeks; the final paper is not due for two months.

7. The university is considering implementing an increase in tuition for the coming year. The students believe that tuition should not be raised, however, the students will most likely not get what they want.

8. The details of the report are confidential, they will not be made public. If want to find out about the report, what you must do it is to file a petition to get hold of the report.

9. My dream house is one that would be in the mountains. It would be surrounded by trees and it would have a view of a gorgeous lake. Moreover, the only noises that could be heard they would be the sounds of birds singing.

10. You must develop your ideas thoroughly. If you make a statement, you should be sure to support that statement. You may use many kinds of ideas to support a statement. For example, you may use details, reasons, or examples.

ERROR CORRECTION/GRAMMAR

It is important when you are producing material on the TOEFL iBT® test that your English be grammatically correct. You should be sure that you know how to use subject/verb agreement, parallel structure, comparatives and superlatives, verb forms, verb uses, passives, nouns, pronouns, adjectives and adverbs, and articles correctly.

Subject/Verb Agreement

Subject/verb agreement is simple: if a subject is singular, then the verb that accompanies it must be singular, and if a subject is plural, then the verb that accompanies it must be plural.

> The <u>student</u> <u>takes</u> many exams.
>
> The <u>students</u> <u>take</u> many exams.

In the first example, the singular subject *student* requires the singular verb *takes*. In the second example, the plural subject *students* requires the plural verb *take*.

Although this might seem quite simple, there are some situations with subject/verb agreement that can be confusing. You should be careful of subject/verb agreement (1) after prepositional phrases, and (2) after expressions of quantity.

Appendix A7: MAKE VERBS AGREE AFTER PREPOSITIONAL PHRASES

Sometimes prepositional phrases can come between the subject and the verb. If the object of the preposition is singular and the subject is plural, or if the object of the preposition is plural and the subject is singular, there can be confusion in making the subject and verb agree.

> Incorrect: The <u>key</u> **to the doors** <u>are</u> in the drawer.
>
> Correct: The key to the doors is in the drawer.
>
> Incorrect: The <u>keys</u> **to the door** <u>is</u> in the drawer.
>
> Correct: The keys to the door are in the drawer.

In the first example, you might think that *doors* is the subject because it comes directly in front of the verb *are*. However, *doors* is not the subject because it is the object of the preposition *to*. The subject is *key*, so the verb should be *is*. In the second example, you might think that *door* is the subject because it comes directly in front of the verb *is*. You should recognize in this example that *door* is not the subject because it is the object of the preposition *to*. Because the subject is *keys*, the verb should be *are*.

The following chart outlines the key information that you should understand about subject/verb agreement with prepositional phrases.

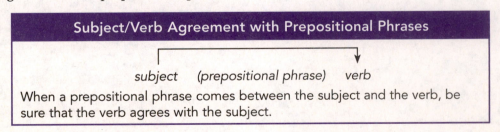

Subject/Verb Agreement with Prepositional Phrases

subject   (prepositional phrase)   verb

When a prepositional phrase comes between the subject and the verb, be sure that the verb agrees with the subject.

Appendix Exercise A7: Each of the following sentences has one or more prepositional phrases between the subject and the verb. Circle the prepositional phrases between the subject and verb. Underline the subjects once and the verbs twice. Then indicate if the sentences are correct (C) or incorrect (I). Correct the errors.

__C__ 1. The forest rangers (in the eastern section) (of the park) have spotted a bear.

__I__ 2. The flowers (on the plum tree) (in the garden) has started to bloom.
   (flowers . . . have started)

_____ 3. The cost of the books for all of his classes are quite high.

_____ 4. The reports prepared by the staff for the manager contain many graphs and charts.

_____ 5. The light from the candles on the end tables provide a soft glow to the room.

_____ 6. The ideas suggested at the meeting of the council was well received by most attendees.

_____ 7. The gemstones in the necklace worn by the actress were beautifully matched.

_____ 8. The speech on a variety of topics of great importance to the citizens are being broadcast this evening.

_____ 9. The new tires for the front of the car are being installed at this moment.

_____ 10. The exams scheduled for the last week of the semester is going to be comprehensive exams.

Appendix A8: Make Verbs Agree after Expressions of Quantity

A particular agreement problem occurs when the subject is an expression of quantity, such as *all, most,* or *some,* followed by the preposition *of.* In this situation, the subject (*all, most,* or *some*) can be singular or plural, depending on what follows the preposition *of.*

> All (of the book) was interesting.
>
> All (of the books) were interesting.
>
> All (of the information) was interesting.

In the first example, the subject *All* refers to the singular noun *book.* In the second example, the subject *All* refers to the plural noun *books,* so the correct verb is the plural verb *were.* In the third example, the subject *All* refers to the uncountable noun *information,* so the correct verb is therefore the singular verb *was.*

The following chart outlines the key information that you should understand about subject/verb agreement after expressions of quantity.

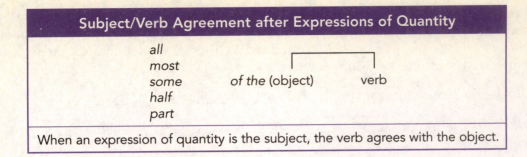

Subject/Verb Agreement after Expressions of Quantity

all
most
some   of the (object)   verb
half
part

When an expression of quantity is the subject, the verb agrees with the object.

Appendix Exercise A8: Each of the following sentences has a quantity expression as the subject. Underline the subjects once and the verbs twice. Circle the objects that the verbs agree with. Then indicate if the sentences are correct (C) or incorrect (I). Correct the errors.

__C__ 1. All of his past (experience) has contributed to his present success.

__I__ 2. Most of the (dishes) served at the banquet was quite spicy.
       (Most of the dishes served at the banquet were quite spicy.)

_____ 3. Some of the details of the plan requires clarification.

_____ 4. Half of the material needs to be completed this week.

_____ 5. All of the homes on this block of town was flooded during the storm.

_____ 6. Most of the children in the class has improved their reading scores tremendously.

_____ 7. Some of the money from the inheritance has to be used to pay taxes.

_____ 8. I bought a carton of eggs yesterday, but half of the eggs in the carton was broken.

_____ 9. For Jane's health to improve, all of the medicine has to be taken on schedule.

_____ 10. At the conference, most of the time allocated for speeches was actually devoted to discussion.

Parallel Structure

In good English, an attempt should be made to make the language as even and balanced as possible. This balance is called "parallel structure." You can achieve parallel structure by making the forms as similar as possible. The following is an example of a sentence that is not parallel.

> Incorrect: I like <u>to sing</u> and <u>dancing</u>.

> Correct: I like to sing and to dance. *OR* I like singing and dancing.

The problem in this sentence is not the expression *to sing*, and the problem is not the word *dancing*. The expression *to sing* is correct by itself, and the word *dancing* is correct by itself. Both of the following sentences are correct.

> I like <u>to sing</u>.

> I like <u>dancing</u>.

The problem in the incorrect example is that *to sing* and *dancing* are joined together in one sentence with *and*. They are different forms where it is possible to have similar forms; the example is therefore not parallel. It can be corrected in two different ways.

> I like <u>to sing</u> and <u>to dance</u>.
>
> I like <u>singing</u> and <u>dancing</u>.

Two issues in parallel structure that you should be familiar with are (1) the use of parallel structure with coordinate conjunctions, and (2) the use of parallel structure with paired conjunctions.

Appendix A9: Use Parallel Structure with Coordinate Conjunctions

The job of coordinate conjunctions (*and, but, or, yet*) is to join together equal expressions. In other words, what is on one side of these words must be parallel to what is on the other side. These conjunctions can join nouns, verbs, adjectives, phrases, or subordinate clauses. They just must join together two of the same thing. Look at the following examples.

> She is not a <u>teacher</u> *but* a <u>lawyer</u>.
>
> He <u>studied</u> hard *yet* <u>failed</u> the exam.
>
> My boss is <u>sincere</u>, <u>friendly</u>, *and* <u>nice</u>.
>
> The papers are <u>on my desk</u> *or* <u>in the drawer</u>.
>
> I am here <u>because I have to be</u> *and* <u>because I want to be</u>.

In the first example, the coordinate conjunction *but* joins two nouns, *teacher* and *lawyer*. In the second example, the coordinate conjunction *yet* joins two verbs, *studied* and *failed*. In the third example, the coordinate conjunction *and* joins three adjectives, *sincere, friendly,* and *nice*. In the fourth example, the coordinate conjunction *or* joins two prepositional phrases, *on my desk* and *in the drawer*. In the last example, the coordinate conjunction *and* joins two clauses, *because I have to be* and *because I want to be*.

The following chart describes the use of parallel structures with coordinate conjunctions.

Parallel Structure with Coordinate Conjunctions			
(same structure)		*and* *but* *or* *yet*	(same structure)
(same structure),	(same structure),	*and* *but* *or* *yet*	(same structure)

Appendix Exercise A9: Each of the following sentences contains words or groups of words that should be parallel. Circle the word that indicates that the sentence should have parallel parts. Underline the parts that should be parallel. Then indicate if the sentences are correct (C) or incorrect (I). Correct the errors.

___I___ 1. The movie <u>was really scary</u> (but) <u>was still quite pleasure</u>.
(*was still quite pleasurable*)

___C___ 2. He said <u>that he was sorry</u> (and) <u>that he would make amends</u>.

_____ 3. The leader spoke of the need for idealism, integrity, and dedicate.

_____ 4. The ball player was not very tall yet was quite athlete.

_____ 5. To contact me, you may call on the phone, write a letter, or send a fax.

_____ 6. This English course is offered in the spring semester but not in the fall semester.

_____ 7. For his job, he travels back and forth between Los Angeles and New York to pick up packages and delivers them.

_____ 8. Sam can work on the report in the library or studies at home.

_____ 9. The news report described the pain, anger, resentment, frustration, and disbelief in the aftermath of the accident.

_____ 10. She gave a well-rehearsed yet natural-sounding speech.

Appendix A10: Use Parallel Structure with Paired Conjunctions

The paired conjunctions *both . . . and, either . . . or, neither . . . nor,* and *not only . . . but also* require parallel structures. Look at the following examples.

> I know *both* <u>where you went</u> *and* <u>what you did</u>.
>
> *Either* <u>Mark</u> *or* <u>Sue</u> has the book.
>
> The tickets are *neither* <u>in my pocket</u> *nor* <u>in my purse</u>.
>
> He *not only* <u>works hard</u> *but also* <u>plays hard</u>.

In the first example, the paired conjunction *both . . . and* is followed by parallel clauses, *where you went* and *what you did*. In the second example, the paired conjunction *Either . . . or* is followed by parallel nouns, *Mark* and *Sue*. In the third example, the paired conjunction *neither . . . nor* is followed by parallel phrases, *in my pocket* and *in my purse*. In the last example, the paired conjunction *not only . . . but also* is followed by parallel verb phrases, *works hard* and *plays hard*.

The following chart describes the use of parallel structure with paired conjunctions.

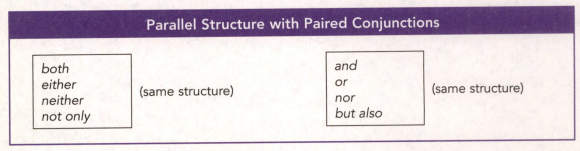

Parallel Structure with Paired Conjunctions			
both either neither not only	(same structure)	and or nor but also	(same structure)

Appendix Exercise A10: Each of the following sentences contains words or groups of words that should be parallel. Circle the word or words that indicate that the sentence should have parallel parts. Underline the parts that should be parallel. Then indicate if the sentences are correct (C) or incorrect (I). Correct the errors.

___I___   1. He (not only) plays football (but also) baseball.
             (plays baseball)

___C___   2. The children were (either) praised (or) scolded for their behavior.

_____   3. There is food to eat both in the refrigerator and the freezer.

_____   4. It has been decided to do neither what you prefer or what I prefer.

_____   5. She not only misplaced her textbook but also couldn't locate her notebook.

_____   6. Either you can work on this committee or join a different one.

_____   7. She was both challenged by and frustrated with her job.

_____   8. Neither the manager nor any members of the staff are staying late today.

_____   9. You can either register for three courses or for four courses.

_____ 10. Both the children as well as the baby-sitter fell asleep.

Comparatives and Superlatives

A comparative (formed with *-er* or *more*) indicates how two items relate to each other, while a superlative (formed with *-est* or *most*) indicates how one item relates to a group.

> My history class is much *harder* than my science class.
>
> My history class is much *more interesting* than my science class.
>
> My history class is *the hardest* of all my classes.
>
> My history class is *the most interesting* of all my classes.

In the first two examples, the comparatives *harder* and *more interesting* show how the history class relates to the science class. In the last two examples, the superlatives *the hardest* and *the most interesting* show how the history class relates to all of the classes.

Comparatives and superlatives are important in academic language. It is important for you to know how to do the following: (1) form the comparative and superlative correctly, and (2) use the comparative and superlative correctly.

Appendix A11: Form Comparatives and Superlatives Correctly

The comparative is formed with either *-er* or *more* and *than*. In the comparative, *-er* is used with shorter (one-syllable and some two-syllable) adjectives such as *tall*, and *more* is used with longer (some two-syllable and all three-or-more-syllable) adjectives such as *beautiful*.

> Rich is *taller than* Ron.
>
> Sally is *more beautiful than* Sharon.

The superlative is formed with *the*, either *-est* or *most*, and sometimes *in*, *of*, or a *that* clause. In the superlative, *-est* is used with shorter adjectives such as *tall*, and *most* is used with longer adjectives such as *beautiful*.

> Rich is *the tallest* man *in* the room.
>
> Sally is *the most beautiful of* all the women in the room.
>
> The spider by the window is *the largest* one *that* I have ever seen.
>
> *The fastest* runner wins the race. (no *in*, *of*, or *that*)

The following chart outlines the possible forms of comparatives and superlatives.

Forms of Comparatives and Superlatives			
Comparative	short adjective + *-er* *more* + long adjective	*than*	
Superlative	*the*	short adjective + *-est* *most* + long adjective	maybe *in*, *of*, *that*
Shorter adjectives are all one-syllable adjectives and some two-syllable adjectives. Longer adjectives are some two-syllable adjectives and all adjectives with three or more syllables.			

Appendix Exercise A11: Each of the following sentences contains a comparative or superlative. Circle the comparative or superlative. Then indicate if the sentences are correct (C) or incorrect (I). Correct the errors.

__I__ 1. This morning I heard (the unusualest) story in the news.
   (*the most unusual*)

__C__ 2. This bicycle is (more expensive than) mine.

_____ 3. Today she became the angriest that I have ever seen her.

_____ 4. This classroom is the hotter than the one next door.

_____ 5. The weather today is much more cloudier today than it was yesterday.

_____ 6. This room houses the most ancient pieces of sculpture in the museum.

_____ 7. The seats on this airline are wider than those on the airline that I took last week.

_____ 8. The building where Nina works is the most tallest in town.

_____ 9. This restaurant has most efficient service of all the restaurants I have visited.

_____ 10. This type of coffee is stronger and more flavorful than my regular coffee.

Appendix A12: Use Comparatives And Superlatives Correctly

The comparative and superlative have different uses, and it is important to understand these differences. The comparative is used to describe two unequal things.

> The math class is *larger than* the philosophy class.
>
> Jean is *more intelligent than* Joan.

In the first example, the *math class* is being compared with the *philosophy class*, and they are not equal. In the second example, *Jean* is being compared with *Joan*, and they are not equal.

The superlative is used when there are more than two items to compare and one of them is outstanding in some way.

> The math class is *the largest* in the school.
>
> Jean is *the most intelligent* in the class.

In the first example, the *math class* is compared with all of the other classes *in the school*, and the math class is larger than each of the other classes. In the second example, *Jean* is compared with all of the other students *in the class*, and Jean is more intelligent than each of the other students.

The following chart outlines the uses of comparatives and superlatives.

Uses of Comparatives and Superlatives	
Comparatives	These words are used to show the relationship between two things, and these two things are not equal.
Superlatives	These words are used to show how one item is outstanding in a group of three or more.

Appendix Exercise A12: Each of the following sentences contains a comparative or superlative. Circle the comparative or superlative. Then indicate if the sentences are correct (C) or incorrect (I). Correct the errors.

_C_   1. We have (the friendliest) pets of all.

_I_   2. This set of problems is (the most difficult of) the last set was.
      (more difficult than)

_____ 3. The grey cat has a nicest disposition than the black cat.

_____ 4. You missed the best party of the year last night.

_____ 5. Her car is the most fuel-efficient of most other cars.

_____ 6. The weather this year is the drier that it has been in a decade.

_____ 7. My boss is not the most understanding of bosses.

_____ 8. This is earlier that I have ever arrived at work.

_____ 9. The scores on the second exam were the highest of those on the first exam.

_____ 10. Cathy is more reticent than the other students in the class to volunteer answers.

Appendix Review Exercise (A7–A12): Indicate if the following sentences are correct (C) or incorrect (I).

_____ 1. The new movie is not only deeply moving but also very well paced.

_____ 2. Some of the rooms were scheduled to be painted this week.

_____ 3. Please drop these letters off at the most near post office.

_____ 4. The man wrote and signed the check, presented it to the cashier, and leaving with cash.

_____ 5. The noises coming from outside the house was frightening the family inside.

_____ 6. Today she has scheduled the more important interview of her career.

_____ 7. Your excuses are neither credible nor acceptable.

_____ 8. Half of your answers on the exam were less than adequate.

_____ 9. Hal is trying to behave in a more honorabler way than he has in the past.

_____ 10. After dinner, we can take a walk, play a game, or go bowling.

_____ 11. The stairs leading to the top floor of the building is blocked now.

_____ 12. This is a more ridiculous plan than you have ever made.

_____ 13. The politician claimed that he had neither asked for nor accepted any illegal donations.

_____ 14. I believe that most of the reasons presented in the report was convincing.

_____ 15. The trip by train is longer but less expensive than the trip by plane.

Verb Forms

You should be familiar with the following verb forms: the base form, the third-person singular, the past, the past participle, and the present participle.

Verb Forms				
Base Form	**Third-Person Singular**	**Past**	**Past Participle**	**Present Participle**
walk	walks	walked	walked	walking
hear	hears	heard	heard	hearing
take	takes	took	taken	taking
begin	begins	began	begun	beginning
come	comes	came	come	coming
think	thinks	thought	thought	thinking

You should be particularly aware of the following three problematic situations with verb forms because they are the most common and the easiest to correct: (1) using the correct form after *have,* (2) using the correct form after *be,* and (3) using the correct form after modals.

Appendix A13: After *have*, Use the Past Participle

The verb *have* in any of its forms (*have, has, had, having*) can be followed by another verb. Whenever you use the verb *have* in any of its forms, you should be sure that a verb that follows it is in the past participle form.

Incorrect: They *had walk* to school.	Correct: They *had walked* to school.
Incorrect: We *have see* the show.	Correct: We *have seen* the show.
Incorrect: He *has took* the test.	Correct: He *has taken* the test.
Incorrect: *Having ate,* he went to school.	Correct: *Having eaten,* he went to school
Incorrect: She *should have did* the work.	Correct: She *should have done* the work.

In addition, you should be sure that if you have a subject and a past participle, you also have a form of the verb *have*.

Incorrect: My friend *sung* in the choir.	Correct: My friend *sang* (or *has sung*) in the choir.
Incorrect: He *become* angry at his friend.	Correct: He *became* (or *has become*) angry at his friend.
Incorrect: The boat *sunk* in the ocean.	Correct: The boat *sank* (or *has sunk*) in the ocean.

The following chart outlines the use of verb forms after *have*.

Verb Forms after *have*
have + past participle

Appendix Exercise A13: Each of the following sentences contains a verb formed with *have*. Underline the verbs twice, and study the forms following *have*. Then indicate if the sentences are correct (C) or incorrect (I). Correct the errors.

__I__   1. Her sisters <u>have came</u> to help plan the party.
            (have come)

__C__   2. I <u>thought</u> that I <u>had told</u> you everything.

_____   3. The girl has wore the same dress to school each day this week.

_____   4. High winds have blown the plane off course.

_____   5. The computer cartridge has running out of ink.

_____   6. Lightning had struck and had knocked the tree down.

_____   7. Perhaps you have drew the wrong conclusion.

_____   8. The professor has taught this course many times before.

_____   9. The surprised student had not knew that there was an exam that day.

_____   10. All the family members have always gotten together to celebrate Thanksgiving.

Appendix A14: After *be*, Use the Present Participle or the Past Participle

The verb *be* in any of its forms (*am, is, are, was, were, be, been, being*) can be followed by another verb. This verb should be in the present participle or past participle form.

Incorrect: We *are do* our homework.   Correct: We *are doing* our homework.

Incorrect: The homework *was do* early.   Correct: The homework *was done* early.

Incorrect: Tom *is take* the book.   Correct: Tom *is taking* the book.

The following chart outlines the use of verb forms after *be*.

Verb Forms after *be*
be + present participle (or) past participle

Appendix Exercise A14: Each of the following sentences contains a verb formed with *be*. Underline the verbs twice, and study the forms following *be*. Then indicate if the sentences are correct (C) or incorrect (I). Correct the errors.

___I___ 1. The new president <u>will be inaugurate</u> next week.
         (will be inaugurated)

___C___ 2. The plans that <u>were presented</u> last week <u>are unchanged</u>.

_____ 3. The photograph was took without her consent.

_____ 4. Vu has been promoted because of her excellent work.

_____ 5. We are always arguing about what is occurs in politics.

_____ 6. He should not have been smoke in the office, but he was.

_____ 7. The telephone was ringing constantly throughout the day.

_____ 8. All of the plants were froze because of the cold weather.

_____ 9. Everyone is wondering when the train will be departing.

_____ 10. The planes were take off and land right on schedule.

Appendix A15: After *will*, *would*, or Other Modals, Use the Base Form of the Verb

Modals such as *will, would, shall, should, can, could, may, might,* and *must* are helping verbs that will be followed by a base form of the verb. Whenever you see a modal, you should be sure that the verb that follows it is its base form.

Incorrect: The boat *will leaving* at
3:00 p.m.   Correct: The boat *will leave* at 3:00 p.m.

Incorrect: The doctor *may arrives* soon.   Correct: The doctor *may arrive* soon.

Incorrect: The students *must taken*
the exam.   Correct: The students *must take* the exam.

The following chart outlines the use of verb forms after modals.

Verb Forms after Modals
modal + base form of the verb

Appendix Exercise A15: Each of the following sentences contains a verb formed with a modal. Underline the verbs twice, and study the forms following the modals. Then indicate if the sentences are correct (C) or incorrect (I). Correct the errors.

_C_ 1. The professor <u>cannot return</u> the papers until tomorrow.

_I_ 2. The tour guide <u>may preferring</u> to leave within an hour.
(may prefer)

_____ 3. The next step in the process will depends on the results of the medical tests.

_____ 4. He asked if you might be coming to the party.

_____ 5. The team members must to try considerably harder in the second half of the game.

_____ 6. My friend told me that he could taken care of the problem.

_____ 7. When do you think the company might announce its decision?

_____ 8. The teaching assistant must not gave the students any more time for the test.

_____ 9. Many of the cars on the lot will going on sale this weekend.

_____ 10. He was angry because his car would not start this morning.

Verb Uses

Many different problems in using verb tenses are possible in English. Three of them occur frequently, so you need to pay careful attention to them: (1) knowing when to use the past with the present, (2) using *had* and *have* tenses correctly, and (3) using the correct tense with time expressions.

Appendix A16: Know When to Use the Past with the Present

One common verb tense problem is the switch from the past tense to the present tense for no particular reason. Often, when a sentence has both a past tense and a present tense, the sentence is incorrect.

Incorrect: He *took* the money when he *wants* it.

This sentence says that *he took the money* (in the past) *when he wants it* (in the present). This sentence does not make sense because it is impossible to do something in the past as a result of wanting it in the present. This sentence can be corrected in several ways, depending on the desired meaning.

Correct: He *took* the money when he *wanted* it.

Correct: He *takes* the money when he *wants* it.

The first example means that *he took the money* (in the past) *when he wanted it* (in the past). This meaning is logical, and the sentence is correct. The second example means that *he takes the money* (habitually) *when he wants it* (habitually). This meaning is also logical, and the second example is also correct.

It is necessary to point out, however, that it is possible for a logical sentence in English to have both a present tense and a past tense.

I *know* that he *took* the money yesterday.

The meaning of this sentence is logical: *I know* (right now, in the present) that he *took the money* (yesterday, in the past). You can see from this example that it is possible for an English sentence to have both a present tense and a past tense. When you see a sentence with both a present tense and a past tense, you must think about whether the meaning is logical.

The following list provides key information about the use of the past tense and the present tense.

Using the Past with the Present

1. If you see a sentence with one verb in the past and one verb in the present, the sentence is probably incorrect.
2. However, it is possible for a logical sentence to have both the past and the present together.
3. If you see the past and the present together, you must check the meaning to determine whether the sentence is logical.

Appendix Exercise A16: Each of the following sentences has at least one verb in the past and one verb in the present. Underline the verbs twice, and decide if the meanings are logical. Then indicate if the sentences are correct (C) or incorrect (I). Correct the errors.

__I__ 1. The audience members <u>need</u> to take their seats because the play <u>was</u> about to start.
(is)

__C__ 2. Today's newspaper <u>has</u> a story that <u>describes</u> what <u>happened</u> during the tragedy.

_____ 3. When he told her the truth, she is pleased with what she heard.

_____ 4. Mrs. Weaver is well aware that the students did not understand the assignment.

_____ 5. I had problems in my last math course, but this one is going much better.

_____ 6. Every morning Rob leaves the house at the same time and took the bus to work.

_____ 7. As the plane was landing, the passengers remain in their seats with their seat belts fastened.

_____ 8. The police are certain that the suspect committed the crime.

_____ 9. On the way home from work, they filled the car up with gas and then heads to the supermarket.

_____ 10. People understand what happened, but they are unclear about why it occurred this way.

Appendix A17: Use *have* and *had* Correctly

Two tenses that are often confused are the present perfect (*have* + past participle) and the past perfect (*had* + past participle). These two tenses have completely different uses, and you should understand how to differentiate them.

The present perfect (*have* + past participle) can refer to the period of time *from the past until the present*.

> Sue *has lived* in Los Angeles for ten years.

This sentence means that Sue has lived in Los Angeles for the ten years up to the present. According to this sentence, Sue is still living in Los Angeles.

Because the present perfect can refer to a period of time from the past until the present, it is not correct in a sentence that indicates past only.

> Incorrect: *At the start of the nineteenth century,* Thomas Jefferson *has become* president of the United States.
>
> Correct: At the start of the nineteenth century, Thomas Jefferson became president of the United States.

In this example, the phrase *at the start of the nineteenth century* indicates that the action of the verb was in the past only, but the verb indicates the period of time from the past until the present. Since this is not logical, the sentence is not correct. The verb *has become* should be changed to *became*.

The past perfect (*had* + past participle) refers to a period of time that *started in the past and ended in the past, before something else occurred in the past.*

> Sue *had lived* in Los Angeles for ten years when she *moved* to San Diego.

This sentence means that Sue lived in Los Angeles for ten years in the past, before she moved to San Diego. She no longer lives in Los Angeles.

Because the past perfect begins in the past and ends in the past, it is generally not correct in the same sentence with the present tense.

> Incorrect: Tom *had finished* the exam when the teacher *collects* the papers.
>
> Correct: Tom had finished the exam when the teacher collected the papers.

This sentence indicates that *Tom finished the exam* (in the past), and that action ended in the past at the same time that *the teacher collects the papers* (in the present). This sentence is not logical, so the sentence is not correct.

The following chart outlines the uses of the present perfect and the past perfect.

Using (*have* + Past Participle) and (*had* + Past Participle)			
Tense	Form	Meaning	Use
present perfect	*have* + past participle	past up to now	not with a past tense*
past perfect	*had* + past participle	before past	not with a present tense
*Except when the time expression *since* is part of the sentence (see Appendix A18).			

Appendix Exercise A17: Each of the following sentences contains a form of *had* or *have*. Underline the verbs twice and decide if the meanings are logical. Then indicate if the sentences are correct (C) or incorrect (I). Correct the errors.

_C_ 1. She <u>is</u> very pleased that her son <u>has graduated</u> with honors.

_I_ 2. After the bell <u>had rung</u>, the students <u>leave</u> class quickly.
(*left*)

_____ 3. I have visited that museum each time that I traveled to the city.

_____ 4. The lawyer suddenly found out that he had made a big error.

_____ 5. Admissions are based on what you have done throughout your high school years.

_____ 6. When all the papers had been collected, the teacher dismisses the class.

_____ 7. The garden was not growing well because there had not been much rain for months.

_____ 8. She knows that you have always tried to be helpful.

_____ 9. I can tell you what I know about what has transpired during the investigation.

_____ 10. We will be able to discuss the situation thoroughly after you have submitted your report.

Appendix A18: Use the Correct Tense with Time Expressions

When a time expression is used in a sentence, it commonly indicates what tense is needed in the sentence.

We <u>moved</u> to New York *in 1998.*

We <u>had left</u> there *by 2002.*

We <u>have lived</u> in San Francisco *since 2004.*

In the first example, the time expression *in 1998* indicates that the verb should be in the simple past (*moved*). In the second example, the time expression *by 2002* indicates that the verb should be in the past perfect (*had left*). In the third example, the time expression *since 2004* indicates that the verb should be in the present perfect (*have lived*).

Some additional time expressions that clearly indicate the correct tense are *ago, last,* and *lately.*

She <u>got</u> a job *two years ago.*

She <u>started</u> working *last week.*

She <u>has worked</u> very hard *lately.*

In the first example, the time expression *two years ago* indicates that the verb should be in the simple past (*got*). In the second example, the time expression *last week* indicates that the verb should be in the simple past (*started*). In the third example, the time expression *lately* indicates that the verb should be in the present perfect (*has worked*).

The following chart lists time expressions that indicate the correct verb tense.

Using Correct Tenses with Time Expressions		
Past Perfect	**Simple Past**	**Present Perfect**
by (1920)	(one century) ago since (1920) last (century)	in (1920) lately

Appendix Exercise A18: Each of the following sentences contains a time expression. Circle the time expressions, and underline the verbs twice. Then indicate if the sentences are correct (C) or incorrect (I). Correct the errors.

__I__ 1. (By 1995) Steve <u>has decided</u> to pursue a different career.
(had decided)

__C__ 2. This university <u>was established</u> (in 1900) at the turn of the last century.

_____ 3. Since I last saw you, I got a job at the United Nations.

_____ 4. Mike has applied to law school a few months ago.

_____ 5. The organization elected new officers just last month.

_____ 6. We experienced problem after problem lately.

_____ 7. By the end of the conference, all of the participants had reached an agreement.

_____ 8. Sara has finally graduated from the university in June.

_____ 9. I am living in the same neighborhood since I was a child.

_____ 10. I was glad that you called me because I tried to call you just a few minutes ago and got a busy signal.

Passive Verbs

In a passive sentence, the subject and object are reversed from where they are found in an active sentence. A passive verb consists of a form of the verb *be* and a past participle, and *by* is used in front of the object in a passive verb.

The teacher <u>graded</u> the papers.   (active)

The <u>papers</u> were graded by the teacher.   (passive)

The first example is an active statement, and the second example is a passive statement. The subject from the active statement (*teacher*) has become the object following *by* in the passive example; the object from the active example (*papers*) has become the subject in the passive example. The verb in the passive example consists of a form of *be* (*were*) and a past participle (*graded*).

It should be noted that, in a passive sentence, *by + object* does not need to be included to have a complete sentence.

> The papers were graded by the teacher.

> The papers were graded.

Each of these examples is a correct sentence. The first example is a passive statement that includes *by the teacher*. The second example is a passive statement that does not include *by*.

You should pay attention to the passive in your English. You should pay attention to (1) the form of the passive, and (2) the use of the passive. Do not use too many passive sentences.

Appendix A19: Use the Correct Form of the Passive

One possible problem with the passive is an incorrect form of the passive. A correctly formed passive will always have a form of *be* and a past participle. The following are examples of common errors in the form of the passive.

> Incorrect: The portrait *was painting* by a famous artist.
>
> Correct: The portrait was painted by a famous artist

> Incorrect: The project *will finished* by the group.
>
> Correct: The project will be finished by the group

In the first example, the passive is formed incorrectly because the past participle *painted* should be used rather than the present participle *painting*. In the second example, the verb *be* has not been included, and some form of *be* is necessary for a passive verb. The verb in the second example should be *will be finished*.

The following chart outlines the correct method to form the passive.

The Form of the Passive
be + past participle

Appendix Exercise A19: Each of the following sentences has a passive meaning. Underline twice the verbs that should be passive. Then indicate if the sentences are correct (C) or incorrect (I). Correct the errors.

__I__ 1. The trees and hedges <u>will be trim</u> this week.
      (will be trimmed)

__C__ 2. That kind of decision <u>is made</u> by the board of directors.

_____ 3. The bank robbed yesterday by a masked gunman.

_____ 4. The plans for the building complex were describing by the architect.

_____ 5. The oil has been changed, and the tires have been filled with air.

_____ 6. Some tickets to the concert have given away by the concert promoters.

_____ 7. As soon as the food was cooked, it was brought to the table.

_____ 8. The money for the purchase was accepted the clerk.

_____ 9. Students will not be allowed to register if their fees have not been pay.

_____ 10. The election is being held, and the results will be posted by the election committee.

Appendix A20: Recognize Active and Passive Meanings

When there is no object (with or without *by*) after a verb, you must look at the meaning of the sentence to determine if the verb should be active or passive. Look at the following examples.

Correct: We <u>mailed</u> the *package* at the post office.

Correct: The letter <u>was mailed</u> *by us* today before noon.

Correct: The letter <u>was mailed</u> today before noon.

Incorrect: The letter <u>mailed</u> today before noon.

The first three examples are all correct. The first example has the active verb *mailed* used with the object *package*; the second example has the passive verb *was mailed* used with *by us*; the third example has the passive verb *was mailed* used without an object. The last example is not correct. The verb *mailed* looks like a correct active verb, but a passive verb is needed. There is no *by* and an object to tell you that a passive verb is needed; instead, you must understand from the meaning that it is incorrect. You should ask yourself *if the letter mails itself* (the letter *does* the action) or if *someone mails the letter* (the letter *receives* the action of being mailed). Since a letter does not mail itself, the passive is required in this sentence. The verb in the last example should be changed from the active *mailed* to the passive *was mailed*.

The following chart outlines the difference in meaning between active and passive verbs.

Active and Passive Meanings	
Active	The subject does the action of the verb.
Passive	The subject receives the action of the verb.

Appendix Exercise A20: Each of the following sentences contains at least one active verb; however, some of the verbs should be passive. Underline the verbs twice. Then indicate if the sentences are correct (C) or incorrect (I). Correct the errors.

_____I_____   1. The game <u>won</u> in overtime.
              (was won)

_____C_____   2. The engine <u>started</u> on the very first try.

_____   3. The photos placed in frames on the mantle.

_____   4. The top students selected to receive scholarships.

_____   5. The store opened right on schedule.

_____   6. The outcome expected because of the lack of effort.

_____   7. The comedian's jokes amused the audience.

_____   8. The policy changes announced late yesterday afternoon.

_____   9. The chair knocked over, and the child fell off.

_____ 10. The surgical procedure lasted for more than six hours.

Appendix Review Exercise (A13–A20): Indicate if the following sentences are correct (C) or incorrect (I).

_____   1. The director may has to cut a few of the more violent scenes from the movie.

_____   2. He feels the way that he does today because of what occurred in the past.

_____   3. The vegetables washed and chopped up for salad.

_____   4. The children have drank all of the milk from the refrigerator.

_____   5. The family did not take any long vacations lately.

_____   6. It is expects that many of the employees will be transferred to new positions.

_____   7. The company was found more than a hundred years ago.

_____   8. The report clearly proved that no one had been treated unfairly.

_____   9. I would like to know when you will be able to give me the money.

_____ 10. The home owner knew that he has paid his insurance premiums on time.

_____ 11. I am worrying about the decisions that I am try to make.

_____ 12. By the end of the final talk, the lecturer has managed to convey his main points.

_____ 13. I am satisfied that you did everything possible to resolve the problem.

_____ 14. I had sought advice from my counselor prior to registering for classes.

_____ 15. The story appeared in the newspaper soon after the politician interviewed.

Nouns

A noun is the part of speech that is used to refer to a person, place, thing (or idea). Two issues related to nouns are (1) whether they are singular or plural, and (2) whether they are countable or uncountable.

Appendix A21: Use the Correct Singular or Plural Noun

A common problem with nouns is whether to use a singular or a plural noun.

Incorrect:	On the table there were many *dish*.
Correct:	On the table there were many dishes.

Incorrect:	The lab assistant finished every *tests*.
Correct:	The lab assistant finished every test.

In the first example, *many* indicates that the plural *dishes* is needed. In the second example, *every* indicates that the singular *test* is needed.

You should watch very carefully for key words such as *each, every, one, single,* and *a* that indicate that a noun should be singular. You should also watch carefully for such key words as *many, several, both, various,* and *two* (or any other number except *one*) that indicate that a noun should be plural.

The following chart lists the key words that indicate to you whether a noun should be singular or plural.

Key Words for Singular and Plural Nouns					
For Singular Nouns	each	every	single	one	a
For Plural Nouns	both	two	many	several	various

Appendix Exercise A21: Each of the following sentences contains at least one key word to tell you if a noun should be singular or plural. Circle the key words. Underline the nouns they describe. Then indicate if the sentences are correct (C) or incorrect (I). Correct the errors.

_____ I 1. (Each) exhibits in the zoo is open today.
           (exhibit)

_____ C 2. (Both) children have (various) assignments to complete tonight.

_____ 3. Would you like a single scoop of ice cream or two scoops?

_____ 4. She must take several pills every days.

_____ 5. Final exam week is an exhausting time for many students.

_____ 6. Various plans for a new community centers have been offered.

_____ 7. Every times that I go there, I run into several acquaintances.

_____ 8. A single serving at this restaurant consists of more food than one people can consume.

_____ 9. One incident last week caused many misunderstandings.

_____ 10. There are several candidates for the position, and each ones of them is extremely qualified.

Appendix A22: Distinguish Countable and Uncountable Nouns

In English, nouns are classified as either countable or uncountable. It is necessary to distinguish countable and uncountable nouns in order to use the correct modifiers with them.

As the name implies, countable nouns can be counted. Countable nouns can come in quantities of one, two, a hundred, and so forth. The noun _book_ is countable because you can have one book or several books.

Uncountable nouns, on the other hand, cannot be counted because they come in some indeterminate quantity or mass. A noun such as _happiness_ cannot be counted; you cannot have one happiness or two happinesses.

It is important for you to recognize the difference between countable and uncountable nouns when you come across such key words as _much_ and _many_.

Incorrect: He has seen _much_ foreign _films._

Correct: He has seen many foreign films.

Incorrect: He did not have _many fun_ at the movies.

Correct: He did not have much fun at the movies.

In the first example, _much_ is incorrect because _films_ is countable. This example should say _many foreign films._ In the second example, _many_ is incorrect because _fun_ is uncountable. This example should say _much fun._

The following chart lists the key word that indicates to you whether a noun should be countable or uncountable.

Key Words for Countable and Uncountable Nouns			
For Countable Nouns	_many_ _number_	_few_	_fewer_
For Uncountable Nouns	_much_ _amount_	_little_	_less_

Appendix Exercise A22: Each of the following sentences contains at least one key word to tell you if a noun should be countable or uncountable. Circle the key words. Underline the nouns they describe. Then indicate if the sentences are correct (C) or incorrect (I). Correct the errors.

_C_ 1. (Many) applicants came to see about the job.

_I_ 2. Today, there is an unusually large (amount) of people in the room. (_number_)

_____ 3. Few suggestions and little assistance were offered.

_____ 4. We need to have more opportunities and less restrictions.

_____ 5. The official gave us much sincere assurances that we would receive assistance.

_____ 6. A large number of the facts in the report are being disputed.

_____ 7. I have less concern than she does about the much unpaid bills.

_____ 8. There are fewer men than women serving on the committee.

_____ 9. Of the many potential problems, only a little have been resolved.

_____ 10. A huge amount of paper was used to prepare the report.

Pronouns

Pronouns are words such as *he, us,* or *them* that take the place of nouns. The following pronoun problems are common: (1) distinguishing subject and object pronouns, (2) distinguishing possessive pronouns and possessive determiners, and (3) checking pronoun reference for agreement.

Appendix A23: Distinguish Subject and Object Pronouns

Subject and object pronouns can easily be confused, so you need to think carefully about these pronouns.

Pronouns	
Subject	**Object**
I	*me*
you	*you*
he	*him*
she	*her*
it	*it*
we	*us*
they	*them*

A subject pronoun is used as the subject of a verb. An object pronoun can be used as the object of a preposition. Compare the following two examples.

> Sally gave the book to John.
>
> *She* gave it to *him.*

In the second sentence, the subject pronoun *she* is replacing the noun *Sally.* The object of the verb *it* is replacing the noun *book,* and the object of the preposition *him* is replacing the noun *John.*

The following are examples of the types of subject or object pronoun errors you might see.

> Incorrect: *Him and me* are going to the movies.
>
> Correct: He and I are going to the movies.

> Incorrect: The secret is between *you and I.*
>
> Correct: The secret is between you and me.

In the first example, the object pronouns *him and me* are incorrect because these pronouns serve as the subject of the verb *are.* The object pronouns *him and me* should be changed to *he and I.* In the second example, the subject pronouns *you and I* are incorrect because these pronouns serve as the object of the preposition *between*. The subject pronouns *you and I* should be changed to *you and me*.

Appendix Exercise A23: Each of the following sentences contains at least one subject or object pronoun. Circle the pronouns. Then indicate if the sentences are correct (C) or incorrect (I). Correct the errors.

__I__   1. (Him) and (me) are going to be taking the early bus today.
        (He and I)

__C__   2. (We) will talk to (them), and (they) will listen to (us).

_____   3. Just between you and I, I think that they made the best decision.

_____   4. He and she have agreed to assist us with the project that we are trying to complete.

_____   5. You and I have to try harder to do more for he and her.

_____   6. It is challenging for we students to complete so many projects.

_____   7. She said that I did not give it to her, but I am sure that she is wrong.

_____   8. They sent you and I an invitation, so I think that we should attend the party.

_____   9. It is not about us; instead, it is all about him and her.

_____ 10. They could not have done any more to help you and I.

Appendix A24: Distinguish Possessive Determiners and Pronouns

Possessive determiners (or adjectives) and pronouns both show who or what "owns" a noun. However, possessive determiners and possessive pronouns do not have the same function, and these two kinds of possessives can easily be confused. A possessive determiner (or adjective) describes a noun: it must be accompanied by a noun. A possessive pronoun takes the place of a noun. It cannot be accompanied by a noun.

> They lent me *their book*.
>
> They lent me *theirs*.

In the first example, the possessive determiner *their* is accompanied by the noun *book*. In the second example, the possessive pronoun *theirs* is not accompanied by a noun.

The following are examples of errors that are possible with possessive determiners and pronouns.

> Incorrect: Each morning they read *theirs* newspapers.
>
> Correct: Each morning they read their newspapers.

> Incorrect: Could you lend me *your*?
>
> Correct: Could you lend me yours?

In the first example, the possessive pronoun *theirs* is incorrect because it is accompanied by the noun *newspapers,* and a possessive pronoun cannot be accompanied by a noun. The possessive determiner *their* is needed in the first example. In the second example, the possessive determiner *your* is incorrect because it is not accompanied by a noun, and a possessive determiner must be accompanied by a noun. The possessive pronoun *yours* is needed.

The following chart outlines the possessives and their uses.

Possessives	
Determiners	**Pronouns**
my	mine
your	yours
his	his
her	hers
its	—
our	ours
their	theirs
Must be accompanied by a noun	May not be accompanied by a noun

Appendix Exercise A24: Each of the following sentences contains at least one possessive pronoun or adjective. Circle the possessives. Then indicate if the sentences are correct (C) or incorrect (I). Correct the errors.

___I___ 1. We must do (our) part to encourage (ours) teammates.
(*our teammates*)

___C___ 2. I will pick up (your) children when I go to pick up (mine).

_____ 3. I am worried about both his response and hers.

_____ 4. She lost her notes, so she asked to borrow my.

_____ 5. Your explanation is, in my opinion, a bit weak.

_____ 6. Why don't you show them where theirs offices are?

_____ 7. It was my error and not your.

_____ 8. He thinks that his argument is more convincing than hers.

_____ 9. If these are not ours keys, then they must be theirs.

_____ 10. Do you think that your answer is better than hers or that her answer is better than ours?

Appendix A25: Check Pronoun Reference for Agreement

After you have checked that the subject and object pronouns and the possessives are used correctly, you should also check each of these pronouns and possessives for agreement. The following are examples of errors of this type.

Incorrect: The *boys* will cause trouble if you let *him*.

Correct: The boys will cause trouble if you let them.

Incorrect: *Everyone* must give *their* name.

Correct: Everyone must give his or her name.

In the first example, the singular pronoun *him* is incorrect because it refers back to the plural noun *boys*. This pronoun should be replaced with the plural pronoun *them*. In the second example, the plural possessive adjective *their* is incorrect because it refers back to the singular *everyone*. This adjective should be replaced with the singular *his or her*.

The following list provides key information about what you should remember about checking pronoun reference.

> ### Pronoun Agreement
> 1. Be sure that every pronoun and possessive agrees with the noun it refers to.
> 2. You generally check back in the sentence for agreement.

Appendix Exercise A25: Each of the following sentences contains at least one pronoun or possessive. Circle the pronouns and possessives. Underline any nouns they refer to. Then indicate if the sentences are correct (C) or incorrect (I). Correct the errors.

___I___ 1. <u>Papers</u> are due today at 5:00 p.m.; be sure to turn (it) in on time.
        (them)

___C___ 2. The <u>party</u> is for (my) neighbors, and (they) know all about (it)

_____ 3. Everyone must submit an application if you want to be considered for the scholarship.

_____ 4. The concert is tonight, and we will be going with our friends to hear them.

_____ 5. The sunshine today is lovely; I enjoy feeling it on my face.

_____ 6. The man has a problem, and he will have to resolve it all by herself.

_____ 7. My friend has a book on that subject, and she said that I could borrow her.

_____ 8. Your brothers have the money, and they know that you want it for yourself.

_____ 9. Each individual has their own individual set of fingerprints.

_____ 10. Your classmates will have to finish the project by yourselves.

Appendix Review Exercise (A21–A25): Indicate if the following sentences are correct (C) or incorrect (I).

_____ 1. She has tried much times to raise a little extra money.

_____ 2. We saw them getting into their car.

_____ 3. Of the two assignments, only one is complete; the other one has many errors in it.

_____ 4. Him and her never even asked us to lend them the money.

_____ 5. She told him about her decision, and he expressed his dissatisfaction with it.

_____ 6. Few issues have raised so many problems.

_____ 7. I have numerous questions about the situation, and I hope you can answer it.

_____ 8. You and I should not open this package because it was not given to you and I.

_____ 9. Many students have tried for perfect grades, but little of them have succeeded.

_____ 10. Our friends are coming to visit us after they visit their parents.

_____ 11. It will take a miracle to meet the various need of each person in the room.

_____ 12. They saw you and me, but we did not see them even though they called out to us.

_____ 13. You have done your part, but they have not done their.

_____ 14. This diet food has less fat and less calories.

_____ 15. We have our reasons, and they have theirs.

Adjectives and Adverbs

An adjective is a modifier that is used to describe a noun or pronoun, while an adverb is a modifier that is used to describe a verb, an adjective, or another adverb.

> Sam is a *nice* man, and he is *generous*.
>
> Sam is *really* generous, and he *almost always* has a smile on his face.

In the first example, the adjective *nice* is describing the noun *Sam,* and the adjective *generous* is describing the pronoun *he.* In the second example, the adverb *really* is describing the adjective *generous,* the adverb *almost* is describing the adverb *always,* and the adverb *always* is describing the verb *has.*

Three issues with adjectives and adverbs that it is important to master are the following: (1) the basic uses of adjectives and adverbs, (2) the correct positioning of adjectives and adverbs, and (3) the use of *-ed* and *-ing* verbal adjectives.

Appendix A26: Use Basic Adjectives and Adverbs Correctly

Adjectives and adverbs have very distinct uses. Adjectives describe nouns and pronouns, and adverbs describe verbs, adjectives, and other adverbs. The following are examples of incorrectly used adjectives and adverbs.

> Incorrect: They were seated at a *largely* table.
>
> Correct: They were seated at a large table.

> Incorrect: The child talked *quick* to her mother.
>
> Correct: The child talked quickly to her mother.

> Incorrect: We read an *extreme* long story.
>
> Correct: We read an extremely long story.

In the first example, the adverb *largely* is incorrect because the adjective *large* is needed to describe the noun *table.* In the second example, the adjective *quick* is incorrect because the adverb *quickly* is needed to describe the verb *talked.* In the last example, the adjective *extreme* is incorrect because the adverb *extremely* is needed to describe the adjective *long.*

The following list provides the important information that you should remember about the basic uses of adjectives and adverbs.

Basic Uses of Adjectives and Adverbs
1. Adjectives describe nouns or pronouns.
2. Adverbs describe verbs, adjectives, or other adverbs.

Appendix Exercise A26: Each of the following sentences has at least one adjective or adverb. Circle the adjectives and adverbs, and indicate which words they describe. Then indicate if the sentences are correct (C) or incorrect (I). Correct the errors.

__I__   1. The race was held under (extreme)(humid) conditions.

         extreme describes humid

         humid describes conditions

         (extremely)

__C__   2. The hungry baby wailed quite plaintively.

         hungry describes baby

         quite describes plaintively

         plaintively describes wailed

_____   3. We saw a real exciting movie with an unexpected ending.

_____   4. The striking workers marched slowly and deliberately outside of the locked front gates of the company.

_____   5. The manager studied the complex issue thoroughly before making the difficultly decision.

_____ 6. The parking lot had recently been resurfaced with thick black asphalt.

_____

_____

_____

_____ 7. We proceeded extremely cautious in order to arrive at a totally acceptable outcome.

_____

_____

_____

_____ 8. The couple decided rather suddenly to alter the plans for their vacation considerable.

_____

_____

_____

_____ 9. The large white building at the end of the circular driveway houses the main office.

_____

_____

_____

_____ 10. Whose brilliantly idea was it to take this supposed shortcut when none of us actually knew where it led?

_____

_____

_____

Appendix A27: Position Adjectives and Adverbs Correctly

It is important to pay attention to the position of both adjectives and adverbs. In English, a one-word adjective comes before the noun. Look at this example of an incorrectly positioned adjective.

Incorrect: The information *significant* is on the first page.

Correct: The significant information is on the first page.

In this example, the adjective *significant* should come before the noun *information* because *significant* describes *information*.

Adverbs can be used in many different positions in English, but there is at least one position where an adverb cannot be used. If a verb has an object, then an adverb describing the verb cannot be used between the verb and its object. Look at these examples.

Correct: The man drove *quickly*.

Incorrect: The man drove *quickly* the car.

Correct: The man drove the car quickly. *OR* The man quickly drove the car.

In the first example, the adverb *quickly* describes the verb *drove*. It is positioned correctly after the verb *drove* because *drove* does not have an object. In the second example, the adverb *quickly* is incorrectly positioned. The adverb *quickly* describes the verb *drove*, but the adverb cannot come directly after the verb because the verb has an object (*car*).

The following chart outlines the key information you should remember about the position of adjectives and adverbs.

The Position of Adjectives and Adverbs	
Adjectives	A one-word adjective comes before the noun it describes.
Adverbs	An adverb can appear in many positions. One place that an adverb cannot be used is between the verb it describes and the object of the verb.

Appendix Exercise A27: Each of the following sentences has at least one adjective or adverb. Circle the adjectives and adverbs, and indicate which words they describe. Then indicate if the sentences are correct (C) or incorrect (I). Correct the errors.

_I_ 1. Can you return (immediately) the necklace?

immediately describes return

(return the necklace immediately)

_____

_C_ 2. He is a (serious) man who (always) works (diligently)

serious describes man

always describes works

diligently describes works

_____ 3. The worried mother gently scolded the little girl.

_____

_____

_____

_____ 4. He uses often his checks to pay for purchases.

_____

_____

_____

_____ 5. The lifeguard attentive jumped quickly into the pool.

_____

_____

_____

_____ 6. In the paper, you need to explain the reasons for your hypothesis more clearly.

_____

_____

_____

_____ 7. The accountant studied carefully the figures before preparing the monthly report.

_____

_____

_____

_____ 8. The lawyer skillfully questioned the hostile witness.

_____

_____

_____

_____ 9. I cannot remember always the number of the account.

_____

_____

_____

_____ 10. The temperature dropped suddenly, and the people local bundled up to face the chilly weather.

_____

_____

_____

Appendix A28: Use -ed and -ing Adjectives Correctly

Verb forms ending in -ed and -ing can be used as adjectives. For example, the verbal adjectives *cleaned* and *cleaning* come from the verb *to clean*.

> The woman *cleans* the car.
>
> The *cleaning* woman worked on the car.
>
> The woman put the *cleaned* car back in the garage.

In the first example, *cleans* is the verb of the sentence. In the second example, *cleaning* is a verbal adjective describing *woman*. In the third example *cleaned* is a verbal adjective describing *car*.

Look at the following examples of incorrectly used -ing and -ed adjectives.

> Incorrect: The *cleaning* car . . .
>
> Correct: The clean car . . .
>
> Incorrect: The *cleaned* woman . . .
>
> Correct: The cleaning woman . . .

The difference between an -ed adjective and an -ing adjective is similar to the difference between the active and the passive (see A19 and A20). An -ing adjective (as when you use the active voice) means that the noun it describes is doing the action. The example above about the *cleaning car* is not correct because a car cannot do the action of cleaning: you cannot say that a car cleans itself. An -ed adjective (as when you use the passive voice) means that the noun it describes is receiving the action from the verb. The example above about the *cleaned woman* is not correct because in this example a woman cannot receive the action of the verb *clean*; this sentence does not mean that *someone cleaned the woman*.

The following chart outlines the key information that you should remember about -ed and -ing adjectives.

Adjectives with -ed and -ing			
Type	Meaning	Use	Example
-ing	active	It does the action of the verb.	. . . the happily *playing* children . . .
-ed	passive	It receives the action of the verb.	. . . the frequently *played* CD . . .

Appendix Exercise A28: Each of the following sentences contains either an -ed or an -ing verbal adjective. Circle the verbal adjectives, and indicate which words they describe. Then indicate if the sentences are correct (C) or incorrect (I). Correct the errors.

__C__ 1. The line is long, but at least it is a (fast-moving) line.

fast-moving describes line

_____

_____

____ 2. The (satisfying) customers thanked the salesperson for the good service.

satisfying describes customers

(satisfied)

____

____ 3. The people felt shocked as they heard the disturbed news.

____

____

____

____ 4. The delighted girl thanked her friend for the unexpected gift.

____

____

____

____ 5. It was such a depressed situation that no one smiled.

____

____

____

____ 6. The snow-capped mountains ringed the charmed village.

____

____

____

____ 7. An annoying guest made a number of rude comments to the frustrated host.

____

____

____

____ 8. The correcting papers are being returned to the waiting students.

____

____

____

_____ 9. An unidentified attacker tried to rob the strolling couple.

_____

_____

_____

_____ 10. The most requesting room in the hotel is the one with the unobstructing view of the lake.

_____

_____

_____

Articles

Articles are challenging to learn because there are many rules, many exceptions, and many special cases. It is possible, however, to learn a few rules that will help you to use articles correctly much of the time.

Nouns in English can be either countable or uncountable. If a noun is countable, it must be either singular or plural. In addition to these general types of nouns, there are two types of articles: definite (specific) and indefinite (general). The following chart demonstrates how to use these articles.

Articles with Different Types of Nouns			
Articles	**Countable Singular Nouns**	**Countable Plural Nouns**	**Uncountable Nouns**
Indefinite	_a_ pen	_____ pens	_____ ink
(General)	_an_ apple	_____ apples	_____ juice
Definite	_the_ pen	_the_ pens	_the_ ink
(Specific)	_the_ apple	_the_ apples	_the_ juice

Appendix A29: Use Articles with Singular Nouns

You can see from the chart that if a noun is either countable plural or uncountable, it is possible to have either the definite article _the_ or no article (indefinite). With all countable singular nouns, however, you must have an article unless you already have another determiner such as _my_ or _each_.

I have _money_. (uncountable—no article needed)

I have _books_. (countable plural—no article needed)

I have _a book_. (countable singular—article needed)

The following chart outlines the key information that you should remember about articles with singular nouns.

Articles with Singular Nouns
A singular noun must have an article (a, an, the) or some other determiner such as my or each. (A plural noun or uncountable noun may or may not have an article.)

Appendix Exercise A29: The following sentences contain different types of nouns. Underline the countable singular nouns. Circle any articles in front of the countable singular nouns. Then indicate if the sentences are correct (C) or incorrect (I). Correct the errors.

___I___ 1. Man wearing stylish hat is standing at door.
     (*A man . . . a . . . hat . . . the door*)

___C___ 2. I am working on Ⓐ difficult task, and I need help with it.

_____ 3. Sam is taking classes in geography, math, and science as well as holding part-time job.

_____ 4. I need advice about problems that I have been having with my neighbors.

_____ 5. She has funny feeling about surprising event that she just witnessed.

_____ 6. We would like to buy a van that has enough space for a family of six.

_____ 7. In the science course, the students must read textbook, take exams, give presentation, and participate in discussions.

_____ 8. The family likes pets; they have turtles, parakeets, snake, cats, and large dog.

_____ 9. She has a strong opinion about a situation involving acquaintances of ours.

_____ 10. Plants need water and air to grow.

Appendix A30: Distinguish *a* and *an*

The basic difference between *a* and *an* is that *a* is used in front of consonant, and *an* is used in front of vowels (*a, e, i, o, u*).

a book	*an* orange
a man	*an* illness
a page	*an* automobile

In reality, the rule is that *a* is used in front of a word that begins with a consonant *sound* and that *an* is used in front of a word that begins with a vowel *sound*. Pronounce the following correct examples.

a university	*a* hand	*a* one-way street	*a* euphemism	*a* xerox machine
an unhappy man	*an* hour	*an* omen	*an* event	*an* x-ray machine

These examples demonstrate that certain beginning letters can have either a consonant or a vowel sound. A word that begins with *u* can begin with the consonant sound *y* as in *university* or with a vowel sound as in *unhappy*. A word that begins with *h* can begin with a consonant *h* sound as in *hand* or with a vowel sound as in *hour*. A word that begins with *o* can begin with a consonant *w* sound as in *one* or with a vowel sound as in *omen*. A word that begins with *e* can begin with either a consonant *y* sound as in *euphemism* or with a vowel sound as in *event*. A word that begins with *x* can begin with either a consonant *z* sound as in *xerox* or with a vowel sound as in *x-ray*.

The following list provides the key information about the use of *a* and *an*.

---

a and *an*

1. *A* is used in front of a singular noun that begins with a consonant sound.
2. *An* is used in front of a singular noun that begins with a vowel sound.
3. Be careful with words beginning with *u, o, e, x,* or *h*. These words may begin with either a vowel or a consonant sound.

Appendix Exercise A30: Each of the following sentences contains at least one *a* or *an*. Circle each *a* or *an*. Underline the beginning of the word that directly follows. Pronounce the word. Then indicate if the sentences are correct (C) or incorrect (I). Correct the errors.

__C__ 1. You have (an) opportunity to attend (a) one-time event.

__I__ 2. He made (a) mistake, but it was (a) honest mistake.
        (an honest mistake)

_____ 3. They are staying in a hotel with a jacuzzi, a sauna, and a heated pool.

_____ 4. It is a honor to be a guest at such a important celebration.

_____ 5. The family is planning a once-in-a-lifetime trip to a faraway country.

_____ 6. Is this a usual occurrence or a unusual occurrence?

_____ 7. The party decorations included a colorful banner, a hand-painted sign, and a helium balloon.

_____ 8. Luisa had an euphoric feeling after she unexpectedly won an huge sum of money.

_____ 9. An individual who is unable to write may use a "X" rather than a signature when signing a document.

_____ 10. The class read a traditional story about a unicorn that saved a helpless child.

Appendix A31: Make Articles Agree with Nouns

The definite article (*the*) is used for both singular and plural nouns, so agreement is not a problem with the definite article. However, because the use of the indefinite article is different for singular and plural nouns, you must be careful of agreement between the indefinite article and the noun. One very common agreement error is to use the singular definite article (*a* or *an*) with a plural noun.

Incorrect: He saw *a* new *movies*.

Incorrect: They traveled to *a* nearby *mountains*.

Incorrect: Do you have *another books*?

In these examples, you should not have *a* or *an* because the nouns are plural. The following sentences are possible corrections of the sentences above.

Correct: He saw a new movie.   (singular)

Correct: He saw new movies.   (plural)

Correct: They traveled to a nearby mountain.   (singular)

Correct: They traveled to nearby mountains.   (plural)

Correct: Do you have another book?   (singular)

Correct: Do you have other books?   (plural)

The following chart outlines the key point for you to remember about the agreement of articles with nouns.

Agreement of Articles with Nouns
You should never use *a* or *an* with a plural noun.

Appendix Exercise A31: Each of the following sentences contains *a* or *an*. Circle each *a* or *an*. Underline the noun that it describes. Then indicate if the sentences are correct (C) or incorrect (I). Correct the errors.

___I___ 1. The team needs ⓐ new uniforms before the start of the season.
(a new uniform OR *new uniforms)*

___C___ 2. I need to buy pens, pencils, ⓐ notebook, and ⓐ textbook.

_____ 3. They are buying a new house with a swimming pool, with a roomy balconies, and with a wonderful views from the balconies.

_____ 4. The visiting professor shared an interesting new theories.

_____ 5. The office has a computer, a phone, a table and chairs, and office supplies.

_____ 6. The mother told her children a bedtime stories, gave them gentle kisses, and then tucked them into bed.

_____ 7. She went shopping and bought a new dress, a new shoes, a new purse, and a new earrings.

_____ 8. I have a good reason for answering questions this way.

_____ 9. The hostess served her guests tea and a vanilla biscuits.

_____ 10. The executive needs a secretary to prepare reports and take phone messages.

Appendix A32: Distinguish Specific and General Ideas

With countable singular nouns, it is possible to use either the definite or the indefinite article, but the definite and indefinite articles will have different meanings. The definite article is used to refer to one specific noun.

> Tom will bring *the* book tomorrow.
> (There is one specific book that Tom will bring tomorrow.)
>
> He will arrive on *the* first Tuesday in July.
> (There is only one first Tuesday in July.)
>
> He sailed on *the* Pacific Ocean.
> (There is only one Pacific Ocean.)

The indefinite article is used when the noun could be one of several different nouns.

> Tom will bring *a* book tomorrow.
> (Tom will bring any one book tomorrow.)
>
> He will arrive on *a* Tuesday in July.
> (He will arrive on one of the four or five Tuesdays in July.)
>
> He sailed on *an* ocean.
> (He sailed on any one of the world's oceans.)

The following chart outlines the key information that you should understand about specific and general ideas.

Specific and General Ideas		
a or *an*	General idea	Use when there are many, and you do not know which one it is. Use when there are many, and you do not care which one.
the	Specific idea	Use when it is the only one. Use when there are many, and you know which one it is.

Appendix Exercise A32: Each of the following sentences contains one or more articles. Circle each article. Underline the noun it describes. Then indicate if the sentences are correct (C) or incorrect (I). Correct the errors.

__I__ 1. We took (a) balloon ride over (an) African continent.
(the African continent)

__C__ 2. Last evening, my friends and I went to see (a) movie that had (a) very unusual ending.

_____ 3. Today there is a big dark cloud in a sky.

_____ 4. The spacecraft that was recently launched is heading toward a planet Mars.

_____ 5. The teacher stood in a middle of the classroom and talked to the students.

_____ 6. Can you think of an idea for a topic for an interesting research paper?

_____ 7. I would like to stay in a same hotel that we stayed in a last time that we visited here.

_____ 8. A hat that you are wearing now is really quite a cute hat.

_____ 9. We won a prize for a best essay in the school's essay contest.

_____ 10. After the man standing over there was punched in a nose, he suffered a bloody nose.

Appendix Review Exercise (A26–A32): Indicate if the following sentences are correct (C) or incorrect (I).

_____ 1. She offered an apology for a unbelievably rude comment.

_____ 2. The recipe calls for sugar, eggs, butter, flour, and vanilla.

_____ 3. The forgetful man misplaces often his keys.

_____ 4. An engine of the car that I am driving is making a funny noises.

_____ 5. The customer became increasingly impatient as she stood in an unmoving line.

_____ 6. A friend of mine works as an orderly in a hospital.

_____ 7. His job provides a good salary and a substantial benefits.

_____ 8. The student triumphantly finished the final part of the project and then turned the completed paper in.

_____ 9. She is taking an undergraduate course at nearby university.

_____ 10. The really angry father explained explicitly why his son's behavior was unacceptable.

_____ 11. It is delight to be a part of such a wonderful organization.

_____ 12. The unmaking beds and the unwashing dishes need some attention.

_____ 13. A dinner guest seated at the table should have a plate, a glass, a napkin, and eating utensils.

_____ 14. The teacher collected swiftly the exams from the anxious students.

_____ 15. At the school assembly this morning, a school principal gave speech to the students.

DIAGNOSIS, ASSESSMENT, AND SCORING

The highest possible score on the TOEFL iBT test is 120. Each of the four sections (Reading, Listening, Speaking, Writing) receives a scaled score from 0 to 30. The scaled scores from the four sections are added together to determine the overall scores.

The following chart shows how overall scores on the TOEFL iBT test can be compared with overall scores on the paper TOEFL test.

iBT	PBT
Internet-Based Test	Paper-Based Test
120	677
115	650
110	637
105	620
100	600
95	587
90	577
85	563
80	550
75	537
70	523
65	513
60	497
55	480
50	463
45	450
40	433
35	417
30	397
25	377
20	350

READING DIAGNOSIS AND SCORING

For the Reading test sections in this book, it is possible to do the following:

- *diagnose* errors in the Pre-Test, Post-Test, Mini-Tests, and Complete Tests sections
- *score* the Pre-Test, Post-Test, Mini-Tests, and Complete Tests sections
- *record* your test results

DIAGNOSING READING ERRORS

Every time you take a Reading test section of a Pre-Test, Post-Test, Mini-Test, or Complete Test, you should use the following chart to diagnose your errors.

Circle the number of each of the questions on the test that you *answered incorrectly* or *were unsure of*. Then you will see which skills you should focus on.

	PRE-TEST	POST-TEST	MINI-TESTS								COMPLETE TEST 1			COMPLETE TEST 2		
			1	2	3	4	5	6	7	8	1–13	14–26	27–38	1–13	14–26	27–39
SKILL 1	3 6 10 17 18 20	2 10 14	2 5 9	1 6 10	2 4	6 8 10	5 7 9	3 9	1 3	3 5 8	1 3 5 9 12	14 16 19 22	29 30 34 36	2 3 6	15 20 24 25	28 30 36
SKILL 2	12 15	6 16	3	12	9	5	11	4	9 11	10	10		31			37
SKILL 3	5	7 11	6	5	12	11	4	12		2	11	24 25	27	9	23	38
SKILL 4	9 19	5 15	8	7	10	9	6	7	7	9	7	21	35	8	18	31
SKILL 5	4 16	9 13 17	1	2 8 11	1 5 8	1 2 12	1 8 12	1 5	2 5	1 6	8	15 20	33	1 5 10 11	14 22	27 29 35
SKILL 6	1 11 14	3 18	4	4	11		2	10	8		2	17	32	4	17 19	32 34
SKILL 7	7 8 21	4 8	7	3 9	3 6	3 7	3	2 6 11	6 10	4 10	4	23	37	7	16	33
SKILL 8	2 13	1 12	10		7	4	10	8	4	11	6	18	28	12	21	
SKILL 9	22	19		13		13	13	13			13	26		13	26	39
SKILL 10		20	11		13				12	12			38			

SCORING THE READING PRE-TEST AND POST-TEST

To determine a scaled score on the Reading Pre-Test or Reading Post-Test, you must first determine the number of points you received in the section. You must determine the number of points you receive on the last two questions before you can determine the total number of points out of a possible 23 points. When you know the total points you received on the Reading Pre-Test or Post-Test, you can refer to the following chart to determine your scaled score out of 30 for this section.

TOTAL POINTS	READING SCALED SCORE	TOTAL POINTS	READING SCALED SCORE
23	30	11	16
22	29	10	14
21	28	9	13
20	26	8	12
19	25	7	11
18	24	6	10
17	23	5	8
16	21	4	7
15	20	3	6
14	19	2	4
13	18	1	2
12	17	0	0

SCORING THE READING MINI-TESTS

To determine a scaled score on a Reading Mini-Test, you must first determine the number of points you received in the section. You must determine the number of points you receive on the last questions before you can determine the total number of points out of a possible 14 points. When you know the total points you received on a Reading Mini-Test, you can refer to the following chart to determine your scaled score out of 30 for this section.

TOTAL POINTS	READING SCALED SCORE	TOTAL POINTS	READING SCALED SCORE
14	30	6	8
13	28	5	7
12	25	4	5
11	22	3	4
10	19	2	2
9	16	1	1
8	14	0	0
7	11		

SCORING THE READING COMPLETE TESTS

To determine a scaled score on a Reading Complete Test section, you must first determine the number of points you received in the section. You must determine the number of points you receive on the last question of each reading passage before you can determine the total number of points out of a possible 42 points. When you know the total points you received on a Reading Complete Test section, you can refer to the following chart to determine your scaled score out of 30 for this section.

TOTAL POINTS	READING SCALED SCORE	TOTAL POINTS	READING SCALED SCORE
42	30	20	9
41	29	19	8
40	28	18	8
39	27	17	7
38	26	16	7
37	25	15	6
36	24	14	6
35	23	13	5
34	22	12	5
33	21	11	4
32	20	10	4
31	19	9	3
30	18	8	3
29	17	7	2
28	16	6	2
27	16	5	1
26	15	4	1
25	14	3	1
24	13	2	0
23	12	1	0
22	11	0	0
21	10		

RECORDING YOUR READING TEST RESULTS

Each time you complete a Reading Pre-Test, a Post-Test, a Mini-Test, or a Complete Test section, you should record the results in the chart that follows. In this way, you will be able to keep track of the progress you are making.

READING TEST RESULTS		
PRE-TEST	_____ out of 23 possible points	**Reading Scaled Score** _____
POST-TEST	_____ out of 23 possible points	**Reading Scaled Score** _____
MINI-TEST 1	_____ out of 14 possible points	**Reading Scaled Score** _____
MINI-TEST 2	_____ out of 14 possible points	**Reading Scaled Score** _____
MINI-TEST 3	_____ out of 14 possible points	**Reading Scaled Score** _____
MINI-TEST 4	_____ out of 14 possible points	**Reading Scaled Score** _____
MINI-TEST 5	_____ out of 14 possible points	**Reading Scaled Score** _____
MINI-TEST 6	_____ out of 14 possible points	**Reading Scaled Score** _____
MINI-TEST 7	_____ out of 14 possible points	**Reading Scaled Score** _____
MINI-TEST 8	_____ out of 14 possible points	**Reading Scaled Score** _____
COMPLETE TEST 1	_____ out of 42 possible points	**Reading Scaled Score** _____
COMPLETE TEST 2	_____ out of 42 possible points	**Reading Scaled Score** _____

LISTENING DIAGNOSIS AND SCORING

For the Listening test sections in this book, it is possible to do the following:

- *diagnose* errors in the Pre-Test, Post-Test, Mini-Tests, and Complete Tests sections
- *score* the Pre-Test, Post-Test, Mini-Tests, or Complete Tests sections
- *record* your test results

DIAGNOSING LISTENING ERRORS

Every time you take a Listening test section of a Pre-Test, Post-Test, Mini-Test, or Complete Test, you should use the following chart to diagnose your errors.

Circle the number of each of the questions on the test that you *answered incorrectly* or *were unsure of*. Then you will see which skills you should focus on.

	PRE-TEST	POST-TEST	MINI-TESTS								COMPLETE TEST 1			COMPLETE TEST 2		
			1	2	3	4	5	6	7	8	1–11	12–22	23–34	1–11	12–22	23–34
SKILL 1	1 6	1 6	1	1 6	1	1 6	1 6	1	1 6	1	1 6	12 18	23 29	1 6	12 18	23 29
SKILL 2	2 4 7	3 8	3 5 8 10 11	3 8 9 10	2 7 8 9 11	3 4 5 7 8 10	2 5 7 10	3 8 9 10 11	3 7 8 9	2 6 7 8 9	2 4 7 9 10 11	15 16 20 21	25 26 27 30 31 32 33	3 4 7 8 9 10 11	13 14 15 16 19 20	24 25 26 27 30 32 33
SKILL 3	5 9	2 4 7	2 6	4 5		2	3 8	7	5 10	10	3 8			2 5	17	28 34
SKILL 4		5	4	2 11	3 4		4	5	2	3 4		13	34		22	
SKILL 5	8 10	10	7 9	7	6	9	9	6	11			14 17	28			
SKILL 6	3 11	11			5 10	11	11	2 4	4	5 11	5	19 22	24		21	31

SCORING THE LISTENING PRE-TEST, POST-TEST, AND MINI-TESTS

To determine a scaled score on the Listening Pre-Test, Listening Post-Test, or the Listening Mini-Tests, you must first determine the number of points you received in the section. You must determine the number of points you receive on the questions that are worth more than one point before you can determine the total number of points out of a possible 13 points. When you know the total points you received on the Listening Pre-Test, Post-Test, and Mini-Tests, you can refer to the following chart to determine your scaled score out of 30 for this section.

TOTAL POINTS	LISTENING SCALED SCORE	TOTAL POINTS	LISTENING SCALED SCORE
13	30	6	12
12	28	5	10
11	25	4	8
10	23	3	6
9	20	2	4
8	17	1	2
7	14	0	0

SCORING THE LISTENING COMPLETE TESTS

To determine a scaled score on a Listening Complete Test section, you must first determine the number of points you received in the section. You must determine the number of points you receive on the questions that are worth more than one point before you can determine the total number of points out of a possible 40 points. When you know the total points you received on a Listening Complete Test section, you can refer to the following chart to determine your scaled score out of 30 for this section.

TOTAL POINTS	LISTENING SCALED SCORE	TOTAL POINTS	LISTENING SCALED SCORE
40	30	19	9
39	29	18	9
38	28	17	8
37	27	16	8
36	26	15	7
35	25	14	6
34	24	13	6
33	23	12	5
32	22	11	4
31	21	10	4
30	20	9	3
29	19	8	3
28	18	7	3
27	17	6	2
26	16	5	2
25	15	4	1
24	14	3	1
23	13	2	1
22	12	1	0
21	11	0	0
20	10		

RECORDING YOUR LISTENING TEST RESULTS

Each time you complete a Listening Pre-Test, a Post-Test, a Mini-Test, or a Complete Test section, you should record the results in the chart that follows. In this way, you will be able to keep track of the progress you are making.

LISTENING TEST RESULTS	
PRE-TEST	_____ out of 13 possible points Listening Scaled Score _____
POST-TEST	_____ out of 13 possible points Listening Scaled Score _____
MINI-TEST 1	_____ out of 13 possible points Listening Scaled Score _____
MINI-TEST 2	_____ out of 13 possible points Listening Scaled Score _____
MINI-TEST 3	_____ out of 13 possible points Listening Scaled Score _____
MINI-TEST 4	_____ out of 13 possible points Listening Scaled Score _____
MINI-TEST 5	_____ out of 13 possible points Listening Scaled Score _____
MINI-TEST 6	_____ out of 13 possible points Listening Scaled Score _____
MINI-TEST 7	_____ out of 13 possible points Listening Scaled Score _____
MINI-TEST 8	_____ out of 13 possible points Listening Scaled Score _____
COMPLETE TEST 1	_____ out of 40 possible points Listening Scaled Score _____
COMPLETE TEST 2	_____ out of 40 possible points Listening Scaled Score _____

SPEAKING ASSESSMENT AND SCORING

For the Speaking test sections in this book, it is possible to do the following:

- *assess* the skills used in the Pre-Test, Post-Test, Mini-Tests, and Complete Tests sections
- *score* the Pre-Test, Post-Test, Mini-Tests, and Complete Tests sections using the Speaking Scoring Criteria
- *record* your test results

ASSESSING SPEAKING SKILLS

After you complete each Speaking task on a Pre-Test, Post-Test, Mini-Test, or Complete Test section, put checkmarks in the appropriate boxes in the following checklists. This will help you assess how well you have used the skills presented in the textbook.

SKILL-ASSESSMENT CHECKLIST Speaking Question 1, Free Choice: Skills 1–2		PRE-TEST, Question 1	REVIEW EXERCISE (Skills 1–2)	POST-TEST, Question 1	MINI-TEST 1, Question 1	MINI-TEST 3, Question 1	MINI-TEST 5, Question 1	MINI-TEST 7, Question 1	COMPLETE TEST 1, Question 1	COMPLETE TEST 2, Question 1
SKILL 1	I read the **question** carefully.									
SKILL 1	I **chose a response** I could support with reasons and examples from **my own experience**.									
SKILL 1	I **noted reasons** that support my opinion and used **personal examples** in my **plan**.									
SKILL 2	I started with an **introduction**.									
SKILL 2	I used **specific examples** from my experience.									
SKILL 2	I used **transitions** to connect my ideas.									
SKILL 2	I used **pauses and intonation** to mark my transitions.									

SKILL-ASSESSMENT CHECKLIST
Speaking Question 2, Paired Choice: Skills 3–4

		PRE-TEST, Question 2	REVIEW EXERCISE (Skills 3–4)	POST-TEST, Question 2	MINI-TEST 2, Question 1	MINI-TEST 4, Question 1	MINI-TEST 6, Question 1	MINI-TEST 8, Question 1	COMPLETE TEST 1, Question 2	COMPLETE TEST 2, Question 2
SKILL 3	I read the **question** carefully.									
SKILL 3	I noted my preference, reasons, and examples in my **plan**.									
SKILL 3	I based the number of points I used in my response on how fast I could deliver my answer.									
SKILL 4	I began with an **introductory statement** that directly answered the question.									
SKILL 4	I used **reasons** for my choice and **examples** to support my choice.									
SKILL 4	I used **transitions** to connect the supporting ideas.									
SKILL 4	I used **transitions** and appropriate **pauses** to make my answer cohesive.									

		PRE-TEST, Question 3	REVIEW EXERCISE (Skills 5–8)	POST-TEST, Question 3	MINI-TEST 3, Question 2	MINI-TEST 5, Question 2	MINI-TEST 7, Question 2	COMPLETE TEST 1, Question 3	COMPLETE TEST 2, Question 3
SKILL 5	I noted the **topic** and **main points** of the **reading passage**.								
SKILL 6	I noted the **opinions** of the two speakers from the **listening passage**.								
SKILL 6	I noted the speakers' reasons for their opinions from the **listening passage**.								
SKILL 7	I read the **question** carefully.								
SKILL 7	I used my notes to find the information necessary and formed a **plan**.								
SKILL 8	I began with an overall **topic statement**.								
SKILL 8	I used my **plan** to **explain** the **speaker's opinion** and the **reasons** for that opinion.								
SKILL 8	I used useful language and **transitions** to connect my ideas.								

		SKILL-ASSESSMENT CHECKLIST Speaking Question 4, Academic Setting Integrated Reading and Listening: Skills 9–12								
		PRE-TEST, Question 4	REVIEW EXERCISE (Skills 9–12)	POST-TEST, Question 4	MINI-TEST 2, Question 2	MINI-TEST 4, Question 2	MINI-TEST 6, Question 2	MINI-TEST 8, Question 2	COMPLETE TEST 1, Question 4	COMPLETE TEST 2, Question 4
SKILL 9	I briefly noted the **topic** and **main points** of the **reading passage**.									
SKILL 10	I noted the **specific examples** of the **listening passage**.									
SKILL 11	I read the **question** carefully.									
SKILL 11	I looked for **connections** between ideas from the reading and listening in my notes.									
SKILL 11	I **organized** my notes to **plan** my response.									
SKILL 12	I began with a **topic statement** that answered the question and stated the relationship between the listening and the reading.									
SKILL 12	I explained the **examples** and main points using my plan.									
SKILL 12	I used **details** from the listening and reading passages.									
SKILL 12	I used useful language and **transitions** to connect my ideas.									

SKILL-ASSESSMENT CHECKLIST
Speaking Question 5, Campus-based Integrated Listening: Skills 13–15

		PRE-TEST, Question 5	REVIEW EXERCISE (Skills 13–15)	POST-TEST, Question 5	MINI-TEST 2, Question 3	MINI-TEST 4, Question 3	MINI-TEST 6, Question 3	MINI-TEST 8, Question 3	COMPLETE TEST 1, Question 5	COMPLETE TEST 2, Question 5
SKILL 13	I focused on listening for the **problems** and the **suggested solutions** in the listening passage.									
SKILL 13	I took **notes** on the problems, solutions, and **reasons** given for the suggested solutions.									
SKILL 14	I read the **question** carefully.									
SKILL 14	I used my notes and added my **opinion** to form a **plan**.									
SKILL 15	I began by explaining the problem.									
SKILL 15	I explained the solution I preferred and gave details to explain my reason for this opinion.									
SKILL 15	I used useful language and **transitions** to connect my ideas.									

SKILL-ASSESSMENT CHECKLIST
Speaking Question 6, Integrated Listening: Skills 16–18

		PRE-TEST, Question 6	REVIEW EXERCISE (Skills 16–18)	POST-TEST, Question 6	MINI-TEST 1, Question 3	MINI-TEST 3, Question 3	MINI-TEST 5, Question 3	MINI-TEST 7, Question 3	COMPLETE TEST 1, Question 6	COMPLETE TEST 2, Question 6
SKILL 16	I noted the **topic**, **main ideas**, and **supporting details** of the listening passage.									
SKILL 17	I read the **question** carefully.									
SKILL 17	I used my notes about the supporting details to form a **plan**.									
SKILL 18	I began by stating the **topic** and a **definition** if necessary.									
SKILL 18	I explained how the main ideas and supporting details answered the question.									
SKILL 19	I used useful language and **transitions** to connect my ideas.									

SCORING THE SPEAKING TESTS USING THE SCORING CRITERIA

You may use the Speaking Scoring Criteria to score your speaking tasks on the Pre-Test, Post-Test, Mini-Tests, and Complete Tests. You will receive a score of 0 through 4 for each Speaking task; this score of 0 through 4 will then be converted to a scaled score out of 30. The criteria for Speaking scores of 0 through 4 are listed below.

	SPEAKING SCORING CRITERIA	
4	ANSWER TO QUESTION	The student answers the question thoroughly.
	COMPREHENSIBILITY	The student can be understood completely.
	ORGANIZATION	The student's response is well organized and developed.
	FLUENCY	The student's speech is generally fluent.
	PRONUNCIATION	The student has generally good pronunciation.
	GRAMMAR	The student uses advanced grammatical structures with a high degree of accuracy.
	VOCABULARY	The student uses advanced vocabulary with a high degree of accuracy.
3	ANSWER TO QUESTION	The student answers the questions adequately but not thoroughly.
	COMPREHENSIBILITY	The student can generally be understood.
	ORGANIZATION	The student's response is organized basically and is not thoroughly developed.
	FLUENCY	The student's speech is generally fluent, with minor problems.
	PRONUNCIATION	The student has generally good pronunciation, with minor problems.
	GRAMMAR	The student uses either accurate easier grammatical structures or more advanced grammatical structures with some errors.
	VOCABULARY	The student uses either accurate easier vocabulary or more advanced vocabulary with some errors.
2	ANSWER TO QUESTION	The student discusses information from the task but does not answer the question directly.
	COMPREHENSIBILITY	The student is not always intelligible.
	ORGANIZATION	The student's response is not clearly organized and is incomplete or contains some inaccurate points.
	FLUENCY	The student's speech is not very fluent and has a number of problems.
	PRONUNCIATION	The student's pronunciation is not very clear, with a number of problems.
	GRAMMAR	The student has a number of errors in grammar or uses only very basic grammar fairly accurately.
	VOCABULARY	The student has a number of errors in vocabulary or uses only very basic vocabulary fairly accurately.
1	ANSWER TO QUESTION	The student's response is only slightly related to the topic.
	COMPREHENSIBILITY	The student is only occasionally intelligible.
	ORGANIZATION	The student's response is not clearly organized and is only minimally on the topic.
	FLUENCY	The student has problems with fluency that make the response difficult to understand.
	PRONUNCIATION	The student has problems with pronunciation that make the response difficult to understand.
	GRAMMAR	The student has numerous errors in grammar that interfere with meaning.
	VOCABULARY	The student has numerous errors in vocabulary that interfere with meaning.
0	The student either says nothing or fails to answer the question.	

The following chart shows how a score of 0 through 4 on a Speaking task is converted to a scaled score out of 30.

SPEAKING SCORE (0–4)	SPEAKING SCALED SCORE (0–30)
4.00	30
3.83	29
3.66	28
3.50	27
3.33	26
3.16	24
3.00	23
2.83	22
2.66	20
2.50	19
2.33	18
2.16	17
2.00	15
1.83	14
1.66	13
1.50	11
1.33	10
1.16	9
1.00	8
0.83	6
0.66	5
0.50	4
0.33	3
0.16	1
0.00	0

Scaled scores on each of the Speaking tasks on a test are averaged to determine the scaled score for the test.

RECORDING YOUR SPEAKING TEST RESULTS

Each time that you complete a Speaking Pre-Test, Post-Test, Mini-Test, or Complete Test section, you should record the results in the chart that follows. In this way, you will be able to keep track of the progress you are making.

SPEAKING TEST RESULTS	
PRE-TEST	Speaking Task 1 _____ Speaking Task 2 _____ Speaking Task 3 _____ Speaking Task 4 _____ Speaking Task 5 _____ Speaking Task 6 _____ **Overall Speaking Score** _____
POST-TEST	Speaking Task 1 _____ Speaking Task 2 _____ Speaking Task 3 _____ Speaking Task 4 _____ Speaking Task 5 _____ Speaking Task 6 _____ **Overall Speaking Score** _____
MINI-TEST 1	Speaking Task 1 _____ Speaking Task 2 _____ Speaking Task 3 _____ **Overall Speaking Score** _____
MINI-TEST 2	Speaking Task 1 _____ Speaking Task 2 _____ Speaking Task 3 _____ **Overall Speaking Score** _____
MINI-TEST 3	Speaking Task 1 _____ Speaking Task 2 _____ Speaking Task 3 _____ **Overall Speaking Score** _____
MINI-TEST 4	Speaking Task 1 _____ Speaking Task 2 _____ Speaking Task 3 _____ **Overall Speaking Score** _____

MINI-TEST 5	Speaking Task 1 _____ Speaking Task 2 _____ Speaking Task 3 _____ **Overall Speaking Score** _____
MINI-TEST 6	Speaking Task 1 _____ Speaking Task 2 _____ Speaking Task 3 _____ **Overall Speaking Score** _____
MINI-TEST 7	Speaking Task 1 _____ Speaking Task 2 _____ Speaking Task 3 _____ **Overall Speaking Score** _____
MINI-TEST 8	Speaking Task 1 _____ Speaking Task 2 _____ Speaking Task 3 _____ **Overall Speaking Score** _____
COMPLETE TEST 1	Speaking Task 1 _____ Speaking Task 2 _____ Speaking Task 3 _____ Speaking Task 4 _____ Speaking Task 5 _____ Speaking Task 6 _____ **Overall Speaking Score** _____
COMPLETE TEST 2	Speaking Task 1 _____ Speaking Task 2 _____ Speaking Task 3 _____ Speaking Task 4 _____ Speaking Task 5 _____ Speaking Task 6 _____ **Overall Speaking Score** _____

WRITING ASSESSMENT AND SCORING

For the Writing test sections in this book, it is possible to do the following:

- *assess* the skills used in the Pre-Test, Post-Test, Mini-Tests, and Complete Tests sections

- *score* the Pre-Test, Post-Test, Mini-Tests, and Complete Tests sections using the Writing Scoring Criteria

- *record* your test results

ASSESSING WRITING SKILLS

After you complete each Writing task on a Pre-Test, Post-Test, Mini-Test, or Complete Test section, put checkmarks in the appropriate boxes in the following checklists. This will help you assess how well you have used the skills presented in the textbook.

SKILL-ASSESSMENT CHECKLIST Writing Question 1, Integrated Task: Skills 1–8		PRE-TEST, Question 1	REVIEW EXERCISE (Skills 1–8)	POST-TEST, Question 1	MINI-TEST 1, Question 1	MINI-TEST 3, Question 1	MINI-TEST 5, Question 1	MINI-TEST 7, Question 1	COMPLETE TEST 1, Question 1	COMPLETE TEST 2, Question 1
SKILL 1	I noted the **topic** of the **reading passage**.									
SKILL 1	I noted the three **main points** of the **reading passage** that are used to support the topic.									
SKILL 2	I noted the **topic** of the **listening passage**.									
SKILL 2	I noted the three **main points** of the **listening passage** that are used to support the topic.									
SKILL 3	I read the question carefully to determine the information requested.									
SKILL 3	I noted the **relationship** between the reading and listening passages in my **plan**.									

	PRE-TEST, Question 1	REVIEW EXERCISE (Skills 1–8)	POST-TEST, Question 1	MINI-TEST 1, Question 1	MINI-TEST 3, Question 1	MINI-TEST 5, Question 1	MINI-TEST 7, Question 1	COMPLETE TEST 1, Question 1	COMPLETE TEST 2, Question 1
SKILL 4	I began with a **topic statement** that shows how the information in the reading passage and the listening passage are related.								
SKILL 4	I wrote **three supporting paragraphs**, with each paragraph detailing one point from the listening passage and its related point from the reading passage.								
SKILL 4	I included **terminology** from the question in the body of my essay.								
SKILL 5	I used an **outline** and included a **topic paragraph** for the **Block method**.								
SKILL 5	I wrote a unified **supporting paragraph** on reading.								
SKILL 5	I wrote a unified **supporting paragraph** on listening.								
SKILL 6	I stated the **relationship** between the listening and reading in my **topic statement**.								
SKILL 6	I used **terminology** in my **topic statement** to indicate the relationship between the passages.								
SKILL 7	I checked the **sentence structure** in my response.								
SKILL 8	I checked the **grammar** in my response.								

		PRE-TEST, Question 2	REVIEW EXERCISE (Skills 9–15)	POST-TEST, Question 2	MINI-TEST 2, Question 1	MINI-TEST 4, Question 1	MINI-TEST 6, Question 1	MINI-TEST 8, Question 1	COMPLETE TEST 1, Question 2	COMPLETE TEST 2, Question 2
SKILL 9	I noted verbs and key words from the **prompt** to **decode** the essay topic.									
SKILL 10	I used an **outline** to **plan** my essay.									
SKILL 11	I wrote unified **supporting paragraphs**.									
SKILL 12	I used **transitions** to connect the supporting paragraphs.									
SKILL 13	I used information to interest the reader in my **introduction**.									
SKILL 13	I stated the **topic** and the organization in my introduction.									
SKILL 13	I summarized the main points in my **conclusion**.									
SKILL 14	I checked the **sentence structure** in my response.									
SKILL 15	I checked the **grammar** in my response.									

SKILL-ASSESSMENT CHECKLIST
Writing Question 2, Integrated Listening: Skills 9–15

SCORING THE WRITING TESTS USING THE SCORING CRITERIA

You may use the Writing Scoring Criteria to score your writing tasks on the Pre-Test, Post-Test, Mini-Tests, and Complete Tests. You will receive a score of 0 through 5 for each Writing task; this score of 0 through 5 will then be converted to a scaled score out of 30. The criteria for Writing scores of 0 through 5 are listed below.

WRITING SCORING CRITERIA		
5	ANSWER TO QUESTION	The student answers the question thoroughly.
	COMPREHENSIBILITY	The student can be understood completely.
	ORGANIZATION	The student's response is maturely organized and developed.
	FLOW OF IDEAS	The student's ideas flow cohesively.
	GRAMMAR	The student uses advanced grammatical structures with a high degree of accuracy.
	VOCABULARY	The student uses advanced vocabulary with a high degree of accuracy.
4	ANSWER TO QUESTION	The student answers the questions adequately but not thoroughly.
	COMPREHENSIBILITY	The student can generally be understood.
	ORGANIZATION	The student's response is adequately organized and developed.
	FLOW OF IDEAS	The student's ideas generally flow cohesively.
	GRAMMAR	The student uses either accurate easier grammatical structures or more advanced grammatical structures with a few errors.
	VOCABULARY	The student uses either accurate easier vocabulary or more advanced vocabulary with some errors.
3	ANSWER TO QUESTION	The student gives a basically accurate response to the question.
	COMPREHENSIBILITY	The student's basic ideas can be understood.
	ORGANIZATION	The student's response is organized basically and is not thoroughly developed.
	FLOW OF IDEAS	The student's ideas flow cohesively sometimes and at other times do not.
	GRAMMAR	The student has a number of errors in grammar or uses only very basic grammar fairly accurately.
	VOCABULARY	The student has a number of errors in vocabulary or uses only very basic vocabulary fairly accurately.
2	ANSWER TO QUESTION	The student discusses information from the task but does not answer the question directly.
	COMPREHENSIBILITY	The student's ideas are not always intelligible.
	ORGANIZATION	The student's response is not clearly organized and is incomplete or contains some inaccurate points.
	FLOW OF IDEAS	The student's ideas often do not flow cohesively.
	GRAMMAR	The student has numerous errors in grammar that interfere with meaning.
	VOCABULARY	The student has numerous errors in vocabulary that interfere with meaning.
1	ANSWER TO QUESTION	The student's response is only slightly related to the topic.
	COMPREHENSIBILITY	The student's ideas are occasionally intelligible.
	ORGANIZATION	The student's response is not clearly organized and is only minimally on the topic.
	FLOW OF IDEAS	The student's ideas do not flow smoothly.
	GRAMMAR	The student produces very little grammatically correct language.
	VOCABULARY	The student uses very little vocabulary correctly.
0	The student either writes nothing or fails to answer the question.	

The following chart shows how a score of 0 through 5 on a Writing task is converted to a scaled score out of 30.

WRITING SCORE (0–5)	WRITING SCALED SCORE (0–30)
5.00	30
4.75	29
4.50	28
4.25	27
4.00	25
3.75	24
3.50	22
3.25	21
3.00	20
2.75	18
2.50	17
2.25	15
2.00	14
1.75	12
1.50	11
1.25	10
1.00	8
0.75	7
0.50	5
0.25	4
0.00	0

Scaled scores on each of the Writing tasks on a test are averaged to determine the scaled score for the test.

RECORDING YOUR WRITING TEST RESULTS

Each time that you complete a Writing Pre-Test, Post-Test, Mini-Test, or Complete Test section, you should record the results in the chart that follows. In this way, you will be able to keep track of the progress you are making.

SPEAKING TEST RESULTS	
PRE-TEST	Writing Task 1 _____ Writing Task 2 _____ **Overall Writing Score** _____
POST-TEST	Writing Task 1 _____ Writing Task 2 _____ **Overall Writing Score** _____
MINI-TEST 1	Writing Task 1 _____ **Overall Writing Score** _____
MINI-TEST 2	Writing Task 1 _____ **Overall Writing Score** _____
MINI-TEST 3	Writing Task 1 _____ **Overall Writing Score** _____
MINI-TEST 4	Writing Task 1 _____ **Overall Writing Score** _____
MINI-TEST 5	Writing Task 1 _____ **Overall Writing Score** _____
MINI-TEST 6	Writing Task 1 _____ **Overall Writing Score** _____
MINI-TEST 7	Writing Task 1 _____ **Overall Writing Score** _____
MINI-TEST 8	Writing Task 1 _____ **Overall Writing Score** _____
COMPLETE TEST 1	Writing Task 1 _____ Writing Task 2 _____ **Overall Writing Score** _____
COMPLETE TEST 2	Writing Task 1 _____ Writing Task 2 _____ **Overall Writing Score** _____